Lecture N[illegible]
Computer Science

Lecture Notes in Computer Science

Vol. 324: M.P. Chytil, L. Janiga, V. Koubek (Eds.), Mathematical Foundations of Computer Science 1988. Proceedings. IX, 562 pages. 1988.

Vol. 325: G. Brassard, Modern Cryptology. VI, 107 pages. 1988.

Vol. 326: M. Gyssens, J. Paredaens, D. Van Gucht (Eds.), ICDT '88. 2nd International Conference on Database Theory. Proceedings, 1988. VI, 409 pages. 1988.

Vol. 327: G.A. Ford (Ed.), Software Engineering Education. Proceedings, 1988. V, 207 pages. 1988.

Vol. 328: R. Bloomfield, L. Marshall, R. Jones (Eds.), VDM '88. VDM – The Way Ahead. Proceedings, 1988. IX, 499 pages. 1988.

Vol. 329: E. Börger, H. Kleine Büning, M.M. Richter (Eds.), CSL '87. 1st Workshop on Computer Science Logic. Proceedings, 1987. VI, 346 pages. 1988.

Vol. 330: C.G. Günther (Ed.), Advances in Cryptology – EUROCRYPT '88. Proceedings, 1988. XI, 473 pages. 1988.

Vol. 331: M. Joseph (Ed.), Formal Techniques in Real-Time and Fault-Tolerant Systems. Proceedings, 1988. VI, 229 pages. 1988.

Vol. 332: D. Sannella, A. Tarlecki (Eds.), Recent Trends in Data Type Specification. V, 259 pages. 1988.

Vol. 333: H. Noltemeier (Ed.), Computational Geometry and its Applications. Proceedings, 1988. VI, 252 pages. 1988.

Vol. 334: K.R. Dittrich (Ed.), Advances in Object-Oriented Database Systems. Proceedings, 1988. VII, 373 pages. 1988.

Vol. 335: F.A. Vogt (Ed.), CONCURRENCY 88. Proceedings, 1988. VI, 401 pages. 1988.

Vol. 336: B.R. Donald, Error Detection and Recovery in Robotics. XXIV, 314 pages. 1989.

Vol. 337: O. Günther, Efficient Structures for Geometric Data Management. XI, 135 pages. 1988.

Vol. 338: K.V. Nori, S. Kumar (Eds.), Foundations of Software Technology and Theoretical Computer Science. Proceedings, 1988. IX, 520 pages. 1988.

Vol. 339: M. Rafanelli, J.C. Klensin, P. Svensson (Eds.), Statistical and Scientific Database Management. Proceedings, 1988. IX, 454 pages. 1989.

Vol. 340: G. Rozenberg (Ed.), Advances in Petri Nets 1988. VI, 439 pages. 1988.

Vol. 341: S. Bittanti (Ed.), Software Reliability Modelling and Identification. VII, 209 pages. 1988.

Vol. 342: G. Wolf, T. Legendi, U. Schendel (Eds.), Parcella '88. Proceedings, 1988. 380 pages. 1989.

Vol. 343: J. Grabowski, P. Lescanne, W. Wechler (Eds.), Algebraic and Logic Programming. Proceedings, 1988. 278 pages. 1988.

Vol. 344: J. van Leeuwen, Graph-Theoretic Concepts in Computer Science. Proceedings, 1988. VII, 459 pages. 1989.

Vol. 345: R.T. Nossum (Ed.), Advanced Topics in Artificial Intelligence. VII, 233 pages. 1988 (Subseries LNAI).

Vol. 346: M. Reinfrank, J. de Kleer, M.L. Ginsberg, E. Sandewall (Eds.), Non-Monotonic Reasoning. Proceedings, 1988. XIV, 237 pages. 1989 (Subseries LNAI).

Vol. 347: K. Morik (Ed.), Knowledge Representation and Organization in Machine Learning. XV, 319 pages. 1989 (Subseries LNAI).

Vol. 348: P. Deransart, B. Lorho, J. Małuszyński (Eds.), Programming Languages Implementation and Logic Programming. Proceedings, 1988. VI, 299 pages. 1989.

Vol. 349: B. Monien, R. Cori (Eds.), STACS 89. Proceedings, 1989. VIII, 544 pages. 1989.

Vol. 350: A. Törn, A. Žilinskas, Global Optimization. X, 255 pages. 1989.

Vol. 351: J. Díaz, F. Orejas (Eds.), TAPSOFT '89. Volume 1. Proceedings, 1989. X, 383 pages. 1989.

Vol. 352: J. Díaz, F. Orejas (Eds.), TAPSOFT '89. Volume 2. Proceedings, 1989. X, 389 pages. 1989.

Vol. 353: S. Hölldobler, Foundations of Equational Logic Programming. X, 250 pages. 1989. (Subseries LNAI).

Vol. 354: J.W. de Bakker, W.-P. de Roever, G. Rozenberg (Eds.), Linear Time, Branching Time and Partial Order in Logics and Models for Concurrency. VIII, 713 pages. 1989.

Vol. 355: N. Dershowitz (Ed.), Rewriting Techniques and Applications. Proceedings, 1989. VII, 579 pages. 1989.

Vol. 356: L. Huguet, A. Poli (Eds.), Applied Algebra, Algebraic Algorithms and Error-Correcting Codes. Proceedings, 1987. VI, 417 pages. 1989.

Vol. 357: T. Mora (Ed.), Applied Algebra, Algebraic Algorithms and Error-Correcting Codes. Proceedings, 1988. IX, 481 pages. 1989.

Vol. 358: P. Gianni (Ed.), Symbolic and Algebraic Computation. Proceedings, 1988. XI, 545 pages. 1989.

Vol. 359: D. Gawlick, M. Haynie, A. Reuter (Eds.), High Performance Transaction Systems. Proceedings, 1987. XII, 329 pages. 1989.

Vol. 360: H. Maurer (Ed.), Computer Assisted Learning – ICCAL '89. Proceedings, 1989. VII, 642 pages. 1989.

Vol. 361: S. Abiteboul, P.C. Fischer, H.-J. Schek (Eds.), Nested Relations and Complex Objects in Databases. VI, 323 pages. 1989.

Vol. 362: B. Lisper, Synthesizing Synchronous Systems by Static Scheduling in Space-Time. VI, 263 pages. 1989.

Vol. 363: A.R. Meyer, M.A. Taitslin (Eds.), Logic at Botik '89. Proceedings, 1989. X, 289 pages. 1989.

Vol. 364: J. Demetrovics, B. Thalheim (Eds.), MFDBS 89. Proceedings, 1989. VI, 428 pages. 1989.

Vol. 365: E. Odijk, M. Rem, J.-C. Syre (Eds.), PARLE '89. Parallel Architectures and Languages Europe. Volume I. Proceedings, 1989. XIII, 478 pages. 1989.

Vol. 366: E. Odijk, M. Rem, J.-C. Syre (Eds.), PARLE '89. Parallel Architectures and Languages Europe. Volume II. Proceedings, 1989. XIII, 442 pages. 1989.

Vol. 367: W. Litwin, H.-J. Schek (Eds.), Foundations of Data Organization and Algorithms. Proceedings, 1989. VIII, 531 pages. 1989.

Vol. 368: H. Boral, P. Faudemay (Eds.), IWDM '89, Database Machines. Proceedings, 1989. VI, 387 pages. 1989.

Vol. 369: D. Taubner, Finite Representations of CCS and TCSP Programs by Automata and Petri Nets. X. 168 pages. 1989.

Vol. 370: Ch. Meinel, Modified Branching Programs and Their Computational Power. VI, 132 pages. 1989.

Vol. 371: D. Hammer (Ed.), Compiler Compilers and High Speed Compilation. Proceedings, 1988. VI, 242 pages. 1989.

Vol. 372: G. Ausiello, M. Dezani-Ciancaglini, S. Ronchi Della Rocca (Eds.), Automata, Languages and Programming. Proceedings, 1989. XI, 788 pages. 1989.

Vol. 373: T. Theoharis, Algorithms for Parallel Polygon Rendering. VIII, 147 pages. 1989.

Vol. 374: K.A. Robbins, S. Robbins, The Cray X-MP/Model 24. VI, 165 pages. 1989.

Vol. 375: J.L.A. van de Snepscheut (Ed.), Mathematics of Program Construction. Proceedings, 1989. VI, 421 pages. 1989.

Vol. 376: N.E. Gibbs (Ed.), Software Engineering Education. Proceedings, 1989. VII, 312 pages. 1989.

Vol. 377: M. Gross, D. Perrin (Eds.), Electronic Dictionaries and Automata in Computational Linguistics. Proceedings, 1987. V, 110 pages. 1989.

Vol. 378: J.H. Davenport (Ed.), EUROCAL '87. Proceedings, 1987. VIII, 499 pages. 1989.

Lecture Notes in Computer Science

Edited by G. Goos and J. Hartmanis

416

F. Bancilhon C. Thanos
D. Tsichritzis (Eds.)

Advances in Database Technology – EDBT '90

International Conference on Extending Database Technology
Venice, Italy, March 26–30, 1990
Proceedings

Springer-Verlag
Berlin Heidelberg New York London Paris Tokyo Hong Kong

Editors

François Bancilhon
ALTAIR
B.P. 105, F-78153 Le Chesnay Cedex, France

Costantino Thanos
I.E.I. – C.N.R.
Via Santa Maria 46, I-56126 Pisa, Italy

Dennis Tsichritzis
Centre Universitaire d'Informatique, Université de Genève
12, rue du Lac, CH-1207 Genève, Switzerland

CR Subject Classification (1987): D.3.3, E.2, F.4.1, H.2, I.2.1, I.2.4

ISBN 3-540-52291-3 Springer-Verlag Berlin Heidelberg New York
ISBN 0-387-52291-3 Springer-Verlag New York Berlin Heidelberg

Printing and binding: Druckhaus Beltz, Hemsbach/Bergstr.
2145/3140-543210 – Printed on acid-free paper

Foreword

This is the second EDBT conference. The first took place in March 1988 in Venice and was such a success that it was decided to create a biannual event and hold the second also in Venice. The intent in creating the conferences has been to provide an international forum appropriate for the exchange of results in research, development and applications which *extend* the scope of database technology. The conferences are designed to facilitate and extend communication among researchers and between academia and industry. They are also intended to be international level European conferences providing a high quality forum for the European database research community.

The program committee received 175 papers. These came from 28 different countries, the largest contributors being the USA, West Germany, France, Italy and the United Kingdom. A wide range of topics was covered, the most popular being object-oriented systems, database and AI, logic and databases, data structures and query processing. From these 175 papers, we had the difficult task of selecting 27 papers. We also selected an invited speaker, Carlo Zaniolo who addresses the issue of deductive databases and their transition from the technology development phase to the system implementation phase.

Two panels were chosen to address some of the most burning issues of the field, the impact of theory on systems in the past and in the future, chaired by David Maier, and the two "competing" fields of object-oriented databases and of deductive databases, chaired by Michele Missikoff.

We are extremely grateful to all the people who helped organize the conference: all the members of the organization committee, all the program committee members, Florence Deshors and Pauline Turcaud for their help in organizing the paper selection and program committee work, Philippe Richard and Paris Kanellakis who helped in the paper handling process.

François Bancilhon
Costantino Thanos
Dennis Tsichritzis

Sponsorship

Promoted by the EDBT Foundation
Sponsored by AFCET - AICA - BCS - ENEA - GI - Comitati Nazionali di Consulenza del CNR
In cooperation with ACM and IEEE
Under the patronage of the Italian Ministry for the University, Research and Technology, the Italian National Research Council, the Commission of European Communities, the Regional Government of Veneto, the University of Venice and UNESCO-ROSTE.

Organization

Conference Chairperson: *D. Tsichritzis (Université de Genève, Switzerland)*
Organization Committee Chairperson: *C. Thanos (IEI-CNR, Italy)*
Program Committee Chairperson: *F. Bancilhon (Altaïr, France)*
Technical exhibitions coordinator: *F. Bonfatti (CIOC-CNR, Italy)*
Tutorial coordinator: *D. Sacca (Universita della Calabria, Italy)*
Conference Secretariat: *M. Mennucci (IEI - CNR, Italy)*
CEC coordinator: *G. Metakides (CEC, Belgium)*
U.S. coordinator: *M. Brodie (GTE Laboratories, USA)*
Far East coordinator: *M. Yoshikawa (Kyoto Sangyo University, Japan)*
Local arrangements coordinator: *F. Dalla Libera (Universita di Venezia, Italy)*
Treasurer: *E. Ricciardi (IEI-CNR, Italy)*
Organization Committee Members : *M. Agostini (Italy), C. Freytag (FRG), K. G. Jeffery (United Kingdom), C. Rolland (France)*

Program Committee

S. Abiteboul (France)
M. Adiba (France)
H. Ait-Kaci (France)
F. Bancilhon (France)
C. Batini (Italy)
C. Bauzer-Medeiros (Brazil)
A. Berre (Norway)
H. Boral (USA)
M. Casanova (Brazil)
S. Ceri (Italy)
K. R. Dittrich (FRG)
C. Freytag (FRG)
G. Grahne (Finland)
T. Hadzilacos (Greece)
M. A. W. Houtsma (The Netherlands)
M. Jarke (FRG)
K. G. Jeffery (United Kingdom)
P. Kanellakis (USA)
M. L. Kersten (The Netherlands)
H. Korth (USA)
R. Kowalski (United Kingdom)
M. Lacroix (Belgium)
M. Leonard (Switzerland)
U. Lipeck (FRG)
P. Lockeman (FRG)
D. Maier (USA)
A. Meier (Switzerland)
A. Mendelzon (Canada)
M. Missikoff (Italy)
R. Morrison (United Kingdom)
G. T. Nguyen (France)
I. Paredaens (Belgium)
F. Rabitti (Italy)
R. Ramakrishnan (USA)
P. Richard (France)
C. Rolland (France)
D. Sacca (Italy)
Y. Sagiv (Israel)
H. Schek (FRG)
J. W. Schmidt (FRG)
O. Shmueli (Israel)
Y. Tanaka (Japan)
J. Ullman (USA)
P. Valduriez (France)
L. Vieille (FRG)
M. Yoshikawa (Japan)
A. V. Zamulin (USSR)
R. Zicari (Italy)

External Referees

C. V.D. Berg
C. Berrut
J. P. Bertrandias
M. F. Bruandet
S. Brass
A. L. Brown
H. J. Buikhardt
G. Cayres Magalhaes
C. Collet
R. C. H. Connor
M. Consens
B. Defude
A. Dearle
C. Delcourt
C. Delobel
U. Deppisch
D. DeWitt
N. Erol
T. Estier
G. Falquet
M. C. Fauvet
M. Freeston
J. P. Giraudin
O. Gruber
R. H. Guting
M. Hofmann
G. Hulin
Y. Ioannidis
M. Jeusfeld
P. Kipelainen
T. Kabas
M. Koubarakis
P. Lavency
C. Lécluse
E. Levy
C. de Maindreville
R. Manthey
H. Martin
F. Mc Cabe
C. Moss
H. B. Pane
M. Rafanelli
D. Rieu
A. Rifaut
T. Rose
J. Rosenberg
G. Saake
M. Sadler
F. Sadri
M. Sakkinen
L. Sbatella
M. H. Scholl
A. Siebes
E. Simon
S. Sippu
G. Speegle
S. Sripada
D. Srivastava
S. Sudarshan
M. Terranova
E. Ukkonen
M. Vanhoedenaghe
P. Velardi
F. Velez
V. Vianu
G. von Bueltzingsloewen
G. Weikum

Contents

Session 1: Opening

Session 2: Data Structures

Session 3: Data Models

Session 4: Deductive Database Systems

Session 5: Query Processing

Session 6: Complex Objects

Session 7: Database Programming Languages

Session 8: Panel

Session 9: Object-Oriented Systems

Session 10: Time, Object-Oriented and Active Systems

Session 11: Rules

Session 12: Panel

Session 11: Rule[illegible]

Deductive Databases–Theory Meets Practice

Carlo Zaniolo

MCC
3500 West Balcones Center Drive
Austin, Texas 78759
USA

Abstract

Deductive Databases are coming of age with the emergence of efficient and easy to use systems that support queries, reasoning, and application development on databases through declarative logic-based languages. Building on solid theoretical foundations, the field has benefited in the recent years form dramatic advances in the enabling technology. This progress is demonstrated by the completion of prototype systems offering such levels of generality, performance and robustness that they support well complex application development. Valuable know-how has emerged from the experience of building and using these systems: we have learned about algorithms and architectures for building powerful deductive database systems, and we begin to understand the programming environments and paradigms they are conducive to. Thus, several application areas have been identified where these systems are particularly effective, including areas well beyond the domain of traditional database applications. Finally, the design and deployment of deductive databases has provided new stimulus and a focus to further research into several fundamental issues. As a result, the theory of the field has made significant progress on topics such as semantic extensions to Horn logic and algorithms for compilation and optimization of declarative programs. Thus, a beneficial interaction between theory and practice remains one of the strengths of Deductive Databases as the field is entering the '90s and the age of technological maturity.

1 Background

Deductive Databases are coming of age with the emergence of efficient and easy to use systems that support *queries, reasoning*, and *application development* on databases through *declarative logic-based* languages.

Interest in the area of Deductive Databases began in the '70s, with most of the early work focusing on establishing the theoretical foundations for the field. An excellent review of this work and the beneficial impact that it had on various disciplines of computing, and the database area in particular, is given in [GMN]. Throughout the '70s and the first part of the '80s, concrete system implementations of these ideas were limited to few ground breaking experiments [Kell]. This situation contrasted quite dramatically with the significant system-oriented developments that were taking place at the same time in two fields very close to deductive databases. The first field was relational databases, where systems featuring logic-based query languages of good performance, but limited expressive power, were becoming very successful in the commercial world. The second field is Logic Programming, where successive generations of Prolog systems were demonstrating performance and effectiveness in a number of symbolic applications, ranging from compiler writing to expert systems.

A renewed interest in deductive database systems came about as a result of the flare-up of attention and publicity generated by the idea of Fifth Generation Computing. It was realized that the rule based reasoning of logic, combined with the capability of database systems of managing and efficiently storing and retrieving large amounts of information could provide the basis on which to build the next-generation of knowledge base systems. As a result, several projects were started that focused on extending Prolog systems with persistent secondary-based storage management facilities [RaSh] or on coupling Prolog with relational databases [JaCV, KuYo, Li, CeGW]. Several commercial systems are now available that support the coupling of SQL databases with Prolog or expert system shells. In particular, is the system described in [Boc, LeVi] provides close integration between Prolog and Database facilities, and smart algorithms for supporting recursive queries against the database.

Yet several other researchers were critical of the idea of using Prolog as a front-end to relational databases. In particular, it was noted that the sequential left-to right execution model of Prolog was a throw-back to navigational query languages used before relational systems. In relational systems, the user is primarily responsible for correct queries, and the system takes care of finding efficient sequencing of joins (query conjuncts), thus optimizing navigation through the database—a special module called the *query optimizer* sees to that [Seta]. In Prolog, instead, the programmer must carefully select the order of rules and of goals in the rules, since the correctness, efficiency and termination of the program depend on it. A second problem follows from the fact that efficient Prolog implementations are based on a abstract machine (WAM) and features (pointers) that rely on the assumption that data resides in main memory rather than secondary store [War]. Thus a number of research projects opted for an approach that builds more on extensions of relational database technology than on adaptations of Prolog technology. While several of these projects limited their interests to extending query languages with specific constructs such as rules and recursion, projects such as NAIL! [Meta] and $\mathcal{LDL}$ [Cetal, NaTs] feature declarative languages of expressive power comparable to Prolog. This paper recounts and summarizes the author's experience in designing, developing and deploying the $\mathcal{LDL}$ system.

2 Overview

The motivation for designing and building the $\mathcal{LDL}$ system was twofold:

- To provide support for advanced database applications, with a focus on expert systems and knowledge based applications.
- To provide better support for traditional database applications by integrating the application development and database queries into one language—thus solving the impedance mismatch problem.

A serious problem with current database applications is due to the limited power of languages such as SQL, whereby the programmer has to write most of the application in a procedural language with embedded calls to the query language. Since the computing paradigm of a procedural language, such as COBOL, is so different from the set-oriented declarative computation model of a relational language, an *impedance mismatch* occurs that hinders application development and can also cause slower execution [CoMa]. Realization of this problem has motivated a whole line of database research into new languages, commonly called *database languages* [BaBu]. The typical approach taken by previous researchers in database languages consisted in building into procedural languages constructs for accessing and manipulating databases [Sch77, RoSh]. Persistent languages, where the database is merely seen as an extension of the programming language, represent an extreme of this emphasis on programming languages. In a sharp departure from these approaches, $\mathcal{LDL}$ focuses on the query language, and extends it into a language powerful enough to support the development of applications of arbitrary complexity. Rather than extending current database query languages such SQL, however, $\mathcal{LDL}$ builds on the formal framework of Horn clause logic—a choice that had less to do with the well-known shortcomings of SQL, than with the influence of Prolog (a language based on Horn clause logic). In fact, we were impressed with the fact that this rule-based language was effective for writing symbolic applications and expert applications as well as being a powerful and flexible database query language [Zan1].

A closer examination on why Horn clauses represent such a desirable rule-based query language reveals the following reasons:

- Horn Clauses are akin to domain relational calculus [Ull], which offer two important advantages with respect to tuple calculus on which languages such as SQL are based—but the two calculi are known to be equivalent in terms of expressive power. One advantage is that domain calculus supports the expression of joins without explicit equality statements; the other is that lends itself to the visualization of queries —both benefits vividly demonstrated by QBE [Ull].
- Horn clauses support *recursion* and *complex terms* (through function symbols) thus eliminating two important limitations of relational query languages and systems.
- Horn clauses have a declarative semantics based on the equivalent notions of minimal model and least fixpoint [Llo, vEKo].
- Horn clauses can also be used effectively as a navigational query language.

As the last two points suggest, Horn clauses can be used effectively as either a declarative query language or navigational one [Zan1]. In the declarative interpretation of Horn Clauses, the order of goals in a rule is unimportant (much in the same way in which the order of conjuncts in a relational query is immaterial). The navigational interpretation of Horn clauses follows from the operational semantics of Prolog. Under this interpretation, goals are executed respectively in a left-to-right order, and the programmer is basically entrusted with the task of using this information to write terminating and efficient programs. For instance, when the goals denote database relations, the order defines a navigation through the database records; the programmer must carefully select the best navigation, e.g., one that takes advantage of access structures and limits the size of intermediate results.

A most critical decision in designing $\mathcal{LDL}$ was to follow the path of relational systems and build on the declarative semantics, rather than on the operational interpretation of Horn clauses. This approach was considered to be superior in terms of data independence and ease of use. Indeed this approach enables the user to concentrate on the meaning of programs, while the system is now entrusted with ordering goals and rules for efficient and safe executions. A further step toward declarative semantics was taken by freeing the user from the concern of whether forward chaining or backward chaining should be used in executing a set of rules. Current expert system shells frequently support only one of these two strategies; when they provide for both, they leave to the programmer the selection of the proper strategy for the problem at hand and its encoding as part of the program. In $\mathcal{LDL}$, the actual implementation is largely based on a forward chaining strategy which is more suitable for database applications [Ceta2]. But the compiler has also the capability of using rule rewrite methods, such as the magic set method or the counting method [BMSU, SaZ1, SaZ2], to mimic backward chaining through a bottom-up computation. Thus the $\mathcal{LDL}$ user is also provided automatically by the system with the functionality and performance benefits of backward chaining. This substantial progress toward declarative programming represents one of the most significant contributions to the technology of rule-based systems brought about by the research on deductive database systems in the recent years.

Another major area of progress for deductive databases is that of semantics. Indeed many other constructs beyond Horn clauses are needed in a language such as $\mathcal{LDL}$ to support application development. In particular, $\mathcal{LDL}$ includes constructs supporting the following notions:

- Negation [ApBW, Naq, Przl],
- Sets, including grouping and nested relations [BNST, ShTZ],
- Updates [NaKr, KNZ]
- Don't-care non-determinism [KrN1].

Most of these constructs (excluding set terms) are also in Prolog—they were added because they were needed for writing actual applications. But, in Prolog, their semantics is largely based on Prolog's operational model. Therefore, a major challenge of the $\mathcal{LDL}$ research was to define a formal declarative semantics for these constructs, in a way that naturally extends the declarative semantics of Horn clauses. The problem of extending the power of declarative logic is in fact the second main area of recent advances promoted by research in deductive databases. Of particular interest is the fact that many open problems in knowledge representation and non-monotonic reasoning have been given a clearer definition, and in some cases brought close a solution by these new advances [MaSu, Prz2]

The combined challenge of designing a powerful and expressive language, with declarative semantics, and efficient techniques for compilation and optimization describes the whole first phase of $\mathcal{LDL}$ research. This began in mid 1984, and culminated in the implementation of the first prototype at the end of 1987. This prototype compile $\mathcal{LDL}$ into a relational algebra based language FAD for a parallel database machine [Bor]. Rule rewriting methods, such as magic set and counting, were used to map recursive programs into equivalent ones that can be supported efficiently and safely by fixpoint iterations [BMSU, SaZ1, SaZ2]. A description of this system is given in [Ceta1].

The implementation of the first $\mathcal{LDL}$ prototype confirmed the viability of the new technology, but did little to transfer this technology from the laboratory to actual users, since FAD is only available on an expensive parallel machine. Seeking a better vehicle for technology transfer, a new prototype system was designed with the following characteristics:

- Portability,
- Efficiency,
- Open System Architecture.

This effort produced a portable and efficient $\mathcal{LDL}$ system under UNIX, called *SALAD*. [1] This implementation assumes a single-tuple, get-next interface between the compiled $\mathcal{LDL}$ program and the underlying fact manager (record manager). This provides for more flexible execution modes than those provided by relational algebra [Ceta1, Zan1]. The new design yields better performance, since the optimizer can now take advantage of different execution modes, and the compiler can cut out redundant work in situations where intelligent backtracking or existential optimization can be used [CGK2, RaBK]. *SALAD* includes a fact manager for a database residing in virtual memory that supports efficient access to the complex and variable record structures provided in $\mathcal{LDL}$. By using *C* as an intermediate target language and an open system architecture, *SALAD* ensures portability, support for modules, and for external procedures written in procedural languages—including controlled access by these routines to internal *SALAD* objects.

The *SALAD* prototype was completed in November 1988, and has undergone improvements and extensions during 1989. By the end of 1989, the system includes a fully functional optimizer, a powerful symbolic debugger with answer justification capability and an X-windows interface. The availability of *SALAD* led to the writing of significant applications and to the emergence of an $\mathcal{LDL}$ programming style. It was found that, in addition to supporting well database applications, $\mathcal{LDL}$ is effective as a rule-based system for rapid prototyping of applications in the *C* environment. Also in 1989, a complete description of the $\mathcal{LDL}$ language with sample applications appeared at bookstores [NaTs], and the first executable copies of *SALAD* were given to universities for experimentation.

I interpret these events as signs of a maturing technology. But, in the end, only the level of satisfaction experienced by users with *SALAD* or similar systems can confirm or disprove my claim that deductive databases are coming of age. To promote this goal, however, this paper will summarize the highlights of my experience with the $\mathcal{LDL}$ system, hoping that the readers will be enticed to experiment with it and then become enthusiastic users of the system. Therefore, the paper focuses on the functionality and usability aspects of the system. The reader interested in the architecture and enabling technology is referred to a recent overview [Ceta2]

3 Declarative Programming and Debugging

A declarative semantics for rules offer several advantages over the operational one, including the following ones:

[1]SALAD—System for Advanced Logical Applications on Data.

- Naturalness,
- Expressive Power,
- Reusability and Data Independence.

Frequently, the most natural definition of a programming object is inductive. For instance, the following $\mathcal{LDL}$ program defines all the integers between zero and K, using Peano's inductive definition (zero is an integer and if J is an integer, so is J+1).

```
int(K,0).
int(K,J) ← int(K,I), I< K, J = I+1.
```

The $\mathcal{LDL}$ compiler has no problem turning this definition into an efficient fixpoint iteration. This pair of rules, or any one obtained by scrambling the order of their goals, cannot be supported by any interpreter or compiler implementing the backward chaining strategy. For instance, in Prolog the user must be go through some interesting contortions to recast this program to fit the operational model.

As the next example, consider the situation where there is a binary tree of atoms. For instance a tree with leaves a and b will be represented by the complex term `tree(a, b)`. Associated with the leaf nodes of a tree there is a weight represented by facts such as

```
node(a, 1).
node(aa, 2).
node(ab, 3).
```

The weight of a tree is inductively defined as the sum of the weights of its two subtrees. We want now to define all the trees with weight less than a certain M. Immediately from these definitions we derive the following rules.

```
w(N, W, M) ← node(N, W), W < M.
w(tree(T1,T2), W, M) ← w(T1,W1), w(T2, W2), W = W1+W2, W < M.
```

This simple definition is not implementable with backward chaining and, unlike the previous example, we do not know of any set of rules that will support this predicate well in Prolog (assuming that the weights of the nodes are not known before hand). While forward chaining is the preferred strategy for these two examples, there are many situations where backward chaining is instead the only reasonable strategy. For instance, say that a tree is at hand and its weight must be computed, as per the the following query goal (where 10000 denotes a value high enough not to be a factor in the computation).

? w(tree(aa,tree(a,ab)), X, 10000).

In this situation, the $\mathcal{LDL}$ compiler simply mimics backward chaining by the use of a rewriting method—the efficient counting method in this particular case [SaZ3]. What is most important here is that the program has not changed. The same program works for different situations and the compiler/optimizer takes care of matching the actual execution method to the problem at hand. The final result is a level of reusability of programs that is well beyond that of Prolog programs. The elimination of cuts, replaced by the `choice` and `if-then-else` constructs, is also very beneficial in terms of reusability [Zan1]. The concept of reusability for database programs is an extension of the notion of data independence, defined as the ability of queries and applications to survive changes in the database physical organization. In relational databases the key instrument in delivering data independence is the optimizer. In $\mathcal{LDL}$ the optimizer ensures data independence, reusability of code and economy of programming, since the user can call the same module or predicate with different set of bindings.

The previous example was inspired by an Alkane Molecules generation problem [Tsur] that was first proposed to illustrate the power of functional languages. The same problem was quite easily formulated in $\mathcal{LDL}$ due to the ability of expressing inductive definitions and to the ease of checking equivalent structures while avoiding cyclic loops, discussed next. Semantically the structures previously discussed are unordered trees. Thus, a given tree is equivalent to those obtained by recursively exchanging the left subtree with the right one. Equivalence can be expressed by following set of rules:

```
eq(T, T).
eq(tree(T1,T2), tree(T2,T3)) ← eq(T3, T1).
```

Thus two trees are equivalent, if they are equal or if their subtrees have been exchanged and possibly replaced with equivalent ones. The problem is that the composition of several exchanges can return the original structure, and the SLD-resolution will cycle. Thus in Prolog the programmer has to carry around a bag of previous solutions and check for cycles at the cost of inefficiency of programming and execution. In $\mathcal{LDL}$ instead, the system can deal with cycles automatically and efficiently. This feature is particularly important in situations involving negations, since it is the key to a complete realization of stratified negation which avoids the floundering problem of negation by failure [Prz1, Llo].

One of the most interesting aspects of programming with a declarative language is debugging. Any trace-based debugger would be a little use in $\mathcal{LDL}$ since the optimizer rearranges the rules to a point that they do not resemble the original program. On the other hand, the logical nature of the system makes it possible to explain and justify the answers, and thus support a truly logical debugger. The current $\mathcal{LDL}$ system provides logical debugging and answer justification capabilities as sophisticated as those of any expert shell or rule-based system available today.

The conceptual basis for the logical debugger consists in combined `why` and `whynot` explanation capabilities, whereby the system carries out a conversation with the user explaining why a certain answer was returned, and why another was not returned.

Thus to a user asking

```
why eq(tree(a, tree(b,c)), tree(a, tree(c,b)).
```

the system will return the instantiated rule that produced it:

```
eq(tree(a, tree(b,c)), tree(a, tree(c,b))) ← eq(tree(c,b),tree(b,c)).
```

If the user is still not convinced and ask

```
eq(tree(c,b),tree(b,c)).
```

then the system returns the unit clause `eq(c,c)`.

In the `whynot` interaction, the user asks an explanation on why some tuple was not returned. This capability is needed for supporting why answers in rules with negation, and yields a level of reasoning about programs which is not possible with traditional debuggers. For instance, if the user ask the question

```
whynot eq(tree(tree(a,b) ,c)), tree(tree(b,a), c))).
```

then, the system request the user to point out the rule that should have produced this answer. When the user does so, the system tries to instantiate this rule. In our example, the user will probably point out the second rule; then, the system reports back that no instantiation is possible since `T2` cannot be unified with both `tree(a,b)` and `tree(b,a)`. That identifies the problem: the given rules do not capture the correct notion of unordered tree.

This was not a contrived example: I had actually written the program above, and, in a attempt to save a rule, combined the switching of arguments and the recursive equivalence of the subtrees into one rule. Only through the debugger I was able to recognize my mistake (which can be fixed by either adding a new `eq` goal or an additional rule). Exploring $\mathcal{LDL}$ programs with the logical debugger is indeed a very interesting experience—further enhanced by an X-window based visualization capability.

4 Open System Architecture

An $\mathcal{LDL}$ program calling a graphic routine or a windowing system calling an $\mathcal{LDL}$ program are two concrete examples that motivated the open system architecture of the system. This architecture also follows from the realization that the combination of a high-level declarative language with a procedural language frequently offers the greatest flexibility and effectiveness in actual applications. Typical situations where this bilingual programming paradigm is useful are as follows:

- *Building on existing software.* Existing libraries are often at hand for performing specific tasks, including computation-intensive operations such as graphics or Fast Fourier Transforms. The natural solution consists in importing these routines into $\mathcal{LDL}$ applications while preserving $\mathcal{LDL}$ amenities such as safety and optimization.

- *Rapid prototyping and hot spot refinement.* As many rule-base systems, $\mathcal{LDL}$ is a good vehicle for the rapid prototyping of applications. Large applications can be easily developed and modified until their functionality and behavior satisfy specifications and clients' requirements. Once this validation is completed, the programmer can turn his attention to the performance problem by identifying the *hot spots.* These are predicates or segments of the $\mathcal{LDL}$ program that, because of taking too long to execute and being executed very often, slow down the execution of the whole program. Then the programmer can re-code these hot spots for efficiency, using a procedural language, such as C.

- *Extensibility.* It is often convenient to use higher order predicates or metalevel predicates. These are not provided as part of $\mathcal{LDL}$; however they can be written as external procedures, say in C. Since external procedures can be given access to the internal objects of *SALAD* and can be made behave exactly as $\mathcal{LDL}$ predicates, this becomes a very effective way to add new built-ins.

Support for an open architecture required the following components to be provided [CGK1]:

1. $\mathcal{LDL}$ language extensions to allow external predicates,
2. An optimization strategy and optimizer extensions to deal with external predicates,
3. Run time interfaces between $\mathcal{LDL}$ and external procedures.

There are actually two kinds of external procedures recognized by $\mathcal{LDL}$. The first kind are *external functions*, which are traditional procedures written in languages such as *C* or FORTRAN that are simply imported by statements such as:

```
import strlen($Str:  string, Len:integer) from C.
```

Then an $\mathcal{LDL}$ rule to select strings of length greater than 80 can be written as follows:

```
long_atom(Str) <- strlen(Str , Len), Len > 80.
```

The second kind of external procedures are *external predicates* which, although written in languages such as *C* or FORTRAN, behave as $\mathcal{LDL}$ predicates: they can fail or return more than one solution. External predicates can manipulate all internal *SALAD* objects, including sets, complex terms and relations. Thus, when invoking an external predicate, the calling $\mathcal{LDL}$ program initializes a temporary relation which is passed to the external procedure. This adds the computed results to the relation, and returns control to $\mathcal{LDL}$ that reads the tuples of this relation as from any other internal relation. Likewise, by creating a temporary relation and calling an $\mathcal{LDL}$ precompiled module, conventional programs can also call $\mathcal{LDL}$. Of course, an impedance mismatch between the procedural language and the underlying system could be a problem for the last situation. This is not the case for the previous situations, where the external module becomes completely integrated into $\mathcal{LDL}$.

The main problem with an open architecture, is to have the optimizer "understand" external predicates and use them effectively in optimization. The first problem, dealing with safety, is directly handled through the notion of finiteness constraint, whereby the finiteness of an argument implies the finiteness of others. For instance in the previous `strlen` relation, the finiteness of the first argument implies that of the second. This information is directly extracted from the `import` statement and used by the optimizer in creating a safe ordering of goals. In order to predict and minimize the execution cost, the optimizer uses descriptors characterizing the selectivity, fan-out and cost of the external predicates. The user has to supply this information that can be deduced either from known properties of the external procedure, or from some experimental runs [CGK1]

An interesting example of the benefits offered by this architecture, is the problem of coupling $\mathcal{LDL}$ with an SQL database. Basically, precompiled SQL modules can simply be imported as externals into $\mathcal{LDL}$. The $\mathcal{LDL}$ system views each precompiled query as another computed relation. Once the usual information about finiteness constraints, cost, selectivity and fan-out is given, the system deal with it without any further complication (at least in those SQL systems where this information is easy to access). The simplicity of this task contrasts with the challenges encountered by various projects coupling Prolog with SQL [JaCV, Boc]. A more interesting problem, which we are now investigating, consists in taking a pure $\mathcal{LDL}$ program using SQL schema relations and translate it into a mixure of $\mathcal{LDL}$ rules and SQL statements. This involves translation of segments of $\mathcal{LDL}$ programs into equivalent SQL queries, and extensions to the $\mathcal{LDL}$ optimizer to determine optimum load sharing between the $\mathcal{LDL}$ front-end and the SQL back-end.

4.1 $\mathcal{LDL}$ Applications

In the end, the utility of the $\mathcal{LDL}$ technology can only be assessed through application development. We first experimented with traditional applications, such as parts explosion, inventory control and job shop scheduling, which are currently implemented by a procedural application program with embedded query calls. Our experience with these applications, has been uniformly positive: we found them easy to write and maintain and extend using $\mathcal{LDL}$. As a result, we moved to more advanced applications, in areas beyond those of traditional DBMSs. Next, we discuss two new areas of particular interest, *data dredging* and *harnessing software*.

4.1.1 Data Dredging

The paradigm that we will describe in this section includes a large class of scientific and engineering problems. The source of the data is typically a large volume of low-level records, collected from the measurement or the monitoring of some empirical process or a system simulation. The objective is to ascertain whether this data lends support to certain abstract concepts where, conceptually, *the level of abstraction of the concepts may be far-removed from the level at which the data was collected.* The procedure adopted to meet the objective is as follows:

1. Formulate hypothesis or concept;

2. Translate (1) into an $\mathcal{LDL}$ rule-set and query;

3. Execute query against the given data and observe the results;

4. If the results do not verify or deny (1) then, reformulate and goto (2); otherwise exit.

Obviously, the decision to exit the process is entirely subjective and is decided by the programmer. At this stage he/she may have either decided that the concept is now properly defined or, that the data does not support this concept and that it should be abandoned or tried out with different data. The use of $\mathcal{LDL}$ over procedural languages offered the advantage of supporting the formulation at a more abstract level where the "iteration time" through reformulations is significantly shortened. With respect to existing database query languages, $\mathcal{LDL}$ supported a more natural expression of higher and higher levels of abstraction via rules, and the ease of incorporating efficient C-based routines for the filtering and preprocessing of low-level data—a demonstration of the two languages programming paradigm. These benefits were observed in experiments with data dredging in two different domains: computer system performance evaluation and scientific data analysis in the area of Molecular Biology. The first application [NaTs] involved the formulation of the "convoy" concept in a distributed computing system. Intuitively, a convoy is a subset of the system entities (processes, tasks) that move together for some time from one node to the other in the network of processors and queues. The recorded data is low-level and consists of arrival/departure records of individual entities at certain nodes. The convoy concept was defined in $\mathcal{LDL}$ using a small set of rules, and actual instances were detected in the simulation data that were used. The second instance of data dredging—performed in collaboration with researchers from the Harvard Medical School and the Argonne National Laboratories—involves the identification of DNA sequences from (very) low-level, digitized autoradiographs, that record the results of the experiments that are performed in the sequencing of the *E.Coli* bacteria [GENE88]. Again, the task is to extract the definitions for the four DNA bases *A*,*C*,*G*,*T* from this low-level, noisy and often imperfect data. Thus, the interpretation proceeds in two phases:

1. An *alignment phase* during which the raw, digitized data is brought to a common base value and smoothed, using standard signal-processing techniques.

2. An *interpretation phase* during which the aligned data is interpreted, using a set of domain-specific heuristics.

This is a good example of the use of the dual language programming paradigm, since the first phase is best supported by procedural routines, mostly library ones, and the second part requires a high-level rule-based language. In fact, a large number of heuristics need to be applied in this case and the use of $\mathcal{LDL}$ has the additional advantage that it is simple to add special definitions, that need to be used within narrow contexts, to the general definitions. It is thus relatively simple to add additional knowledge to the system as the experience with its use increases. The problem just described can also be viewed as that of writing an expert application to do gel-interpretation. However, the approach is more data-driven than in a typical expert application: the focus has been on extracting knowledge from data, rather than capturing human expertise in the area.

4.1.2 Harnessing Software

We mentioned that external *C* procedures can be used in the definition of $\mathcal{LDL}$ programs. In the $\mathcal{LDL}$ context, these are regarded as evaluable predicates. While normally we expect the use of external code to be the exception rather than the rule (reserved for special purposes e.g., graphical routines), we can think of situations that lay at the other extreme: the bulk of the software is written in standard, procedural code and only a small fraction of it is rule-based and encoded in $\mathcal{LDL}$. In this situation the rule-set forms the "harness" around which the bulk of the code is implemented. The rule portion forms a knowledge base that contains:

1. The definition of each of the C-module types used in the system.

2. A rule set that defines the various ways in which modules can be combined: inheritance and export/import relationships between modules, constraints on their combinations, etc.

The advantage of this organization becomes apparent in information systems where most new service requests can be supported by building on a Lego-set of basic, reusable modules. The knowledge base and rule-based harness externally encode the logic of module interaction and subsets of instances of the existing module types can now be recombined, subject to the rule-restrictions, to support different task-specifications. An added advantage is that each of the individual module-types can be verified using any of the existing verification methods and their global behavior is controlled by the rule-set. We are currently experimenting with such an application in the domain of banking software.

5 Looking Ahead

Coming of age also means having to accept the limitations of reality. Foremost among these is that the novelty of a technology and the soundness of the underlying theory will not ensures the acceptance a new system or, even less, or a new paradigm for application development. For acceptance, there must be commercial potential, and obvious benefits to the users— the theory must meet practice. Perhaps the most significant aspect of $\mathcal{LDL}$ research is a serious determination of bridging the gap between theory and practice. This is demonstrated by the fact that a team of six to eight people with a wide spectrum of interests and backgrounds—from very theoretical ones to very applied ones—closely collaborated during the last five years in the design and implementation effort. The result is a system that supports the declarative semantics of $\mathcal{LDL}$ and its underlying theory completely and efficiently.

An healthy interaction between theory and practice remains a distinctive mark of some of the most recent developments in $\mathcal{LDL}$. On the theory side, the focus is still on defining key semantic concepts, in areas such as negation and non-monotonic logic [SaZ3], higher order extensions [KrN2], and support for object identity and inheritance [Zan3, BNS]. In the longer term, we expect many of these concepts will become an integral par of the next generation of deductive database systems. The shorter term focus, however, is on deploying the current technology and on developing application areas particularly suitable for deductive databases. Among these we find the area of rapid prototyping and development development of applications—an important area poorly served by existing systems. In fact, the most popular use of rapid prototyping relies on SQL, often enhanced with 4GL facilities [CoSh, DM89, Gane]. Because of its power, open architecture, and support of Knowledge based programming, $\mathcal{LDL}$ can be used in this role much more effectively than SQL, which has obvious the functionality limitations. To further extend the capabilities of the $\mathcal{LDL}$ system in this domain, we are enhancing its environment, (e.g., by providing a standard interface to SQL databases) and addressing the ease-of-use problem. In terms of ease of use, the challenge is not doing better than SQL. Standard relational queries are normally easier to express in $\mathcal{LDL}$ than in SQL. The real research challenge is make it easier and more natural to express the much more complex applications which can now be written in $\mathcal{LDL}$; e.g., those which require complex terms and non-linear recursion. We are currently exploring with the use of visualization, since Horn clauses provide a good conceptual basis on which to support visual programming and debugging. Clearly the conceptual task of solving a complex problem will remain complex; but we expect that the task of coding or debugging the solutions can be greatly facilitated by these interfaces. Our first experience with a visual debugger is encouraging in this respect.

Acknowledgments

The author would like to recognize the following persons for their contribution to the $\mathcal{LDL}$ project: Brijesh Agarwal, Danette Chimenti, François Bancilhon, Ruben Gamboa, Fosca Giannotti, Charles Kellogg, Ravi Krishnamurthy, Tony O'Hare, Shamim Naqvi, Kayliang Ong, Oded Shmueli, Leona Slepetis, Carolyn West, and, last but not least, Shalom Tsur on whose work the section on Applications is based.

References

[ApBW] Apt, K., H. Blair, A. Walker, "Towards a Theory of Declarative Knowledge," in Foundations of Deductive Databases and Logic Programming, (Minker, J. ed.), Morgan Kaufman, Los Altos, 1987.

[BaBu] Bancilhon, F. and P. Buneman (eds.), "Workshop on Database Programming Languages," Roscoff, Finistere, France, Sept. 87.

[BNS] Beeri, C., R. Nasr and S.Tsur, "Embedding *psi*-terms in a Horn-clause Logic Language", *Procs. Third Int. Conf. on Data and Knowledge Bases—improving usability and responsiveness*, Jersualem, June 28-30, pp. 347-359, 1989

[Bor] Boral, H. "Parallelism in Bubba," Proc. Int. Symposium on Databases in Parallel and Distributed Systems, Austin, Tx, Dec. 1988.

[BNST] Beeri C., S. Naqvi, O. Shmueli, and S. Tsur. "Set Constructors in a Logic Database Language", to appear in the Journal of Logic Programming.

[BMSU] Bancilhon, F., D. Maier, Y. Sagiv, J. Ullman, "Magic sets and other strange ways to implement logic programs", Proc. 5th ACM SIGMOD-SIGACT Symp. on Principles of Database Systems, 1986.

[Boc] Bocca, J., "On the Evaluation Strategy of Educe," Proc. 1986 ACM-SIGMOD Conference on Management of Data, pp. 368–378, 1986.

[Ceta1] Chimenti, D. et al., "An Overview of the LDL System," Database Engineering Bulletin, Vol. 10, No. 4, pp. 52-62, 1987.

[Ceta2] Chimenti, D. et al., "The LDL System Prototype," IEEE Journal on Data and Knowledge Engineering, March 1990.

[CeGW] Ceri, S., G. Gottlob and G. Wiederhold, "Interfacing Relational Databases and Prolog Efficiently," Expert Database Systems, L. Kerschberg (ed.), Benjamin/Cummings, 1987.

[CG89] Chimenti, D. and R. Gamboa. "The *SALAD* Cookbook: A User's Guide," MCC Technical Report No. ACA-ST-064-89.

[CGK1] Chimenti, D., R. Gamboa and R. Krishnamurthy. "Towards an Open Architecture for LDL," Proc. 15th VLDB, pp. 195-203, 1989.

[CGK2] Chimenti, D., R. Gamboa and R. Krishnamurthy, "Abstract Machine for LDL," Proc. 2nd Int. Conf on Extending Database Technology, EDBT'90, Venice, Italy, 1990.

[CoMa] Copeland, G. and Maier D., "Making SMALLTALK a Database System," Proc. ACM SIGMOD Int. Conf. on Management of Data, pp. 316–325, 1985.

[CoSh] Connell, J.L. and Shafer, L.B., "Structured Rapid Prototyping", Prentice Hall, 1989.

[DM89] "The Rapid Prototyping Conundrum", DATAMATION, June 1989.

[Fost] Foster, R.K. "Feature Comparison of LDL and SQL", Control Data Corporation Interoffice Memorandum, March 23, 1987.

[Gane] Gane, C. "Rapid System Development," Prentice Hall, 1989.

[GMN] Gallaire, H.,J. Minker and J.M. Nicolas,"Logic and Databases: a Deductive Approach," Computer Surveys, Vol. 16, No. 2, 1984.

[GENE88] R. Herdman, et al. "MAPPING OUR GENES Genome Projects: How Big, How Fast?" Congress of the United States, Office of Technology Assessment. The John Hopkins University Press, 1988.

[JaCV] Jarke, M., J. Clifford and Y. Vassiliou, "An Optimizing Prolog Front End to a Relational Query System," Proc. 1984 ACM-SIGMOD Conference on Management of Data, pp. 296–306, 1986.

[Kell] Kellogg, C., "A Practical Amalgam of Knowledge and Data Base Technology" Proc. of AAAI Conference, Pittsburg, Pa., 1982.

[KNZ] Krishnamurthy, S. Naqvi and Zaniolo, "Database Transactions in $\mathcal{LDL}$", Proc. Logic Programming North American Conference 1989, pp. 795-830, MIT Press, 1989.

[KrN1] Krishnamurthy and S. Naqvi, "Non-Deterministic Choice in Datalog," Proc. 3rd Int. Conf. on Data and Knowledge Bases, June 27–30, Jerusalem, Israel.

[KrN2] Krishnamurthy and S. Naqvi, "Towards a Real Horn Clause Language," Proc. 1988 VLDB Conference, Los Angeles, California, August 1988.

[KrZa] Krishnamurthy, R. and C. Zaniolo, "Optimization in a Logic Based language for Knowledge and Data Intensive Applications," in Advances in Database Technology, EDBT'88, (Schmidt, Ceri and Missikoff, Eds), pp. 16–33, Springer-Verlag 1988.

[KuYo] Kunifji S., H. Yokota, "Prolog and Relational Databases for 5th Generation Computer Systems," in Advances in Logic and Databases, Vol. 2 (Gallaire, Minker and Nicolas eds.), Plenum, New York, 1984.

[Li] Li, D. "A Prolog Database System," Research Institute Press, Letchworth, Hertfordshire, U.K., 1984

[LeVi] Lefebvre, A. and Vieille, L. "On Deductive Query Evaluation in the DedGin System," Proc. 1st Int. Conf. on Deductive and O-O Databases, Dec. 4-6, 1989, Kyoto, Japan.

[Llo] Lloyd, J. W., Foundations of Logic Programming, Springer Verlag, (2nd Edition), 1987.

[MaSu] Marek, V. and V.S. Subramanian, "The Relationship between Logic Program Semantics and Non-Monotonic Reasoning," Proc. 6th Int. Conference on Logic Programming, pp. 598-616, MIT Press, 1989.

[Meta] Morris, K. et al. "YAWN! (Yet Another Window on NAIL!), Data Engineering, Vol.10, No. 4, pp. 28–44, Dec. 1987.

[Mi68] Michie, D. "'Memo' Functions and Machine Learning" in Nature, April 1968.

[NaKr] Naqvi, S. and R. Krishnamurthy, "Semantics of Updates in logic Programming", Proc. 7th ACM SIGMOD–SIGACT Symp. on Principles of Database Systems, pp. 251–261, 1988.

[Naq] Naqvi, S. "A Logic for Negation in Database Systems," in Foundations of Deductive Databases and Logic Programming, (Minker, J. ed.), Morgan Kaufman, Los Altos, 1987.

[NaTs] S. Naqvi, and S. Tsur. "A Logical Language for Data and Knowledge Bases," W. H. Freeman Publ., 1989.

[Przl] Przymusinski, T., "On the Semantics of Stratified Deductive Databases and Logic Programs", in Foundations of Deductive Databases and Logic Programming, (Minker, J. ed.), Morgan Kaufman, Los Altos, 1987.

[Prz2] Przymusinski, T., "Non-Monotonic Formalism and Logic Programming," Proc. 6th Int. Conference on Logic Programming, pp. 656-674, MIT Press, 1989.

[RaBK] Ramakrishnan, R., C. Beeri and Krishnamurthy, "Optimizing Existential Datalog Queries," Proc. 7th ACM SIGMOD–SIGACT Symp. on Principles of Database Systems, pp. 89–102, 1988.

[RaSh] Ramamohanarao, K. and J. Sheperd, "Answering Queries in Deductive Databases", Proc. 4th Int. Conference on Logic Programming, pp. 1014-1033, MIT Press, 1987.

[RoSh] Rowe, L. and K.A. Shones, "Data Abstraction, Views and Updates in RIGEL", Proc. ACM SIGMOD Int. Conf. on Management of Data, pp. 71-81, 1979.

[SaZ1] Saccá D., Zaniolo, C., "Implementation of Recursive Queries for a Data Language based on Pure Horn Logic," Proc. Fourth Int. Conference on Logic Programming, Melbourne, Australia, 1987.

[SaZ2] Saccá D., Zaniolo, C., "The Generalized Counting Method for Recursive Logic Queries," Journal of Theoretical Computer Science, 61, 1988.

[SaZ3] Saccá D., Zaniolo, C., "Stable Models and Non-Determinism in Logic Programs with Negation," MCC Tech. Rep., ACT-ST-202, 1989.

[Sch77] Schmidt, J., "Some High Level Language Constructs for Data of Type Relations", ACM Transactions on Database Systems, 2(3), pp. 140-173, 1977.

[Seta] Selinger, P.G. et al. "Access Path Selection in a Relational Database Management System," Proc. ACM SIGMOD Int. Conf. on Management of Data, 1979.

[ShNa] Shmueli, O. and S. Naqvi, "Set Grouping and Layering in Horn Clause Programs," Proc. of 4th Int. Conf. on Logic Programming, pp. 152–177, 1987.

[ShTZ] Shmueli, O., S. Tsur and C. Zaniolo, "Rewriting of Rules Containing Set Terms in a Logic Data Language (LDL)," Proc. 7th ACM SIGMOD-SIGACT Symp. on Principles of Database Systems, pp. 15–28, 1988.

[Tsur] Tsur S., "Applications of Deductive Database Systems," Proc. IEEE COMCON Spring '90 Conf., San Francisco, Feb 26-March 2.

[Ull] Ullman, J.D., Database and Knowledge-Based Systems, Vols I and II, Computer Science Press, Rockville, Md., 1989.

[vEKo] van Emden, M.H., Kowalski, R., "The semantics of Predicate Logic as a Programming Language", JACM 23, 4, 1976, pp. 733–742.

[War] Warren, D.H.D., "An Abstract Prolog Instruction Set," Tech. Note 309, AI Center, Computer Science and Technology Div., SRI, 1983.

[Zan1] Zaniolo, C. "Prolog: a database query language for all seasons," in Expert Database Systems, Proc. of the First Int. Workshop L. Kerschberg (ed.), Benjamin/Cummings, 1986.

[Zan2] Zaniolo, C. "Design and implementation of a logic based language for data intensive applications. *Proceedings of the International Conference on Logic Programming*, Seattle, 1988.

[Zan3] Zaniolo, C. "Object Identity and Inheritance in Deductive Databases: an Evolutionary Approach," Proc. 1st Int. Conf. on Deductive and O-O Databases, Dec. 4-6, 1989, Kyoto, Japan.

An Adaptive Overflow Technique for B-trees *

(Extended Abstract)

Ricardo A. Baeza-Yates

Departamento de Ciencias de la Computación
Universidad de Chile
Casilla 2777, Santiago, CHILE

Abstract

We present a new overflow technique for the B-tree. The technique is a hybrid of partial expansions and unbalanced splits. This technique is asymmetric and adaptive. Considering a growing file (only insertions), the storage utilization is 77% for random keys, 70% for sorted keys, and over 75% for non-uniform distributed keys. Similar results are achieved when we have deletions mixed with insertions. One of the main properties of this technique is that the storage utilization is very stable with respect to changes of the data distribution. This technique may be used for other bucket-based file structures, like extendible hashing or bounded disorder files.

1 Introduction

The B^+-tree is one of the most widely used file organizations. In a B^+-tree all the information is stored at the lowest level (*buckets*), and the upper levels are a B-tree index. File growth is handled by bucket splitting, that is, when a bucket overflows, a new bucket is allocated and half of the records from the overflowing bucket are moved to the new bucket.

*This work was supported by an Ontario Graduate Scholarship.

This provides a worst-case utilization of 50%, and an average utilization of 69% for random keys [Yao78].

To improve the storage utilization, several overflow techniques have been proposed. The most important are the so-called B*-method [BM72] and the method of partial expansions [Lom87]. In the B*-method, if a bucket overflows, we scan the right or left brother to see if there is any free space. If so, we move one key to that node. Otherwise, we split two full buckets into three buckets. This provides a minimum storage utilization of 67% in a growing file. However, the number of accesses during an insertion increases substantially (30% in most cases).

On the other hand, the method of partial expansions uses different bucket sizes. The idea is to increase the size of the overflowing bucket instead of splitting it. When the maximum size is reached, we split the bucket into two buckets of minimum size. In practice, only two bucket sizes are used with the ratio of sizes being 2/3. As in B*, this provides a minimum storage utilization of 67%, but without substantially increasing the insertion time[1]. However, disk space management is more difficult, because of the two bucket sizes. On average, low external fragmentation can be achieved [BYL89].

In this paper we introduce an overflow technique that also uses different bucket sizes, but performs unbalanced splits. The main feature of this method is that it is *adaptive* and very stable. This method results in approximately the same storage utilization for arbitrary data. Although storage utilization is slightly lower than that of previous overflow methods, the insertion time is better than in the B* case, and disk space management is simpler and more stable than in partial expansions. Table 1 shows a comparison the complexities involved.

---

[1]We assume that the seek time of an access is much bigger than the transfer time, thus the size of the bucket is not relevant.

Technique	Storage Utilization			Acc. per Insertion
	Worst case	Random Data	Sorted Data	(20000 keys)
Simple	.50	.69	.50	3.6
B^*	.67	.81	.67	4.7
Partial Expansions	.67	.81	.67	3.4
Adaptive ($\alpha = .68$)	.50	.76	.68	3.7
Adaptive ($\alpha = .75$)	.50	.75	.75	3.6

Table 1: Comparison of different overflow techniques

2 A New Overflow Technique

Let b be the *page block* size (one or more physical pages). We use two bucket sizes: b and $2b$. The overflow technique works as follows:

- If a bucket of size b overflows, the bucket is expanded to one of size $2b$. Therefore, the worst case utilization is 50%. Case (a) in Figure 1.
- If a bucket of size $2b$ overflows, we create a new bucket of size b, and $\alpha(2b+1)$ keys remain in the old bucket, while $(1-\alpha)(2b+1)$ keys are moved to the new bucket. The value of α is chosen such that $1/2 \leq \alpha \leq 3/4$, to maintain a 50% worst case utilization, and $\alpha(2b+1)$ is an integer.

  Because the split is asymmetric, we place the new bucket to the right (left) of the old bucket, if the key that produced the overflow is greater than (less than or equal to) the $b+1$-st larger element in the bucket. In other words, the split tries to be adaptive, according to the last insertion point. Case (b) in Figure 1.

The first consequence of the adaptive rule is that a sorted sequence will produce a storage utilization of α, instead of .5 for normal B-trees. A reasonable value for α is 2/3. In this case, the storage utilization in both buckets after the split is 2/3. However,

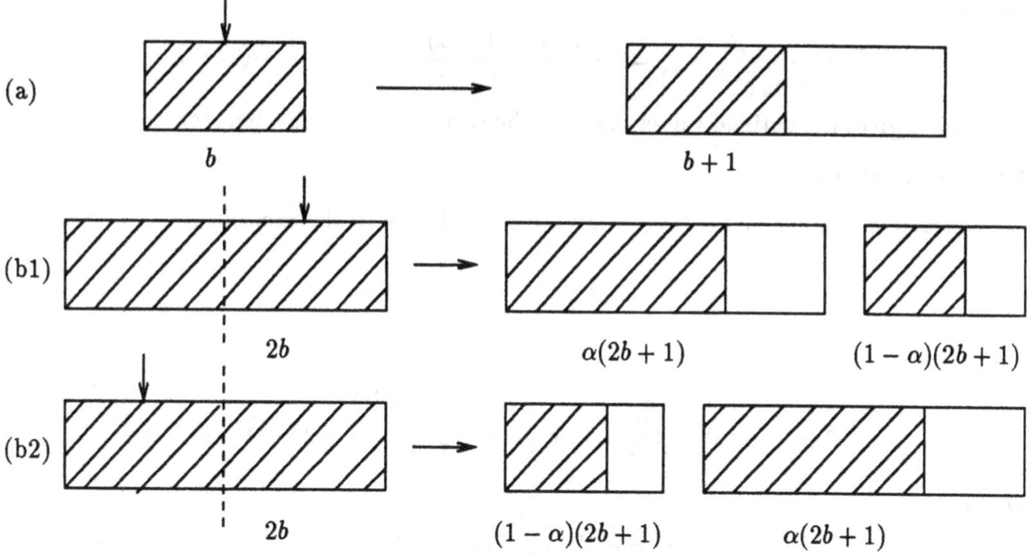

Figure 1: New adaptive overflow technique

depending on the data distribution, there is an optimal value for α such that the expected storage utilization is maximized. In the following paragraphs we assume a uniform random distribution and a growing file (only insertions). We study non-uniform distributions and deletions in subsequent sections.

Let $A_i(n)$ be the expected number of buckets with i keys in a random B-tree with n keys. In [BY89b], by using fringe analysis [Yao78, EZG+82, BY89a] it was shown that the asymptotic value for $A_i(n)$ when asymmetric splitting is used is

$$\frac{A_i(n)}{n} = \begin{cases} \frac{1-\alpha}{i(i+1)\beta} & i = (1-\alpha)(2b+1), ..., \alpha(2b+1)-1 \\ \frac{1}{i(i+1)\beta} & i = \alpha(2b+1), ..., 2b \end{cases}$$

with $\beta = H_{2b+1} - \alpha H_{\alpha(2b+1)} - (1-\alpha)H_{(1-\alpha)(2b+1)}$.

The storage utilization is defined as the ratio between the space used by the keys (n) and the total space used by the buckets. Because we have two bucket sizes, the asymptotic expected storage utilization is

$$\overline{U} = \frac{n}{b\sum_{i=(1-\alpha)(2b+1)}^{b} A_i(n) \ + \ 2b\sum_{i=b+1}^{2b} A_i(n)} \ .$$

Hence

$$\overline{U} = \frac{\beta}{b(\frac{1}{2b+1} + \frac{1-\alpha}{b+1})} = \frac{-\alpha \ln \alpha - (1-\alpha)\ln(1-\alpha)}{\frac{3}{2} - \alpha} + O(1/b) .$$

Table 2 gives the optimal values of α and the corresponding expected storage utilization for some values of b.

For large b, the optimal α is given by the real solution to the equation

$$\alpha^3 + \alpha - 1 = 0 ;$$

namely

$$\alpha_{opt} = \left(\frac{1}{2} + \frac{1}{6}\sqrt{\frac{31}{3}}\right)^{1/3} + \left(\frac{1}{2} - \frac{1}{6}\sqrt{\frac{31}{3}}\right)^{1/3} \approx 0.682378 ,$$

giving

$$\overline{U} = -2 \ln \alpha_{opt} \approx 0.764490 .$$

The experimental results are shown in Table 3.

3 Disk Space Management

Our problem now is how to allocate buckets of size b. We use chunks of size $2b$ and we allocate buckets of size b boundary aligned (that is, we place the bucket at the beginning of the chunk or at the middle). We also assume that buckets allocated in the same chunk will have a similar lifetime. Note that, in a growing file, a bucket of size $2b$ is never freed. Experimental results show that on average, the external fragmentation is less than 1% (see Table 3). For partial expansions the external fragmentation is about 3%.

The allocation algorithm is straightforward:

- If a bucket of size $2b$ is needed, we use an empty chunk. Otherwise, we allocate a new one.
- If a bucket of size b is needed, we use a chunk that already has a bucket of size b, and between all possible ones, the most recently used (buckets have similar life time). Otherwise, we use an empty bucket or we allocate a new chunk.

When a bucket is released, we update the state of the corresponding chunk accordingly. Note that a bucket of size $2b$ can only be freed if we have deletions.

The worst expected case is when each bucket of size b is in a chunk of size $2b$. That is

$$\overline{U}_{ext} = f_b \frac{u_b}{2} + f_{2b} u_{2b} ,$$

where f_x denotes the fraction of buckets of size x, and u_x denotes the expected storage utilization in buckets of size x. Using the results of the previous section, we obtain

$$\overline{U}_{ext} = \frac{2b+1}{2b} \beta .$$

Namely, the optimal α from this point of view is as near to $1/2$ as possible; in particular, $\alpha = (b+1)/(2b+1)$. However, experimental results show that a bucket of size b will usually share a chunk with another bucket of the same size.

4 Adaptability

Through extensive simulations we have found that this technique is very adaptive, particularly when loading the file (transient behaviour), and when the data has a non-uniform distribution or changes over time.

The transient behaviour is very stable with respect to other overflow techniques (see Figure 2), because the variance of the storage utilization is reduced. When a large bucket splits, the storage utilization remains near the average, and does not drop to 50%. When a small bucket is expanded, on average the large bucket that created the small bucket is almost full, and again the utilization is closer to the average. From Figure 2 we see that there is a very fast convergence to the steady state with almost no oscillations. This results in uniform search and insertion costs while the file is growing.

For the case of non-uniform data the storage utilization is approximately the same for several distributions (for example, normal, exponential, etc.). A similar behaviour occurs when the distribution changes over time.

Finally, we can set the value of α to our current data. For example, if we load the file from sorted data, we start with a high value of α. If we know that there are insertions of

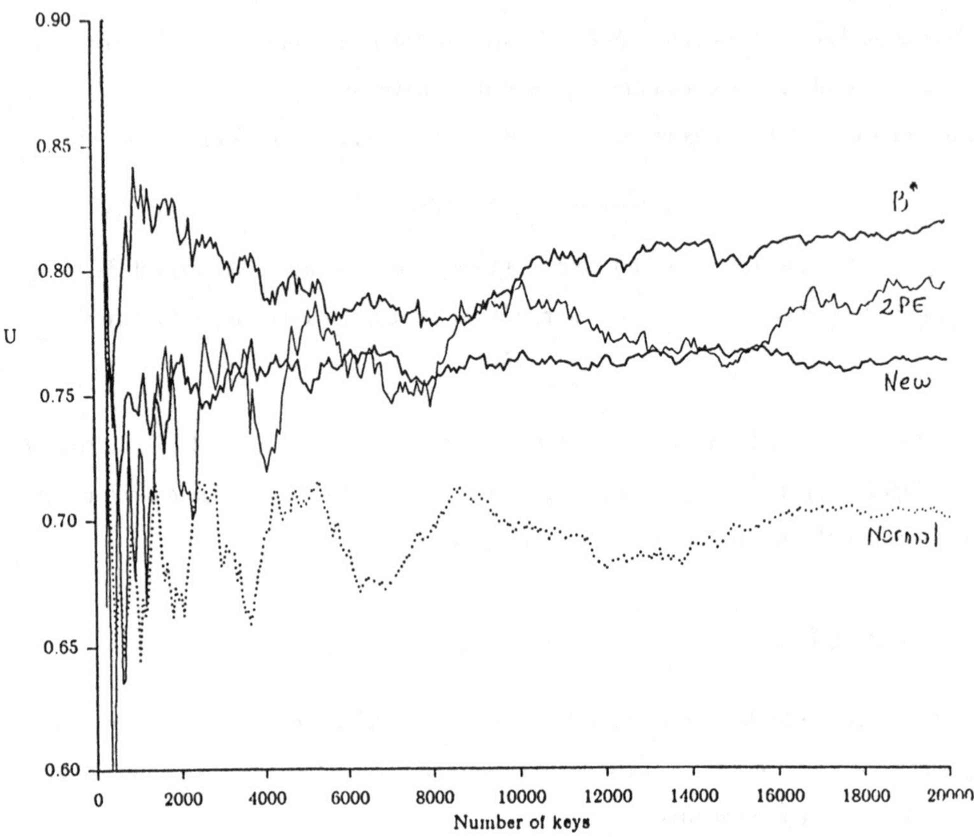

Figure 2: Experimental results for transient phase when loading the file

semi-sorted data, we can use $\alpha = 0.74985$ (with this value the storage utilization for random data is the same as that for sorted data). The value of α may be changed dynamically.

5 Deletions

Deletions are handled in a similar fashion. Although in many cases it is not necessary to have an underflow mechanism (growing file), merging is very simple in this case. If we delete a key from a bucket, and the bucket has storage utilization less than ϵ (a parameter with value less than or equal to the possible minimum storage utilization), we try to merge the bucket with an adjacent bucket. We have two cases:

- The number of keys does not fit in a bucket of size $2b$. We then shift some keys to the underflowed bucket, until the storage utilization in both buckets is roughly the same.
- Merge both buckets into the smallest bucket size possible.

The analysis of deletions in search trees in the model presented in previous sections is an open problem. It is possible to analyze the behaviour of a B-tree using a linear model [Miz79], where we assume that insertion is still random after a random deletion. However, it appears that the linear model under-estimates the storage utilization [JS89]. Nevertheless, this model may be used to compare different overflow/underflow techniques under random insertions and deletions.

Following Mizoguchi [Miz79], when insertions and deletions are equally likely, the storage utilization for our overflow technique is

$$\overline{U} = \frac{2(2\alpha - 1)(2\alpha^5 - \alpha^4 - \alpha + 1)}{2\alpha(\ln 2 - 1 - \ln(1-\alpha) + 2\ln\alpha) + 1} + O(1/b)$$

where $1/2 < \alpha \leq 3/4$. The optimal α is $(b+1)/(2b+1)$, and we obtain an asymptotic value of

$$\overline{U} = \frac{2}{1 + 4\ln 2} \approx 0.5301 .$$

This figure should be compared with $\overline{U} = 1/(4\ln 2) \approx 0.3607$ for B-trees [Miz79, JS89] and $\overline{U} = 9/(12\ln 6 - 4) \approx 0.5143$ for B-trees with 2 partial expansions [BY87]. The analysis of this case for B^*-trees is still an open problem, even using the linear model. Thus, it appears that the adaptive overflow technique performs better. Simulations agree with this result.

6 Generalization

We can generalize the overflow technique to $r - q + 1$ different bucket sizes, from qb to rb $(1 \leq q < r)$.

The worst-case storage utilization is computed using

$$\min((\alpha + U_m)/2, U_m) ,$$

where $U_m = \min(q/(q+1), (1-\alpha)r/q)$ is the minimum storage utilization in a bucket of size qb. This is due to the fact that for each bucket of size rb there is at least one bucket of size qb (the converse is not true).

For a uniform distribution we have the following result

$$\overline{U} = \frac{\beta}{b(\frac{q}{2b+1} + (1-\alpha)\sum_{j=q}^{r-1}\frac{1}{jb+1})} = \frac{-r(\alpha\ln\alpha + (1-\alpha)\ln(1-\alpha))}{q + r(1-\alpha)(H_{r-1} - H_{q-1})} + O(1/b) .$$

The optimal values for α and q are the solutions of the following equations:

$$\alpha^{q+r(H_{r-1}-H_{q-1})} - (1-\alpha)^q = 0 \quad \text{and} \quad r(1-\alpha)\psi'(q) = 1$$

where $\psi(x) = \frac{d}{dx}(\ln\Gamma(x))$ (see [AS72, page 258]).

The optimal storage utilization ($b \to \infty$) for optimal α and q is given by

$$\overline{U} = -\frac{r}{q}\ln\alpha = -\frac{r}{q}\ln(1 - \frac{1}{r\psi'(q)}) .$$

Some optimal values for α and q are given in Table 4 which also shows the corresponding average and worst case storage utilization. For large r, the optimal α and $\overline{U}$ tends to 1.

7 Concluding Remarks

We have presented a new overflow technique that is *adaptive*. Changing the parameter α dynamically we can improve storage utilization while loading the file, or when the input data changes (semi-sorted sequences, etc.). The storage utilization is not as good as it is for the methods of partial expansions or B^*. However, it is more stable and with respect to B^*, the insertion cost is significantly lower, being B^* 30% more expensive (see Figure 3). Compared with partial expansions, insertion time is almost the same, but the storage utilization is much more stable during the transient phase. For these reasons, this technique is a viable choice for database systems with a high frequency of updates.

Finally, this overflow technique may be used in any file structure based in buckets, like extendible hashing files, grid files, bounded disorder files, etc. In all these cases, the same disk storage allocation algorithm can be used.

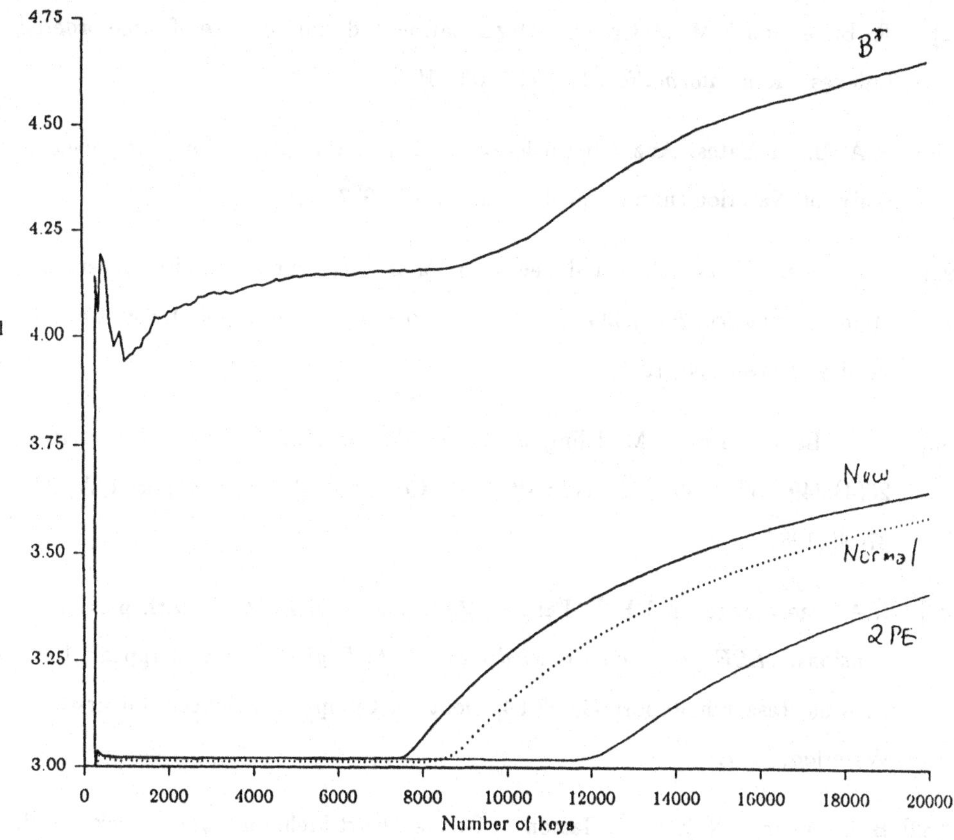

Figure 3: Expected number of accesses per insertion.

Acknowledgements

We wish to acknowledge the helpful comments of José Blakeley, Tony Gahlinger and Gaston Gonnet.

References

[AS72] M. Abramowitz and I. Stegun. *Handbook of Mathematical Functions.* Dover, New York, 1972.

[BM72] R. Bayer and E.M. McCreight. Organization and maintenance of large ordered indexes. *Acta Informatica*, 1(3):173–189, 1972.

[BY87] R.A. Baeza-Yates. Analyzing deletions in B-trees. Dept. of Computer Science, Univ. of Waterloo (unpublished manuscript), 1987.

[BY89a] R.A. Baeza-Yates. Expected behaviour of B^+-trees under random insertions. *Acta Informatica*, 26(5):439–472, 1989. Also as Research Report CS-86-67, University of Waterloo, 1986.

[BY89b] R.A. Baeza-Yates. Modeling splits in file structures. *Acta Informatica*, 26(4):349–362, 1989. Also as Institute for Computer Research Report UW/ICR 87-08, 1987.

[BYL89] R.A. Baeza-Yates and P-Å. Larson. Performance of B^+-trees with partial expansions. *IEEE Trans. on Knowledge and Data Engineering*, 1:to appear, 1989. Also as Research Report CS-87-04, Dept. of Computer Science, University of Waterloo, 1987.

[EZG+82] B. Eisenbarth, N. Ziviani, Gaston H. Gonnet, Kurt Mehlhorn, and Derick Wood. The theory of fringe analysis and its application to 2-3 trees and B-trees. *Information and Control*, 55(1):125–174, Oct 1982.

[JS89] T. Johnson and D. Shasha. Utilization of B-trees with inserts, deletes and modifies. In *PODS'89*, pages 235–246, 1989.

[Lom87] D. Lomet. Partial expansions for file organizations with an index. *ACM TODS*, 12:65–84, 1987. Also as tech report, Wang Institute, TR-86-06, 1986.

[Miz79] T. Mizoguchi. On required space for random split trees. In *Allerton Conference*, pages 265–273, Monticello, IL, 1979.

[Yao78] A.C-C. Yao. On random 2-3 trees. *Acta Informatica*, 9(2):159–170, 1978.

b	α		$\overline{U}$	b	α		$\overline{U}$
1	2/3	.6667	1.	18	25/37	.6757	.7771
2	3/5	.6000	.8750	19	2/3	.6667	.7761
3	5/7	.7143	.8296	20	28/41	.6829	.7757
4	2/3	.6667	.8220	21	29/43	.6744	.7752
5	7/11	.6364	.8082	22	2/3	.6667	.7745
6	9/13	.6923	.8005	23	32/47	.6809	.7743
7	2/3	.6667	.7971	24	33/49	.6735	.7739
8	11/17	.6471	.7915	25	35/51	.6863	.7733
9	13/19	.6842	.7893	26	36/53	.6792	.7732
10	2/3	.6667	.7872	27	37/55	.6727	.7728
11	15/23	.6522	.7839	28	13/19	.6842	.7725
12	17/25	.6800	.7833	29	40/59	.6780	.7723
13	2/3	.6667	.7818	30	41/61	.6721	.7719
14	20/29	.6897	.7800	40	55/81	.6790	.7701
15	21/31	.6774	.7796	50	69/101	.6832	.7690
16	2/3	.6667	.7784	60	82/121	.6777	.7682
17	24/35	.6857	.7775	∞		.6823	.7645

Table 2: Optimal value of α and $\overline{U}$ for some values of b

Smallest Bucket size	Internal		External
	Experimental	Theoretical	Experimental
12 (40000 keys)	.78327 ± .00053	.78329	.78288 ± .00053
60 (150000 keys)	.76827 ± .00064	.76823	.76771 ± .00066

Table 3: Experimental results for the storage utilization (95% confidence interval)

r	q	α	$\overline{U}$	U_{wc}
2	1	.6823	.7645	.5000
3	2	.5959	.7766	.6010
4	3	.5634	.7650	.5728
5	3	.6157	.8082	.6281
6	3	.6582	.8365	.6709
7	3	.6928	.8562	.7048
8	3	.7214	.8707	.7321
9	3	.7453	.8818	.7477
10	3	.7656	.8905	.7500
15	4	.7844	.9106	.7922
20	4	.8307	.9276	.8000
25	5	.8295	.9347	.8314
30	5	.8546	.9429	.8333

Table 4: Optimal values of α and q for large b

Single Table Access Using Multiple Indexes: Optimization, Execution, and Concurrency Control Techniques

C. Mohan

Data Base Technology Institute, IBM Almaden Research Center, San Jose, CA 95120, USA
mohan@ibm.com

Don Haderle*
Yun Wang
Josephine Cheng*

*Data Base Technology Institute
IBM Santa Teresa Laboratory, San Jose, CA 95150, USA

Abstract Many data base management systems' query optimizers choose at most one index for accessing the records of a table in a given query, even though many indexes may exist on the table. In spite of the fact that there are some systems which use multiple indexes, very little has been published about the concurrency control or query optimization implications (e.g., deciding how many indexes to use) of using multiple indexes. This paper addresses these issues and presents solutions to the associated problems. Techniques are presented for the efficient handling of record ID lists, elimination of some locking, and determination of how many and which indexes to use. The techniques are *adaptive* in the sense that the execution strategies may be modified at run-time (e.g., not use some indexes which were to have been used), if the assumptions made at optimization-time (e.g., about selectivities) turn out to be wrong. Opportunities for exploiting parallelism are also identified. A subset of our ideas have been implemented in IBM's DB2 V2R2 relational data base management system.

1. Introduction

1.1. Indexes and Queries

A data base management system (DBMS) user specifies the data to be retrieved via a query, generally in a high level language, which contains predicates to identify which records are to be retrieved from a single stored table or from the result of joining multiple tables.[1] The optimizer component of the DBMS determines an execution strategy for the query, determining in what order and how the tables should be accessed. The most common access method in today's DBMSs is an index. Typically, an index is implemented using a variant of the B-tree and the ***key*** of an index is the set of fields of the table over which the index is defined. A key is a ***simple key*** if it consists of only one field of the table. A key is a ***complex key*** if it is constructed by concatenating multiple fields of the table. Each entry in the index leaf page consists of a key value followed by a RID, where the ***RID*** is the record identifier of the record

---

1 In this paper, we use the relational terminology, but it should be noted that almost all of our ideas are applicable to nonrelational systems also.

containing that key value. In a ***nonunique index***, multiple RIDs may be associated with the same key value. In general, most of the tables in a data base will have multiple indexes defined on them. One of the indexes of a table may be designated as the ***clustering index*** (i.e., this index is consulted during a record insert to pick a candidate data page for the insert - the candidate page is the page which contains other records which have the same key value or neighboring key values).

An index is an ***eligible index*** for use in answering a given query if its key includes at least one of the fields referenced in the predicates of the query. If a predicate is going to be applied via any indexes at all, then it is possible that there are multiple eligible indexes for applying that predicate, but only one of them needs to be chosen. One of the important problems in query optimization is determining how many and which of the eligible indexes to use. If a complete table scan is to be avoided, then, depending on the predicates, certain eligible indexes may definitely have to be accessed in order to get the correct answer. The ***selectivity*** of a predicate is the fraction of records in the table that satisfy the predicate.

When many predicates are specified in a query, the predicates are linked together by the Boolean operators *AND* and *OR*. Those predicates which are linked by ANDs are called ***conjunctive predicates***. Those predicates which are linked by ORs are called ***disjunctive predicates***. In some systems, the predicates are converted to the ***Conjunctive Normal Form*** (***CNF***). A CNF expression consists of a set of predicates (called ***Boolean factors*** or conjuncts) connected by ANDs. Each conjunct may be a nondecomposable predicate (***simple predicate***) or a set of simple predicates connected by ORs. Therefore, a CNF set of predicates is a conjunct of disjuncts. We do not require that the predicates be converted to CNF.

As an example, an SQL query that finds those employees who have qualified for retirement (age older than 65 or more than 30 years of service) may appear as follows:

```
SELECT EMP_NAME
FROM   EMPLOYEE
WHERE  AGE > 65 OR
       SERVICE > 30;
```

If the DBMS were not capable of using more than one index for a table, and a single index with a complex key that included both AGE and SERVICE did not exist,[2] then the only way to find the answer to the query is to scan every record of the EMPLOYEE table and to check the predicates against each record. This may turn out to be a terribly inefficient execution plan. If in fact 2 indexes were to exist, where one index's key included AGE and the other index's key included SERVICE, then it is possible to use the first index to find those employees with AGE > 65 and use the second index to find those employees with SERVICE > 30. The final answer is the union of these two partial answer sets.

In spite of the fact that there are some systems (e.g., CCA's MODEL 204 [Onei87, Onei89]) that use multiple indexes, very little has been published [BlEs76, BlEs77, RoRe82] about the

---

2 If such an index were to exist, then it may be profitable to look at every key in that index to check if it qualifies rather than do a complete table scan. Even though System R did not consider such an index scan, DB2 does consider it as a potential execution strategy and costs it. Depending on the sizes of the keys and the data records, the number of index pages that need to be scanned may be much smaller than the number of data pages. Furthermore, since the index manager typically reduces, due to key compression, the number of key compares when there are many duplicate key values, doing predicate checking against index entries may be much cheaper than performing them against fields in the records.

concurrency control or query optimization implications (e.g., deciding how many indexes to use) of using multiple indexes. Some performance numbers are provided in [Onei87, Onei89] which convincingly demonstrate the advantages of using multiple indexes. A CPU advantage of 400 to 1 and an elapsed time advantage of 30 to 1 are reported. In this paper, we do not report any performance numbers. Instead, we concentrate on the optimization and execution strategies and describe how a system can choose to exploit all or a subset of the eligible indexes on a table to apply as many predicates as possible in a query so that the answer to the query can be derived in the most efficient way.

We use the technique of ***index intersection*** (i.e., the intersection of the qualifying RIDs from the different indexes) for evaluating conjunctive predicates and the technique of ***index union*** (i.e., the union of the qualifying RIDs from the different indexes) for disjunctive predicates. For a query with both conjunctive and disjunctive predicates, both index intersection and index union are applied. The papers in the literature have generally taken an inefficient approach to handling queries with disjunctions (see, e.g., [Daya87], which suggests splitting the query into multiple queries, each with a disjunct, and then taking the union of the results of those queries). An exception is the work reported in [Mura88]. Index intersection and index union are not new ideas. What are new are the approaches that we present for deciding *how many* and *which* indexes to use given (1) a query, (2) statistics about the indexes and the table, and (3) cost information relating to I/Os and CPU processing. Our techniques concerning run-time adaptation and locking are also new.

1.2. Organization

The rest of the paper is organized as follows. Section 2 describes the handling of conjunctive predicates, while section 3 deals with disjunctive predicates. Accesses to the data pages using RID lists is the topic of section 4. Then, section 5 discusses the interactions between use of multiple indexes and the avoidance of data page accesses using index-only scans. The implications of the use of multiple indexes on locking and the different consistency levels are presented in section 6. Section 7 discusses the use of parallelism to improve the response time of complex queries. Finally, section 8 describes the status of the implementation of our ideas in DB2.

2. Index Intersection for Conjunctive Predicates

In this section, we discuss the evaluation of conjunctive predicates via index intersection. We present techniques used at optimization time as well as at execution time.

When there are predicates involving key fields of an index, the RIDs of the records that satisfy those predicates are found using the index. When there exist other conjunctive predicates on key fields of another index, then, rather than evaluating those additional predicates by accessing the records in the data pages, it is preferable to (1) generate another RID list using the second index, (2) intersect the two RID lists, and (3) access the records using the resulting RID list.

The index intersection technique *may* reduce I/O and CPU costs for the following reasons:

- The index structure is more compact and clustered than the data pages of a table's file. Therefore, it may be cheaper, in terms of the number of I/Os and CPU usage, to obtain the RID list by using an eligible index, since the sum of the number of index pages that need to be accessed and the number of data pages with qualifying records that need to be accessed *may be* much smaller than the total number of data pages occupied by the table's records.

- The intersected RID list *may be* much smaller than either of the original RID lists. In any case, the former cannot be larger than the first list. Therefore, substantially fewer data pages and records may need to be accessed. The former saves I/Os and the latter reduces CPU usage. Of course, an increase in the number of indexes accessed increases the number of index pages that are accessed and the CPU usage for searching the index pages for the qualifying RIDs.

- The sort-merge technique may be used to intersect the RID lists so that the final RID list has the RIDs in order, which allows the data page I/Os to be performed in page number sequence and asynchronous prefetch [CLSW84, TeGu84] to be enabled to reduce the number of synchronous I/O requests. This essentially provides clustered access to the data and also allows overlapping of CPU processing and I/Os. The asynchronous I/Os help bridge the ever-growing speed mismatch gap between CPUs and I/O devices [PMCLS89]. While considering using multiple indexes, in addition to the costs associated with accessing the multiple indexes, the cost of performing the sort-merge operations on the RID lists must also be taken into account.

This method may also reduce the impact of the severe problems caused by uncertainties about data value distributions [Lync88, MuDe88, Mura88], if one were to be restricted to using only one index. For example, the key values of an index may be assumed to be uniformly distributed and thus an index access to match a key may be inferred to be relatively cheap. In the traditional approach (e.g., as proposed for System R [SACL79]), the data pages would be accessed as and when a qualifying RID is retrieved from the index (as opposed to generating a list of RIDs first and then accessing the data pages in increasing RID sequence). If the assumptions turn out to be wrong (e.g., 20% of the records have this index key), then the costs could be very high, especially if the chosen index is a nonclustering index. Building in some run-time adaptation (see below) and being able to use multiple indexes would make the effects of wrong guesses less severe. In addition to doing the optimizations outlined below at the time of optimization of the query, we also introduce some checks to be performed at the time of execution of the query. The latter is done so that if any of the estimates that were made at optimization time turn out to be drastically in error, then corrective actions could be taken. The corrective actions may be (1) avoiding accessing some indexes entirely or (2) giving up using certain indexes after having retrieved some RIDs through those indexes since the additional indexes turn out not to be very beneficial. We first describe the optimization-time steps and then the run-time steps.

In order to avoid an exponential growth in the strategy space, we avoided adopting an approach, like the one described in [RoRe82], in which (1) every index is treated very much like a table, (2) accessing a table via an index is treated very much like a join, and (3) even joining indexes of different tables is considered. Our approach even avoids considering all possible combinations and permutations of the indexes of a single table. As we describe below, we essentially use a greedy heuristic. Without perturbing the existing logic flow in the optimizer too much, we added the support for considering using multiple indexes by appending some additional logic to the optimizer.

1. **Selection and Sequence of Indexes for Intersection** (*Optimization-Time*)

   a. For each index, search among the simple conjunctive predicates to see if one or more of these predicates can be applied by the index, as is done for example in System R [SACL79]. For each eligible index, compute the selectivity and the cost of using that index.

   b. For each conjunct that is made up of disjuncts, use the method presented in section "3. Index Union for Disjunctive Predicates" to find the best strategy for unioning indexes to satisfy the disjunctive predicates.

   c. The single-index strategies from step a) and index union strategies from step b) are ordered by their selectivity. The strategy with the *most selectivity* and the *least cost* is chosen as the first strategy.

   d. Then, the strategy which, when combined with the already chosen strategies, produces the *most overall selectivity* and the *least cost* will be chosen as the next strategy.

   e. Step d) is repeated until either there are no indexes left or using an additional index cannot improve the performance (i.e., the cost of using the additional index is greater than the savings resulting from a shorter RID list).

It should be noted that there may not necessarily be a direct relationship between the *selectivity* of an index and the *cost* of using that index. For example, if index I1 is known to be more selective than index I2, then it does not necessarily mean that the cost of using I1 is less than that of I2. Assume that I1 is defined on the fields F1,F2,F3 and I2 is defined on F2 and that the predicate is F2 = 20 AND F3 = 30. While the cost of using I2 might be small compared to that of I1 since all keys in I1 have to be checked, the selectivity of I1 will be better than that of I2 since with the former two conditions can be checked rather than just one.

2. **Execution of Index Intersection** (*Run-time*)

   a. Each RID list is obtained by following the strategies determined at the time of query optimization, as described above.

   b. As each RID list is being built, abandon its construction if it is noticed that the number of qualifying RIDs exceeds a certain ***upper bound threshold*** that was determined by the query optimizer, based on the statistics on the table size. The RID list from this index will not be intersected with those from the other indexes because it is suspected that the intersection probably will not filter out many RIDs. If we give up for this reason, we go back to step a) for the next strategy; otherwise, we go to the next step.

   c. The new RID list is intersected with the current RID list to derive a new current RID list.

   d. If the resulting RID list is shorter than the ***lower bound threshold*** that was determined by the query optimizer, based on the statistics on the table size, no more intersection is needed because the RID list is short enough so that further intersections will not be beneficial. Otherwise, go back to step a) for the next strategy.

The values for the upper and lower bound thresholds may also take into account factors like the number of pages that are prefetched in one start I/O operation, the cost of a full table scan, the cost of evaluating predicates using records in data pages versus keys in index pages, the cost of sorting RIDs, number of data pages occupied by the records, etc.

If a condition like $F1 \neq 10$ is present in the predicates and there is an index on F1, then one way to handle the condition would be to do the following:

1. Access the index on F1 and obtain the RIDs of records having $F1 = 10$.

2. From the list of RIDs obtained by accessing the other indexes for other conjuncts, *eliminate* those RIDs obtained in the previous step.

3. Index Union for Disjunctive Predicates

In this section, we discuss the evaluation of disjunctive predicates via index union. Again, we present techniques used at optimization time as well as at execution time.

When **all** the disjunctive predicates can be fully checked efficiently using one or more eligible indexes, it is probably preferable to union the RID lists from the different indexes and then access the records using the unioned RID list, rather than doing a full table scan. If any disjunctive predicate cannot be checked by any index, then a full scan of all the data records is inevitable to check for this disjunctive predicate. Since a full scan on all data records is needed, it usually won't be advantageous to use indexes to check the other predicates, but there are cases when it will. For example, for the query given before, let us assume that an index exists only on AGE and that only a small percentage of the records in the table satisfy the predicates. In this case, it may still be beneficial from a *CPU usage* point of view to do the following (call it the ***full scan with RID list*** strategy):

1. Access the AGE index and obtain the RIDs of qualifying records and sort the RIDs.

2. Access the table sequentially, examine the records whose RIDs do *not* appear in the RID list from the previous step, and check the predicate on SERVICE.

3. Retrieve the required fields from those records that qualified in the first or the second step.

The advantage of following this *full scan with RID list* execution plan, instead of avoiding using the AGE index and using a full scan without a RID list, is that with the latter approach, for every record that did not satisfy the predicate on SERVICE, we would have had to check the predicate on AGE. If the selectivities are good, then the cost of identifying those records that satisfy the predicate on AGE via the index would have been much cheaper than doing it by checking that predicate against every record (in the table) which did not satisfy the predicate on SERVICE. This could happen for a number of additional reasons also: (1) Gaining access to the AGE field in the record may be very expensive if the field follows one or more varying length fields and the System R-type record formats are used. (2) Indexes generally store duplicate keys very efficiently (e.g., keeping in each page only one instance of the key followed by a list of RIDs of records with that key value - see [Moha89, MoLe89]). After one compare in each index leaf, a large number of RIDs may be retrieved, assuming there are many duplicates.

The index union technique *may* reduce I/O and CPU costs for reasons similar to the ones that we listed earlier for index intersection.

1. **Selection and Sequence of Indexes for Union** (*Optimization-Time*)

   a. For each disjunct that is a simple predicate, search among the indexes to look for the best index against which the predicate can be checked. If, for some simple predicate, there exists no such index, then this method of index union cannot be be used, unless we choose to follow the *full scan with RID list* strategy described above. Otherwise, a single index strategy is produced for each simple predicate.

   b. For each disjunct that is made up of conjunctive predicates, use the method of section "2. Index Intersection for Conjunctive Predicates" to find the strategy of index intersection. If such an index intersection strategy cannot be found for this disjunct, this method of index union cannot apply, unless we choose to follow the *full scan with RID list* strategy described above.

   c. The single-index strategies from step a) and the index intersection strategies from step b) are ordered by their selectivity. The strategy with the *most selectivity* and the *least cost* is chosen as the first strategy for execution. Then, the next strategy is chosen among the remaining strategies.

   d. All the strategies will be used together to generate the unioned RID list.

2. **Execution of Index Union** (*Run-Time*)

   a. Each RID list is obtained by following the strategies determined at the time of query optimization, as described above.

   b. Completion of building the next RID list can be bypassed whenever its size exceeds the upper bound threshold. The union will not be performed because the unioned RID list will be even longer. The execution of index union terminates, and we resort to another strategy (e.g., a table scan).

   c. The new RID list is unioned with the current RID list to derive a new current RID list.

   d. If the resulting RID list is longer than the upper bound threshold, then no more union is needed because the RID list is too long so that further unions will not be beneficial. Otherwise, go back to step a) for the next strategy.

In step 1c above, we could have used the criterion of *least* selectivity rather than *most* selectivity for ordering the strategies. There is a trade-off involved in this decision. If the assumptions about selectivities are likely to be wrong, resulting in more than the expected number of RIDs being retrieved and the upper bound threshold being reached in step 2d, then we would prefer accessing the indexes in the order of *least* selectivity to most selectivity so that the "bad news" is found out early. The negative side of this is that when we merge RID lists the most optimal way of merging is to start from the smallest list and keep merging longer lists. That is, it is better to postpone merging the longer lists as late as possible. If we want to minimize the cost of merging, then we must access the indexes in the order of *most* selectivity to least selectivity.

4. Access Records by Unioned/Intersected RID List

The final RID list, which is obtained from multiple indexes through unions and intersections, is a candidate list that includes the answer of the query as a subset. The answer to the query may consist of only a subset of the records whose RIDs are in the RID list because there may be some additional conjuncts that were not checked using the indexes.

It is possible that a RID list was not produced, since it was suspected that the list would be too long. In this case, a full scan will be performed because most of the records would have qualified and a full sequential scan is indeed a good strategy. Another possibility is the *full scan with RID list* strategy discussed in section "3. Index Union for Disjunctive Predicates".

If the final RID list is sorted on the RID value, then data pages can be prefetched using this list.

The unions and intersections are performed only when they are beneficial. Therefore, not all the candidate indexes are necessarily exploited, nor are all the predicates on key columns of the accessed indexes necessarily checked. These predicates will be checked again when the data records are accessed via the final RID list, which is usually very short. If all the predicates had eligible indexes, all the predicates were checked using indexes during this execution, and RR locking was used, then predicates do not necessarily need to be rechecked (see also section "6.2. Repeatable Read").

5. Index-Only Accesses

For some queries, all the fields to be retrieved in the result may be distributed over the keys of one or more of the indexes to be accessed in generating the list of RIDs, as determined in the previously described algorithms, and no predicates may remain to be checked after all the index accesses are executed and the final list of RIDs is generated. Under these conditions, accesses to the data pages may be completely avoided by extracting from those indexes not only the qualifying RIDs but also the result fields. A simplest case of this is when the result needed is the count of the qualifying records (i.e., COUNT(*) in SQL). This kind of query execution is termed ***index-only accesses***.

A combination of the indexes-only accesses, and data and indexes accesses is also possible. That is, for some records, the result fields are available from the accessed indexes and for others they have to be retrieved from the data pages. This may turn out to be the case if index union is necessary and only a subset of the indexes participating in the union have the result fields in their keys. For the RIDs qualifying from the other indexes, the data pages would have to be accessed to retrieve the result fields.

If only index intersection is involved for determining the qualifying records of a table and the table's records are needed in the key sequence of a particular index participating in the intersection, then a sort of the retrieved records can be avoided by (1) choosing that index as the last index and (2) accessing the qualifying records in the order in which their RIDs appear in that index.

6. Locking and Bit Vectors

A ***bit vector*** strategy, instead of the use of RID lists, may be employed to keep track of qualifying RIDs [Onei87, Onei89]. A one-to-one correspondence will be established between a bit position in the vector and a RID. Based on various values like minimum record size, the maximum number of RIDs that would be used in a page can be computed. Using the current file size plus an expansion factor, the size of the bit vector can be computed.[3] If that number is too large, then the RID space can be divided into multiple ranges. Using a shorter bit vector and multiple passes of the indexes with intervening data accesses, the answer to the query may be computed. During each pass, different ranges of RIDs are dealt with.

For each index accessed, a separate bit vector is generated, and when dealing with conjunctive predicates, the bit vectors are ANDed together in an incremental fashion.

For disjunctive predicates, a single bit vector can be used. As the different indexes are accessed and qualifying RIDs are found, the corresponding bits can be set in the same vector.

In the following discussion, it is assumed that the locking done while accessing the indexes is such that all the locks obtained are on the underlying data pages or RIDs (i.e., the index entry locks are not different from the locks on the corresponding data). This is called ***data-only locking***. It is implemented in the OS/2 Extended Edition[4] data base manager and is described in detail in [MoLe89]. Whether the data page or the RID is locked will depend on the granularity of locking in effect for the table. This data-only locking approach must be differentiated from the ***index-specific locking*** approach in which the index locks are different from data locks (e.g., DB2 locks index pages, System R locks index pages or key values, and the ARIES/KVL method of [Moha89] locks key values).

Traditionally, there has been very little discussion in the query optimization and query execution literature on the impact of different levels (degrees) of consistency (isolation) on execution strategies and predicate evaluations. The rest of this section discusses some of the subtle problems that arise in these areas when (1) multiple indexes are going to be used or (2) only one index is going to be used but the RID list is first going to be materialized before the data pages are accessed.

6.1. Latches and Locks

Before we delve into the interactions between locking and the use of multiple indexes for single table access, this subsection introduces some of the concepts relating to concurrency control.

Normally latches and locks are used to control access to shared information. Locking has been discussed to a great extent in the literature. Latches, on the other hand, have not been discussed that much. ***Latches*** are like semaphores. Usually, latches are used to guarantee physical consistency of data, while ***locks*** are used to assure logical consistency of data. Latches are usually held for a much shorter period of time than are locks. Also, the deadlock

---

3 During the execution of the query, if the file expands beyond the anticipated range and RIDs which are not covered by the bit vector are encountered, then those few RIDs alone can be handled specially using RID lists.

4 OS/2 is a trademark of the International Business Machines Corporation.

detector is not informed about latch waits. Latches are requested in such a manner so as to avoid deadlocks involving latches alone, or involving latches and locks.

Acquiring a latch is much cheaper than acquiring a lock (in the no-conflict case, 10s of instructions versus 100s of instructions), because the latch control information is always in virtual memory in a fixed place, and direct addressability to the latch information is possible given the latch name. Since each transaction holds at most 2 or 3 latches simultaneously (see, e.g., the protocols presented in [Moha89, MoLe89]) the *latch request blocks* can be permanently allocated to each transaction and initialized with transaction ID, etc. right at the start of that transaction. On the other hand, storage for individual locks may have to be acquired, formatted, and released dynamically, and more instructions need to be executed to acquire and release locks. This is because, in most systems, the number of lockable objects is many orders of magnitude greater than the number of latchable objects. Typically, all information relating to locks held is stored in a single, central table; addressability to a particular lock's information is gained by first hashing the lock name to get the address of the hash anchor and then, possibly, following a chain of pointers. Usually, in the process of trying to locate the *lock control block*, due to the fact that multiple transactions may be simultaneously reading and modifying the contents of the lock table, one or more latches will be acquired and released. Generally, one latch on the hash anchor and, possibly, one on the specific lock's chain of holders and waiters will be acquired.

Locks may be obtained in different ***modes*** such as S (Shared), X (eXclusive), IX (Intention eXclusive), IS (Intention Shared), and SIX (Shared Intention eXclusive), and at different ***granularities*** such as record (tuple), table (relation), and file (tablespace, segment, dbspace). The S and X locks are the most common ones. S provides the read privilege and X provides the read and write privileges. Locks on a given object can be held simultaneously by different transactions only if those locks' modes are ***compatible***. X is compatible with none of the modes. S is compatible with S and IS only. IX is compatible with IX and IS only. IS is compatible with IX, IS, S, and SIX only. SIX is compatible with IS only. With ***hierarchical locking***, the intention locks (IX, IS, and SIX) are generally obtained on the higher levels of the hierarchy (e.g., table), and the S and X locks are obtained on the lower levels (e.g., record). The nonintention mode locks (S or X), when obtained on an object at a certain level of the hierarchy, *implicitly* grant locks of the corresponding mode on the lower level objects of that higher level object. The intention mode locks, on the other hand, only give the privilege of requesting the corresponding nonintention mode locks on the lower level objects (e.g., SIX on a table implicitly grants S on all the records of that table, and it allows X to be requested *explicitly* on the records). For more details, the reader is referred to [Gray78].

Lock requests may be made with the *conditional* or the *unconditional* option. A ***conditional*** request means that the requestor is not willing to wait if the lock is not grantable immediately at the time the request is processed. An ***unconditional*** request means that the requestor is willing to wait until the lock becomes grantable. Locks may be held for different *durations*. An unconditional request for an ***instant duration*** lock means that the lock is not to be actually granted, but the lock manager has to delay returning the lock call with the *success* status until the lock becomes grantable. ***Manual duration*** locks are released some time after they are acquired and, typically, long before transaction termination. For each transaction, a count is kept of the number of times a lock was acquired in the manual duration. Such a lock is considered to be no longer held by a transaction, at a point in time before transaction termination, only after as many unlocks are issued by the transaction. ***Commit duration*** locks are released only at the time of termination of the transaction, i.e., after commit or abort is completed. The lock manager chains together all the locks acquired by a transaction, and at the time of transaction termination, all the commit and manual duration locks still held are released via a single call to the lock manager. Once a lock is obtained for commit duration, it stays at commit duration, irrespective of whether it had been acquired as a manual duration lock initially or it is requested in manual duration later on. A special lock manager call could still be used to release a commit duration lock before transaction termination. The above discussions concerning conditional calls, S and X modes, and durations, except for commit duration, apply to latches also. Generally, to minimize the overhead, all the latches held by a transaction at any time are not chained together.

Transactions may request different ***levels of consistency*** (or ***isolation***) with respect to each other. In the context of System R, levels 0, 1, 2, and 3 were discussed [Gray78]. The IBM products SQL/DS, the OS/2 Extended Edition Database Manager, and DB2 support the consistency levels ***cursor stability*** (*consistency level 2* of System R) and ***repeatable read*** (*consistency level 3* of System R). They are referred to as ***CS*** and ***RR***, respectively. Both return only committed data to the transactions, unless the accessed data is uncommitted data belonging to the accessing transaction. When the chosen level is CS, as long as an *updateable* SQL cursor is positioned on a record, a lock will continue to be held on the record and the record will be guaranteed to exist in the data base, unless the current transaction itself deletes the record after the cursor is positioned on it. As soon as the cursor is moved to a different record, the lock may be released on the previous record. We say *may be* because, with page locking, if the previous record and the current record were to be on the same page, then the lock would continue to be held. With RR, locks are held on all the accessed records until the end of the transaction. Actually, locks are somehow held even on nonexistent records, which would have satisfied the query (see [Moha89, MoLe89] for discussions about how this is done when the accesses are made via indexes). If a certain query is posed at a certain point in a transaction, and a little later the same query is posed within the same transaction, then the response to the query would be the same, even if it were a negative response like *not found*, unless the same transaction had changed the data base to cause a difference to be introduced in the responses. If all the transactions are run with RR, then their concurrent executions would be ***serializable*** in the sense of [EGLT76]. That is, the concurrent execution would be equivalent to some *serial* execution of those transactions. With CS, only the locks on data modified by the transaction are held for commit duration and so, repeating a query *may* give a different response due to other concurrent transactions' activities.

6.2. Repeatable Read

With the bit vector strategy, if the consistency level chosen for locking is RR and the locking granularity is record level, then, while doing the bit settings for disjunctive predicates, unnecessary locking can be avoided by doing locking only if a qualifying RID's bit position is not already set (i.e., only if the RID had not already qualified through another index). Similar optimization can be made with the RID list approach also, but the cost of checking the RIDs that have already qualified is much cheaper with the bit vector approach. With page locking, this optimization can be performed even more efficiently by having a separate bit vector for locks. In this bit vector, each bit will correspond to a particular data page.

When processing a query with conjunctive predicates only and RR, it is sufficient if locking is done only while accessing the first index. This is because the subsequent indexes can only subset the RID list obtained as a result of accessing the first index and locks would have been obtained on those RIDs (or the data pages) during the access to the first index due to data-only locking. To take an example, if the predicates are *F1 = C1 AND F2 = C2 AND ...*

AND Fk=Ck, where the *Ci*s are constants and the *Fi*s are fields, then assuming that there are separate indexes on each of the referenced fields and that the predicate on *F1* is the most restrictive, locking will be done while accessing *F1*'s index. This will permit other transactions to insert records which do not satisfy the query's predicates, including those records which satisfy the predicate *F1* ≠ *C1 AND (F2 = C2 OR ... OR Fk = Ck)*. Without our optimization of avoiding locking on all the indexes except the index on F1, the latter records would not have been insertable by other transactions.

The above idea concerning locking can easily be extended to the case where a mixture of conjunctive and disjunctive predicates are involved. If index-specific locking is used, then (1) locking would have to be done during accesses to all the indexes or (2) locking needs to be done only while accessing one of the indexes, but when the data pages are accessed and the records are locked, the predicates already checked using the other indexes must be checked again. The latter is necessary since the keys in the other indexes may be in the uncommitted state. The fact that locking was done during the accesses of the first index does not guarantee that the corresponding records are in the committed state since the index locks are different from data locks.

With RR, when the final RID list is obtained and the data pages are accessed to retrieve the corresponding records, there is no need to do any further locking, since all the qualifying data would have already been locked during the index accesses. Furthermore, no predicates that were already checked need to be reevaluated. These optimizations could result in substantial path length savings, especially in the case of disjunctive predicates for which the number of qualifying RIDs may be large.

If, between the time the RID list is generated and the time a certain record (whose RID was in the list) is accessed for retrieval, the same transaction could perform some updates to the same table, then it is possible for those updates to affect the record under consideration in such a way as to disqualify the record. In such an event, it would be erroneous to return that record. This is possible in SQL since we would expect (1) the RID list to be materialized at the time of the OPEN of the cursor defining the query under consideration and (2) the records to be retrieved from the data pages using the RID list one at a time, as the FETCH calls are issued. Between the time of the OPEN and the FETCH call involving the record under consideration, many other SQL statements could have been executed by the transaction. In such a case, the predicates already checked would also have to be rechecked when the record is accessed using the RID in the list. In fact, it is even possible for the record not to exist anymore due to its earlier deletion by the same transaction. It is possible that new records have been inserted which satisfy the predicates. Such records will not be retrieved. Note that only the current transaction could have inserted those records and the nonretrieval of those records is not a violation of RR.

6.3. Cursor Stability

If the consistency level requested is CS, then, as long as latches are used to provide physical consistency while accessing the index pages, no locking needs to be done during the index accesses. When the final RID list is obtained and the data pages are accessed to retrieve the corresponding records, locking is done and **all** the predicates are reevaluated if the record still belongs to the table of interest. The records that do not qualify anymore (or those that have been deleted) are ignored. Note that in spite of the need for reevaluation of all the predicates, it *may* still be worthwhile performing the *full scan with RID list* (see section "3. Index Union for Disjunctive Predicates").

For read-only CS retrievals, during the RID list scan, by S latching the data page before requesting a lock on a qualifying RID on that page (or lock on the page itself if page locking is in effect), the lock duration can be made to be instant instead of manual. This is because, for such scans, we are only trying to make sure that the record does not contain uncommitted changes of another transaction and we are not trying to prevent future updates. Only for updateable CS cursors is the record under the cursor guaranteed to be nonupdateable by other transactions until the cursor is moved. Changing the duration from manual to instant reduces the number of interactions with the lock manager from two to one. In order to avoid deadlocks involving latches, the instant duration lock must be requested conditionally. If the conditional lock request is not granted, then the latch must be released and the lock rerequested *unconditionally* for *manual* duration. With page locking, if all the qualifying RIDs on the page are not returned in one access (i.e., in one latch-unlatch interval) to the page, then it is better to request the page lock for manual duration rather than for instant duration. This is because the latch should not be held while returning to the caller. If performance rather than ultra-high concurrency is the greater concern, then it is better to get the page lock once for manual duration rather than getting it for instant duration as many times as there are qualifying records on the page (i.e., during every latch-unlatch interval).

Not doing the locking during the index accesses could result in substantial path length savings. It will also increase the level of concurrency and reduce the impact of ad hoc queries on online transactions. The concurrency advantages would be especially significant if page locking is used, instead of record locking. Such savings will occur even when the requested consistency level is RR.

7. Parallelism

With the availability of cheap and powerful microprocessors, exploitation of parallelism has become enormously important [Bora88, PMCLS89]. If multiple indexes are going to be used for a single table access, then we can exploit parallelism conveniently by using one process for each index access. Of course, partitioning the work in this way does not guarantee balancing of the load across the different processes. Accesses to the data pages can also be performed in parallel using multiple processes, thereby gaining I/O parallelism and computation parallelism. If multiple processes are involved and a shared-memory architecture is used, then the bit vector approach will make it easier to gain the reductions in locking described in section "6. Locking and Bit Vectors" and also to do index unions. This is because sharing of information between processes is easier with bit vectors than with RID lists. In a nonshared-memory architecture, the RID list approach is the right one. If the RID list approach is used, parallelism can be exploited during the sorting and the merging of the different RID lists also ([LoYo89, ValH88] describe algorithms for performing merges in parallel).

When parallelism is used, supporting dynamic adaptation via the use of the upper and lower bound thresholds requires more work. In the shared-memory architecture, one or more global counters may be used to communicate amongst the processes information about the number of RIDs that each process has retrieved. During the processing of conjunctive predicates, if one process has retrieved less RIDs than the lower bound threshold, then that process can terminate the other processes. A process which has reached the upper bound threshold can terminate itself.

8. Summary

In this paper, we concentrated on techniques for deciding how many and which indexes to use for accessing the records of a table, while minimizing the cost of evaluating the query. We also discussed techniques to minimize the cost of locking and to avoid, when records are accessed, unnecessary reevaluations of the predicates which had already been checked during index accesses. A subset of the ideas of this paper have been implemented in Version 2 Release 2 of DB2 [Alur89]. The ideas relating to locking are not implemented, since, in today's DB2, the smallest granularity of locking is a page and no latching support exists for pages. The only way to guarantee physical consistency of the data in a page is via locking. The current DB2 index manager does index-specific locking. The bit vector ideas have not been implemented in DB2. Readers interested in performance numbers will find convincing evidence of the advantages of using multiple indexes in [Onei87, Onei89].

In systems which use at most one index for each table, the users who would like to let the optimizer choose an index to check multicolumn predicates are forced to define indexes with complex keys. Defining the latter is a nontrivial data base design problem since it requires deciding which fields to include and in which order. Once a system begins to support use of multiple indexes, then there is considerably less motivation for defining indexes with complex keys. Thus, the former eases a data base design problem.

Some of the ideas of this paper, like run-time adaptation and sorting RIDs before accessing data pages, are useful even if only one index is going to be used. Unclustered indexes are likely to be chosen more frequently now than before, since even when using unclustered indexes data accesses are made clustered by accessing the data in RID sequence. Prefetching of the data pages containing the records of interest is also made possible.

Acknowledgements We would like to thank Mike Carey, Laura Haas, Bala Iyer, Pat Selinger and, especially, Guy Lohman for their valuable comments.

9. References

Alur89 Alur, N. *A Look at Version 2.2's Performance Enhancements*, **The Relational Journal for DB2 Users**, Volume 1, Number 3, November 1989.

BlEs76 Blasgen, M., Eswaran, K. *On the Evaluation of Queries in a Relational Data Base System*, **IBM Research Report RJ1745**, IBM San Jose Research Laboratory, April 1976.

BlEs77 Blasgen, M., Eswaran, K. *Storage and Access in Relational Databases*, **IBM Systems Journal**, Vol. 16, No. 4, 1977.

Bora88 Boral, H. *Parallelism in Bubba*, **Proc. International Symposium on Databases for Parallel and Distributed Systems**, Austin, December 1988.

CLSW84 Cheng, J., Loosely, C., Shibamiya, A., Worthington, P. *IBM Database 2 Performance: Design, Implementation, and Tuning*, **IBM Systems Journal**, Vol. 23, No. 2, 1984.

Daya87 Dayal, U. *Of Nests and Trees: A Unified Approach to Processing Queries that Contain Nested Subqueries, Aggregates, and Quantifiers*, **Proc. 13th International Conference on Very Large Data Bases**, Brighton, September 1987.

EGLT76 Eswaran, K.P., Gray, J., Lorie, R., Traiger, I. *The Notion of Consistency and Predicate Locks in a Database System*, **Communications of the ACM**, Vol. 19, No. 11, November 1976.

Gray78 Gray, J. *Notes on Data Base Operating Systems*, In **Operating Systems - An Advanced Course**, R. Bayer, R. Graham, and G. Seegmuller (Eds.), Lecture Notes in Computer Science, Volume 60, Springer-Verlag, 1978.

LoYo89 Lorie, R., Young, H. *A Low Communication Sort Algorithm for a Parallel Database Machine*, **Proc. 15th International Conference on Very Large Data Bases**, Amsterdam, August 1989.

Also Available as **IBM Research Report RJ6669**, IBM Almaden Research Center, February 1989.

Lync88 Lynch, C. *Selectivity Estimation and Query Optimization in Large Data Bases with Highly Skewed Distributions of Column Values*, **Proc. 14th International Conference on Very Large Data Bases**, Los Angeles, August-September 1988.

MHLPS89 Mohan, C., Haderle, D., Lindsay, B., Pirahesh, H., Schwarz, P. *ARIES: A Transaction Recovery Method Supporting Fine-Granularity Locking and Partial Rollbacks Using Write-Ahead Logging*, To Appear in **ACM Transactions on Database Systems**. Also Available as **IBM Research Report RJ6649**, IBM Almaden Research Center, January 1989.

Moha89 Mohan, C. *ARIES/KVL: A Key-Value Locking Method for Concurrency Control of Multiaction Transactions Operating on B-Tree Indexes*, **IBM Research Report RJ7008**, IBM Almaden Research Center, September 1989.

MoLe89 Mohan, C., Levine, F. *ARIES/IM: An Efficient and High Concurrency Index Management Method Using Write-Ahead Logging*, **IBM Research Report RJ6846**, IBM Almaden Research Center, August 1989.

MuDe88 Muralikrishna, M., DeWitt, D. *Equi-depth Multidimensional Histograms*, **Proc. ACM-SIGMOD International Conference on Management of Data**, Chicago, June 1988.

Mura88 Muralikrishna, M. *Optimization of Multiple-Disjunct Queries in a Relational Database System*, **PhD Thesis**, Computer Science Technical Report #750, University of Wisconsin at Madison, February 1988.

Onei87 O'Neil, P. *MODEL 204 Architecture and Performance*, **Proc. 2nd International Workshop on High Performance Transaction Systems**, Asilomar, September 1987. Also in **Lecture Notes in Computer Science Vol. 359**, D. Gawlick, M. Haynie, A. Reuter (Eds.), Springer-Verlag, 1989.

Onei89 O'Neil, P. *A Set Query Benchmark for Large Databases*, **Proc. CMG Conference**, Reno, December 1989.

PMCLS89 Pirahesh, H., Mohan, C., Cheng, J., Liu, T.S., Selinger, P. *Parallelism in Relational Data Base Systems: Architectural Issues and Design Approaches*, **IBM Research Report**, IBM Almaden Research Center, December 1989.

RoRe82 Rosenthal, A., Reiner, D. *An Architecture for Query Optimization*, **Proc. ACM-SIGMOD International Conference on Management of Data**, Orlando, June 1982.

SACL79 Selinger, P., Astrahan, M., Chamberlin, D., Lorie, R., Price, T. *Access Path Selection in a Relational Database Management System*, **Proc. ACM-SIGMOD International Conference on Management of Data**, Boston, June 1979.

TeGu84 Teng, J., Gumaer, R. *Managing IBM Database 2 Buffers to Maximize Performance*, **IBM Systems Journal**, Vol. 23, No. 2, 1984.

ValH88 Varman, P., Iyer, B., Haderle, D. *Parallel Merge on an Arbitrary Number of Processors*, **IBM Research Report RJ6632**, IBM Almaden Research Center, December 1988.

Optimization of Queries using Nested Indices

Elisa Bertino*
Istituto di Elaborazione dell'Informazione
Via S.Maria 46 - 56100 Pisa (Italy)

Abstract

The notion of nested object is a basic concept of the object-oriented paradigm. It allows the value of an object attribute to be another object or a set of other objects. This means that a class consists of a set of attributes, and the values of the attributes are objects that belong to other classes; that is, the definition of a class forms a hierarchy of classes. All attributes of the nested classes are nested attributes of the root of the hierarchy. In a previous paper [Bert 89], we have introduced the notion of nested index that associates the values of a nested attribute with the objects instances of the root of the hierarchy. In that paper, we have evaluated the performance of this indexing mechanism in the case of queries containing a single predicate. In the present paper, we consider the usage of nested indices in the framework of more general queries containing several predicates.

1 Introduction

Object-oriented databases have recently emerged as the new database generation. Their overall goal is to provide data management facilities for advanced applications, such as CAD/CAM, software engineering, office automation, that need handling objects more complex than tuples of relations. This has resulted in the development of several object-oriented DBMSs. These systems, because of the increased complexity of the data model, have had to address new issues and requirements in the design and analysis of suitable access mechanisms [Ditt 86]. In fact, to be viable an object-oriented approach to data management must be supported by an architecture that directly implements the basic concepts of the object-oriented paradigm.

One important element in the object-oriented paradigm is the view that the value of an attribute of an object is an object or a set of objects. A class C consists of a number of attributes, and the value of an attribute A of an object belonging to the class C is an object or a set of objects belonging to some other class C'. The class C' is the domain of the attribute A of the class C. The class C' in turn consists of a number of attributes, and their domains are other classes. In other words, in object-oriented databases a class is in general a hierarchy of classes. This hierarchy is called a *class-attribute hierarchy* in [Kim 88]. Figure 1 is an example class-attribute hierarchy; the hierarchy is rooted at the class Vehicle, and the * symbol next to an attribute indicates that the attribute is multi-valued. An attribute of any class in a class-attribute hierarchy is logically an attribute of the root of the hierarchy, that is, the attribute is a *nested attribute* of the root class. For example, in Figure 1, the Location attribute of the class Division is a nested attribute of the class Vehicle.

In normalized relational databases, the search conditions in a query are expressed as a boolean combination of predicates of the form <attribute operator value>. The query is directed to one or more relations, and the attribute specified in a predicate is an attribute of one of the relations.

*This work was partially performed while the author was visiting the Microelectronics and Computer Technology Corporation, Austin (Texas)

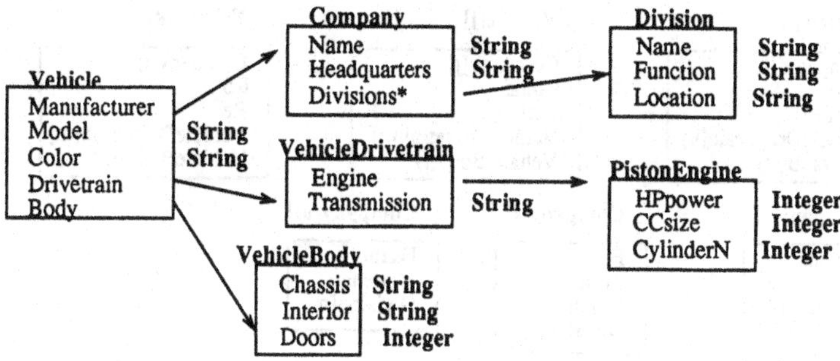

Figure 1: A class-attribute hierarchy

In object-oriented databases, the search conditions in a query on a class can still be expressed as a boolean combination of predicates of the form <attribute operator value>. However, the attribute may be a nested attribute of the class. For example, the following is a query that may be issued against the class Vehicle as defined in the class-attribute hierarchy of Figure 1.

Retrieve all 2-doored red vehicles manufactured by Fiat (Q1).

The query consists of a predicate against the non-nested attribute Color, and two predicates against the nested attributes Name and Doors. We call a predicate on a nested attribute a *nested predicate* and a predicate on a non-nested attribute a *simple predicate*. An important issue in supporting queries in object-oriented databases is the efficient evaluation of queries involving nested predicates.

Given a branch, or *path*, in a class-attribute hierarchy a nested index provides a direct association between the objects (or values) at the end of the path and the objects instances of the class which is the root of the path. For example, a nested index on the path P=Vehicle.Manufacturer.Name will associate a distinct value of the Name attribute with a list of object identifiers of Vehicle whose Manufacturer is an instance of the Company class whose Name is the key value. For the objects shown in Figure 2, the nested index will contain the following entries:
(Fiat, {Vehicle[i], Vehicle [j]}) (Renault, {Vehicle[k]}).

The attribute Name is the *ending attribute* of path P.

In [Bert 89], the performance and update costs of the nested index have been evaluated and compared with the costs of other organizations. The nested index has the best retrieval performance, while the update costs may be quite high depending on how the updates are distributed on the classes along the path. An overall conclusion was that the nested index organization can be convenient, compared to others, for path lengths 2 or 3 provided that reverse references among objects are supported. For greater path lengths, however, it is better to split a path into several subpaths and allocate a nested index on each path if the frequency of updates is not negligible.

In [Bert 89], however, the performance of the nested index has been evaluated in the case of queries containing a single predicate. In the present paper, we provide an analysis of the usage of the nested index when queries contain several predicates. In particular, we identify the types of queries for which a nested index is more suited. The goals of this analysis are: (1) to show additional opportunities provided by the usage of nested indices in optimizing queries; (2) to derive useful indications for index configuration strategies in the framework of object-oriented DBMSs. The remainder of this paper is organized as follows. In Section 2, we summarize query processing strategies in object-oriented DBMSs from [Kimk 88] and we introduce a graphical representation of query strategies that will be used throughout the paper. In Section 3 we present the analysis of query strategies where the nested index is used.

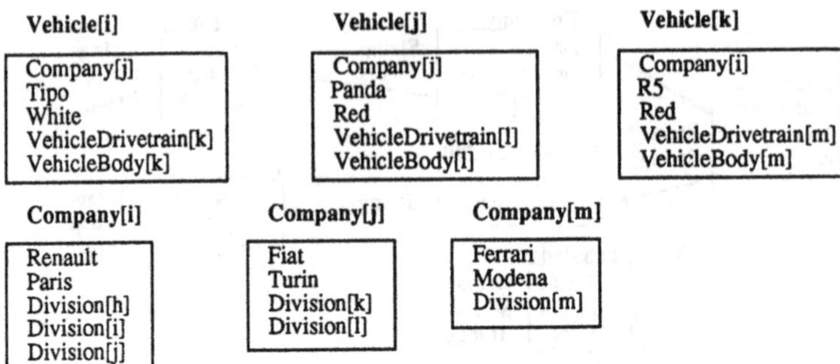

Figure 2: Instances of classes of Figure 1

2 Query Processing Strategies

The queries that we will consider throughout the discussion are single-target queries. A single-target query retrieves objects from only one class (called target class). Other classes, however, may be used in the query based on their relationships with the target class. Therefore, only implicit joins (i.e. joins based on the class-attribute hierarchy) may occur in the qualification part of the query. A qualification clause of a typical query will contain several predicates on both simple and nested attributes of the query target class.

As discussed in [Kimk 88], a query can be conveniently represented by a *query graph*. A detailed description of query graphs is presented in [Kimk 88]. The query execution strategies described in [Kimk 88] vary along two dimensions. The first dimension concerns the method used to traverse the query graph. The second dimension is the technique used to retrieve data from the classes that are traversed for the evaluation of nested predicates. There are three traversal methods [Kimk 88]:

- *Forward traversal*: the first class visited is the target class of the query (root of the query graph). The remaining classes are traversed starting from the target class in any depth-first order. Possible forward traversal strategies for query Q1 are (Vehicle VehicleBody Company) (Vehicle Company VehicleBody).
- *Reverse traversal*: the traversal of the query graph begins at the leaves and proceeds bottom-up along the graph. Possible reverse traversal strategies for query Q1 are (VehicleBody Company Vehicle) (Company VehicleBody Vehicle).
- *Mixed traversal*: this method is a combination of the previous two. Possible mixed traversal strategies for query Q1 are (Company Vehicle VehicleBody) (VehicleBody Vehicle Company).

In [Kimk 88] two methods are considered for retrieving data from a visited class. The first method is called *nested-loop* and consists of instantiating separately each qualified instance of a class. The instance attributes are examined for qualification, if there are simple predicates on the instance attributes. If the instance qualifies, it is passed to its parent node (in the case of reverse traversal) or to its child node (in case of forward traversal). The second method is called *sort-domain* and consists of instantiating all qualified instances of a class at once. Then all the qualifying instances are passed to their parent or child node (depending on the traversal strategy used).

We assume that the query returns the object-identifiers (UIDs) of the selected instances. Then the user can send messages to these instances to retrieve specific attributes or invoke methods.

A query execution strategy represents the decomposition of a query into a set of basic operations with a partial ordering among them. Basic operations are: index scan (I), nested-loop join (NJ), sort-merge join (SJ), intersection ($\bigcap$), selection (S), projection (P), sort-order (O). The selection is the operation of applying one or more simple predicates to a set of objects. The projection is the operation of extracting one or more attributes from an instance. We assume

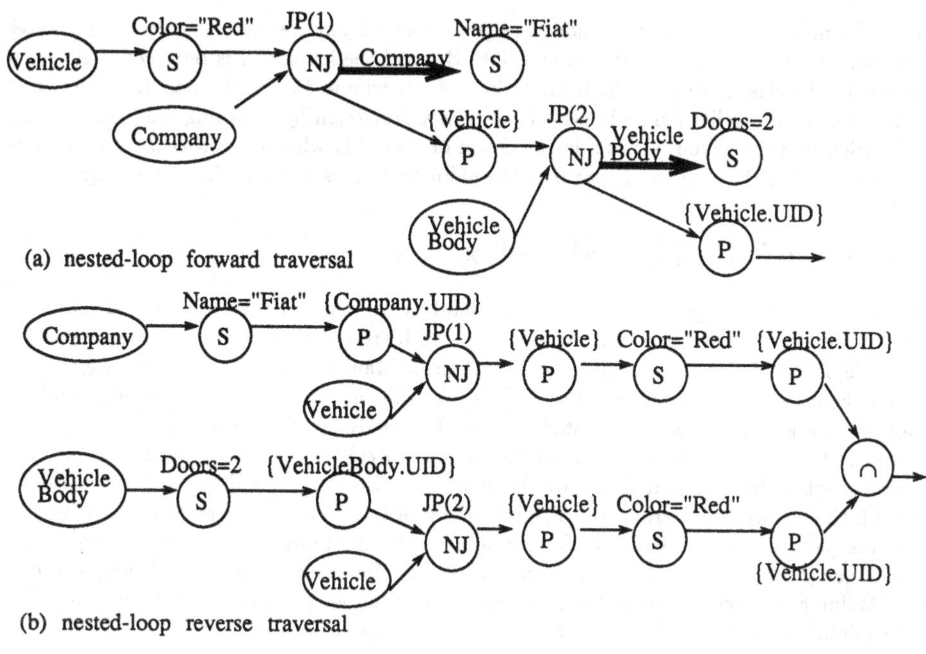

Figure 3: Example of graphical representation of nested-loop strategies

that the projection eliminates the duplicates. A special attribute name, UID, prefixed by a class name indicates that the object identifiers of the instances of the class must be returned by the projection.

We will represent a query execution strategy by using a *query execution graph* (QEG). Each node in a QEG is labeled with the name of the operation it represents. A node representing a selection operation has also associated the selection predicate. Similarly, a node representing an index scan operation has associated the predicate which is solved by the index scan. If a node represents a sort-order operation, the name of the sort attribute is associated with the node. Nodes are also used to represent the classes to which the query applies. In this case, the node is labeled with the name of the class it represents.

Arcs in a QEG are oriented. An arc from node N to node N' indicates that the result of the operation (or the instances of the class) represented by node N is the input to the operation represented by node N'. Using this graphical representation some of possible execution graphs for the query Q1 are represented in Figure 3. A node representing a join (either nested-loop or sort-merge) has associated a join predicate. In addition it may have a conditional exiting arc (represented in bold in the graphs). The meaning of this conditional arc is the following. Once a join is executed, the instance of the class whose name labels the conditional arc is passed to the node which follows the conditional edge and the predicate represented by this node is evaluated. If the instance verifies this predicate, the join result is passed to the (non-conditional) arc following the join node. For example, in the query strategy in Figure 3(a), an instance I of class Vehicle is accessed. If attribute Color of I has value "red", the value of the attribute Manufacturer of I is retrieved (node NJ). This value is an instance J of the class Company. Then the attribute Name of J is examined (conditional node S following the join). If the Name is equal to "Fiat", the result of the operation NJ, that is, the pairs of instances (I,J) is passed to the non-conditional node following the node NJ. The following node is a project operation that retains only the instances of class Vehicle, i.e. I. Then the value of attribute Body of the instance I is retrieved. This is an instance K of the class Autobody. If K has value 2 for attribute Doors, the pair (I,K) is passed to the following non-conditional node, which executes a projection by returning the identifier of I. The execution of a query consists of a linearization of the QEG where the ordering relationships are preserved. Since the ordering is partial, several linearizations can exist for a given QEG.

3 Usage of the Nested Index

In general the usage of nested index appears useful in the case of reverse traversal or mixed traversal strategies, since several accesses to classes can be replaced by the scan of a single index. For example, if an index is defined on the path P=Vehicle.Manufacturer.Name, in a strategy using this index the class Company needs not to accessed. In this section we provide a detailed analysis of query processing strategies using nested indices. The analysis will be restricted to the case of predicates of the form: key=value (i.e. *single-key* predicates). Also, we assume that a query is directed against a class without including its subclasses. However, the discussion can be easily extended if these restrictions are lifted. The remainder of this section is organized as follows. We first list the parameters used in the evaluation and the assumptions made. Then we discuss the cases of a query containing a nested predicate and a simple predicate in conjunction, and of a query containing two nested predicates in conjunction. Then we generalize our discussion to the case of conjunctive queries containing more than two predicates.

3.1 Parameters

Given a path $P = C_1.A_1.A_2.\ldots.A_n$, such that the corresponding classes along P are $\{C_1, C_2, \ldots, C_n\}$, we have the following parameters that describe characteristics of the classes and attributes:

- D_i number of distinct values for attribute A_i, $1 \leq i \leq n$. In particular, when $1 \leq i < n$, this parameter defines the number of distinct references from instances of class C_i to instances of class C_{i+1} through attribute A_i.
- N_i cardinality of class C_i, $1 \leq i \leq n$.
- k_i average number of instances of class C_i, assuming the same value for attribute A_i; $k_i = \lceil N_i/D_i \rceil$.
- $UIDL$ length of the object-identifier.
- $PC(C_i)$, $1 \leq i \leq n$, number of disk pages containing instances of class C_i. $1 \leq i \leq n$,
- NIA cost of access to a nested index. For this cost, we use the formulation presented in [Bert 89].
- SIA cost of access to a simple (non-nested) index. Also for this cost, we use the formulation presented in [Bert 89].

The parameters k_i $(1 \leq i \leq n)$ model the degree of reference sharing, which impacts the costs most significantly. Two objects share a reference if they reference the same object.

To simplify our model, we make a number of assumptions.

1. Each instance of a class C_i is referenced by instances of class C_{i-1}, $1 < i \leq n$. This implies that $D_i = N_{i+1}$.
2. All key values have the same length. As discussed in [Bert 89], this implies that all non-leaf node index records have the same length in all indices.
3. The values of attributes are uniformly distributed among instances of the class defining the attributes.

4. All attributes are single-valued.
5. The indices are not clustered. This means that in general instances are not stored according to the same order in which their UIDs are stored in the leaf-node index records. This assumption is to simplify the presentation of the model. However, the model can be easily extended to the case of clustered indices.

3.2 Nested predicate and simple predicate

Let us consider the path $P = C_1.A_1.A_2.\ldots.A_n$. Suppose that a nested index (NI) is defined on this path. Suppose also that class C_1 has in addition to A_1 another attribute A' which has as domain a primitive class. Suppose that a query is issued on class C_1 having a predicate P on the nested attribute A_n and a predicate P' on A'. We distinguish two cases depending on whether or not an index is defined also on A'.

no index on A'

In this case, we consider four strategies. The first two are based on reverse traversal with the usage of the nested index. They consist of evaluating the nested predicate by using the nested index, and then accessing the selected objects to evaluate the predicate on A'. In the first strategy (NL-RT-NI) a UID is retrieved from the index. Then the physical address of the corresponding object is determined, the object is accessed and the remaining predicate is evaluated on the object, according to the nested loop method. This is executed for all objects that are retrieved from the index search. The second strategy (SD-RT-NI) differs from the first in that all UIDs from the index are retrieved at once. Their physical addresses are determined and sorted. This method avoids accessing twice the same page if two objects retrieved from the index are stored in the same page. The third strategy (NL-FT) consists of accessing all objects of class C_1 evaluating first the predicate on A' and then evaluating the nested predicate by using the nested-loop method. The fourth strategy (SD-FT) is similar to the third except that sort-domain method is used. Both the third and fourth strategies use the forward traversal. Note that in the third and fourth strategies the nested index is not used. We do not consider in this case reverse traversal strategies without using the index, since it is obvious that the strategy using the index is more efficient. In order to compare the strategies we provide an estimate of their cost in terms of page accesses.

cost(NL-RT-NI)$= NIA + 2 \times nr$

where $nr = k_1 \times k_2 \times \ldots \times k_n$ is the number of UIDs retrieved by the index scan. For each of them one access must be executed to determine the physical address of the object and then another access to evaluate the predicate on A'.

In the case of the SD-RT-NI, we determine the number of class pages to be accessed by using a formula developed in [Yao 77]. This formula determines the number of page hits when accessing k records randomly selected from a file containing n records grouped into m pages:

$$H(k,m,n) = m \times [1 - \prod_{i=1}^{k} \frac{n-(n/m)-i+1}{n-i+1}].$$

Therefore **cost(SD-RT-NI)** $= NIA + nr + sort(nr \times UIDL) + H(nr, PC(C_1), N_1)$

In the previous expression the number of page accesses needed to sort a list nr of UIDs is given by $TP \times (log_2 TP)$ where TP is the number of bytes needed to store the list of UIDs. We are assuming that two-way sorting is performed.

cost(NL-FT) $= PC(C_1) + 2 \times k(A') \times (n-1)$.

In the previous expression $k(A')$ represents the average number of instances of C_1 having the same value for A' and therefore satisfying a single-key predicate on A'. For each of these objects a forward traversal must be performed until the value of the nested attribute A_n is determined. Note that if there is high degree of reference sharing, this strategy may cause accessing several times the same object.

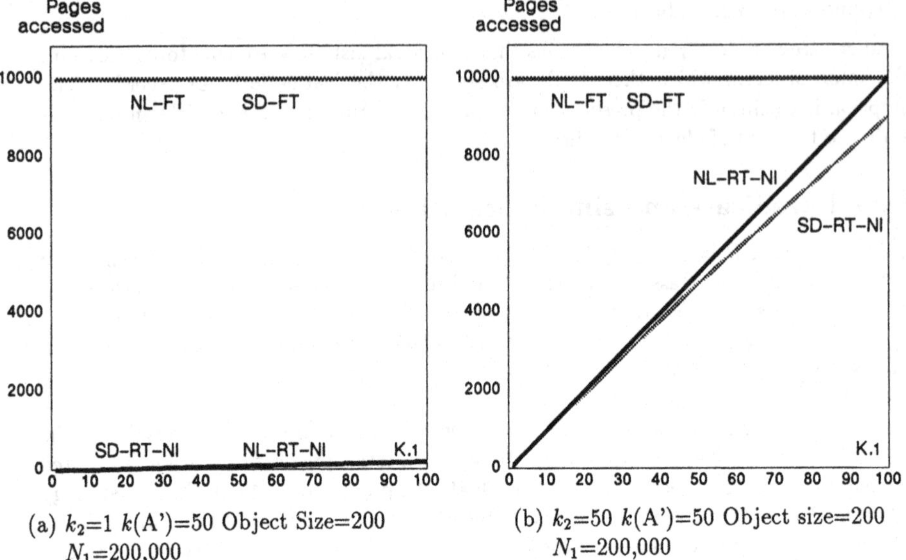

(a) k_2=1 k(A')=50 Object Size=200 N_1=200,000

(b) k_2=50 k(A')=50 Object size=200 N_1=200,000

Figure 4: Query costs

In evaluating the cost of the sort-domain forward traversal, we must determine the number of objects of class C_{i+1} that must be accessed (without repetition), once a number no_i of objects of class C_i have been selected. The objects of class C_{i+1} that must be accessed are those that are values of attribute A_i of class C_i. Under the assumption that attributes are single-valued, this number is evaluated by using the formula developed in [Yao 77].

Therefore, given $k(A')$ the number of objects of class C_1 verifying the predicate on A', no_i is evaluated as follows

$no_2 = H(k(A'), D_1, N_1)$ $no_i = H(no_{i-1}, D_{i-1}, N_{i-1})$ for $i = 3, n$.

cost(SD-FT) $= PC(C_1) + \sum_{i=2}^{n}[no_i + sort(no_i \times UIDL) + H(no_i, PC(C_i), N_i)]$.

index on A'

In this case, we have the same strategies as before. The only difference is that the predicate on A' is now evaluated by using the index, rather than accessing all instances of class C_1. Therefore, one strategy (RT-NI-SI) consists of scanning the two indices, and then intersecting the results of the index scans. We assume that UIDs in the index records are kept ordered, so that there is no need to execute a sort before performing the intersection. Other two strategies (NL-FT-SI and SD-FT-SI) are similar to strategies NL-FT and SD-FT. The only difference is that here the predicate on attribute A' is evaluated by using the simple index on attribute A'. The costs are as follows:

cost(RT-NI-SI) $= NIA + SIA$ **cost(NL-FT-SI)** $= SIA + 2 \times k(A') \times n$.

cost(SD-FT-SI) $= SIA + k(A') + sort(k(A') \times UIDL) + H(K(A'), PC(C_1), N_1) + \sum_{i=2}^{n}[no_i + sort(no_i \times UIDL) + H(no_i, PC(C_i), N_i)]$.

comparison

When there is no index on attribute A', the strategies using the index (i.e. NL-RT-NI and SD-RT-NI) have a better performance in most of the cases. However, when there is a high degree of reference sharing along the path on which the nested index is defined and the number of pages occupied by the class C_1 is small, the strategies using the index have a cost which is very close to the cost of the strategies that do not use the index (i.e. NL-FT and SD-FT). Figure 4 presents an example of the cost in term of page accesses for the case of a nested index defined on a path $P = C_1.A_1.A_2$ (of length 2).

We note that when the product $k_1 \times k_2$ is equal to 5000 (see Figure 4.b) the cost of the strategy NL-RT-NI is equal to the cost of the strategies NL-FT and SD-FT. This is explained by observing

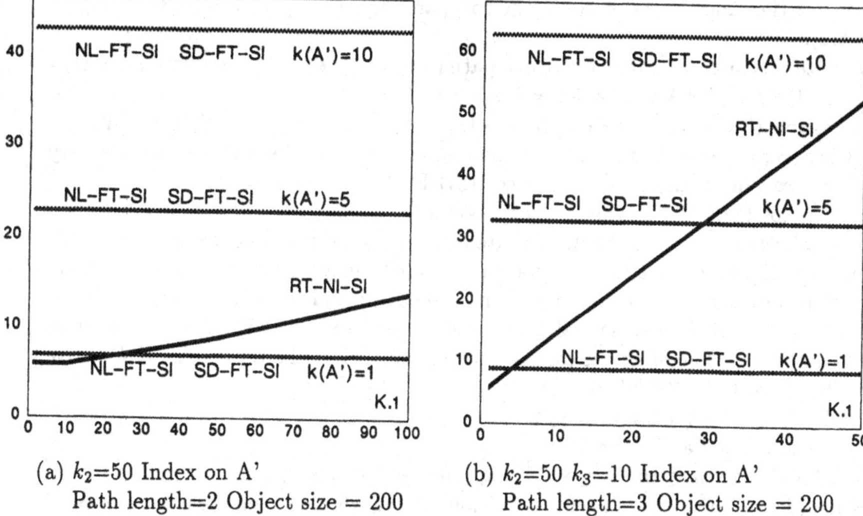

(a) k_2=50 Index on A'
Path length=2 Object size = 200

(b) k_2=50 k_3=10 Index on A'
Path length=3 Object size = 200

Figure 5: Query costs

that the number of UIDs that are returned by the nested index scan is given by the product $k_1 \times k_2$. For each of the returned UIDs, the physical address of the object must be determined and then the object accessed. Therefore, for each UID returned from the index scan two accesses must be executed. The SD-RT-NI performs slightly better when a large number of UIDs are returned, since it avoids accessing the same page twice. We observe that the strategies using the nested index would have half of the cost, if the object physical addresses were stored in the index records. However, in environments where objects change sizes and structures dynamically, storing the object physical addresses in the index records may be rather expensive.

We now generalize this discussion to the case of a path length n for the case when nested loop is used. We have that cost(NL-FT) > cost(NL-RT-NI) (1) if

$PC(C_1) + 2 \times k(A') \times (n-1) > NIA + 2 \times k_1 \times k_2 \times \ldots \times k_n$ (2) where

cost(NIA) $= 2 + \lceil k_1 \times k_2 \times \ldots \times k_n / 500 \rceil$ (3)

We assume that the cost of the index scan is equal to the cost of traversing the non leaf-nodes of the index is 2 (which is a common case) plus the cost of accessing the leaf-node record. The derivation of the last cost is summarized in Appendix from [Bert 89]. Therefore expression (2) becames

$PC(C_1) + 2 \times k(A') \times (n-1) > 2 + \lceil k_1 \times k_2 \times \ldots \times k_n/500 \rceil + 2 \times k_1 \times k_2 \times \ldots \times k_n$.

From the previous expression, we obtain that the inequality (1) holds if:

$PC(C_1) > 2 + \lceil k_1 \times k_2 \times \ldots \times k_n/500 \rceil + 2 \times k_1 \times k_2 \times \ldots \times k_n - 2 \times k(A') \times (n-1)$ (4).

When there is an index on attribute A', the strategy RT-NI-SI performs in general better than the strategies that do not use the nested index (i.e. NL-FT-SI and SD-FT-SI). However, when there is a high degree of reference sharing along the path on which the nested index is defined and $k(A')$ is small, the strategy RT-NI-SI (using both the nested index and the index on attribute A') has a higher cost than the strategies that do not use the nested index. Figure 5 presents some examples of the cost for the cases of a nested index defined on a path $P_1 = C_1.A_1.A_2$ (of length 2) and on a path $P_2 = C_1.A_1.A_2.A_3$ (of length 3).

This is explained by observing that when the degree of reference sharing along the path is high, a leaf-node record occupies more than one page (cf. expression for record size in Appendix). This increases the cost of the nested index access. If in addition, the value of $k(A')$ is small, the number of object accesses in the strategies that do not use the nested index is quite low. This number depends on $k(A')$ and on the path length (cf. expression for NL-FT-SI and SD-FT-SI).

This explains why for the same values of $k(A')$, the costs are higher for path length 3 (cf. Figure 5.a with Figure 5.b).

We now generalize this discussion to the case of a path length n. We have that cost(RT-NI-SI)> cost(NL-FT-SI) (4) if $NIA + SIA > SIA + 2 \times k(A') \times n$ (5).

By using expression (3) for NIA we obtain $2 + \lceil k_1 \times k_2 \times \ldots \times k_n/500 \rceil > 2 \times k(A') \times n$ (6). Therefore, whenever expression (6) holds it is preferable not using the nested index in query execution. Furthermore, since cost(NL-FT-SI) $\geq$ cost(SD-FT-SI), we have that

cost(RT-NI-SI) > cost(SD-FT-SI) whenever expression (6) holds.

We now discuss whether it is preferable to allocate a simple index or a nested index on a given class. In fact, in several situations allocating too many indices may increase the cost of object updates and therefore a careful choice must be performed about the indices to be allocated. This is an important point since it provides some useful indications for the problem of index configuration in object-oriented databases. Therefore, we compare strategies NL-FT-SI and NL-RT-NI. We have that cost(NL-FT-SI) $\geq$ cost(NL-RT-NI) if

$SIA + 2 \times k(A') \times n \geq NIA + 2 \times k_1 \times k_2 \times \ldots \times k_n$ (7).

Expression (7) is developed as follows:

$\lceil k(A')/500 \rceil + 2 \times k(A') \times n \geq \lceil k_1 \times k_2 \times \ldots \times k_n/500 \rceil + 2 \times k_1 \times k_2 \times \ldots \times k_n$ (8).

From expression (8) we derive the following condition stating whether a simple index or nested index must be allocated.

Proposition 1 *Given a path* $P = C_1.A_1.A_2.\ldots.A_n$ *and an attribute* A' *of class* C_1, *such that* $k_1 \times k_2 \times \ldots \times k_n = k(A')/\alpha$, *cost(NL-FT-SI)* $\geq$ *cost(NL-RT-NI) if*
(i) $\alpha \geq 1$ *or (ii)* $0 < \alpha < 1$ *and* $n > (1 + 1/1000) \times 1/\alpha$.
The derivation of the condition is presented in [Bert 89a].

3.3 Two nested predicates

Let us consider two paths $P_1 = C_1.A_1.A_2.\ldots.A_n$ and $P_2 = C_1.A'_1.A'_2.\ldots.A'_m$ ($n \geq 2$ and $m \geq 2$) both originating from the same class. Let us assume that the classes associated with the paths are as follows:

Class(P_1) = $\{C_1, C_2, \ldots, C_n\}$ Class(P_2) = $\{C_1, C'_2, \ldots, C'_m\}$.

We consider a query with two predicates: $Pred_n$ on the nested attribute A_n, and $Pred_m$ on the nested attribute A'_m. Suppose that a nested index (NI) is defined on P_1. We discuss first the case when the two paths are not overlapping. Examples of non overlapping paths are Vehicle.Manufacturer.Name, Vehicle.Body.Chassis, while examples of overlapping paths are Vehicle.Manufacturer.Name, Vehicle.Manufacturer.Headquarters.

3.3.1 Non overlapping paths

As for the previous case, we distinguish two cases depending on whether or not a nested index is defined also on P_2.

no nested index on P_2

In this case, we consider four strategies. The first two are based on reverse traversal with the usage on the nested index. They consist of evaluating the predicate on the nested attribute A_n by using the nested index defined on P_1. The predicate on the nested attribute A'_m is evaluated by using a reverse traversal, starting from last class on path P_2. The difference between the two strategies is that the first (NL-RT-NI(P_1)) uses a nested-loop while the second (SD-RT-NI(P_1)) uses the sort-domain strategy. The third and fourth strategies are mixed strategies. They consist of evaluating the predicate on the nested attribute A_n by using the nested index defined on P_1. The predicate on the nested attribute A'_m is evaluated by using a forward-traversal strategy. The difference between the two strategies is that the third (NL-FT-NI(P_1)) uses a nested-loop while the fourth (SD-FT-NI (P_1)) uses the sort-domain strategy. In the following we list the cost formulae

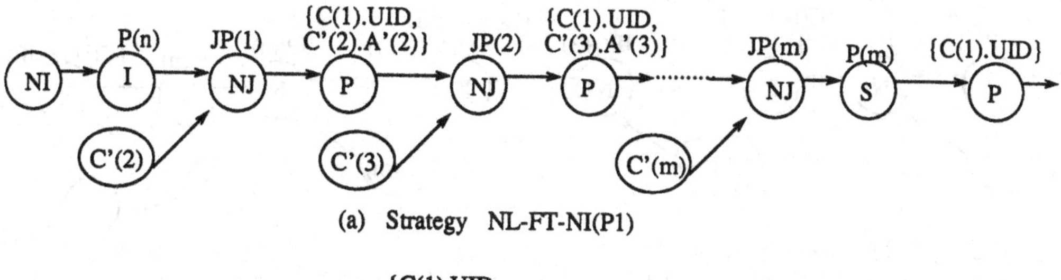

(a) Strategy NL-FT-NI(P1)

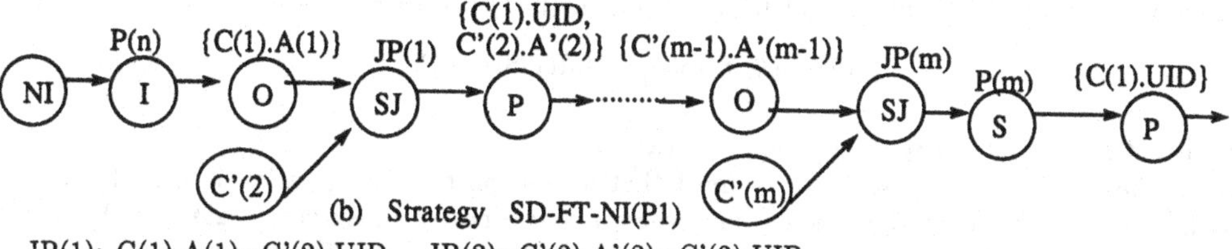

(b) Strategy SD-FT-NI(P1)

JP(1): C(1).A(1)=C'(2).UID JP(2): C'(2).A'(2)=C'(3).UID ....
JP(m): C(m-1).A'(m-1)=C'(m).UID

Figure 6: Strategies for queries containing two nested predicates

only for third and fourth strategies, since the strategies based on reversal traversal have greater costs in most cases. The NL-FT-NI(P_1) and SD-FT-NI(P_1) strategies are graphically represented in Figure 6.

cost(NL-FT-NI(P_1)) $= NIA(P_1) + 2 \times nr \times m$ (9)

where $nr = k_1 \times k_2 \times \ldots \times k_n$ is the number of UIDs retrieved by the index scan. For each UID retrieved from the index scan, the corresponding object is fetched and its value for attribute A'_1 is determined. The object which is value of attribute A'_1 is fetched and its value for attribute for attribute A'_2 is determined, and so forth until the value of attribute A'_m is obtained.

cost(SD-FT-NI(P_1)) $= NIA(P_1) + nr + sort(nr \times UIDL) + (nr, PC(C_1), N_1) + \sum_{i=2}^{m}[no_i + sort(no_i \times UIDL) + H(no_i, PC(C'_i), N'_i)]$

where no_i is evaluated as follows

$no_2 = H(nr, D'_1, N_1)$ $no_i = H(no_{i-1}, D'_{i-1}, N'_{i-1})$ for $i = 3, m$.

nested index on P_2

In this case we consider the strategy where both indices are used. This strategy (NI(P_1)-NI(P_2)) has the following cost: **cost(NI(P_1)-NI(P_2))** $= NIA(P_1) + NIA(P_2)$.

comparison

In general the strategy based on the usage of both indices has lower costs than the strategies where only one index is used. However, in certain situations the latter may perform better. Using the previous expressions we have that cost(NI(P_1)-NI(P_2)) > cost(NL-FT-NI(P_1)) if the following inequality holds:

$NIA(P_1) + NIA(P_2) > NIA(P_1) + 2 \times nr \times m.$

The previous inequality is developed as follows

$2 + \lceil nr'/500 \rceil > 2 \times nr \times m$ where $nr' = k'_1 \times > k'_2 \times \ldots \times k'_m$, that is

$nr' > 500 \times nr \times (2 \times m - 2/nr)$ (10).

Therefore, using the strategy based only on the nested index on P_1 is better if there is a high degree of reference sharing on path P_2, while there is a low or no degree of reference sharing on path P_1. For example, if $nr = 1$ (no reference sharing) and $m = 3$, the strategy that uses only the nested index on P_1 is less costly than the strategy using both indices if $nr' > 2000$.

3.3.2 Overlapping paths

We consider now the case of overlapping paths originating from the same class. That is, given $P_1 = C_1.A_1.A_2.\ldots.A_n$ and $P_2 = C_1.A'_1.A'_2.\ldots.A'_m$, a subscript j ($j < \min\{m, n\}$ and$j > 1$) exists

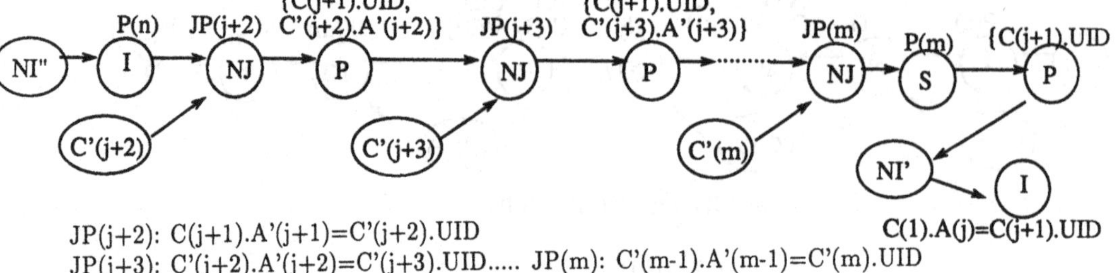

Figure 7: Strategy NL-RT-SNI(P_1)

such that $A_i = A'_i$ $(1 \leq i \leq j)$ and $A_i \neq A'_i$ for $i > j$.

In the previous cases, we have assumed that a non-splitted configuration is used for the paths. A non-splitted configuration is one where a single nested index is allocated on the entire path. However for certain types of queries, it may be more cost effective to split the path into several subpaths and allocate a nested index on each subpath. For example, given the path P=Vehicle.Manufacturer.Divisions.Location a possible splitted configuration is the following:

P'=Vehicle.Manufacturer, P"=Company.Divisions.Location.

In this case, the path has been split into two subpaths. The first has length 1 and associates with each company the set of vehicles manufactured by that company. The second has length 2 and associates with each value of location, the set of companies having a division at that location. In this case a query like

Retrieve all vehicles manufactured by a company having a division located in Milan

is processed as follows. The nested index defined on P" is accessed to determine all companies having a division located in Milan. Then the index on P' is accessed to determine all vehicles that are manufactured by one of the companies returned by the previous index lookup.

While it is clear that a non-splitted organization is more efficient in all the previous types of queries, for queries with nested predicates on overlapping paths a splitted organization may be more efficient. Therefore, a result of this analysis is to determine in which cases a splitted configuration is more efficient that the non-splitted index configuration.

no nested index on P_2

Given the path P_1, the splitted configuration that we consider is the following:

$P'_1 = C_1.A_1.A_2.\ldots.A_j, P"_1 = C_{j+1}.A_{j+1}.\ldots.A_n$. Two nested indices NI' and NI" are allocated respectively on subpaths P'_1 and $P"_1$.

Note that if we consider path P_2, a subpath of P_2 defined as $P"_2 = C_{j+1}.A'_{j+1}.\ldots.A'_m$ is non-overlapping with path $P"_1$, while $P'_2 = C_1.A'_1.A'_2.\ldots.A'_j$ is equal to P'_1. This is by definition of j. Class C_{j+1} is called the *splitting class.*

When the non-splitted configuration on path P_1 is used, the execution strategies are the same as in the case of non overlapping paths (cf. subsection 3.3.1). If the splitted configuration is used, an additional strategy (NL-RT-SNI(P_1)) is possible. It is based on first evaluating both nested predicates with respect to class C_{j+1}. Since the paths $P"_1$ and $P"_2$ starting from C_{j+1} are non-overlapping or one of them could reduce to a simple attribute, the strategies seen in the previous cases can be used. For instance, the predicate on the nested attribute A_n could be evaluated by using the nested index on path $P"_1$. Then the predicate on the nested attribute A'_m could be evaluated by using a forward traversal strategy. Once the set S of qualifying instances of class C_{j+1} is determined, a lookup is executed for each one of them in the nested index defined on path P'_1. The index lookups determine the instances of class C_1 having as value of the (nested) attribute A_j one of the elements of set S. The set of instances of class C_1 returned by these index lookups is the set of instances verifying the query. The strategy is graphically represented in Figure 7.

As an example, we consider the case of the query

Retrieve all vehicles manufactured by a company with headquarters located in Milan and with at least one division located in Rome. (Q2)

Given this query, we have that P_1=Vehicle.Manufacturer.Divisions.Location and P_2=Vehicle. Manufacturer.Headquarters. In this case $j = 1$ and a splitted organization for P_1 is P_1'=Vehicle. Manufacturer, $P"_1$=Company.Divisions.Location. On each subpath a nested index is defined. P_2 is also splitted into P_2'=Vehicle.Manufacturer, and $P"_2$=Company.Headquarters. Note that with respect to the class Company, $P"_2$ reduces to a simple attribute. Company is the splitting class.

The query execution strategy consists of the following steps. First, the companies that have at least a division located in Rome are determined by looking up the nested index on $P"_1$. Then the selected instances of the class Company are accessed to evaluate the predicate on the attribute Headquarters. For each of the qualifying instances of class Company, an index lookup is executed in the index defined on P_1' to determine the vehicles having as manufacturer that instance. A variation of this strategy is to order all the qualifying instances and execute a single index lookup with key range. For simplicity, we do not present here the cost formulae for this variation. They can be found in [Bert 89].

The cost of the strategy NL-RT-SNI(PI) is derived as follows:

cost(NL-RT-SNI(P_1)) = cost(C_{j+1}) + $nr(C_{j+1}) \times NIA(P_1')$ (11) where:

- cost(C_{j+1}) is the cost of evaluating the query with respect to class C_{j+1};
- $nr(C_{j+1})$ is the number of instances of class C_{j+1} that qualify the query;

  $nr(C_{j+1}) = k_{j+1} \times k_{j+2} \times \ldots \times k_n / D'_m$

  (D'_m is the cardinality of the domain of attribute A'_m).
- $NIA(P_1')$ is the cost of index lookup for the index defined on path P_1';

  $NIA(P_1') = 2 + \lceil k_1 \times k_2 \times \ldots \times k_j / 500 \rceil$.

comparison

In order to compare the splitted versus the non-splitted configuration, we assume that the forward traversal with nested loop using the nested index on $P"_1$ is used (cf.subsection 3.3.1) to evaluate the query on class C_{j+1}. Therefore

cost(C_{j+1}) = cost(NL-FT-NI($P"_1$)) = $NIA(P"_1) + 2 \times k_{j+1} \times k_{j+2} \times \ldots \times k_n \times (m - j) =$
$2 + \lceil k_{j+1} \times k_{j+2} \times \ldots \times k_n / 500 \rceil + 2 \times k_{j+1} \times k_{j+2} \times \ldots \times k_n \times (m - j)$.

We also assume that when the non-splitted configuration is used for P_1, the strategy NL-FT-NI(P_1) is used to evaluate the query. The following proposition holds:

Proposition 2 *Given two overlapping paths P_1 and P_2,*
query-cost(non-splitted configuration) $\geq$ query-cost(splitted configuration) always for nested loop strategies.

Proposition 2 is demonstrated by showing that expression (9) (cf. Subsection 3.3.1) is always greater or equal to expression (11). The demonstration is presented in [Bert 89a].

nested index on P_2

In this case we consider three types of strategy for the nested index on P_1 and P_2. The first (NI(P_1)-NI(P_2)) is when the non-splitted index configurations are used on both paths. In this strategy both nested predicates are evaluated by using the indices and then intersecting the results of the two index lookups. The second (NI(P_1)-SNI(P_2)) is when a non-splitted index configuration is used on P_1, and a splitted configuration on P_2. This strategy is similar to the first, except that the evaluation of the predicate on the nested attribute A'_m requires to use two indices. We assume that the splitting class for P_2 is a class C'_i $(i > 1)$.

The third ((SNI(P_1)-SNI(P_2)) is one where a splitted configuration is used for both paths. In this configuration a nested index is allocated on each of the following subpaths

$P_1' = C_1.A_1.A_2.\ldots.A_j$, $P"_1 = C_{j+1}.A_{j+1}.\ldots.A_n$, $P"_2 = C_{j+1}.A'_{j+1}.\ldots.A'_m$.

The evaluation of the query consists of the following steps. The nested predicate on A'_m is evaluated with respect to the splitting class C_{j+1} by using the nested index defined on path $P"_2$. Similarly the nested predicate on A_n is evaluated with respect to C_{j+1} by using the nested index defined on path $P"_2$. The results of the two index lookups are intersected, generating a set S of instances of class C_{j+1} that qualify the query. For each instance in S a lookup is executed on the nested index defined on path P'_1. The index lookups determine the instances of class C_1 having as value of the (nested) attribute A_j on of the element of set S. The set of instances of class C_1 returned by these index lookups is the set of instances verifying the query.

The costs of the previous strategies are derived as follows

cost(NI(P_1)-NI(P_2)) $= NIA(P_1) + NIA(P_2)$ (11)

cost(NI(P_1)-SNI(P_2)) $= NIA(P_1) + NIA(P"_2) + nr(P"_2) \times NIA(P'_2)$ (12)

where $nr(P"_2) = k'_{i+1} \times k'_{i+2} \times \ldots \times k'_m$ is the number of instances of class C'_i that are returned from the lookup of the index on path $P"_2$.

cost(SNI(P_1)-SNI(P_2)) $= NIA(P"_1) + NIA(P"_2) + nr(C_{j+1}) \times NIA(P'_1)$ (13)

where $nr(C_{j+1})$ is as in expression (10).

comparison

The following propositions hold.

Proposition 3 *Given two overlapping paths P_1 and P_2, cost(NI(P_1)-SNI(P_2)) > cost(NI(P_1)-NI(P_2)) always.*

Proposition 3 is demonstrated by showing that expression (12) (cf. Subsection 3.3.1) is always greater or equal to expression (11). This proposition states that if a non-splitted configuration is used for path P_1, then a non-splitted configuration should be used also for path P_2.

Proposition 4 *Given two overlapping paths P_1 and P_2, such that*

- *C_{j+1} is the splitting class*
- $k_{j+1} \times k_{j+2} \times \ldots \times k_n = \alpha \times k_1 \times k_2 \times \ldots \times k_j \quad \alpha > 0$
- $k'_{j+1} \times k'_{j+2} \times \ldots \times k'_m = \beta \times k_1 \times k_2 \times \ldots \times k_j \quad \beta > 0$

cost(NI(P_1)-NI(P_2)) > cost(SNI(P_1)-SNI(P_2)) if the following condition holds:

$k_1 \times k_2 \times \ldots \times k_j \geq (\alpha \times (1 + 1000/D'_m) + \beta)/(\alpha(1 - 1/D'_m) + \beta)$.

For example, for $D'_m = 100$ and $\alpha = \beta = 10$, we obtain that strategy NI(P_1)-NI(P_2) has a higher cost if $k_1 \times k_2 \times \ldots \times k_j \geq 12$. Therefore, given two overlapping paths a splitted configuration is in general more efficient if the degrees of reference sharing on the common subpath are high.

3.4 Generalization

We first observe that if a query contains a nested predicate and several simple predicates, the results of section 3.2 can be easily extended to this case. Given a path $C_1.A_1.A_2.\ldots.A_n$ on which a nested index is defined, and given $B_1, B_2, \ldots, B_m$ simple attributes, we have that:

1. if no index is defined on any of the simple attributes,

   cost(NL-FT) > cost(NL-RT-NI) if

   $PC(C_1) > 2 + \lceil k_1 \times k_2 \times \ldots \times k_n/500 \rceil + 2 \times k_1 \times k_2 \times \ldots \times k_n - [2 \times N_1 \times (n-1)]/(D(B_1) \times D(B_2) \times \ldots \times D(B_m))]$

   where $D(B_i)$ is the number of distinct values of attribute B_i, $i = 1, ..., m$.

   Therefore the nested index should be used only if the previous inequality is verified.

2. if indices are defined on some of the simple attributes, for instance on $B_1, B_2, \ldots, B_k$, $1 < k \leq m$, then cost(NL-RT-NI) > cost(NL-FT-SI) if $2 + \lceil k_1 \times k \times 2 \times \ldots \times k_n/500 \rceil > 2 \times N_1/(D(B_1) \times D(B_2) \times \ldots \times D(B_k) + [2 \times N_1 \times (n-1)]/(D(B_1) \times D(B_2) \times \ldots \times D(B_m))$

   where $D(B_i)$ is the number of distinct values of attribute B_i, $i = 1, ..., m$.

   Therefore a strategy that uses the nested index and the simple indices is less costly of a strategy that uses only the simple indices if the previous inequality is verified.

Now we consider the case of several non overlapping paths originating from the same class. If nested indices are defined only on some paths, the best strategy in most cases is to use all the nested indices to restrict the target class (by performing an intersection of the results of the index lookup) and then to use a forward strategy to solve the nested predicates that have not been evaluated by using the nested indices. Note that in certain cases this strategy may not be optimal as we discussed in the case of two paths. This happens when a path P_i has a high degree of reference sharing, while the degree of reference sharing on the other paths is low. In this case, a strategy which uses all nested indices except the one on path P_i has a lower cost than the strategy using all nested indices. Conditions similar to condition (10) presented in Section 3.3.1 can be derived for the case of several non overlapping paths.

If there is only one nested index and all paths are overlapping then a splitted configuration is more efficient than a non-splitted configuration. Note however that in this case the indexed path may be split in more than two subpaths. As an example we consider the case of four paths:

$P_1 = C_1.A_1.A_2.A_3.A_4.A_5$ $P_2 = C_1.A_1.A_2.B_3.B_4$ $P_3 = C_1.A_1.A_2.B_3.D_4$ $P_4 = C_1.A_1.A_2.A_3.E_4$.

Let us assume that P_1 is the indexed path and also that C_3 is the class domain of attribute A_2 in P_1 and C_4 is the class domain of A_3. In this case, there are two splitting classes with respect to P_1: C_3 and C_4. Therefore an index configuration for P_1 is the following:

$P_{1_1} = C_1.A_1.A_2$, $P_{1_2} = C_3.A_3$, $P_{1_3} = C_4.A_4.A_5$. On each subpath a nested index is allocated. Note that when the subpath length is one, as for subpath P_{1_2}, the nested index coincides with a simple index (like in relational databases).

When there are both overlapping and non overlapping paths, the best index configuration for each path depends only on the overlapping subpaths, but it is independent from the non overlapping subpaths.

Finally we consider the case of a query on a class C having predicates on simple attributes, and predicates on the ending attributes of both overlapping and non overlapping paths. Suppose also that at least one nested index is defined. In this situation, the strategy with the lowest cost in most cases is the following:

1. evaluate with respect to class C all nested predicates that can be solved using nested indices and all predicates on non indexed paths overlapping with some of the indexed paths;
2. evaluate with respect to class C all simple predicates on attributes on which an index is defined;
3. intersect the results of the index lookups executed at the previous steps;
4. access the instances of class C obtained at step (3);
5. evaluate on each selected instance of C, the predicates on simple attributes that have not been evaluated at step (2);
6. evaluate on each instance selected at the previous step the predicates on nested attributes that have been not evaluated at step (1).

As an example, we consider the paths (originating from a class C) illustrated in Figure 8. Suppose that a nested index is defined on path $C.A_1.A_2.A_3$ and a simple index on B_1. We consider a query containing in the qualification clause the conjunction of predicates shown in Figure 8. Note that since path $C.A_1.A_2.A_3$ is overlapping with path $C.A_1.A_4$, a splitted configuration is used on $C.A_1.A_2.A_3$, that is:

$C.A_1$, $C_2.A_2.A_3$, where C_2 is the class domain of attribute A_1. Let NI_1 and NI_2 be the indices defined on these subpaths. NI_1 is a simple index, while NI_2 is a nested index.

Using the previous strategy, the query is evaluated as follows:

1. Predicate Pr1 is evaluated with respect to class C_2 using $N1_2$. Each of the selected instances of C_2 is accessed and predicate Pr2 is evaluated. Let $S(C_2)$ be the set of instances of class C_2 that satisfy both Pr1 and Pr2. For each instance in $S(C_2)$ an index lookup of NI_1 is executed. Let $S(A_1)$ be the set of instances of class C returned by the index lookups.

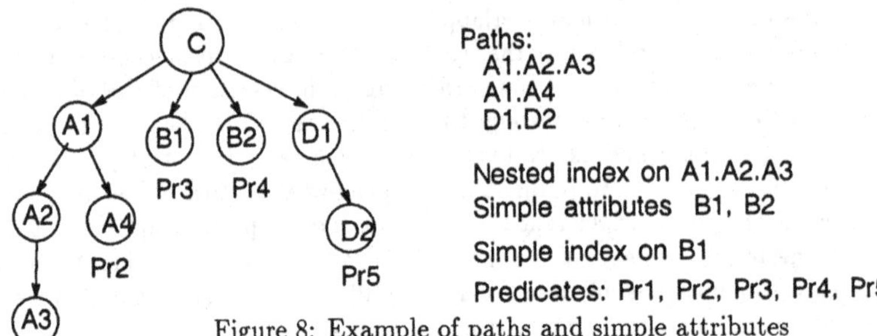

Figure 8: Example of paths and simple attributes

2. Predicate Pr3 is evaluated by using the index defined on B_1. Let $S(B_1)$ be the set of selected instances.
3. Sets $S(A_1)$ and $S(B_1)$ are intersected. Let S be the resulting set.
4. For each instance I in S the following steps are executed:

   (a) access I and evaluate predicate Pr4;

   (b) if I verifies Pr4, then evaluate Pr5 (using a forward traversal strategy);

   (c) if I verifies Pr5, then I qualifies the query.

In the previous example, we have assumed that nested loop is used. However, sort-domain can also be used.

4 Conclusions

In this paper, we have discussed the usage of an index organization for complex objects in the framework of different query patterns. The organization considered is called nested index and has been defined in [Bert 89]. Given a class C and a nested attribute A of C, a nested index associates with a given value of A the instances of C having that value for A. It is similar to a conventional index. The only difference is that the indexed attribute is a nested attribute.

We have evaluated the performance of this index organization under different query patterns. Based on our results, we can conclude that this organization provides competitive query execution strategies in most cases. In particular, we have shown that strategies based on the nested index are nearly always very efficient for queries having a predicate on deeply nested attribute of the target class and several predicates on simple attributes. When a query contains several predicates on nested attributes, the nested index organization is very efficient when paths are not overlapping. However, for overlapping paths different index configurations may be more efficient. In general these index configurations consist of splitting the indexed path into several subpaths and allocating a nested or a simple index on each subpath.

The results of this paper provide useful indications for the problem of index configuration in object-oriented databases. This problem is in general very complex and requires to take into account the update costs. However, we have identified cases where the nested index does not provide efficient execution strategy. This is useful, since it allows us to limit the complexity of the problem of index configuration.

Acknowledgments The author is indebted with Dr. Won Kim director of the OODS laboratory at MCC for suggesting the topics discussed in this paper.

References

[Bert 89] Bertino, E., W.Kim, Indexing Techniques for Queries on Nested Objects, to appear in *IEEE Trans. on Knowledge and Data Engineering*, 1989, also MCC Technical Report Number: ACT-OODS-132-89, March 1989.

[Bert 89a] Bertino, E., Optimization of Queries using Nested Indices, Technical Report (available from the author), November 1989.

[Ditt 86] Dittrich, K., Object-Oriented Database Systems: the Notion and the Issues, in *Intl. Workshop on Object-Oriented Database Systems*, Asilomar (Calif.), Sept. 23-26, 1986.

[Kim 88] Kim, W., A Foundation for Object-Oriented Databases, MCC Technical Report, No. ACA-ST-248-88, Aug. 1988.

[Kimk 88] Kim, K-C., W.Kim, D. Woelk, and A. Dale, Acyclic Query Processing in Object-Oriented Databases, in *Proc. Entity-Relationship Conference*, Rome (Italy), November 1988.

[Vald 87] Valduriez, P., Optimization of Complex Database Queries using Join Indices, MCC Technical Report Number: ACA-ST-265-87, August 1987.

[Yao 77] Yao, S.B., Approximating Block Accesses in Database Organizations, *ACM Commun.*, Vol.20, Apr. 1977.

Appendix A

An index record in a leaf node consists of the record-length, key-length, key-value, the number of elements in the list of unique identifiers (UIDs) of the objects which hold the key value in the indexed attribute, and the list of UIDs. Therefore, given a path $P = C_1.A_1.A_2.\ldots.A_n$, the size XN of a leaf-node record is

$$XN = k_1 \times k_2 \times \ldots \times k_n \times UIDL + kl + kll + rl + nuid$$

where:

- $UIDL$ is the length of the object-identifier;
- kl is the average length of a key value for the indexed attribute;
- kll is the size of the key-length field;
- rl is the size of the record-length field;
- $nuid$ is the size of the no. uids field.

For some parameters we have adopted values from the B-tree implementation of indices in ORION. Also we have assumed that the average length of a key value is equal to the size of a UID. The values for these parameters are: $UIDL = 8$; $kl = 8$; $kll = 2$; $rl = 2$; $uid = 2$.

The access cost AR for a leaf-node record, expressed in terms of pages accessed, is $AR = \lceil XN/P \rceil$. By assuming that $P = 4096$, we have that $AR \simeq \lceil k_1 \times k_2 \times .... \times k_n/500 \rceil$.

A Probabilistic Relational Data Model

Daniel Barbara´
Hector Garcia-Molina
Daryl Porter

Department of Computer Science
Princeton University
Princeton, New Jersey 08544

Abstract

It is often desirable to represent in a database entities whose properties cannot be deterministically classified. We develop a new data model that includes probabilities associated with the values of the attributes. The notion of missing probabilities is introduced for partially specified probability distributions. This new model offers a richer descriptive language allowing the database to reflect more accurately the uncertain real world. Probabilistic analogs to the basic relational operators are defined and their correctness is studied.

1. Probabilistic Model

Entities with stochastic attributes abound in real database applications. For example, Toyota might have demographic information indicating that customers living in a certain region are likely to purchase a Corolla with probability 0.7 or a Celica with probability 0.3. An oil company might have a database of potential *Oil Sites* with probabilistic projections as to the *Type* and *Quantity* of oil at each site. In a military application, there may be entities such as *Military Bases* where hardware at the camp is uncertain or an entity set like *Spies* whose *Location* attribute is the product of guesswork. In a traditional database application, *Employees*, the qualitative attributes *Work Quality*, or *Enthusiasm* could be introduced. The stock market features *Companies* with many attributes that are notoriously non-deterministic. Finally, *Medical Records* describing, say, a patient's *Susceptibility to Heart Attack* or the *Causes of a Disease* could be stochastic in nature.

In this paper we develop the Probabilistic Data Model (PDM), an extension of the relational model [Dat, Ull] that lets one represent probabilities associated with the values of attributes. In this model, relations have deterministic keys. That is, each tuple represents a known real entity. The non-key attributes describe the properties of the entities and may be deterministic or stochastic in nature.

EXAMPLE 1.1. To illustrate, consider the following probabilistic relation:

Key	Independent Deterministic	Interdependent Stochastic	Independent Stochastic
EMPLOYEE	DEPARTMENT	QUALITY BONUS	SALES
Jon Smith	Toy	0.4 [Great Yes] 0.5 [Good Yes] 0.1 [Fair No]	0.3 [$30-34K] 0.7 [$35-39K]
Fred Jones	Houseware	1.0 [Good Yes]	0.5 [$20-24K] 0.5 [$25-29K]

The relation describes two entities, "Jon Smith" and "Fred Jones." Attribute DEPARTMENT is deterministic. e.g., it is certain that Jon Smith works in the Toy department. In this example, QUALITY and BONUS are probabilistic and jointly distributed. The interpretation is that QUALITY and BONUS are random variables whose outcome depends on the EMPLOYEE in consideration. For instance,

$$\text{Prob}[\text{ QUALITY} = \text{"Great" AND BONUS} = \text{"Yes"} \mid \text{EMPLOYEE} = \text{"Jon Smith"}] = 0.4$$

It makes sense to consider QUALITY and BONUS jointly distributed if, as the example implies, QUALITY functionally determines BONUS. The last attribute, SALES, describes the expected sales in the coming year by the employee. The SALES values are given as disjoint ranges, e.g., $30-34K means 30,000 to 34,999 dollars. This attribute is probabilistic but independent of the other non-key attributes. For instance,

Prob[SALES = "$35-39K" | EMPLOYEE = "Jon Smith"] = 0.7.

In our model, each stochastic attribute is handled as a discrete probability distribution function [Mey]. This means that the probabilities for each attribute (in a tuple) must add up to 1.0. This is why the probabilities in Example 1.1 have this property. This requirement could be a problem in practice because it may be difficult to know the exact probabilities for all possible domain values. For example, say $30-34K and $35-39K are the two most likely sales ranges for Jon Smith, with probabilities 0.3 and 0.5 respectively. However, suppose that there are many other ranges that are possible but unlikely. It would be inconvenient to have to assign probabilities to all of them.

The most important feature of our model is the inclusion of *missing probabilities* to account for such incompletely specified probability distributions. For example, the Jon Smith tuple of Example 1.1 could instead be:

EXAMPLE 1.2.

EMPLOYEE	DEPARTMENT	QUALITY BONUS	SALES
Jon Smith	Toy	0.3 [Great Yes] 0.4 [Good Yes] 0.2 [Fair *] 0.1 [* *]	0.3 [$30-34K] 0.5 [$35-39K] 0.2 [*]

Here, 0.2 probability has not been assigned to a particular sales range. It is assumed that this missing probability is distributed over all ranges in the domain, but we make *no assumptions* as to how it is distributed. This situation could arise if, for instance, 10 people are polled to estimate Jon Smith's sales for the upcoming year. Three people have estimated sales of 30,000 to 34,999 (e.g., similar to last year's sales); five of 35,000 to 39,999 (e.g., last year plus inflation). Two people have not been reached and give rise to the 0.2 missing probability. Since the missing probability could or could not go to the range $30-34K, the probability that the sales will be $30-34K next year is actually between 0.3 and 0.3 + 0.2. In this sense, the probability 0.3 associated with the sales range $30-34K is a lower bound. Similarly, 0.5 is a lower bound for the probability associated with $35-39K. Notice that the 0.2 is *not* a lower bound. The tuple 0.2 [*] states how much probability could be assigned to tuples with no wildcards.

The missing probability for QUALITY, BONUS is interpreted similarly. A probability of 0.1 is distributed in an undetermined way over all possible quality, bonus pairs, while 0.2 is distributed only over pairs that have a "Fair" quality component. Thus, the probability that Smith is rated as "Great" and gets a bonus is between 0.3 and 0.3 + 0.1.

We believe that missing probability is a powerful concept. It allows the model to capture uncertainty in data values as well as in the probabilities. It facilitates inserting data into a probabilistic relation, i.e., it is not necessary to have all information before some tuple can be entered. It also makes it possible to eliminate uninteresting information when displaying relations. For example, a user may only be interested in seeing values with probability greater than 0.5; the rest can be ignored. Finally, as we will see later on, missing probability arises naturally during relational operations, even when the base relations have no missing probability.

We have chosen the *no assumptions* interpretation for missing probabilities for two main reasons. One, we believe it is very natural and powerful. Second, manipulating such missing probabilities as relations are projected, joined, and so on, is surprisingly easy (see Section 2). Other interpretations of missing probabilities are possible, for example, one may wish to consider the missing probabilities to be distributed over domain values not explicitly listed in the relation. Another possibility is to consider probabilities not listed in the relation to be *uniformly* distributed. In this case, the probability distribution is known but not enumerated in the relation. We do not want to rule out other interpretations, but due to space limitations, we will only study the no assumptions interpretation. The full system we envision, however, will allow multiple interpretations.

A central premise of our model is that keys are deterministic. This is not the only choice, but we feel that deterministic keys are very natural and lead to simple relational operators. Furthermore, it is still possible to represent stochastic entities with our model. For instance, suppose that we are not certain whether Jon Smith and Fred Jones are employees in company Acme of Example 1.1. Say the probability that Jon Smith "exists," i.e., works for Acme, is at least 0.7. To represent this, we can include an attribute COMPANY in our relation, making its distribution for Jon Smith assign 0.7 probability to "Acme," the rest missing.

Before continuing, we will discuss briefly where the "probabilistic data" for our relations come from.† There are actually many possibilities. One is to have users assign the probabilities according to their "confidence" or "belief" in the values [Pea]. Thus a user, after reading recommendation letters for a job candidate, may say that he is 80% confident that this is a good candidate.

A second option is to compute the probabilities from an underlying sample. For example, a conventional deterministic relation may contain the evaluations of Fred Jones made by 100 people. Say 15 people find Jones "Very Good", 85 find him "Good". The relative frequencies can lead to probabilities of 15/100 for "Very Good," 85/100 for "Good". Our extended model includes a new operator (Stochastic) that will automatically generate a probabilistic relation out of an underlying deterministic relation containing samples (see Section 6).

Probabilities can also be assigned to data according to their timeliness. For instance, suppose that at 9:00am the position of a ship is reported as X. As time progresses, the likelihood that the ship is still at X decreases, so the user may provide a time decreasing function to generate the probabilities attached to positions. (Note that missing probability is useful once again to cover the unknown locations of the ship.)

Incidentally, in this paper we will focus exclusively on discrete probability distribution functions. Although we do not discuss it here, it may be possible to extend our model to continuous probabilities, and this opens the door to other sources of probabilistic data. For example, we may know that a given radar has a normally distributed error with standard deviation of one mile. Thus, the position of an airplane will be given by a normal distribution.

In presenting our probabilistic model in a relatively short conference paper, we are faced with a dilemma. On the one hand, the power of the model is best appreciated if we describe the full range of operators and facilities. On the other hand, we must also present the formal underpinnings of the model. Although the PDM seems very intuitive and the operations appear straightforward, there are some subtle issues regarding missing probabilities. It is true that missing probabilities can be manipulated in a straightforward fashion, but *proving* that these manipulations are correct and make sense in a probabilistic sense is not trivial.

In this paper we have chosen to limit the scope to the basic model and the three fundamental relational operators, project, select, and join. This makes it possible to write a self-contained paper that provides a solid theoretical foundation to the model. Then, at the end (Section 6) we briefly summarize PDM components not covered here, hopefully convincing the reader that the basic core can be expanded into a full and very practical system.

We start by introducing the basic relational operators via examples in Section 2. Section 3 contains a formalization of our model, plus a precise definition of the operators. Section 4 looks at the "correctness" of the operators on missing probability. In Section 5 we explain the differences between the PDM and previous ideas.

---

† Strictly speaking, probabilities cannot be determined from a finite set of observations [Mey]. Our approach is to estimate the probability distribution function and then to treat the estimate as the true distribution.

2. Examples

In this section we present illustrative examples for the three basic operators in the PDM. The formal definitions are presented later. Let us begin with the project operator. For the project examples we use the following relation.

PROJECT EXAMPLE Relation STOCKS

NAME	DIV PRICE	RATING
P.J.	0.3 [10 200] 0.2 [20 250] 0.2 [10 250] 0.1 [0 *] 0.1 [* 100] 0.1 [* *]	0.9 [AAA] 0.1 [AA]
CONTI	1.0 [0 50]	0.5 [BBB] 0.5 [CCC]

Relation STOCKS predicts next year's stock dividends, price, and rating. Dividends and prices represent ranges, but for simplicity are shown as single values. We assume that dividends and prices are dependent attributes, but that the rating of a stock is independent (it is related to company's indebtedness and financial policy rather than to market conditions). For instance, our analysts tell us that P.J.'s stock will remain at this year's level, with dividends in the range 10-20 and prices in the 200-250 dollar range, with probability 0.3. The next two entries for DIV, PRICE indicate likely scenarios where the stock price will go up into the 250-300 range. With probability 0.1 it is possible that the company will yield no dividends, and in this case, the stock price is unpredictable. Similarly, it is also possible for the stock prices to collapse into the 0-100 range, and it is difficult to predict what dividends the company will declare. Finally, the last entry covers unexpected scenarios. Company CONTI is just going on the market so we can be confident that the initial offering will be at 50 dollars and that the company will not have dividends its first year.

Notice how the missing probabilities give us great flexibility. We reiterate that the probabilities of the *fully specified tuples* in a distribution are lower bounds. For example, for stock P.J., the scenario DIV = 10, PRICE = 200 occurs with at least probability 0.3. Its maximum probability is 0.4, occurring if the last scenario (DIV = *, PRICE = *) happens to cover the first. The scenario DIV = 0, PRICE = 100 may occur with probability ranging from zero to 0.1 + 0.1 + 0.1. Tuples within a probability distribution containing a wildcard are not lower bounds; they are used in delimiting the upper bounds.

EXAMPLE 2.1 PROJECT STOCKS ONTO NAME, DIV.

This amounts to computing the marginal probability distribution for DIV. The result shows the expected dividends for the various stocks:

NAME	DIV
P.J.	0.5 [10] 0.2 [20] 0.1 [0] 0.2 [*]
CONTI	1.0 [0]

Note that operationally the wildcard value * is treated as if it were simply another DIV attribute value. Intuitively, this appears to be correct: In the resulting tuple for P.J., 0.2 probability is distributed over all possible DIV values because that was the amount spread over [*, 100] and [*, *] values in STOCKS. In Section 4 we will prove that treating * as another domain value is the correct way to perform projects.

EXAMPLE 2.2 PROJECT STOCKS ONTO NAME, PRICE, RATING.

The result is:

NAME	PRICE	RATING
P.J.	0.3 [200] 0.4 [250] 0.1 [100] 0.2 [*]	0.9 [AAA] 0.1 [AA]
CONTI	1.0 [50]	0.5 [BBB] 0.5 [CCC]

The next operator is select. The select condition can refer to the attribute values, their probabilities, or both. A condition refers to a single attribute group, but several conditions can be joined together. Each individual condition is of the form

group_name: value condition, probability condition

A condition can be of two types. In a *certainty condition* we require that the condition hold with absolute certainty in order for a tuple to appear in the result relation. In a *possibility condition* we request that the condition hold at least under one interpretation of the missing probabilities. We use **V**, **P** to refer to the value and probability components of a certainty condition, and **v**, **p** to the components of a possibility condition.

For our examples we use the following relation:

SELECT EXAMPLE Relation APPLICANTS

STU	GPA	INTEREST	ACC EVAL
Adam	3.8	0.7 [theory] 0.3 [*]	0.6 [Y A] 0.1 [N A] 0.3 [* *]
Eve	3.9	0.6 [database] 0.4 [systems]	0.5 [Y A] 0.3 [Y B] 0.2 [Y C]

This relation is used by the graduate admissions committee at some Computer Science department. Attribute STU is the name of the student and GPA is the grade point average at his or her undergraduate institution. Attribute INTEREST describes the potential student's interests. This distribution is assigned by a professor who reads the applicants essay and description of what he or she might want to do. In the last group, ACC indicates whether the applicant will accept (Y) or not (N) an offer of admission, if made. (This information is critical in knowing how many offers to make.) Attribute EVAL represents the evaluation of the admissions committee (A, B, or C). The two attributes are not independent since a good student is less likely to accept an offer (he will be accepted by more schools) than a poor one. To obtain the distributions for ACC, EVAL, everybody on the committee ranks applicants and predicts whether they would accept an offer. The distribution in APPLICANTS reflects the distribution of opinions (see operator STOCHASTIC in Section 6).

EXAMPLE 2.3 SELECT APPLICANTS WHERE ACC_EVAL: **V** = [Y, *], **P** > 0.7.

This query selects all tuples that certainly have a value of Y in their ACC component with probability greater than 0.7. Tuple Eve satisfies this condition, i.e., we are sure that Eve will accept our offer with probability greater than 0.7. That is, if we project out the "do not care" attribute in the group (EVAL), we see that in Eve, ACC = Y occurs with probability 0.5 + 0.3 + 0.2 which is greater than 0.7. For tuple Adam, we *cannot* be certain that Y occurs with probability larger than 0.7; this may or may not be the case, depending on how the missing probability is distributed. Thus, the result is:

STU	GPA	INTEREST	ACC EVAL
Eve	3.9	0.6 [database] 0.4 [systems]	0.5 [Y A] 0.3 [Y B] 0.2 [Y C]

EXAMPLE 2.4. SELECT APPLICANTS WHERE ACC_EVAL: **v** = [Y, *], **p** > 0.7.
This is similar to example 2.3, except that we now select tuples where it is possible that ACC is Y with probability greater than 0.7. Here, both tuples satisfy the condition and the result is the entire relation. (In tuple Adam we *cannot* rule out the possibility that Y occurs with probability greater than 0.7.)

EXAMPLE 2.5. SELECT APPLICANTS WHERE INTEREST: **v** = [A.I.], **p** > 0.
This selects applicants we cannot rule out are interested in A.I. The result is tuple Adam of APPLICANTS. This example illustrates Lipski's upper bound select (see [Lip],[Lip2]).

EXAMPLE 2.6. SELECT APPLICANTS WHERE ACC_EVAL: **V** = [Y, *], **P** = 1.0.
This finds all applicants where it is absolutely certain they will accept an admission offer. The result contains only tuple Eve. This query implements Lipski's lower bound select ([Lip], [Lip2]). Note that we do not require any additional operators for Lipski's upper and lower bounds. Our probabilistic model is general enough so that these particular conditions can be expressed very naturally.

Let us continue with the join operator. Consider the following two relations:

SHIPS

NAME	TYPE
Maria	0.6 [Frigate] 0.4 [Tugboat]

DESCR

TYPE	MAX-SPEED
Frigate	0.7 [20-knots] 0.3 [30-knots]
Tugboat	1.0 [15-knots]

We are 40% sure the Maria is a Tugboat. We know that Tugboats have a maximum speed of 15 knots, so it makes sense to say that we are 40% sure the Maria's maximum speed is 15 knots. Similarly, we are 60% sure she is a Frigate, and Frigates have a maximum speed of 20 knots with probability 0.7, so it is reasonable to expect the Maria to have a maximum speed of 20 knots with probability 0.6 times 0.7. This motivates the natural join operator.

EXAMPLE 2.7. JOIN SHIPS, DESCR.
There must be a common attribute, in this case TYPE. That attribute must be the key of one of the relations. The resulting relation is as follows. (We show the resulting probabilities as products, e.g., 0.6×0.7, to show how they are derived.)

NAME	TYPE MAX-SPEED
Maria	0.6×0.7 [Frigate 20-knots] 0.6×0.3 [Frigate 30-knots] 0.4×1.0 [Tugboat 15-knots]

EXAMPLE 2.8.
Natural join can generate missing probabilities, even where the initial relations have none. Suppose that the DESCR relation given earlier does not contain a tuple for Tugboat. The result of the join in this case would be:

NAME	TYPE MAX-SPEED
Maria	0.6×0.7 [Frigate 20-knots] 0.6×0.3 [Frigate 30-knots] 0.4 [Tugboat *]

The resulting relation has 0.4 missing probability. The interpretation is quite natural. With probability 0.4 the TYPE_MAX-SPEED attribute takes on a value [Tugboat *], where "*" is some speed value. The distribution of this probability over all possible [Tugboat *] values is unknown.

Note, incidentally, that the join operator is not commutative. This is inherent from what join means in a probabilistic database. Also note that join works in the same fashion if the join group has multiple attributes. For instance, say ship TYPES consists of CLASS and LENGTH. Relation DESCR would need to have CLASS, LENGTH as key. If Maria was [frigate, long] with probability 0.2, then we would multiply 0.2 by the MAX-SPEED distribution of [frigate, long] in DESCR.

3. Probabilistic Relational Algebra

In this section we formalize our probabilistic model and relational operators. Our goal is to specify what constitutes a probabilistic relation and exactly how the operators function. We start by defining relations with a *single group* of jointly distributed attributes, and their operators. At the end of this section we then show how multi-group relations (what we will call multi-relations) can be viewed simply as a collection of single-group relations.

Definition 3.1. *Probabilistic Relation.* Let K be a set of attributes $K_1, K_2, \ldots, K_n$ and A be a set of attributes $A_1, A_2, \ldots, A_m$. The domains are given by $dom(K_i)$ and $dom(A_i)$. A probabilistic relation r (on K, A) is a function (many to one) from $dom(K_1) \times \cdots \times dom(K_n)$ into **PF**. The set **PF** is a set of probability functions for A. Each $\beta \in$ **PF** is a function (many to one) from $dom(A_1) \cup \{*\} \times \cdots \times dom(A_m) \cup \{*\}$ into the real number interval [0,1]. The symbol $* \notin dom(A_i)$ for $1 \le i \le m$, represents instances in which the value of the attribute A_i is unknown, i.e., acts as a wildcard. (The symbol * is not allowed in any key domain $dom(K_i)$.) Every β must satisfy the following property:

$$\sum_a \beta(a) = 1 \quad \bigcirc$$

Probabilistic relations are displayed in table form in the obvious way. Note that the mappings of probability functions into 0 are not displayed in the table. For example, the table

KEY	A B
k1	0.6 [a1 b1] 0.2 [a1 b2] 0.1 [a1 *] 0.1 [* *]
k2	1.0 [a1 b2]

is equivalent to the relation $r(k1) = \beta_1, r(k2) = \beta_2$, where β_1 and β_2 are defined as follows:

$\beta_1([a1\ b1]) = 0.6$ $\quad\quad$ $\beta_1([a1\ b2]) = 0.2$

$\beta_1([a1\ *]) = 0.1$ $\quad\quad$ $\beta_1([*\ *]) = 0.1$

$\beta_2([a1\ b2]) = 1.0$

and all other values are mapped by β_1 and β_2 to 0. We refer to the probabilistic functions of a relation as *rows* since they correspond to tuples in the table representation. For instance, we call $r(k1)$ $(= \beta_1)$ and $r(k2)$ $(= \beta_2)$ rows.

Definition 3.2 *Cover* We say that $a' = (a'_1, a'_2, \ldots, a'_m)$ covers $a = (a_1, a_2, \ldots, a_m)$ if for all i, $1 \le i \le m$, either $a'_i = a_i$ or $a'_i = *$. ○

3.1 Semantics of Probabilistic Relations

A probabilistic relation r on K, A defines the probabilities of certain events. One can think of the K and A attributes as random variables. If there are no missing probabilities

$$r(k)(a) = Prob[A = a \mid K = k]$$

where $k = <k_1, \ldots, k_n>$, $a = <a_1, \ldots, a_m>$, $k_i \in dom(K_i)$ and $a_i \in dom(A_i)$. Note that the expression $A = a$ above is shorthand for the event "$A_1 = a_1$ and $A_2 = a_2$ and ... and $A_m = a_m$." The event $K = k$ has similar meaning.

With missing probabilities, and a containing no wildcards,

$$r(k)(a) \le Prob[A = a \mid K = k] \le \sum_{a' \text{ covers } a} r(k)(a')$$

That is, the function $r(k)(a)$ gives a lower bound of the probability assigned to a. The upper bound is found by adding probabilities assigned to all a's that cover a.

In the rest of this section, we will continue to refer to tuples k and a as we have just defined. We will also use the shorthand $A = a$ for events as described above.

Whenever a probabilistic relation is defined, there is an *implicit independence assumption.* In other words, we assume that the probabilities given in r are *independent* of any other possible database attributes. So, the existence of r in the database indirectly implies that

$$Prob[A = a \mid K = k \text{ and } B = b] = Prob[A = a \mid K = k]$$

for any set of attributes B appearing in other relations such that $B \cap K = B \cap A = \emptyset$.

3.2 Project

Before discussing the project operator, we need to make the following definition:

Definition 3.3. *Restriction of a tuple.* Let a be a tuple over a set of attributes A, and let B be a subset of these attributes. Then $a[B]$ is the sub-tuple that contains the corresponding B elements. For example, if $A = A_1, A_2, A_3$ and $B = A_2, A_3$, then $<a_1, a_2, a_3>[B] = <a_2, a_3>$. ○

Consider $r' =$ PROJECT r ONTO α, where r is a probabilistic relation over K, A, and α is a set of attributes $\alpha_1, \alpha_2, \ldots$. Let $A' = A \cap \alpha$, the non-key attributes that remain in r'. In what follows we assume that $A' \ne \emptyset$ (the case where A' is empty is trivial; we simply project out all attributes except the key).

With no missing probabilities, the interpretation of r' is that $r'(k)(a') = Prob[A' = a' \mid K = k]$. From basic probability theory, we know that this probability can be computed as follows:

$$Prob[A' = a' \mid K = k] = \sum_{\text{all } a \text{ s.t. } a[A'] = a'} Prob[A = a \mid K = k]$$

This equation tells us immediately how to define r', at least for the case with no missing probabilities. In Section 2 we argued that with missing probabilities, * can be treated simply as another attribute value. This is what the next definition does, but we leave the formal proof that this is correct for Section 4.

Definition 3.4. *Project.* The project of r over α is the following probabilistic relation r' (over K, A'). If $r(k)$ is not defined, then $r'(k)$ is not defined either. If $r(k)$ is defined, then $r'(k)$ is the function β defined by

$$\beta(a') = \sum_{\text{all } a \text{ s.t. } a[A'] = a'} r(k)(a) \quad ○$$

To check that the function β given in Definition 3.4 is valid, we compute

$$S = \sum_{a'} \beta(a') = \sum_{a'} \sum_{\text{all } a \text{ s.t. } a[A']=a'} r(k)(a)$$

Consider an arbitrary tuple $z = <z_1,...,z_m>$ (where $z_i \in dom(A_i) \cup \{*\}$). It will be included in the S sum when $a' = z[A']$ and $a = z$ (and in no other case). So, since all z tuples are being considered once in the sum, $S = \sum_a r(k)(a) = 1$. Hence, the β functions of Definition 3.4 are valid.

3.3 Select

We now turn our attention to selects. A select condition $C(k,r)$ evaluates to true if row k of r satisfies the selection. In this paper we consider a simplified syntax for these conditions. (It could be extended in several useful ways. The extensions are straightforward and are not discussed here.) We assume that conditions are of the form **V** $= a$, **P** $op\ p$ (or **v** $= a$, **p** $op\ p$), where a is a tuple with possible *'s, op is an operator like $=$, $<$, etc., and p is a real number in [0, 1]. Recall that **V**, **P** are used for certainty conditions, **v**, **p** for possibility conditions. As we saw in Example 2.3, the "do not care" fields in a have to be projected out in order to select the appropriate rows. This implicit project is included in the following definitions.

Definition 3.5. The conditions $C(k,r)$: **V** $= a$, **P** $op\ p$ when op is $>, \geq, =$; and $C(k,r)$: **v** $= a$, **p** $op\ p$ when op is $<, \leq$ are evaluated as follows. Let A' be the attributes of r where a has no *'s, and let $a' = a[A']$. Let r_j = PROJECT r OVER A'. Then $C(k,r)$ is true if $r_j(k)(a')\ op\ p$ is true. ○

Definition 3.6. The conditions $C(k,r)$: **v** $= a$, **p** $op\ p$ when op is $>, \geq, =$; and $C(k,r)$: **V** $= a$, **P** $op\ p$ when op is $<, \leq$ are evaluated as follows. Again, let A' be the attributes of r where a has no *'s, and let $a' = a[A']$. Let r_j = PROJECT r OVER A'. Then $C(k,r)$ is true if $\sum_{\text{all } x \text{ s.t. } x \text{ covers } a'} r_j(k)(x)\ \ op\ p$ is true. ○

Definition 3.7 *Select.* Let r' = **SELECT** r **WHERE** C be the target relation obtained by the operation select over the probabilistic relation r defined on K, A. Probabilistic relation r' is also defined on K, A. If $r(k)$ is undefined or if $C(k,r)$ is false, then $r'(k)$ is undefined. Otherwise, $r'(k) = r(k)$. ○

3.4 Join

Definition 3.8. *Natural Join.* Consider two relations, r on K, A, and s on A, B. Let r' be the natural join of r and s. Relation r' is over K, AB. If $r(k)$ is not defined, then $r'(k)$ is not defined. Otherwise the function is defined as follows:

if $s(a)$ is defined then

$$r'(k)(ab) = r(k)(a) \times s(a)(b)$$

else if $s(a)$ is not defined then

$$r'(k)(a*) = r(k)(a)$$

$$r'(k)(ab) = 0 \text{ for all } b \text{ other than } *.$$

Note that if $a = <a_1,...,a_m>$ and $b = <b_1,...,b_o>$, then ab is the tuple $<a_1,...,a_m,b_1,\ldots,b_o>$. The tuple $a*$ represents $<a_1,...,a_m,*,...,*>$. ○

If no missing probabilities are present, this definition is justified by basic probability theory. The value $r'(k)(ab)$ should be equal to $Prob[AB = ab \mid K = k]$. Using Bayes' theorem, we get:

$$Prob[AB = ab \mid K = k] = Prob[B = b \mid K = k \text{ and } A = a]\, Prob[A = a \mid K = k]$$

Because of our independence assumption, the probability of $B = b$ only depends on A, not on K. Thus,

$$Prob[AB = ab \mid K = k] = Prob[B = b \mid A = a]\, Prob[A = a \mid K = k]$$

This is the formula that is used in Definition 3.8. We discuss the correctness of Definition 3.8 under missing probabilities in Section 4. It is straightforward to check that the probability functions given in Definition 3.8 are valid. We omit the proof here.

3.5 Multi-Relations

Definition 3.9. *Multi-Relation.* A table with multiple groups is represented by a multi-relation. A multi-relation R on attributes $K, A_1, ..., A_q$ is a tuple $<r_1,...,r_q>$ where each r_i is a probabilistic relation on K, A_i. There is one condition (we call it the "same keys" constraint) that must be satisfied by the relations: if $r_i(k)$ is defined, then for all j, $1 \leq j \leq q$, $r_j(k)$ must also be defined. ○

A multi-relation is displayed in table form by concatenating the individual relations. However, the key attribute column is only displayed once, on the left. The condition in Definition 3.9 ensures that in every row of the table, the probability function will be defined. As an example, consider multi-relation r_1 used for the project examples of Section 2. (It was called a relation then since we had not introduced multi-relations.) It is composed of a relation on K, AB and another on K, C. Attributes A and B are jointly distributed, but because of our independence assumption (Section 3.1), C and A, as well as C and B, are independent.

Relational operators on such a multi-relation can now be defined in terms of the operators on the component relations.† Let $R = <r_1, \ldots, r_q>$ be a multi-relation on $K, A_1, ..., A_q$.

- *Project.* PROJECT R ONTO $\alpha = <r'_1,...,r'_q>$ where r'_i = PROJECT r_i ONTO α.
- *Select.* The select condition c for R has $q+1$ components, $c_0, c_1, ..., c_q$. The condition c_i is intended to select within relation r_i. Condition c_0 selects keys. If no selection is desired for r_i, then c_i is set to "true."

SELECT R WHERE $c_0,c_1,...,c_q = <r'_1,...,r'_q>$ where r'_i = SELECT r_i WHERE d. Condition $d(k,r_i)$ is true if and only if $c_0(k)$ and $c_1(k,r_1)$ and ... and $c_q(k,r_q)$. (Note that implements a logical AND of the conditions. More general multi-relation selects could be defined in a similar fashion.)

- *Natural Join.* Let $S = <s_1, \ldots, s_t>$ be a second multi-relation on $A_i, B_1, ..., B_t$.

JOIN $R, S = <r'_1, \ldots, r'_{i-1}, r'_{i+1}, \ldots, r'_q, s'_1, \ldots, s'_t>$, where $r'_j = r_j$ $(j \neq i)$, and s'_j = JOIN r_i, s_j.

For each of the above definitions, it is relatively simple to show that result is a valid multi-relation, i.e., that the same-keys constraint holds. Finally, in Section 1 we introduced deterministic attributes. Deterministic attributes are just like probabilistic ones except that the probability functions always assign probability 1.0 to a single value. When such attributes are displayed in table form, the probabilities are stripped away.

4. Lossy Operations

The project and join operators generate new probability distribution functions in the result. In Section 3 we showed that these new functions were correct when no missing probabilities were involved. In this section we address the issue of whether the new functions are still meaningful when missing probabilities are involved.

We start by showing that in certain cases join yields functions that are "unexpected." Consider the following:

EXAMPLE 4.1.

r

K	A
k	0.4 [a1] 0.6 [*]

s

A	B
a1	0.7 [b1] 0.3 [b2]

Join *r*, *s*

K	AB
k	0.28 [a1 b1] 0.12 [a1 b2] 0.6 [* *]

In the resulting join, the probability of tuple [a1 b1] ranges from 0.28 to 0.88. (This last value is obtained when all the missing probability of 0.6 is assumed to fall on [a1 b1].) However, if we look at the original relations, there is no way we can obtain a probability of 0.88 for [a1 b1]. Even if in r we assume all of the 0.6 missing

† Equivalently, we could convert a multi-relation into a single-group one, performing a cross-product of the attribute probabilities. Then the multi-relation operators could be defined in terms of the single-group ones acting on the converted multi-relation.

probability is given to [a1], when we join we obtain at most 1.0×0.7 for [a1 b1]. Thus, the result we have shown does not accurately represent the join.

Another way of looking at this problem is that the missing probability of 0.6 [* *] in the result is not correct. It is not the case that we know nothing about the distribution of this 0.6 probability over all possible A, B tuples. If the first component happens to be a1, then the missing probability should be assigned according to the a1 distribution shown in s. Hence, the most of the 0.6 probability that could be assigned to [a1 b1] is 0.6×0.7. However, all of the 0.6 can be assigned to say [a2 b1]. Our PDM is not rich enough to capture this subtlety in the missing probabilities.

It would be possible to extend the model for missing probabilities to represent "partially unknown" distributions, but this would lead to a cumbersome model and language. Instead we have stayed with the simple interpretation of missing probabilities. There are several good reasons for this. First, the problem illustrated in this example only occurs with joins when the first relation has missing probabilities. It never occurs with projects or selects. (We will formally prove this in this section.) So a system implementing our model could simply refuse to perform joins that have the problem.

Second, the "problem" is not necessarily bad. The data in the resulting relation can still be useful. It provides a simplified but "diffused" view of the join. The probability ranges are larger than should be, but the minimum value is still correct. (We will prove this later.) For example, as we indicated above, the range for [a1 b1] is given as 0.28 to 0.88, but it should be 0.28 to 0.7. The range for [a1 b2] is shown as 0.12 to 0.72, but should be 0.12 to 0.3.

In a sense, the problem illustrated here causes "information loss." The resulting relation has less information about the probabilities involved that what could be inferred form the original relations. If a user does not want to lose information, then he should not replace two relations by their join when the first relation has missing probabilities. An analogy can be drawn to lossy-join decompositions in conventional relational algebra [Ull]. When a relation is decomposed in certain ways, information is lost. Such decompositions should be avoided. Similarly, we must avoid certain compositions, i.e., replacing two relations by their join.

In the rest of this section we formalize the notion of probabilistic information loss. We only consider single attribute relations; the generalization to multi-relations is straightforward.

Definition 4.1 *Potential Set.* Given a tuple with key k in a probabilistic relation r, the potential set of $r(k)$, or simply $PSET(r(k))$, is defined as the set of all functions (without missing probabilities) that can be obtained from $r(k)$, each one by assuming a particular distribution of the missing probabilities. More formally, $PSET(r(k))$ is the set of all valid probabilistic functions β such that

(i) for all tuples a with *'s, $\beta(a) = 0$;

(ii) for all tuples a with no *'s, $r(k)(a) \leq \beta(a) \leq \sum_{a' \text{ covers } a} r(k)(a')$ ○

To illustrate, consider relation r of Example 4.1. The function that maps [a1] to a probability of 0.5 and [a2] to 0.5 is in $PSET(r(k))$. No function that maps [a1] to 0.2 could be in $PSET(r(k))$.

It is clear from Definition 4.1 that for any row with key k in which there are no missing probabilities $PSET(r(k)) = \{r(k)\}$. By extension, the PSET of a relation r is simply

$$PSET(r) = \{r' \mid r'(k) \in PSET(r(k)) \text{ for all } k\}$$

Definition 4.2 *Probabilistically Lossless Operations.* Let $\oplus$ be an operation over relations $r_1, r_2, \ldots, r_n$ such that $r = \oplus(r_1, r_2, \ldots, r_n)$. The operation is probabilistically lossless if for all k such that $r(k)$ is defined either

(i) $r(k) = r_i(k)$ for some i, $1 \leq i \leq n$; or

(ii) $PSET(r(k)) = \bigcup_{\text{all } r'_i \in PSET(r_i)} PSET[\oplus(r'_1, \ldots, r'_n)(k)]$ ○

An operation that is not lossless is called lossy. Definition 4.2 states that for an operation to be lossless the probability function assigned to every tuple in the result must be meaningful. This occurs if the function was in the original set of functions, or if it has a potential set that can be reproduced by the potential sets of tuples in the operand relations. In part (ii) of the definition, notice that even though $r'_1, ..., r'_n$ have no missing probabilities, $\oplus(r'_1, \ldots, r'_n)(k)$ may have missing probabilities (in particular if $\oplus$ is a join, see Definition 3.8). This makes necessary the application of the *PSET* function to $\oplus(r'_1, \ldots, r'_n)(k)$.

In [Bar] we show that project and select are always probabilistically lossless operations. As was shown in Example 4.1, join can be lossy in some cases. To determine in what cases it is not, we introduce the following definition and state two lemmas. The proofs of the lemmas can be found in [Bar].

Definition 4.3. A relation *r* has property *NMP* if no row in *r* is a function with missing probabilities.

Lemma 4.1 If a relation *r* has property *NMP*, then JOIN *r*, *s* is probabilistically lossless, for any relation *s*.

In the cases where r' = JOIN *r*, *s* is lossy, the result is still of partial use because the lower bounds for probabilities are correct.

Lemma 4.2. Let r' = JOIN *r*, *s*, where *r* is over *K*, *A*, and *s* is over *A*, *B*. Say $r'(k)(ab) = p$, where *ab* has no *'s. Then $Prob\,[AB = ab \mid K = k]$ is indeed greater than or equal to *p*.

5. Related Work

The PDM we are proposing here was inspired by many of the prior ideas relating to uncertain information [Cav, Gel, Imi, Imi2, Imi3, Lip, Lip2, Liu, Men, Mor, Raj, Rei, Vas]. However, our model is distinguished by two critical aspects: (a) the use of probabilities to describe uncertainty, as opposed to other mechanisms such as fuzzy sets, possibilities, sets of alternatives, null values, and so on; and (b) the introduction of missing probabilities.

To understand aspect (a), let us briefly compare the PDM to Fuzzy Relations [Raj]. Both models may look similar on the surface, but there are important differences. A fuzzy relation is viewed as a fuzzy set, with tuples that may or may not be in a relation *r*. A *Possibility Distribution Function*, μ_r is defined to map each tuple *t* to a value over $[0,1]$. Additionally, the domain of an attribute can also be expressed as a fuzzy set, defining a possibility distribution function for it.

EXAMPLE 5.1 Consider the following fuzzy relation.

EMPLOYEE	SALES	μ
Jon Smith	\$30,000 / 0.3 \$40,000 / 0.6 \$50,000 / 0.4	0.70
Jim Jones	\$10,000 / 0.8	0.8

The numbers next to the sales figures indicate the values of the possibility function for the sales attribute. For instance, Possibility(Sales of Jon Smith = *\$30,000*) = 0.3. The value of μ = 0.7, associated with the tuple of Jon Smith, indicates that the possibility that this tuple belongs to the relation is 0.7. Note that the values of a possibility function do not have to sum to 1.0.

Possibilities and probabilities are obviously different concepts. One major difference is that it is hard to represent with possibilities attributes like SALES that have a single outcome. In other words, the example above implies that SALES for Jon Smith can take on several values at once (i.e., it is a fuzzy set). This is not the case for SALES (and for a large number of common database attributes, we think). A probabilistic function, on the other hand, captures this exactly: SALES can take on a single value out of the listed ones, and each probability gives the likelihood that it happens. In addition to being able to represent single outcome attributes, the PDM can still model fuzzy sets if necessary. (See the example of the employee working at Acme in Section 1.) Although possibilities and fuzzy sets have been carefully studied, probabilities are much more widely known and have strong intuitive appeal. Thus, they seem like a good basis for building a *general purpose* incomplete information model.

Probabilities have been used in one database model we know of [Cav]. In it, each tuple is assigned a probability, representing the likelihood that the tuple appears in the relation.

EXAMPLE 5.2. The following is a relation in the [Cav] model. A,B $\in$ {0, 1}

A	B	p(Tuple = .)
0	0	0.35
0	1	0.25
1	0	0.01
1	1	0.39

For instance, the probability that tuple <0,0> exists is 0.35. The PDM we propose provides a richer structure, allowing probabilities to be assigned to individual attributes. As described in the introduction, we think deterministic keys (which do not exist in [Cav]) are very useful, especially in applications where the entities in question clearly exist (e.g., a patient in a hospital, a military base). Finally, and most importantly, the PDM provides for missing probabilities. As we have argued, this provides for substantial flexibility in modeling real applications.

In closing this section, we briefly discuss two research areas that are also related to our work. One is statistical databases. For example, in [Won], Wong views queries as statistical experiments in which information was incomplete because, for example, it was old. His method centered around computing the query response as those tuples which minimized the two types of statistical errors. In another paper [Gho], Ghosh discusses statistical relational tables. Although there are similarities (see for instance the operator Stochastic in Section 6), our main interest in this paper is on uncertain, not statistical information.

Our work is also related to the current efforts with non-first normal form relations [Dad, Rot, Rot2]. As a matter of fact, our probabilistic relations are simply nested relations with depth two. Each attribute in the top level relation can be a relation that gives the probability distribution function for the attribute. Our focus in this paper will be on the probabilistic operators and not on the non-first normal form issues.

6. Conclusions

We have presented a probabilistic relational data model where tuples have deterministic keys and both probabilistic and deterministic attribute groups. We believe that the major strengths of our model are its generality and naturalness. Most existing incomplete information models can be encompassed by ours. For example, a null value can be represented by a 1.0 [*] distribution. A list of alternate values [Lip] can be represented by a distribution that assigns each value an equal probability. As discussed in Section 5, fuzzy sets can also be represented in our model. At the same time, these other models cannot represent the full range of probabilities we can. Another important strength, in our opinion, is the concept of missing probability. Not only does this concept make it easier to input probabilistic data, but it also makes joins feasible when join attribute values are missing.

In this paper we have focused on the three basic operators project, select, and join. There are of course many additional issues that we cannot cover here due to the limited space. These include implementation and user-interface issues, plus additional operators and interpretations for missing probabilities. Here we briefly summarize other operators and interpretations, to illustrate that our basic model can be naturally extended and enhanced. (Some of these ideas are described in more detail in [Gar].)

Conventional Operators Applied to Probabilistic Relations. The basic set operators INTERSECT, UNION, MINUS work as in a conventional system. The only complication is that UNION may produce a relation containing two rows with the same key but different functions. The COMBINE operator, discussed below, can be used to produce a single probability function. In addition, INSERT, DELETE, and UPDATE operators can be introduced to modify existing relations.

Operators for Multi-Relations. Our system provides operators for manipulating multi-relations. GLUE produces a multi-relation out of a collection of simple relations. CUT is used to break a multi-relation into its components. The GROUP operator combines two groups into a single one, computing the joint probability distribution.

New Operators. The following operators do not have a counterpart in relational databases:

(a) *STOCHASTIC* : This operator takes as input a deterministic relation containing samples and a probabilistic schema, returning a probabilistic relation based on that schema. (The probabilistic schema describes what attributes comprise the KEY, and which of the dependent attributes are jointly distributed or independent.) The probabilities are computed as relative frequencies of the samples.

This operator can be used to obtain the distributions for group ACC, EVAL in our graduate admissions example (Section 2). Each committee member evaluates each applicant (EVAL) and rates the chances that he will accept an admission offer. The evaluations are collected in a conventional relation. The STOCHASTIC operator then computes the probabilistic relation APPLICANTS.

(b) *DISCRETE*. The DISCRETE operator transforms a probabilistic relation into a deterministic one. Each probability distribution is replaced by the expected value of the attributes. If the domains are not numeric, a conversion function must be provided. For example, if student "Fred" is expected to get "A" with probability 0.7 and "B" with probability 0.3, then the DISCRETE relation would show "Fred" with a grade of $0.7 \times 4 + 0.3 \times 3 = 3.7$, assuming "A" is mapped to a numeric grade of 4 and "B" to 3.

In our STOCKS example (Section 2), we could use the DISCRETE operator to compute the expected dividends (DIV) for each stock. Using other operators, we could then compute the expected income from a particular portfolio.

(c) *COMBINE* : This operator can be used to combine two probability distributions. For example, suppose that two independent observers keep track of the distance of objects to a given site. Each observer generates a probabilistic relation for his data. If two such relations are available, it may be desirable to perform a union to combine the information. In the union there may be two distributions for the same object. The two distributions can be combined into a single one, possibly giving a different weight to each observer.

(d) *CONDITIONAL*. Say we have a relation r with key K and attributes AB. CONDITIONAL can convert r into r' with key KA and attribute B. The value $r'(ka)(b)$ will then equal $Prob[B=b \mid K=k \text{ and } A=a]$.

(e) *ε-JOIN* : This operator acts like the natural join, except the attributes for which the tables are joined are both probabilistic. The corresponding tuples are joined if the two distributions are less than ε apart according to a predetermined distance function.

(f) *ε-SELECT* : This operator selects tuples for which the distribution function is less than epsilon apart from a given distribution, again according to a pre-defined distance function.

Finally, it is possible to allow other interpretations for missing probabilities. Instead of assuming that missing probabilities are distributed over *all* domain values (as we did in this paper), one can for example assume that they are distributed over values not explicitly listed in the relation. This may be more natural in some applications. The relational operators work differently in these other cases. It is also possible and useful to pre-define common probability distribution functions. For example, the notation 0.4 U[a2 ... a5] can be used in a relation instead of assigning 0.1 probability to each of a2, a3, a4, a5. Wildcards can also be used. For instance, 0.3 U[*] uniformly distributes 0.3 probability among all possible domain values. This is simply shorthand notation: the relational operators should manipulate a relation with uniform distributions simply as if they had been expanded.

7. References

[Bar] Barbara, D., Garcia-Molina, H., Porter, D., "A Probabilistic Relational Data Model," Technical Report CS-TR-215-89, Department of Computer Science, Princeton University, January 1989.

[Cav] Cavallo, R. & Pittarelli, M., "The Theory of Probabilistic Databases," *Proceedings of the 13th Conference on Very Large Databases*, 1987.

[Dad] Dadam, P., Kuespert, K. et al, "A DBMS Prototype to Support Non-First Normal Form Relations: An Integrated View on Flat Tables & Hierarchies", *SIGMOD Proceedings*, 1986.

[Dat] Date, C., *An Introduction to Database Systems Vol. 1,* Addison-Wesley, 4th Edition, 1986.

[Gar] Garcia-Molina, H & Porter, D., "Supporting Probabilistic Data in a Relational System," Technical Report TR-147, Department of Computer Science, Princeton University, February 1988.

[Gel] Gelenbe, E. & Hebrail, G., "A Probability Model of Uncertainty in Databases," *Proceedings of the International Conference on Data Engineering*, Feb. 1986.

[Gho] Ghosh, S., "Statistical Relational Tables for Statistical Database Management," *IEEE Transactions on Software Engineering*, Dec. 1986.

[Imi] Imielinski, T., "Query Processing in Deductive Databases with Incomplete Information," Rutgers Technical Report DCS-TR-177, Mar. 1986.

[Imi2] Imielinski, T., "Automated Deduction in Databases with Incomplete Information," Rutgers Technical Report DCS-TR-181, Mar. 1986.

[Imi3] Imielinski, T. & Lipski, W., "Incomplete Information in Relational Databases," *Journal of the ACM*, Vol. 31, No. 4, Oct. 1984.

[Lip] Lipski, W., 'On Semantic Issues Connected with Incomplete Information Databases," *ACM Transactions on Database Systems*, Vol. 4, No. 3, Sep. 1979.

[Lip2] Lipski, W., "On the Logic of Incomplete Information," *Proceedings of the 6th International Symposium of Mathematical Foundations of Computer Science*, September 1977.

[Liu] Liu, Ken-Chih & Sunderraman, R., "On Representing Indefinite & Maybe Information in Relational Databases," *Proceedings of the 4th International Conference on Data Engineering*, February 1988.

[Men] Mendelson, H. & Saharia, A., "Incomplete Information Costs & Database Design," *ACM Transactions on Database Systems*, Vol. 11, June 1986.

[Mey] Meyer, P. *Introductory Probability & Statistical Applications,* Addison-Wesley, 2nd Edition, 1970.

[Mor] Morrissey, J. & van Rijsbergen, C., "A Formal Treatment of Missing & Imprecise Information," *Proceedings of SIGIR*, 1987.

[Pea] Pearl, Judea, "Fusion, Propagation, and Structuring in Belief Networks," *Artificial Intelligence* 29, 1986, pp 241-288.

[Raj] Raju, K.V.S.V.N., & Majumdar A., "Fuzzy Functional Dependencies and Lossless Join Decomposition of Fuzzy Relational Database Systems," *ACM Transactions on Database Systems*, Vol. 13, No. 2, June 1988.

[Rei] Reiter, R., "A Sound & Sometimes Complete Query Evaluation Algorithm for Relational Databases with Null Values," *Journal of the ACM*, Vol. 33, No. 2, Apr. 1986.

[Rot] Roth, M., Korth, H., & Silberschatz, A., "Extended Algebra & Calculus for Non-1NF Relational Databases," University of Texas at Austin Technical Report TR-84-36, Jan. 1985.

[Rot2] Roth, M., Korth, H., & Silberschatz, A., "Null Values in Non-1NF Relational Databases," University of Texas at Austin Technical Report TR-85-32, Dec. 1985.

[Ull] Ullman, J. D., *Principles of Database and Knowledge-Base Systems*, Computer Science Press, 1988.

[Vas] Vassilou, Y., "Functional Dependencies & Incomplete Information," *Proceedings of the 6th International Conference on Very Large Databases*, Montreal, Oct. 1980.

[Won] Wong, E., "A Statistical Approach to Incomplete Information in Database Systems," *ACM Transactions on Database Systems*, Vol. 7, No. 3, Sep. 1982.

EXTENDING THE FUNCTIONAL DATA MODEL TO COMPUTATIONAL COMPLETENESS

Alexandra Poulovassilis and Peter King

Department of Computer Science, Birkbeck College
University of London, Malet Street
London WC1E 7HX, U.K.

Abstract

We introduce the functional database language FDL which extends the functional data model to computational completeness while also supporting the persistence of any function, whether extensionally or intentionally defined. FDL improves on previous implementations of the functional data model by providing a uniform formalism both for modelling data and for computation, by supporting arbitrarily nested data types which are all persistent, and by allowing for the representation of incomplete and default knowledge. All functions are updated incrementally by the insertion and deletion of individual equations and an integrity sub-system verifies updates against the declared semantic integrity constraints.

1. Introduction

Functions have provided an underlying formalism for data models from as early as Abrial's *access functions* for representing binary relationships between entities [ABRI74] and Florentin's *property functions* for representing the attributes of entities [FLOR74]. The integration of these two uses for functions leads to a so-called *functional data model*. With such a data model, the universe of discourse is represented by means of *entities* and *functions* between them. Entities may be *scalar*, for example strings, integers and booleans, or *abstract*, for example students, teachers and enrollments. The scalar and abstract entity types of a functional data model correspond to the *lexical* and *non-lexical* object types identified in the information analysis method NIAM [VERH82]. We use both terminologies interchangeably in this paper.

One of the desirable properties of a functional data model is that abstract entities are identified by means of unique surrogates. Thus there is no requirement for keys or for maintaining referential integrity and the update semantics of all functions are of equal complexity (or simplicity!). However, the need to maintain referential integrity is replaced by the need to detect and manage dangling references to deleted entities.

Sibley and Kershberg demonstrated that a functional data model can provide a unifying formalism for the network and relational data models [SIBL77] and Hammer and McLeod showed that intentionally defined functions can be used as derivation rules [HAMM78]. Shipman integrated these ideas in the database language DAPLEX [SHIP81]. In parallel, Buneman *et al.* developed the functional query language FQL [BUNE82]. More recently, it has been shown that a functional data model is well-suited to modelling complex objects [DAYA87, BANC87]. If entity identifiers are independent of time and physical location, the evolution and physical distribution of the database can also be readily supported [KHOS86]. Finally, it has been shown that functions can provide an underlying formalism for object-oriented data models [HEIL88, BEEC88].

1.1 Previous Implementations of the Functional Data Model

Despite the advantages of a functional data model outlined above, previous implementations of it have suffered from a number of drawbacks which we identify below.

FQL [BUNE82] and the related functional query language GENESIS [BATO88] rely on a relational back-end DBMS for data storage and update facilities. Only functions which are extensionally defined can be stored in the database. In particular, although a later version of FQL [NIKH85] allows for the definition of intentional functions in the style of the functional programming language ML [MILN84], these functions cannot be stored.

In DAPLEX [SHIP81] and the languages which derive from it [SMIT83, KULK86, GRAY88], functions are either purely extensionally defined (*base* functions) or defined intentionally by a single equation (*derived* functions). It is not possible for a function to be partly extensionally defined but also to contain an equation for the general case. Thus, information about the application domain which takes the form of *default* knowledge cannot be represented.

DAPLEX is not computationally complete. Thus, in the DAPLEX-related languages the functional data model is either embedded in a procedural programming language (ADAPLEX [SMIT83]), or extended with procedural features (EFDM [KULK86,87]), or embedded in Prolog (P/FDM [GRAY88, PATO88]). Later functional systems such as PROBE [DAYA87] and FAD [BANC87] assume that intentional functions are coded in an external programming language and not stored in the central database. All these solutions give rise to different formalisms for modelling real-world data and for computation.

The *persistent data types* [ATKI87] of the DAPLEX-related languages are scalar types, abstract types, and unions, products and sets thereof. No nesting of types is possible and function composition results in "flattened" sets; hence these languages are *type incomplete* [ATKI87]. With respect to the persistence of functions, ADAPLEX supports only base functions; P/FDM stores procedural data in the form of Prolog source code all of which is asserted at the start of every session; EFDM stores derived functions in the form of an abstract syntax tree but the functional component of the language is computationally incomplete and so arbitrary functions cannot be stored.

1.2 Outline of Our Work

Our work has been motivated by the considerable potential of a functional data model on the one hand and the above limitations of previous functional data models on the other. We have designed and implemented the functional database language FDL which extends the functional data model to computational completeness while also supporting the persistence of any function, whether extensionally or intentionally defined. Thus, FDL improves on previous implementations of a functional data model as follows :

- The language is formally based on the λ calculus and so any recursive function can be defined [HIND86]. Furthermore, all functions are stored in the database.
- All functions, whether used for data modelling purposes or for computation, are treated uniformly with respect to their definition, evaluation, update and persistence.
- The data types of the language include arbitrarily nested lists, sums and products and all of them are persistent.
- Functions can be partly extensionally defined, partly intentionally defined and so default knowledge can be represented.
- All procedural data is stored in a pre-interpreted form ready for subsequent evaluation by a λ calculus evaluator.

We discuss these and other features of FDL in Sections 3 and 4 below. In the next section we give a brief introduction to *functional programming* [PEYT87, FIEL88] which forms the theoretical basis of FDL. Since all functional languages are largely syntactic variants of each other, we use the syntax of FDL in Section 2.

2. Functional Programming

We commence this section with an introduction to the λ calculus in Section 2.1. We continue in Section 2.2 with a description of how functional programming languages extend the λ calculus into a high-level programming language. Most importantly, in Section 2.3 we note several ways in which existing functional languages are deficient for use as database languages with a functional data model, thus providing further motivation for the development of FDL. Our general references for all italicised terms in Sections 2.1 and 2.2 are Hindley & Seldin [HIND86], Peyton Jones [PEYT87] and Field & Harrison [FIEL88].

2.1 The λ Calculus

The theoretical foundation of any functional programming language is the *λ calculus.* The syntax of expressions in this calculus is

$$E ::= I \mid K \mid E_1E_2 \mid \lambda I.E \mid (E)$$

where I is a member of an infinite set of distinct variables and K is a member of a finite (possibly empty) set of predefined constants. By convention, capital roman letters are used to denote expressions and small roman letters to denote distinct variables. Expressions of form E_1E_2 are termed *applications.* Application associates to the left, so MNP denotes the expression ((MN)P). Expressions of form λx.E are termed *abstractions*; E is the *lambda body* and x is the *formal parameter* which will be bound to any argument to which the abstraction is applied. For example, the function f such that f(x) = x * (x – 1) is defined by the abstraction

λx. * x (– x 1)

(by convention, all operators are written prefix in the λ calculus).

The λ calculus can be used as a rudimentary programming language. A program in this language is an expression which is evaluated by repeated simplification. Simplification consists of the repeated selection of a *reducible sub-expression* (or *redex*) until there are none left. Applications of λ abstractions are simplified by means of *β reduction,* a transformation whereby all occurrences of the formal parameter in the lambda body are substituted by the argument to the abstraction. Applications of predefined functions are simplified by means of *δ reduction,* a transformation whereby the application is replaced by the result of executing the built-in code for the function for the given arguments. For example, given the function

g = λ x. λ y. * x (– y 1)

the expression g 2 3 is evaluated as follows, recalling that application associates to the left :

```
g 2 3 =                            /* definition of g */
(λ x. λ y. * x (– y 1)) 2 3 →      /* β reduction */
(λ y. * 2 (– y 1)) 3 →             /* β reduction */
* 2 (– 3 1)                        /* δ reduction */
* 2 2 →                            /* δ reduction */
4
```

An expression, such as the constant 4 above, which contains no redexes is said to be in *normal form.* In general, there may be a choice of reduction steps to reach a normal form. Fortunately, the *Church-Rosser Theorem* implies that if an expression E reduces to two normal forms, M and N, then M and N are identical up to a renaming of variables.

2.2 Functional Programming Languages

Functional programming languages extend the λ calculus into a high level programming language by including a number of primitive types and functions, a set of type-forming operators for the definition of further types, and facilities for the definition of further functions. FDL supports all of these features.

Functions can be *polymorphic*, that is their declarations may include one or more *type variables* (FDL's type variables are named alpha, alpha1, alpha2, ...). Examples of polymorphic functions are "member" which tests for the membership of an element in a list, and the higher order function "map" which applies a function to each element of a list in turn :

```
member      : alpha  (list alpha)  → bool
member       x []          ⇐ false
member       x [y|z]       ⇐ (x = y)  or  (member  x  z)
map    : (alpha1 → alpha2)  (list alpha1)  →  (list alpha2)
map  f  []     ⇐ []
map  f  [x|y]  ⇐  [(f x) | map  f  y]
```

In FDL, the notation [ ] is equivalent to the empty list, NIL, the notation [x|y] is equivalent to the list with head x and tail y, CONS x y, the notation $[x_1, ..., x_n]$ is equivalent to the list CONS x_1 (CONS x_2...(CONS x_n NIL)...), and the symbol ⇐ is used for function definition.

The functions "map" and "member" above are defined by means of multiple equations rather than by a single equation. Given the application of such a multiply-defined n-ary function, f, to a set of arguments, (f E_1 ... E_n), a *pattern-matching algorithm* determines which of the equations of f applies for the given arguments. A common pattern-matching algorithm is the "top-to-bottom" one adopted by Miranda [PEYT87] which examines each equation in turn until one is found whose left hand side matches the given arguments - if no such equation is found, the program terminates with an error message. An alternative pattern-matching algorithm is the "best-fit" one adopted by HOPE [FIEL88]. Unlike top-to-bottom pattern matching, which picks the *first* matching equation, best-fit pattern matching picks the *most specific* matching equation and is independent of the order in which equations are examined. However, best-fit pattern matching can only guarantee to find a single most specific match if the equations are *unambiguous* [FIEL88]. For example, the definition

```
amb : integer  integer  → integer
amb  0  v      ⇐ 1
amb  v  1      ⇐ 2
amb  v  w      ⇐ 3
```

is ambiguous since the first two equations are equally specific matches for (amb 0 1). In order to disambiguate this definition, a further equation which is a more specific match for (amb 0 1) must be added, namely an equation whose left hand side is amb 0 1.

Whichever pattern-matching algorithm is adopted, when an n-ary function is defined by m≥ 1 equations,

$$
\begin{aligned}
&f\ p_{1\,1} \cdots p_{1\,n} \Leftarrow R_1\\
&f\ p_{2\,1} \cdots p_{2\,n} \Leftarrow R_2\\
&\cdots\\
&f\ p_{m\,1} \cdots p_{m\,n} \Leftarrow R_m
\end{aligned}
$$

code must be generated (i) for encapsulating the semantics of the pattern-matching algorithm, and (ii) for binding the variables in the left hand sides of the equations to the appropriate argument components. The resulting function definition is of the form :

$f = \lambda x_1 . \lambda x_2 ... \lambda x_n .$
case *pattern-matching-code* **of**
1 : (*binding-code*$_1$ R_1)
2 : (*binding-code*$_2$ R_2)
....
m : (*binding-code*$_m$ R_m)
other : error
end-case

2.3 Suitability of Functional Languages for Use as Database Languages

Referential transparency, a rich set of data types, and higher order functions make functional programming a very powerful high-level programming paradigm. However, existing functional languages are not suitable for use as database languages with a functional data model for a number of reasons.

Firstly, in functional programming languages functions are assumed to be defined completely at one time and are "updated" by their complete redefinition. Such an update is affected either by recompiling the entire program with the new definition replacing the old (as in Miranda [TURN85]) or by creating a new version of the function while previous references to the function continue to use the old version (as in ML MILN84]). Neither approach is feasible in a database environment where data is amassed incrementally and where small-grain (i.e. equation-based) update facilities are necessary.

Secondly, functions are assumed to be totally defined over their argument domain. Thus, a failure to match a set of arguments against the equations for a function is treated as an error. This is not suitable for database querying where the evaluation of a query should not be aborted as the result of incomplete information in some sub-query.

Thirdly, given that functions are to be defined incrementally by the insertion and deletion of individual equations, pattern-matching algorithms which rely upon an ordering of the equations (such as the top-to-bottom algorithm of Miranda) or on an examination of all the equations to check for unambiguity (such as the best-fit algorithm of HOPE) are not suitable. Rather, the pattern-matching algorithm should be independent of the order in which equations are inserted and retrieved. Furthermore, updates to functions should not require the retrieval of any existing equations to verify that unambiguity is maintained.

Fourthly, functional programming languages do not provide dynamically extensible data types corresponding to real-world entity types. Neither do they include integrated meta data and so the powerful facilities available at the object level cannot be used to formulate metalevel queries.

Finally, the long-term storage of functions as source or object code and their run-time representation by a main memory data structure is not adequate for large volumes of data. Instead, functions must *persist* [ATKI87] on secondary storage and the run-time management of data on secondary storage is required.

Two functional languages do support the persistence of data on secondary storage, namely Amber [CARD85] and Galileo [ALBA85]. However, these languages do not assume a functional data model and share the drawbacks of functional programming languages regarding function updates and pattern-matching semantics. Galileo and Amber integrate database and programming language technology by extending a programming language with persistent data. In contrast, FDL extends a functional data model to computational completeness. Both approaches may be regarded as "tight" couplings of the two technologies and are in contrast to "loose" couplings where a DBMS is used as a back-end to a programming or query language.

3. The Functional Database Language FDL

In the previous section we gave a necessarily brief introduction to functional programming and noted several ways in which existing functional languages are deficient for use as database languages with a functional data model. In the present section we show how FDL overcomes these deficiencies, as well as those of previous implementations of a functional data model which we identified in Section 1.1.

The first part of this section concerns the expressiveness of FDL. We commence with a description of FDL's data types (Section 3.1) and with the declaration and definition of functions both for modelling data and for computation (Section 3.2). In Sections 3.3, 3.4 and 3.5 we consider how FDL handles database closure, null data and default data, respectively. In Section 3.6 we discuss inverse functions. Finally, in Section 3.7 we consider how the semantic integrity of the database in maintained in FDL and identify a further category of information which can be expressed in FDL, namely semantic integrity constraints.

We then consider database updating and querying. In Section 3.8 we note how function updates in FDL differ from those in the DAPLEX-related languages. In Section 3.9 we discuss the formulation and storage of queries. Finally, in Section 3.10 we give a description of query evaluation. We reserve implementation considerations for Section 4.

3.1 Data Types

The data types of FDL are the arbitrarily nested lists, products and sums of the functional programming languages. In addition, abstract entity types, which we term *non-lexical* types [VERH82], can be declared. Examples of type declarations are

```
person :: nonlex                                          (1)
constituency :: nonlex                                    (2)
result :: nonlex                                          (3)
election :: nonlex                                        (4)
party :: LABOUR ++ CONSERVATIVE ++ OTHER string           (5)
votes == integer                                          (6)
name == string                                            (7)
date == (integer ** integer ** integer)                   (8)
```

(1)-(4) are declarations of new non-lexical types and (5) is a declaration of a new sum type. In (5), the identifiers in capitals are termed *constructor functions* and serve as tags for the components of the sum type. Sum types can be defined recursively, for example the built-in, polymorphic, list type :

list alpha :: NIL ++ CONS alpha (list alpha)

(6)-(8) above declare synonyms for existing types. Thus, FDL's type checker regards "votes" as being synonymous with "integer", "name" as being synonymous with "string", and "date" as being synonymous with the product type (integer ** integer ** integer). Three similar types which are *not* synonyms of existing types can be declared as single-component sum types :

```
new_votes :: VOTES integer
new_name :: NAME string
new_date :: DATE (integer ** integer ** integer)
```

Non-lexicals (that is, abstract entities) are created and deleted via **create** and **delete** commands e.g.

```
create person $p1 $p2 $p3
delete $p2
```

The $x are transient global variable aliases which allow non-lexicals to be referenced directly without resorting to their actual values. For any non-lexical type, t, the zero-argument *generator function* All_t:→(list t) is available and returns the current non-lexicals of type t in the form of a list. Generator functions are non-deterministic with respect to the *order* in which non-lexicals are returned; for example, given the above creations and deletion, the query

All_person

returns either the list [$p1, $p3] or the list [$p3, $p1].

FDL's use of global variables to reference non-lexicals is in contrast to FQL and the DAPLEX-related languages which have no means of referencing abstract entities globally. These languages therefore require that abstract entities be identifiable by means of unique scalar-valued keys during any batch loading of data. In contrast, FDL imposes no requirement for keys since non-lexicals can be referenced by global variables during a batch load just as during an interactive session. However, semantic integrity constraints can be optionally declared for enforcing uniqueness constraints on attributes of entities (see Section 3.7 below). In fact, in contrast to E/FDM and P/FDM, FDL's Load Utility is identical to its interactive interface except that no prompts are written to the output file and that all error messages display the line number of the offending command in the input file.

FDL's non-lexicals provide attribute-independent identity for objects. Thus, arbitrarily complex objects can be represented, including recursive objects. This feature, together with FDL's unified functional model for both data and computation, imply that the language is well-suited to the implementation of an *object-oriented* [BANC88, DITT88] database language. Such a language would have a uniform functional semantics for the construction of objects from component objects, for the representation of relationships between objects, and for the implementation of query methods. As yet, FDL does not provide explicit primitives for the definition of inheritance lattices or for the encapsulation of information and these are areas of on-going research.

3.2 Functions

Properties of entities and relationships between entities are represented by functions in FDL. For example, given the type declarations (1)-(8) of Section 3.1, the names of people, the names of constituencies and the dates of elections are modelled by the functions

```
name_of      : person → name
const_name   : constituency → name
date_of      : election → date
```

the results of an election at a constituency are modelled by the 2-ary function

```
results_of   : constituency  election → (list result)
```

and the details of a particular result by the functions

```
candidate_of : result → person
party_of     : result → party
votes_of     : result → votes
```

We note from "results_of" above that FDL's bulk data type is the list, hence multi-valued functions are represented by list-valued functions in FDL.

Equations can be inserted for functions which have been declared. For example, to record the U.K. General Election of 11th June 1987 :

```
create election $e
date_of $e   ⇐ <87,6,11>
```

to record the Finchley constituency :

```
create constituency $c
const_name $c     ⇐ "Finchley"
```

and to record the results at Finchley in 1987 :

```
create result $r1 $r2 $r3
results_of $c $e ⇐ [$r1, $r2, $r3]
create person $p1 $p2 $p3
name_of $p1 ⇐ "M.H.Thatcher"
candidate_of $r1 ⇐ $p1; party_of $r1 ⇐ CONSERVATIVE; votes_of $r1 ⇐ 21603
name_of $p2 ⇐ "J.Davies"
candidate_of $r2 ⇐ $p2; party_of $r2 ⇐ LABOUR; votes_of $r2 ⇐ 12690
name_of $p3 ⇐ "D.Howarth"
candidate_of $r3 ⇐ $p3; party_of $r3 ⇐ OTHER "Liberal"; votes_of $r3 ⇐ 5580
```

Functions which are used for computation can be declared and defined. Such functions are stored in the database in the same way as functions modelling real-world data (see Section 4 below). Since FDL is computationally complete, counting and aggregation functions such as "count", "max", "min", "average", "append" need not be built in but can be defined in the language itself. We have already defined "member" in Section 2.2 and as further examples we define "append" and "max" below. In the first equation for max, the constant @ is a null value denoting "undefined" which we discuss further in Section 3.3.

```
append: (list alpha) (list alpha) → (list alpha)
append[ ] z ⇐ z
append[x|y] z      ⇐ [x | append y z]
max    : (list integer) → integer
max    [ ]    ⇐ @
max    [x]    ⇐ x
max    [x|y]  ⇐ let prev_max == max y in if (x > prev_max) x prev_max
```

In the last equation for max, the **let** construct associates the value of (max y) with the new variable prev_max. Thus, the repeated evaluation of (max y) which could occur with the equivalent equation

```
max    [x|y]  ⇐ if (x > max y) x (max y)
```

is avoided.

Higher order functions can also be defined and stored, for example the function map of Section 2.2. Further examples are trans_clos which computes the transitive closure of functions of type t→t :

```
trans_clos : (alpha → alpha) alpha → (list alpha)
trans_clos f a ⇐ let b == f a in if (b = @) [ ] [b | trans_clos f b]
```

and ltrans_clos which computes the transitive closure of functions of type t→(list t) :

```
ltrans_clos : (alpha → (list alpha)) alpha → (list alpha)
ltrans_clos f a ⇐ let b == f a in append b [y || x ← b & y ← ltrans_clos f x]
```

Here, the construct [... || ...] is a *list abstraction* [PEYT87] and may be read as "the list of values, y, such that x is in the list b and y is in the list (ltrans_clos f x)". In general, the syntax of list abstractions is [E || Q_1 & ... & Q_n], where each Q_i is termed a *qualifier* and has the syntax Q ::= E | I←E. Each qualifier of the form I←E is termed a *generator* and E is a list-valued expression which generates successive values for the variable I. Each qualifier of the form E is termed a *filter* and is a boolean-valued expression which must be satisfied by the instantiations of variables generated by the generators.

3.3 Database Closure

Functions will frequently not be exhaustively defined over their argument domains. However, a lack of information for a particular entity should not cause the abortion of a query over a number of entities. Rather, a departure from the pattern matching of functional programming languages is required in that a failure to match some sub-expression (f E_1 ... E_n) of a query Q against the equations for f should not be considered an error. Instead, some default value should be *assumed* for the sub-expression. In FDL, a null value $@_t$ is included in every type t, whether simple or structured, for precisely this reason (we often write @ without its subscript since its type can be inferred from the context). Thus, if no equation exists whose left hand side matches (f E_1 ... E_n), the value @ is substituted for this sub-expression in Q.

In other words, we have adopted a @-as-failure assumption to "close" the database, analogous to negation-as-failure for logic-based languages [CLAR78] or to the Closed World Assumption [REIT78]. For example, consider the function

salary : person ⟶ integer

and the people $p1, $p2, $p3, $p4. Then, given the following definition for "salary"

```
salary $p1  ⇐ 40000
salary $p3  ⇐ 50000
salary $p4  ⇐ 75000
```

the query

[p ‖ p ← [$p1, $p2, $p3, $p4] & (salary p) > 45000]

returns [$p3,$p4] as opposed to aborting at (salary $p2).

The penalties paid for the @-as-failure rule are that errors become more difficult to trace and that the potentially expensive evaluation of a query may proceed only to yield @ as its final outcome. For example, given the "sum" function :

```
sum : (list integer) ⟶ integer
sum [ ]      ⇐ 0
sum [x|y]    ⇐ x + (sum y)
```

the query

sum [salary p ‖ p ← [$p1, $p2, $p3, $p4]]

returns @, since the built-in function + returns @ if either of its arguments is @. The user then has to examine both the definition of "sum" and that of "salary" to track down the reason for @ being returned. However, FDL does provide a built-in function error:string⟶alpha whose effect is to abort computation, outputing its argument as an error message. Thus, the "error-as-failure" assumption of the functional programming languages can be programmed for specific functions, if required. For example, the second equation for "sum" above could be replaced by

```
sum [x|y]    ⇐ if ((x = @) or (x = ?)) (error "null value passed to sum") (x + (sum y))
```

3.4 Null Data

In addition to the value $@_t$, a second null value, $?_t$, is also included in every type t in order to provide a means of representing defined but as yet unknown information. These two nulls are not to be confused with the least element of each type, $\perp_t$, which denotes "no information" and results from non-terminating computations. The values $@_t$ and $?_t$ are bona fide members of t and can be used just as the non-null values of type t. In particular, they can appear

(a) in any position in nested structures

(b) in equations, and

(b) as arguments to functions.

Characteristic (a) allows partially known structures to be modelled to arbitrary granularity. This is in contrast to the DAPLEX-related languages which have a single undefined value, no unknown value and no means of representing partially known sets. Characteristic (b) allows the value of a function applied to a null value to be defined just as it is for non-null values. For example, consider the function :

```
salary : person → integer
salary $p1   ⇐ 45000
salary $p2   ⇐ @
salary $p3   ⇐ 50000
salary $p4   ⇐ ?
```

Then, we can define the function

```
sum_salaries : (list integer) → integer
sum_salaries [ ]    ⇐ 0
sum_salaries [@|y]⇐ sum_salaries y
sum_salaries [?|y]  ⇐ 10000 + (sum_salaries y)
sum_salaries [x|y]  ⇐ x + (sum_salaries y)
```

in which values of 0 and 10000 are assumed for undefined and unknown salaries, respectively, whence the query

sum_salaries [salary p || p ← [$p1, $p2, $p3, $p4]]

returns 45000 + 0 + 50000 + 10000 ≡ 105000, rather than 45000 + @ + 50000 + ? ≡ @.

3.5 Default Data

FDL employs a modified form of best-fit pattern matching to evaluate function applications (see Sections 3.10 and 4 below). With this algorithm, variables are considered a less specific match for a constant than the constant itself. Thus, equations with variables on their LHS can be used to define *default rules*. Examples are the rule that unless known to the contrary the number of votes for a candidate is 0 :

votes_of r ⇐ 0

and the rule that unless known to the contrary a candidate is a member of the Conservative party if he/she represents the Conservative party :

```
con_party_member : person → bool
con_party_member p ⇐
        (count [r || r ← inv_candidate_of p & (party_of r) = CONSERVATIVE]) > 0
```

This last rule states that a person is a Conservative party member if there is at least one result for which he/she is a candidate and represents the Conservative party. The inverse function "inv_candidate_of" (see Section 3.6 below) generates the results pertaining to the candidate, and the (user-defined) function count:(list alpha)→integer counts these results.

3.6 Inverse Functions

For any first-order function f:t→s such that t is a non-lexical type and s is a non-list type, the inverse function inv_f:s→(list t) is available. The equation defining this inverse function may be assumed to be :

inv_f x ⇐ [y || y ← All_t & (f y) = x]

Similarly, for any f:t→(list s) such that t is a non-lexical type and s is any non-function type, the "converse" function inv_f:s→(list t) is available and its definition may be assumed to be :

inv_f x ⇐ [y || y ← All_t & member x (f y)]

3.7 Maintaining Semantic Integrity

Like most functional languages, FDL is *polymorphic* and *strongly typed* [MILN78, CARD87]. All type checking is performed at compile time. Thus, queries containing type errors are never run and equations which do not conform to the function declarations are never stored.

A final category of information which can be expressed in FDL are ***semantic integrity constraints*** over extensionally defined functions of type $t_1 \ldots t_n \rightarrow s$, where $n \geq 1$, the t_i are non-lexical types and s is any type. Integrity constraints are zero-argument boolean-valued functions, f, which must always evaluate to "true" and are defined by an equation of the form

$$f \Leftarrow [\, \langle v_1, \ldots v_n \rangle \parallel v_1 \leftarrow All\_t_1 \;\; \& \;\; \ldots \;\; \& \;\; v_n \leftarrow All\_t_n \;\; \& \;\; \textit{list of filter expressions}] = [\,]$$

For the example, the constraint that each election must have a date is expressed by the function:

```
e_dates :→ bool
e_dates ⇐ [e || e ← All_election  &  (date_of  e) = @] = [ ]
```

and the constraint that each constituency must have a unique name is expressed by the function:

```
const_names :→ bool
const_names ⇐ [<c1, c2> || c1 ← All_constituency  &  c2 ← All_constituency  &
                 not (c1 = c2)  &  (const_name c1) = (const_name c2)] = [ ]
```

The validity of the integrity constraints is checked after every database update (unless the update occurs within a transaction in which case the integrity constraints are checked at the end of the transaction with respect to the accumulated updates). Only the integrity constraints whose value may be changed by the given update (or set of updates) are checked. Also, the constraints are only evaluated over "changed" data as opposed to over the entire database.

3.8 Function Updates

Functions are defined and updated incrementally by the insertion and deletion of individual equations. At any time there can be no two equations with the same left hand side (LHS). Thus, if an equation is specified which has the same LHS as an existing equation, the new right hand side (RHS) replaces the old. As in DAPLEX, an enumerated list on the RHS of an equation can be updated by means of two primitives **include** and **exclude** which insert and remove individual elements from the list, respectively.

If the RHS of a new equation contains no variables, and could therefore be evaluated before insertion, it is not in fact evaluated. This is in contrast to DAPLEX and related languages where the single equation which defines a derived function is stored as entered but where any expression on the RHS of an assignment to a base function is first evaluated and the resulting value stored. To illustrate this difference between FDL and the DAPLEX-related languages, consider the function

```
sponsored_by  : person → (list name)
sponsored_by  $p1        ⇐ ["T.G.W.U.", "N.U.M."]
```

where $p1 is an alias for a non-lexical of type person. The information that a further person, with alias $p2, is sponsored by the same organisations as $p1 can be recorded in two different ways in FDL :

```
sponsored_by  $p2 ⇐  ["T.G.W.U.", "N.U.M."]          (1)
sponsored_by  $p2 ⇐  sponsored_by  $p1               (2)
```

If the sponsors of $p1 are subsequently updated by the request

```
sponsored_by  $p1 ⇐ exclude "N.U.M."
```

with (1) the value of (sponsored_by $p2) remains unchanged whereas with (2) the value of (sponsored_by $p2) is now also ["T.G.W.U."]. In contrast, only the semantics of case (1) can be captured with DAPLEX since "sponsored_by" is a base function and the RHS of any assignment to it will be evaluated before being stored.

3.9 Formulation and Storage of Queries

A query in FDL is an expression to be evaluated with respect to the equations in the database. For example, to find the details of the winning result at Finchley in 1987 we can pose the query

```
let [ e ] == inv_date_of <87,6,11> in                /* find the election on <87,6,11> */
let [ c ] == inv_const_name "Finchley" in            /* find the Finchley constituency */
let max_vote ==
   max [votes_of r || r ← results_of  c  e]  in      /* find the winning vote */
   (<party_of r, name_of candidate_of r, votes_of r> || r ← results_of  c  e  &
    (votes_of r) = max_vote)                 /* print details of the result with the winning vote */
```

which returns the answer <CONSERVATIVE, "M.H.Thatcher", 21603>. We note that *patterns* [e] and [c] are used in the **let** clauses above rather than simple variables. These patterns have the effect of extracting the single element e and c from within the list returned by inv_date_of and inv_const_name, respectively. We also note the use of the construct (E || Q_1 & ... & Q_n), which is semantically equivalent to

head [E || Q_1 & ... & Q_n]

Any query can be stored on the RHS of a zero-argument function. For example, the above query can be stored on the RHS of the function

```
Result_at_finchley  : → (party ** name ** votes)
Result_at_finchley  ⇐ let  [ e ]  == ...
```

Generic queries can be expressed as functions of one or more arguments. For example, the generic query requesting the details of the winner of a constituency on a particular date can be stored on the RHS of a function of two arguments :

```
Winning_info  : name  date  → (party ** name ** votes)
Winning_info  nm  dt  ⇐
   let [ e ]  ==  inv_date_of  dt in
   let [ c ]  ==  inv_const_name  nm in
   let max_vote  == max [votes_of r || r ← results_of  c  e]  in
      (<party_of r, name_of candidate_of r, votes_of r> || r ← results_of  c  e  &
       (votes_of r) = max_vote)
```

Specific results for generic queries can be stored explicitly to avoid future repeated evaluation. For example, the following equations can be added to the definition of Winning_info above :

```
Winning_info  "Finchley"  <87, 6, 11>  ⇐  <CONSERVATIVE, "M.H.Thatcher", 21603>
Winning_info  "Monklands East"  <87, 6, 11>  ⇐  <LABOUR, "J.Smith", 22649>
```

This choice of whether to store only specific results, or only the generic query, or some specific results together with the generic query as a default rule has not been available in previous languages with a functional data model where functions have had to be either purely intentionally defined or purely extensionally defined.

3.10 Evaluation of Queries

An FDL query is first represented as a directed graph, and then evaluated by the technique of *graph reduction* which repeatedly simplifies reducible sub-graphs of the query graph until a graph representing a normal form expression is obtained [PEYT87, FIEL88]. A reducible sub-graph is

(i) a λ abstraction applied to an argument, or

(ii) a built-in n-ary function applied to n arguments, or

(iii) a user-defined n-ary function applied to n arguments.

In cases (i) and (ii), graph reduction simulates β and δ reduction respectively. In case (iii), FDL's pattern matcher is invoked to retrieve the appropriate equation from the database and the function application in the query graph is replaced by the RHS of this equation. Since FDL's pattern matcher differs from those outlined in Section 2.2 above, we consider it further below and in Section 4.

At any time, a function f is defined by a (possibly empty) list of equations, which we denote by $Eqns_f$. No two equations in $Eqns_f$ can have the same LHS, and no variable can appear more than once on the LHS of the same equation. FDL's pattern-matching algorithm is a *left-to-right best-fit* one : given a function application (f E_1 E_2 ... E_n), the equation which defines the n-ary function f for the arguments E_1 ... E_n is determined by matching each E_i in turn against $Eqns_f$ and any equation whose i^{th} parameter is not a left-to-right best-fit match for E_i is not considered when matching the remaining E_{i+1}, E_{i+2}, ..., E_n. For example, given the function "amb" of Section 2.2, the expression (amb 0 1) evaluates to 1. We give the definition of FDL's pattern matcher in Section 4.2 below.

4. Implementation

The current implementation of FDL is in 'C' and runs on a MicroVax II under VMS. This implementation relies on a 3-key Grid File implemented by Derakhshan [DERA89] for the placement of data on secondary storage and for the retrieval of data. In particular, all FDL data, including meta data, is stored as a number of triples, $<x_1, x_2, x_3>$, where the x_i are the three key fields. A set of triples is logically identified by a partial-match query of the form *set_id = set(*a_1,a_2,a_3*)*, where each a_i is either a constant or the wildcard value, *. The triples in this set are retrieved one at a time by a series of requests *triple = get_another(set_id)* until the set is exhausted or until no more triples are required. Only the data page containing the next triple is retrieved from the database (if it does not already reside in the buffer pool); this page is then "fixed" in the buffer pool so that it does not get paged out before the next *get_another(set_id)* request [DERA89]. A significant feature of the Grid File is that triples corresponding to neighbouring points in the 3-dimensional key space tend to be clustered onto the same data pages [NIEV84].

The main requirements for the implementation of any database language derive from the assumption that the language will be accessing data structures which do not reside in main memory. Thus, the minimisation of I/O activity during query processing is crucial. In particular

- virtual storage must be utilised for buffering I/O
- main memory should be utilised for caching data structures which are accessed frequently
- constructor functions such as CONS should be evaluated lazily, that is one argument at a time
- "bulk" data should be retrieved according to need

In our case, all I/O is ultimately handled by the underlying Grid File which does incorporate a Buffer Manager. Main memory is utilised during query evaluation and integrity constraint enforcement (the most recently used equations are cached as are the semantic integrity constraints). Constructor functions are indeed evaluated lazily since query evaluation only proceeds to *weak head-normal form* (WHNF) as opposed to full normal form, where an expression is in WHNF if it has no outer-level redexes but may have inner-level ones [PEYT87]. Finally, our implementation supports the lazy retrieval of enumerated lists on the RHS of equations, extents of non-lexical types, lists returned by inverse functions, and the LHS of equations during pattern matching.

4.1 Storage of FDL's Persistent Structures

Every non-lexical value is stored as a triple of the form <ALL,type,value>, where ALL is an unique predefined identifier. Hence, non-lexicals are clustered according to their type and the extent of a non-lexical type, t, is identified by the query *set(ALL, t, *)*.

The equations constituting a function definition have a natural representation as a labelled tree whose root is the function itself, whose inner arcs represent components of the LHS of equations, and whose leaves uniquely identify the RHS of equations. We term this tree the function's *match tree*. For example, the match trees for the functions "name_of", "results_of" and "max" of Section 2 are shown in Figure 1, where the v_i are normalised names for the variables appearing in any equation and the t_i are unique, system-generated, identifiers which implement the connections of the match tree. In particular, t_1 uniquely identifies the list on the RHS of the equation

results_of $c $e ⇐ [$r1, $r2, $r3]

and t_4 uniquely identifies the expression on the RHS of the equation

max $[v_0|v_1]$ ⇐ **let** prev_max == max v_1 **in** if (v_0 > prev_max) v_0 prev_max

In general, a RHS which is not a constant or enumerated list is stored as a binary tree of the same form as a query graph. The binary tree is constructed from triples which are all assigned the same unique identifier in their first field. This identifier serves to link the RHS of the equation to the LHS and also to cluster the triples constituting the RHS. Thus, the potentially expensive fragmentation of expressions on disk is reduced. Also, the replacement of a function application in the query graph by the RHS of an equation in the database simply consists of retrieving the set of triples *set(RHS-id, *, *)* and reconstituting the triple tree in the query graph, branch for branch.

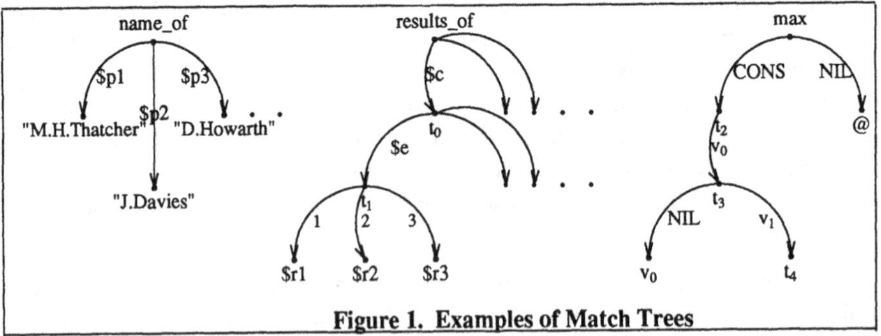

Figure 1. Examples of Match Trees

The conversion of match trees into sets of triples is straight-forward, each arc $N \to^{Label} M$ being stored as one triple <N,Label,M>. The insertion (or deletion) of an equation in a function's match tree is implemented by traversing the match tree from the root to a leaf, inserting (or deleting) arcs as necessary.

4.2 FDL's Pattern Matcher

Given an application of an n-ary function, (f E_1 ... E_n), FDL's pattern matcher chooses a single path from the root of f's match tree to a leaf without back-tracking, at the same time setting up a binding for each variable in the path. In Figure 2 we define the pattern matcher as a 3-ary function, Match, which is initially called with the list of arguments $[E_1,...,E_n]$, with an empty list of bindings, and with the root of f's match tree. Match returns a node which uniquely identifies an RHS, and a list of bindings for the variables in this RHS. In Figure 2, the notation $N \rightarrow^{Label} M$ can be read as "there is an arc $N \rightarrow^{Label} M$ in f's match tree". We note that Match treats constants as constructor functions of arity 0.

```
Match(Args,Bindings,Node)
if Args = [ ]
      return {Node,Bindings}
else  let [A | Rest] == Args in
      case A of
        a constant, C, or a constructor function application, C A1 ... Am, where m≥0 :
          if Node→C M
                return Match(append [A1,...,Am] Rest,Bindings,M)
          else  if Node→vi M  for some i
                return Match(Rest,[{vi,A} | Bindings],M)
          else  return {@,[ ]};
        an expression not in WHNF :
          if the only arc from Node is  Node→vi M  for some i
                return Match(Rest,[{vi,A} | Bindings],M)
          else  evaluate A to WHNF and return Match([A|Rest],Bindings,Node)
```

Figure 2. FDL's Pattern Matcher

Match has the following desirable properties :

- The semantics of a function, f, are captured by its physical representation and no pattern-matching code need be generated.
- The semantics of f are independent of the order in which its equations are inserted into or retrieved from $Eqns_f$ (since at each call of Match *all* the equations which are a best-fit match for the current argument are effectively selected).
- No update can give rise to an ambiguous definition for f (since, by the uniqueness of the LHSs of equations, Match will terminate at a unique leaf).

5. Concluding Remarks

In this paper we have introduced the functional database language FDL. We have shown how FDL improves on other implementations of a functional data model by being computationally complete while retaining a single functional model for both data and computation. Any computable function can be stored, as can arbitrarily nested data objects. Default knowledge can be represented and FDL's treatment of null data is richer than in previous functional models. Finally, all procedural data is translated into a graph which is stored physically clustered and ready for subsequent evaluation.

We have also shown how FDL modifies the functional programming paradigm for database applications by providing equation-oriented update facilities, and a left-to-right best-fit pattern-matching algorithm with an @-as-failure assumption. In addition, non-lexical types allow real-world entities to be represented and semantic integrity constraints over such types can be expressed as zero-argument boolean-valued functions. Finally, a set of built-in metalevel functions (not described here) allow meta data to be queried in the same functional formalism as data.

Further details regarding the meta language, updates, query evaluation, and the enforcement of semantic integrity constraints may be found in [POUL89]. FDL provides the Level 1 functionality of the 3-level TRISTARP system [KING89] whose Level 0 is the 3-key Grid File referred to in Section 4, and whose Level 2 consists of a variety of end-user interfaces.

Acknowledgements

We would like to thank our colleagues Mark Levene and Carol Small for their pertinent remarks on this paper. Alexandra Poulovassilis has been financially supported by the Greek State Scholarships Foundation (I.K.Y.) and by I.B.M. U.K. Laboratories Ltd.

References

[ABRI74] Abrial J.R., *Data Semantics*, in "Data Base Management", pp 1-59, J.W. Klimbie and K.L. Koffeman (eds.), North Holland, 1974

[ALBA85] Albano A., Cardelli L. and Orsini R., *Galileo : A Strongly Typed, Interactive Conceptual Language*, A.C.M. Trans. on Database Systems, 10(2) 1985, pp 230-260

[ATKI87] Atkinson M.P. and Buneman P., *Types and Persistence in Database Programming Languages*, A.C.M. Computing Surveys, 19(2) 1987, pp 105-190

[BANC87] Bancilhon F., Briggs T., Khoshafian S. and Valduriez P., *FAD, A Powerful and Simple Database Language*, Proc. of the 13th VLDB Conference, September 1987, pp 97-105

[BANC88] Bancilhon F., *Object-Oriented Database Systems*, Proc. of the 11th A.C.M. Symposium on Principles of Database Systems, pp 152-162

[BATO88] Batory D.S., Leung T.Y. and Wise T.E., *Implementation Concepts for an Extensible Data Model and Data Language*, A.C.M. Trans. on Database Systems, 13(3) 1988, pp 231-262

[BEEC88] Beech D., *A Foundation of Evolution from Relational to Object Databases*, in [SCHM88]

[BUNE82] Buneman P., Frankel R.E. and Nikhil R., *An Implementation Technique for Database Query Languages*, A.C.M. Trans. on Database Systems, 7(2) 1982, pp 164-186

[CARD85] Cardelli L., *Amber*, in "Combinators and Functional Programming Languages", G. Cousineau *et al.* (eds.), Springer-Verlag, 1985

[CARD87] Cardelli L., *Basic Polymorphic Typechecking*, Science of Computer Programming, 8(2) 1987, pp 17-172

[CLAR78] Clark K.L., *Negation as Failure*, in [GALL78]

[DAYA87] Dayal U. *et al.*, *Simplifying Complex Objects : The PROBE Approach to Modelling and Querying Them*, presented at the International Workshop on the Theory and Applications of Nested Relations and Complex Objects, Darmstadt, West Germany, April 1987

[DERA89] Derakhshan M. *A Development of the Grid File for the Storage of Binary Relations*, Ph.D. Thesis, Birkbeck College, University of London, March 1989

[DITT88] Dittrich K.R. (ed.), *Advances in Object-Oriented Database Systems*, Lecture Notes in Computer Science, No. 334, Springer-Verlag, September 1988

[FIEL88] Field A.J. and Harrison P., *Functional Programming*, Addison Wesley, 1988

[FLOR74] Florentin J.J., *Consistency Auditing of Databases*, The Computer Journal, 17(1) 1974, pp 52-58

[GALL78] Gallaire H. and Minker J. (eds.), *Logic and Databases*, Plenum Press, 1978

[GRAY88] Gray P.M.D., Moffat D.S., and Paton N.W., *A Prolog Interface to a Functional Data Model Database*, in [SCHM88]

[HAMM78] Hammer M.M. and McLeod D.J., *The Semantic Data Model : A Modelling Mechanism for database applications*, Proc. of the A.C.M. SIGMOD Conference, 1978, pp 26-35

[HEIL88] Heiler S. and Zdonik S., *Views, Data Abstraction and Inheritance in the FUGUE Data Model*, in [DITT88]

[HIND86] Hindley J.R. and Seldin J.P., *Introduction to Combinators and the Lambda Calculus*, Cambridge University Press, 1986

[JOUA85] Jouannaud J.-P. (ed.), *Functional Programming Languages and Computer Architectures*, Lecture Notes in Computer Science No. 201, Springer-Verlag, 1985

[KHOS86] Khoshafian S.N. and Copeland G.P., *Object Identity*, Proc. of the A.C.M. OOPSLA Conference, October 1986, pp 406-416

[KING89] King P., Derakhshan M., Poulovassilis A. and Small C., *TRISTARP - An investigation into the development and exploitation of Binary Relational Storage Structures*, submitted for publication.

[KULK86] Kulkarni K.G. and Atkinson M.P., *EFDM : Extended Functional Data Model*, The Computer Journal, 29(1) 1986, pp 38-46

[KULK87] Kulkarni K.G. and Atkinson M.P., *Implementing an Extended Functional Data Model Using PS-Algol*, Software Practice and Experience, 17(3) 1987, pp 171-185

[MILN78] Milner R., *A Theory of Type Polymorphism in Programming*, Journal of Computer and System Sciences, Vol 17, 1978, pp 348-375

[MILN84] Milner R., *A Proposal for Standard ML*, Proc. of the A.C.M. Symposium on LISP and Functional Programming, 1984, pp 184-197

[NIEV84] Nievergelt J., Hinterberger H. and Sevcik K.C., *The Grid File : An Adaptable Symmetric Multikey File Structure*, A.C.M. Trans. on Database Systems, 9(1) 1984, pp 38-71

[NIKH85] Nikhil R., *Practical Polymorphism*, in [JOUA85]

[PATO88] Paton N.W. and Gray P.D.M., *Object Storage in Databases*, Research Report AUCS/TR8803, Department of Computing Science, University of Aberdeen

[PEYT87] Peyton Jones S.L., *The Implementation of Functional Programming Languages*, Prentice Hall International, 1987

[POUL89] Poulovassilis A., *The Design and Implementation of FDL, a Functional Database Language*, Forthcoming Ph.D. Thesis, Birkbeck College, University of London, 1989

[REIT78] Reiter R., *On Closed World Databases*, in [GALL78]

[SCHM88] Schmidt J.W., Ceri S. and Missikof M. (eds.), *Advances in Database Technology - EDBT 88*, Lecture Notes in Computer Science, No. 303, Springer-Verlag, March 1988

[SHIP81] Shipman D., *The Functional Data Model and the Data Language DAPLEX*, A.C.M. Trans. on Database Systems, 6(1) 1981, pp 140-173

[SIBL77] Sibley E.H. and Kershberg L., *Data Architecture and Data Model Considerations*, Proc. of the AFIPS National Computer Conference, 1977, pp 85-96

[SMIT83] Smith J.M, Fox S. and Landers T., *ADAPLEX Rationale and Reference Manual*, Computer Corporation of America, CCA-83-08

[TURN85] Turner D.A., *Miranda : A non-strict functional language with polymorphic types*, in [JOUA85]

[VERH82] Verheijen G.M.A and Van Bekkum J., *NIAM : An Information Analysis Method*, in "Information Systems Design Methodologies : A Comparative Review", T.W. Olle *et al.* (eds.), North Holland, 1982, pp 537-589

METHODS AND TOOLS FOR EQUIVALENT DATA MODEL MAPPING CONSTRUCTION

Leonid A. Kalinichenko
Institute of Problems of Informatics
of the USSR Academy of Sciences
Vavilova 30/6, Moscow, V-334, 117900

Abstract

The paper contributes to the elaboration of a methodological framework for solving the problem of data model heterogeneity in multidatabase systems.

It presents an approach to rigorous definition of data models and to the handling of them as formal objects provided for the development of data model mappings in the process of design of heterogeneous multidatabase systems. The paper defines strict principles and specific techniques facilitating verifiable design of commutative data model mappings. The methods introduced make it possible to construct generalized data model kernel extensions equivalent to various internal data models and to develop and verify algorithms of the generalized level DML interpreters.

1. Introduction

Recently substantial attention in the DBMS area has been attracted to the problem of heterogeneous database integrating systems design [13-17,21]. The practical importance of this direction consists in development of tools making possible coexistence of different DBMS supporting various data models meeting applications requirements. The methodological importance of this direction arises from the fact that integration of heterogeneous databases requires methods of equivalent data model transformation and methods of constructing unifying data models and languages promoting generalization of various approaches to the development of DBMS languages.

This paper has been motivated by the 1989 CRAI school on heterogeneous database integration and is based on the experience in the development and application of one of the first implementations of a heterogeneous database integrating system [1,10,17] in which a strict formal basis for data model transformation and a set of well-defined architectural principles of system design were applied. The principal results of this research were obtained in the period of 1977 - 1981 [17] and only part of them were published in English [10].

Heterogeneous database integration is defined as an approach to database design, application and management providing for the achievement of the following objectives:

1) joint usage of data from several heterogeneous databases as

from a logically single database;

2) multidatabase management (homogeneous presentation for an application program of a collection of various databases, maintenance of its integrity, provision of a common data manipulation language);

3) data descripton and data manipulation language unification for various data models;

4) maintenance of DBMS-independent generalized level of an application domain description;

5) provision of application program independence of DBMS;

6) continuous embracement of an extending spectrum of data representations and operations in computers.

In most of the known systems the above goals were only partly achieved.

For ultimate solution of the problem it is necessary to create a formal theory in which a data model would play the role of the main object under analysis. Such a theory should contain a system of concepts, languages, metalanguages to treat existing data models and data models developed on the basis of formal semantics, with a view to expressing of the properties of a data model as a whole and operations on them (e.g., transformation of one data model into another). Examples of the properties mentioned are data model equivalence, data model inclusion and intersection.

Some of the interesting results published in the area of data model mapping in the same period as the research by the author are summarized below.

The notion of database state equivalence was analyzed in several papers [8,9]. In [8] it was shown that it is not possible to give a complete formal description of a specific database system if the reality should be taken into account and it's necessary to rely on common understanding of natural language. But with respect to an abstract model the semantics of a database can be formally defined.

The notion of data model equivalence (isomorphic or based on compound operations) was introduced in [9].

In [2,4] the concepts of denotational semantics were used to define the CODASYL data model.

The approaches to data model mapping based on some kind of formal model were studied in several papers.

In [5] the notion of mapping based on the concepts of the category theory was introduced. In [6] the formalism for data model mapping was proposed, databases were represented by many-sorted algebras and mappings were treated as homomorphisms.

In-depth theoretical analysis of data model mapping was undertaken in [11]. Here the problem of preserving by the mapping of consistency constraints was investigated. It was shown that the general problem of determinacy of consistent mapping is unsolvable. The positive contribution of the study was that it looked for languages for which it would be possible to decide on the desirable properties of data structure mappings. For that purpose the relational structure mappings were analyzed. It was shown that algorithms can be written which can decide when relational structure mapping preserves functional dependency and subsets constraints and when operation mapping correctly interprets the operations. The results of the study are applicable to other data models if the mapping of such data model can be expressed in terms of relational mappings.

In [12] an algorithm was presented for designing relational views over CODASYL schemas to support query capability, preserve the information content of the data base and provide independence from its physical organization.

This paper presents an approach for rigorous definition of data models and for handling of them as formal objects in the process of development of data model mappings provided for the design of heterogeneous multidatabase systems. The paper contributes to development of strict principles and specialized techniques for verifiable design of commutative [10] data model mappings.

2. Basic principles of heterogeneous database integration

The basic idea of heterogeneous database integration consists in the introduction of DBMS-independent generalized level of data representation and manipulation - **virtual database level** - and a generalized model of an integrating system corresponding to this level. Data models (DM) supported by DBMS with respect to this common DM are internal ones.

Each DM is completely defined by data description language (DDL) and data manipulation language (DML) semantics. Construction of an integrating system becomes possible on the basis of methods of data model mapping (while speaking about mapping, the DM being mapped will be called a **source** DM and the DM into which the mapping is carried out - a **target** one).

The notions of "mapping" and "transformation" will be distinguished further. By "mapping" we shall denote the abstract mechanism of conversion of one model into another and by "transformation" - implementation of the mapping in a computer. A software processor performing such mapping will be called "a data model transformer".

In transition from internal to generalized DM it's necessary to preserve the information and operators. This requires that the internal DM be equivalently represented in the generalized one in the process of DM mapping. A notion of **data model equivalence** is introduced in the following manner.

Database states in source and a target DM are equivalent if they are mapped into the same state in the content of an **abstract data metamodel** . Such a state mapping should be "isomorphic" - i.e. each element of a composite state in one model should correspond to an equivalent element in the other model. It is assumed that equivalent database states represent one and the same collection of facts.

Database schemas are equivalent if they produce sets of database states of equal power related by bijective dependency in such a way that the states being in one-to-one correspondence are equivalent. Two data models are **equivalent** if each database schema in one model can be put into a one-to-one correspondence with the equivalent schema in the other model (and vice versa), while providing completeness of the DML operator set in each data model.

A DML operator set is functionally complete if for each type of DDL objects the actions of retrieving, putting, deleting and updating of objects are expressible in DML and for each initial state b_1 of a database with the schema s_1 it's possible to define a sequence of DML operators transferring the database into any given state b_2 correct in frame of schema s_1.

It is assumed that DML operator sets of the data models which will be considered further are functionally complete.

Formal definitions.

For data model M_i the set af all schemas expressible in DDL of M_i is denoted by S_i, set of all data manipulation statements which may be constructed by DML of M_i is denoted by O_i.

The **database state** corresponding to schema s_i belonging to S_i is a function b_{si}: $Id_{si} \rightarrow V_i$, defining for each data type in the schema denoted by identifier **Id** its value v_i taken from the set of permissible values V_i of the data type. It is essential that v_i can also be a function. A set of permissible states corresponding to some schema s_i belonging to S_i is a set of functions B_{si}: $[Id_{si} \rightarrow V_i]$.

A **space of states** expressible in M_i is a set of functions B_i: $[Id_i \rightarrow V_i]$, which may be considered as union of sets B_{si} for all s_i belonging to S_i.

Data model M_i is a quadruple $<S_i, Ms_i, O_i, Mo_i>$ where Ms_i: $S_i \rightarrow B_i$ is a semantics function of M_i DDL, Mo_i: $O_i \rightarrow [B_i \rightarrow B_i]$ is a semantics function of M_i DML.

The following set of mappings constitutes the mapping **f** of data model M_j into data model M_i :

-the database state space of M_j into the database state space of M_i

$$\theta : B_j \rightarrow B_i,$$

-database schema of M_j into database schema of M_i

$$\sigma : S_j \rightarrow S_i,$$

-DML operators of DML of M_i into the sequence of operators of DML of M_j

$$\beta : O_i \rightarrow P_j,$$

where $p_j \in P_j$ is a procedure in DML of M_j.

The following propositions form the basis of a heterogeneous database integration conception.

The **data model axiomatic extension principle.** Generalized data model in the integrating system should be **extensible** while new data models are included into the system. Such an extension is implemented **axiomatically**. Axiomatic in this context means that such an extension of target DM is carried out by addition to its DDL of a system of axioms determining (in terms of a target model) logical dependencies of the source data model and the altered semantics of DML operators of the target DM. The result of the extension should be equivalent to the source data model.

Construction of a target DM axiomatic extension is considered as a new language design (DDL and DML) on the basis of the target DM.

The **data model commutative mapping principle**. In the process of mapping the DM of a specific DBMS into a generalized one it's necessary to preserve information and operators. This requirement is satisfied if DM mapping is **commutative**.

Mapping $f=<\sigma, \theta, \beta>$ of data model M_j into extension M_{ij} of data model M_i is commutative if the following conditions hold:

- schema mapping diagram is commutative:

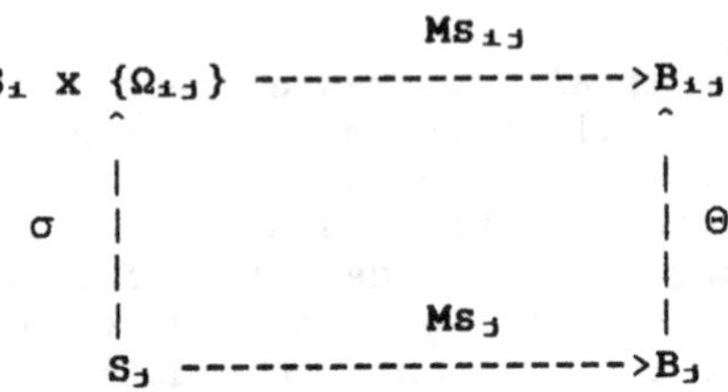

- DML operators mapping diagram is commutative:

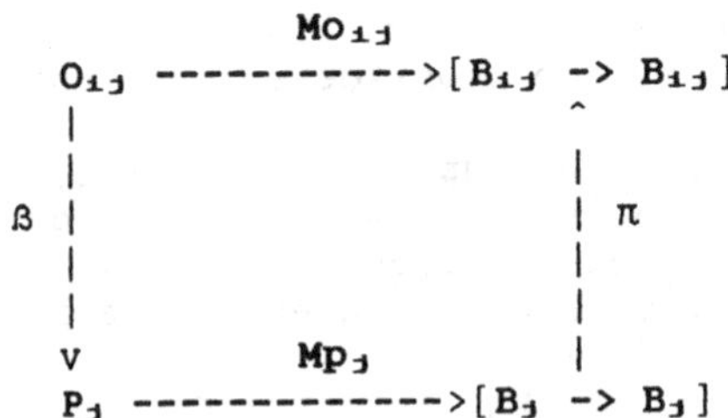

- Θ mapping is bijective.

Here Ω_{ij} denotes a set of axiom schemas expressing the data dependencies of M_j in terms of M_i; P_j denotes sequences of M_j DML operators (procedures).

The **unifying generalized data model synthesis principle.** Generalized data model synthesis is a process of construction of generalized data model kernel extensions equivalent to data models of DBMS embraced by the integrating system and a process of the merging of such extensions in a generalized data model. In such a way a unifying generalized data model is formed in which data models of various DBMS have homogeneous equivalent representations (by the subsets of a unifying data model).

3. Commutative data model mapping characterization

Axioms a_{ij} ε Ω_{ij} by which inherent consistency rules fixed in data model M_j and defined in terms of M_i are expressed will be referred to as data base **invariants**.

Actions of database state modification **induced by axiom** a_{ij} ε Ω_{ij} on the execution of database update statement o_{ij} ε O_{ij} is such minimal additional actions with respect to the statement o_i ε O_i of the target data model M_i which provide for a_{ij} to become an invariant with respect to o_{ij}.

In axiomatic extensions of M_i complete sets of invariants are considered which on the one hand completely define for data types of M_{ij} inherent consistency rules of M_j and on the other - completely define the changes of DML M_{ij} statements semantics with respect to analogeous statements of M_i.

Data model M_i **is included** in data model M_j if all axioms schemas Ω_{ri} of some reference M_r data model extension M_{ri} equivalent to M_i are included (not strictly perhaps) into the set of axiom schemas Ω_{rj} of reference M_r data model extension M_{rj} equivalent to M_j.

Proposition of existence.

If database schema mapping diagram for the M_j to M_{ij} mapping commutes, a set of M_j DML statements is functionally complete and if semantics function Mo_{ij} is defined, then the mapping $\beta:O_{ij} \to P_j$ exists which makes DML statement mapping diagram commutative.

Proposition of equivalence.

Data model M_j is equivalent to M_i iff there exists commutative mapping of M_j to M_i.

Proposition of constructiveness.

Commutative mapping of data model M_j into extension of data model M_i can be constructed if target data model (M_i) is included into the source one (M_j).

The properties of commutative data model mappings defined above influence greatly the methods of commutative DM mapping design. In particular, from proposition of existence it follows that the process of the design of generalized data model kernel axiomatic extensions equivalent to data models of the set of DBMS and the process of the design of the algorithms of extended target data model DML statements interpretation by means of the source one can be separated. Thus, it is allowed to separate and treat independently the process of the generalized unifying data model synthesis from the process of the definition of the algorithms of the DML interpreters.

More about properties of commutative DM mappings can be found in [20].

4. Method of formal definition of data model semantics

4.1. Semantical model

The main reason for formal definition of the data models is to obtain their compact and precise description, making possible manipulation by different data models as by mathematical objects. The metalanguage used for the formal definition of the data models is called the **data metamodel** (DMM). DMM should be general (i.e., independent of particular data models concepts), allowing precise expression of semantics properties of different data models, of their similarity or difference on the basis of one and the same language.

The main purpose of formal definition of a data model is the development of a common discipline for the design of data model mappings, according to which the construction of the algorithm of data model mapping and of the proof of it's correctness should be done simultaneously.

In developing DMM it is natural to use results obtained in the domain of programming languages semantics description. Generally, the definition of programming language L semantics is mechanism **M**, which relates the syntactical constructions or programs of the language to their content (or denotation - an object corresponding to its own name). In other words $M : P \to D$, where **P** is syntactical domain of **M** (the set of all syntactically correct programs in L), **D** - semantical domain of **M** (the set of the program denotations).

The existing methods for defining the programming language semantics are usually classified according to the type of domain **D** as:

-compiler based in which **D** is the set of target language programs and **M** is expressed as translation defined on a certain abstract representation of the syntax of the language (e.g., in the form of a parse tree);

-**operational** or **interpretative** in which **D** is the set of calculations (of sequences of abstract machine states), induced by the programs;

-**axiomatic** in which **D** is a relation defined on the sets of pre- and post- conditions, defining the allowable set of initial and final program states;

-**functional** or **denotational** in which the denotation of the program is a partially recursive function.

Generally, operational methods are mostly convenient for language implementors. Axiomatic methods mostly correspond to the process of programming. Denotational methods are generally convenient for language designers. Among the methods of semantics definition mentioned only the functional method has the remarkable property of combining program treatment as mathematical objects (functions) with flexible facilities for data types formal definition (in the form of partially-ordered sets).

Such considerations and the fact that during the design of data model mappings it is necessary to go into construction of the languages (in the process of data model extension) leads to the choice of denotational method as the basis for the design of data metamodel which will be defined further.

4.2. Data types as partially-ordered sets

The cornerstone of the denotational semantics is introduction of the class of "data types" - domains of functions - as partially-ordered sets and of a class of functions (generally recursive) for creation of a natural and precisely defined computational model. Foundations of such a model were created through research of D.Scott, C.Strachey, D.deBakker, Z.Manna, devoted to the theory of computations, methods of program analysis, programming language semantics. In essence, this results are based on the theory of the fixpoint of partially-recursive functions developed by S.Kleene.

Generalization of the above theory for programming became possible due to a special extension of the notions of monotonicity and continuity of functions in case of complexly structured program domains. Such an extension is achieved by introduction of several conditions which should be satisfied by the functions and their domains in order that the methods of classical theory could be applied. The approaches mentioned constitute the data metamodel basis.

In sequel functions **f** with domain D_1 and range D_2 are in general considered to be partial (undefined for some of domain values). Such functions are considered as abstract objects treated extensionally (being completely defined by set of pairs (argument, value)). In particular, it means that **f=g** if **f(x)=g(x)** for all **x**. In case of partial functions extensions of such functions to total ones are considered. These extensions are created by addition to domains D_1, D_2 of undefined value $\perp$ in such way that if function **f** is undefined on d_1 belonging to D_1 then $f(d_1)=\perp$. Besides, function **f** is defined also in point $\perp$. The class of all functions mapping D_1 into D_2 is denoted further as $[D_1\text{->}D_2]$.

Relation $\sqsubseteq$ ("less defined or equal") is a partial order on domain D such that for all d belonging to D the following relationships hold : $\perp \sqsubseteq d$ and $d \sqsubseteq d$. Different elements d_1, d_2 from D **minus** $\{\perp\}$ are not linked by relation $\sqsubseteq$.

Data type (domain) in the data metamodel is a set partially ordered by relation $\sqsubseteq$.

5. Data metamodel description

5.1. Data metamodel content

Abstract data metamodel consists of:

- a set of elementary domains D_1, D_2, ... corresponding to primary sets of objects;
- operations allowing construction of complex domains (data types) from simpler ones and facilities for data type formal definition;
- a set of data types defined on the basis of elementary domains by means of data type constructing operations;
- a set of primitive functions and predicates, defined on the data types;
- a set of functional forms, used for new function definition and facilities for formal definition of functions;
- a set of function definitions;
- a set of rules of equivalent function transformations.

The choice of DMM constructs was influenced by [2,3,4].

5.2. DMM data types

5.2.1. Primary domains and domain constructing operations

Elementary domain

Let **E** denote arbitrary set $\{e_i;\ i \in I\}$. Elementary domain D is created by addition of element $\perp$ to **E** and setting on a created set of a partial order $\sqsubseteq$:

for all $e_i \in \mathbf{E}$ it holds that $\perp \sqsubseteq e_i$;

for all e_i, $e_j \in \mathbf{E}$ it holds that $e_i \sqsubseteq e_j \leftrightarrow e_i = e_j$.

Operation of elementary domain creation from arbitrary set is denoted as

$D=\{e_i;\ i \in I\}^\circ$.

E.g., N= { ..., -2, -1, 0, 1, 2, ...}°, B= {true, false}°, C= {'a', 'b', 'c', ... }° - domains of integer, boolean and symbolic values.

Production domain

If D_1 and D_2 are domains then $D= D_1 x D_2$ is a domain - cartesian product of domains consisting of the pairs $\langle d_1,d_2\rangle, d_1 \in D_1, d_2 \in D_2$. It is essential that $\langle d_1, d_2\rangle \sqsubseteq \langle d_1', d_2'\rangle$ iff $d_1 \sqsubseteq d_1'$ in D_1 and $d_2 \sqsubseteq d_2'$ in D_2.

Let D_i $(1 \le i \le n)$ be a number of domains. $D=D_1 x D_2 x \dots x D_n$ is new domain consisting of n-ary tuples of elements of D_1, D_2, ... ,D_n. Special case when D_i is one and the same domain is denoted by $D=D_i^n$.

Domain of sum

If D_1 and D_2 are domains then $D= D_1+D_2$ is a domain - sum including arbitrary elements of initial domains. Elements **d,d'** ε **D'** are related by ⊑ iff **d,d'** belong to one of initial domains D_1 or D_2 and in this domain this relation between **d,d'** holds. For large number of domains the domain-sum is denoted as $D=D_1+D_2+ \dots +D_n$.

Functional domain

A class of monotonic continuous functions $[D_1 \to D_2]$ where D_1 and D_2 are domains creates domain with respect to partial ordering ⊑ in such a way that $f \sqsubseteq g$, $(f,g \in [D_1 \to D_2])$ iff for all $d \in D_1$ it holds that $f(d) \sqsubseteq g(d)$.

List domain

If D is any domain then $D^{*}= D + D^2 + D^3 + \dots$ denotes a list domain which includes all possible tuples of arbitrary order composed of the elements of D.

5.2.2. Data type construction

Any data type (domain) **T** is constructed recursively from data types (domains) D_i $(1 \le i \le n)$ using domain constructing operations **OP= +|x|->** (operation -> leads to the creation of functional domain) according to the following definition:

$T=D_i$ (any domain is a data type),

$T=T^{*}$,

$T=T^{n}$,

T= T OP T.

In domain constructing expressions parentheses may be used : **T=(T OP T)**. For readability the functional domain is inserted into square brackets: **T=[T->T]**.

5.2.3. Data type definition

Data type definition in the metamodel is the following construction:

<data type definition>::=<identifier>=<data type>

<data type>::= T|<predicate>--><data type>, <data type>

Data type definition connects its identifier with the definition of domain T, or with a list of alternative domains, in which the predicate expressing condition of one or another domain choice is included. If the predicate is true then the data type which immediately follows --> is used, otherwise the second data type will be used.

5.3. Functions

5.3.1. Function types and function application

New functions in data metamodel are introduced by means of definitions including functional forms - expressions containing free variables. In the metamodel the set of basic primitive functions and predicates is fixed. The main operation of data metamodel is function application denoted by $f(a_1, a_2, \dots ,a_n)$ where a_1, a_2, ... , a_n is an ordered set of function arguments.

5.3.2. Primitive functions and predicates

The range of predicates is a domain of {T,F}°. The range of primitive function is scalar value or a primary set of objects. In function definitions $p \dashrightarrow f_1, f_2$ is a conditional choicing f_1 if p=T and f_2 if p=F.

Functional domain analysing functions
domain(f) $\equiv$ f ε [D -> D'] --> {d ε D; f(d) $\neq$ |}, $\perp$
range(f) $\equiv$ f ε [D -> D'] --> {d ε D'; f^{-1}(d') $\neq \perp$}, $\perp$

Element length function
length(d) $\equiv$ d ε D^* & d=<d_1,d_2, ... ,d_n>--> n, $\perp$

Projection function
s-D_j $\equiv$ d=<d_1,d_2, ... ,d_n> & d ε $D_1 x D_2 x \ldots x D_n$ &
($1 \le j \le n$) --> d_j, $\perp$
It is allowed to write also j(d) or j·d if the structure of d is obvious.

Selector function
This function is used for analysis of the components of structured functional domains [D_1 -> [D_2 -> ... [D_{k-1} -> D_k] ...]] :
$d_1 \cdot d_2 \cdot \ldots \cdot d_{k-1}(f)$ $\equiv$ f ε [D_1 -> [D_2 -> ... [D_{k-1} -> D_k] ...]] & (d_1 ε D_1 & ... & d_{k-1} ε D_{k-1}) & ($f_1 \neq \perp$ & ... & $f_{k-1} \neq \perp$) --> f_{k-1}, $\perp$
Here f_1, f_2, ... ,f_{k-1} denotes:
$f_1=f(d_1)$ ε [D_2 -> ... [D_{k-1} -> D_k] ...]
$f_2=f_1(d_2)$ ε [D_3 -> ... [D_{k-1} -> D_k] ...]
.
.
.
$f_{k-1}=f_{k-2}(d_{k-1})$ ε [D_k -> D_{k+1}]
The notation $d_1 \cdot d_2 \cdot \ldots \cdot d_{k-1} \cdot f$ is also allowed.

Sum domain analysis predicate

is-D_j(d) $\equiv$ d ε $D_1+D_2+ \ldots +D_n$ -->(d ε D_j & ($1 \le j \le n$) & d $\neq \perp$ --> T,F), $\perp$

5.4. Functional forms

A functional form in a data metamodel is an expression denoting function. The function is defined by the functions included into the functional form and their arguments. Here the basic functional forms used in data metamodel for construction of complex forms as a composition of simpler ones will be defined.

Conditional form
p-->f,g $\equiv$ p=T --> f, p=F --> g, $\perp$

Form-functional substitution
Let f ε [D -> D'], d ε D, v ε D'. Then f[d/v] is a functional form, describing new function f', obtained from f by substitution of value f on the argument d equal to v. In case D and D' are complex domains (e.g., $D=D_1 x D_2 x \ldots x D_n$, $D'=D_1 x D_2 x$

... xD_m) the substitution is denoted in the following way:

$f[d_1,d_2,\ldots,d_n/v_1,v_2,\ldots,v_m]$

Here $\langle d_1,d_2,\ldots,d_n\rangle \in D$, $\langle v_1,v_2,\ldots,v_m\rangle \in D'$.

Composition

Let $f \in [D \to D']$, $g \in [D' \to D'']$. The composition (left composition) of functions is the form $g\cdot f \in [D \to D'']$ defined by the rules $(g\cdot f)(d) \equiv g(f(d))$ for all $d \in D$. The composition of n functions $f_1,f_2,\ldots,f_n$ is the form

$O_{i=1}^{n} f_i \equiv f_n\cdot f_{n-1}\cdot\ldots\cdot f_1$

Form - constant

If $d \in D$ - an arbitrary element of some domain, $d^{\sim}$ denotes a constant function such that for all arguments **a** the value of $d^{\sim}(a) \equiv a = \perp \to \perp, d$.

5.5. Definition of functions

Definition of function in the data metamodel is a construction of one of the following possible forms. If the domains of the arguments of the function are obvious the function f with the arguments $x_1,x_2,\ldots,x_n$ is defined as

$f(x_1,x_2,\ldots,x_n)=$ <functional form>

If the domains of the function arguments is to be defined explicitly, the function definition takes the form:

$f(x_1:D_1,x_2:D_2,\ldots,x_n:D_n)=$ <functional form>

Such functions belong to the class of functions $[D_1xD_2x\ldots xD_n \to D]$ where D is an arbitrary data type.

5.6. Rules of equivalent function transformations

Equivalent function transformation is a useful tool to demonstrate the commutativity of the data model mappings being constructed. Some basic transformations are shown below. Naturally, this list is not complete and can be extended.

In definitions of rules of equivalent functions transformations f,g,h will be used to denote arbitrary functions, p,q - to denote any predicates, $f \equiv g$ will denote equivalence of functions .

It is well known [7] that the following equations hold:

$\perp^{\sim}\cdot f \equiv f\cdot \perp^{\sim} \equiv \perp^{\sim}$ (1)

$(p \to f,g)\cdot h \equiv p\cdot h \to f\cdot h,\ g\cdot h$ (2)

$h\cdot(p \to f,g) \equiv p \to h\cdot f,\ h\cdot g$ (3)

$p \to (p \to f,g),h \equiv p \to f,h$ (4)

6. Structure of data model formal definition

The definition of DDL of data model M_i consists of the following partitions:

1) **Abstract DDL syntax**. Abstract DDL syntax is defined as a domain of all proper schemas Sch_i expressible in M_i;

2) **DDL semantics domains**. DDL semantics domains are data types which may be represented in the data model. Every data type is interpreted by elementary or recursively defined data type of data metamodel;

3)**DDL semantics function schemas**. DDL semantics function schemas are definitions of functional domains of the form **Id -> V** establishing for each M_i data type correspondence of possible identifiers of the schemas of this type to the set of the data type values - semantics domain. Thus a data base state is described as a product of functional domains defined in such a way.

4)**Functions of DDL constructions interpretation**. Functions expressing exactly the correspondence of M_i DDL constructions to semantical domains are given.

The definition of DML semantics of data model M_i consists of the following partitions:

1)**Abstract DML syntax**. Abstract DML syntax is defined as a domain of all DML operators expressible in M_i ;

2)**DML semantics domains**. DML semantics domains are DDL semantics domains and additional data types, characterizing the state of the program communicating with the database;

3)**DML semantics function schemas**. DML semantics function schemas define the general view of the interpretation function of the program, including DML statements, and of the separate DML statements;

4)**Primitive function schemas**. Primitive function schemas fix the domains and ranges of the primitive undefinable functions which are characteristic for particular M_i;

5)**Standard functions definition**. Here definitions of general functions and predicates useful for specification of functional forms of different DML statement interpretation functions are given;

6)**DML statement interpretation functions definition**. For each DML statement there is a corresponding functional form which interpretes the changes of database and program on DML statements execution in the context of a particular database schema.

While defining DML semantics of M_i data model it is convenient to keep to the following agreement.

Primitive functions, standard functions and DML interpretation functions are generally treated as $f:Ar_f x B_i x Sch_i \rightarrow B_i$, where Ar_f is a set of values of function **f** arguments. In particular, if **f** is a DML statement interpretation function then the element of Ar_f domain is tuple of this statement parameter values defined by DML syntax. Everywhere further it is assumed that **f** is executed in the state **b** ε B_i in the context of schema **s** ε Sch_i. So in the definition of functions Sch_i and B_i as the function domains are usually omitted, and in the range only the components of B_i as objects of the function action are included.

Applications of **f** to the arguments of the function **ar** ε Ar_f are represented everywhere as **f(ar)** instead of more complete notation **f(ar,b,s)**.

If function application **f(ar)** is included into the composition of the function, e.g., **f(ar)** · **g(ar')** where **ar'** ε Ar_g , all free variables of functional form **f(ar)** - components of Ar_f- are bound to the values from **ar**, all free variables denoting Sch_i components are bound to their values from **s**, all free variables denoting B_i components are bound to their values from the state **b** = **g(ar)**.

The meaning of $b^{\sim}$ is a constant function which, if applied to the state $b \in B_i$ in the context of the schema $s \in Sch_i$ gives b as a value. The meaning of b everywhere is a database state formed at the moment of constant function application.

7. Data model mapping and unifying technique

While constructing commutative data model mappings formal tools are essential for :

- definition of rules of database schema mapping of the source DM into database schemas of the target one;
- definition of the semantics of DML operators of extended target DM;
- consistency of extended DM axiom operational semantics with DML operator semantics of the extended data model;
- definition and verification of algorithms of interpretation of extended data model DML operators by means of the source DM.

The only possible way to solve above problems is their transformation into an abstract language environment in order that the use of formal methods becomes possible. Note that for obtaining practically useful results it's necessary to take into account all essential details of DDL and DML semantics of the source and target data models.

Method of commutative data model mapping construction [10,17] is oriented towards the solution of two different problems. The first one consists in construction of generalized DM kernel extensions equivalent to internal data models, that is in construction and formal fixation of generalized DM level languages (DDL and DML) and their semantics. The second one consists in the development and verification of generalized DM level DML interpretors

To solve such problems systematic procedures independent of data model types were defined. The procedures fix the order of operations, the tools and techniques used at each step by the person constructing data model mapping .

The process of commutative data model mapping construction is shown on Fig. 1.

It is important to note that in this process it is sufficient to consider only database update statements. Database retrieval facilities do not influence commutative data model construction (though efficient algorithms for interpretation of data selection statements of the target data model by means of the source one should be found).

Method of unifying generalized data model(UGDM) synthesis. UGDM contains arbitrary data models of different DBMS types reduced to homogeneous representations equivalent to them. Process of UGDM synthesis consists of the following stages :

1) source data models set selection: $W = \{M_1, M_2, \dots, M_n\}$;

2) setting of partial order on the **W** set by the relation of inclusion of one data model into another ($\leq$);

3) UGDM kernel (M_g) selection. "Minimal" data model M_i, (i= 1, 2, ... ,n) is selected so that

FOR ALL $j_{1 \leq j \leq n}$ $(M_{ri} \leq M_{rj})$

Here M_{ri} (or M_{rj}) denotes mapping of M_i (or M_j) data models into fixed reference data model (e.g., a relational one);

4) construction of extensions M_{gj} of the kernel M_g

equivalent to M_j;

5) UGDM construction as a union of all M_{gj}.

Formal definition of the target (M_t) and the source (M_s) DM by DMM tools (semantics functions construction for DDL **Ms: Sch -> B** and DML **Mo -> [B -> B]**)

v

Construction of DDL_s mapping into DDL_t (definition of $\sigma:Sch_s \rightarrow Sch_t$, $\theta:B_s \rightarrow B_t$, θ is injective

v

Axiomatic extension of M_t to M_{ts}: axiom schemas Ω_{ts} selection, construction of $\sigma:Sch_s \rightarrow Sch_t \times \{\Omega_{ts}\}$, definition of operational interpretation of axioms, checking of bijectivity of $\theta:B_s \rightarrow B_{ts}$

v

DML semantics definition of M_{ts}: $Mo_{ts}:O_t \rightarrow [B_{ts} \rightarrow B_{ts}]$. The expression of axioms operational semantics in terms of functions in Mo_{ts}. Checking of the fact of consistency of operational axioms interpretation with their semantics in Mo_{ts}

v

DML statements interpretation function construction :

$Mo_{ts}^{s}: P_s \rightarrow [B_s \rightarrow B_s]$

v

Verification of commutativity of DML statement mapping diagram (transformation of $Mo_{ts}^{s}(o_t)$ into $Mo_{ts}(o_t)$)

Fig. 1

8. Example: fragments of network to relational data model mapping construction

8.1. Formal definition of source and target data models

8.1.1. Network data model formal definition

Here only fragments of mapping of the subset of a network into a relational data model are considered. A complete description of the mapping may be found in [17].

DDL definition

Abstract syntax

The following subset of the CODASYL DDL will be used.

```
    Schema entry
SCHEMA NAME IS name-of- schema;
    Record entry
RECORD NAME IS record-name;
LOCATION MODE IS CALC USING identifier-1 [,identifier-2]...
    DUPLICATES NOT ALLOWED;
    Data subentry
data-name TYPE IS { FIXED | FLOAT | CHARACTER[integer-1] }
    Set entry
SET NAME IS set-name;
OWNER IS record-name;
    Member subentry
MEMBER IS record-name
    { MANDATORY AUTOMATIC | OPTIONAL MANUAL }
    DUPLICATES ARE NOT ALLOWED FOR identifier-1 [,identifier-2]...
 SET SELECTION IS THROUGH set-name OWNER
    IDENTIFIED BY KEY
         [identifier-1 EQUAL TO identifier-2]...
    [THEN THROUGH set-name OWNER
     IDENTIFIED BY [identifier-3 EQUAL TO
     identifier-4]...]
```

Abstract syntax

Database schema

Sch_n = Scn x Ren x Sen product of schema names, record and set entries

Record entry

Ren = Re*

Re = Rna x Loc x De product of record names, location phrases, data subentries

Rna = |N

Loc = CALC x Di*

Di = |N x |N

Di - is a data identifier, which consists of a record type name and a data element name. **|N** = {1,2,3,...}° domain of positive integers. Elements of **|N*** will be used to represent data structure names in the schema. In the sequence of numbers in **n ε |N*** the first one usually denotes the record type, the next one the data element type.

De = Dse*

Dse = Type

Type = {FIXED, FLOAT, CHARACTER}° + **Char**

Char = CHARACTER x **|N**

Usage of the reserved word of the language in abstract syntax denotes a domain and is defined as, e.g. {FIXED}°

Set entry

Sen = Se*

Tm = {MA, OM}°

MA,OM - MANDATORY AUTOMATIC, OPTIONAL MANUAL for short.

Se = Sna x Owner x Member

Sna = |N

Owner = Rna

Member=Rna x Tm x Dup x Sos

Dup = Di*

Sos = Calckey x Sna x Pseudo

Calckey = (|N x |N)*

Pseudo = **Di***
DDL semantics domain

CHAR = {'a','b','c',...}°
NR = {set of **numbers representable** in the **database**}°
DBK = |**N** — data base keys
Vo = **NR** + **CHAR*** — elementary values
Vrec = [K -> **Ds**] — record values
K = {1,2, ... , **length(de)**}°
Here **de** = **s-De** · **i(ren)**, **ren** = **s-Ren(s)** - set of record entries in the schema s.
Ds = **Dse** -> Vo
dse = **j(de)** — data subentry j
Ds(dse) = (**is-FIXED(s-Type(dse))** --> **NR**,
is-FLOAT(s-Type(dse)) --> **NR**,
is-CHARACTER(s-Type(dse))-->**CHAR**,
is-Char(s-Type(dse))-->**CHAR**$^{2\cdot s\text{-}Type(dse)}$, ⊥)
Vr = [|**N** -> Vrec] — set of records
Vs = [**Nm** -> **No**] — set of sets
Nm = |**N**
No = |**N**
Ms_n = Sch_n -> Sdb_n
Sdb_n = **Rs** x **Ss** = [**Rna** -> **Vr**] x [**Sna** -> **Vs**]

Notation :
Vr_j = |**N** -> **Vrec** — set of instances of record type j ε **Rna**
Vs_i = Nm_i -> No_i — set of instances of set type i ε **Sna**

Fragments of DML definition

Abstract syntax

Prog = **On***
On = **Sts** + **Ers** + **Mods** + **Con** + **Dsc**
DML statements: store, erase, modify, connect, disconnect; e.g., **Ers** = ERASE x **Rna**

DML semantics domains

Suwa = [**Rna** -> **Vuwa**] — user working area
Vuwa = |**N** x **Rna** x **Vrec**
Cis = [(**Rna** + **Sna** + **Cri**) -> **Kb** x **Rna**]
Cri - indicator of current record of run-unit;Cis - currency state indicators
Kb = |**N** — data base key
Spb = **Cis** x **Suwa**
B_n = Sdb_n x **Spb** — set of states

DML primitive functions

ckey : **Rna** x **Vl** -> |**N**
Vl = **Vo***
ownr : **Rna** -> ℬ(**Sna**) - set of set types in which record type i ε **Rna** is defined as an owner

DML statements semantics

Erase statement
$Mo_n(ers) = Cis[Cri/ \perp , \perp] \cdot erase(n,h)$
ers ε Ers; h=1 · Cis(Cri) current record of run unit
$erase(n,h) = Vr_n[h/ \perp] \cdot O_{i \in ownr(n)}(O_m \in vs_i^{-1}(h)$
$(s\text{-}Tm \cdot s\text{-}Member \cdot set = MA \dashrightarrow erase(s\text{-}Rna \cdot s\text{-}Member(set),m),$
$Vs_i[m/ \perp]))$
set=i·s-Sen(s) - i-set type entry in the schema

8.1.2. Relational model formal definition

DDL definition
Simple relational model schema definition language:
RELATIONAL SCHEMA <schema name>;
DOMAIN <domain description> {;<domain description>};
DATABASE VAR <relation description> {;<relation description>} END
<domain description> ::= <identifier> : <type>
<type> ::= INTEGER | REAL | CHAR | CHAR(<integer>)
<relation description> ::= <identifier> : RELATION <list of domain identifiers> KEY <identifier list> END

DML statements:

Cursor definition
(<label>) CURSOR <relation identifier> COND <selection expression>
Delete statement (enforces deletion of current tuple defined by cursor with the same label)
DELETE <label>

Abstract syntax
Sch_r = Rsn x Domain x Rd
Domain = Rtype*
Rtype = {INTEGER, REAL, CHARACTER}° + Char
Char= CHARACTER x |N
Rd = Rel*
Rel = Rena x Rkey x Rdom
Rkey = |N*
Rdom = |N*

DDL semantics domains
Vrel = [|N -> Vt]
Vt = [K -> Dos]
K = {1,2, ... , length(dom)}°, dom = s-Rdom · i(rd),
rd = s-Rd(rs)
d = j(dom) d - name of attribute j
Dos = Rdom -> Vo, tp = d · s-Domain(rs),
rs - name of relational database schema
Dos(d) = (is-INTEGER(tp) --> NR,
is-REAL(tp) --> NR,
is-CHARACTER(tp)-->CHAR,
is-Char(tp)-->$CHAR^{2 \cdot tp}$, ⊥)
Res = [Rena -> Vrel]

Sdb_r = Res
$Ms_r : Sch_r \to Sdb_r$

Fragments of DML definition
Abstract syntax

Prog = Or*
Or = Pt + Upd + Dlt — PUT, UPDATE, DELETE statements
Dlt = DELETE x Cl — Cl - cursor label

DML semantics domains

Isa = [Rena -> |N x Vt] — tuple with unique number in working area

Cp = [Cl -> |N x Rena] — state of cursors (cursor label defines number and type of current tuple of cursor)

Spb = Cp x Isa — program state with respect to DBMS

$B_r = Sdb_r \times Spb$

DML statement semantics

Delete statement (dlt ε DLT)

h = 2 · dlt — value of h is cl ε Cl - cursor label
t = 1 · Cp(h) — current tuple of the cursor
$Mo_r(dlt) = Cp[h/nxt(i,t),i] \cdot Vrel_i[t/ \perp]$
Here i=2·Cp(h), nxt: Rena x |N -> |N - primitive function giving for any tuple number of relation i ε Rena the number of the next tuple in the relation.

8.2. Construction of database schema mapping

Database schema mapping σ: $Sch_n \to Sch_r$ may be represented by the following collection of mappings:

1) Mapping of scalar data types :
tmap: Type -> Rtype;

2) Bijective mapping of record type names into the relation type names:
nmap: [Rna -> Rena];

3) Correspondence of relation domain names to the data element names of the record types:
syn: [|N* -> |N*];

4) Correspondence of each record type to a set of selective keys making possible identification of selective paths leading to the record through sets and owner - member record instances in the paths. The schema of each relation will include attributes mapped from data elements of the corresponding record type and additional attributes from all selective keys for the record type. Such selective keys make it possible to define functional dependency of relation type A from relation type B corresponding in the network schema to record type A'(owner in some set) and record type B' (member in the same set). In such a way the correspondence of selective keys for each record type in the network schema to the foreign keys for the corresponding relation type in relational schemas will be provided;

5) Function defining a key for each relation in the schema:
rk: Rena -> (|N x |N)*.

Formally the schema mapping described may be defined by

transformational schema language which will be defined now in an abstract form.

Abstract syntax of transformational schema language

Sch_{nr} = Rdm x Nmap x Syn x Rd
Rdm = Domain
Rd = Rel* definition of relation in transformational schema
Rel = Rena x Rkey x Rdom x Rna x Sel

Here : **Rkey** = **|N*** - key of the relation, **Rdom** = **|N*** - attribute list, **Rna** - names of the record types corresponding to the relation types.

Sel = (Rim x Ftype x Rsna x Pak x Pseudo)*

rs denotes relational schema . To each relation which is functionally dependent on relation **s-Rena** · **i** · **s-Rd(rs)** the component **j(sel)** in **sel** = **s-Sel** · **i** · **s-Rd(rs)** will be put into correspondence. In **sel** :

- **s-Rim** · **j(sel)** denotes the relation name which is functionally dependent on relation **i**;
- **s-Ftype** · **j(sel)** - class of functional dependency which may be total, corresponding to MANDATORY AUTOMATIC set membership, and partial corresponding to OPTIONAL MANUAL set membership;
- **s-Rsna** · **j(sel)** - set name;
- **s-Pseudo** · **j(sel)** - pseudokey of this functional dependency - collection of attributes whose values are sufficient for identification of tuples of relation i corresponding to member type record instances. The pseudokey identifies the tuple among other tuples of relation i connected to one and the same tuple (corresponding to owner record) of relation **s-Rim·j(sel)** corresponding to owner record type in the set **s-Rsna** · **j(sel)**;
- **s-Pak** · **j(sel)** - selective path, selective and secondary keys.

Formal definitions of **Sel** components:

Rim = Rena
Ftype = {TOTAL, PARTIAL}°
Rsna = Sna
Pak = Cs x Pa x Kc
Pa = Fst x Nxtr selective path
Fst = Rna
Nxtr = Rna x Sna
Cs = Kc = Fkey x Nst Cs - selective key, Kc- secondary key
Fkey = Dn*
Nst = Pseudo
Pseudo = Dn*

Now it is obvious that in the schema mapping defined the function Θ is injective. One example. According to network data model semantics in network database only such states are allowed in which every member record may be connected to only one owner record in any given set. There is no equivalent restriction on the relational level.

8.3. Axiomatic extension of relational DM

On the basis of studying differences in the sets of states of source and target data models using DDL schema mapping formal description, the axiom schemas (in this example - Ω_{rn}) are introduced which express additional logical dependencies of target DM data and provide for removal of the differences mentioned above. Each axiom should express some atomic (elementary) fact.

In the example being developed axioms covering equivalent to set dependencies on the level of target data model will be introduced.

System of axioms of total functional dependency

Main axiom :

$R_i(Cs_j)$ -> $R_j(Kc_j)$ expresses a fact of total functional dependency of relation R_j on relation R_i. Cs_j here denotes attributes of R_i constituting a selective key (which is a foreign key of R_j). Kc_j is a secondary key of R_j, attributes of the Kc_j being in one-to-one correspondence to the attributes of Cs_j.

Invariants of R_i:

UNIQUE Es_j — collection of attribute values given in UNIQUE axiom should uniquely identify the tuple of the relation R_i

OBLIGATORY Es_j — collection of attributes given by OBLIGATORY axiom should have nonnull values

Es_j is a key of R_i formed as the union of attributes of Cs_j and of attributes of R_i pseudokey in this functiònal dependency.

Invariants of R_j

UNIQUE Kc_j

OBLIGATORY Kc_j

System of axioms of partial functional dependency

Main axiom :

$R_i(Cs_j)$ => $R_j(Kc_j)$ expresses fact of partial functional dependency of relation R_j on relation R_i.

Invariants of R_i:

UNIQUE NONNULL Es_j — collection of attribute values given in UNIQUE NONNULL axiom should uniquely identify the tuple of the relation in case all such values are nonnull

SYNCHRONOUS NONNULL Cs_j — the axiom expresses the requirement that the attributes of Cs_j should obtain nonnull values or should all "disappear"

Invariants of R_j

UNIQUE NONNULL Kc_j

By introduction of such a set of axioms Ω_{nr} the schema mapping will be extended to σ: $Sch_n \rightarrow (Sch_r \times \{\Omega_{rn}\})$, function Θ becomes bijective and the schema mapping diagram becomes commutative. To show that it is sufficient to consider in the injective Θ each fact of bijectivity violation and for such a case to find a set of axioms removing of the violation.

Operational semantics of the axioms

For each axiom, each DML statement receives the description of axiom-induced minimal actions which are sufficient to provide for this axiom to become database invariant. Only delete statement will be considered here.

Axiom	DELETE (R_i,t_i)	DELETE (R_j,t_j)
Total functional dependency		
$R_i(Cs_j)$ -> $R_j(Kc_j)$	-	Delete all $t_i \in R_i$ such that $t_i[Cs_j] = t_j[Kc_j]$. Apply such deletions recursively to the hierarchy of the functional dependencies having R_i as a root
UNIQUE Es_j	-	-
. . .		
Partial functional dependency		
$R_i(Cs_j)$ => $R_j(Kc_j)$	-	In all $t_i \in R_i$ such that $t_i[Cs_j] = t_j[Kc_j]$ values of all attributes in Cs_j should become null
UNIQUE NONNULL Es_j	-	-
. . .		

8.4. Semantics of DML statements of extended relational data model M_{rn}

Here functional forms to express the semantics of DML statements of extended relational data model will be defined. These forms should take into account the schema mapping and logical dependencies introduced by the axioms.

Delete statement

$Mo_{rn}(dlt) = Idlt(n,t)$

$Idlt(n,t) = Cp[h/nxt(n,t),n] \cdot rmv(n,t)$

Here $h = 2 \cdot dlt$ - cursor index; $n = 2 \cdot Cp(h)$ - relation name; $t = 1 \cdot Cp(h)$ - number of current tuple of cursor.

$rmv(n,t) = Vrel_n[t/\perp] \cdot (0_{n1 \in Iim(n)}$

$0_{m=1}^{length(sel1)}$(s-Rim $\cdot$ m(sel1) = n -->

$(0_{p \in seek(n1,con)}$ (s-Ftype $\cdot$ m(sel1) =TOTAL -->

rmv(n1,p), (s-Ftype $\cdot$ m(sel1) = PARTW -->

ch(p,n1,cs1, $\perp$), b˜))),b˜))

Here $Iim(R_j) = \{ R_i \mid R_j$ is functionally dependent on $R_i\}$,

sel1= **s-Sel·n1·s-Rd(rs)**, **ch(t,n,a,v)** - function making such modification of tuple **t** of relation **n** that the values of t attributes defined by the list **a** ε Dn* will be substituted by **v** ε Vo*.

seek: Rena x Con -> ß(|N) puts into correspondence to each search condition applied to the given relation subset of the numbers of its tuples relevant to such a condition.

Condition **con** ε **Con** is expressed by the functinal domain **cond: Dn* x Vo* -> Con** in which the range consists of the lists of data element names **id** ε **Dn*** and data values **vo** ε **Vo*** corresponding to them . In functional form for **rmv con** means list of selective key attribute names of **n1** relation and values of the secondary key attributes of **n** relation corresponding to them .

Now operational semantics of the axioms may be formally defined.

Axiom	DELETE (R_i,t_i)	DELETE (R_j,t_j)
Total functional dependency		
$R_i(Cs_j)$ -> $R_j(Kc_j)$	-	$rmv(R_j,t_j)$
Partial functional dependency		
$R_i(Cs_j)$ => $R_j(Kc_j)$	-	$ch(p,n1,cs1, \perp)$ in the expression for **rmv**

It is easy to see that the set of axioms introduced is **operationally complete** with respect to the set of statements of M_{rn} data model. It means that each action of database state modification made by some DML statement of M_{rn} follows from this statement semantics of the target data model or is induced by some axiom of target DM extension included into the definition of the data type - argument of the statement.

Now the system of axioms extending M_r and semantics of M_{rn} DML are in **well-defined correspondence**.

8.5. Construction of functions of M_{rn} interpretation by means of M_n

For each o_{rn} ε O_{rn} interpretation functions by means of M_n DML should be defined. These functions are based on the mapping σ and Θ defined above. Only the delete statement function will be considered here. The functions will be given directly in the form Mo_{rn}: O_r -> $[B_n$ -> $B_n]$.

$Mo_{rn}{}^n(dlt) = Cp[h/nxtn(n\hat{},t)] \cdot Mo_n(ERASE,n\hat{}) \cdot$
$Cis[Cri/t,n\hat{}]$

Here $n\hat{} = nmap^{-1}(n)$ - the result of mapping the corresponding data type of the network (relational) data model into the relational (network) one.

8.6. Verification of the commutativity of DML mapping diagram

This is the crucial moment in data model mapping construction. Commutativity of a DML mapping diagram is a necessary condition to guarantee exact correspondence of the definition of semantics of extended target data model DML to its interpretation by the source data model DML. Thus the correctness of a complete system of invariants expressing for users the exact meaning of logical data dependencies of internal databases on the target level and DML statements semantics of the extended DM will be approved. Finally, the equivalence of the source data model to the extension of the target data model will be shown.

To verify the commutativity of DML mapping diagram the following constructive approach will be used :

1) For each o_{rn} ε O_{rn} on the basis of the function $\mathbf{Mo_{rn}^{n}(o_{rn})}$ the function $\mathbf{Vo_{rn}(o_{rn})}$ expressing an equivalent to $\mathbf{Mo_{rn}^{n}(o_{rn})}$ actions by means of $\mathbf{M_{rn}}$ data model will be constructed. This transformation is done in the following way:

- each argument of the $\mathbf{Mo_{rn}^{n}(o_{rn})}$ function which is the semantics domain of the source data model is substituted by the semantics domain of the target data model whose components are in one-to-one correspondence with respect to σ and Θ mappings to the components of such a source DM domain;
- every function $\mathbf{f_{rn}}$ in $\mathbf{Mo_{rn}^{n}(o_{rn})}$ definition is substituted by the function $\mathbf{vf_{rn}}$ expressing an equivalent to $\mathbf{f_{rn}}$ modifications of objects of $\mathbf{M_{rn}}$ which are in one-to-one correspondence to the $\mathbf{M_n}$ objects modified by $\mathbf{f_{rn}}$.

It is expected that due to such construction functions $\mathbf{Mo_{rn}^{n}(o_{rn})}$ and $\mathbf{Vo_{rn}(o_{rn})}$ applied to any pair of equivalent states of source and target databases will again produce equivalent database states.

2) The equivalence of functions $\mathbf{Mo_{rn}(o_{rn})}$ and $\mathbf{Vo_{rn}(o_{rn})}$ should be demonstrated. To achieve that the function $\mathbf{Vo_{rn}(o_{rn})}$ will be transformed to the function $\mathbf{Mo_{rn}(o_{rn})}$ by means of rules of equivalent function transformation.

This approach will be demonstrated for DELETE statement interpretation.

Verification function construction

```
Vo_rn(dlt) = Cp[h/nxtn(n^,t)] · verase(n,h)
verase(n^,t) = Vren_n[t/ ⊥ ] · (0_{n1 ε Tim(n^)}
    0_{m=1}^{length(sel1)} (s-Rim · m(sel1) = n -->
    (0_{p ε seek(n1,con)} s-Ftype · m(sel1) = TOTAL -->
    verase(n1,p),ch(p,n1,cs1, ⊥ )), b~))
```

Function transformation

In $\mathbf{Mo_{rn}(dlt)}$ function **rmv** will be transformed (taking into account that **s-Ftype** · **m(sel1)** may take only two values - **TOTAL** or **PARTW**):

```
rmv(n,t) = Vrel_n[t/ ⊥ ] · (0_{n1 ε Tim(n)}
    0_{m=1}^{length(sel1)}(s-Rim · m(sel1) = n -->
```

$(0_{p \in seek(n1,con)}$ (s-Ftype · m(sel1) =TOTAL -->
rmv(n1,p), (s-Ftype · m(sel1) = TOTAL -->
b˜,ch(p,n1,cs1, ⊥)))),b˜))

Now to the function (s-Ftype · m(sel1) =TOTAL --> rmv(n1,p), (s-Ftype · m(sel1) = TOTAL --> b˜,ch(p,n1,cs1, ⊥))) the rule (4) for equivalent function transformation may be applied : p-->(p-->f,g),h ≡ p-->f,h. In our case we have p-->h,(p-->f,g) ≡ p-->h,g. After application of this rule we obtain:

rmv(n,t) = $Vrel_n$[t/ ⊥] · $(0_{n1 \in Iim(n)}$
$0_{m=1}^{length(sel1)}$(s-Rim · m(sel1) = n -->
$(0_{p \in seek(n1,con)}$ (s-Ftype · m(sel1) =TOTAL -->
rmv(n1,p), ch(p,n1,cs1, ⊥))),b˜))

Now it is clearly seen that verase and rmv functions are the same.

9.Unifying generalized data model (UGDM) synthesis

On the basis of systematic application of the commutative data model mapping method and of the method of UGDM synthesis the following results were obtained.

Axiomatic extensions of relational DM equivalent to DM of different classes (network,hierarchical,binary,descriptor) were constructed. An example of such an extension equivalent to CODASYL network data model is given in fig. 2. The axioms shown here sometimes are not atomic facts as axioms given in 8.3. For user convenience axioms of functional dependencies represent combined semantics of all of the axioms given in 8.3 for expressing total and partial functional dependencies.

Simple axioms (for relation Ri; Ai,Aj,Ak - collection of attributes of Ri)

1.Axiom of uniqueness
UNIQUE Ai

2.Axiom of constancy
CONSTANT Ai

3.Axiom of definiteness
OBLIGATORY Ai

4.Axiom of conditional uniqueness
UNIQUE NONNULL Ai

5.Axiom of order
Ri[RESTRICTED BY Ai] IS ORDERED[<order>]
[BY <direction> Aj {,<direction> Ak}]

Compound axioms (for relations Ri, Rj)

6.Axiom of total functional dependency(f.d.)
Rj(Aj)->Ri(Ai)

7.Axiom of partial functional dependency(p.f.d.)
Rj(Ai)=>Ri(Ai)

8.Axiom of partial strong functional dependency
Ri(Ai)=S=>Ri(Ai)

9.Axiom of partial functional dependency with initial connection
Rj(Aj)=L=>Ri(Ai)

Fig.2

A set of UGDM facilities obtained as a result of generalized data model synthesis during SISYPHUS system design is shown in fig. 3. A list of selected source data models is also shown here. Some of them correspond to DBMS described in [19]. Complete description of the axioms given in fig. 3 is presented in [17]. An important property of the process of synthesis consists in relatively fast saturation of the generalized data model when consideration of new source data model introduces no new axioms on target DM level. The resulting generalized data model with respect to the known DM is a saturated one. This circumstance allows to consider the resulting model to be a **unifying** one.

UGDM facilities	Data models											
	1	2	3	4	5	6	7	8	9	10	11	12
Kernel of generalized data model												
Normalized relations	*	*	*	*	*	*	*	*	*	*	*	*
Hierarchical relations		*				*	*	*		*		*
Positional aggregates							*	*				
Kernel extension												
Axiom of uniqueness		*	*	*	*				*		*	*
Axiom of constancy		*	*	*	*				*			*
Axiom of definiteness		*	*	*	*				*		*	*
Axiom of conditional uniqueness		*										
Axiom of conditional constancy		*										
Axiom-function											*	
Axiom-partial function											*	
Axiom of order		*	*	*		*	*		*	*		
Axiom-predicate											*	
Axiom of total f.d.		*	*	*					*	*	*	*
Axiom of partial f.d.		*									*	*
Axiom of strong p.f.d.		*										
Axiom of p.f.d.with initial connection		*										
Axiom of total f.d. with backward connection			*									
Axiom of p.f.d. with backward connection											*	
Axiom of stable total f.d.(s.t.f.d.)			*									
Axiom of s.t.f.d. with backward connection			*									
Axiom of of duplex dependency					*	*						

Data models denotation

1. Codd relational DM (1970)
2. CODASYL network DM
3. IMS Hierarchical DM
4. IDS Network DM
5. DM of DBMS PALMA
6. ADABAS DM
7. Descriptor DM of DBMS BASIS
8. DM of DBMS POISK
9. TOTAL network DM
10. Hierarchical DM of DBMS INES
11. Binary relational DM
12. Codd relational DM (1979)

Fig. 3

The generalized DM kernel expressed by DDL should provide facilities for management of a mixed database including both structured and unstructured data.

The main structured data types of the kernel are the types of normalized and hierarchical relations. The database is unstructured if every new fact about the application domain has its own structure and the schema of such objects cannot be fixed. Unstructured data are represented in database by means of semantic nets included into positional aggregates.

Complete description of the UGDM DDL and DML is given in [17].

10. Conclusion

The paper contributes to the creation of a methodological basis for solving the problem of data model heterogeneity in multidatabase systems.

The data model axiomatic extension principle, the data model commutative mapping principle, the unifying generalized data model synthesis principle based on the notion of data model equivalence were proposed to create the necessary ground for the design of a heterogeneous database integrating systems architecture.

Specific techniques oriented towards applications of such principles were developed. In particular, a technology for commutative [10] data model mapping construction was proposed. According to the technology the main steps of the mapping design are :

- formal definition of target and source data model semantics (on the basis of an abstract data metamodel);
- formal definition and verification of the rules of database schema mapping;
- definition of the semantics of DML operators of extended target data model;
- checking of consistency of the axioms operational semantics with the DML operators semantics of the extended data model;
- definition and verification of the algorithms of interpretation of extended data model DML operators by means of the source data model.

Thus the methods introduced make it possible to construct the generalized data model kernel extensions equivalent to the internal data models and to develop and verify the algorithms of the target level DML interpretors.

These methods, together with a carefully defined set of architectural principles of multidatabase systems design were used as a methodological basis during implementation of SISYPHUS heterogeneous database integrating system in the early '80s [17]. In accordance with the methods CODASYL, hierarchical, textual and others DM transformers to the extended relational one were designed. Still, these methods seem to be among very few complete generalized techniques for formalized development of data model mapping, analysis and classification.

Application of the systematic approach to the design of the architecture of heterogeneous database integrating system allowed to develop a system which is distinguished from other known similar projects by the following main features:

- a unifying generalized data model was synthesized making it possible to represent equivalently data models of various DBMS; due to this result updating of integrated data base is supported;

- the spectrum of data models embraced by the integrating system includes structured as well as unstructured models;

- heterogeneous modular multidatabase management is implemented on the basis of a specially designed metabase of data and on the usage of two level representation of conceptual schema;

- a technology of developing generic parameterized application programs independent of DBMS was created [22].

Commutative data model mapping methods may be used in case when for the kernel of generalized data model an object-oriented data model is chosen. Alongside with the axiomatic extension of such data model the design of extensions of the algorithms of the methods supporting modification of the object instances of a class should be developed. All other ideas and techniques presented in the paper will be preserved.

Acknowledgements

The author wishes to thank Michael Brodie, John Mylopoulos and Witold Staniszkis for their helpful suggestions leading to a more readable paper.

References

1. Kalinichenko L.A., Ryvkin V.M., Chaban I.A. Design principles and architecture of SISYPHUS - a system for integrated storage of information.-Programmirovanie, 1975, N4. (Translated into English in Programming and Computer Software, Consultants Bureau, New York, 1975, N4).

2. Biller H., Glatthaar W. On the semantics of data bases: the semantics of data definition language, Institut f. Informatik, Univesity of Stuttgart, Nov. 1975, p. 1-19.

3. Tennent R.D. The denotational semantics of programming languages.- CACM, 1976, v. 19, N8, p.437-453.

4. Biller H., Glatthaar W., Neuhold E.J. On the semantics of data bases : the semantics of data manipulation languages. - In Proc. IFIP TC-2 Working Conference on Modelling in DBMS. Amsterdam: North-Holland, 1976, p. 239-267.

5. Maibaum T.S. Mathematical semantics and a model for data bases. Information Processing 77, North Holland, 1977, p. 133 - 138.

6. Paolini P., Pelagatti G. Formal definition of mappings in a data base.- ACM Sigmod Proc., August 1977, p. 40-46.

7. Backus J. Can programming be liberated from the von Neumann style ? A function style and its algebra of programs. - CACM, 1978, v.21, N8.

8. Biller H., Neuhold E.J. Semantics of data bases: the semantics of data models. Information systems, vol. 3, 1978, p. 11 - 30.

9. Borkin S.A. Data model equivalence. Proc. of the 4-th International Conference on VLDB, West Berlin, N-Y.:IEEE, 1978 , p. 526 - 534.

10. Kalinichenko L.A. Data model transformation method based on axiomatic data model extension.-In Proc. of the 4-th International Conference on VLDB. West Berlin, N-Y.:IEEE, 1978.

11. Klug A.C. Theory of database mappings. Technical report CSRG-98, Dec. 1978, University of Toronto.

12. Zaniolo C. Design of Relational Views over Network Schemas. SIGMOD 1979 Conference Proceedings, May 1979, p. 179- 189.

13. Adiba M. et al. POLYPHEME: an experience in distributed database system design and implementation.-In Proc. of the International Symposium on Distributed Data Bases. Paris, Amsterdam: North-Holland, 1980, p.67-84.

14. Cardenas A.F., Pirahesh M.H. Data Base Communication in a heterogeneous DBMS network.-Information Systems, 1980, v.5,p.55-79.

15. Landers T. Rosenberg R.L. An overview of Multibase.-In Proc. of the 2-nd International Symposium on Distributed Data Bases. Amsterdam: North-Holland, 1982, p.153-184.

16. Litwin W. Logical model of a distributed data base.-In Proc. of the Second International Seminar on Distributed Data Sharing Systems. Amsterdam: North-Holland, 1982, p. 173-208.

17. Kalinichenko L.A. Methods and Tools for Integration of Heterogeneous Databases.-Moscow.:Science Publ., 1983, 423p. (in Russian).

18. Gligor V.D., Luckenbaugh G.L. Interconnecting Heterogeneous Database Management Systems.- Computer, 1984, N1, p. 33-43.

19. Data Base Management Systems for ES computers: the guide.-Moscow, Finance and Statistics, 1984, 224p (in Russian).

20. Kalinichenko L.A. Properties of commutative data model mappings.- Cybernetics, N5, 1985, p. 37-40 (in Russian).

21. Staniszkis W. Integrating Heterogeneous Databases.- Infotech State of the Art Report: Relational databases, 1986, p. 229-247.

22. Kalinichenko L.A. Reusable database programming independent of DBMS.- In Proc. of the 10th International Seminar on Data Base Management Systems, Poland, 1987, p. 281-296.

The Many Faces of Query Monotonicity *

Catriel Beeri † Yoram Kornatzky ‡
The Hebrew University
Jerusalem 91904, ISRAEL

Abstract

Monotonicity, based on the partial order defined by the 'is a subset of' relation, is a well understood property of queries. For nested relations, other partial orders leading to different notions of monotonicity are possible. Monotonicity can be used for simple negative comparison of the expressive power of two languages by showing that one is monotone and the other is not. Using this approach we study three questions related to the expressive power of practically useful subsets of well known programming languages for nested relations. First, we show that logic programming languages over nested relations can be regarded as Datalog with user-defined algebraic expressions. This leads to a modular integration of recursion with the monotone subset of the algebra. Second, we prove that the equivalence of the powerset algebra and the complex object Datalog breaks down for their monotone subsets. Third, for the class of positive existential queries over nested relations, which generalize the relational tableau set queries, we show that the use of intermediate types does not enhance their expressive power, in contrast to the known result for general existential queries. We also show that this class does not contain the powerset operator, hence it is a candidate for a tractable tableau query system for nested relations. Finally, the (monotone) Bancilhon-Khoshafian calculus for complex objects is shown to be incomparable to the monotone subsets of most known languages.

1 Introduction

New database applications have emerged in the last decade in fields such as CAD and software engineering. The deficiencies of the relational model for supporting these applications are well documented. This has led to the development of more general data models, in particular the nested relational model that generalizes the flat relational model by allowing relation-valued attributes. The languages proposed for this model are either algebraic [1,24], calculus-like [1,15], or deductive [7,9,17,18].

While a hierarchy of database queries in terms of complexity and expressive power is well established for the relational model [10], the power of query languages over nested relations and complex objects is less well understood. Results reported so far are mainly concerned with the high end of the complexity hierarchy. Two important classes of queries from flat databases to flat relations with intermediate nested types were identified: the computable queries ($\mathcal{C}$) [11], and the elementary queries ($\mathcal{E}$), computable in hyper-exponential time and space respectively [15]. Most of the languages for nested relations suggested in the literature were shown to be equivalent to the class of elementary queries when typed sets are used. These languages include the safe complex

*Research partially supported by grant 2545/3/89 of Israel National Council for Research and Development.

†Department of Computer Science
‡Leibniz Center for Research in Computer Science

object calculus [1], the powerset algebra and its augmentations by programming constructs such as loops [14], COL [2], stratified Datalog over sets [9] and ELPS [19].

Practically, the lower end of the complexity and expressiveness hierarchy, consisting of limited hence efficiently tractable sublanguages, is more important. It is well known that the restricted classes of conjunctive, existential, and tableau queries form the backbone of the query processing and optimization strategies of most relational systems [26]. Complex objects database systems built so far, are also founded on efficiently implemented subsets of the nested relational algebra [8,12,22]. This paper is concerned with the expressive power of such limited, hence practically interesting, subsets of the full languages mentioned above, especially those that generalize practically useful relational languages. We avoid measuring expressive power through queries over flat relations, as this blurs the essential issues in manipulating nested relations especially for the sublanguages of interest here.

A relational query is monotone if increasing its input relations produces an equal or larger result. Thus, the partial order of set inclusion underlies the monotonicity definition. However, for nested relations or more general complex objects, other partial orders naturally arise. Indeed, deductive query languages for complex objects use a variety of lattices for defining their operational semantics [4,7,17]. In this paper, we investigate the expressive power of languages using monotonicity concepts defined by several partial orders. It turns out that for these partial orders monotonicity is preserved under two common operations for constructing queries: composition and least fixed point. Languages whose basic operations define monotone queries and in which queries are constructed using only composition or least fixed point, define only monotone queries and cannot express any non-monotone query. This argument provides a simple technique for deriving a negative comparison of the expressive power of languages.

In both algebraic and logic programming languages, queries can be applied to relation valued attributes of tuples. We show that nesting of queries yields only monotone queries. It follows that one can view Datalog over nested relations as the incorporation of user-defined algebraic expressions into Datalog. We study this combination of the procedural (algebraic) and declarative views of manipulating nested relations, and prove that the expressive power of Datalog is indeed enhanced by the introduction of user-defined expressions. This contrasts the fact that, for the powerset algebra, adding the nested application of functions is redundant [1]. We also show that the equivalence of the powerset algebra and the stratified complex object Datalog breaks down for their monotone subsets: the monotone algebra is strictly contained in the complex object Datalog.

Positive existential queries over nested relations generalize the useful relational tableau set queries [23]. These queries can involve quantification of variables ranging over intermediate types not appearing in the database or the output. For both general calculus queries and for existential ones, it is known that the set-height of intermediate types induces a strict hierarchy of query classes in terms of expressive power and computational complexity [15,20]. We prove that for positive existential queries the hierarchy collapses to its lowest level (not using intermediate types), and it cannot express the powerset operation. Hence, this class is a tractable useful sublanguage that can serve the same role for nested relations as that of tableau queries for flat ones.

The Bancilhon-Khoshafian calculus [7] is a deductive language for manipulating untyped complex objects. It can be regarded as the bare core of many others based on the notion of an object lattice, e.g. [4,17]. Its exact expressive power is unknown except that it is data-complete for the class of Turing computable data functions [16]. Its queries are monotone w.r.t. one of the partial orders we consider. We prove that it is incomparable to the monotone subsets of the languages mentioned above. This suggests that a straightforward compilation of this language into algebraic or logic programming ones is infeasible.

The plan of the paper is as follows. In section 2 we present the basic definitions of the nested relational model, the powerset algebra, and the calculus. Notions of monotonicity are discussed in section 3 and the operators of the algebra are characterized as (non) monotone with respect to these notions. In section 4 we discuss logic programming languages over nested relations. Section 5 examines positive existential queries over nested relations. Section 6 discusses the Bancilhon-Khoshafian calculus for complex objects.

2 A Model for Nested Relations

2.1 Nested Relations

Our definition of nested relations follows that of [14]. We briefly explain what are attributes and values, relation schemes, relation instances and databases.

Assume an infinitely enumerable set U of *elementary attributes*. Attributes are either elementary or composite, where a composite attribute is a set of elementary or composite attributes.

Definition 2.1 *The set of all attributes $\mathcal{U}$ is the smallest set containing U such that every finite subset X of $\mathcal{U}$, in which no elementary attribute appears more than once, is in $\mathcal{U}$.*

Elements of U are called *elementary*; those of $\mathcal{U} - U$ are called *composite* (or relation-valued). We denote elementary attributes by $A, B, C, \cdots$, composite attributes by $X, Y, Z \cdots$, and general attributes, also called *types*, by $T_1, T_2, \cdots$. A *relation scheme* Ω is a composite attribute, i.e. an element of $\mathcal{U} - U$. The structural complexity of types is measured by the depth of set constructs in their definition. The *set-height* of a type T, denoted $sh(T)$, is defined as 0 for $T \in U$, and $1 + \max\{sh(X) : X \in T\}$ for $T \in \mathcal{U} - U$.

Next we define simultaneously the notions of value, tuple and instance. Assume an infinitely enumerable set V of *elementary values*.

Definition 2.2 *The set $\mathcal{V}$ of all values, the set $\mathcal{I}_X$ of all instances over $X \in \mathcal{U} - U$, the set $\mathcal{T}_X$ of all tuples over $X \in \mathcal{U} - U$, and the set $\mathcal{I}$ of all instances are the smallest sets satisfying:*
1. $\mathcal{V} = V \cup \mathcal{I}$;
2. $\mathcal{I} = \cup_{X \in \mathcal{U}-U} \mathcal{I}_X$;
3. $\mathcal{I}_X$ *consists of all finite subsets of* $\mathcal{T}_X$;
4. $\mathcal{T}_X$ *consists of all mappings t from X into $\mathcal{V}$, called tuples, such that $t[A] \in V$ for all $A \in X \cap U$ and $t[Y] \in \mathcal{I}_Y$ for all $Y \in X - U$.*

Definition 2.3 *A* (nested) relation *is a pair (Ω, ω) where $\Omega \in \mathcal{U} - U$ and $\omega \in \mathcal{I}_\Omega$. Ω is called the scheme of the relation and ω is called the instance of the relation.*

A relation is a set of tuples over its scheme. Assume an infinitely enumerable set $\mathcal{R}$ of *relation (predicate) names*. A *database schema* is a sequence $D = [R_1 : \Omega_1, \ldots, R_n : \Omega_n]$, where $R_i \in \mathcal{R}$, and Ω_i is a relation schema. A *database instance* of D is a sequence $d = [R_1 : \omega_1, \ldots, R_n : \omega_n]$, where $\omega_i \in I_{\Omega_i}$. [1] The family of instances of D is denoted $\mathcal{I}_D$.

The traditional (non-nested) relational model consists of the restriction of relation schemes to sets of elementary attributes. In the sequel, we call the traditional relational model the *flat* relational model, and refer to the above defined concepts in its context with the adjective flat.

[1] Formally, the domain of the database, the set U, should be included.

2.2 Queries

The active domain of a tuple t (relation instance ω, database instance d), denoted $adom(t)$ ($adom(\omega), adom(d)$), is the set of all elementary values appearing in t (ω, d).

Definition 2.4 *A query from a database scheme D to a relations scheme Ω, denoted $f : D \to \Omega$, is a (partial) mapping from $\mathcal{I}_D$ to $\mathcal{I}_\Omega$, such that for some finite set $C \subseteq V$ the following holds:*
1. f is domain preserving w.r.t. C: $\forall d \in \mathcal{I}_D$, $adom(f(d)) \subseteq adom(d) \cup C$;
2. f is C-generic [11]: for each permutation σ over V (extended in the natural way to $\mathcal{I}$ and $\mathcal{V}$), such that $\forall x \in C, \sigma(x) = x$, $f \circ \sigma = \sigma \circ f$.

Two query languages L_1, L_2 are *equivalent*, denoted by $L_1 \equiv L_2$, if each query expressible in L_1 is expressible in L_2 and vice versa. A language L_1 is *strictly contained* in L_2, denoted $L_1 \subset_{\neq} L_2$, if all queries expressible in L_1 are expressible in L_2, but there are queries expressible in L_2 inexpressible in L_1. In the sequel, we abusingly speak of expressions as queries.

2.3 The Algebraic Languages

Algebraic languages for nested relations are obtained from the relational algebra by extending its operators to deal with nested relations, and adding restructuring operators. The main new operators are nest, unnest and powerset. To define the operators we need the following. Two attributes are *compatible* if there is a permutation over U (naturally extended to $\mathcal{U}$), such that one is a permutation of the other. Intuitively, this means that they have isomorphic structures.

Definition 2.5 (Operators)

- *The classical relational operators of* **union, intersection, difference, projection,** *and* **cartesian product.** *Cartesian product is applicable only to relations whose schemes are built from disjoint sets of elementary attributes. Required renaming of attributes is performed by the* **rename** *operator.*
- **Selection** *of tuples from a relation (Ω, ω) is defined relative to a predicate φ on tuples as $(\Omega, \omega') = \sigma_\varphi(\Omega, \omega) = \{t \mid t \in \omega \ \& \ \varphi(t) = True\}$. We consider the following predicates:*
  Elementary attributes equality, *$A = B$, for $A, B \in \Omega \cap U$.*
  Composite attributes equality, *$X = Y$, for compatible attributes $X, Y \in \Omega - U$.*
  Membership of attributes, *$X \in Y$, for $X \in \Omega$, and $Y \in \Omega - U$, such that $Y = \{X'\}$, where X and X' are compatible.*
  Composite attributes containment, *$X \subseteq Y$, for compatible $X, Y \in \Omega - U$.*
  In all predicates one of the attributes can be replaced by a constant.
- *Let $X \subseteq \Omega$. The* **nesting** *$\nu_X(\Omega, \omega)$ equals (Ω', ω') where $\Omega' = (\Omega - X) \cup \{X\}$ and*

$$\omega' = \{t \in \mathcal{T}_{\Omega'} \mid \exists t' \in \omega : t|_{\Omega - X} = t'|_{\Omega - X} \ \& \ t[X] = \{t''|_X \mid t'' \in \omega \ \& \ t'|_{\Omega - X} = t''|_{\Omega - X}\}\}$$

- **singleton**(Ω, ω) *is* $(\{\Omega\}, \{\omega\})$.
- *Let $X \in \Omega - U$. The* **unnesting** *$\mu_X(\Omega, \omega)$ equals (Ω', ω') where $\Omega' = (\Omega - \{X\}) \cup X$ and $\omega' = \{t \in \mathcal{T}_{\Omega'} \mid \exists t' \in \omega : t|_{\Omega - \{X\}} = t'|_{\Omega - \{X\}} \ \& \ t|_X \in t'[X]\}$.*
- *The* **set-collapse** *$collapse(\{\Omega\}, \omega)$, is (Ω, ω'), where $\omega' = \{t \mid \exists t' \in \omega : t \in t'\}$.*
- **scons**$((\Omega, \omega), (\{\Omega\}, \omega_1))$ *is* $(\{\Omega\}, \omega_1 \cup \{\omega\})$.
- *Let 2^ω denote the set of all subsets of ω. The* **powerset** *$P(\Omega, \omega)$ equals $(\{\Omega\}, 2^\omega)$.*

We have defined a redundant set of operators as we are interested in characterizing the power of individual ones.

The **powerset algebra** $\mathcal{P}$ is defined by expressions built from typed relation variables and constant relations using the operators above. The **nested relational algebra** $\mathcal{N}$ is the the subset of $\mathcal{P}$ not using the powerset operator. If $E(x, y, \ldots)$ is an algebraic expression, then $E(r, s, \ldots)$ denotes its 'application' to the arguments $r, s, \cdots$, which are assumed to be of the appropriate types. The scheme of the output of E is denoted by Ω^E.

2.4 A Calculus for Nested Relations

The calculus uses typed variables ranging over tuples. The *terms* are constants, variables, and expressions of the form $x.Z$, where $Z \in \mathcal{U}$. The *atomic formulas* are (well-typed) expressions of the form $t_1 = t_2, t_1 \subseteq t_2, t_1 \in t_2$, and $R(t_1)$, where t_1, t_2 are terms and R is a predicate (relation) name. Formulas are built using connectives and quantifiers in the usual manner. A *calculus query* from a database schema $D = [R_1 : \Omega_1, \ldots, R_n : \Omega_n]$ to a type T is an expression $Q = \{y \mid \phi\}$, where ϕ is built from the predicate symbols in D, has only y free, and y has type T.

3 Monotonicity

3.1 Partial Orders, Monotonicity, and Queries

Monotonicity of functions is defined relative to a partial order on their arguments and result.

Definition 3.1 *Let $\mathcal{D}, \mathcal{E}$ be partially ordered domains. A function $f : \mathcal{D} \rightarrow \mathcal{E}$ is* **monotone** *if for all $x_1, x_2 \in \mathcal{D}$, if $x_1 \leq x_2$, then $f(x_1) \leq f(x_2)$.*

Recall that queries are functions from databases to relations. Hence, it is natural to consider their monotonicity with respect to partial orders defined over relations. Queries are expressed in a query language by combining the basic operators using combining operations, e.g. composition [10], or the least fixed point operator, defined by Tarski's Fixpoint Theorem [25] for monotone functions. Note that the least fixed points of a function, monotone relative to different partial orders, are not necessarily equal. These combining operations preserve monotonicity of queries.

Theorem 3.2 (Monotonicity Preservation) *The composition of monotone queries and the least fixed point of a monotone query are monotone.*

It follows that to show that two query languages are not equivalent, it suffices to find a partial order such that one of the languages is monotone for that order but the other is not.

3.2 Partial Orders on Nested Relations

Traditionally, monotonicity of queries was considered with respect to the partial order defined by set inclusion between relation instances [26]. Nested relations and more generally complex objects have a richer structure which gives rise to other natural partial orders.

Definition 3.3 *Given two instances S and R in $\mathcal{I}_\Omega$,*

- *S is smaller than R in the* **inclusion order**, *denoted $S \subseteq R$, if S is contained in R;*

- *S is smaller than R in the* **attribute-wise order**, *denoted* $S \leq_a R$, *iff*

$$(\forall s \in S)(\exists t \in R)(\forall X \in \Omega \cap U : s[X] = t[X] \ \& \ \forall X \in \Omega - U : s[X] \subseteq t[X])$$

- *The* **sub-object order** *(dominance), denoted* $R \leq_{obj} S$, *is defined recursively as:*
  For every value O, $O \leq_{obj} O$.
  For tuples O *and* O', $O \leq_{obj} O'$ *if* $O.A \leq_{obj} O'.A$ *for all attributes* A.
  For sets (instances) O *and* O', $O \leq_{obj} O'$ *if* $\forall o_1 \in O \exists o_2 \in O'(o_1 \leq_{obj} o_2)$.

We extend the definitions coordinate-wise to vectors of relations.

Example 1: The following relationships hold between the given instances over the scheme $\{A, \{B\}\}$:

$$\{[1,\{2,3\}],[4,\{5,6\}]\} \subseteq \{[1,\{2,3\}],[4,\{5,6\}],[7,\{8,9\}]\}$$

$$\{[1,\{2,3\}],[4,\{5,6\}]\} \leq_a \{[1,\{2,3\}],[4,\{5,6,7\}]\}$$

However, the relationship $\subseteq$ does not hold in the second case in any direction. □

Proposition 3.4 $\subseteq, \leq_a$ *and* $\leq_{obj}$ *are partial orders* [2]. *Further,* $\subseteq$ *is strictly contained in* $\leq_a$, *which in turn is strictly contained in* $\leq_{obj}$.

Note that for flat relations $\subseteq$ coincides with $\leq_a$, and $\leq_{obj}$ coincides with $\leq_a$ for for single-level nested relations. We define **monotone, attribute-wise monotone**, and **object-monotone** queries, as queries that are monotone relative to the partial orders $\subseteq, \leq_a$, and $\leq_{obj}$, respectively. Until section 6, we use only the first two notions.

3.3 The Monotone Subset of the Algebra

The next theorem characterizes the operators of the powerset algebra in terms of monotonicity and attribute-wise monotonicity:

Theorem 3.5
1. The following operators fail to be monotone or attribute-wise monotone: nest, scons, difference, and singleton.
2. The following operators are monotone: powerset, intersection, selection by membership, selection by attributes containment, and composite equi-select. However, they fail to be attribute-wise monotone.
3. The following operators are attribute-wise monotone and monotone: unnest, set-collapse, projection, union, Cartesian product, and elementary equi-select.

Corollary 3.6 *When combining operators only by composition and least fixed point: (a) the operators in groups (2) and (3) cannot express those in group (1), and (b) The operators in group (3) cannot express those in group (2).*

This shows that elementary equi-select alone is less expressive than the selection by predicates on composite attributes.

Let $\mathcal{N}_+$ and $\mathcal{P}_+$ denote the monotone subsets of the nested relational algebra and the powerset algebra which use only the monotone operators (groups (2) and (3) in Theorem 3.5). Corollary 3.6 shows that $\mathcal{N}_+ \subset\neq \mathcal{N}$ and $\mathcal{P}_+ \subset\neq \mathcal{P}$.

[2]The sub-object order is a lattice and can be defined for complex objects with untyped (heterogeneous sets) [7].

3.4 Nested Application of Functions

The recursive structure of nested relations encourages a recursive mode of expression in which queries operate on composite attributes of each tuple in a relation. This is expressed by different means in algebraic and logic programming languages. The former employ expressions whose arguments are named attributes of a relation scheme [1,24], while the latter use built-in predicates and functions on variables denoting arguments of database predicates [9,18].

Example 2: The complex object algebra uses replace specifications for nested application of functions [1]. Given a relation r over the scheme $\{\{A\},\{B\}\}$, the expression $s := \rho < \{A\} \cup \{B\} >$ (r) denotes a new relation s over the scheme $\{\{C\}\}$, which contains a tuple for each tuple in r, such that the $\{C\}$ attribute of the former is the union of the $\{A\}$ and $\{B\}$ attributes of the latter.

The following LDL program [9] computes the same function for database predicates (relations) r and s, $s(Z)\ :-\ r(X,Y) \wedge union(X,Y,Z)$. □

Following [1], we define a general form of nested function application:

Definition 3.7 *Let $E(x_1,\ldots,x_n)$ be an algebraic expression over attributes, where the scheme of x_i is Ω^{x_i}, and let Ω be a scheme that contains each of Ω^{x_i}. The* **nested application** *of E to the relation (Ω,ω), denoted $\rho < E > (\Omega,\omega)$, is $(\{\Omega^E\},\omega')$, where ω' equals $\{E(t[\Omega^{x_1}],\ldots,t[\Omega^{x_n}]) \mid t \in \omega\}$. We extend the definition to sequences of expressions by having the tuple of their results as the target.*

Nested application of functions is an operation for constructing new queries. Surprisingly, it yields only monotone queries.

Proposition 3.8 *For every expression E as above,*
1. $\rho < E >$ is monotone;
2. If E is monotone, then $\rho < E >$ is attribute-wise monotone.

Proof: 1. This follows directly from the definition of $\rho < E >$.
2. If $R \leq_a S$, then for every tuple $t \in R$, there is a tuple $s \in S$, such that for all $X \in \Omega - U$, $t[X] \subseteq s[X]$, and for all $X \in \Omega \cap U$, $t[X] = s[X]$. Hence, because E is monotone and its arguments are attributes of tuples in t or s, $E(t) \subseteq E(s)$. Consequently, $E(r) \leq_a E(s)$. □

4 Logic Programming with Nested Relations

Logic programming languages for nested relations generalize Horn clause programs by using set-theoretic predicates and constructs. We consider languages over some first-order language L, which includes the interpreted (built-in) predicate symbols, $\in$, $=$,**union**,**singleton**, and the interpreted function symbols **scons**, and $\{\}$ (set enumeration). We assume that L does not include uninterpreted function symbols. We consider three types of clauses (rules):

Definition 4.1 *Let $A, B_1, \ldots, B_m$ be atomic formulas in L, where A is not an interperted predicate and all variables in A appear in one of the B_i's.*

- *A Horn clause over L is a formula of the form*

$$A\ :-\ B_1 \wedge \cdots \wedge B_m$$

- *An ELPS clause is a formula of the form*

$$A \;:-\; (\forall x_1 \in X_1)\cdots(\forall x_n \in X_n)(B_1 \wedge \cdots \wedge B_m)$$

for $n \geq 0$.

- *An LDL grouping clause over L is a formula of the form*

$$A(x_1,\ldots,x_n,<x>) \;:-\; B_1 \wedge \cdots \wedge B_m$$

Its meaning is that $A(a_1,\ldots,a_n,a)$ *must hold whenever a is the set of all the values of x for which the body of the clause holds (for the values* $a_1,\ldots,a_n$ *of* $x_1,\ldots,x_n$*).*

A program is a finite set of clauses. We consider the following languages: (a) Datalog uses Horn clauses with no interpreted predicates except equality, (b) Complex object Datalog (denoted CO-Datalog) uses Horn clauses, (c) LDL uses LDL grouping clauses and Horn clauses, and (d) ELPS uses ELPS clauses. Datalog is the primary logic programming language studied for flat relational databases.

The semantics of programs is defined like that of Horn programs [6], as the least fixed point of a relational operator defined by the program. When the operator fails to be monotone, e.g negation of predicates is used in the body of the rules, or the LDL grouping clause is used [9], a decomposition of the program into strata defines the program semantics as a composition of least fixed point computations [5]. We call the languages with stratification the *stratified* languages.

Proposition 4.2
1. Datalog and CO-Datalog programs are monotone. However, they fail to be attribute-wise monotone.
2. Programs in the stratified languages fail to be monotone or attribute-wise monotone.

Proof: The positive side follows from Proposition 3.8. A Datalog rule can be viewed as an algebraic expression using the interpreted predicates, and projection (or more generally, a restructuring operation). Given a tuple in the cross product of the relations mentioned in the rule's body, the expression produces a tuple for the rule's head, by applying the predicates of the body, then a projection (or restructuring). Applying the rule once to a collection of relations has the same effect as applying $\rho < E >$ to their cross product. It follows that the immediate consequence operator associated with the program is monotone, hence so is the least fixed point operator associated with it. The negative side with respect to attribute-wise monotonicity results from Theorem 3.5 due to the use of composite equi-select (through identical variables refering to sets) in all languages. □

4.1 A Modular View of Programs over Nested Relations

The languages defined above can be alternatively viewed as Datalog augmented with nested and regular application of algebraic operators. This is clearly the case with predicates used in the bodies of rules, including the interpreted predicates such as union. As explained above, the body of a rule can be viewed as an expression applied to each tuple in a set of tuples. Grouping in LDL clauses applies a nest operator to the result of the application of the rule with grouping removed. This is a regular, rather than a nested, application of nesting. Likewise, an ELPS clause can be viewed as first applying the rule without the quantifiers, and then checking that the result contains the cross product of the X_i's. Proposition 3.8 suggests we could use a larger class of algebraic expressions in the body of rules. Any nested application of an algebraic expression, even a non-monotone one, does not destroy monotonicity.

Example 3: A CO-Datalog program for computing the difference between the two composite attributes in each tuple of a relation r, using a nested application of difference is:

$$s(Z)\ :-\ r(X,Y), \mathbf{difference}(X,Y,Z)$$

Expressing this program in existing languages with the built-in predicates as described above requires stratification. □

As remarked above it is possible to apply tuple-wise algebraic expressions in logic programs while maintaining the standard semantics, by viewing such an expression as an interpreted predicate. The opposite direction of invoking logic programs as part of algebraic expressions is also useful in two respects. First, even though the powerset algebra is equivalent to the stratified CO-Datalog, inherently recursive queries are more elegantly expressed and efficiently implemented as logic programs than as algebraic expression. For example, computing transitive closure in the algebra requires exponential time [1]. A second way to embed logic programs into the algebra is by applying them to composite attributes of tuples, in the same way we have defined nested application of algebraic expressions. Linnemann [21] considered a similar approach of a nested computation of least fixed points of algebraic expressions. This leads to succinct and more efficient expression of some recursive queries than their application to the nested relations themselves.

All these observations suggest that integrating the monotonic subsets of the algebra and CO-Datalog allows for clearer expression of some queries, and to faster evaluation of queries by expressing each in the language inherently suited for it. Such an integration can be carried in a modular and simple way by generalizing the concept of an expression to include logic programs. As observed by Fitting [13] logic programs can be packaged into modules whose semantics is that of an operator from given input relations (predicates) to a distinguished output relation. The external interface of the module can be thus described as an algebraic expression $E(x_1, \ldots, x_k)$ whose arguments are the input relations, and its result the output relation. In the reverse direction, we can regard an algebraic expression E as defining a logic program module with the above semantics and use it as a clause in a logic program. Alternatively, it can be used in the body of a clause as a user-defined interpreted predicate. We thus arrive to the following definition of program over nested relations:

Definition 4.3 *A program over nested relations is a logic program module.*
A logic program module, is either an extended CO-Datalog program without negation, or an algebraic expression.
An algebraic expression is either an expression in $\mathcal{P}_+$ or a nested application of a program.
An extended CO-Datalog program is a CO-Datalog program with interpreted predicates which are either the built-in predicates, or are defined by an expression in $\mathcal{P}$.

Since the outermost level of a program uses a monotone algebraic expression, or clauses without negation, meaning can be assigned to programs within the conventional semantics of logic programming and the algebra. This modular framework should clearly enhance programmer productivity and database performance due to the freedom from the constraints of a particular programming paradigm, and the ability to capture each query in the most efficient formalism for its evaluation. The next section investigates in detail the implications on the expressive power of languages of the suggested enhancements.

4.2 The Power of the Monotone Sublanguages

Datalog programs, when applied to nested relations, are unable to restructure them as they cannot decompose composite values because of the lack of any built-in set-theoretic predicates. Hence,

Theorem 4.4 *(stratified) Datalog* $\subset\neq$ *(stratified) CO-Datalog.*

Proof: The proof follows from:
Claim: *The values of all composite attributes in the result of a (stratified) Datalog program appear in the database relations or in the program.*
The claim is proved by induction on the number of rule applications. Consider now the CO-Datalog program: $q(Z)\ :-\ r(X,Y) \wedge$ **union(X, Y, Z)** or for that matter any restructing operation applied to the variables in the body. From the claim the value of q cannot be computed in Datalog. □

This theorem should be contrasted with the nested relational algebra and the powerset algebra for which the addition of nested application of functions does not enhance their expressive power [1]. For the monotone subset of the algebra, the lack of a nest or singleton operator, that can be used to convert results of queries into composite attributes of tuples, causes the nested application of functions to actually increase its power.

Proposition 4.5 *The augmentation of* $\mathcal{N}_+$ *or* $\mathcal{P}_+$ *with nested application of functions increases their expressive power.*

Proof: For $\mathcal{N}_+$ this follows from a claim analogous to that used in Theorem 4.4 above.

The powerset operator can create composite attributes whose values did not appear in the input. However, consider performing the union of two composite attributes of each tuple by $\rho < \{A\} \cup \{B\} >$. We show that the new composite values created by powerset cannot be filtered without the nested application of functions, to contain exactly the values we need.

Take the two tuples relation $r = \{t_1, t_2\}$ over the scheme $\Omega = \{\{A\}, \{B\}\}$, where $t_i = [\alpha_i, \beta_i]$, and for $i = 1, 2$: $\gamma_i = \alpha_i \cup \beta_i$, $\gamma_i \neq \alpha_i$, $\gamma_i \neq \beta_i$, and $\gamma_1 \cap \gamma_2 = \emptyset$. We prove the stronger claim that we cannot create a relation s with an attribute Y, whose values are γ_1, γ_2 and possibly subsets of one of these. First, we have to use the powerset operator because,
Claim: *The values of all composite attributes in the result of an expression without powerset appear in the database relations or as constants in the expression.*
Because of genericity we cannot separate $adom(t_1)$ and $atom(t_2)$:
Claim: *An expression applied to* r *whose result has a tuple* t *with* $adom(t) \subseteq \gamma_1$*, has a tuple* t' *with* $adom(t') \subseteq \gamma_2$.
Hence, because all but the highest level attributes in the powerset result come from the input, we have to apply powerset to $adom(r)$.
Claim: *The result of that powerset has a tuple* t'' *with attribute* X*, such that* $\gamma_1 \cup \gamma_2 = t.X''$.
Let us consider the attribute Y of the result. It results from X through a sequence of operator applications. Wlog assume the sequence does not contain intersection or set-collapse. It cannot use unnest on X or a projection which will omit X. Otherwise, Y is obtained from another powerset operation, and in that case our argument applies to that operation. Hence, assume that creating X is the last application of powerset in the expression. The tuple t'' of the previous claim can be deleted only through a selection operation.
Claim: *The result of a selection on a relation with a tuple* t'' *as in the previous claim, has some tuple* t_3 *with the same property as* t''.
Let us consider each selection predicate. First, the instance chosen guarantees that any test of

equality (containment) of attribute X to (in) the attributes of r would remove γ_i, and containment in the other direction does not remove t''. To perform selection w.r.t. other attributes in order to delete t'' we need a relation w with an attribute whose values are γ_i and (perhaps) smaller sets. But then w is the required result, in contrast to X resulting from the last powerset application. Testing membership of X in another attribute, again has to use such a relation w. From the second claim, any relation with scheme $\{C\}$ (for some C) will contain values from both γ_1 and γ_2, and hence a membership test $C \in X$ will not remove $t''.X$. □

In the sequel, we consider the nested application of functions to be part of the algebra.

We mentioned that the powerset algebra is equivalent to the stratified CO-Datalog. It would seem that the parallel restriction to CO-Datalog and the monotone powerset algebra would preserve that equivalence as both are monotone subsets of the languages. This conjecture is false.

Theorem 4.6 $\mathcal{P}^+ \subset\neq$ *CO – Datalog.*

Proof: Containment follows by observing that the equivalence proof of the full languages does not involve negation for the monotone algebraic operators [1]. For strict containment, by examining the equivalence proof we see that the algebra can express the transitive closure (in contrast to the classical result [3]), by using the powerset to create arbitrary sets of node pairs. Selection is used jointly with nest and difference to filter the desired set. However, the restriction to monotone operators prevents the construction of such a filtering expression. We need the following classical claim.

Claim: *Given an undirected graph with edge relation R, no algebraic expression E not using powerset can compute a relation of all pairs of nodes whose distance is greater than $\mid E \mid$.*

Hence, we are forced to apply powerset to some relation over pairs of nodes. If the diameter of R is large enough, this relation cannot be R or a subset of the pairs of nodes connected by R. Otherwise, the claim applies for the composite attributes created by the powerset. Consequently, we create sets of node pairs which do not necessarily contain R or nodes connected in the graph. Testing for containment of R is a non monotone query and hence inexpressible in the algebra, and any subsequent restructuring of the result of the powerset cannot guarantee to create a relation with just pairs connected in the graph. □

A consequence of this theorem is that when integrating CO-Datalog with the algebra, one can delimit the use of the powerset operator without loosing expressive power.

The algebraic analogue of the logic programming languages is the least fixed point closure of the algebra, obtained by adding the application of the least fixed point operator to expressions (obtaining lfp expressions [14]). We denote the least fixed point closure of the powerset (nested relational) algebra by $\mathcal{P}^*$ ($\mathcal{N}^*$), and similarly for their monotone subsets $\mathcal{P}^*_+$ ($\mathcal{N}^*_+$). The following lemma states the known results about the power of these languages:

Lemma 4.7 ([1,14,19]) *The following languages are equivalent: $\mathcal{P}$, $\mathcal{N}^*$, $\mathcal{P}^*$, stratified CO-Datalog, and stratified ELPS. ELPS is equivalent to CO-Datalog.*

The next proposition completes the picture for the monotone languages (see Fig. 1):

Proposition 4.8

(1) $\mathcal{N}_+ \subset\neq \mathcal{N}^*_+ \subset\neq \mathcal{P}^*_+$

(2) $\mathcal{P}_+ \subset\neq \mathcal{P}^*_+$

(3) $\mathcal{P}_+$ *and* $\mathcal{N}^*_+$ *are incomparable*

(4) *ELPS* $\subset\neq$ *stratified LDL*

(5) $\mathcal{P}_+$, *CO – Datalog, and ELPS are each incomparable with* $\mathcal{N}$

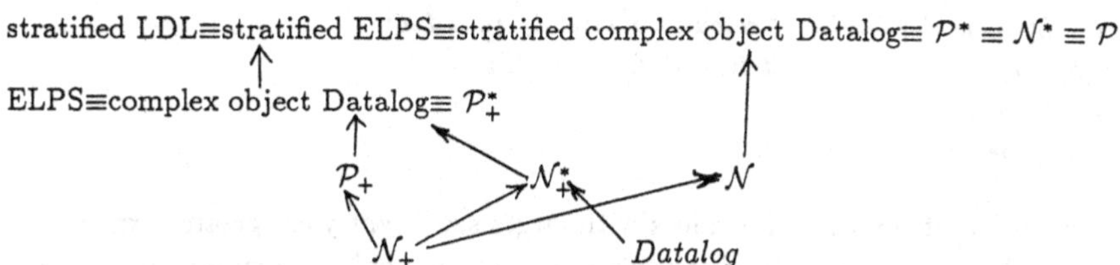

Figure 1: **Expressive power of monotone Languages.** (An upward arrow denotes strict containment)

Proof:
1. The operators included in $\mathcal{N}_+$ cannot increase the set-height of relations whereas powerset can.
2. and 3. From $\mathcal{P}_+$ use the proof of Theorem 4.6. In the other direction, see item 1.
4. Follows from Lemma 4.2.
5. The nested relational algebra cannot express powerset [14]. All the other languages are unable to perform nesting because they compute only monotone queries. □

The expressiveness of stratified ELPS was determined by Kuper to be at least that of stratified LDL [19]. We next prove their equivalence.

Proposition 4.9 *stratified LDL* $\equiv \mathcal{P}^*$

Proof: From LDL to $\mathcal{P}^*$, we attach a lfp expression equivalent to the set of rules in each stratum. Negation and grouping separating stratas are translated into difference and nesting, respectively, on these expressions.

For the other direction, we translate from $\mathcal{P}$ to LDL, using the equivalence of $\mathcal{P}^*$ and $\mathcal{P}$. The transformation is done bottom-up adding a new strata whenever nest or difference is encountered. As there are no recursive expressions this ensures that the resulting program is stratified. □

5 Positive Existential Queries over Nested Relations

The tableau formalism is widely accepted as a tool for optimizing relational algebra expressions. A generalization of tableau queries are the tableau set queries [23]. In this section we investigate the expressive power of these over nested relations. We use their relational calculus formulation as positive existential formulas. A **positive existential query** is a calculus query defined from the atomic formulas using only conjunction, disjunction, and existential quantification.

Proposition 5.1 ([23]) *Tableau set queries (over flat relations) are equivalent to the monotone subset of the flat relational algebra and to the class of positive existential queries in the flat relational calculus.*

Quantification in the relational calculus is only over flat tuples. In contrast, the calculus we have defined over nested relations allows the quantification over variables ranging over types with arbitrary set-height. These variables can store values with set-height greater than any appearing in the input and output of a query. Intuitively, it is clear that such values can be used as scratch area for computations. Let τ_k denote the collection of all types of set-height k.

Definition 5.2 *If* $D = [R_1 : T_1, \ldots, R_n : T_n]$ *is a database schema, and* $Q : D \rightarrow T$ *a query on* D *where* $Q = \{x/T \mid \phi(x)\}$, *then* S *is an intermediate type of* Q, *if there is a variable of type* S *in* $\phi(x)$ *and* $S \not\in \{T_1, \ldots, T_n, T\}$.

Definition 5.3 *$CALC_{k,i}$ is the family of calculus queries Q such that:*
1. for some $D = [R_1 : T_1, \ldots, R_n : T_n]$ and type T, $Q : D \to T$;
2. $\{T_1, \ldots, T_n, T\} \subseteq \cup_{j \le k} \tau_j$;
3. each intermediate type of Q is in $\cup_{j \le i} \tau_j$.

Hull and Su have proved that intermediate values with larger set-height yield greater expressive power [15]. Kuper and Vardi have considered the subclasses that use only existentially quantified variables over intermediate types, denoted $CALC_{k,\exists i}$, and proved the existence of a similar strict hierarchy citekn:KV88. These results are summarized in the next theorem.

Theorem 5.4 *For every $0 \le k \le i$, $CALC_{k,i} \subset\neq CALC_{k,(i+1)}$ and $CALC_{k,\exists i} \subset\neq CALC_{k,\exists(i+1)}$.*

It is desirable to avoid the use of intermediate types in positive existential queries, possibly without losing any (or much) expressive power. This would make the extension of the conventional tableau formalism to nested relations a rather direct task. Intuitively, the lack of universal quantification and negation in the queries we consider implies that values over intermediate types are under specified. Namely, a query can assert what will belong to such a set but cannot specify what will not be there. Exploiting this intuition we prove below that the use of intermediate types is indeed redundant and moreover cannot express the expensive powerset operation. We denote the class of positive existential queries in $CALC_{k,\exists i}$ by $CALC^+_{k,\exists i}$.

Theorem 5.5 *For every $k \ge 0$, $CALC^+_{k,\exists k} \equiv \cup_{k \le i} CALC^+_{k,\exists i}$.*

Proof: As remarked above queries in these classes assert only a finite amount of information about the contents of variables ranging over intermediate types. Hence, we can eliminate these variables by using as *witnesses* terms built using set-enumeration and tuple constructors. These witnesses contain just the finite set of values required to be in those variables.

Let φ be a query in $CALC^+_{k,\exists i}$. Let us call variables ranging over intermediate types intermediate variables. Rename all bound variables to be distinct and replace equality predicates by identical variables. Wlog assume the formula is in prenex normal form, and the body is a disjunction of conjuncts. We consider each disjunct separately, and show how to eliminate all intermediate variables without changing its meaning. The following procedure replaces intermediate variables, in order of increasing set-height $i > k$, by witnesses from an expanded set of terms which uses set enumeration $\{\}$ (as in logic programming languages) and tuple constructors.

1. If an intermediate variable x appears in atomic formulas of the form $y_1 \in x, \ldots, y_l \in x$, for terms y_i not containing intermediate variables, we use $\{y_1, \ldots, y_l\}$ instead of x.

2. Similarly, for atomic formulas of the form $y_1 = x.X_1, \ldots, y_l = x.X_l$, use a tuple term $[X_1 : y_1, \ldots, X_l : y_l]$ as a witness for x, with any constant for attributes not specified in the query. In case, two terms y_j, y_k should be equal to the same attribute rename one of them to the other everywhere in the query.

3. Any intermediate variable left can be replaced by a constant witness.

Having constructed the witnesses as above, they are guaranteed to satisfy the quantifiers over the intermediate variables and hence these quantifiers can be eliminated. Hence, we obtain a query in $CALC^+_{k,\exists k}$. □
Note the procedure used in the proof can be used to effectively remove intermediate types from $CALC^+_{k,\exists i}$ queries.

Theorem 5.6 *Positive existential queries over nested relations cannot express the powerset operator.*

Proof: The proof is similar to the previous one in using the fact that subsets of a relation constructed by a positive existential queries are under-specified. Hence, satisfiability of a formula is preserved when increasing all sets mentioned in the the query with set-height larger than that of the input relations. In particular, this includes the target variable of a positive existential query expressing the powerset operator. The powerset of the relation $(\{A\}, \{d\})$ is $\{\emptyset, \{d\}\}$. From the argument above the answer of any positive existential query expressing the powerset should also include $\{d, d'\}$ for any $d \neq d'$ in the active domain of the database, which is a contradiction.

To formally prove the preservation property of positive existential queries we consider mappings on the values. An *increasing mapping* h is a one-to-one mapping on the set of values, which is: (a) scheme preserving, (b) increases composite values in the inclusion order, and (c) preserves membership and subset predicates, i.e. if $x \in y$ then $h(x) \in h(y)$, and if $x \subseteq y$ then $h(x) \subseteq h(y)$.

Wlog consider a query in $CALC^{+}_{k,\exists k}$ whose input has set-height $k-1$ to be in prenex normal form, i.e. $\psi(y) = \exists\vec{x}\varphi(\vec{x}, y)$. For each answer a, there is an assignment $\vec{a}_x$ to the quantified variables. Apply an increasing mapping h which is identity on all values with set-height smaller than k and strictly increasing for all others. In particular, for a query expressing the powerset operator for relations over scheme with set-height $k-1$ the target variable is of the latter kind. The next claim implies the preservation property:

Claim: $\varphi(\vec{a}_x, a) \Longrightarrow \varphi(h(\vec{a}_x), h(a))$

The proof is by induction on the structure of φ. Atomic formulas can be either $R(\vec{z})$ for some relation name R, or one of $z_1 \in z_2$ or $z_1 \subseteq z_2$. For $R(\vec{z})$ preservation follows the fact that h is identity on the database relations, whereas for the others it follows from the definition of increasing mappings. The induction step for formulas built using sentential connectives is immediate. □

These two theorems show that the sublanguage of the calculus defined by the positive existential queries is not too expressive as to make its practical use prohibitive expensive.

6 The Bancilhon-Khoshafian Calculus

The Bancilhon-Khoshafian calculus for complex objects (BK) [7] is a deductive language that allows untyped sets, with no restriction on the types of their members. The complex objects thus obtained form a significantly larger class than nested relations. A lattice over complex objects is defined by the sub-object order (see Definition 3.3). Computation of rules in the language is defined in terms of operations over the lattice. In this section we consider the relationship between BK and subsets of the languages we have defined. For lack of space we omit the definition of the language and refer the reader to [7].

Lemma 6.1 *All queries computed by the Bancilhon-Khoshafian complex object calculus are object-monotone. However, they fail to be generally monotone or attribute-wise monotone.*

Proof: For the positive side see [7]. To see the negative side consider the two rules: $[R' : \{X\}] \ :- \ [R : X]$ and $[R' : \{\{X\}\}] \ :- \ [R : \{X\}]$, which compute $R' := singleton(R)$, and $R' := \rho < singleton(X) > (R)$, respectively. □

To compare algebraic and logic programming languages with BK we allow the application of algebraic operators and logic programs to untyped set objects, for example, the formation of union of sets of different types. Also, horizontal operators such as selection "ignore" elements not having the right shape. The following theorem shows that indeed monotonicity has many faces:

Theorem 6.2 *BK is incomparable with the following languages: the complex object Datalog without negation, the monotone subset of the powerset algebra, and ELPS.*

Proof: All these languages include composite equi-select which is not expressible in BK because it is not object-monotone. In the other direction, use Lemma 6.1. □
By lemma 6.1, since difference is not object-monotone , it follows that BK is strictly contained in the stratified complex object DATALOG (equivalent to $\mathcal{C}$ over untyped sets [16]). Thus, a syntactic characterization of BK in terms of more conventional languages does not exist.

References

[1] S. Abiteboul and C. Beeri. *On the Power of Languages for the Manipulation of Complex Objects.* Technical Report 846, INRIA, May 1988.

[2] S. Abiteboul and S. Grumbach. COL: a logic-based language for complex objects. In *Proc. of the Workshop on Database Programming Languages*, pages 253–276, Roscoff, France, September 1987.

[3] A.V. Aho and J.D. Ullman. Universality of data retrieval languages. In *Proc. Sixth ACM Symp. on Principles of Programming Languages*, pages 110–117, January 1979.

[4] H. Ait-Kaci and R. Nasr. LOGIN: a logic programming language with built-in inheritance. *Journal of Logic Programming*, 3:185–215, 1986.

[5] K. Apt, H. Blair, and A. Walker. Towards a theory of declarative knowledge. In J. Minker, editor, *Foundations of Deductive Databases and Logic Programming*, pages 89–184, Morgan Kaufman Publishers, 1987.

[6] Krzysztof R. Apt and M.H. Van Emden. Contributions to the theory of logic programming. *Journal of the ACM*, 29(3):841–862, July 1982.

[7] F. Bancilhon and S. Khoshafian. A calculus for complex objects. In *Proc. Fifth ACM Symp. on Principles of Database Systems*, pages 53–59, 1986.

[8] F. Bancilhon, P. Richard, and M. Scholl. On line processing of compacted relations. In *Proc. Intl. Conf. on Very Large Data Bases*, pages 263–269, 1982.

[9] C. Beeri, S. Naqvi, R. Ramakrishnan, O. Shmueli, and S. Tsur. Sets and negation in a logic database language (LDL1). In *Proc. Sixth ACM Symp. on Principles of Database Systems*, pages 21–37, March 1987.

[10] A. Chandra and D. Harel. Structure and complexity of relational queries. *Journal of Computer and System Sciences*, 25(1):99–128, 1982.

[11] A.K. Chandra and D. Harel. Computable queries for relational datbase systems. *Journal of Computer and System Sciences*, 21(2):156–178, 1980.

[12] P. Dadam et. al. A DBMS prototype to support extended NF^2 relations: an integrated view on flat tables and hierarchies. In *ACM SIGMOD Intl. Conf. on Management of Data*, pages 356–367, 1986.

[13] M. Fitting. Enumeration operators and modular logic programming. *J. of Logic Programming*, 4:11–21, 1987.

[14] M. Gyssens and D. Van Gucht. The powerset algebra as a result of adding programming constructs to the nested relational algebra. In *ACM SIGMOD Intl. Conf. on Management of Data*, pages 225–232, 1988.

[15] R. Hull and J. Su. On the expressive power of database queries with intermediate types. In *Proc. Seventh ACM Symp. on Principles of Database Systems*, pages 39–51, 1988.

[16] R. Hull and J. Su. Untyped sets, invention, and computable queries. In *Proc. Eighth ACM Symp. on Principles of Database Systems*, 1989.

[17] M. Kifer and J. Wu. A logic for object-oriented logic programming (Maier's O-Logic revisited). In *Proc. Eighth ACM Symp. on Principles of Database Systems*, 1989.

[18] G.M. Kuper. Logic programming with sets. In *Proc. Sixth ACM Symp. on Principles of Database Systems*, pages 11–20, 1987.

[19] G.M. Kuper. On the expressive power of logic programming with sets. In *Proc. Seventh ACM Symp. on Principles of Database Systems*, pages 10–14, 1988.

[20] G.M. Kuper and M.Y. Vardi. On the complexity of queries in the logical data model. In D. Van Gucht M. Gyssens, J. Paredaens, editor, *2nd International Conference on Database Theory*, pages 267–280, Springer-Verlag, Bruges, Belgium, August 1988.

[21] V. Linnemann. Non first normal form relations and recursive queries: an SQL-based approach. In *Proc. Intl. Conf. on Data Engineering*, pages 591–598, 1987.

[22] H.-B. Paul, H.-J. Schek, M.H. Scholl, G. Weikum, and U. Deppisch. Architecture and implementation of the Darmstadt database kernel system. In *ACM SIGMOD Intl. Conf. on Management of Data*, 1987.

[23] Y. Sagiv and M. Yannakakis. Equivalence among relational expressions with the union and difference operators. *Journal of the ACM*, 27(4):633–655, 1980.

[24] H. -J. Schek and M.H. Scholl. An algebra for the relational model with relation-valued attributes. *Information Systems*, 11(2):137–147, 1986.

[25] A. Tarski. A lattice theoretical fixpoint theorem and its applications. *Pacific J. Math.*, 5(2):285–309, 1955.

[26] J.D. Ullman. *Principles of Database and Knowledge-Base Systems*. Computer Science Press, 1988.

File Access Level Optimization Using Page Access Graph on Recursive Query Evaluation

Yuki KUSUMI *
Kansai Information and Communications Research Laboratory
Matsushita Electric Industrial Co., Ltd.
1006 Kadoma, Kadoma-shi, Osaka, 571 Japan

Shojiro NISHIO †
Department of Information and Computer Sciences, Osaka University
Toyonaka, Osaka, 560 Japan

Toshiharu HASEGAWA
Department of Applied Systems Science, Kyoto University
Kyoto, 606 Japan

ABSTRACT

As the performance measure for recursive query evaluation algorithms in the deductive database system, the largest amount of necessary storage space for intermediate results measured by the number of tuples has been usually employed. In this paper, using a practical performance evaluation measure based on the physical file access; namely, the number of pages accessed, we will investigate a general framework of efficient file access strategies for the transitive closure computation, which is one of performance bottlenecks in the recursive query evaluation. We introduce the page access graph for representing the page structure of a given file, and this graph provides the basis for considering the optimization of page access scheduling. Under the assumption that whole or a part of this graph is processed in the main memory, if the graph is acyclic, our algorithm provides the optimal page access scheduling, i.e., each page has to be fetched at most once.

1 Introduction

Recently, many evaluation algorithms of queries for recursively defined predicates have been proposed in studies on the *deductive database system* (DDBS) [4]. As the evaluation measure for these algorithms, the largest amount of necessary storage space for intermediate results measured by the number of tuples has been usually employed. However, considering the practical file access mechanism in the database system, the performance of algorithms should be also measured by the access times to a physical access unit of files in the system, i.e., the number of *pages* (or *segments*) accessed in the algorithm. The performance of recursive query evaluation algorithms based on the physical file access have been discussed in several papers (see, e.g., [1][6]), and some algorithms in these

*E-mail: kusumi@sws.cpd.mei.co.jp
†E-mail: nishio@osaka-u.ac.jp

papers have considered to utilize the full information obtained from the pages which are temporarily stored in the main memory. But these algorithms do not care about any page accessing schedule for realizing the minimum number of pages accessed.

In this paper we will investigate efficient page access scheduling algorithms useful to the computation of transitive closure, a typical evaluation problem in recursive queries. Under the performance measure of the number of pages accessed, our algorithms aim at further optimization of the conventional algorithms which have been proposed under different performance measures, for instance, the number of tuples of the intermediate results. Though we will describe the algorithms only for the transitive closure problem, by an appropriate rule analysis for a given query, the idea proposed in this paper can be applicable to a wide variety of rules having complicated recursive structures.

In Section 2, we sketch past works relevant to this paper. Then in Section 3 we introduce the *page access graph* for representing the page structure of a given file. This graph is the basis for considering the optimization of page access scheduling in Section 4 for both bound and unbound recursive queries. We discuss in the rest of the paper various aspects of the proposed algorithms considering their application to practical DDBSs. Finally, concluding remarks as well as several open problems are given in Section 7.

2 Sketch of Relevant Past Works

Like most researchers, we assume that a deductive database system consists of an *extensional database* (EDB) and an *intensional database* (IDB), where the former is a set of *facts*, and the latter is a set of *deduction rules*. In the rest of the paper, we adopt *Prolog* convention of denoting rules. A fact is represented as a ground clause (i.e., a clause whose body is empty) which contains no variables. A predicate which appears both in the EDB and in the head of IDB clause can be removed with adequate procedure. Thus, we can assume that predicates appeared in a database are decomposed into the *EDB predicate* and the *IDB predicate*. Since an EDB predicate corresponds to a *relation* of a relational database system, let us assume in the rest of the paper that a set of facts for an EDB predicate is stored as an *EDB relation*.

Example 1 *Let us introduce the set of rules (*or logic program*), to obtain the ancestor relationship for the given parenthood relation in the EDB. It is a typical example of* transitive closure rules.

$$\begin{aligned} &anc(X,Y) :- par(X,Y). \\ &anc(X,Y) :- anc(X,Z), par(Z,Y). \end{aligned} \tag{1}$$

Here let us assume as follows; EDB relation $par(X,Y)$ means that Y is a parent of X, and IDB predicate $anc(X,Y)$ means that Y is an ancestor of X. ■

Queries for the predicate defined with such rules can be divided into two classes. One is the class of *bound queries* where at least one argument in the query is constant, and the other is the class of *unbound queries* where no argument in the query is constant. For example, for the rules in Example 1, the query $?-anc(a,X)$ that finds all ancestors of particular individual a is a bound query, where a is called *query constant.* On the other hand, the query $?-anc(X,Y)$ that finds the entire ancestor relation is an unbound query. Query evaluation algorithms for these two classes of queries have been studied separately.

For evaluating the bound query, the main objective of optimization is avoiding the access to facts (or tuples) which are irrelevant to the query constant. One way to achieve such objective is the top down evaluation starting with the query constant in the given query [5][6][7][8]. Another way is to reduce the size of intermediate results by means of cutting down irrelevant part of EDB relations through adequate top-down binding propagation[3].

For unbound queries, one objective is to reduce the cost of massive join operations often appearing in the computation. Another objective is preventing the redundant access to the same tuple. Many algorithms have been proposed in order to attain these objectives[1][2][9][10][11]. In particular, Agrawal and Jagadish [1] analyzed the problem through the adjacent matrix of the graph constructed from given EDB relations, and developed an evaluation algorithm for reducing the amount I/O traffic by means of adequate clustering of relations as well as gimmicky ordering of computation on the matrix.

3 Page Access Graph (PAG)

The optimization with respect to the page I/O cost is called *page access level optimization* so that we can distinguish it from optimization methods measured by the tuple I/O cost. Different from the optimization techniques regarding the tuple I/O cost, the page access level optimization concerning the EDB relation may require new optimization methods. For discussing such techniques, we will show an example.

Example 2 *Let us consider the ancestor rules (1) in Example 1. Assume that the EDB relation is given in Figure 1 along with its* database graph. *The database graph represents a tuple (a, b) in the relation as an arc (a, b). Note that this sample EDB is often referred to in the rest of this paper if necessary. For the query $?-anc(a, X)$, a well optimized* Breadth First Search *(BFS) will find answers as follows:*

1. *Fetch P_1, find $\{b\}$ that is parent of a.*
2. *Fetch P_1, find $\{c, f\}$.*
3. *Fetch P_2 and P_3, find $\{i, e, d\}$.*
4. *Fetch P_2 and P_3, find $\{g, h, j\}$.*

For the above computation, if the system has the buffer for only one page, 4 or 5 pages are fetched in amount. However, if we compute the answer set in the following way, only 3 pages are fetched.

1. *Fetch P_1, find $\{b, c, f\}$.*
2. *Fetch P_3, find $\{e, i, j\}$.*
3. *Fetch P_2, find $\{d, g, h\}$.*

In this computation we happened to choose P_3 in Step 2, however, without any information a priori, it is not deterministic which page P_2 or P_3 to be fetched first. ■

For most of query evaluation algorithms optimized at the tuple I/O level, further optimization is possible at the page access level. Here, we model an EDB relation as follows:

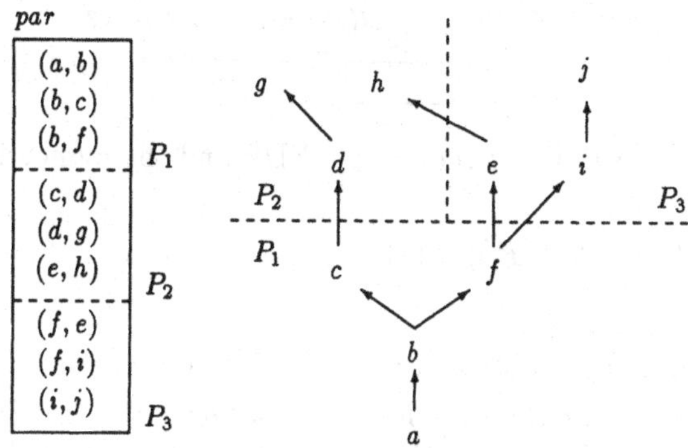

Figure 1: The sample EDB relation and its database graph.

Definition 1 *Let each of $P_1, P_2, \ldots, P_n$ be an arbitrary partition of an EDB relation P. Each of $P_1, P_2, \ldots, P_n$ is called* page *if and only if number of tuples included in each of P_i is at most m.* ■

As an important graphical tool for our proposing algorithms, now let us introduce the *page access graph*, which is useful to formalize the access to pages in EDB relations and to exclude such a non-determinicity as was mentioned in Example 2.

Definition 2 *Let P be an EDB relation and $P_1, P_2, \ldots, P_n$ be pages in P, then the* page access graph *(PAG) $G = (V, E)$, where V is a set of nodes and E is a set of arcs, for the transitive closure computation of P is defined as follows:*

$$V = \{P_1, P_2, \ldots, P_n\}$$
$$E = \{(P_i, P_j) \mid \exists p, q, r \text{ such that tuple } (p, q) \in P_i,\ \text{tuple } (q, r) \in P_j,\ i \neq j\}$$

■

In the database graph, if a tuple of relation is represented in a way such that the corresponding arc is from the first attribute value of the tuple to its second attribute value, then a PAG describes how the paths in a database graph cross over the pages. Therefore, if the second attribute of a query is bound with respect to the predicate defining ancestor rules in Example 1, we should either traverse arcs conversely in the PAG, or construct a PAG each of whose arcs is given in the opposite direction as compared with the above PAG. Note that our PAG becomes an undirected graph for unbound queries, and that it is identical to the *join index* [12] if only one tuple is stored in a page.

The numbering on nodes in the PAG is given as follows, which is useful in considering page access schedules.

Definition 3 *Let P_i and P_j be nodes in PAG G, then* distance *between P_i and P_j, denoted by $D(P_i, P_j)$, is the maximum length of path from P_i to P_j.* ■

Definition 4 *Let $G = (V, E)$ be an acyclic PAG, and $V = \{P_1, P_2, \ldots, P_n\}$, then numbering on node $N(P_i)$ is defined as follows:*

1. *$N(P_i) = 1$, if P_i has no preceding node.*

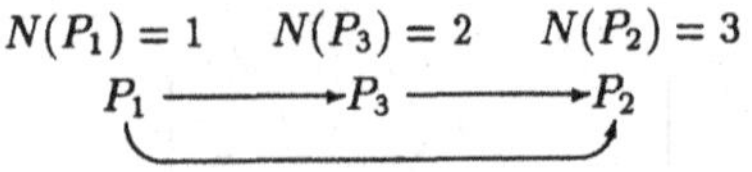

$$\begin{array}{ccc} N(P_1)=1 & N(P_3)=2 & N(P_2)=3 \\ P_1 \longrightarrow & P_3 \longrightarrow & P_2 \end{array}$$

Figure 2: The PAG for the sample EDB and the numbering on pages.

2. $N(P_j) = N(P_i) + D(P_i, P_j)$, *if* $(P_i, P_j) \in E$.

■

Note that this numbering is obtained by the conventional *Depth First Search* (DFS).

Example 3 *The PAG for the sample EDB relation given in Figure 1 is illustrated in Figure 2, where the numbering $N(P_i)$ is associated with each node.* ■

If it is possible to construct the PAG efficiently, and if sufficient space for storing whole or a part of the graph is available in the main memory, we can take advantage of it to obtain efficient page access scheduling algorithms for query evaluation.

First, we consider the procedure to construct a PAG. It seems to take a cost for searching all of combinations of arbitrary two tuples in a relation. However, to construct a PAG efficiently we can make use of an index or a hash table, which is usually associated with a relation.

Algorithm 1 *(Construction of PAG)*

input *EDB relation P.*
An index for the first attribute of P, which records all of page numbers in which each key appears.

output *PAG for the transitive closure computation of P.*

1. $E = \phi$;
2. **for** *each page* P_i $(1 \leq i \leq n)$
   which contains keys $q_1, \ldots, q_m$ *in its second attribute* **do**

2.1 *Find all pages* $P_{j_1}, \ldots, P_{j_s}$
   such that $q_1, \ldots, q_m$ *appears in the first attribute using the index.*

2.2 $E := E \cup \{(P_i, P_{j_1}), \ldots, (P_i, P_{j_s})\}$

endfor

■

Now let us consider the computational complexity of the algorithm. If we use the *B-Tree* index, the total number of nodes visited in Step 2.1 is $O(N(1 + \log(N + 1)/2))$, where N is the number of tuples in the relation. The number of arcs generated in Step 2.2 will be $mn(n - 1)$ in the worst case, where m is the number of tuples in a page and n is that of pages in the relation. However, as will be discussed in Section 5, under the assumption that EDB relation is sorted (i.e., clustered) so that all of tuples whose first (or second) attribute have the same value are stored in the same page, total number of arcs generated will be at most mn. Furthermore, if the PAG is always stored in the main memory and is updated together with the change of EDB relation (such updation of the PAG can be easily done), it is not necessary to construct the PAG expressly at every time when a new query comes in, it means no overhead for the construction of PAG.

Next, we will estimate the size of PAG in case a PAG is stored as a relation. According to the above assumption on clustering, the number of arcs in the PAG is mn, which is equivalent to the number of tuples N in the relation in case that each page is utilized to the fullest. Let us assume that B_{tuple} (B_{arc}) bytes are necessary for representing a tuple in the EDB relation (an arc in the PAG), respectively, then the number of pages necessary for storing the PAG is nB_{arc}/B_{tuple}.

Example 4 *Let us assume that* $B_{tuple} = 128 bytes$, $B_{arc} = 4 bytes$, *and a page consists of* $8192 bytes$. *For a relation of 2000 tuples (i.e., 32 pages), the number of pages for storing the PAG is at most one.* ■

We assumed in the above that a PAG is stored as a relation. However, it becomes more effective to represent a PAG by a boolean matrix. See Section 5 for further discussion for such a case.

4 PAG for the Transitive Closure Computation

Let us assume in the rest of this paper that whole or a part of the PAG can be loaded into the main memory whenever necessary. On this assumption, the optimal page access level scheduling for the EDB relation can be obtained. We will deal with only the computation of transitive closure defined by IDB rules (1) for binary EDB relations $par(X,Y)s$, nevertheless, as was mentioned in [6], a similar discussion is applicable to the query for the IDB predicates defined by more complicated rules.

4.1 PAG for the Evaluation of Bound Queries

While *Magic Set Method, Counting Method* [3], *Henshen-Naqvi's Algorithm* [8], *δ-Wavefront Algorithm, Level Cycle Merge Method* [6][7], et al. are well known algorithms to evaluate bound queries, these algorithms did not care about the page level access optimization.

Han et al. [6][7] demonstrated that the strict BFS is not required in case that the iteration level of recursive evaluation is not important (e.g., transitive closure queries) or that the exact recursive level information is registered in intermediate results. According to this observation, they proposed the *Level Relaxed δ-Wavefront Algorithm*, which is at present one of the most efficient algorithms for transitive closure computation. First, let us give the original δ-Wavefront Algorithm in Algorithm 2 and its Level Relaxed version in Algorithm 3.

Algorithm 2 δ-Wavefront Algorithm [7]
input *EDB relation* $P(X,Y)$.
IDB rules (1).
Query $?-A(a,X)$ *where* a *is query constant.*
output *Answer set for the query.*

1. $WAVE := \{a\}; ANSWER := \phi;$
2. **while** $WAVE \neq \phi$ **do**
2.1 $WAVE := \pi_3(WAVE \bowtie P);$
2.2 $WAVE := WAVE - ANSWER;$
2.3 $ANSWER := ANSWER \cup WAVE;$
endwhile.

Note: *(1) The semijoin,* $WAVE \rtimes P$, *is the projection onto the attributes of* P *of the natural join of* $WAVE$ *and* P. *(2) The unary relation* $WAVE$ *is called* wavefront relation. *(3) Each key in the* $WAVE$ *is called* driver *because it drives the next step of derivation.* ■

The above algorithm is considered to be a well optimized BFS shown in Example 2.

Algorithm 3 Level Relaxed δ-Wavefront Algorithm [7]
We describe this algorithm unlike the one in [7] under the assumption for simplicity that the buffer with the capacity of only one page is available. The algorithm's input and output are the same as ones of Algorithm 2.

1. $WAVE := \{a\}$; $ANSWER := \phi$;

2. **while** *there exists derivable page for drivers in* $WAVE$ **do**

2.1 *Fetch derivable page;*

2.2 **while** *drivers in* $WAVE$ *can generate new keys in the main memory* **do**

2.2.1 $NEW\_ANS := \pi_3(WAVE \rtimes P_i)$;

2.2.2 $live\_driver := NEW\_ANS - ANSWER$;

2.2.3 $WAVE := WAVE \cup live\_drivers - drivers$;

2.2.4 $ANSWER := ANSWER \cup live\_drivers$;

endwhile

endwhile

Note: *(1)* P_i *in Step 2.2.1 is the page fetched in Step 2.1. (2) Step 2.2.1 is implemented as a main memory algorithm. (3)* The drivers accessed *in Step 2.2.3 are excluded from the* $WAVE$ *based on the assumption that the drivers for the same value reside in the same page.* ■

This algorithm derives the answer by an efficient page accessing, just as we demonstrated in Example 2. However, *Level Relaxation* is only a lower level optimization of δ-Wavefront Algorithm, and further optimization is possible because the algorithm has still non-determinicity regarding the order of page access, which we will find under the comparison between Example 2 and the following one.

Example 5 *Let us consider query* $?{-}anc(a, X)$ *for ancestor rules (1) and the sample EDB illustrated in Figure 1. As was shown in Example 2, immediately after the derivation in* P_1 *is finished, drivers in the* $WAVE$ *are given by* $\{c, f\}$. *If* P_2 *for* c *is chosen, the subsequent derivation will be proceeded as follows:*

1. Fetch P_2, find $\{d, g\}$.
2. Fetch P_3, find $\{e, i, j\}$.
3. Fetch P_2, find $\{d, g, h\}$.

In the above procedure, the total number of pages fetched is 4, while 3 pages are fetched in the optimal case as was demonstrated in Example 2. ■

Such non-determinicity in Level Relaxed δ-Wavefront Algorithm is generally inevitable unless a priori information about the join selectivity between pages is available. However, for queries in a certain restricted class, we can solve this problem by means of the PAG.

Theorem 1 *Let us consider a bound query that finds a part of transitive closures of the database graph for a binary relation* P *whose starting node is query constant* a. *Constructing the PAG for the database graph, and if the connected component of the PAG (CCPAG) starting from the page where the query constant* a *appears in the first attribute* *is acyclic, then we can obtain the optimal page access level schedule such that each page is fetched at most once.*

Proof: *From the assumption that $CCPAG = (V_c, E_c)$ is acyclic, we can make the numbering (see Definition 4) on each node in V_c. Now, let us consider a schedule which always fetches a page having the smallest number among requested pages (i.e., pages which will be derivable from drivers in WAVE). According to the acyclicity of CCPAG as well as the definition of PAG, this scheduling will not request any page access to those with smaller numbers than that of the current page. Consequently, a page is fetched after the processing for all of preceding pages in the PAG since, otherwise, pages with smaller numbers will be left unprocessed. This discussion holds for all steps in the derivation, and thus we can show that this schedule fetches each page at most once.* ■

According to Theorem 1, under the condition that CCPAG is acyclic, the access schedule which fetches pages in increasing order of node numbers in the PAG leads to an optimal one as long as the number of pages accessed is employed as the evaluation measure. Now, we note that the PAG may have cycle(s) even though the database graph is acyclic. Thus, it is important to extend our scheduling method to a more general class of PAGs.

In case that a given PAG is cyclic, an access schedule which processes a strongly connected component (SCC) of CCPAG at a time is reasonable, because such an access plan can compute all of drivers in the cycle at a time and excludes any redundant fetching. This idea can be realized by means of adapting the numbering on each node of the CCPAG in Theorem 1 to each SCC of the CCPAG. Based on the above consideration, we will give an access scheduling algorithm applicable to the PAG with cycles.

Algorithm 4 Level Relaxed δ-Wavefront Algorithm with PAG

input *EDB relation $P(X, Y)$.*
IDB rules (1).
Query $? - A(a, X)$ where a is query constant.

output *Answer set for the query.*

1. *Get $CCPAG$ for the query constant a;*
2. *Decompose $CCPAG$ into SCCs, namely, $V_1, \ldots, V_r$;*
3. *Number each SCC in CCPAG;*
4. *$WAVE := \{a\}$; $ANSWER := \phi$;*
5. **while** *there exist derivable pages for drivers in WAVE* **do**

5.1 *Decide derivable SCC V_i with* the smallest number among requested SCCs ;

5.2 *Derive $ANSWER$ and $WAVE$ in V_i* using ordinary Level Relaxed δ-Wavefront Algorithm

endwhile

■

Example 6 *Let us consider the query in Example 2 again. The CCPAG for the query constant a becomes the PAG itself (see Figure 2) and it is acyclic. Thus, the numbering for each node exactly follows the way shown in Figure 2. After the completion of derivation in P_1, our algorithm always request the access to P_3 preceding to P_2, and this gives the optimal access scheduling.* ■

The correctness of our algorithms is straightforward because our algorithm is a variation of Level Relaxed δ-Wavefront Algorithm (our algorithm has additionally a page access ordering mechanism). However, our numbering does not always guarantee the minimality concerning intermediate results. Numbering for the minimal intermediate results is still an open problem. This problem is considered to be difficult to solve unless another information is provided a priori.

4.2 PAG for the Evaluation of Unbound Queries

For the unbound query evaluation, unlike the bound query evaluation, no irrelevant set to be cut down is explicitly provided because no query constant is given. In other words, we can not obey the principle "*selection before join*" for achieving efficient page access schedules, and the objective of optimization is to eliminate duplicated access in the process of the derivation for obtaining the answer set for a given recursive query.

Semi-Naive Evaluation [2], *Blocked Warshall and Blocked Wallen* [1], *Logarithmic Algorithm* [11], *Hybrid Algorithm* [10], *Depth First Transitive Closure Algorithms* [9], et al. are well known as efficient algorithms for recursive unbound queries. The efficiency of these algorithms is achieved by reducing duplicate computations caused by cycles and/or irregular paths in the database graph. However, their performance is not stable due to different characteristics of the EDB relation[10] and to different storing structures of tuples into pages.

One way to stabilize their performance is to further optimize these algorithms using additional information, such as the information provided by the PAG. In this section, we will consider for simplicity an application of our PAG to Semi Naive Evaluation. Note that the idea proposed in the following is applicable to other BFS algorithms based on Semi Naive Evaluation. First of all, we shall give a brief description of Semi Naive Algorithm, which has a similar control structure to δ-Wavefront Algorithm.

Algorithm 5 Semi Naive Algorithm *[2].*

input *EDB relation* $P(X,Y)$.
IDB rules (1).
Query $?-A(X,Y)$.

output *Answer relation* $A(X,Y)$ *for the query.*

1. $A := P;\ \Delta A := P;$
2. **while** $\Delta A \neq \phi$ **do**
2.1 $\Delta A := \pi_{14}(\Delta A \bowtie_{2=3} P);\ \Delta A := \Delta A - A;$
2.2 $A := A \cup \Delta A;$
endwhile

■

Example 7 *Let us consider the query* $?-anc(X,Y)$ *for the rules and the EDB relation given in Example 2. Semi Naive Algorithm finds the answer set by the following steps:*

1. *Initialization (Read* $P_1,\ldots,P_3$*).*

$$\Delta A = \{(a,b),(b,c),(b,f),(c,d),(d,g),(e,g),(f,e),(f,h),(h,i)\}$$
$$A\ = \{(a,b),(b,c),(b,f),(c,d),(d,g),(e,g),(f,e),(f,h),(h,i)\}$$

2. *Read* $P_1,\ldots,P_3$

$\Delta A = \{(a,c),(a,f),(b,d),(b,e),(b,h),(c,g),(f,g),(f,i)\}$
$A \;= \{(a,b),(b,c),(b,f),(c,d),(d,g),(e,g),(f,e),(f,h),(h,i),(a,c)(a,f),(b,d),$
$(b,e),(b,h),(c,g),(f,g),(f,i)\}$

3. *Read* P_2, P_3
$\Delta A = \{(a,d),(a,e),(a,h),(b,g),(b,i)\}$
$A \;= \{(a,b),(b,c),(b,f),(c,d),(d,g),(e,g),(f,e),(f,h),(h,i),(a,c),(a,f),(b,d),$
$(b,e),(b,h),(c,g),(f,g),(f,i),(a,d),(a,e),(a,h),(b,g),(b,i)\}$

4. *Read* P_2, P_3
$\Delta A = \{(a,g),(a,i)\}$
$A \;= \{(a,b),(b,c),(b,f),(c,d),(d,g),(e,g),(f,e),(f,h),(h,i),(a,c),(a,f),(b,d),$
$(b,e),(b,h),(c,g),(f,g),(f,i),(a,d),(a,e),(a,h),(b,g),(b,i),(a,g),(a,i)\}$

In this example, if the buffer for EDP relation has the capacity of only one page, at least 7 pages are accessed in total. ∎

If the PAG for EDB relation P is sparse, i.e., it consists of sufficiently small number of arcs, then the page access level is possible by means of applying the discussion in the previous section to the whole of PAG. As the result, Theorem 1 is satisfied for the computation of all transitive closures in the PAG.

Corollary 1 *Let us consider the computation of all transitive closures P^+ for an EDB relation P. If the PAG for P is acyclic, then there exists an access scheduling which fetches each page P_i in P at most once.*

Proof: *From the definition of PAG and the numbering on the nodes, all the pages having non-zero join selectivity with the first attribute of P_i precede the node P_i on the PAG. Because of this fact and the discussion similar to the proof of Theorem 1, any page access schedule which fetches the pages in increasing order of node numbers never accesses a page twice.* ∎

By this corollary, we can compute the transitive closure according to the optimal page access schedule for the EDB relation under the assumption that the PAG is acyclic. For a general EDB relation for which the PAG is cyclic, it is difficult to guarantee the optimality of page access scheduling. However, in a way similar to that given in Algorithm 4; namely, numbering is done for each SCC of the CCPAG, we can obtain an algorithm applicable to cyclic PAGs.

Algorithm 6 Level Relaxed Semi Naive Method

input *EDB relation* $P(X,Y)$.
PAG for P *with SCCs* $V_1,\ldots,V_r$ *such that* $N(V_1) \leq \cdots \leq N(V_r)$.
IDB rules (1).
Query $?-A(X,Y)$.

output *Answer relation* $A(X,Y)$ *for the query.*

1. $A := \phi$;
2. **for** $i := 1$ **to** r **do**
2.1 **solve** (
$A_i(X,Y) :- V_i(X,Y).$
$A_i(X,Y) :- A_i(X,Z), V_i(Z,Y).$
);

2.2 **if** $\exists$succ(V_i) **then**
2.2.1a $\quad\quad \Delta A_i := A_i$;
2.2.2a $\quad\quad$ **for** $\forall k$ *such that* pred$(V_i) = V_k$ **do**
$\quad\quad\quad\quad \Delta A_i := \Delta A_i \cup \pi_{14}(\Delta A_k \bowtie_{2=3} A_i)$
$\quad\quad$ **endfor** ;
2.2.3a $\quad\quad \Delta A_i := \Delta A_i - A$;
2.2.4a $\quad\quad A := A \cup \Delta A_i$;
$\quad$ **else**
2.2.1b $\quad\quad A := A \cup A_i$;
2.2.2b $\quad\quad$ **for** $\forall k$ *such that* pred$(V_i) = V_k$ **do**
$\quad\quad\quad\quad A := A \cup \pi_{14}(\Delta A_k \bowtie_{2=3} A_i)$
$\quad\quad$ **endfor** ;
$\quad$ **endif** ;
endfor ;

Note: *This algorithm fetches each page at most once as long as Step 2.1 is processed on the main memory*[1]. ■

Example 8 *Let us consider the query evaluation in Example 7 again. The process of query evaluation by Level Relaxed Semi Naive Method is given as follows:*

1. *Fetch* P_1.

$$A_1 = \{(a,b),(b,c),(b,f),(a,c),(a,f)\}$$
$$\Delta A_1 = \{(a,b),(b,c),(b,f),(a,c),(a,f)\}$$
$$A = \{(a,b),(b,c),(b,f),(a,c),(a,f)\}$$

2. *Fetch* P_3.

$$A_3 = \{(f,e),(f,h),(h,i),(f,i)\}$$
$$\Delta A_3 = \{(f,e),(f,h),(h,i),(f,i),(b,e),(b,h),(b,i),(a,e),(a,h),(a,i)\}$$
$$A = \{(a,b),(b,c),(b,f),(a,c),(a,f),(f,e),(f,h),(h,i),(f,i),(b,e),(b,h),(b,i),(a,e),(a,h),(a,i)\}$$

3. *Fetch* P_2.

$$A_3 = \{(c,d),(d,g),(e,g),(c,g)\}$$
$$A = \{(a,b),(b,c),(b,f),(a,c),(a,f),(f,e),(f,h),(h,i),(f,i),(b,e),(b,h),(b,i),(a,e),(a,h),(a,i),(c,d),(d,g),(e,g),(c,g),(a,d),(b,d),(a,g),(b,g),(f,g)\}$$

In this example, irrespective of the maximum path length in the database graph, three pages in the EDB relation are fetched in total, and this is obviously the minimum as far as accessing to the EDB relation is concerned. As for the intermediate results, the total size of ΔA_i is slightly smaller than that of ΔA for the ordinary Semi Naive Algorithm, because our algorithm does not generate any intermediate result for the page having no successor. Consequently, it is conclusive that our algorithm outperforms the ordinary Semi Naive Algorithm on the assumption that the PAG is acyclic and each ΔA_i is processed in the main memory, or on the assumption that Step 2.1 of Algorithm 6 is processed in the main memory.

■

[1] This algorithm is applicable to the case where the PAG has cycles, though we can not guarantee that each page is fetched at most once by the algorithm.

Here, let us prove the correctness of Algorithm 6.

Lemma 1 *Let $V_1, \ldots, V_r$ be SCCs of the PAG for EDB relation P that satisfies $N(V_1) \leq \cdots \leq N(V_r)$. And let A_i be a relation defined by the following rules:*

$$A_i(X,Y) \quad :- \quad V_i(X,Y).$$
$$A_i(X,Y) \quad :- \quad A_i(X,Z), V_i(Z,Y).$$

Then, transitive closure A of relation P can be computed correctly by the following procedure:

$A := \phi$
for $i := 1$ **to** r **do**
  $\Delta A := A_i \cup \pi_{14}(A \bowtie_{2=3} A_i)$
  $A := A \cup \Delta A$
endfor

Proof: *Let us consider the induction on r. Assuming that the lemma holds for $r-1$, then A is correct transitive closure of the $P - V_r$, at the end of the $r-1$th iteration. Thus, if we compute*

$$\Delta A \quad := \quad A_r \cup \pi_{14}(A \bowtie_{2=3} A_r) \cup \pi_{14}(A_r \bowtie_{2=3} A)$$
$$A \quad := \quad A \cup \Delta A$$

at the rth iteration, then A becomes the correct transitive closure of relation P. Furthermore, the third term in the right-hand side of the expression for ΔA becomes empty, otherwise, V_r must have successor nodes, which contradicts the assumption $N(V_1) \leq \cdots \leq N(V_r)$. Thus the procedure indeed computes the correct transitive closure for relation P.

■

Theorem 2 *Algorithm 6 computes the correct transitive closure for EDB relation P.*
Proof: (Sketch) *From Lemma 1, it is only required to prove that each ΔA_i at the ith iteration is the sufficient and correct set. This is easily proved from the definition of PAG.*

■

The idea of Level Relaxation is applicable to the computation of transitive closure of each SCC in Step 2.1 in the following way; namely, starting the evaluation from a certain page, and employ the DFS at every new page, where no fixed point operation is required for the pages that have not been previously visited.

In closing this section, we would like to discuss how to execute Step 2.1 of Algorithm 6 in the main memory. Let m be the number of keys in SCC V_i, and B_{tuple} be the number of bytes necessary to store a tuple. Then the size of result A_i will be $m^2 B_{tuple}$ (bytes) in the worst case. Therefore, it is advantageous to handle this step by the adjacent matrix as compared with handing it by the tuple based algorithm. In case of adopting the matrix based algorithm, an index table is necessary for keeping the information on the mapping from a key to its corresponding column (row) in the matrix, whose size is $m(B_{tuple}/2+2)$ (bytes) if $m \leq 65535$. Also, the size of matrix becomes m^2 bytes even if each boolean variable is allocated in one byte area.

Example 9 *Let us compute the following T_{tuple} and T_{matrix} for several values of m.*

$$T_{tuple} \quad = \quad m^2 B_{tuple}$$

$$T_{matrix} \quad = \quad m(B_{tuple}/2+2)+m^2$$

m	T_{tuple}	T_{matrix}
10	10^4	620
100	10^6	15200
1000	10^8	1052000

In the above, B_{tuple} is assumed to be 100 bytes. From these numerical results, it becomes clear that Step 2.1 can be executed in the main memory as long as the number of nodes in each V_i is smaller than that of the PAG, and that extraordinary large capacity is required to compute transitive closures of the whole EDB relation P in the main memory even if matrix based algorithms are adopted. ∎

5 Improvement of Page Structure

The size of PAG and the performance of algorithms proposed in the previous section will obviously vary according to the *page structure of EDB*; namely, how to store tuples of relational files into pages. If the PAG becomes dense, the efficiency of the algorithm is deteriorated. The following two reasons are considered for a given PAG to become a dense graph.

First one is unclustered EDB relation file; namely, tuples $(q,r_1),\ldots,(q,r_k)$ are stored in different pages. In such case, multiple arcs are issued from node P_i which contains tuple (p,q), which results in a dense graph. We shall consider the above situation in more details. Let m be the number of tuples in a page, and n be the number of pages in a relation file. Reminding that m is a constant value determined by the number of bytes for a page as well as that for a tuple, we can assume without loss of generality that $m<n$. In the PAG for unclustered file, the number of arcs starting from a page is $\min(n-1,m(n-1))=n-1$ in the worst case, therefore, the total number of arcs in PAG is $n(n-1)$. On the other hand, if the file is clustered, and tuples with the same key with respect to their first (or second) attributes are stored in the same page, then the number of arcs starting from a page is $\min(n-1,m)=m$. Thus the total number of arcs in the PAG is mn, i.e., linear with respect to the number of pages.

Example 10 *Let us consider the two logically equivalent EDBs with $n=6$ and $m=2$ illustrated in Figure 3, where* (a) *is not clustered and* (b) *is clustered. The number of arcs in the PAG for* (a) *is 24, while that for* (b) *is 12(= mn).* ∎

The second reason for dense PAGs is paths in the database graph which traverse multiple pages. Such a path causes not only an increase of the number of arcs in the PAG but also an increase of SCCs in the PAG. It is difficult to exclude a priori such paths traversing multiple pages completely, and it may take almost the same cost as that for computing the entire transitive closures.

Example 11 *The number of arcs in the PAG for the EDB* (a) *in Figure 4 is 2, while that for* (b) *is 0. The arcs in the PAG for* (a) *are caused by paths $a\rightarrow d\rightarrow e$ and $b\rightarrow c\rightarrow f$, both of which are stored over two pages.* ∎

A dense PAG may cause access to some pages of EDB more than once, along with the increase of cost for processing the PAG itself. It is required to eliminate cycles in PAG

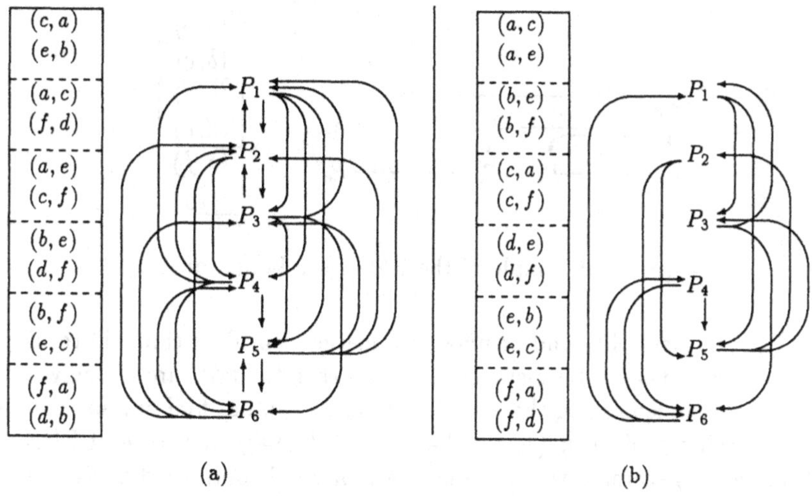

Figure 3: Clustering of EDB relation for realizing better PAG.

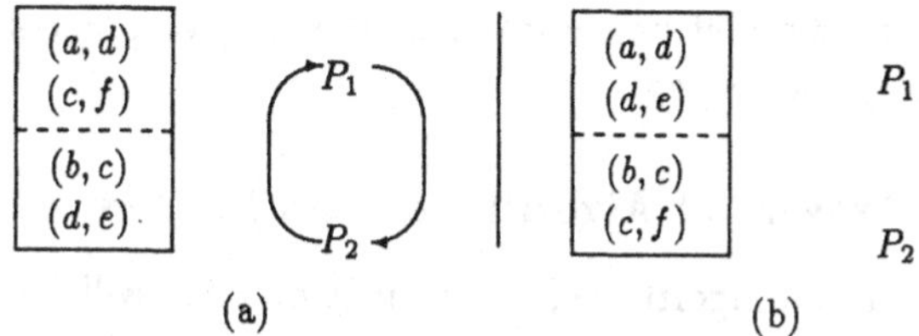

Figure 4: Paths traversing multiple pages.

and reduce the degree of each node for attaining the optimal access schedule to the EDB file. Nevertheless, for realizing a PAG with good property, the higher cost is necessary for sorting the EDB file. Consequently, the optimization level for the page structure depends on the characteristics of EDB as well as the ratio of update requests to query requests among access operations in the system.

6 Performance Comparison

According to the discussions in Section 4, the relative superiority of algorithms is expected to be:

Level Relaxed δ-Wavefront Algorithm without PAG
$\geq$ Level Relaxed δ-Wavefront Algorithm with PAG

for bound query evaluation algorithms, and

Semi Naive Algorithm
$\geq$ Level Relaxed Semi Naive Algorithm with PAG

for unbound query evaluation algorithms, where $A \geq B$ indicates that B outperforms A. However, any quantitative performance comparison is considered to be difficult for such an optimization technique employed in this paper, as was mentioned in [7][10].

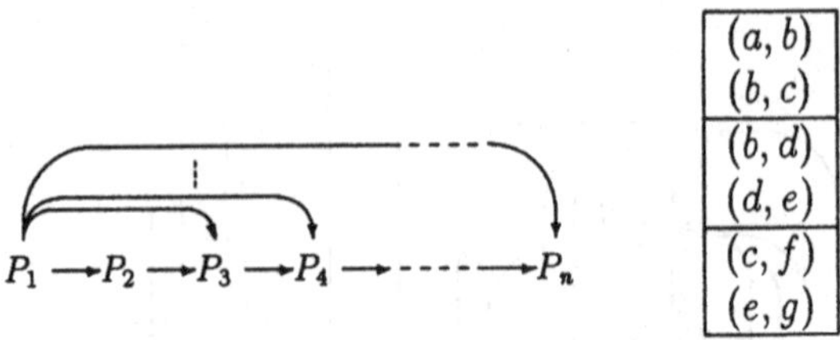

Figure 5: Example of the PAG for a bound query.

Especially, regardless of bound or unbound queries, our algorithm will result in overhead for some unsound cases, for instance, all of nodes in the PAG are strongly connected. In such a case, for implementing the actual system, we can not find out any good suggestion on the following problems: (1) to what extent the page structure of EDB must be optimized, (2) more generally, whether query evaluation is optimized using the information from the PAG or not.

Considering the above difficulty for performance evaluation, in the following, we will employ a typical example by which we can easily find the advantage of using the PAG for simplicity of discussion. Here let us assume that the cost for processing PAG is much smaller than that for query processing.

6.1 Level Relaxed δ-Wavefront Algorithms: with PAG vs. without PAG

As for bound query evaluation algorithms, the benefit of PAG will be clear in the case that $CCPAG = (V_c, E_c)$ is given by:

$$
\begin{aligned}
V_c &= \{P_1, P_2, \ldots, P_n\} & \\
E_c &\ni (P_{i-1}, P_i) & (2 \leq i \leq n) \\
E_c &\ni (P_1, P_i) & (3 \leq i \leq n)
\end{aligned}
$$

The numbering for the nodes in V_c is given by $N(P_i) = i$. Let us assume that all of arcs in E_c are related to the answer, and that answer values obtained from different paths are different (see Figure 5).

Considering that the cost of processing the intermediate results as well as the answer set does not depend on the access schedule, we will only take care of the cost for fetching EDB.

The best access schedule for given CCPAG is $P_1 \rightarrow P_2 \rightarrow \cdots \rightarrow P_n$, where the total number of fetched pages is n. On the contrary, the worst scheduling is $P_1 \rightarrow P_n \rightarrow P_{n-1} \rightarrow P_n \rightarrow P_{n-2} \rightarrow P_{n-1} \rightarrow P_n \cdots P_2 \rightarrow P_3 \rightarrow \cdots \rightarrow P_n$, where the total number of fetched pages is $(1 + n(n-1)/2)$ if the buffer has the only one page capacity in the main memory. Consequently, the number of pages fetched in the execution of ordinary Level Relaxed δ-Wavefront algorithm varies from n to $(1 + n(n-1)/2)$, while our proposed algorithm always fetches n pages in total.

$$P_1 \rightarrow P_2 \rightarrow P_3 \rightarrow P_4 \rightarrow \cdots \rightarrow P_n$$

Figure 6: Example of the PAG for an unbound query.

6.2 Semi Naive Algorithms without PAG vs. Level Relaxed Semi Naive Algorithms with PAG

We shall compare Level Relaxed Semi Naive algorithm with the ordinary Semi Naive Evaluation. Under the assumption that each A_i of Level Relaxed Algorithm is computed in the main memory, it is reasonable to compare the size of ΔA_i in Level Relaxed Method with that of ΔA in Semi Naive Evaluation, as far as intermediate results concern. According to the discussion of Example 8, the following relationship is satisfied.

$$\begin{array}{l} \bigcup \Delta A_i \text{ in Level Relaxed Algorithm} \\ \subseteq \bigcup \Delta A \text{ in each iteration of Semi Naive} \end{array}$$

Therefore, we can consider that the cost of processing intermediate results and the answer set through Level Relaxed Algorithm is not greater than that of Semi Naive Evaluation.

Now let us focus on the cost of fetching EDB relation again. As an example which is simple but may give a remarkable performance difference between the two algorithms, we consider the following $PAG = (V, E)$ (see Figure 6):

$$\begin{array}{lcll} V & = & \{P_1, P_2, \ldots, P_n\} & \\ E & \ni & (P_{i-1}, P_i) & \qquad (2 \leq i \leq n). \end{array}$$

As for Semi Naive Evaluation, the number of iteration depends on the maximum path length h in the database graph. Thus the total number of pages fetched by Semi Naive Algorithm is estimated as $(h+1)n$ (note that this value varies depending on the implemented join algorithm). On the other hand, our algorithm fetches n pages in total for given EDB relation. By such evaluation, we can recognize the benefits of PAG.

7 Conclusion

In this paper, for a typical recursive query evaluation problem; namely, the transitive closure computation in deductive databases, we have proposed algorithms that minimize the number of pages accessed in the EDB. The page access graph (PAG) was proposed, which represents the existence of join selectivity among pages and plays a key role to find efficient page access scheduling algorithms. In a special case that the page access graph is acyclic, we showed that our proposed algorithm became the optimal page access schedule.

As the results of this paper, the proposed algorithms much contribute to the performance improvement of recursive query evaluation strategies on condition that the whole or a part of the page access graph can be stored in the main memory. In view of this fact, by implementing our algorithms on deductive database machines on the hardware level, the processing speed of recursive queries will be considerably improved.

Finally, as several of future research topics, we shall list up the followings:

1. For simplicity, we did not deal with the processing of SCCs in PAG. The detailed description of algorithm to handle SCC is important to obtain the strategy with fairly good performance.
2. Investigation of the efficient sorting algorithm for realizing a more useful PAG is practically important.
3. Application of the notion of PAG to the join algorithm is interesting, and it is considered that the algorithm will be similar to the hash-based algorithm.

References

[1] R.Agrawal and H.V.Jagadish, "Direct Transitive Closure Algorithms: Design and Performance Evaluation", *Technical Memorandum, AT&T Bell Laboratories,* Murray Hill, New Jersey, 1987.

[2] F.Bancilhon, "Naive Evaluation of Recursively Defined Relations", *On Knowledge-base Management Systems (M.Brodie and J.Mylopoulos eds.),* Springer-Verlag, New York, 1986, pp.165-178.

[3] F.Bancilhon, D.Maier, Y.Sagiv and J.Ullman, "Magic Set and Other Strange Ways to Implement Logic Programs", *Proc. 5th ACM SIGMOD-SIGACT Symposium on Principles of Database Systems,* Cambridge, Massachusetts, 1986, pp.1-15.

[4] F.Bancilhon and R.Ramakrishnan, "An Amateur's Introduction to Recursive Query Processing Strategies", *Proc. ACM-SIGMOD Int'l Conf. on Management of Data,* Washington D.C., 1986, pp.16-52.

[5] J.Han and L.J.Henschen, "Processing Linear Recursive Database Queries by Level and Cycle Marging", *Tech. Rep. 87-05-DBM-01,* North Western Univ., Chicago, 1987.

[6] J.Han and L.J.Henschen, "Handling Redundancy in the Processing of Database Queries", *Proc. of ACM SIGMOD Int'l Conf. on Management of Data,* San Francisco, California, 1987, pp.73-81.

[7] J.Han, G.Qadah and C.Chaou, "The Processing and Evaluation of Transitive Closure Queries", *LCCR Tech. Rep. 88-1,* Simon Fraser Univ., Canada, 1988.

[8] L.J.Henschen and S.Naqvi, "On Compiling Queries in Recursive First-Order Databases", *J.ACM, 31(1),* 1984, pp.47-85.

[9] Y.E.Ioannidis and R.Ramakrishnan, "Efficient Transitive Closure Algorithms", *Proc. 14th Int'l Conf. Very Large Data Bases,* Los Angels, California, 1988, pp.382-394.

[10] H.Lu, "New Strategies for Computing the Transitive Closure of Database Relation", *Proc. 13th Int'l Conf. on Very Large Data Bases,* Brighton, England, 1987, pp.255-266.

[11] P.Valduriez and H.Boral, "Evaluation of Recursive Queries Using Join Indices", *Proc. the 1st Int'l Conf. on Expert Database Systems,* Charleston, South Carolina, 1986, pp.197-208.

[12] P.Valduriez, "Join Indices", *ACM Transactions on Database Systems, 12(2),* 1987, pp.218-246.

Abstract Machine for $\mathcal{LDL}$

Danette Chimenti Ruben Gamboa Ravi Krishnamurthy
MCC, 3500 West Balcones Center Drive, Austin, Texas 78759
danette@mcc.com,ruben@mcc.com,ravi@mcc.com

Abstract

We propose an abstract machine for $\mathcal{LDL}$ that maintains a high-level view of an $\mathcal{LDL}$ program while incorporating aspects of its execution that make a performance difference. A canonical AND/OR graph corresponding to the $\mathcal{LDL}$ program provides the skeleton of its execution. The nodes in the AND/OR graph are annotated to specify relevant details of the execution, such as access methods, join methods, execution strategies, intelligent backtracking etc. We formalize four execution methods (top-down, bottom-up as well as two hybrid methods that incorporate memoing) and two recursive computations (fixpoint and stack-based). The two computations and four execution methods are combined to cater to a rich variety of recursive techniques. This annotated AND/OR graph represents a declarative program for the abstract machine. The set of all possible annotated AND/OR graphs constitutes the execution space that defines the abstract machine.

To prove the feasibility of this declarative abstract machine, we demonstrate an actual realization by presenting a code generation algorithm that proceeds by translating each node in the annotated AND/OR graph into a sequence of imperative statements that include calls to a tuple-level interface of an underlying DBMS. The $\mathcal{LDL}$ compiler — which supports Datalog, sets, updates, negation, non-deterministic choice and other advanced features — has been implemented using this approach.

1 Introduction

The Logic Data Language, $\mathcal{LDL}$, is a declarative language for data-intensive and knowledge-based applications built upon the experience of both the relational database and logic programming communities [NT89]. The user need only supply the declarative program and the compiler is expected to devise an efficient execution strategy. In order to provide efficient executions for $\mathcal{LDL}$ programs, the compiler must be capable of reasoning about the program at a high level while still retaining knowledge of the underlying system.

In the context of relational programs, join, selection and projection methods together with join ordering provides such a framework. In a sense, the join, selection, and projection methods are instructions in an abstract relational machine. A composition of these instructions that encodes the join ordering constitutes an imperative program to the abstract machine. The program can be viewed as a model of an actual execution, representing the important run-time aspects affecting performance in the underlying system.

Abstract machines have been proposed for logic programming (e.g., the WAM, [Wa83]) by enumerating the instruction set. However, these abstract machines were never intended to provide the same level of abstraction as in the relational approach. Consequently, they do not directly provide a framework to exploit techniques proven successful in database technology, such as effective use of compilation (optimization), use of bottom-up as well as top-down executions, and independence of data through a tuple level interface.

We propose an abstract machine for $\mathcal{LDL}$ that is in the spirit of the relational abstract machine, that is, it incorporates aspects that make a performance difference in execution, while maintaining a high-level of abstraction. We formalize the abstract machine, not by enumerating the instruction set, but by declaring the execution space — the set of all executions that are allowed by the machine. This is achieved by modeling an execution as follows. A canonical AND/OR graph corresponding to an $\mathcal{LDL}$ program provides the skeleton of the execution. Then, the nodes in the AND/OR graph are annotated to specify relevant details of the execution, such as access methods, join methods, execution strategies, etc. This annotated AND/OR graph represents a program for the abstract machine (i.e., an execution model). The set of all possible annotated AND/OR graphs constitutes the execution space that defines the abstract machine.

One of the major contributions of this approach is to present four distinct execution methods — top-down, bottom-up as well as two hybrid methods that incorporate memoing [Mi68] and to demonstrate the usefulness of each. Further, two recursive computations are formalized: the fixpoint (e.g., semi-naive, [Ba85]) and stack-based (e.g., Prolog). These two computations and the four execution methods are combined to cater to a rich variety of recursive techniques ranging from bottom-up using magic sets [B*86] to query-subquery using memoing [Vi89] and pure top-down. All these methods are given as declarative annotations to the AND/OR graph. Even though the execution model is proposed in a declarative paradigm, procedural aspects such as intelligent backtracking are also incorporated. To prove the feasibility of this declarative approach, we demonstrate an actual realization by presenting the code generation algorithm used in the $\mathcal{LDL}$ compiler. The algorithm proceeds by translating each node in the annotated AND/OR graph into a sequence of imperative statements that include calls to a tuple-level interface of an underlying DBMS.

The $\mathcal{LDL}$ compiler has been implemented using this abstract machine not only for Datalog, but also to support advanced language features such as sets, updates, negation and non-deterministic choice. In this paper, however, we restrict our attention to Datalog. We develop the abstract machine for Datalog in two steps: first, for nonrecursive Datalog and then for complete Datalog. The treatise for nonrecursive Datalog is sufficiently encompassing that the recursive case is shown as a natural extension. Thus, the majority of the paper details the nonrecursive case.

2 Definitions

We assume the reader is familiar with Datalog and the associated semantics, as well as definitions for rule, base/derived predicate, predicate occurrence, and mutual recursion. Throughout this paper, we follow the notational convention that p_i's and b_i's are predicates and base predicates, respectively. We define a *clique* to be a maximal set of mutually recursive predicates.

A query with marked bound/unbound arguments (binding pattern) will be called a *query form*. Throughout this paper we use capital letters to denote variables and the lower case letter c to denote a constant. Thus, $p1(c, Y)$? is a query form with the first argument bound and the second unbound. In a departure from previous approaches to compilation of logic, we make our compilation specific to a given query form. For instance, the query form, $p1(X, Y)$?, will be compiled and optimized separately from $p1(c, Y)$?.

In general, given a query form and, for each rule, a specific permutation of the literals in the body, we can define the notion of a binding pattern for any predicate, using sideways information passing (SIP) as defined in [Ull85]. Each argument of the predicate can be either bound, free, or existential. A variable, say X, appearing in a given argument is *bound* if it is instantiated to a particular constant value at runtime. X is *free* if the current predicate occurrence will instantiate it at run-time. Finally, it is *existential* if it does not appear elsewhere in the rule, except possibly in the head as an existential argument. We can construct an *adorned program,* where every argument of each predicate is marked as either b (bound), f (free), or e (existential) [Ull89,RBK88]. Note that for a given query form and permutation of the literals in each rule, there is a unique adornment for the program.

3 Non-Recursive Datalog

In this section we develop an abstract machine for non-recursive Datalog (NRD) programs in a declarative fashion. First, we represent the skeleton of the execution by a canonical AND/OR graph, where each OR node represents a predicate occurrence and each AND node represents the head of a rule [Nil80]. Then, we superimpose a set of annotations on the AND/OR nodes which are used to specify the details of the execution, while still retaining the declarative nature of the program. The purpose of the annotated AND/OR graph is to represent those aspects of the execution that can make a performance difference.

Obviously, there are many annotated AND/OR graphs for a given program, all of which can faithfully model the bottom-up semantics of the original NRD program. We define the execution space to be the set of all such faithful executions and use this execution space to define the abstract machine. Any implementation that is capable of computing all the executions in the execution space is a valid implementation of the abstract machine. In order to show that such an implementation exists, we outline the code generation algorithm used in the $\mathcal{LDL}$ compiler.

3.1 Non-recursive Execution Structure

We can view an NRD program as an AND/OR graph [Nil80]. We first make the assumption that the graph is a tree, possibly by replicating some rules in the program. This assumption is relaxed in section 3.8. As the AND/OR tree and the program have a one-to-one correspondence, we use these terms interchangeably.

In keeping with our relational algebra execution model, we map each AND node into a join and each OR node into a union. Strictly speaking, the relational join operator is binary and a rule containing more than two literals is computed by a sequence of joins. As the order of joins will reflect on the efficiency of the execution, we define a normal form, called *Chomsky Normal Form* or *CNF* of the program. The CNF program has at most two literals in the body of any rule, which we order left-to-right. It is obvious that such an equivalent program exists. The AND/OR tree corresponding to the CNF program, called the *execution structure*, forms the skeleton of the final execution.

All variables in the program are assumed to have global scope. That is, when the program is viewed as a logical formula, there is only one (existential or universal) quantifier for each variable. The $\mathcal{LDL}$ compiler achieves this requirement by renaming as few variables as possible.

3.2 Execution Method Annotations

In this subsection we present four execution methods that capture the notions of bottom-up and top-down, as well as two hybrid executions that incorporate memoing [Mi68]. We also delineate advantages and disadvantages of each method, in order to show that all of these methods are important in the execution model. Each predicate occurrence (i.e., OR node) is annotated with an execution method.

Let $p(\ldots)$ be the query with the following rule, where $p1$ and $p2$ are derived predicates:

$$p(X,Y) \leftarrow p1(X,Z), p2(Z,Y).$$

The four execution methods are described using $p2$ as an example.

Pipelined Execution chooses a tuple for $p1$ which instantiates a value for the variable Z. Only tuples having this Z-value in $p2$ are computed *one tuple at a time* to get the tuples for p.

Lazy Pipelined Execution is a pipelined execution in which, as the tuples are generated for $p2$, they are stored in a temporary relation, say $rp2$, for subsequent use. For each tuple in $p1$, $rp2$ is checked to see if the corresponding tuples in $p2$ have already been computed. If so, the tuples are read from $rp2$ as if it were a base relation; otherwise, the tuples are computed one at a time, as in the pipelined execution. As the set of tuples computed for a given value for the bound arguments, i.e., Z-value, can be incomplete due to intelligent backtracking (see section 3.6), a *done* indicator is associated with each Z-value to denote the completion of the computation. This also allows for the efficient reuse of *negative information* in the case that no tuple in $p2$ has this Z-value.

Lazy Materialized Execution proceeds as in the lazy pipelined case except that, for a given Z-value, all tuples in $p2$ having that Z-value are computed and stored in $rp2$ before proceeding. The *done* indicator is also used in this case to allow the reuse of negative information.

Materialized Execution computes *all* tuples in $p2$ and stores them in the relation $rp2$. Then, the computation proceeds, using the tuples from $rp2$.

Note that the above discussion can be generalized to any OR node with a (possibly empty) set of bound arguments. We refer to the above executions using the acronyms P, LP, LM and M, respectively. Their relative advantages (+) and disadvantages (−) are summarized in the following table:

	P	LP	LM	M
Amortized Work	−	+	+	+
Superfluous Work	+	+	+	−
Backtrackable	+	+	−	−
Reentrant	−	−	+	+
Space Required	++	−	−	−−

Amortized Work: The materialized (as well as LM and LP) execution computes a tuple, in $p2$ exactly once and uses it as many times as needed to join with tuples from $p1$, whereas the pipelined execution must recompute the tuple each time. This savings is termed *amortized work*.

Superfluous Work: A tuple, may be computed for $p2$ that is never used to join with any tuple in $p1$. This is referred to as *superfluous work*. The pipelined (as well as LP and LM) execution avoids this by using the SIP property, which specifies that $p2$ tuples are computed for a given value of Z. The materialized execution, however, computes all $p2$ tuples and, hence, may perform superfluous work.

Backtrackable: The ability to compute the tuples of $p2$ one tuple at a time (as in P and LP) has the advantage that if the binding from $p1$ does not join with other predicates to produce an answer, the computation for other tuples of $p2$ with the same Z-value can be avoided. This advantage is called *backtrackable advantage*. The lazy materialized (and M) execution computes all the tuples for a Z-value and is not capable of avoiding such useless computations.

Reentrant: If a predicate is used in more than one rule, the code generated for it may be shared in both occurrences. Conceptually, this can be done if the code generated is *reentrant*. In the case of pipelined (and LP) execution, the state of the computation is needed to get the next tuple on backtracking. Therefore, in order to make the code reentrant, the state needs to be managed, resulting in some run-time overhead. The materialized (and LM) execution, however, completes the computation of a predicate before proceeding, allowing multiple occurrences to share the materialized relation.

Space Required: The pipelined execution has the least space requirement, whereas the materialized execution has the most. The lazy executions can be better than the materialized one if there are lots of superfluous tuples, but are not better in the worst case.

In conclusion, the pipelined execution is useful if the joining column is a key for *p*1, whereas the materialized execution is the best if all the Z-values of *p*2 are joined with some *p*1 tuple. Note that in both of these cases, the respective lazy evaluation incurs more overhead due to the checking that is needed for each *p*1 tuple as well as the *done* indicator that must be maintained. The reentrant property is especially useful if the predicate is in the scope of a recursive query that is being computed top-down. In such cases, LM is preferred over LP. LP is preferable, otherwise, to exploit the backtrackable property.

Interestingly, many researchers assume the computation of a logic program with bottom-up semantics (e.g., $\mathcal{LDL}$) is necessarily computed bottom-up. In $\mathcal{LDL}$, the resulting execution need not be bottom-up. It is usually some combination of top-down and bottom-up. In fact, for NRD programs, the execution is almost always top-down.

3.3 Dataflow Annotations

In this section, we introduce the concept of *dataflow points* to a CNF program. Each node of the corresponding AND/OR tree has dataflow points, which represent different states of computation in the node.[1] These points are connected by *dataflow destinations*[2]. The dataflow points and destinations together describe how tuples are combined to produce an answer to a query.

The dataflow points associated with each node of the AND/OR tree and their corresponding state are given in the following table:

DF Pt.	Computation State
entry	getting first tuple of node
backtrack	getting next tuple of node
success	a tuple has been generated
fail	no more tuples can be generated

A dataflow point of one node can be directed to a dataflow point of a different node by a dataflow destination. The *entry destination (e_dest)* of a given node is the dataflow point to which its entry point is directed. Similarly, *backtrack (b_dest), success (s_dest),* and *fail destinations (f_dest)* can be defined. The dataflow destinations represent logical operations between the nodes involved; for example, a join of the two nodes.

The dataflow points and destinations of a node describe how the tuples of that node are combined with tuples from other nodes, not how these tuples are generated in the first place. That is, they describe the dataflow of the program, without assuming an execution method (i.e., P, LP, LM or M). In the following description, we use the intuition of a pipelined execution. However, we emphasize that neither the dataflow points nor the destinations are changed for a different execution method.

Figures 1 and 2 show the dataflow points and destinations of a typical OR node and AND node, respectively. In a CNF program, each rule has at most two OR nodes, which are ordered left-to-right, so as to define first and second node. We arbitrarily order the AND node successors of a given OR node, so that the notions of first, next, and last AND node are also defined.

Intuitively, to get the first tuple from an OR node, we get the first tuple from its first successor AND node. To get the next tuple, we get the next tuple from the AND node that generated the previous tuple. Note that the currently "active" AND node must be determined at run-time. Clearly, when a tuple is generated by any AND node, we get a tuple for the OR node. When no more tuples can be generated for a given AND node, we try to generate tuples from the next AND node, until the last such node is reached. At this point, no more tuples can be generated for the OR node.

The execution of an AND node is conceptually less complicated. Intuitively, the execution corresponds to a nested loop, where, for each tuple of the first OR node, we generate all matching tuples from the

[1] The dataflow points are analogous to the ports in Byrd's Prolog execution model [By80].

[2] referred to in the literature as continuations [Wa71].

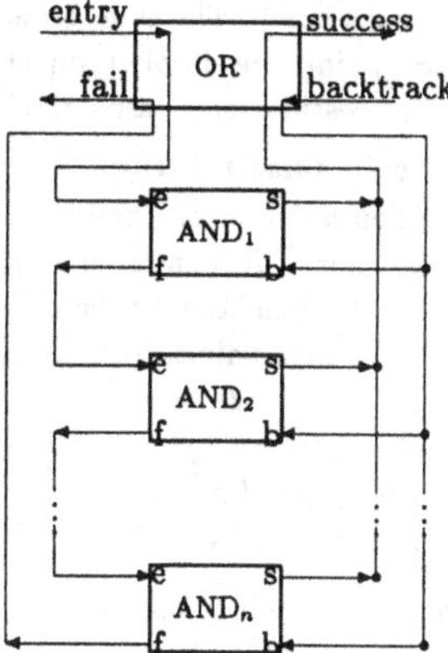

Figure 1: Dataflow Annotations for OR Node

second OR node. Thus, when generating the next tuple of an AND node, we generate the next matching tuple from the second OR node. If there are no more matching tuples, we generate the next tuple from the first OR node. When there are no more tuples for this OR node, we can generate no more tuples for the AND node.

The execution described above is nicely captured by the following list of destination annotations:[3]

- **OR node:**
  - *e_dest:* entry point of first AND successor
  - *b_dest:* backtrack point of "active" AND succ.
  - *f_dest:* if node is first OR node in a rule then fail point of parent AND node else backtrack pnt of previous OR node
  - *s_dest:* if node is last OR node in a rule then success point of parent AND node else entry point of next OR node
- **AND node:**
  - *e_dest:* entry point of first OR successor
  - *b_dest:* backtrack point of last OR successor
  - *f_dest:* if node is last AND successor then fail point of parent OR node else entry point of next AND node
  - *s_dest:* success point of parent OR node

3.4 Code Generation

So far, we have provided a model for the execution of an NRD program by describing an adorned CNF program that is annotated with execution methods and dataflow destinations. The annotated CNF program is a declarative representation of the final execution. In this section, we turn to an operational view in order to provide the rationale for the particular model chosen, as well as to provide a conceptual view of an actual execution. We show how a CNF program can be compiled into an imperative language by demonstrating that procedural code can be generated which, in fact, reflects all the declarative notions that have been described and is faithful to the dataflow paradigm. We also demonstrate that the annotated CNF program encodes all the information necessary to generate code locally with respect to each node in our execution structure and, thus, allows for a simple, elegant, recursive algorithm to generate efficient run-time code.

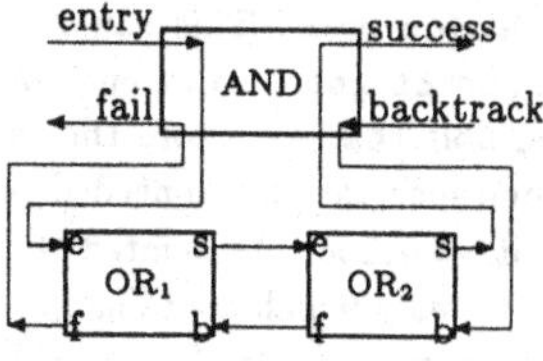

Figure 2: Dataflow Annotations for AND Nodes

We will first outline the conventions necessary to map an annotated CNF program into procedural code. Then we describe the code generation for a pipelined execution, followed by the changes necessary to realize lazy pipelined, lazy materialized and materialized executions.

3.4.1 Conventions:

The specific target language of the compiler is largely irrelevant; we assume only that it have `goto` and `indirect goto` statements, as well as other procedural and data representation capabilities available in most imperative programming languages.[4]

A dataflow point of a node corresponds to a label in the compiled program. This label can be chosen with a simple naming convention; for example, *node_e* and *node_s* are the entry and success points of *node*. The *node* portion of the label can be constructed by combining the predicate name and some unique identifier.[5] Thus, the entry point of an AND node for predicate *p* may be called p_and_31_e, where and_31 is the unique identifier for the AND node. Dataflow destinations can be implemented as simple `goto` statements that jump to the specified dataflow point. However, recall that in the case of an OR node, it is necessary to alter the backtrack

[3] Note that for a base relation, the entry and backtrack destinations are not used and, thus, need not be defined.

[4] Our implementation compiles into *C*, substituting a `switch` statement for the non-existent *C* `indirect goto`.

[5] The unique identifier is necessary because there may be multiple occurrences of the predicate.

destination at run-time. This can be achieved by using an `indirect goto` statement. We need only choose a variable that will store the indirect label. Since only one such variable is needed per OR node, we can call it *node*_loc. Associated with each node is a *node table* entry which contains information relevant to that node. The *node*_loc to be used by a particular node may be stored in the node table entry for that node. Other information stored in the node table will be discussed in the context of recursive Datalog.

Variables in the CNF program are mapped into variables in the compiled program using a simple approach — for example, `X` can be compiled into `var_X`. Recall that all variables in a CNF program have global scope. Thus, this simple naming scheme avoids name conflicts. Moreover, it conveys the global dataflow of the program in a localized manner, since the node assigning `var_X` does not need to be aware of the node that uses this variable in order to store a value. One advantage of our approach is that all variables to be used in the program are known at compile-time, and, hence, space for them can be allocated statically.

Finally, we assume a tuple-level interface to the database. This is achieved through a set of library routines, such as `open_cursor`, `get_tuple`, `create_index`, etc.

3.4.2 Pipelined Execution: We can completely describe the code generation for the pipelined execution of an NRD program by outlining the code that is generated at each of the four dataflow points for a base relation and a derived relation. For a base relation, we need only outline the code for an OR node, while in the case of the derived relation, we outline the code for both an OR node and an AND node.

The code generated at the entry point for a base relation must first initialize a cursor (pointer) on the base relation and then get a tuple from the relation. The code must continue getting tuples until one is found that matches all arguments adorned as bound for this OR node. After obtaining a valid tuple, any arguments which are adorned as free are assigned values from the tuple and a jump to the success point for this node is executed.[6] If no valid tuples are found, then a jump to the fail point for this node is executed. The code to actually get a tuple from the relation is also needed at the backtrack point. Hence, the entry point simply opens the cursor and then falls into the backtrack point. The code generated for the fail and success points are simply jumps to the node's fail and success destinations, respectively.

- **OR node — base relation:**

```
node_e: open a cursor on the base relation
node_b: get next tuple satisfying all bnd args
        if a tuple is found then
            assign values to free arguments
            goto node_s
        else goto node_f
node_f: goto f_dest for node
node_s: goto s_dest for node
```

At each dataflow point for both a derived relation OR node and an AND node, the code generated is simply a jump to the label for that dataflow destination. The only exception occurs at the backtrack point of the OR node. Here the jump is an indirect jump through the node's backtrack location variable, *node*_loc, as described in section 3.3. This variable is set at run-time at the entry points for each AND node successor to the OR node so that the rule which generated the last tuple will become the backtrack destination for the OR node. Note that each AND node successor must have access to the name of the parent's backtrack location variable. The node table can be used to obtain this information.

- **OR node — derived relation:**

```
node_e: goto e_dest for node
node_b: goto node_loc; i.e., indirect
node_f: goto f_dest for node
node_s: goto s_dest for node
```

- **AND node:**

```
node_e: set parent_node_loc to be node_b
        goto e_dest for node
node_b: goto b_dest for node
node_f: goto f_dest for node
node_s: goto s_dest for node
```

Figure 3 shows an annotated CNF program, the node table and the corresponding code that is generated for the program. We assume an adornment of `bf` for `p1`. In the annotated CNF program, AD is the adornment and LABEL is the unique identifier. The remaining annotations are the dataflow destinations. Note that the execution method has been omitted from the annotations since we are pipelining all OR nodes.

3.4.3 Lazy Pipelined Execution: The lazy pipelined execution is useful only for derived relations and, thus, only changes to the code generated for a derived OR node and AND node need to be discussed. Furthermore, we can localize all necessary

[6] Note that arguments marked as existential in the adornment are not assigned from the tuple.

Annotated CNF

	AD	LABEL	E_DEST	B_DEST	F_DEST	S_DEST
p1(X,Z) <-	bf	p1_and_1	p2_or_2_e	b1_or_7_b	*parent_f*	*parent_s*
p2(X,Y),	bf	p2_or_2	p2_and_3_e	p2_or_2_loc	p1_and_1_f	b1_or_7_e
b1(Y,Z).	bf	b1_or_7	—	—	p2_or_2_b	p1_and_1_s
p2(X,Y) <-	bf	p2_and_3	b2_or_4_e	b2_or_4_b	p2_and_5_e	p2_or_2_s
b2(X,Y).	bf	b2_or_4	—	—	p2_and_3_f	p2_and_3_s
p2(X,Y) <-	bf	p2_and_5	b3_or_6_e	b3_or_6_b	p2_or_2_f	p2_or_2_s
b3(X,Y).	bf	b3_or_6	—	—	p2_and_5_f	p2_and_5_s

Node Table

NODE	LOC
p2_and_3	p2_or_2_loc
p2_and_5	p2_or_2_loc

Generated Code

```
p1_and_1_e: goto p2_or_2_e
p1_and_1_b: goto b1_or_7_b
p1_and_1_f: goto parent_f
p1_and_1_s: goto parent_s

p2_or_2_e:  goto p2_and_3_e
p2_or_2_b:  indirect goto p2_or_2_loc
p2_or_2_f:  goto p1_and_1_f
p2_or_2_s:  goto b1_or_7_e

p2_and_3_e: set p2_or_2_loc = p2_and_3_b
            goto b2_or_4_e
p2_and_3_b: goto b2_or_4_b
p2_and_3_f: goto p2_and_5_e
p2_and_5_s: goto p2_or_2_s

b2_or_4_e:  open a cursor on b2
b2_or_4_b:  get next tuple with 1st arg = X
            if a tuple is found then
                    assign Y
                    goto b2_or_4_s
            else    goto b2_or_4_f
b2_or_4_f:  goto p2_and_3_f
b2_or_4_s:  goto p2_and_3_s

p2_and_5_e: set p2_or_2_loc = p2_and_5_b
            goto b3_or_6_e
p2_and_5_b: goto b3_or_6_b
p2_and_5_f: goto p2_or_2_f
p2_and_5_s: goto p2_or_2_s

b3_or_6_e:  open a cursor on b3
b3_or_6_b:  get next tuple with 1st arg = X
            if a tuple is found then
                    assign Y
                    goto b3_or_6_s
            else    goto b3_or_6_f
b3_or_6_f:  goto p2_and_5_f
b3_or_6_s:  goto p2_and_5_s

b1_or_7_e:  open a cursor on b1
b1_or_7_b:  get next tuple with 1st arg = Y
            if a tuple is found then
                    assign Z
                    goto b1_or_7_s
            else    goto b1_or_7_f
b1_or_7_f:  goto p2_or_2_b
b1_or_7_s:  goto p1_and_1_s
```

Figure 3: Annotated CNF, Node Table and Generated Code

changes to the OR node and keep the same code for the AND node as shown in section 3.4.2.

In order to generate code for a lazy pipelined execution, a temporary relation (referred to below as the materialized relation) must be used to store and access tuples. In addition, we need to introduce a secondary relation to store a *done* indicator for each binding pattern that has been completely materialized, i.e., all possible tuples with this binding pattern have been computed and stored.

The code at the entry point for the OR node checks to see if the *done* indicator exists for the given bound arguments. If so, a state variable, *node_state*, is set to indicate that tuples are being read from the materialized relation, and a cursor into this relation is opened. Then, the code proceeds to the backtrack point and reads the first tuple from the relation. If, however, the *done* indicator does not exist, *node_state* is set to indicate that tuples are being materialized and there is a jump to the entry destination.

The code at the backtrack point checks *node_state* and, if the materialized relation is currently being read, it reads the next tuple from the relation just as at the backtrack point for a base relation. If the tuples are being materialized, there is an indirect jump to *node*_loc as described in section 3.4.2.

In the case where tuples are being materialized, they are stored at the success point of the OR node. Likewise, the *done* indicator is stored at the fail point of the OR node. Note that the fail and success points will only be reached during materialization since the fail and success destinations have been incorporated into the entry and backtrack points where appropriate. Note also that even if no tuples are found for a particular binding pattern, the *done* indicator will be stored at the fail point and subsequent attempts to get tuples with this binding pattern (at the entry point of the OR node) will result in immediate failure. Thus, the *done* indicator also provides ***negative information***, avoiding unnecessary computation.

- **OR node:**

```
node_e: if done materializing for given bnd args
            set node_state to reading
            open a cursor on the materialized rel.
        else
            set node_state to materializing
            goto e_dest for node
node_b: if node_state is reading
            get next tuple satisfying all bnd args
            if a tuple is found
               assign values to free arguments
               goto s_dest for node
            else goto f_dest for node
        else goto node_loc (indirectly)
node_f: store done for current binding in
            secondary relation
        goto f_dest for node
node_s: assemble a tuple from global variables
        store that tuple in the materialized rel.
        goto s_dest for node
```

3.4.4 Lazy Materialized Execution: As with the lazy pipelined case, lazy materialization makes sense only for derived relations and we can localize all changes to the derived OR node. In fact, for the lazy materialized execution, the entry and backtrack points are identical to those given for the lazy pipelined execution. The success and fail points, however, must be altered so that all the tuples corresponding to the given binding pattern are generated before going to the success destination. This is accomplished by jumping to the backtrack point after storing the computed tuple in the materialized relation at the success point. After storing the *done* indicator at the fail point, a jump is made back to the entry point so that the stored tuples may be read.

```
node_f: store done for current binding in
                   secondary relation
        goto node_e
node_s: assemble a tuple from global variables
        store that tuple in the materialized rel.
        goto node_b
```

3.4.5 Materialized Execution: The materialized execution may be viewed simply as a special case of the lazy materialized execution where no arguments are bound. Therefore, no changes need be made to the code outlined for lazy materialization except to note that storing a *done* indicator is superfluous for the materialized execution.

3.5 More Annotations: Access methods

In the last section we digressed to impart the operational view of the declarative execution model consisting of the CNF program attributed with the annotations. Let us return to the declarative model of execution and discuss other annotations that are needed to fully describe the execution.

The CNF program encodes the ordering of joins but not the choice of access methods. We can associate other annotations that detail the choice of access methods with the nodes in the AND/OR tree [Ull88]. We discuss some of these to exemplify the aspects of the computation that are modeled as annotations. It is easy to see that the join method to be used can be annotated. Similarly, the set of arguments that are to be postselected, after a tuple is computed, can also be annotated to that node. Certain preprocessing information can also be annotated to the node. For example, the preselection of the subset of tuples that satisfy a condition or creation of an index for subsequent use in the join are such cases. Needless to say, that the code generator produces the appropriate imperative statements to reflect the necessary inflexion implied by the associated annotations.

In short, we have provided a sample of annotations that can be attributed to an execution structure (i.e., CNF program) to flesh out the details of the actual execution. The choice of modeling an aspect of the execution as an annotation, as opposed to in the execution structure, has not been arbitrary. Obviously, preselect and postselect can be modeled in the execution structure by rewriting the program. This was not done because of the following observation:

> Given an execution structure, the specific annotation can be chosen using a greedy algorithm. This implies that the optimal choice of the annotations does not require an exponential search, whereas the optimal choice of the execution structure does.

Therefore, the desiderata that is proposed for the choice of modeling any aspect of execution is to guarantee the existence of an efficient algorithm for the optimal choice.

3.6 More on Dataflow Annotations: Intelligent Backtracking

One important aspect of the execution that needs to be represented in the execution model is the capability of intelligent backtracking. This is easily done in the context of the dataflow paradigm by changing the dataflow destinations.

Intelligent backtracking as proposed in the context of Prolog has been known to require too much runtime overhead [PP82]. As a result, in most cases, it does not reduce the execution time. This is because intelligent backtracking is not applicable for most joins. Consequently, even a small overhead to detect that intelligent backtracking is unnecessary will add up to total more than the savings. For this reason, in $\mathcal{LDL}$ we incorporate backtracking techniques by doing compile-time analysis such that little (if any) overhead is incurred at run-time.

Intelligent backtracking consists of avoiding useless computation that cannot generate new tuples. Initially, we assume only a single rule per predicate. We can classify the useless computations as follows. Consider the following rule, with all three OR nodes to be pipelined:

$$p(X,Y) \leftarrow p1(X,Z), p2(Y,Z), p3(X,U).$$

Get-First Optimization: If the attempt to get the first tuple in $p3$ fails, it is unnecessary to backtrack to $p2$, since it does not change the bound argument for $p3$, i.e., X. The only way this value can be changed is by backtracking to $p1$. In general, on entry to an OR node, if no tuples are found, we need to backtrack to the OR node where the bound variable is instantiated (i.e., is adorned as free).

Get-Next Optimization: After computing a tuple for p, backtracking to get the next tuple for $p3$ is unnecessary, since it will not yield any new tuples for p. A new p tuple can only be generated by backtracking to $p2$. In general, when backtracking from an AND node, the computation should resume at the last OR node that binds a variable occurring in the head.

These two optimizations can be incorporated into the dataflow annotations by providing two fail destinations for each node: one for the entry and the other for the backtrack point of the node. We define these dataflow destinations as follows:

Entry Fail Destination: For an OR node with exactly one bound argument,[7] the entry fail destination is the backtrack point of the first OR node where the argument is adorned as free, if it occurs in the same rule, and the entry fail destination of the head, otherwise. For an AND node, it is the entry destination of the parent OR node.

Backtrack Fail Destination: For an OR node, the backtrack fail destination is the backtrack point of the previous OR node in the rule that binds a variable occurring in the head, if such an OR node exists, and the backtrack fail destination of the parent AND node, otherwise. For an AND node, it is the backtrack point of the last OR node in the rule that binds a variable occurring in the head if such an OR node exists, and the backtrack fail destination of the parent OR node, otherwise.

Note that the backtrack fail destination corresponds to the previous notion of fail destination, which is now subsumed. Also note that, the entry

[7] We make this assumption for ease of exposition. The $\mathcal{LDL}$ compiler allows arbitrary binding patterns in the OR node.

fail destination can only be used if we detect failure of the node at the entry point as well as the backtrack point for the node.

It is easy to show that the above annotations result in an execution that faithfully models the bottom-up semantics of the program. Note that there is absolutely no run-time overhead involved in the above changes and that these changes will result in improved executions.

Allowing more than one rule per predicate poses the problem of detecting the get-first failure for all rules of the derived predicate. This can be achieved by keeping a count of all AND nodes that register an entry fail, so that the last AND node can determine if get-first optimization is applicable. This incurs a marginal overhead (a single assignment per rule).[8] This overhead is only incurred for derived predicates with multiple rules. No additional overhead is incurred for get-next optimization. We note that compile-time analysis can be used to avoid intelligent backtracking in cases where it is of little (or no) advantage, for example, when the entry and backtrack fail destinations of a node are the same.

3.7 Execution Space: The Declarative Abstract Machine

Using the annotations described in the previous subsections we can now define an *annotated CNF program* to be a CNF program with a valid[9] set of annotations. Note that the dataflow annotations capture procedural notions such as intelligent backtracking, while still retaining a declarative nature. The set of all annotated CNF programs is termed the *execution space*. The declarative *abstract machine* for NRD programs is specified by the set of all possible executions — the execution space. Any implementation capable of realizing the entire execution space is a valid implementation of the abstract machine.

In particular, an interpreter for executing directly from the annotated CNF programs can be devised. This is evident since code generation was possible using only information local to each node. Therefore, we can modify the code generator proposed in section 3.4 to obtain an interpreter that actually implements the semantics instead of generating code. Such an interpreter is a faithful implementation of the abstract machine. Needless to say, the compilation approach has performance advantages.

[8] The overhead was observed to be insignificant in the $\mathcal{LDL}$ implementation.

[9] The validity of an annotation is being used in an informal sense; e.g., preselect on a pipelined execution is invalid.

In summary, we have proposed an abstract machine using annotated CNF programs, which retain the structure of the original program while encoding performance-critical aspects of the execution.

3.8 Relaxing the Tree Assumption

Up to this point, we have assumed the AND/OR graph generated from the CNF program is actually a tree. If the program contained common subexpressions (subtrees), we simply replicated the entire subexpression at each point where it was needed. We now present other techniques to deal with common subexpressions. In section 4, we show how these techniques can also be used to implement recursion.

We can eliminate common subexpressions by treating the subtree as a subroutine called from each occurrence. The subroutine analogy is useful; however, it is limited in that we need two return pointers instead of one (i.e., success and fail destinations) and in that the subroutine can return multiple solutions. Our implementation simply sets the return destinations and then jumps to the entry point of the subtree — no actual subroutines are used.

We need to be careful to prevent two invocations of this subtree from interfering with each other, for example, by changing the value of a variable or a relation cursor. One way of doing this is to guarantee that two calls to the subtree cannot be active at the same time. That is, each call to the subtree must compute all results before proceeding to the success point, i.e., use the LM or M execution methods.

Another approach is to assign each invocation its own environment. This is easily accomplished by declaring each variable in the subtree as a member of a structure and having each occurrence of the subtree declare its own local structure. The environment contains not only the variables of the CNF program, but also all variables that store state information, such as *node*_loc, relations, cursors, etc. This allows us to pipeline tuples out of the subtree, resulting in P and LP executions.[10] Since the number of occurrences of the subtree is known at compile-time, we can still allocate all the space for the program statically. However, variable references now involve a base-address plus displacement computation.

3.9 Implementation Notes

For the sake of convenience and brevity, we have chosen to limit our discussions in this paper to pure

[10] Since the LM and M execution methods are reentrant, the environment need only contain the state information up to a frontier of the subtree, delineated by such nodes.

Datalog and, therefore, have not included complex terms. The actual $\mathcal{LDL}$ implementation, however, does handle complex terms and the abstract machine outlined here can easily be modified as in the actual implementation to include them. Additional preselect and postselect annotations for AND nodes are used to handle unification in the presence of complex terms, and the postselect annotations for OR nodes are also extended. To process the annotations, capabilities for constructing and checking structures, as well as accessing structure arguments must be provided. These capabilities also provide the facilities needed for assigning to free variables in complex terms and constructing indices when complex terms are involved. Note that arguments within a complex term need to be adorned as discussed in section 2.

A few details relevant to the code generation implementation are worth noting. First of all, a symbol table must be constructed and maintained during the code generation process to facilitate the correct assignment of names to variables (global and temporary), constants (including those from the query form), complex terms, indices, and relations (temporary and base). The use of a symbol table also facilitates the generation of declarations and initializations for variables. Secondly, it is imperative that before entering into a full materialization, the values currently assigned to bound variables (if any) be saved into temporary variables so that the values are not lost during the materialization process. The correct values may then be restored to the variables upon completion of the materialization.

It is interesting to note that the name of the *node*_loc variable may be passed down from an OR node to its successor AND nodes during code generation, obviating the need for the node table described in section 3.4.1. This is the approach taken in the $\mathcal{LDL}$ implementation. It requires non-local information (with respect to a single node) but is easy to incorporate (along with other node table information used in recursion) into the simple recursive AND/OR tree (graph) traversal algorithm used during code generation.

It is apparent from the code descriptions presented in this section that the generated code will contain many goto statements which could be condensed or folded to provide a more succinct and efficient program. In the $\mathcal{LDL}$ implementation, this is performed in a postprocessing pass.

Finally, we point out that the $\mathcal{LDL}$ compiler does not actually construct a fully annotated CNF prior to code generation. The compiler extracts only those rules relevant to the current query form from the original $\mathcal{LDL}$ program and constructs the corresponding AND/OR tree. The $\mathcal{LDL}$ optimizer then chooses the CNF structure and encodes it directly in the AND/OR tree. After choosing the structure, the optimizer annotates the node of the tree to provide most of the access method annotations discussed using a greedy algorithm.

The simple, naive code generator outlined in this paper was based on the existence of a fully annotated CNF which provided all the information necessary to generate code locally with respect to each node in the AND/OR tree. The actual $\mathcal{LDL}$ code generator, however, is quite sophisticated, essentially computing argument adornments and providing the dataflow destinations, intelligent backtracking destinations, as well as some of the postselect and preselect annotations on the fly as the target language code is generated.

4 Recursive Datalog

We now extend our model to include recursive Datalog programs. Our goal is to show that the techniques presented so far are, in fact, sufficient to compile recursive queries.

4.1 Execution Method Annotations

We extend the AND/OR graph to include two new types of OR nodes: *clique-entry* and *clique* nodes. These nodes correspond to recursive predicate occurrences. A clique node corresponds to a predicate occurrence in the rule of a predicate from the same recursive clique. A clique entry node corresponds to all other recursive predicate occurrences, i.e. the initial point of invocation of a recursive clique. The successors of a clique-entry node are the rules for all predicates in the recursive clique. Note that this may include rules for predicates other than the invoked predicate, because of mutual recursion. Clique nodes have no successors. The distinction between clique and clique-entry nodes is easily motivated by the desire to have a finite, non-cyclic representation of the clique.

The main challenge in implementing recursion is to keep multiple invocations of the recursive predicate from interfering with each other. This is essentially the same problem solved in section 3.8 in the context of common subexpressions, so we would expect the same solutions to apply. Briefly, the solutions were to make the code reentrant by using a relation to store all results of the computation or a complex structure to keep a unique environment for each entry point into the subtree.

If we choose to use a relation, we end up with a semi-naive, fixpoint approach to recursion [Ba85]. Note the materialized relation avoids having multiple invocations of the recursive predicate occurrence active at the same time by replacing the recursive subquery with the tuples computed in the previous iteration. By assuming the overhead of duplicate elimination, we are guaranteed to terminate.

If we choose to use separate environments, we have to allocate space for them dynamically, since we cannot tell how many recursive calls will be made a priori. This allocation can be based on a stack.[11] This approach does not incur the overhead of duplicate checking, but cannot guarantee termination.

Regardless of whether we choose the semi-naive or stack-based approach, the four execution methods are still applicable. That is, we can pipeline a semi-naive computation, lazy pipeline a stack-based computation, etc. The resulting combinations provide a rich mixture of execution strategies. However, note that if we pipeline a semi-naive computation, the clique node is not reentrant. If there is more than one entry point into this clique, we can simply treat it as a common subexpression, and any of the techniques in section 3.8 apply.

4.2 Dataflow Annotations

We briefly discuss the dataflow annotations of clique nodes, clique-entry nodes and their immediate successors. It is not necessary to introduce new dataflow points, only to describe how the dataflow destinations are modified for each of the new types of nodes.

A clique-entry node is simply a new type of OR node, and its dataflow destinations are similar to those of the OR node. The successors to the clique-entry node are the rules of the recursive clique. We group the rules for each recursive predicate together, and assume that the first group contains the rules for the predicate associated with the clique-entry. We choose an arbitrary order for the rules in each group, so that the notion of first, next, and last rule in the group are defined. The entry destination of the clique-entry node is the entry point of the first rule in the first group. The dataflow destinations for each group of rules are identical to those of the AND node successors to an OR node. In particular, the fail destination of the last rule for each recursive

[11] This is essentially the way Prolog implements recursion.

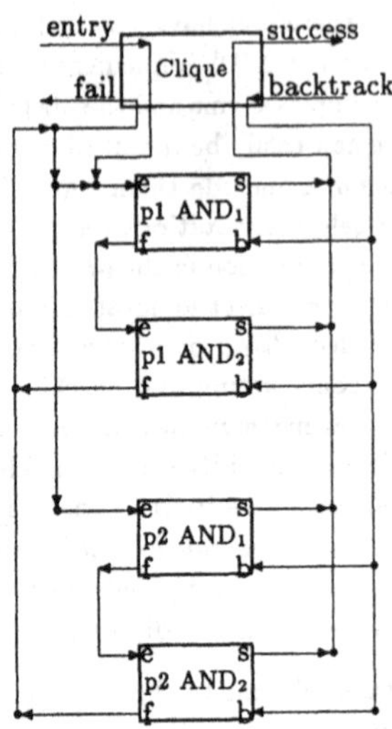

Figure 4: Dataflow Annotations for Clique Nodes

predicate is the fail node of the parent clique-entry node. The fail destination of the clique-entry node is different. It is easier to understand in the context of semi-naive computation. After all tuples for a recursive predicate have been found, we must find all tuples for the next recursive predicate. Thus, the fail destination of the clique-entry node can be the entry point of the first rule for any of the recursive predicates. Of course, it can also be the regular fail destination for an OR node. The decision of whether to go to the regular fail destination or to one of the rule entry points can be viewed as the fixpoint check in the computation.

By definition, clique nodes have no successors. Conceptually, however, a clique node is the same as a clique-entry node. Hence, we would expect that its dataflow destinations are the same as for the corresponding clique-entry node. We note here that the fail destination of the last AND node for a given clique predicate is no longer simply the fail point of the clique-entry node, but the fail point of one of the clique-entry or clique nodes. Again, the specific node destination may have to be determined at run-time.

Figure 4 illustrates the dataflow points and destinations for a specific recursive clique, with two recursive predicates, p1 and p2, and two rules for each predicate. We assume the clique-entry node refers to the predicate **p1**. The general case is easier to infer than to draw, so it is left up to the reader.

4.3 Code Generation

In this section, we describe how code can be generated to implement both semi-naive and stack-based recursive computations. We first mention some conventions necessary to compile recursive queries. Then, we describe the code generated for a pipelined execution, and briefly outline the changes necessary to realize lazy pipelined, lazy materialized, and materialized executions.

4.3.1 Conventions: First of all, we assume the adornment algorithm has taken care of *stability transformations* [HN84]. This is necessary, since we compile each clique only once, so the adornment of the clique-entry node must be subsumed by the clique nodes. It is not strictly necessary that the converse be true, since any extra bound arguments can be post-selected.

For semi-naive computation, we assume that the rules have been rewritten into a form amenable for bottom-up processing. That is, magic-set , counting-set or some other rewriting transformation has taken place [Ba85,SZ86,B*86,BR87]. These rewriting techniques normally transform a recursive clique into two phases or fixpoint computations. We note that the first phase can be viewed simply as a clique embedded in the second phase. Hence, we need only discuss how code is generated for a single fixpoint.

In the semi-naive computation of a recursive clique, the clique-entry node must know which recursive predicate is currently being computed, in much the same way that an OR node needs to know the rule that is currently active. The name of the current predicate is stored in a variable called *node*_pred.

The semi-naive computation consists of repeatedly executing the recursive rules, where the results of each iteration are used in the subsequent pass. Thus, we need to manage the tuples generated at each iteration. For efficiency, we assume the *fact manager* (i.e., the underlying DBMS with a tuple-at-a-time interface) supports this model directly, by keeping the tuples generated in the current iteration separate from the entire relation. A cursor can then be declared as either a *delta* cursor, selecting only those tuples generated in the previous iteration, or a *total* cursor, which selects all tuples in the relation. The clique nodes in the recursive rules read the tuples in this *semi_naive* relation. For each clique node, we assume an annotation to determine whether a delta or total cursor should be used.[12]

[12]A total cursor is needed for non-linear recursion.

In the stack-based approach, we use the stack, not the fact manager, to store temporary computations. This includes partial results, as well as the execution environment. Hence, all variable accesses must be resolved as offsets from a stack frame. The offsets can be computed easily if the stack frame is declared as a structure type, in which case the type name is sufficient to compute them. The type name of the stack frame used at each node can be found in the node table.

For each recursive invocation, we create a new environment in the stack. Since an environment remains active after a solution is found, the current environment is not necessarily at the top of the stack. Thus, we must assume two different pointers: one to the current environment and one to the top of the stack. Note that each environment must keep a pointer to its calling environment, since the two environments are not necessarily adjacent in the stack.

4.3.2 Semi-Naive Computation: In a pipelined execution, we would like to go to the success destination of the node every time we generate a tuple. Moreover, we do not wish to store the tuples generated in a relation — that is, at subsequent invocations we start work from scratch. In semi-naive recursion, however, it is necessary to store the tuples into a relation as they are generated. To be consistent with the pipelined approach, we must clear the relation after we generate all possible tuples. While this may seem strange at first, it is desirable in precisely the same cases where pipelining is, e.g., there is little duplication in the incoming binding pattern, and we wish to conserve memory.

We now describe the code generation for the clique and clique-entry nodes. As stated previously, the clique nodes are treated as base relations. It is only necessary to know the name of the relation being read and whether to open a delta or total cursor. This information is stored in the annotations for the clique node. Thus, the code for clique nodes is virtually identical to that for base relations in the nonrecursive case.

A clique-entry node is a bit more complicated. Intuitively, the semi-naive execution consists of repeatedly "firing" each rule in the recursive predicate until no more tuples from it can be found. When all rules have been tried, we determine whether we have reached a fixpoint. If we have, then no more tuples can be generated for the clique, and so we go to the normal fail destination for the node. Otherwise, we proceed to "fire" each of the rules one more time.

Clearly, upon entry to the clique, there is no need to try any of the recursive rules in the clique, since these cannot possibly produce any tuples. Also, in the remaining iterations, it is unnecessary to try any of the non-recursive (exit) rules, since these cannot produce any new tuples. For brevity, we do not make this distinction in the following code description, but clearly this is something any implementation would use to its advantage (as does ours).

- **Clique-Entry:**

```
node_e: set node_pred to first clique predicate
        goto e_dest for node
node_b: goto node_loc (indirectly)
node_f: if node_pred is last clique predicate
          indicate new semi-naive phase
          if last phase generated new tuples
            set node_pred to first clique pred
            goto entry point of first rule for
                  first clique pred
          else
            clear all clique relations
            goto f_dest for node
        else
          set node_pred to next clique pred
          goto entry point of first rule
                  for next clique pred
node_s: construct and store a tuple in
                  appropriate clique relation
        if node_pred is clique-entry predicate
          if tuple matches input bindings
            goto s_dest for node
        goto node_b
```

Two things should be noted. First of all, since there may be more than one clique predicate, at the success of the clique-entry node, we may have to store into more than one relation. We can determine the correct relation by looking at the value of *node*_pred. Secondly, before going to the success destination, we must determine whether the tuple just generated matches the input bindings. In the non-recursive case, this was unnecessary, because only matching tuples were generated. However, in the recursive case, this is not so. For example, to find the ancestors of mary, we may have to find the ancestors of john as well. However, we should not go to the success destination with one of john's ancestors.

As in the non-recursive case, it is easy to modify the pipelining code to do lazy pipelining. The approach is to modify the entry point so that it can determine whether we are *done* computing the tuples for a particular binding pattern. The backtrack point is modified so that it can either read from the materialized relation or proceed to the normal backtrack destination of the node. The success point stores any new tuples generated into the materialized relation, and the fail point marks the materialization for the current binding pattern as *done*. Since we are already storing tuples into a relation, these changes are easier to incorporate for the recursive case than for the non-recursive case. In fact, we simply have to avoid deleting the clique relations at the fail point. The tests for the *done* indicator are the same as in the non-recursive case.

As was the case with non-recursive queries, lazy pipelining can be converted into lazy materialization simply by changing the code for the success and fail points. In particular, at the success point we jump to the backtrack point rather than the success destination, and at the fail point we jump to the entry point rather than the fail destination.

Finally, the materialized execution can be viewed as a special case of lazy materialization, where no arguments are bound. For brevity, we do not include the code for the last three executions.

4.3.3 Stack-Based Computation:

In a stack-based execution, there is no distinction between clique-entry and clique nodes. Essentially, they both consist of a subroutine call, where we pass parameters, set up a new execution environment, and receive answers after the subroutine returns.

The main difficulty lies in setting up a new environment. When an environment is created, we need to set up the bound variables in this environment. That is, we must copy them from the previously active environment to the newly created one. Similarly, when an answer is found, the return variables must be copied to the environment of the caller. Finally, note the return address is also stored in the environment. Actually, two return addresses are required in our approach — the success and fail destinations for the current invocation.

As with the semi-naive computation, no changes are necessary to the AND nodes, so we omit them entirely in this description. We present the code for both clique-entry and clique nodes.

- **Clique or Clique-Entry:**

```
node_e: allocate space for new environment
        copy bnd vars from prev. to new env.
        set fail dest. of env. to node_f
        set success dest. of env. to node_s
        set frame ptr of env. to old frame ptr
        set frame pointer to new env.
        goto e_dest for node
```

node_b: set frame pointer to be new env.
goto *node*_loc of env. (indirect)
node_f: release space for new env.
set frame pointer to be previous env.
goto *f_dest* for *node*
node_s: copy results from new to previous env.
set frame pointer to be previous env.
goto *s_dest* for *node*

A few points from the above code should be noted. Since each recursive call produces only tuples that match the bound arguments, it is not necessary to check the tuples at the success point. This should be contrasted to the semi-naive case. Also, note that we only execute the rules for the predicate that is actually being invoked. This simplifies the code generated at the fail point considerably.

The transformations from pipelining to lazy pipelining, lazy materialization and materialization are the same as in the semi-naive case, and hence are not described here. However, some things should be noted. Recall that in a top-down execution there is no fundamental difference between a clique-entry node and a clique node. Thus, it is quite natural to achieve common subexpression elimination within the recursive calls. That is, after all the ancestors of mary have been discovered, there is no need to recompute them, even if the tuples are needed deep within the recursive computation. We expect this will lead to considerable savings in certain queries, for example, finding connected components of a graph.

4.4 Implementation Notes

As was the case for NRD, complex terms have been handled in the actual $\mathcal{LDL}$ implementation and the model for recursive Datalog that is presented here can easily be modified simply using preselect and postselect annotations. The name of the stack frame may be passed down from the clique entry node to its successor AND nodes during code generation just as was possible with the backtrack location variable, again obviating the need for the node table. All other implementation details outlined for the NRD case also carry over for the recursive case. However, there are some points where recursion adds a level of complexity to the normal processing. These complications, as well as some necessary assumptions, are briefly discussed below.

Garbage collection is a traditional problem associated with recursion. In the semi-naive approach, the fact manager becomes responsible for garbage collection. This is accomplished when the clique relations are deleted. In the stack-based approach, on the other hand, the garbage collection problem is addressed when the stack is popped.

In section 3.6, we showed that intelligent backtracking can be implemented with no overhead for non-recursive queries. In the presence of recursion, intelligent backtracking is more complicated. Our experience with the $\mathcal{LDL}$ implementation, however, has proven that intelligent backtracking can be implemented in the presence of recursion with little or no overhead. The solution outlined in section 3.6 carries over to the semi-naive approach with no changes. It is sufficient to note that when we are pipelining, we must clear the clique relations at the entry point, not the fail point, of the clique, since the fail point may be bypassed during intelligent backtracking. In the stack-based approach, however, we must clean up the stack after backtracking over a clique.

In this section we assumed that the fact manager supports the semi-naive model directly. This required adding a fact manager routine to declare when we enter a new phase of the computation — that is, a new iteration in our fixpoint computation. In return, the fact manager supports delta cursors, where only the tuples generated in the previous phase are returned. We chose to add these concepts to the fact manager, rather than to emulate them at the inference engine level, purely for efficiency. In fact, we store tuples in such a way that only a "high-water mark" is necessary to implement a semi-naive scan.

Essential to our ability to extend the Abstract Machine to handle recursive Datalog is the existence of two preprocessing phases, one which analyzes the rules and groups all strongly connected components into recursive cliques and one which generates the annotated CNF for the recursive cliques. In the latter processing phase, non-trivial transformations must take place to map the program into an equivalent one where, for the semi-naive case, constants are pushed through the recursion [B*86,BR87,SZ86]. Both processing phases exist as part of the current $\mathcal{LDL}$ implementation.

5 Conclusions

In this paper, we proposed an abstract machine for $\mathcal{LDL}$ that maintains a high-level view of an $\mathcal{LDL}$ program while incorporating aspects of its execution that make a performance difference. The abstract machine is defined by the execution space, i.e., the set of all annotated CNF programs, each of which models an actual execution. The CNF program provides the skeleton of the execution, and the annotations specify other relevant details, such as access methods, join methods, execution strategies, intelligent backtracking etc. We formalized four execution methods (top-down, bottom-up and two hybrid methods that incorporate memoing) and two recursive computations (fixpoint and stack-based). The two computations and four execution methods provide a rich variety of recursive techniques.

We presented a realization of this abstract machine by describing the code generation algorithm used in the $\mathcal{LDL}$ compiler. This algorithm proceeds by translating each node in the annotated CNF program into a sequence of imperative statements, including calls to a tuple-level interface of an underlying DBMS. In this paper we presented the abstract machine in the context of Datalog. The experience in implementing the compiler for $\mathcal{LDL}$ has shown that this abstract machine is sufficient to support advanced features, such as sets, negation, updates and non-deterministic choice.

There are many aspects of execution that have not been explicitly addressed in the above proposal. The use of parallelism and peep-hole optimization, for example, are of special interest to us. Further, the abstract machine provides a framework for comparison of various techniques proposed in the literature. For example, many recursive query processing techniques can be modeled and compared using this abstract machine.

Acknowledgements: The ideas in this paper were greatly influenced by an earlier proposal by Carlo Zaniolo. We are also thankful to Kevin Greene, Manuel Hermenegildo, and Roger Nasr for providing a forum for preliminary discussions leading to this abstract machine.

References

[Ba85] Bancilhon, F.D. "Naive Evaluation of Recursively Defined Relations," in *On Knowledge Base Management Systems*, edited by M. Brodie and J. Mylopoulos, Springer-Verlag, 1985.

[B*86] Bancilhon, F.D., D. Maier, Y. Sagiv, and J. Ullman. "Magic Sets and Other Strange Ways to Implement Logic Programs," in *Proc. SIGACT-SIGMOD Principles of Database Systems Conference (PODS)*, 1986.

[BR86] Bancilhon, F.D. and R. Ramakrishnan. "An Amateur's Introduction to Recursive Query Processing Strategies," in *Proc. SIGACT-SIGMOD Int. Conf. on Management of Data (SIGMOD)*, Washington D.C., 1986.

[BR87] Beeri, C. and R. Ramakrishnan. "On the Power of Magic," in *Proc. SIGACT-SIGMOD Principles of Database Systems Conference (PODS)*, 1987.

[By80] Byrd, L.. "Understanding the Control Flow of Prolog Programs," in *Proc. of the Logic Programming Workshop*, 1980.

[HN84] Henschen, L. and S. Naqvi "On Compiling Queries in Recursive First-Order Databases," in *J. ACM 31*, 1(Jan. 1984), pp. 47-85.

[KZ88] Krishnamurthy, R., and C. Zaniolo. "Optimization in a Logic Based Language for Knowledge and Data Intensive Applications," *Extending Data Base Technology*, Venice, 1988.

[Ll84] Lloyd, J.W. *Foundations of Logic Programming*, Springer Verlag, 1984.

[Me82] Mellish, C. "An Alternative to Structure Sharing in the Implementation of a Prolog Interpreter," in *Logic Programming*, edited by K.L. Clark and S.A. Tärnlund, Academic Press, 1982.

[Mi68] Michie, D. "'Memo' Functions and Machine Learning," in *Nature*, April 1968.

[Nil80] Nilson, N.J. *Principles of Artificial Intelligence*, Tioga Publishing Company, 1980.

[NT89] Naqvi, S. A. and S. Tsur. *A Language for Data and Knowledge Bases*, W.H. Freeman, 1989.

[PP82] Pereira, L.M. and A. Porto. "Selective Backtracking," in *Logic Programming*, edited by K.L. Clark and S.A. Tärnlund, Academic Press, 1982.

[RBK88] Ramakrishnan, R., C. Beeri, and R. Krishnamurthy. "Optimizing Existential Queries," in *Proc. SIGACT-SIGMOD Principles of Database Systems Conference (PODS)*, Austin, April 1988.

[SZ86] Sacca, D. and C. Zaniolo. "The Generalized Counting Method for Recursive Logic Queries," in *Proc. 1st Int. Conf. on Database Theory*, Rome, 1986.

[Ull85] Ullman, J. "Implementation of Logical Query Languages for Databases," in TODS, Vol. 10, No. 3, pp. 289-321, 1985.

[Ull88] Ullman, J. *Database and Knowledge Systems, Vol. I*, Computer Science Press, 1988.

[Ull89] Ullman, J. *Database and Knowledge Systems, Vol. II*, Computer Science Press, 1989.

[Vi89] Vieille, L. "Recursive Query Processing: The Power of Logic," to appear in *Theoretical Computer Science*, 1989.

[Wa71] Wadsworth, C.P.. "Semantics and Pragmatics of the Lambda-Calculus," D. Phil. Thesis, University of Oxford, 1971.

[Wa83] Warren, D.H.D. "An Abstract Prolog Instruction Set," Technical Note 309, SRI International, 1983

Query Processing In Distributed ORION

B. Paul Jenq, Darrell Woelk, Won Kim, Wan-Lik Lee

Microelectronics and Computer Technology Corporation
3500 West Balcones Center Drive
Austin, TX 78759

Abstract

In this paper we describe query processing strategies we have developed and implemented in the distributed version of the ORION object-oriented database system. The ORION query model is based on the ORION object-oriented data model. Further, we have adopted the response time as the primary objective function for query optimization. The query-processing strategies we have developed reflect our solutions to these requirements. In particular, our strategies are based on a dataflow execution model which represents a plan for executing a query concurrently at multiple sites. One important observation we bring out in our description of the ORION query-processing strategies is that most of the important techniques developed for optimizing and processing a relational query apply directly to an object-oriented query, despite the differences in the underlying data models.

1. Introduction

One of the areas of extensive research during the past decade has been query optimization and processing for both centralized and distributed database systems. However, the research has been focused almost exclusively on the relational model. Only recently, efforts have begun to extend this research into object-oriented databases and nested-relational databases. A query model for object-oriented databases has been proposed in [BANE88, KIM89b]. Query optimization and processing strategies used in the centralized version of the ORION object-oriented database system [KIM88] were reported in [BANE88, KIMK88].

In this paper, we describe the query optimization and processing strategies we have developed and implemented in the distributed version of ORION. The shared database is distributed across multiple sites on a local-area network. A query may originate at any site. Each site maintains a global directory that contains the object-distribution information.

Two key factors influenced our solutions to the new problems of optimizing and processing an object-oriented query in a distributed environment. One is that the ORION query model is based on an object-oriented data model. One facet of an object-oriented data model is the nesting of objects; that is, the value of an attribute of an object may be a reference to (object identifier of) another object. This is similar to complex objects [LORI83, KIM87] or nested relations [IEEE88, MAKI77, ABIT84]. The nested structure of the schema, corresponding to the nested objects, offers an opportunity to structure the query optimization and processing strategies differently from those used for relational queries. In a distributed system, an object and objects it references may reside in different sites, adding another twist to query processing.

Another key factor which influenced our approach to query processing in distributed ORION is the fact that we have adopted the minimal response time as the primary objective. In contrast, most systems we are aware of have attempted to minimize the total processing time, for example, R* [LOHM85]. The application environment ORION aims to support is often highly interactive, and explicitly minimizing the response time of a query seems more appropriate than minimizing the total system utilization. To minimize the response time of a query, we have had to develop a dataflow execution model which exploits parallelism inherent in a distributed query; the execution model is a representation of a query execution plan which captures a strategy to decompose a query into a set of subqueries for concurrent execution at multiple sites.

One important conclusion we have reached in developing our solutions to the problems of optimizing and processing queries for an object-oriented database is that much of the results of research into relational query optimization and processing applies directly to object-oriented queries. This observation is reported in [KIMK88] in the context of a centralized database. The description in this paper of our approach to query optimization and processing in distributed ORION is intended to further articulate on this observation by extending the discussion to distributed databases. The similarities mean in particular that the rich set of solutions developed for distributed relational queries [APER83, CHAN83, DANI82, LOHM85, MACK86, YU87] can be used for object-oriented queries.

The adoption of an object-oriented query model and the response-time optimization criterion represents primary differences between our approach and that used in R* [LOHM85, MACK86]; however, much of the results from the query-processing research in R* is directly applicable to our context. Query processing in the Bubba parallel-database machine is aimed at minimizing the response time [VALD88]. However, query processing in Bubba assumes a uniform distribution of data across sites; further, the data model Bubba implements is a nested-relational model, essentially a subset of an object-oriented data model.

2. Queries in ORION

In this section, we start by giving an example of an ORION query, both as a means of introducing the reader to the concept of a query for an object-oriented database, and for use in illustrating key concepts in query processing throughout the remainder of this paper. Next, we briefly introduce the query-graph formalism for ORION queries; the query graph is not only a convenient means of representing a query, but also the basis of formulating our query-execution model. Then we provide a comparison of object-oriented queries to relational queries; using the query-graph formalism, we will show the fundamental similarities (and some differences as well) in query optimization and processing for the two types of queries. The reader should see [KIM89b] for a full description of the query model for object-oriented databases.

2.1 Example Query

Figure 2.1 is a schema for a simple object-oriented database using the ORION data model [BANE87]. As the figure shows, a class consists of a set of attributes; and the *domains*(type) of an attribute may be a class with its own set of attributes. There is a solid line between an attribute name and its domain class. For example, the class Vehicle has the attributes owner and manufacturer; and the domain of the manufacturer attribute is the class Company, which means that the value of the manufacturer attribute is an instance (or a set of instances) of the class Company. The names of classes are in bold type and the names of the attributes are in normal type. Since the domains of the attributes of a class are, in general, classes which may have their own sets of attributes, the definition of a class forms a directed graph of classes rooted at the class; such a graph is called a *class-attribute hierarchy* in [KIM89b]. For example, Figure 2.1 may be viewed as a class-attribute hierarchy rooted at the class Vehicle; in particular, all other classes in the figure are direct or indirect domains of the class Vehicle.

The class Automobile is a subclass of the class Vehicle. This relationship is shown using a dashed line. A subclass inherits all attributes and methods from its superclass. In this example, the subclass Automobile inherits the attributes owner and manufacturer from the class Vehicle and also defines an additional attribute called model.

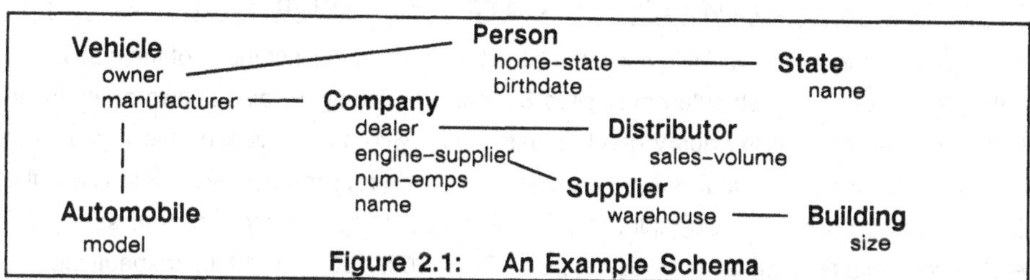

Figure 2.1: An Example Schema

Queries in ORION are formulated using the query language defined in [BANE88]. The following example query may be formulated against the schema of Figure 2.1. Normal Lisp syntax is used for queries in ORION. The quote preceding Vehicle indicates to Lisp that Vehicle is a symbol name and not a variable name. The quote preceding the **and** expression indicates that Lisp should not evaluate this expression.

```
(select 'Vehicle
        '(and (path Owner Home-state (equal name "Texas"))
              (path Manufacturer
                    (or  (path Engine-Supplier Warehouse (> size 10000))
                         (Dealer (> sales-volume 800)))))
```

In this query, the class Vehicle is called the *target class* of the query. The Vehicle class is qualified by an and-expression. A query subexpression beginning with the keyword "path" specifies a path along the class-attribute hierarchy in the schema. The select query shown here returns a list of the unique identifiers (UIDs) of the qualified instances of the target class. Alternatively, a select* query can be used to return the UIDs of the qualified instances of the target class and also the qualified instances of its subclasses.

This query returns the UIDs of all vehicle instances that are owned by a person whose home-state is Texas and were manufactured by a company that either has an engine-supplier with a warehouse of greater than 10000 square feet, or has a dealer with sales-volume greater than 800 vehicles.

2.2 Query Graph

As in most database systems, an ORION query is parsed into a query graph. Figure 2.2 shows the query graph representing our example query. The query involves seven classes distributed across three sites S_1, S_2, and S_3. The target class is Vehicle. The query is assumed to originate at

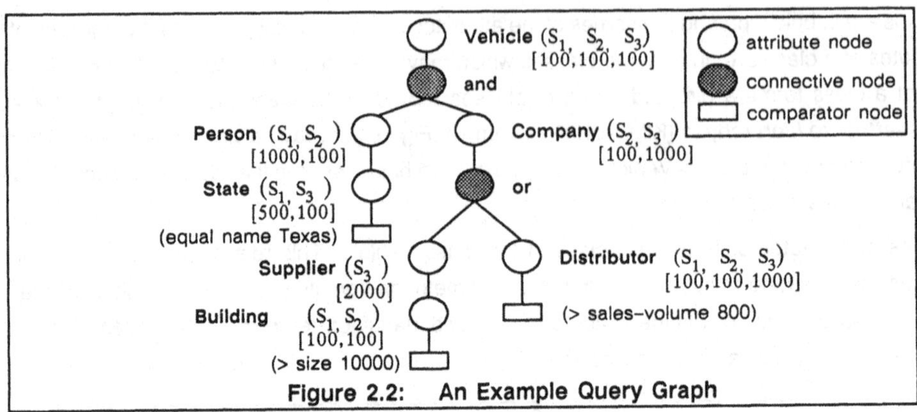

Figure 2.2: An Example Query Graph

S_2. For each class in the graph, we also show the sites that contain the instances of the class. For instance, the Person class is distributed over sites S_1 and S_2. This figure also shows an example data distribution; each node in the query graph is associated with a list indicating the numbers of instances that satisfy *simple predicates* (i.e., a comparator node represented by a rectangle in the graph), if any, at each site. For example, the numbers of Distributor instances that satisfy the predicate (> sales-volume 800) at sites S_1, S_2, and S_3 is 100, 100, and 1000, respectively.

There are three types of node in a query graph: an *attribute* node, a *connective* node, and a *comparator* node. An attribute node refers to either the target class or an attribute of a class. The domain of an attribute node can be a class or a set of instances of a class. We will call a site where the domain of an attribute node resides in a *resident site* of that node. A connective node can have an attribute node or a connective node as its parent node in a query graph. A connective node qualifies its parent attribute node by one or more query expressions. There are three types of connective node: *AND*, *OR*, and *NOT*, for conjunction, disjunction, and negation, respectively, of the query expressions represented by the child nodes of a connective node. A comparator node is a simple predicate applied to its parent attribute node to restrict the attribute values in the domain of the parent node. Since the domain of an attribute can be a set of objects, an attribute may have one of two types of quantifier: *Some* and *All*. A query quantified by the expression (*some* attribute-name), for example, (select 'Person '(equal (some hobby) "golf")), returns true if there exists at least one instance that satisfies the predicate; while a query quantified by the expression (*all* attribute-name), for example, (select 'Person '(path (all College) (equal name "Harvard"))), returns true only if all instances in the domain satisfy the predicate.

A query may be cyclic or acyclic. A *cyclic query* has at least one cyclic path of nodes in the graph. A tree query is an acyclic query in which each node has at most one parent node. An *acyclic query* is always a tree query if there is no common subexpression in the query. In this paper, we focus on tree queries. Note that a cyclic query can be transformed into an equivalent tree query by simply making each reference to a domain a separate node in the query graph. For example, a cyclic query may have three classes: Vehicle, Person, and State such that the owner attribute of a vehicle contains an instance of Person, the home-state attribute of a person contains an instance of State, and the violation-vehicle attribute of a state contains a set of vehicles. The Vehicle->Person->State->Vehicle cycle in the query graph can be broken by introducing two separate nodes for the Vehicle class, i.e., Vehicle'->Person->State->Vehicle''. Since our query expressions are inherently tree-structured, such a transformation is always possible, although it is not necessarily an efficient way to process a cyclic query.

2.3 Object-Oriented vs. Relational Query Processing

We began our research into query optimization and processing for object-oriented databases with the expectation that we would end up with solutions that are significantly different from those developed for relational queries. However, after much effort, we have concluded that most of the important techniques developed for relational query optimization and processing are directly applicable to object-oriented queries against a single target class. An object-oriented query against a single-target class retrieves nested objects belonging to the class. (We note that the existing techniques need to be augmented with some new techniques and storage structures, especially if more than one nested target classes are to be 'joined'; we do not address these issues in this paper.) The techniques that directly apply to both relational and object-oriented queries include the computation of reasonable permutations of the classes (relations), estimating their costs by using a cost model, maintenance of statistics to aid the cost estimation, matching instances of a class (tuples of a relation) with instances of another class, and, in the case of a distributed database, the generation of a global query plan as a collection of local query plans.

In retrospect, the extent of similarities between relational and object-oriented query processing should not have come as a surprise, if we recognized that, regardless of data models, query processing is essentially a process of mapping a declarative query expression into a sequence of procedural executions. In particular, the query-graph formalism can be used to show that there exists a mapping from an object-oriented query to a semantically equivalent relational query. An intuitive argument was given in [BANE88].

An object-oriented query with a single target class differs from a relational query in a few ways. Perhaps the most important difference is that the scope of an attribute node in an object-oriented query graph can be a class hierarchy rooted at the domain of that attribute node. Therefore, a class-hierarchy index [KIM89a], that is, an index on an attribute common to all classes on a class hierarchy rooted at some user-specified class, can be an effective access method in processing an object-oriented query.

A relational system may allow a virtual attribute to be defined in a relation. The value of a virtual attribute, instead of being physically stored, is computed based on other attributes of the relation. This is a less powerful concept compared to methods in an object-oriented system. In an object-oriented database, a message is sent to an object (e.g., the owner message to a vehicle object) and the method associated with its class is invoked to return values for the message. There can be different methods invoked for the same message sent to different classes. This makes maintaining statistics and thus cost estimation for query optimization more difficult. In this paper, we do not attempt to address this issue.

3. Overview of ORION Query Processing

As in most database systems which support queries, query processing in ORION proceeds in two phases: query optimization and query execution. The inputs to the optimizer are a query graph and a global directory. For query optimization, we also maintain statistics. We chose to have each site maintain a copy of the global directory with statistics for the entire shared database. That is, for each class in the database, the global directory at each site contains a vector of two-tuples (s,r), where s is a resident site of the class and r is a list containing per-site statistics such as the cardinality of the class at that site. Query optimization determines an optimal *global query plan* for a query at the *query-originating site*.

Given a query graph, the query optimizer searches the solution space for the best solution. It proceeds by enumerating solutions. The cost of a solution is estimated using a cost model, as in System R [SELI79], R*, and other systems. The solution with the minimum cost is selected and used to construct an optimal *global-query plan*.

A global query plan is composed of a set of *local query plans*, one for each participating site. There are two phases in executing a query. In the first phase, each participating site is sent a local query plan by the query-originating site. In the second phase, each site begins to execute its query plan in parallel with other participating sites. Executions of the query plans are synchronized only by the sending and receiving of data among participating sites. The results are sent to the query-originating site, which in turn returns the final result to the user.

4. ORION Query-Processing Strategies

There are four major elements in a query-processing strategy for distributed ORION: *the query-graph traversal order, object matching, parallelism in processing query-graph branches, and query-execution site selection*. Thus, the search space has four dimensions. A combination of the solutions for these four elements is called a query-processing strategy or a query-execution plan. The query optimizer enumerates all plausible plans and selects an optimal plan. As we will show in this section, the first two elements in an ORION query-processing strategy correspond to the join order and concatenation of tuples in a pair of relations, respectively, in relational query processing. The third element is important in distributed ORION, since our optimization criterion is the response time of a query, and thus it is essential for the optimizer to exploit parallelism inherent in distributed query execution. The fourth element is found in a distributed query-processing strategy, regardless of the data model.

4.1 Query-Graph Traversal Orderings

A query graph with n class nodes in it is roughly equivalent to a relational query which joins n relations [BANE88]. Just as there are potentially n! permutations of n relations, there are potentially n! ways of 'joining' n classes in a query graph. Thus the problem of determining the traversal orderings of n classes in a query graph is equivalent to the problem of determining the join orders for n relations in an n-relation query.

In our query optimization algorithm, we decompose a query graph into clusters of nodes and enumerate traversal orderings for these clusters iteratively. This approach allows us to enumerate traversal orderings systematically on the basis of the query-graph representation of a query. Further, it obviates the need to explicitly screen orderings that lead to computing the cartesian product of classes in a query graph.

Given a query graph G, there exist several levels of transformed graph as follows:

(1) G' is a transformation of G in which the connective and comparator nodes are combined with their parent attribute nodes such that G' is a graph consisting of only attribute nodes. We call G' a level-0 graph.

(2) A level-i graph (i >=0) is *transformed* to a level i+1 graph by replacing each cluster of nodes at the level-i graph with its root node.

A cluster in a level-i graph is rooted at a node whose child nodes are all leaf nodes in a level-i graph. The cluster consists of that root node and its child nodes. Typical clusters, Person-State, Company-Supplier-Distributor, or Vehicle-Person-Company, are shown in Figure 4.1. We will distinguish a *chain cluster* (e.g.,Person-State) and a *tree cluster* (e.g., Company-Supplier-Distributor). Further, there can be two types of tree cluster, AND-cluster and OR-cluster, depending on the connective node. To evaluate a cluster, we aim to *reduce* its root node (i.e., filter its instances) using the restrictions represented by the links to its parent and child nodes. For instance, evaluating the AND-cluster Vehicle-Person-Company reduces the attribute node Vehicle using its child attribute nodes Person and Company, which in turn are reduced by evaluating the clusters Person-State and Company-Supplier-Distributor (an OR-cluster), respectively.

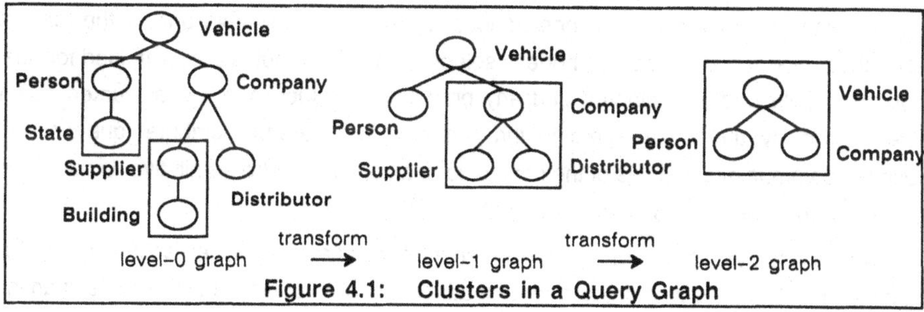

Figure 4.1: Clusters in a Query Graph

Within a cluster, there are two basic methods for traversing its nodes: forward and reverse. A combination of these two basic methods is called a mixed-traversal method.

(a) *Forward Traversal.* Traversing of a cluster begins at its root node and proceeds in a top-down fashion. A forward traversal of a cluster requires two phases: *propagate-down* and *percolate-up*. In the first phase, the values of an attribute (UIDs of the child class), after projection to remove duplicates, propagate down from the parent node to the child nodes. In the second phase, UIDs of qualified instances percolate up from a child to its parent. At the parent node, the child UIDs are used to filter instances in the parent's class.

An alternative is to send UID-pairs consisting of (parent-UID child-UID), instead of child UIDs only, from a parent to a child. In this case, there is no need for the second phase, since the filtering of the parent-UIDs can be done at the sites where the child nodes reside. However, the amount of data to be sent might become significantly larger.

(b) *Reverse Traversal*. Traversing of a cluster begins at its leaves and proceeds in a bottom-up fashion. A list of UIDs of qualified instances, filtered at the leaves, flows from the leaves to the root node; at each node the UIDs in the list are matched with the attribute values of the class of the node. Obviously, the cost for a reverse traversal can be significantly reduced if there exists an index on the attribute of the parent's class. One might note that this traversal performs a semi-join operation over the UIDs of the attribute. There is no need for a projection over the UID lists, however, since a UID is unique.

(c) *Mixed Traversal*. In a mixed traversal, some links are forward traversed, while the rest are reverse traversed. For example, given a root node T and a set of child nodes $\{C_i, i = 1, 2, 3\}$, C_1->T can be reverse traversed, while T->C_2 and T->C_3 are forward traversed.

4.2 Object Matching

Object matching refers to the process of matching objects belonging to one class with objects in another class. This is similar to the concatenation of tuples in one relation with tuples in another relation in a relational join. Under the ORION query model, an object A is matched with another object B, if object B is a value of an attribute of object A. Two basic algorithms have been used in relational databases for concatenating tuples: sort-merge and nested loop [SELI79]. These algorithms apply equally well to matching objects for object-oriented queries.

In the sort-merge algorithm, the UIDs selected from a node in the query graph are sorted and then passed to its parent node (in the case of a reverse traversal) or its child nodes (in the case of a forward traversal) for matching. The nested-loop algorithm is applicable only in the forward-traversal method. First, an instance of a node is selected and its attributes are examined for qualification. Next, a child node is selected and any predicates on the node are evaluated against its attributes. Obviously, the sort-merge algorithm is more appropriate for distributed query processing because the communication costs of the nested-loop algorithm can be prohibitive. In our implementation, we do not use the nested-loop algorithm.

ORION supports the creation of an index on an attribute of a class. When an index is created for the attribute of a class, it is also created for that attribute in all subclasses of the class. If an index is available, it will be used to enhance performance during reverse traversal.

4.3 Parallel Processing of the Query-Graph Branches

A query graph has three types of logical connective: *AND*, *OR*, and *NOT*. An *AND* or *OR* node has two or more branches. The branches can be processed in parallel or serially.

(a) *Parallel AND/OR*. Branches of an AND or OR node are processed in parallel to exploit parallelism. We call the methods *AND-Parallel* and *OR-Parallel*, respectively. Obviously, the response time for a cluster is determined by the maximum time required to traverse the links.

(b) *Serial AND*. Even though our optimization criterion is the response time, a serial "branch-by-branch" processing might be beneficial for an AND node, since the amount of data that need to be sent in processing a branch might be reduced by pre-filtering some other branches and thus incur less communication cost. In this case, the order in evaluating the children of an AND node is important. Given a cluster with a root node T and a set of child nodes {C_i, 1<=i<=n}, the number of permutations of {C_i} for a serial traversal is n!, where n is the number of child nodes. This might significantly expand the search space if the number of permutations is large. Therefore, when n is larger than 3, we reduce the search space by selecting the next child node to process on the basis of the selectivities of the child nodes. That is, given an AND cluster, its branches are ordered such that the most selective one is the first in a depth-first search; serial traversals of the cluster using other ordering are eliminated. However, since an *OR* node returns a "union" of the qualified UIDs, *OR-Serial* is necessarily inferior to *OR-Parallel*. Thus we always process *OR* branches in parallel.

We will pause at this point to illustrate query-processing strategies that result from combining the elements of a query-processing strategy discussed thus far. The following five strategies result from combining two elements, namely, the query-graph traversal orderings and parallel processing of the query-graph branches. Note that we use the notation "||" to indicate parallel execution of operations enclosed by square brackets; and an arrow "->" to indicate a precedence relation, for example, A->B indicates A is reduced before B. We will illustrate these strategies using the AND cluster Company-Supplier-Distributor shown in Figure 4.2. The class Company is the root of the cluster. Case 1 and Case 4 will be described in detail.

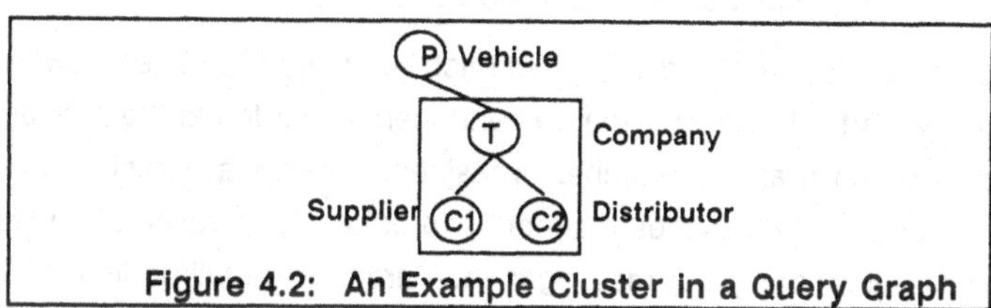

Figure 4.2: An Example Cluster in a Query Graph

Case 1. Reverse-Parallel (R-P) ([C_1||C_2]->T)
Case 2. Forward-Parallel (F-P) (T->[C_1||C_2]->T)
Case 3. Mixed-Parallel (M-P) ([C_1->T||T->C_2->T] or [C_2->T||T->C_1->T])
Case 4. Forward-Serial (F-S) (T->C_1->T->C_2->T)
Case 5. Mixed-Serial (M-S) (C_1->T->C_2->T)

For the Reverse-Parallel case (Case 1), C_1 and C_2 are reduced in parallel (using predicates represented by their child nodes, if any) and the UIDs of the reduced C_1 and C_2 are sent to reduce T. Concurrently, the node T processes any simple predicates (comparator nodes) on T and then waits for UIDs from C_1 and C_2. For example, the Distributor node is reduced using the simple predicate (> sales-volume 800), and the Supplier node is concurrently reduced using the strategy chosen for the Supplier-Building cluster and the simple predicate on the Building node. The resulting UIDs of the classes Distributor and Supplier are used to filter the instances in the class Company.

For the Forward-Serial case (Case 4), C_1's UIDs are sent from node T to C_1 which is then reduced and UIDs of the reduced C_1 are sent back to node T where T's instances are filtered. The attribute values (UIDs of instances of C_2) of the reduced T node are then sent to the second child node C_2 which is then reduced and a reduced list of C_2's UIDs is sent back to node T for further reduction.

For each of the above cases, we have assumed that the parent node P of the root T of the cluster is reduced after T. However, P may also be reduced before T. For example, the attribute values (UIDs of the instances of T) of node P are projected and sent to node T in parallel with the reduction of T's child nodes C_1 and C_2. Before node T is reduced, it must receive UIDs from all links.

4.4 Selection of Subquery-Evaluation Sites

In a distributed system, the communication costs of a query depend to a significant extent on the sites chosen to execute a query. Thus, site selection has an impact on the response time of a query. In ORION, we consider two basic methods, *Parent-Site/Children-Site* and *Originating-Site*, and one heuristic called *Largest-Data-Site*.

(a) *Parent-Site/Children-Site.* The Parent-Site method can be used in conjunction with the reverse-traversal method, while the Children-Site method is used with the forward-traversal method. With a reverse traversal, data are sent from each resident site of an attribute node in the query graph to all the resident sites of its parent node. For example, if the tree cluster Vehicle-Person-Company in the query graph of Figure 2.2 is reverse traversed, the UIDs of the instances of Company at sites S_2 and S_3 are sent to all the resident sites, S_1, S_2, and S_3, of Vehicle. Similarly, when forward traversal is used, data from each resident site of an attribute node are sorted by the site-id and then sent to the resident sites of its child node.

(b) *Originating-Site.* In this method, the result of each subquery of a node is always sent to the originating site where the partial results are merged and then forwarded to the resident sites of its parent or child node. If p and q are the number of resident sites for a parent and a child node, respectively, then the number of messages that needs to be sent in a reverse traversal is (p+q). (p+q) is generally smaller than the (p*q) messages the Parent-Site method incurs. The effect is more obvious if total time is used as the optimization criterion. However, even when response time is used, it can still be profitable because each site has less work to do (i.e., each child site sends one message to the originating site instead of sending p messages in serial, if no broadcast mechanism exists, to each parent site.)

(c) *Largest-Data-Site.* To minimize the amount of network communication needed to process a query, it is sometimes better to choose a site with the largest estimated data in a cluster to process a subquery. We call such a site a *pivot site* for the cluster. For each site in a cluster, we calculate the cardinalities of instances in the site, and pick the site with the largest number of instances as the pivot site. For example, given the data distribution shown in Figure 2.2, the pivot sites for the Company-Supplier-Distributor cluster and the Person-State cluster are site S_3 and S_1, respectively. Other participating sites send relevant data to the pivot site where the subqueries are evaluated. We will illustrate this method using an example in Section 6.

4.5 Consideration of Migrated Objects

In object-oriented databases, each object contains its UID. In distributed ORION, the UID of an object includes an identification of the site in which it was created (called the *birth* site). If a request for the object originates at some other site later, ORION routes the request to the birth site of the object. If one site makes many references to an object, the user may wish to migrate the object to that site. If an object is migrated to another site (called the *store* site), however, the UID of the object continues to hold the birth-site identifier. When the object is later requested, the request will be made to the birth site. The birth site will then forward the request to the store site of the object. During query processing, this may cause many short messages between sites.

Migrated objects cause no extra burden for query processing when the reverse-traversal method is used. This is because instances are referenced associatively according to a value of one or more attributes. For example, instances of the class Person in Figure 2.2 are qualified by a comparison of the value of their home-state attribute with a list of State UID values received from the execution of a previous subquery on the class State. Therefore, the list of State UID values must be sent to all sites containing Person instances. Even if there is an index on the home-state attribute of the person class, in ORION an individual index will be maintained at each site containing Person instances. This index will only contain references to the Person instances at that site. Therefore, the list of State uid values must still be sent to all of these sites.

However, problems may arise when the forward-traversal method is used. For example, if the forward-traversal method is used for Figure 2.2, values of the attribute home-state of Person instances will be sent to the next lower node in the query graph during the propagate-down phase. The values sent are UIDs of the instances of the class State. Only these instances of the class State will be considered, rather than all instances of the class State. Since these UIDs have a birth-site identifier included in them, it would seem that a UID could be sent only to its birth site, thus avoiding the overhead of sending all UIDs to all sites containing instances of the class State. However, if an object has migrated from the birth site, an extra message will be needed to retrieve the object from the new store site. This may cause many extra messages to be sent during the execution of a query.

There are two ways to deal with migrated objects when a query is executed using forward-traversal. One is to send the UIDs only to their birth sites during the propagate-down phase. A site which is processing a subquery will then retrieve migrated objects from their new store sites whenever they are encountered. Another way is to send all UIDs to all sites during the propagate-down phase. A site which is processing a subquery will not have to retrieve migrated objects from the new store sites, because equivalent subqueries executing at the store sites will evaluate the objects. We plan to investigate the merits of these alternatives during optimizer validation.

5. Query Optimization

As mentioned earlier, the classes in a query-graph representation of a query are grouped into clusters, and query-processing strategies are enumerated for these clusters in a bottom-up fashion. To avoid re-enumerating strategies (solutions), we have introduced the notion of *independent* and *dependent* solutions for a cluster. The independent solution for a cluster is the optimal strategy when the cluster is evaluated without input from its parent node. The dependent solution for a cluster is the optimal strategy when the cluster is evaluated with input from its parent node to the root of the cluster. We will use the notation QI and QD to denote the optimal costs for the independent and dependent solutions for a cluster, respectively. Note that, given a strategy for a cluster, we know whether a QI or a QD of each of the child nodes is needed to calculate the cost of reducing the root node of the cluster, since the direction of the link between a child node and the root node is fixed by the chosen strategy. For example, if the strategy uses the reverse-traversal method such as R-P-ParentSite, then QI's of the child nodes are needed, because the links in the cluster is reverse traversed. On the other hand, traversing a link using forward traversal needs the QD of the child node. During query optimization, if the QI/QD at a child node was known (i.e., has been calculated in a previous iteration), the value is simply returned and no calculation is needed. Since QD is generally a function of f (the number of instances input to a cluster from its parent node), a list of (QD,f) is maintained at each node to avoid re-calculation.

Let Σ denote the search space for a cluster and σ denote a member of Σ. Let Φ = {R-P, F-P, M-P, F-S, M-S} (i.e., the set of traversal methods), and Γ = {Parent-Site, Originating-Site, Largest-Data-Site}. We have $\Sigma = \Phi \times \Gamma$. For a given cluster, let T denote its root node and H = $\{C_1, C_2, \ldots, C_i, \ldots\}$ denote its child nodes. Each node has associated with it a six-tuple (QI, σ-QI, QD, σ-QD, Ω, S), where QI is the optimal cost to evaluate the node independently of its parent node, that is, without input from its parent; QD is the optimal cost to evaluate the node when there are data input from its parent; σ-QI and σ-QD are the selected solutions for QI and QD, respectively; Ω represents the statistics of the domain (and the class hierarchy rooted at it) of the node. The statistics include the cardinality and the number of distinct values at each site; and S is the selectivity of that node.

Step 1. Search the graph in a depth-first order to obtain site-ids and statistics (Ω) for the class hierarchy rooted at the domain of each node; and to calculate the selectivity (S) for each node.

Step 2. Beginning with the cluster at the root node (called the *root cluster*) in the query graph, choose a strategy $\sigma \in \Sigma$ that has not been enumerated. On the basis of the chosen strategy σ, mark each child node $C_i \in H$ of the cluster with a QI or QD to indicate that the cost of reducing the root node depends on the QI or QD of that child node. Also, on the basis of the selectivity, calculate the number of instances, denoted as f, that need to be communicated over each link for forward traversal.

Step 3. Repeat step 2 for each cluster in a depth-first search of the query graph.

Step 4. Calculate QI/QD based on the cost model. The calculation is bottom-up, that is,
(a) when a leaf cluster is reached, the QI/QD of the root node of the cluster is calculated.
(b) for a non-leaf cluster, the QI/QD of the root node of the cluster is calculated based on the QI's/QD's of its child nodes.

Step 5. Enumerating σ's in Σ, repeat step 4 recursively in a bottom-up fashion on the query graph. That is, for each cluster, each σ in Σ is enumerated before its parent node is given the next σ. When the σ's in Σ are exhausted for a given cluster, the σ with the least cost is associated with its node as σ-QI or σ-QD (i.e., the local optimal solution for a cluster). When the cost of σ for the root cluster is obtained, we have found the cost of a solution for the query, which is optimal under the condition that the σ was chosen for the root cluster.

Step 6. The enumeration stops when the search space Σ for the root cluster is exhausted. The solution with the least cost for the root is selected as the optimal solution, which is represented as a collection of σ-QI's or σ-QD's associated with each cluster in the graph.

As an example, let us look at the query graph in Figure 2.2. First, the query graph is walked through and, for each node, statistics are obtained and selectivity is calculated. Next, we choose a strategy, R-P-ParentSite, for the cluster Vehicle-Person-Company. Using this strategy, both links are traversed in reverse direction, that is, Person->Vehicle and Company->Vehicle. Thus, we need the QI costs of the child nodes, Person and Company, to calculate the cost to reduce its root node, Vehicle. To find the QI cost of Person, we consider the cluster Person-State and choose first the strategy R-P-ParentSite to reduce the Person node. The cost is calculated based on the statistics and the predicate on State. Then the cost to reduce the Person node using the strategy, F-P-ParentSite, is calculated and compared with the cost using the first strategy, R-P-ParentSite. We then proceed with the next strategy for the Person-State cluster. Eventually, the solution space for the Person-State cluster is exhausted and the optimal cost (and its strategy) is assigned as QI (σ-QI) for the Person node. The QI for Company is calculated in a similar way. We can now calculate the cost to reduce the Vehicle node using R-P-ParentSite. Then the next strategy, F-P-ParentSite, for the root cluster is chosen. Since the links are traversed in forward direction, that is, Vehicle->Person and Vehicle->Company, under F-P-ParentSite, we need to calculate the QDs of the child nodes, Person and Company, which are then calculated by enumerating the strategies for Person-State and Company-Supplier-Distributor clusters. After the cost for the root cluster using F-P-ParentSite is obtained, we proceed with other strategies until the solution space is exhausted and the solution with a minimum cost is chosen. Note that a QI and one or more QDs are associated with each node after they have been calculated to avoid re-calculation. For instance, when we wish to calculate the cost for the root cluster using the M-P-ParentSite strategy (after R-P-ParentSite and F-P-ParentSite have been considered) with a reverse link, Person->Vehicle, and a forward link, Vehicle->Company, the QI for Person and QD for Company are available, and there is no need to re-calculate them.

On the basis of the algorithm, we can show the size of the search space. Let β be the number of non-leaf nodes in a given query graph G. By definition, the number of clusters is β. Also, let γ be the cardinality of the search space Σ for a cluster, we have $\gamma = 15$ for a tree cluster and $\gamma = 6$ for a chain cluster (in which Φ = {R-P, F-P}, since there is only one link.) Thus, the search space for G in our algorithm is $\prod_{i=1}^{\beta} \gamma_i$, where γ_i =15 or 6, which is exponential in the number of non-leaf nodes. However, the complexity of our algorithm is significantly lower, since there is no need to re-calculate QI or QD when they are known.

6. Query-Execution Model

In this section, we will describe the query-execution plan, and illustrate it using an example. We will also outline the cost model that the query optimizer uses. (A discussion of the cost model logically belongs to Section 5; however, the cost model is based on the query-execution model, and thus is presented here.)

6.1 The QXP Model

Our query-execution model is a dataflow-based graphical representation of a global query plan, and is abbreviated as the QXP model. The following is a precise definition of the model.

Definition: A query-execution-plan is a quadruple QXP = (N,S,D,R), where N is a finite set of operations called subqueries, each of which is defined on the domain class of a query-graph node (Section 7 describes the subquery types);
S is a finite set of sites where the domain classes of the query-graph nodes reside;
D is a partial order relation (dependency relation) defined on N, that is, $D \subseteq N \times N$; and
R is a binary relation on $N \times S$, representing a partition of the subquery nodes into their resident sites.

Besides representing an optimal global-query plan, the QXP serves a number of useful purposes. First, a QXP is partitioned into a set of local query plans, one for each participating site. Thus it is the basis for distributing subquery plans to participating sites. Second, it makes it easy to determine parallelism in a query plan, since control and synchronization are determined only by data dependency. Third, it provides a conceptual framework in which the correctness of the query execution can be traced using a small number of well-defined subquery types. Fourth, as we will show, it is used as a framework for cost estimation by the query optimizer; costs are associated with the nodes and links in a QXP.

In Figure 6.1, we show an example QXP. Data flows from the leaves of the graph to the root. A subquery is indicated by a node; and nodes are connected by links. The nodes are partitioned into a set of local query plans on the basis of the sites where they will be executed. The links represent dependency relations; they indicate data flow and synchronization. A vertical link within a subquery plan for a site represents a local precedence order of the subqueries. The QXP is depicted as several levels of nodes connected by links. The nodes connected by a "thick" link represent the same subquery, and does not indicate any data flow. The links across sites also indicate inter-site communication. Note that each subquery in a QXP is labeled with a subquery number and the class it operates on.

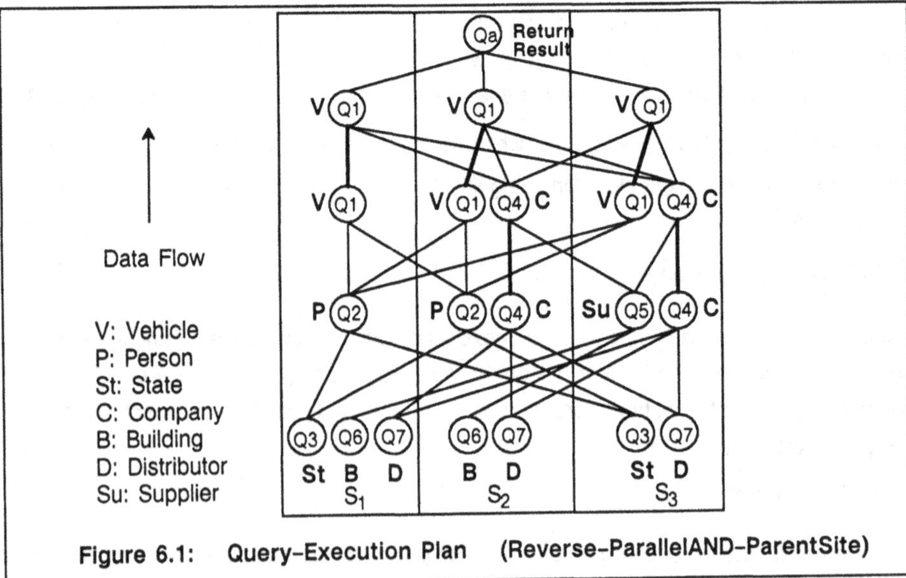

Figure 6.1: Query-Execution Plan (Reverse-ParallelAND-ParentSite)

The QXP of Figure 6.1 uses reverse traversal with the Parent–Site method for each cluster of the query graph. Let us describe the local query plan executed at site S_1. In the local query plan, Q_7, Q_6, and Q_3 are subqueries on Distributor, Building, and State, respectively. The subqueries evaluate a predicate that corresponds to a comparator node. These subqueries are processed in parallel and their results are sent to the resident sites of their parent nodes, Company, Supplier, and Person, respectively. Next, upon receiving the results of Q_3, that is, the UIDs of State from Site S_1 and Site S_3, subquery Q_2 evaluates Person's instances and selects those with matching home–state attributes. After receiving the results from Q_2 and Q_4, subquery Q_1 executes an *AND* operation that selects instances of Vehicle by matching the owner and manufacturer attributes in each Vehicle instance with the UIDs of Person and Company classes received from Q_2 and Q_4, respectively. The results of Q_1 are sent to the query–originating site S_2 where subquery Q_a merges the results from sites S_1, S_2 and S_3 and returns them to the user.

6.2 Cost Estimation

For each candidate query plan (a solution), the optimizer has to estimate its cost, which corresponds to an estimate of the response time in ORION. Cost estimation in a distributed query has two parts: local processing and communication. Local processing includes CPU and disk I/O costs. The communication cost has two factors: CPU time and communication delay. In this section, we describe briefly our cost estimation for a cluster; detailed cost formulae for local and communication costs are omitted. Note that we do not currently consider the effects of possible overlapping between local processing and inter–site communication, and we assume that there is no overlapping between CPU and I/O execution.

The cost to reduce the root node of a cluster is determined by three factors: the local processing cost at the root node, the communication cost to/from its children, and the costs associated with its children. A convenient way to calculate these costs is to construct conceptually a QXP for the cluster based on the selected strategy. To estimate the cost of a solution, each node in the QXP is associated with a local processing cost; and each edge is associated with a communication cost. A *path cost* is calculated by summing up these costs along a path in the QXP. The path with the maximum path cost to the root is the critical path. The cost of a solution is determined by the estimated cost of the critical path in its corresponding QXP.

We assume that each of the resident sites of a node sends its data in parallel and the processing and communication costs are increasing functions of the amount of data at each site, (which is true if the same access methods can be applied at each site). Also, the selectivity at node N_i (S_{Ni}) is assumed to be the same among the resident sites. Under these assumptions, the critical path in a QXP for a given cluster is determined by the site with the largest amount of data among the resident sites of each node in the cluster. We will use $C_{Ni,m}$ to denote the maximum of C_{Ni} (the cardinality of the domain class for node N_i) over the resident sites of node N_i.

For example, we have the following equation for a cluster using the Reverse–Parallel–ParentSite strategy. In this case, all the *l* links are in reverse direction. Therefore, to calculate the QI of node N from the QI's of its child nodes $\{N_i$, $i = 1,l\}$, we have

$QI_N = Max_i\ [QI_{Ni} + CM_{Ni\text{->}N}(D_{i,m})] + LC_N$,

where $CM_{Ni\text{->}N}$ is the communication cost from N_i to N based on $D_{i,m}$, the maximum amount of data sent from a site of node N_i to node N ($D_{i,m} = C_{Ni,m} * S_{Ni}$). LC_N is the local processing cost at node N (i.e., the maximum of the local processing costs of the resident sites of node N). Local processing at node N involves the filtering of the instances of the class of node N using the UIDs received. Thus, the local cost includes, for each link i, the merging cost of the D_i instances from the resident sites of N_i, the sorting cost (if needed) of the UID lists, and the selection cost through index search or segment scan, depending on whether there exists an index for the attribute (represented by N_i) of the class of node N.

In case there are instances input from the parent node of N, then we need to calculate the QD of node N. The equation for QD is similar to that of QI except the local processing cost. In this case, the local processing at each site of node N needs to check each of the f instances (that were input from N's parent node) to see if it qualifies using the received UIDs from N_i's. The local processing cost (a function of f) includes costs for merging the instances from participating sites, sorting the UID lists (if needed) and a scan of the f instances to check each attribute value against the UID lists received.

7. Query Execution

As we have seen, the query optimizer generates an optimal global-query plan. A global-query plan consists of a number of local-query plans for executing subqueries at local sites. A global-query plan is distributed to participating sites for execution. In this section, we will first describe elements of a global-query plan, that is, the types of subquery. Then we will discuss execution of the local-query plans.

7.1 Subquery Types

Figure 7.1 enumerates the types of subquery that may be used in a global-query plan. The query-processing strategy with which the subquery is associated is also shown in the figure. The first seven subqueries are *evaluation subqueries* which are used to reduce a node of the query-

SUBQUERY TYPE	STRATEGY
reverse-leaf	Reverse Parallel-AND (for leaf nodes)
reverse	Reverse Parallel-AND (for non-leaf nodes)
forward-start	Forward Parallel-AND/OR Forward/Mixed Serial-AND
forward	Forward Parallel-AND/OR Forward Serial-AND
forward-leaf	Forward Parallel-AND/OR Forward Serial-AND
forward-up	Forward/Mixed Parallel/Seral-AND Parallel-OR
forward-to-reverse	Reverse Parallel-AND (when parent cluster is forward-traversed)
merge-orig-reverse	Originating Site
merge-orig-forward	Originating Site
merge-large	Largest Data Site
merge-results	All

Figure 7.1: Table of Subquery Types

execution–plan using a predicate on the instances of the class represented by the node. The last four subqueries are *merge subqueries* which are used to merge the results of evaluation subqueries which were executed at multiple sites.

The reverse–leaf and reverse are used for the reverse–traversal method. The rest of the evaluation subqueries are necessary for execution of the forward–traversal method. As we described in Section 4.1, the forward–traversal method requires a propagate–down phase and a percolate–up phase. The forward–start, forward, forward–leaf subqueries are used during the propagate–down phase and the forward–up subquery is used during the percolate–up phase. The forward–start subquery is used in the propagate–down phase if reverse–traversal was used for the parent node or if there was no parent node. The forward subquery is used in the propagate–down phase if forward–traversal was used for the parent node. The forward–leaf subquery is used for a leaf node of the query–execution–plan. The forward–to–reverse subquery is used for the root node, T, of a cluster when it is processed using the reverse–traversal method and the link from its parent node, P, to T is forward traversed. The forward–start and forward subqueries must save intermediate results (temporary tables) that are used later during the percolate–up phase of the execution. The table contains two entries: the value of an attribute that was sent down to the next lower node of the query–execution–plan; and the value of the UIDs of the instances having that value for the attribute. Note that the forward–start subquery can also have incoming data in the form of qualifying values of an attribute of the class in order to implement the mixed serial strategy. Once the propagate–down phase is completed, the forward–up subquery is used to percolate up the results. The input data for a forward–up subquery are qualifying values (from one or more sites) of an attribute of the class at the node. Note that the forward–up subquery is similar to the reverse subquery except that instead of evaluating all of the instances of the class, the table from a previously executed forward–start or forward subquery contains the information to be evaluated.

The last four subqueries in Figure 7.1 are used for merging the results of evaluation subqueries which were executed at multiple sites. The merge–results subquery is executed at the originating site of the query and is used to merge the final results of the query to be returned to the user. If the optimizer selects the Originating–Site method, the results from the execution of a reverse or reverse–leaf subquery at multiple sites must all be sent to the originating site of the query. The merge–orig–reverse subquery is executed at the originating site to assemble the results. The merge–orig–forward serves a similar purpose when a forward–start or forward subquery is executed. When the optimizer selects the Largest–Data–Site method, the merge–large subquery is executed to bring relevant information about the instances of a class from all other sites.

7.2 Execution of a Local Query Plan

The local query plan is implemented as a table of subquery entries. Each entry represents a subquery that is waiting to receive input results from subqueries at its own site and other participating sites. When all necessary input data have been received, the subquery will execute some function on the local partition of the database. Note that a subquery operates only on a class or classes in a class hierarchy. The output results from this function serve as input data for other subqueries.

The subquery-execution control subsystem is invoked at the query-originating site through a procedure call. The subquery-execution control subsystem at remote sites are invoked through a message from the originating site to the remote sites. This message also contains the local query plan for the site to execute. Each site then begins to execute its own local query plan. First, all subqueries are executed that require no input data. Next all subqueries are executed that require only input data from the local site. Then, the subquery-execution control subsystem calls the ORION communication subsystem to receive data from any of the other sites participating in the query. If no data has been received and there is no executable subquery, the execution of this subsystem for the query will be blocked. When a message is received from a subquery at some other site, the subquery-execution control subsystem will examine the local query plan to see if any of the subqueries have received all of the input data necessary for execution. If an executable subquery is found, it is executed. This continues until all subqueries have been executed at the site.

8. Conclusions

In this paper, we described the query optimization and processing strategies we have developed and implemented for the distributed version of the ORION object-oriented database system at MCC. Most of the research in the area of query processing thus far has been focused on relational databases, both centralized and distributed. The new problems we had to address include the ORION query model which is based on an object-oriented data model, and the requirement to minimize the response time of a query rather than the total processing time. Our approach was to use a query-graph representation of an object-oriented query as the basis for systematically generating a complete set of alternative query-processing strategies. The optimizer selects an optimal global query-processing strategy (global-query plan) from the set of strategies it generates; the optimal solution is selected on the basis of cost estimation for each of the alternative strategies. The global-query plan is represented in a form that we call a query-execution model; the model explicitly represents a global query in terms of subqueries that must be executed at local sites in parallel.

In the discussion of our solutions to the problems of query processing for object-oriented databases, we showed that most of the important techniques developed for query optimization and processing in the context of relational databases apply directly to object-oriented queries. This is an important conclusion, since this means that with relatively minor efforts implementors of object-oriented database systems (and nested-relational systems) can support queries.

We plan to continue the current research into object-oriented queries in two directions. Our research thus far has been focused on processing object-oriented queries with single target classes. More general queries involving joins of multiple target classes may require some new techniques and data structures for efficient query processing. Further, now that we have implemented sophisticated query-processing strategies, we need to validate them through extensive experimentation. In particular, we expect to fine-tune our cost model, and introduce additional heuristics to reduce the search space for an optimal query plan.

References

[ABIT84] Abiteboul, S., and N. Bidoit. "Non First Normal Form Relations to Represent Hierarchically Organized Data," in *Proc. ACM SIGACT-SIGMOD Symposium on Principles of Database Systems*, 1984, pp. 191-200.

[APER83] Apers, P., Hevner, A., and Yao, S.B. "Optimization Algorithms for Distributed Queries," *IEEE Transactions on Software Engineering*, Vol. SE-9, No. 1, January 1983.

[BANE87] Banerjee, J., et al. "Data Model Issues for Object-Oriented Applications," *ACM Trans. on Office Information Systems*, January 1987.

[BANE88] Banerjee, J., Kim, W., and Kim, K.C. "Queries in Object-Oriented Databases," in *Proc. of the International Conference on Data Engineering*, Los Angeles, February 1988.

[CHAN83] Chan, A., et. al. "Overview of an Ada Compatible Distributed Database Manager," *Proc. of ACM SIGMOD*, 1983.

[DANI82] Daniels, D., et. al. "An Introduction to Distributed Query Compilation in R*," *IBM Research Report* RJ3497, June 1982.

[IEEE88] IEEE Computer Society, *Database Engineering*, special issue on Non-First Normal Form Relational Databases (ed. Z.M. Ozsoyoglu), Sept. 1988.

[KIM87] Kim, W., et al. "Composite Object Support in an Object-Oriented Database System," in *Proc. 2nd Intl. Conf. on Object-Oriented Programming Systems, Languages, and Applications*, Orlando, Florida, Oct. 1987.

[KIM88] Kim, W., et al. "Integrating an Object-Oriented Programming System with a Database System," in *Proc. 2nd Intl. Conf. on Object-Oriented Programming Systems, Languages, and Applications*, San Diego, Calif., Sept. 1988.

[KIM89a] Kim, W., Kim, K-C., and Dale, A. "Indexing Techniques for Object-Oriented Databases," to appear in *Object-Oriented Concepts, Databases, and Applications*, Addison-Wesley, 1989.

[KIM89b] Kim, W. "A Model of Queries for Object-Oriented Databases, *Proc. of the 15th International Conference on Very Large Data Bases*, 1989.

[KIMK88] Kim, K-C., Kim, W., and Woelk, D. "Acyclic Query Processing in Object-Oriented Databases," *Proc. Entity-Relationship Conference*, Italy, November 1988.

[LOHM85] Lohman, G., et al. "Query Processing in R*," *Query Processing in Database Systems*, (eds. W. Kim, D. Reiner, and D. Batory), Springer-Verlag, 1985.

[LORI83] Lorie, R. and W. Plouffe. "Complex Objects and Their Use in Design Transactions," *in Proc. Databases for Engineering Applications*, Database Week 1983 (ACM), May 1983, pp. 115-121.

[MAKI77] Makinouchi, A. "A Consideration of Normal Form of Not-necessarily Normalized Relations in the Relational Data Model," in *Proc. Intl Conf. on Very Large Data Bases*, 1977, pp. 447-453.

[MACK86] Mackert, L., and Lohman, G. "R* Optimizer Validation and Performance Evaluation for Distributed Queries," *Proc. of the 12th International Conference on Very Large Data Bases*, 1986.

[SELI79] Selinger, P.G. et. al. "Access Path Selection in a Relational Database Management System," in *Proc. ACM SIGMOD Intl. Conf. on Management of Data*, Boston, Mass. pp 23-34, 1979.

[VALD88] Valduriez, P., and Danforth S. "Query Optimization in FAD," *MCC Technical Report* ACA-ST-316-88, September 1988.

[YU87] Yu, C., et. al. "Algorithms to Process Distributed Queries in Fast Local Networks," *IEEE Transactions on Computer*, Vol. C-36, No. 10, October 1987.

A LOCALIZED APPROACH TO DISTRIBUTED QUERY PROCESSING

Arbee L.P. Chen
Bell Communications Research
444 Hoes Lane, Piscataway, NJ 08854
U.S.A.

ABSTRACT

To process queries against a global schema in a distributed multidatabase system, query transformation which maps the query against the global schema to the local schemas is necessary. In this paper, a *localized approach* is presented which optimizes distributed query processing. This approach transforms a query to subqueries. Each subquery references data contained at a local site and therefore can be locally processed. It reduces data transmission time and query response time due to local processing and parallel processing. It can therefore be applied in distributed database systems implemented in either long-haul or local networks. Moreover, semantic information can be incorporated with this approach to process distributed queries at a single site. Data fragmentation and schema and data conflicts exist in the multidatabase environment, which are treated in a uniform framework in this approach.

1. INTRODUCTION

Many distributed query processing algorithms have been proposed [4], [22], [29]. Some make use of *semijoins* to reduce the amount of data transfer [1], [3], [4], [10] - [14], [31], [36]; some make use of the *fragment and replicate* strategy to allow parallel processing [7], [22], [37], [38]; some integrate these two strategies for adapting to various network environments [9], [39]; some use *operation grouping* as the heuristic [15], [16]; some consider query transformation for multidatabases [17], [19], [27]; moreover, some apply semantic information for fast query processing [26], [28], [32], [40].

In a distributed database system (homogeneous or heterogeneous) [6], [21], [33], [35], data are often partitioned and distributed at multiple sites. Data can be horizontally or vertically partitioned. These partitions provide portions of the data close to the users who use them most often. For existing databases, data can be virtually integrated horizontally or vertically to represent the global database. That is, data exist as partitions naturally in the multidatabase environment.

Views are defined in multidatabase systems to provide data fragmentation, data distribution and schema difference transparencies [2], [5], [18], [20], [24]. To process queries against these views, modification of queries [34] from against the view to against the underlying local schemas is needed. This paper addresses the query transformation and optimization issues, considering various data fragmentation schemes and schema integration conflicts. None of the algorithms mentioned above considered the data fragmentation issues completely, and few papers discussed the query optimization for a multidatabase system, where schema integration conflicts need be resolved.

Our approach for query optimization is to transform a global query to subqueries which reference data fragments at local sites and to process these subqueries locally. At this stage of query processing, no data movement is needed. Moreover, since these subqueries are processed at different sites, they can be processed in parallel. After the results are generated at local sites, final processing will be performed to get the answer. Final processing may include a union operation, or additional join operations. In some cases, no final processing is needed. We call this approach *localized query processing*. Localized query processing reduces the data transmission cost when the local processing reduces the size of data fragments, and increases the query processing parallelism which reduces the query response time. This localized approach is therefore suitable for query processing in distributed database systems employing either long-haul or local networks. Moreover, since we consider localized processing, the information of the query semantics and data distribution can be used to check whether a query can be processed at a single site (i.e., only data fragments at a single site are needed and therefore no data movement is required for processing this query). This semantic query optimization approach could significantly save the query processing cost.

Various data fragmentation schemes including horizontal fragmentation, vertical fragmentation and mixed fragmentation will be considered in this localized query processing approach. Also, schema and data conflicts in the mutidatabase environment will be considered in the same data fragmentation framework.

This paper is organized as follows. Section 2 discusses data fragmentation and schema mapping. Section 3 provides the conditions and properties for localized query processing for various data fragmentation schemes. Incorporating mapping of inconsistent data and different schema structures in the fragmented database environment, the query optimization tactics discussed in Section 3 are revisited in Section 4. Section 5 concludes this work.

2. DATA FRAGMENTATION AND SCHEMA MAPPING

In this section, an example schema will be used to discuss the problems of data fragmentation, fragment distribution and schema mapping.

The example schema consists of two relations:

EMP (E#, Ename, D#, Rank, Salary)
DEPT (D#, Dname, Mgr#, Budget)

where E# and Mgr# are in the same domain, so are EMP.D# and DEPT.D#.

2.1 Data fragmentation with constraints

There are two types of data fragmentation, namely, horizontal fragmentation and vertical fragmentation [8]. Horizontal fragmentation partitions the tuples of a relation into disjoint subsets. This is useful in distributed databases, where each subset can contain data which have common geographical properties. For example, relation EMP can be partitioned into subsets, where each subset contains data for employees who work at the same location. These subsets can be stored at their associated locations. For existing databases, data stored at different sites may have the same schema, and may be disjoint. These data can be viewed as subsets of a global relation. In this situation, "Location" can be added as a new attribute in the global schema, whose value is implicitly known for the local users, and is not stored in local databases.

The fragmentation could be represented by a select qualification over the relation. The relation can be reconstructed by unioning the subsets. The disjointness of the subsets will be referred to as the *key disjointness constraint.*

Vertical fragmentation partitions the attributes of a relation into groups. This is useful in distributed databases, where each group of attributes can contain data which have common geographical properties. For example, attributes of relation DEPT can be grouped into $DEPT_1$ (D#, Dname, Mgr#) and $DEPT_2$ (D#, Budget), where $DEPT_1$ stores personnel data and resides at site 1 while $DEPT_2$ stores budget data and resides at site 2.

The fragmentation could be represented by a project qualification over the relation. In order to be able to reconstruct the relation, we require that the key attribute be included in each group, and its values be duplicated in each fragment of the relation. The reconstruction of the relation can be done by joining all the fragments on the key attribute. The key value duplication in each fragment will be referred to as the *key duplication constraint.*

Denote F_{ij} as a fragment of R_i, which resides at site j. Also, let F_{ij} be H_{ij} if the fragmentation is horizontal, or V_{ij}, if it is vertical. Define a *configuration* of data distribution as a set of fragments denoted as above. In Section 3, we will discuss the processing of queries which retrieve data from the following three configurations: C_1 = $\{H_{11}, H_{12}, H_{21}, H_{22}|$ with key disjointness constraint$\}$, C_2 = $\{V_{11}, V_{12}, V_{21}, V_{22}|$ with key duplication constraint$\}$, and C_3 = $\{H_{11}, H_{12}, V_{21}, V_{22}|$ with key disjointness constraint and key duplication constraint$\}$. C_1 represents two horizontally partitioned relations, C_2 represents two vertically partitioned relations, and C_3 represents a horizontally partitioned relation and a vertically partitioned relation in the distributed database.

2.2 Data fragmentation without constraints

In this subsection, we discuss the relaxation of the key disjointness and the key duplication constraints for the horizontal fragmentation and vertical fragmentation, respectively. This constraint relaxation is especially necessary in the environment where multiple databases could be pre-existing.

In the horizontal fragmentation situation, the key disjointness constraint is relaxed by allowing tuples in different fragments to have the same key value but different values for other attributes. This is called "conflicting data" or "inconsistent data" in the multidatabase literature. The functional dependency constraint that the key value functionally determines the other values in a tuple is satisfied in each fragment but not in the global relation. The resolution of this conflict can be to show the different attribute values, to pick one presumably more reasonable value, or to give the aggregate of these conflicting values when the same key value is globally queried. Referring to the example schema, assume different Salary values exist, say, 50 and 10, for the same E# value in different fragments. When this E# value is queried, the Salary values obtained could be both 50 and 10, or just 50, presumably more reasonable, or the aggregate, say, SUM (50, 10) = 60 (this may be explained as two salaries for two jobs for one person, and each salary value is stored in one fragment).

In the vertical fragmentation situation, the key duplication constraint is relaxed by allowing the key values in one fragment to be different from those in another fragment. In order to present all the data stored in these fragments for the global relation, an outerjoin on the common key attribute over all the fragments is usually performed. The result of the outerjoin is the result of the join expanded with unmatched tuples from each fragment padded with null values for the attributes not in the fragment under consideration. This is called "missing data" or "schema structural differences" in the multidatabase literature. For example, if we outerjoin $DEPT_1$ and $DEPT_2$ in pre-existing databases, some departments in $DEPT_1$ may not have Budget values while some departments in $DEPT_2$ may not have Dname and Mgr# values.

By relaxing the two constraints, we have three more configurations to consider. Namely, $C_4 = \{H_{11}, H_{12}, H_{21}, H_{22}|$ without key disjointness constraint$\}$, $C_5 = \{V_{11}, V_{12}, V_{21}, V_{22}|$ without key duplication constraint$\}$, and $C_6 = \{H_{11}, H_{12}, V_{21}, V_{22}|$ without key disjointness constraint and key duplication constraint$\}$.

3. LOCALIZED QUERY PROCESSING WITH CONSTRAINED DATA FRAGMENTATION

In this section, we consider localized query processing with constrained data fragmentation. The queries considered are of the form [target:qualification], where the target represents a set of attributes to appear in the answer, and the qualification represents a set of join and select clauses. The attributes in the target and in the select clauses will be called *target attribute* and *select attribute*, respectively (we consider select clauses of the form: "X θ constant" to simplify the discussion, where X is a select attribute and θ represents any valid scalar comparison operator).

Define *join-preserving local processing* as the preprocessing of a join at each site which contains fragments of the joining relations such that the results of this processing can be postprocessed to compute the join. The postprocessing can involve a union or a join operation. In the following, we consider each data fragmentation configuration and identify the possibility of the join-preserving local processing for each case.

The select and target attributes will be considered to identify the situations where not every fragment of the joining relations need be processed. In these situations, the localized query processing approach may be still applicable even the join-preserving property is not satisfied. Moreover, as a result of this consideration, the query could actually be processed at a single site without data movement involved, which significantly reduces the cost for query processing.

3.1 Queries referencing horizontally fragmented relations

Consider the configuration $C_1 = \{H_{11}, H_{12}, H_{21}, H_{22}\}$. The join $R_1 \overset{A}{\infty} R_2$ can be processed as follows.

$$\begin{aligned} & R_1 \overset{A}{\infty} R_2 \\ &= (H_{11} \cup H_{12}) \overset{A}{\infty} (H_{21} \cup H_{22}) \\ &= (H_{11} \overset{A}{\infty} H_{21}) \cup (H_{11} \overset{A}{\infty} H_{22}) \cup (H_{12} \overset{A}{\infty} H_{21}) \cup (H_{12} \overset{A}{\infty} H_{22}) \end{aligned}$$

When $H_{11} \overset{A}{\infty} H_{22}$ and $H_{12} \overset{A}{\infty} H_{21}$ produce null results, this join can be processed by first performing $H_{11} \overset{A}{\infty} H_{21}$ at site 1 and $H_{12} \overset{A}{\infty} H_{22}$ at site 2 then unioning the results. That is, the join-preserving property is satisfied when the results of $H_{11} \overset{A}{\infty} H_{22}$ and $H_{12} \overset{A}{\infty} H_{21}$ are null.

In the following, the concept of *partition dependency* will be introduced, which guarantees the join-preserving property for queries referencing horizontally partitioned relations.

3.1.1 Join processing

Denote P_i as the set of sites which contain a fragment of the relation R_i.

Definition 1: A *horizontal partition* of a relation R_i is a set of fragments $\{H_{ij}\}$ where $H_{il} \cap H_{im} = \varnothing$ for l ≠ m, and $R_i = \cup H_{ij}$.

Definition 2: A relation R is *horizontally partitioned by attribute A* if there exists a horizontal partition of R such that all tuples of R having the same value of A belong to the same fragment; A is named *fragment attribute* (FA). An FA could also be a set of attributes.

Property 1: A key is a fragment attribute if the relation is horizontally partitioned.
Proof: A key is a unique identifier of a relation. That is, no two tuples of the relation contain the same value of the key. Therefore, if a relation is horizontally partitioned, by Definition 2, its key is an FA. □

Property 2: If A is a fragment attribute of a horizontally partitioned relation R, and B is a set of attributes in R, which contain A then B is also a fragment attribute.
Proof (by contradiction): If B is not an FA, then tuples of R, which have the same value of B could exist in different fragments. However, since A is contained in B the same value of A could therefore exist in different fragments, contradicting the assumption that A is an FA. □

Definition 3: Let R_1 and R_2 both be horizontally partitioned by attribute A, and $\{H_{1j}\}$ and $\{H_{2k}\}$ be their associated partitions. There is a *partition dependency* between R_1 and R_2 on A if for every a ∈ H_{1j}.A, a ∉

H_{2k}.A where k $\neq$ j, and vice versa.

Denote partition dependency between R_1 and R_2 on attribute A as $\langle R_1,R_2|A\rangle$.

Property 3: If $\langle R_1,R_2|A\rangle$ exists then the join $R_1 \overset{A}{\infty} R_2$ can be processed locally at sites $P_1 \cap P_2$.
Proof: Since $\langle R_1,R_2|A\rangle$ exists, $H_{1j} \overset{A}{\infty} H_{2k} = \emptyset$ for j $\neq$ k, where j $\in P_1$ and k $\in P_2$. Therefore, $R_1 \overset{A}{\infty} R_2 = \cup$ $(H_{1i} \overset{A}{\infty} H_{2i})$ for i $\in P_1 \cap P_2$. That is, it can be processed locally at sites $P_1 \cap P_2$. □

Property 4: If $\langle R_1,R_2|A\rangle$ exists and B is a set of attributes in both R_1 and R_2, which contain A then there also exists $\langle R_1,R_2|B\rangle$.
Proof (by contradiction): From Property 2, B is an FA for R_1 and R_2. If $\langle R_1,R_2|B\rangle$ does not hold then for a value, say b, in H_{1j}.B (accordingly, H_{2k}.B), it could also exist in H_{2k}.B (accordingly, H_{1j}.B) for j $\neq$ k. Since A is contained in B, the value of A in b could therefore exist in both H_{1j}.A and H_{2k}.A, contradicting the assumption of $\langle R_1,R_2|A\rangle$. □

Partition dependencies exist in databases whether they are recognized or not. For example, in an employee database, records about an employee may be located at the headquarter of the employee's division. This results in a logical dependency between the employee's records and the division records. It is therefore important to discover the partition dependency semantic and apply it when possible for the distributed query optimization. We extend the partition dependency concept to more than two relations in the following.

Property 5: If $\langle R_1,R_2|A\rangle$ and $\langle R_2,R_3|B\rangle$ hold then $\langle R_{12},R_3|B\rangle$ and $\langle R_1,R_{23}|A\rangle$ hold, where R_{12} and R_{23} represent the sets $\{H_{12i}\}$ and $\{H_{23j}\}$, respectively, where $H_{12i} = H_{1i} \overset{A}{\infty} H_{2i}$, i $\in P_1 \cap P_2$, and $H_{23j} = H_{2j} \overset{B}{\infty} H_{3j}$, j $\in P_2 \cap P_3$.
Proof: We prove "if $\langle R_1,R_2|A\rangle$ and $\langle R_2,R_3|B\rangle$ hold then $\langle R_{12},R_3|B\rangle$ holds" first. Since $\langle R_2,R_3|B\rangle$ holds, R_2 and R_3 are both horizontally partitioned by B. Since R_2 is horizontally partitioned by B, R_{12} is also horizontally partitioned by B. For a value, say b, in H_{12i}.B, it must also be in H_{2i}.B since $H_{12i}.B \subset H_{2i}.B$. Since $\langle R_2,R_3|B\rangle$ holds, b cannot be in H_{3j}.B for j $\neq$ i. That is, for each value in H_{12i}.B, it cannot be in H_{3j}.B for i $\neq$ j. Now, for a value, say b', in H_{3j}.B, it cannot be in H_{2i}.B for i $\neq$ j due to $\langle R_2,R_3|B\rangle$. Since $H_{12i}.B \subset H_{2i}.B$, b' cannot be in H_{12i}.B. That is, for each value in H_{3j}.B, it cannot be in H_{12i}.B for i $\neq$ j. We conclude that $\langle R_{12},R_3|B\rangle$ holds. Similarly, we can prove "if $\langle R_1,R_2|A\rangle$ and $\langle R_2,R_3|B\rangle$ hold then $\langle R_1,R_{23}|A\rangle$ holds." □

Property 6: if $\langle R_1,R_2|A\rangle$ and $\langle R_2,R_3|B\rangle$ hold then $R_1 \overset{A}{\infty} R_2 \overset{B}{\infty} R_3$ can be processed locally at sites $P_1 \cap P_2 \cap P_3$.

Proof: Since $\langle R_1,R_2|A\rangle$ holds, from Property 3, $R_1 \overset{A}{\infty} R_2$ can be processed locally at sites $P_1 \cap P_2$. Denote P_{12} as $P_1 \cap P_2$. Denote R_{12} as the set $\{H_{12i}\}$ where $H_{12i} = H_{1i} \overset{A}{\infty} H_{2i}$, i $\in P_{12}$. From Property 5, we have $\langle R_{12},R_3|B\rangle$. Again, from Property 3, $R_{12} \overset{B}{\infty} R_3$ can be processed locally at sites $P_{12} \cap P_3$. That is, $R_1 \overset{A}{\infty} R_2 \overset{B}{\infty} R_3$ can be processed locally at sites $P_1 \cap P_2 \cap P_3$. □

The partition dependency semantic can be generalized to process n joins locally in a small subset of the sites containing fragments of the joining relations.

3.1.2 Select processing

If a select attribute in a query is a fragment attribute (there could be more than one select clauses), then we can check the fragmentation predicate to determine the fragments which are involved in the select. If there exists partition dependency on this fragment attribute then only these selected fragments need be processed to get the answer.

3.2 Queries referencing vertically partitioned relations

Consider the configuration $C_2 = \{V_{11}, V_{12}, V_{21}, V_{22}\}$. Vertical partitioning requires that the key values be duplicated in each fragment such that the relation can be reconstructed by joining all fragments on the key attribute. The localized join processing on two vertically partitioned relations R_1 and R_2 on attribute A is discussed by the following three cases. k_1 and k_2 are key attributes of R_1 and R_2, respectively (we assume that A, k_1 and k_2 could each be a set of attributes for the discussion).

1. $A \subset (k_1 \cap k_2)$.

   The localized approach transforms the join processing as follows. σ denotes select and $\times$ denotes Cartesian product.

$$
\begin{aligned}
& R_1 \overset{A}{\infty} R_2 \\
&= (V_{11} \overset{k_1}{\infty} V_{12}) \overset{A}{\infty} (V_{21} \overset{k_2}{\infty} V_{22}) \\
&= (\sigma_{k_1=k_1} (V_{11} \times V_{12})) \overset{A}{\infty} (\sigma_{k_2=k_2} (V_{21} \times V_{22})) \\
&= \sigma_{k_1=k_1}\, \sigma_{k_2=k_2}\, \sigma_{A=A}\, (V_{11} \times V_{12} \times V_{21} \times V_{22}) \\
&= \sigma_{k_1k_2=k_1k_2}\, \sigma_{A=A}\, \sigma_{A=A}\, (V_{11} \times V_{12} \times V_{21} \times V_{22}) \\
&= (\sigma_{A=A}\, (V_{11} \times V_{21})) \overset{k_1k_2}{\infty} (\sigma_{A=A}\, (V_{12} \times V_{22})) \\
&= (V_{11} \overset{A}{\infty} V_{21}) \overset{k_1k_2}{\infty} (V_{12} \overset{A}{\infty} V_{22})
\end{aligned}
$$

   $V_{11} \overset{A}{\infty} V_{21}$ and $V_{12} \overset{A}{\infty} V_{22}$ can be processed locally at site 1 and site 2, respectively. The results are then joined on k_1k_2 to compute the final result of the join.

   Select can be done locally. The query can be further simplified considering the locations of the fragments which contain the target or select attributes. If these fragments reside at the same site then the query can be processed at a single site.

2. $A \subset k_2$ and $A \not\subset k_1$.

We assume that only key values are duplicated for the vertical partitioning. Since A $\not\subset k_1$, only one fragment of R_1 contains the attribute A. Assume V_{12} is the fragment which contains A. The join over R_1 and R_2 on A is transformed as follows.

$$R_1 \overset{A}{\infty} R_2$$
$$= (V_{11} \overset{k_1}{\infty} V_{12}) \overset{A}{\infty} (V_{21} \overset{k_2}{\infty} V_{22})$$
$$= V_{11} \overset{k_1}{\infty} (V_{12} \overset{A}{\infty} V_{22}) \overset{k_2}{\infty} V_{21}$$

The only possible local processing is $V_{12} \overset{A}{\infty} V_{22}$. Since V_{11} and V_{21} cannot be processed at site 1, the join-preserving property is not satisfied. However, the join on k_1 or k_2 is needed only when V_{11} or V_{21} contains either select or target attributes. Therefore, when all the select and target attributes are contained in the fragments at site 2 (i.e., V_{12} and V_{22}), this query can be processed at a single site. In all cases, the select can be processed locally.

3. A $\not\subset k_1$ or k_2.

   As in case 2, we assume that only key values are duplicated. Since A $\not\subset k_1$ or k_2, A can only exist in one fragment of R_1 and R_2. If R_1.A and R_2.A reside at the same site, then the analysis is the same as that in case 2. When R_1.A and R_2.A do not reside at the same site, the localized approach is not applicable.

3.3 Queries referencing horizontally and vertically partitioned relations

The data fragmentation configuration considered here is $C_3 = \{H_{11}, H_{12}, V_{21}, V_{22}\}$. Two cases follows based on the relationship between the joining attribute A and the key of R_2, say k.

1. A $\subset$ k.

$$R_1 \overset{A}{\infty} R_2$$
$$= (H_{11} \cup H_{12}) \overset{A}{\infty} (V_{21} \overset{k}{\infty} V_{22})$$
$$= (H_{11} \overset{A}{\infty} (V_{21} \overset{k}{\infty} V_{22})) \cup (H_{12} \overset{A}{\infty} (V_{21} \overset{k}{\infty} V_{22}))$$
$$= ((H_{11} \overset{A}{\infty} V_{21}) \overset{k}{\infty} V_{22}) \cup ((H_{12} \overset{A}{\infty} V_{22}) \overset{k}{\infty} V_{21})$$

$H_{11} \overset{A}{\infty} V_{21}$ and $H_{12} \overset{A}{\infty} V_{22}$ can be performed locally while the other two joins cannot. Thus, the join-preserving property is not satisfied. Let T_1 and T_2 denote the result of $H_{11} \overset{A}{\infty} V_{21}$ and $H_{12} \overset{A}{\infty} V_{22}$, respectively. By the operation of join, T_1.k $\subset$ V_{21}.k, and T_2.k $\subset$ V_{22}.k. Since there exists key duplication between V_{21} and V_{22}, V_{21}.k = V_{22}.k. Therefore, the joins $T_1 \overset{k}{\infty} V_{22}$ and $T_2 \overset{k}{\infty} V_{21}$ cannot change the results in T_1 and T_2 except that the non-key attribute values in V_{22} and V_{21} can be associated with tuples in T_1 and T_2, respectively, where the key values match. Therefore, if the target attributes are not in the non-key attributes of R_2, this query can be processed locally. That is,

$\Pi_{R_1 k}(R_1 \overset{A}{\infty} R_2)$

$= (H_{11} \overset{A}{\infty} \Pi_k(V_{21})) \cup (H_{12} \overset{A}{\infty} \Pi_k(V_{22}))$, where Π denotes project.

Again, select on V_{21} or V_{22} can be done locally. Also, if only H_{11} or H_{12} is involved in the select, and the target attributes are either in R_1 or in the fragment of R_2, which resides at the same site with the selected fragment of R_1, then this query can be processed at a single site.

2. A $\not\subset$ k (assume A is in V_{21}).

$$R_1 \overset{A}{\infty} R_2$$
$$= (H_{11} \cup H_{12}) \overset{A}{\infty} (V_{21} \overset{k}{\infty} V_{22})$$
$$= ((H_{11} \cup H_{12}) \overset{A}{\infty} V_{21}) \overset{k}{\infty} V_{22}$$
$$= ((H_{11} \overset{A}{\infty} V_{21}) \cup (H_{12} \overset{A}{\infty} V_{21})) \overset{k}{\infty} V_{22}$$

If H_{11} is selected by a select clause, then $H_{12} \overset{A}{\infty} V_{21}$ need not be performed. By the same reason as in case 1, $(H_{11} \overset{A}{\infty} V_{21}).k \subset V_{22}.k$. If the target attributes are not in the non-key attributes of V_{22}, the join on k need not be performed. That is, if H_{11} is the selected fragment, and the target attributes are not in the non-key attributes of V_{22} then this query can be processed at a single site.

4. LOCALIZED QUERY PROCESSING WITH UNCONSTRAINED DATA FRAGMENTATION

In this section, the constraints of horizontal and vertical data fragmentation are relaxed for considering localized query processing in multidatabase systems. As in Section 3, the conditions for localized query processing are discussed based on three categories, namely, queries referencing horizontally partitioned relations, queries referencing vertically partitioned relations, and queries referencing both horizontally and vertically partitioned relations.

4.1 Queries referencing horizontally partitioned relations

Since we relax the key disjointness constraint, the same key value could appear in different fragments. Denote the key which does not satisfy the key disjointness constraint as κ. Also, we assume that there is only one relation with such a key κ.

A value of κ may associate different values for some attributes in different fragments. Define these attributes as *aggregate attribute* (since an aggregate function will be specified for each such attribute). There are three cases for the consideration of the aggregate attribute. They are (1) the aggregate attribute is the joining attribute, (2) the aggregate attribute is the select attribute, and (3) the aggregate attribute is the target attribute. If the aggregate attribute is not in the above three cases, then the analysis of the localized query processing for the configuration C_4 is as that for C_1 in Section 3.

For our example relation DEPT(D#,Dname,Mgr#,Budget), assume that departments can have separate budgets at different locations. That is, (D002,CTT,E200,152) and (D002,CTT,E200,357) can exist in $DEPT_1$ and $DEPT_2$, respectively. Then, κ is D# and Budget is the aggregate attribute.

Based on the identity of κ and the joining attribute A, the localized query processing for the configuration C_4 is discussed in the following.

4.1.1 κ is not the joining attribute

If there exists a partition dependency between R_1 and R_2 on the joining attribute A, then as in the configuration C_1, the join can be processed locally. If the target includes the aggregate attributes, then the results of all locally processed joins can be unioned and the aggregate function applied to the aggregate attribute values for the same κ value. If the select attribute is the aggregate attribute then it can be processed after all the join results are unioned. The values for the select attribute can be computed by the associated aggregate function. The select can then be performed. Under certain conditions the select can be processed locally. Refer to [17] for details.

4.1.2 κ is the joining attribute

Since the same value of κ can exist in different fragments, the concept of partition dependency need be extended. We discuss the extension as follows.

Let R_2 be the relation containing κ. Define

$H_{21} = PH_{21} \cup NH_{21}$, and
$H_{22} = PH_{22} \cup NH_{22}$

where PH_{2j} is a subset of H_{2j}, which satisfies the key disjointness constraint, and $NH_{2j} = H_{2j} - PH_{2j}$, which represents tuples with the same κ values in different fragments. Notice that $PH_{21}.\kappa \cap PH_{22}.\kappa = \emptyset$, and there is a one-to-one correspondence between the values in $NH_{21}.\kappa$ and $NH_{22}.\kappa$.

Also, define

$H_{11} = PH_{11} \cup NH_{11}$, and
$H_{12} = PH_{12} \cup NH_{12}$

where NH_{1j} is a subset of H_{1j}, which represents tuples with the A-values corresponding to the κ-values in NH_{2j} (the name, A, of the joining attribute will be used for κ hereafter), and $PH_{1j} = H_{1j} - NH_{1j}$.

We have the following property for the localized query processing approach.

Property 7: If there exists partition dependency between PH_{1j} and PH_{2j} on attribute A, and NH_{1j} contains at least one tuple which has the same A-value for each A-value in NH_{2j} then the join $R_1 \overset{A}{\infty} R_2$ can be processed locally.

Proof: Use NH_i to denote $NH_{i1} \cup NH_{i2}$, $R_1 \overset{A}{\infty} R_2$ can be transformed as follows.

$$R_1 \overset{A}{\infty} R_2$$
$$= (PH_{11} \cup PH_{12} \cup NH_1) \overset{A}{\infty} (PH_{21} \cup PH_{22} \cup NH_2)$$
$$= (PH_{11} \overset{A}{\infty} PH_{21}) \cup (PH_{11} \overset{A}{\infty} PH_{22}) \cup (PH_{11} \overset{A}{\infty} NH_2)$$
$$\cup (PH_{12} \overset{A}{\infty} PH_{21}) \cup (PH_{12} \overset{A}{\infty} PH_{22}) \cup (PH_{12} \overset{A}{\infty} NH_2)$$
$$\cup (NH_1 \overset{A}{\infty} PH_{21}) \cup (NH_1 \overset{A}{\infty} PH_{22}) \cup (NH_1 \overset{A}{\infty} NH_2)$$
$$= (PH_{11} \overset{A}{\infty} PH_{21}) \cup (PH_{12} \overset{A}{\infty} PH_{22}) \cup (NH_1 \overset{A}{\infty} NH_2)$$

(by the partition dependency and the definitions of PH and NH)

$PH_{11} \overset{A}{\infty} PH_{21}$ and $PH_{12} \overset{A}{\infty} PH_{22}$ can be processed locally. Now, consider $NH_1 \overset{A}{\infty} NH_2$.

$$NH_1 \overset{A}{\infty} NH_2$$
$$= (NH_{11} \cup NH_{12}) \overset{A}{\infty} (NH_{21} \cup NH_{22})$$
$$= (NH_{11} \overset{A}{\infty} NH_{21}) \cup (NH_{11} \overset{A}{\infty} NH_{22}) \cup (NH_{12} \overset{A}{\infty} NH_{21}) \cup (NH_{12} \overset{A}{\infty} NH_{22})$$

There is a one-to-one correspondence between the A-values in NH_{21} and NH_{22}. For the same A-value, the tuples in NH_{21} and NH_{22} may contain different values for the aggregate attribute. Since these values can be obtained by performing $NH_{11} \overset{A}{\infty} NH_{21}$ and $NH_{12} \overset{A}{\infty} NH_{22}$, $NH_{11} \overset{A}{\infty} NH_{22}$ and $NH_{12} \overset{A}{\infty} NH_{21}$ are therefore redundant and can be eliminated. Now,

$$H_{11} \overset{A}{\infty} H_{21}$$
$$= (NH_{11} \cup PH_{11}) \overset{A}{\infty} (NH_{21} \cup PH_{21})$$
$$= (NH_{11} \overset{A}{\infty} NH_{21}) \cup (NH_{11} \overset{A}{\infty} PH_{21}) \cup (PH_{11} \overset{A}{\infty} NH_{21}) \cup (PH_{11} \overset{A}{\infty} PH_{21})$$
$$= (NH_{11} \overset{A}{\infty} NH_{21}) \cup (PH_{11} \overset{A}{\infty} PH_{21}) \text{ (by the definitions of PH and NH)}$$

and

$$H_{12} \overset{A}{\infty} H_{22}$$
$$= (NH_{12} \cup PH_{12}) \overset{A}{\infty} (NH_{22} \cup PH_{22})$$
$$= (NH_{12} \overset{A}{\infty} NH_{22}) \cup (NH_{12} \overset{A}{\infty} PH_{22}) \cup (PH_{12} \overset{A}{\infty} NH_{22}) \cup (PH_{12} \overset{A}{\infty} PH_{22})$$
$$= (NH_{12} \overset{A}{\infty} NH_{22}) \cup (PH_{12} \overset{A}{\infty} PH_{22}) \text{ (by the definitions of PH and NH)}$$

Therefore,

$$R_1 \overset{A}{\infty} R_2$$
$$= (PH_{11} \overset{A}{\infty} PH_{21}) \cup (PH_{12} \overset{A}{\infty} PH_{22}) \cup (NH_{11} \overset{A}{\infty} NH_{21}) \cup (NH_{12} \overset{A}{\infty} NH_{22})$$
$$= H_{11} \overset{A}{\infty} H_{21} \cup H_{12} \overset{A}{\infty} H_{22}$$

That is, $R_1 \overset{A}{\infty} R_2$ can be processed locally. □

4.2 Queries referencing vertically partitioned relations

The key duplication constraint is relaxed by allowing the key values in one fragment to be different from those in another fragment. Outerjoins on the common key attribute over all the fragments are needed to obtain all the data represented by the global relation scheme.

Define the outerjoin between R_1 and R_2 on attribute A as follows.

$$R_1 \underset{o}{\overset{A}{\infty}} R_2$$
$$= R_1 \overset{A}{\infty} R_2 \cup R_1' \cup R_2'$$

where the attributes of R_i' are those produced by the join of R_1 and R_2, and the tuples in R_i' are those of R_i which do not have matching values in the join. For a tuple in R_i', null values are padded for the attributes not in R_i. As the consideration of the configuration C_2 in Section 3, we discuss the localized approach by the following three cases. k_1 and k_2 are keys of R_1 and R_2, respectively.

1. $A \subset k_1 \cap k_2$.

$$R_1 \overset{A}{\infty} R_2$$
$$= (V_{11} \underset{o}{\overset{k_1}{\infty}} V_{12}) \overset{A}{\infty} (V_{21} \underset{o}{\overset{k_2}{\infty}} V_{22})$$
$$= ((V_{11} \overset{k_1}{\infty} V_{12}) \cup (V_{11}' \cup V_{12}')) \overset{A}{\infty} ((V_{21} \overset{k_2}{\infty} V_{22}) \cup (V_{21}' \cup V_{22}'))$$
$$= ((V_{11} \overset{k_1}{\infty} V_{12}) \overset{A}{\infty} (V_{21} \overset{k_2}{\infty} V_{22})) \cup ((V_{11} \overset{k_1}{\infty} V_{12}) \overset{A}{\infty} (V_{21}' \cup V_{22}'))$$
$$\cup ((V_{11}' \cup V_{12}') \overset{A}{\infty} (V_{21} \overset{k_2}{\infty} V_{22})) \cup ((V_{11}' \cup V_{12}') \overset{A}{\infty} (V_{21}' \cup V_{22}'))$$
$$= ((V_{11} \overset{A}{\infty} V_{21}) \overset{k_1 k_2}{\infty} (V_{12} \overset{A}{\infty} V_{22})) \cup ((V_{11} \overset{k_1}{\infty} V_{12}) \overset{A}{\infty} V_{21}')$$
$$\cup ((V_{11} \overset{k_1}{\infty} V_{12}) \overset{A}{\infty} V_{22}')) \cup (V_{11}' \overset{A}{\infty} (V_{21} \overset{k_2}{\infty} V_{22}))$$
$$\cup (V_{12}' \overset{A}{\infty} (V_{21} \overset{k_2}{\infty} V_{22})) \cup (V_{11}' \overset{A}{\infty} V_{21}') \cup (V_{11}' \overset{A}{\infty} V_{22}')$$
$$\cup (V_{12}' \overset{A}{\infty} V_{21}') \cup (V_{12}' \overset{A}{\infty} V_{22}')$$

$V_{11} \overset{A}{\infty} V_{21}$ and $V_{12} \overset{A}{\infty} V_{22}$ can be computed locally. However, others cannot. Since not all tuples in the answer can be obtained locally, the localized approach is not applicable no matter what the target attributes are.

Without key duplication constraint, the key values in all the fragments of a vertically partitioned relation have to be unioned for processing a join on this key attribute. This makes the localized approach not applicable. We have the following property:

Property 8: If a query contains a join in which one joining relation is vertically partitioned without key duplication constraint, and the joining attribute is the key of that relation, then the localized query processing approach cannot be applied.

2. $A \subset k_1$ and $A \not\subset k_2$.

   Since $A \subset k_1$, by Property 8, no localized query processing is possible.

3. $A \not\subset k_1$ or k_2 (assume the fragments containing A reside at the same site, say, site 1; otherwise, the localized approach is not applicable).

   $R_1 \overset{A}{\infty} R_2$

   $= (V_{11} \underset{o}{\overset{k_1}{\infty}} V_{12}) \overset{A}{\infty} (V_{21} \underset{o}{\overset{k_2}{\infty}} V_{22})$

   These two outerjoins cannot affect the values of the joining attributes in V_{11} and V_{21}. Therefore, if the select and target attributes are contained in the fragments at site 1 (i.e., V_{11} and V_{21}), the query can be processed at a single site by performing the join $V_{11} \overset{A}{\infty} V_{21}$ (refer to the join transformation derived in case 1).

4.3 Queries referencing horizontally and vertically partitioned relations

As the consideration of the configuration C_3 in Section 3, we discuss the localized approach based on the following two cases. Assume k is the key of the vertically partitioned relation R_2.

1. $A \subset k$.

   By Property 8, the localized approach cannot be applied.

2. $A \not\subset k$.

   Since R_1 contains κ, both H_{11} and H_{12} need to be joined with the fragment of R_2 containing A, no localized query processing is possible.

5. CONCLUSIONS

We have presented a localized approach to optimize query processing in a distributed multidatabase environment. This localized approach transforms a global query such that a local site can be utilized to process a subquery referencing the data fragments contained at that site. Various data fragmentation schemes were considered. The schema and data inconsistencies in multidatabases were discussed in the same framework of the data fragmentation. This localized approach reduces the data transmission cost, and increases the processing parallelism which reduces the query response time. Semantic information was used to process queries at a single site.

This semantic query optimization by the localized processing approach can be incorporated in a semantic query optimizer, or be used as transformation rules for the query optimizer generator as proposed in [23], [25], [30].

REFERENCES

[1] Apers, P., A. Hevner, S.B. Yao, "Optimization Algorithm for Distributed Queries," in *IEEE Transactions on Software Engineering*, January 1983.
[2] Batini, C., M. Lenzerini and S. Navathe, "A comparative analysis of methodologies for database schema integration," *ACM Computing Surveys*, Dec. 1986.
[3] Bernstein, P. and D.M. Chiu, "Using Semi-joins to Solve Relational Queries," in *JACM*, January 1981.
[4] Bernstein, P., N. Goodman, E. Wong, C. Reeve, J. Rothnie, "Query Processing in a System for Distributed Databases (SDD-1)," in *ACM Transactions on Database Systems*, December 1981.
[5] Breitbart, Y., P. Olson and G. Thompson, "Database integration in a distributed heterogeneous database system," Proc. IEEE International Conference on Data Engineering, 1986.
[6] Breitbart, Y. and L. Tieman, "ADDS - Heterogeneous distributed database system," *Distributed Data Sharing Systems*, Schreiber, F. and W. Litwin (Ed's), North Holland, 1984.
[7] Brill, D., M. Templeton, C.T. Yu, "Distributed Query Processing Strategies in Mermaid, A Frontend to Data Management Systems," in Proc. IEEE International Conference on Data Engineering, 1984.
[8] Ceri, S. and G. Pelagatti, *Distributed Databases: Principles and Systems*, McGraw-Hill, 1984.
[9] Chen, A.L.P., D. Brill, M. Templeton and C. Yu, "Distributed query processing in a multiple database system," *IEEE Journal on Selected Areas in Communications*, special issue on Databases in Communications Systems, Apr. 1989.
[10] Chen, A.L.P. and V.O.K. Li, "Optimizing Star Queries in a Distributed Database System," in Proc. of VLDB, 1984.
[11] Chen, A.L.P. and V.O.K. Li, "Improvement Algorithms for Semijoin Query Processing Programs in Distributed Database Systems," in *IEEE Transactions on Computers*, November 1984.
[12] Chen, A.L.P. and V.O.K. Li, "An Optimal Algorithm for Processing Distributed Star Queries," in *IEEE Transactions on Software Engineering*, October 1985.
[13] Chiu, D.M., P. Bernstein, Y.C. Ho, "Optimizing Chain Queries in a Distributed Database System," in *SIAM J. Comput.*, February 1984.
[14] Chiu, D.M. and Y.C. Ho, "A Method for Interpreting Tree Queries into Optimal Semi-join Expressions," in Proc. of ACM SIGMOD, 1980.
[15] Chu, W. and P. Hurley, "Optimal query processing for distributed database systems," *IEEE Trans. on Computers*, Sep. 1982.
[16] Czejdo, B., M. Rusinkiewicz and D. Embley, "An approach to schema integration and query formulation in federated database systems," Proc. IEEE International Conference on Data Engineering, 1987.
[17] Dayal, U., "Query processing in a multidatabase system," *Query Processing in Database Systems*, Kim, Reiner and Batory (Ed's), 1985.
[18] Dayal, U. and H. Hwang, "View definition and generalization for database integration in multibase: A system for heterogeneous distributed databases," *IEEE Trans. Softw. Eng.*, Nov. 1984.
[19] Deen, S.M., R.R. Amin and M.C. Taylor, "Query decomposition in PRECI*," *Distributed Data Sharing Systems*, Schreiber and Litwin (Ed's), 1985.
[20] Deen, S., R. Amin and M. Taylor, "Data integration in distributed databases," *IEEE Trans. Softw. Eng.*, Jul. 1987.
[21] Deen, S. et al., "The architecture of a generalized distributed database - PRECI*," *Comput. J.*, Jul. 1985.
[22] Epstein, R., M. Stonebraker, E. Wong, "Distributed Query Processing in a Relational Database System," in Proc. of ACM SIGMOD, 1978.
[23] Freytag, C.F., "A ruled-based view of query optimization," in Proc. of ACM SIGMOD, 1987.
[24] Gamal-Eldin, M., G. Thomas and R. Elmasri, "Integrating relational databases with support for updates," in Proc. IEEE International Symposium on Databases for Parallel and Distributed Systems, 1988.

[25] Graefe, G. and D. DeWitt, "The EXODUS optimizer generator," in Proc. of ACM SIGMOD, 1987.
[26] Hammer, M. and S. Zdonik, "Knowledge-Based Query Processing," in Proc. of VLDB, 1980.
[27] Hwang, H., U. Dayal and M.G. Gouda, "Using semiouterjoins to process queries in multidatabase systems," in Proc. of ACM PODS, 1984.
[28] King, J., *Query Optimization by Semantic Reasoning*, UMI Research Press, 1984.
[29] Lohman, G., C. Mohan, L. Hass, D. Daniels, B. Lindsay, P. Selinger, P. Wilms, "Query Processing in R*," *Query Processing in Database Systems*, Kim, Reiner and Batory (Ed's), 1985.
[30] Lohman, G.M., "Grammar-like functional rules for representing query optimization alternatives," in Proc. of ACM SIGMOD, 1988.
[31] Luk, W. and L. Luk, "Optimizing Semi-join Programs for Distributed Query Processing," in Proc. International Conference on Databases, 1983.
[32] Shenoy, S.T. and Z.M. Ozsoyoglu, "A system for semantic query optimization," in Proc. of ACM SIGMOD, 1987.
[33] Smith, J. et al., "Multibase - Integrating heterogeneous distributed database systems," in Proc. of AFIPS NCC, 1981.
[34] Stonebraker, M., "Implementation of integrity constraints and views by query modification," in Proc. of ACM SIGMOD, 1975.
[35] Templeton, M., D. Brill, A.L.P. Chen, S. Dao, E. Lund, R. MacGregor, P. Ward, "Mermaid - A Front-end to Distributed Heterogeneous Databases," *Proceedings of the IEEE*, May, 1987.
[36] Yu, C.T., C.C. Chang, M. Templeton, D. Brill, E. Lund, "On the Design of a Query Processing Strategy in a Distributed Database Environment," in Proc. of ACM SIGMOD, 1983.
[37] Yu, C.T., C.C. Chang, M. Templeton, D. Brill, E. Lund, "Query Processing in a Fragmented Relational Distributed System: MERMAID," *IEEE Transactions on Software Engineering*, August 1985.
[38] Yu, C.T., K. Guh, D. Brill, A.L.P. Chen, "Partition Strategy for Distributed Query Processing in Fast Local Networks," *IEEE Trans. on Software Engineering*, June 1989.
[39] Yu, C., K. Guh and A.L.P. Chen, "An integrated algorithm for distributed query processing," in Proc. IFIP Conference on Distributed Processing, 1987.
[40] Yu, C.T., L. Lilien, K. Guh, M. Templeton, D. Brill, A.L.P. Chen, "Adaptive Techniques for Distributed Query Optimization," in Proc. IEEE International Conference on Data Engineering, 1986.

Retrieval of Multimedia Documents by Imprecise Query Specification

F. Rabitti

Istituto di Elaborazione dell' Informazione - CNR
Via S. Maria 46, 56100 Pisa (Italy)

P. Savino

Olivetti DOR
Via Palestro 30, 56100 Pisa (Italy)

ABSTRACT

The retrieval process in multimedia document systems is inherently different from the retrieval process in traditional (record oriented) database systems. While the latter can be considered an exact process (records either satisfy the query or not), the former is not an exact process and the system must take into account the uncertainty factor (i.e. the answer is not only "true" or "false" but is often in between them).
Uncertainty is mainly introduced in evaluating how images and text components in documents are relevant to user's queries. Moreover, it may be useful to give the user some flexibility in specifying the query on multimedia documents (i.e. the "importance" of different parts of the query). The possibility to specify imprecise queries in a system can significantly increase the effectiveness and the precision in the retrieval process on multimedia documents.
This approach is being tested extending the MULTOS system, a prototype system for the storage and retrieval of multimedia documents.

This work has been funded in part by the Commission of the European Communities as ESPRIT-Project No. 28. Partner in this Project are Ing. C. Olivetti S.p.A. (I), Cretan Research Center (GR), IEI-Consiglio Nazionale delle Ricerche (I), TA Triumph-Adler AG (D), Battelle Institut e.V. (D), Epsilon Ltd. (GR) Estudios y Realizaciones en Informatica Aplicada, S. A. (E)

1. INTRODUCTION

A key problem in all application environments where documents have to be managed is the increasing amount of information that is being generated with wide use of documents in electronic form. This amount of data is likely to increase with the introduction of new tools dealing with multimedia documents.

A multimedia document can be defined as a collection of components which may contain different information in form of text, formatted attributes, images and voice. The components can be mixed and interrelated, and they may have an internal structure. As a result, these documents have complex structures which tend to differ from one document to another.

Editors for multimedia document creation and formatting [Hora86] are actually available, while multimedia document exchange is simplified by new tools for multimedia mail exchange [Thom85] and standards for document transmission [ODA85]. Many information systems are currently being developed that address the problem of multimedia document management (e.g. [Gibb87, Chri86]). In this paper we are particularly interested to analyze the problem of *efficient* and *effective* retrieval of these documents.

The retrieval process has different characteristics in DataBase Management Systems (DBMS) and in Information Retrieval Systems (IRS). Retrieval in DBMSs is based on the exact evaluation of a boolean combination of predicates on attributes. Each attribute has a well defined domain and predicates which can be applied to it. It is possible to exactly determine in a DBMS when the query is satisfied or not. The answer to a query is the set of database records for which the query condition (i.e. the boolean combination of predicates on record attributes) evaluate to "true".

The Information Retrieval approach to document retrieval consists in retrieving all documents whose properties are similar to those present in the query. In the past, IRS research has focused on the problem of retrieving unstructured text document from large document archives [Salt83]. Text retrieval techniques can be classified in two broad classes: *exact match* techniques and *partial match* techniques. The *exact match* retrieval techniques provide a basic token matching capability in that only the documents that exactly match with the specified query can be retrieved. The *partial match* retrieval techniques allow to retrieve the documents that match only partially with the query. However the exact match retrieval techniques have some disadvantages [Belk87] since:

a) documents whose representations match the query only partially are missed

b) retrieved documents cannot be ranked in relevance order

c) the relative importance of concepts either within the query or text cannot be taken into account.

These problems can be solved if partial match techniques are used. These techniques are more powerful that the exact match techniques as far as the effectiveness of the query results are concerned.

The IRS approach (better than the DBMS approach) could be applied also to structured multimedia documents. In fact, document retrieval may be viewed, in general, as a process of plausible inference [Rijs86] where the documents which can be plausibly implied by the query are retrieved. For example if D is a document that contains the phrase *"MULTOS is an ESPRIT Project in the Office Systems area"* and Q = *"ESPRIT Projects dealing with multimedia document retrieval"* is a query, then Q can be inferred from D. This is usually an imprecise implication since, as in the previous example, documents rarely imply the query precisely. This approach is particularly useful if document components such as text and images, characterized by unprecisely defined semantics, are used in document retrieval.

In case of multimedia documents, queries will be more complex with respect to text only documents. The document structure and the document image content can also be used in query formulation. More sources of evidence will then be used in measuring the probability of inference, but the model is similar. The measure of the plausibility of inference between a document and a query is dependent on the uncertainty of the query representation, on the matching degree between document structure, content and the query restriction and also on the uncertainty of document representation [Morr87]. A ranking function, which includes all these sources of evidence may be defined, so that retrieved documents can be ranked in decreasing relevance order.

In order to try this approach in the retrieval of multimedia documents, we decided to modify an existing prototype system, MULTOS [Bert88, Bert88a]. It supports the management of structured multimedia documents with a retrieval process based on exact matching techniques. In this paper, we first describe (in Sec.2) the main features of the MULTOS prototype as it is now, then we discuss the extensions to the MULTOS system which we foresee for supporting imprecise queries (in Sec.3).

2. MULTOS FILING AND RETRIEVAL CAPABILITIES

MULTOS (MULtimedia Office Server) is an ESPRIT Project in the area Office Systems. The system supports basic filing operations, such as creation, modification, and deletion of multimedia documents, and the ability to process queries on documents. Documents are stored in data bases (integrating also Optical Disk media, allowing storage of very large amounts of data) and may be shared by several users, while facilities like authorization, version, and concurrency control are supported. MULTOS is based on a client/server architecture. Three different types of document servers are supported, *current server, dynamic server and archive server* which differ in storage capacity and document retrieval speed. They allow filing and retrieval of multimedia documents based on document collections, document types, document attributes as well as document text and images.

In order to support a fast document retrieval process, the MULTOS system must be able to answer queries at a high level of abstraction, where conditions on different documents components, such as free text, formatted attributes and images, are intermixed. An example of a typical query in an office environment is:

> *Find all the offer letters on PCs with a price of approximately $ 5,000 produced by Olivetti. These PCs are described as products having good ergonomics. I am rather sure about the producer and the price but not about the description. Moreover, the offer letter should contain a picture of the PC, complete of screen and keyboard, with at least two floppy drives.*

To provide support for expressing this query, it is necessary to provide a model that allows: (i) to represent high level concepts (e.g. price) present in the documents contained in the database; (ii) to group documents into classes of documents having similar content and structures (e.g. offer letter); (iii) to express conditions on free text (e.g. good ergonomics) and on image content.

The MULTOS document model has been developed with the purpose to support operations such as editing, presentation, transmission and retrieval of multimedia documents. Each document is described by logical, layout and conceptual structures [Barb85]. The *logical structure* determines arrangements of logical document components (e.g. title, introduction, chapter, section, etc.). The *layout structure* defines the layout of document content in output. It contains components such as pages, frames, etc. The *conceptual structure* allows a semantic oriented description of the document content as opposed to a syntax oriented description provided by logical and layout structures. The logical and layout structures are defined according to the ODA [ODA85] document representation. The conceptual structure has been added to provide support for document retrieval by content.

Documents having similar conceptual structures can be grouped into classes (conceptual types). In order to handle types in an effective manner, these are maintained in a hierarchy of generalization, where a subtype inherits from its supertype the conceptual structure which will then be further refined (only simple inheritance is supported).

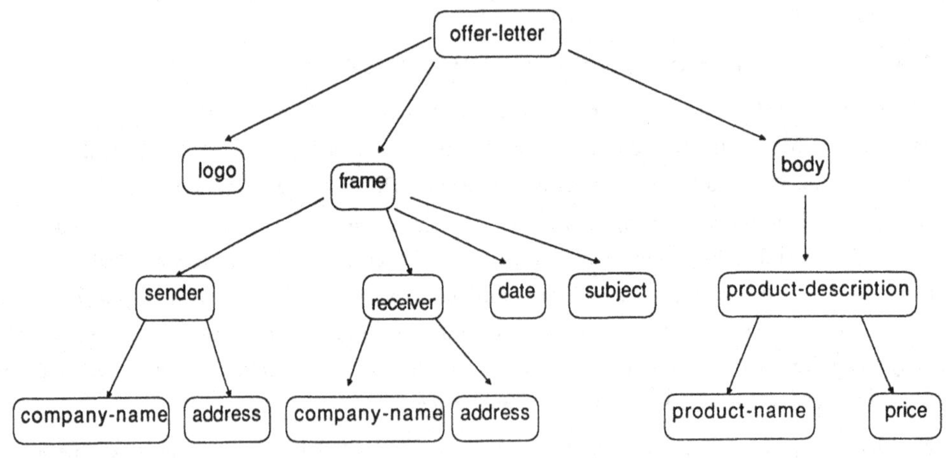

Figure 1. Example of the offer-letter type

For *document retrieval* the conceptual types play the role of the DataBase schema which enables the maintenance of efficient access structures. It is the basis for formulating queries on an abstract level. In Figure 1 an example of the type *offer-letter* is given.

An open system must be able to handle documents from arbitrary sources, including documents without a conceptual structure. A stepwise construction of this structure by an editor during the creation of the document is not sufficient. Therefore the MULTOS system provides a knowledge based classification subsystem (in this context "classification" not only comprises the association of a document to a class but also the generation of the conceptual structure from raw documents) that analyses the document's content and automatically constructs a conceptual structure based on a given set of type definitions [Bert88a, Eiru88].

In MULTOS, document retrieval is based on a boolean query language that allows one to specify restrictions on document collections, document types, and document content. Document content is constituted by the document structure, attributes, text and images. The problem of *image retrieval* by content cannot be approached by trying to perform, at query execution time, picture recognition. This is based on very expensive pattern recognition routines which are effective only on specific application domains. Furthermore it is very difficult for the user to precisely specify the content of the picture he wants. These difficulties can be somewhat bypassed by retrieving image data through associated text or attribute information and through some of their broad characteristics (e.g. position of an image, etc.). However, some type of content addressability for image data is a desirable goal since most of document's meaning may be contained in its image part.

The user query previously presented, expressed in the MULTOS Query Language [1], becomes:

> FIND DOCUMENTS SCOPE = PC-documentation TYPE = offer-letter WHERE
> product-price BETWEEN (4000,6000) AND company-name = Olivetti
> AND TEXT CONTAINS good ergonomics
> AND WITH IMAGE;

It can be observed that the user query cannot be exactly translated in the actual MULTOS query language. In particular the range used for translating the user condition *"approximately equal to $ 5000"* is completely arbitrary. Documents having a price exactly equal or very close to $ 5000 are considered as relevant as documents whose price is quite different from $ 5000. Moreover, the user uncertainty on some attribute values cannot be expressed. The condition on the image content cannot be expressed: only the presence of one image in the document may be requested.

The retrieval approach adopted in MULTOS provides a fast retrieval and makes possible, during the formulation of the query, to express many of the user needs. However the approach has the disadvantages typical of the methods based on exact matching; if a small error in matching occurs, the document is not retrieved. No evaluation of the different relevance of the retrieved documents is provided to the user. It is not possible to express the uncertainty that the user has on part of the query he is formulating. It often happens that the user is able to express only imprecise requests. To improve the quality of retrieval it is important to provide the possibility to express this user uncertainty and to measure, for each document, its relevance to the query. The retrieved documents can be then returned to the user in decreasing relevance order.

---

[1] We assume that the type described in Figure 1 is defined in the type catalog. Furthermore we consider that a collection named *PC-documentation* has been defined (a collection is a user defined set of documents, even belonging to different types).

3. UNCERTAINTY MANAGEMENT

Multimedia documents have a more complex structure than usual database objects. They contain attributes, represented in MULTOS through the conceptual structure, on which exact match can be performed, but also components such as text, graphics and raster images on which partial match is more appropriate. The retrieval of multimedia documents is more complex than retrieval in a DBMS. The user usually, has only an imprecise knowledge of the characteristics of documents he is seeking and it is also difficult, with features offered by available query languages, to express queries which help in discriminating between relevant and non relevant documents.

It is possible to improve the quality of retrieval [Crof88, Morr87]. It has been observed that the quality of the output of the retrieval process is strictly dependent from the quality of the input, i.e. the query. This means that a query language should offer the user the possibility of expressing as much the knowledge he has as possible on the characteristics of the documents to be retrieved. In section 2 we have seen how a query expressed in natural language can be represented in the MULTOS query language. Many of user's needs have been expressed; indeed the queries may contain restrictions on document collections, document types, presence of conceptual components (and presence of images), values associated to conceptual components and text in the documents. In the MULTOS query language, however, it is not possible to express uncertain user knowledge. Furthermore, exact and partial match query constructs are treated the same.

The expressive power of the MULTOS query language can be enhanced by allowing the user to explicitly express uncertainty in the query. Query components may have different *importance* for the user (e.g. it is more important that retrieved documents satisfy the Date attribute than the Author attribute). The values associated to a query component could have different *preference* (e.g. retrieved documents should have been written at the end of June, but possibly even at the beginning of July). The *preference* values associated to each attribute value and the *importance* values associated to each attribute can then be used for ranking retrieved documents. Further uncertainty may derive from queries involving the document structure. Indeed the user may be uncertain or he can make errors in specifying these structures. For example, in the query "body.product_description.price = 5000" [2], the restriction on the component can be verified by a document D for document.price; the actual MULTOS prototype does not retrieve D at all, so treating it exactly as any document *D* it does not match the restriction at all. It is more correct to retrieve D and to associate a "score" (i.e. a quantification of the relevance of the document to the query) to it which takes into account how large is the difference between the path specified by the user and that is present in D. If the restriction involves a conceptual component of type text or image (e.g abstract CONTAINS "Information Retrieval") a different type of partial matching is possible. A document D can match the text or image specified in the query, but not in the required component (e.g. "Information Retrieval" is contained in the body of the document and not in the abstract). In MULTOS this restriction is treated "as not verified" by the document D; it should instead be possible to retrieve D and to associate

[2] This indicates that the complex component "body" contains (in a PART-OF relationship) the component "product_description", which, in turn, contains the component "price".

it a score that considers that the restriction only partially has been matched. After the retrieval operation, the set of documents may then be presented to the user as an ordered list. The ordering is given by a score associated to each document. This score gives a measure of the matching degree between each document and the query. It is obtained as a combination of preference values, partial matching uncertainty values and importance values associated to each predicate in the specified query based on probabilistic models [Rijs79, Crof81].

3.1. Query Language

We now present in more detail the extensions necessary to the query language that provide for the formulation of imprecise queries. A query contains restrictions on document collections (SCOPE clause), on document types (TYPE clause) and on document content (WHERE clause). The latter is composed of conditions on formatted conceptual components (whose data types are string, integer, date), on conceptual components of type text and image and on restrictions on the whole textual and image document content. In the following a partial definition of the query syntax is given (expressions between square brackets are optional, while words in capital letters are tokens of the language):

```
FIND   [<nb-of-docs>] DOCUMENTS
       [SCOPE <scope-clause>]
       [TYPE  <type-clause>]
[WHERE [<comp-restriction-clause>]
        [<text-restriction-clause>]
        [<image-restriction-clause>]]
```

The possibility of limiting the number of retrieved documents through the `<nb-of-docs>` value, allows one to reduce the problem of document overloading typical of classical boolean document retrieval systems. It must be noted that this is possible because the retrieved documents are ranked in decreasing relevance order. The SCOPE clause specifies the domain against which the query is applied (e.g. SCOPE PC-documentation): either a list of documents or one or more document collections can be used. The TYPE clause (e.g. TYPE offer-letter) allows to restrict the search to documents that are instances of the specified types and their specializations in the type hierarchy. The `<comp-restriction-clause>` is a combination of conditions on formatted conceptual components (`<form-comp-restriction-clause>`), and on conceptual components of type text (`<text-comp-restriction-clause>`) and image (`<image-comp-restriction-clause>`). The `<form-comp-restriction-clause>` is a combination in AND/OR of simple conditions each one having the form `<component><restriction><importance>`. The logical operator NOT is not permitted because it would introduce severe complications in handling uncertainty during query processing (see section 3.2). However, in the experiences with the actual MULTOS prototype, we have noticed that boolean queries with NOT operator are very seldom used by the users (and they could be transformed into equivalent queries without NOT). The conditions on collections, types and formatted conceptual components must be verified by all retrieved documents. The `<text-comp-restriction-clause>` and `<image-comp-restriction-clause>` are relative to textual and image basic document components, respectively. They are composed of a list of restrictions of the form `<component><restriction><importance>`. Retrieved documents will verify with a given certainty these restrictions.

The `<component>` is expressed through a pathname which has the form

$$[*]n_1[er_1][.|*]n_2 \ldots n_{m-1}[er_{m-1}][.|*]n_m.$$

where each n_i $(i = 1,...,m)$ is a component name. If n_i and n_{i+1} are separated by "." then n_{i+1} is directly contained in n_i; if n_i and n_{i+1} are separated by "*" then n_{i+1} is contained in n_i either directly or indirectly. As mentioned, the condition may be verified on the specified path or on a different path having n_m as terminal component; the er_i values (which must be between 0 and 1) are used for computing the score associated to this partial matching. If n_m is a conceptual component of type text or image, then it is possible that the restriction is not verified in the component n_m but in the whole document content. The values l_t (for textual components) and l_{im} (for image components) are used as document ranking scores (l_t and l_{im} are real numbers in the range [0,1]). The `<restriction>` allows to express restrictions on values associated to the conceptual component together with a *preference* degree, while the *importance* of the whole condition is expressed through the `<importance>` value. The importance values allowed are HIGH, MEDIUM and LOW (or a numeric value between 0 and 1) while an attribute value may have the preference degrees PREFERRED or ACCEPTABLE (or, again, a numeric value between 0 and 1).

Restrictions on all the textual parts of the document are given in `<text-restriction-clause>`. They have the form `TEXT CONTAINS <list-of-terms><importance>`. The text restriction contains a list of words that specify the text content of retrieved documents.

The text retrieval process is based on the algorithm presented in [Crof88a]. This algorithm consists in a variation of well known signature algorithms [Chri84] (as a result signatures remain the main access structures for text retrieval) allowing the computation of a score associated to each retrieved document. For each word in the query the frequency in whole document collection and in the retrieved document is used to evaluate the score. Also the use of dependent groups of words in the text is considered. The score is a numeric value between 0 and 1. It gives a measure of the matching degree between document textual content and query textual restriction.

Restrictions on the whole image document content are given in the `<image-restriction-clause>`. They have the form `IMAGE MATCHES <list-of-image-restrictions>` where each `<image-restriction>` has the form `[<domain-name>]<object-clause><importance>` The content of an image is described on the ground of objects therein contained. The image restriction retrieves all documents that satisfy at least one of the restrictions in the list. The `<object-clause>` contains the name of an object (for the specific application domain, if `<domain-name>` is specified), an object quantifier (es. AT LEAST n, with n=1 by default) and the lowest recognition degree required in order to recognize the object in the image interpretation. The score associated to each document is determined by using a recognition degree associated to the recognition of each object, as resulting from the image analysis process (this is explained in [Cont87] and [Cont89]). The image analysis process is separated from the image retrieval process: in the actual implementation the image analysis process is working on some specific application domains (described in advance to the system in term of basic objects, using an ARG based approach, and in term of complex objects, using a rule-based approach) and only for two dimensional images with non-overlapping complex objects. Image interpretation, in terms of all the objects recognized in the image with associated belief and plausability, is based on the Dempster-Shafer theory of evidence [Barn81] [Gord84]. The results of each image interpretation is stored in the image indices which will then be used by the system in processing queries on image content [Cont89].

Retrieved documents are ranked in decreasing relevance order, by using *importance* and *preference* values and through the ranking scores obtained for restrictions on text and image components.

The query used as example in section 2 can now be extended with conditions on the content (in terms of contained objects) of the image required in the documents to be retrieved and with the specification of importance of condition and preference of values:

```
FIND 20 DOCUMENTS
     SCOPE = PC-documentation
     TYPE = offer-letter
WHERE (*product-price BETWEEN (4000,4500) ACCEPTABLE,
                      BETWEEN (4501,5500) PREFERRED,
                      BETWEEN (5501,6000) ACCEPTABLE) HIGH OR
      (*company-name = "Olivetti") HIGH
      (TEXT CONTAINS "good ergonomics") LOW
      (IMAGE MATCHES
             screen HIGH
             keyboard HIGH
             AT LEAST 2 floppy_driver LOW) HIGH
```

We may observe that the extended query language made it possible to express the uncertainty the user had. It is indeed possible to specify that the *product-price* is approximately equal to $ 5,000 and that the values around $ 5,000 are preferred; furthermore in the query it is stated that the condition on the *company-name* and *product-price* is more important than the others.

3.2. Query Processing

A query is composed of five elements, as seen in the previous subsection: `Q = (S, T, C, FT, IM)` where S is the SCOPE restriction, T is the TYPE restriction, C is the `<conc-restriction-clause>`, FT is the restriction on full text and IM is the restriction on all images. The C restriction is composed of three different parts: CC, TC and IC. CC is a boolean combination (in AND/OR) of conditions on conceptual components of different data types (string, integer, date, etc.), TC is a list of restrictions on conceptual components of type text, IC is a list of restrictions on conceptual components of type image.

Retrieved documents are determined by evaluating the S, T and CC restrictions first. The other restrictions are evaluated on the set of documents determined through this process. Each retrieved document is then ranked assigning it a score calculated through a ranking function **g**.

Let us suppose that CC has l elements, TC has m elements and IC has k. Let us denote with pr_i the preference value of the i-th query term and with im_i the importance of i-th query term. r_i is a measure of the matching between the path specified in the query and that present in the document. All these values are real numbers in the range [0,1].

The ranking function **g** for CC is given by

$$g = \sum_{i=1}^{l} pr_i \times im_i \times r_i \tag{1}$$

with $r_i = \prod_{j=1}^{n_j} er_j^{\,q_j}$

where n_j = number of conceptual components specified in the path, and

$$q_j = \begin{cases} 1 & \text{if } j\text{-th element of the path is correctly specified} \\ 0 & \text{otherwise} \end{cases}$$

As mentioned, TC and IC are restrictions on conceptual components of type text and image, respectively. However we consider also the possibility that the restriction is verified on the whole document content but not for the conceptual component specified in the query. The ranking function, for these documents, is multiplied by a factor l_t (for textual components) and l_{im} (for image components), with l_t and l_{im} real numbers in the range [0,1]. In this situation g is given by

$$g = \sum_{i=1}^{m} pr_i \times im_i \times l_t^{\,q_i} + \sum_{i=1}^{k} pr_i \times im_i \times l_{im}^{\,q_i} \tag{2}$$

with $q_i = \begin{cases} 1 & \text{if } i\text{-th restriction is verified only on whole document content} \\ 0 & \text{if } i\text{-th restriction is verified on the specified conceptual component} \end{cases}$

(note that only the query elements that satisfy a matching, either exact or partial are included in (1) and (2)).

The ranking function for FT and IM query components is given by

$$g = \sum_{i=1}^{r} c_i \times pr_i \times im_i$$

where c_i is the score (in the range [0,1]) associated to each document that verifies the conditions FT or IM; r is the number of query elements in FT and IM. For FT query components no preference value is specified.

The query Q can be viewed as a boolean combination of its elements as follows:

```
Q = S AND T AND CC AND (TC OR IC OR FT OR IM)
```

This indicates that retrieved documents must verify the S restriction, the T restriction and the CC restrictions. The restrictions TC, IC, FT and IM may optionally be verified by retrieved documents and they are mainly used for ordering retrieved documents in decreasing relevance order. However if the number of documents that verify the S, T and CC restrictions is significantly higher then the maximum number of documents to be retrieved, then these restrictions are essential for evaluating the documents that will compose the retrieved set.

The execution of the query is performed with the following steps:

1. The S and T query components are executed; a set $L_1 = (d_1,...,d_n)$ of n documents is determined. If $n = 0$ then the query process stops.
2. The CC condition is executed using indices defined on attributes. The set L_2 of documents that satisfy the CC query component is intersected with the set L_1, by giving the set L_2'. If L_2' is empty then the query process stops. The other restrictions are executed on the set of documents belonging to L_2'. If card(L_2') $>N$ (N = maximum number of documents to be returned to the user) then it is possible to optimize the retrieval process by trying to reduce the number of documents used for the execution of the other restrictions. Let us order L_2' in decreasing relevance order. Then L_2' is given by $(d_1,...,d_M)$ with the corresponding scores (ordered) $(s_1,...,s_M)$ where $s_i \geq s_j$ iff $i<j$. The process used to reduce the number of documents in L_2' is as follows. We calculate s_{max} as the maximum score that a document verifying all the remaining restrictions can obtain. Then, if a document d_R with a score s_R exists in L_2' such that $s_{max}+s_R<s_N$ (R>N) then the set L_2' can be reduced to $L_2''=(d_1,...,d_N,\ldots,d_{R-1})$ since the documents $(d_R,...,d_M)$ cannot enter in the set of the N top ranked documents even if they will verify all the remaining conditions. This computation is performed after the execution of each of the other restrictions.
3. For each one of the k IC restrictions, the score to be assigned to the documents that verify it is estimated by using the importance and the preference values. Then the restrictions are ordered by decreasing estimated scores and executed in that order. After the execution of each restriction the evaluation described in 2 is repeated and the set L_2'' is determined again. The same process is repeated for the m TC restrictions, for the IM restrictions and for the FT restrictions.
4. The set of documents L_2'' is returned to the user in decreasing relevance order.

Further improvement of the query execution can be obtained if the execution of IC, TC, IM and FT restrictions is intermixed; the exact execution order is determined by considering the score that each restriction assigns to retrieved documents and the cost of the execution of the restriction is considered.

3.2.1. Query Execution Example

The query execution process can be better understood through the use of an example. Let us consider the query used in the previous sections. With the notation introduced it becomes:

```
N = 20
S = PC-documentation
T = offer-letter
CC1  = (*.product-price BETWEEN (4000,4500) 0.3
        *.product-price BETWEEN (4501,5500) 1.0
```

```
        *.product-price BETWEEN (5501,6000) 0.3) 1.0
CC2 = (company_name = "Olivetti" 1.0) 1.0
TC and IC are empty
FT1 = good ergonomics 0.3
IM1 = (screen 0.3) 1.0
IM2 = (keyboard 1.0) 1.0
IM3 = (2 floppy 0.3) 1.0
```

Note that the numbers associated to the restrictions are the importance and preference values (we assumed that the preference values are 0.3 when ACCEPTABLE is specified and 1.0 for PREFERRED, while the importance values are 0.3 for LOW, 0.6 for MEDIUM and 1.0 for HIGH). Note that the assignment of these values is heuristic. An evaluation of the prototype system will allow to determine the most appropriate values.

The query processing steps are as follows:

1. The system tables are accessed and the list of documents NC_1 belonging to the collection PC-documentation is determined. Then the system tables containing the list of document instances associated to each type are accessed to determine the instances of the type offer-letter, whose number is NT_1. The two sets are intersected and the list of documents L_1 is determined.
2. The CC_1 and CC_2 restrictions are executed. For the conceptual components representing formatted data, the system maintains an index table which is accessed during query execution. The set of documents whose *product-price* is between 4000 and 4500 (set L_{21}), between 4501 and 5500 (set L_{22}) and between 5501 and 6000 (set L_{23}) are determined. A score is assigned to each document in L_{21}, L_{22} and L_{23}, given by the corresponding importance and preference values. Thus documents in L_{21} have a score equal to 0.3, those in L_{22} have a score equal to 1.0 and those in L_{23} have a score equal to 0.3; these scores are maintained in L_{21}, L_{22} and L_{23} together with the document identifiers. The set of documents whose conceptual component *company-name* has a value equal to "Olivetti" is determined and maintained in L_{24}, together with the scores assigned to each document (it is equal to 1.0). The set of documents $L_2=(L_{21} \cup L_{22} \cup L_{23}) \cup L_{24}$ is determined. The possible scores of documents belonging to L_2 are 2.0, 1.3, 1.0, 0.3 (we assume that L_{21}, L_{22} and L_{23} are disjunct sets). The set L_1 is intersected with L_2 and gives L_2'. Let us suppose that card(L_2')=100, so that it is higher than N (N=20). A reduction of the number of documents on which FT_1, IM_1, IM_2 and IM_3 restrictions are verified can be tried. The documents in L_2' are ordered in decreasing relevance order. Let us suppose that 15 documents have the maximum score 2.0, 20 documents have a score of 1.3, 10 have a score of 1.0, and the remaining documents have a score of 0.3. The estimation of the maximum score assigned to documents that verify the FT restriction is s_{FT}=0.3 (obtained for c_i=1 and im_i=0.3). The estimation for documents that verify the IM restrictions is s_{IM}=0.53 (obtained for c_i=1). This means that $s_{\max}=s_{FT}+s_{IM}=0.83$ (the estimation is obtained by multiplying the importance and precision factors and dividing by the number of restrictions). This implies that the FT and IM restrictions must be verified on the set of documents $L_2''=(d_1, \ldots, d_{45})$ since documents in $(d_{46},\ldots,d_{100})$ will never obtain a score higher than the score of d_{20} (which is 1.3).

3. The score of documents that verify IM_1, IM_2, IM_3 is estimated through the importance and preference values. Thus the values 0.1 for IM_1, 0.33 for IM_2 and 0.1 for IM_3 are obtained (the estimated score for IM_i is given by $\frac{im_i \times pr_i}{n}$, where n is the number of image restrictions). IM_2 is the restriction having higher estimated score. It is executed first and on the set L_2''. Let us suppose that 20 documents satisfy the IM_2 restriction. After execution the exact score is determined; let us suppose that it is equal to 0.2 (the maximum score that documents satisfying IM_2 is 0.33). The scores of documents belonging to L_2'' are modified by using the new scores and the process that tries to reduce the number of documents in L_2'' is repeated again, using IM_1, IM_3 and FT for the estimation of the maximum scores that documents can obtain. The same process is repeated again, after the evaluation of IM_1 and IM_3. Finally FT is evaluated.

3.3. Query Formulation

The query is formulated by direct interaction with the user; the query formulation tool is driven by the query language syntax and the user is helped in all stages of the process.

The following steps are part of the query formulation process:

1. A window with all system collections is displayed. The user can click with the mouse on one of the collection names, which is then included in the S part of the query. More collections can be specified, repeting the process.

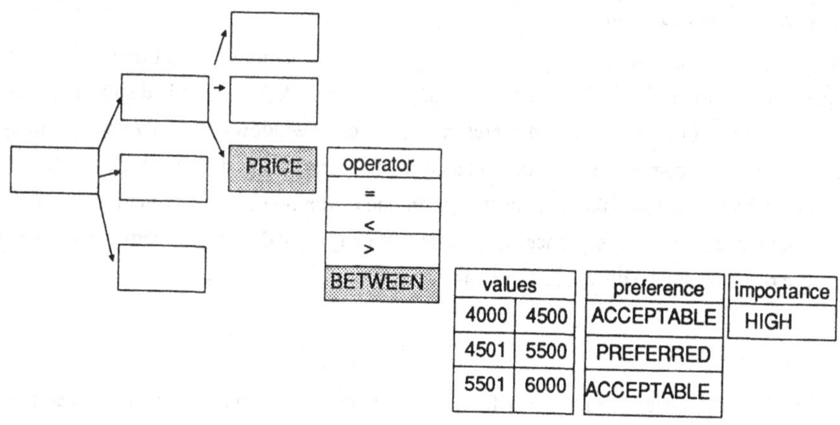

Figure 2. Query Formulation Tool - Conceptual component restrictions

2. A window with all system types is displayed. If no type restriction is expressed then step 3.2 is executed. The user can select one of the system types through the use of the mouse; the type is included in the T part of the query and then step 3.1 is executed. After that step 2. is executed again,

and one more type can be selected (if no type is selected at this stage step 4. is executed).

3. Restrictions on conceptual components are expressed. Firstly, CC components are considered. Two different user interfaces are possible, depending on whether a type has been specified (3.1) or not (3.2).

   3.1 The type description is displayed and the user is enabled to express restrictions involving conceptual components contained in the type (Figure 2). By clicking with the mouse on one conceptual component, the operator, the value(s) of the restriction together with their preferences and importance are requested. If the conceptual component name is given through a path, then different plausibility degrees can be associated to each element of the path (the *er* values).

   3.2 If no type has been specified, then the list of all conceptual components present in the system is displayed. The restrictions are expressed as in 3.1 by clicking on the conceptual component name. By pressing the "execute" button the process stops and step 4. is activated.

   This step is repeated for TC components and then for IC components. In each case the values associated to conceptual components of type text and image are introduced as in 4 (in case of TC components) or as in 5 (in case of IC components).

4. Free text restrictions are expressed by inserting lists of words. An importance value can be associated to the restriction.

5. For the image restriction a menu with all image domains is displayed. If a domain has been chosen, then the possible objects contained in the domain are displayed in a menu. After that, some of these objects are selected and a preference value is expressed. An importance value can be expressed for the whole image restriction.

After the execution of the query, the results are displayed by presenting a list of document names, document types plus an indication of the relevance of the document. A document is displayed by clicking on its name. The document and the query are presented in two subwindows. The elements of the query that are satisfied for the document are put in evidence as the parts of the document that matched with the query. To exit from this phase the user must click in one of the two buttons at the bottom of the screen; in this way he can express his relevance judgments that can be used by the system for a relevance feedback (the use of relevance feedback, however, is not described in this paper).

4. FINAL REMARKS

The problem of managing uncertainty for attaining better results in retrieving multimedia documents is discussed in this paper. The user can specify imprecise queries to express his uncertain knowledge about the content of the documents he is seeking. The user can also query text and image document components and, during query processing, the significance of these components is evaluated in relation to the query. Therefore, text and image components play an active role in the document retrieval process. The approach presented in this paper for the retrieval of multimedia documents allows the ranking of the retrieved documents in order of relevance to the query. This leads to a better understanding by the system of the user needs.

The techniques presented for supporting user's imprecise queries and managing uncertainty in the document retrieval process are applied in the MULTOS system. We have also presented the essential characteristics of the actual MULTOS prototype system which is a system intended to support powerful content based retrieval and efficient storage of large numbers of multimedia documents. A first MULTOS prototype has been developed since September 1987. The implementation was initially based on a network (Ethernet with TCP/IP) of SUN workstations with UNIX operating system. Then the prototype has been ported on Olivetti machines (LSX 30XX minicomputers family, as server and M380-XP5 as client); the UNIX System V was used as operating system and X11 as window system. The extension of the MULTOS system, to incorporate the new techniques described in the paper is now in progress. A first step has been completed, with the implementation of an intermediate prototype enabling the analysis of images (only for graphic images belonging to one application domain [Cont87]) and the processing of queries on them (i.e. IC and IM). The final prototype implementation is expected by early 1990. Evaluation of effectiveness of multimedia document retrieval will be crucial in tuning the techniques described in this paper.

REFERENCES

Barb85. F. Barbic and F. Rabitti, "The Type Concept in Office Document Retrieval,," *Proc. VLDB Conference*, Stockholm (August 21-23, 1985).

Barn81. J. Barnett, "Computational Methods for a Mathematical Theory of Evidence," *Proc. 7th International Joint Conference on Artificial Intelligence*, Vancouver, B.C., pp. 868-875 (1981).

Belk87. N.J. Belkin and W.B. Croft, "Retrieval Techniques," *Annual Review of Information Science and Technology (ARIST)* **22**, pp. 109-145 (1987).

Bert88. E. Bertino, S. Gibbs, and F. Rabitti, "Query Processing in a Multimedia Document System," *ACM Transactions on Office Information Systems* **6**(1), pp. 1-41 (1988).

Bert88a. E. Bertino, A. Converti, H. Eirund, K. Kreplin, F. Rabitti, P. Savino, and C. Thanos, "MULTOS - A filing server for Multimedia Documents," *Proc. of the 1st EURINFO '88 Conf.*, pp. 435-442 (1988).

Chri84. S. Christodoulakis and C. Faloutsos, "Design Consideration for a Message File Server," *IEEE Transactions on Software Engineering* **SE-10**(2), pp. 201-210 (1984).

Chri86. S. Christodoulakis, M. Theodoridou, J. Ho, M. Papa, and A. Parthia, "Multimedia document presentation, information extraction and document formation in MINOS: A Model and a System.," *ACM Transactions on Office Information Systems* **4** (October 1986).

Cont87. P. Conti and F. Rabitti, "Retrieval of Multi-Media Document Images in MULTOS," *Fourth Esprit Conference*, New York-Amsterdam, pp. 1389-1412, North Holland (1987).

Cont89. P. Conti and F. Rabitti, "Image Retrieval by Semantic Content," *Multimedia Office Filing and Retrieval: the MULTOS paradigm*, New York-Amsterdam, pp. 290-320, North Holland (1989).

Crof81. W.B. Croft, "Document Representation in Probabilistic Models of Information Retrieval," *Journal of the American Society of Information Science* **32**, pp. 451-457 (1981).

Crof88. W.B. Croft and R. Krovetz, ''Interactive retrieval of office documents,'' *Proc. Conf. on Office Information Systems*, pp. 228-235 (1988).

Crof88a. W.B. Croft and P. Savino, ''Implementing Ranking Strategies using Text Signatures,'' *ACM Transactions on Office Information Systems* **6**(1), pp. 42-62 (1988).

Eiru88. H. Eirund and K. Kreplin, ''Knowledge based document classification supporting integrated document handling,'' *Proc. Conf. on Office Information Systems*, pp. 189-196 (1988).

Gibb87. S. Gibbs, D. Tsichritzis, A. Fitas, D. Konstantas, and Y. Yeorgaroudakis, ''MUSE: A Multimedia Filing System,'' *IEEE Software* (March 87).

Gord84. J. Gordon and E. Shortliffe, *The Dempster-Shafer Theory of Evidence in Rule-Based Expert Systems,* Addison - Wesley Publishing Company (1984), pp. 272-292. Buchanan B., Shortliffe E., (edt.)

Hora86. W. Horak and G. Kronert, ''An Interactively Formatting Document Editor Based on the Standardised Office Document Architecture,'' *Proc. of IFIP Conf. OFFICE SYSTEMS: Methods and Tools*, pp. 287-300 (1986).

Morr87. J.M. Morrissey and C.J. Van Rijsbergen, ''A Formal Treatment of Missing and Imprecise Information,'' *Proc. of the 10th Annual International ACMSIGIR Conference on Research and Development in Information Retrieval*, pp. 149-156 (1987).

ODA85. ODA, *Office Document Architecture,* ECMA-101 (1985).

Rijs79. C.J. Van Rijsbergen, *Information Retrieval,* McGraw-Hill, London: Butterworths (1979). 2nd Edition

Rijs86. C.J. Van Rijsbergen, ''A Non-Classical Logic for Information Retrieval,'' *Computer Journal*(29), pp. 481-485 (1986).

Salt83. G. Salton and M. McGill, *Introduction to Modern Information Retrieval,* McGraw-Hill, London: Butterworths (1983). 2nd Edition

Thom85. R.H. Thomas, H.C. Forsdick, T.R. Crowley, R.W. Schaaf, R.S. Tomlinson, V.M. Travers, and G.G. Robertson, ''Diamond: A multimedia message system built on a distributed architecture,'' *Computer* **18**(12), pp. 65-77 (Dec. 1985).

A Lock Technique for Disjoint and Non-Disjoint Complex Objects

U. Herrmann[1,2], *P. Dadam*[1], *K. Küspert*[1], *E. A. Roman*[1], *G. Schlageter*[2]

[1] IBM Heidelberg Scientific Center,
Tiergartenstr. 15, D-6900 Heidelberg

[2] University of Hagen, Department of Computer Science,
Feithstraße 140, D-5800 Hagen

Abstract

Using database systems in the field of non-standard applications like engineering, robotics, etc. leads to many new requirements. Some of the major ones are support of (disjoint and non-disjoint) complex objects and of long transactions. These requirements disclose severe drawbacks of traditional concurrency control techniques: Transactions are either serialized unnecessarily or the concurrency control overhead grows drastically. Furthermore, traditional lock protocols cannot be applied in a straightforward way to *non-disjoint* complex objects.

In this paper, a new concurrency control technique is proposed which is derived from the well-known DAG-locking mechanism of System R. The proposed technique avoids most disadvantages of traditional methods. Accesses to non-disjoint complex objects and to their common data can be properly synchronized. Furthermore, a high degree of concurrency with acceptable overhead is achieved on disjoint and non-disjoint, non-recursive complex objects. All this is attained by the use of appropriate lock granules within the structure of complex objects, by a special protocol for requesting locks, and by the anticipation of lock escalations. Lock granules within the structure of complex objects are represented in object-specific lock graphs; query-specific lock graphs show the anticipation of lock escalations. The benefits of the proposed technique are evaluated qualitatively.

1 Introduction

Traditional database systems are primarily designed for use in commercial and business applications. Recent trends in the field of database systems, however, lead to the support of so-called non-standard applications, such as CAD/CAM, robotics, artificial intelligence, etc. [DiDa86, Ditt88]. The use of database systems in non-standard applications poses new demands on such systems. Some of the most important demands are the support of (disjoint and non-disjoint) *complex objects* and of *workstation-server environments* with *long transactions* [HaLo82, LoPl83, BaBu84, Lori85, KDG87, Paul87, HHMM88].

A ***complex object*** is a collection of "flat" (simple) structured objects (usually called "tuples") which has a specific well-defined structure; also, complex objects can be handled as a whole (structural, operational, and behavioral object orientation in the sense of [Ditt86]). Different complex objects need not necessarily be disjoint. It is very useful if different complex objects may share some data, especially for non-standard applications (part libraries with component parts or with standard parts like bolts and nuts or ICs). The discussion in this paper is based on a data model which supports at least disjoint, non-recursive as well as non-disjoint, non-recursive complex objects. Examples of such data models are the extended NF^2 data model [PiAn86, ScSc86] with an additional reference concept, the molecule-atom data (MAD) model [HMMS87], the design object data model (DODM) of DAMOKLES [Rehm88], or the object-oriented data model for CAD/CAM databases introduced in [WKS89]. In the following, the extended NF^2 data model with an additional reference concept is used to describe disjoint and non-disjoint complex objects.

For the purposes of this paper a ***transaction*** is defined as widely accepted (cf. [Date85]). Furthermore, it is assumed that multiple reads of the same data during one transaction lead to the same result (degree 3 of consistency [GLPT76]). Transactions in traditional applications are usually short (most last seconds or a few minutes). In non-standard applications like VLSI-design, however, the duration of a transaction can last up to days or even weeks (*long transactions* [KLMP84, KSUW85], *conversational transactions* [LoPl83]). In this paper, the term *short transactions* is used for transactions in a conventional centralized database system whereas the term *long transactions* is used for transactions in a "conversational" (e.g. workstation-server) environment.

In non-standard applications different users or user groups may *check-out* complex objects of a central database onto ***workstations***. Data which are checked out can be regarded (at least temporarily) as private, local databases. A *check-in* back into the central database may be done for data which have been changed on a workstation. Nowadays, different users or user groups often work on private databases in an independent way, e.g. in automotive industry. Therefore, special actions must be taken to guarantee that the private databases are always in a consistent or at least in a well-known state among one another and with the central database. In such an environment, traditional concurrency control techniques reveal some severe drawbacks, especially with regard to the synchronization of long transactions on disjoint and, in particular, on non-disjoint complex objects.

Optimistic methods [KuRo81] do not lend themselves to long transactions since these methods do not reveal access conflicts before the end of a transaction, and the rollback of a long transaction which may have lasted for some weeks is not acceptable. If ***locking techniques*** [GLPT76] are applied, conflicts are detected much earlier, i.e. usually when the corresponding data are accessed. So, in this paper synchronization techniques based on the use of locks are examined exclusively. The term "lock" will always be used in the sense of *transaction-oriented locks*; *action-oriented locks*, e.g. on indexes [BaSc77], are not addressed.

A database system which supports complex objects should also be able to synchronize access to *parts* of complex objects. If ***traditional lock techniques*** are used such synchronization leads to unsatisfactory results: Locking complex objects as a whole (including existing common data, if any) prohibits a high degree of concurrency, because a lot of data are usually blocked unnecessarily for a long time. On the other hand, locking each single tuple individually (i.e. the basic elements of complex objects) leads to immense overhead caused by the administration of locks and conflict tests. These disadvantages are of particular importance to long transactions since long transactions need long locks, and to non-disjoint complex objects since the potential conflict rate on shared (possibly "high traffic") data grows drastically. In addition to the size of the lock granules, the corresponding lock modes heavily influence the possible degree of concurrency. Hence, in an environment with long transactions and non-disjoint complex objects it is very important to lock data in the least restrictive way necessary.

Consequently, a synchronization technique for disjoint and non-disjoint complex objects should support appropriate lock granules *within* the structure of complex objects, and also, should satisfy the special requirements of non-disjoint complex objects. Furthermore, a *mechanism to determine the "optimal" lock requests automatically* (i.e. the lock mode which is requested for a certain granule during query execution) should be provided because it is not acceptable that database system users themselves have to set "optimal" locks which meet the requirements pointed out above. The criterion for optimization should be the overall throughput of a database system.

In ***this paper*** a lock technique is proposed which is well-suited to the needs of complex objects in non-standard applications. The proposed technique is based on the use of lock granules of different sizes within complex objects. Complex objects with common data are handled by the proposed lock protocol in a way which allows a high degree of concurrency with an acceptable overhead. In *section 2*, a possible classification and representation of complex objects is shown. At the beginning of *section 3*, traditional lock techniques are described. The lock technique of System R is used as an example and will be discussed in some detail. Then, the lock requirements of non-standard applications as well as the problems arising from the use of traditional lock techniques in non-standard applications are discussed. *Section 4* is the central part of this paper. First, a general lock graph for disjoint and non-disjoint complex objects as well as object-specific lock graphs are introduced. Then, rules for explicitly requesting locks on disjoint and non-disjoint complex objects are proposed. After a short discussion on how to determine "optimal" lock requests automatically, a qualitative evaluation of the proposed lock technique completes section 4. Conclusions in *section 5* round off the paper.

2 Classification and Representation of Complex Objects

In [BaBu84] a classification of complex objects into disjoint or non-disjoint and recursive or non-recursive complex objects was proposed. In contrast to *disjoint* complex objects, *non-disjoint* complex objects may share some data. Complex objects are *recursive* if they contain other complex objects of the same type. Otherwise, complex objects are *non-recursive.*

Disjoint, non-recursive complex objects are the best examined class of complex objects. They have hierarchical structure. To describe such structures the NF^2 or extended NF^2 data model can be used. The extended NF^2 data model allows an attribute of a relation to be again table-valued (a set or a list), or to be tuple-valued (i.e. a (complex) tuple).

Redundant storing of data is the only way to avoid common data. Redundancy, however, causes problems with regard to storage space and the preservation of consistency after updates. Hence, at least in centralized databases, data sharing is usually superior to redundant storing of data. Especially in non-standard applications, there exists a wide spectrum of applications for ***non-disjoint, non-recursive*** complex objects. Examples of such complex objects are part libraries with component parts or standard parts. Common data may again contain common data. In the present paper, it is assumed that data which may be shared are stored in relations of their own, i.e. *a reference*[1] *to common data always refer-*

[1] The discussion in this paper makes no assumptions on the implementation of these references; they can be implemented e.g. under use of key values, surrogates [MeLo83], etc.

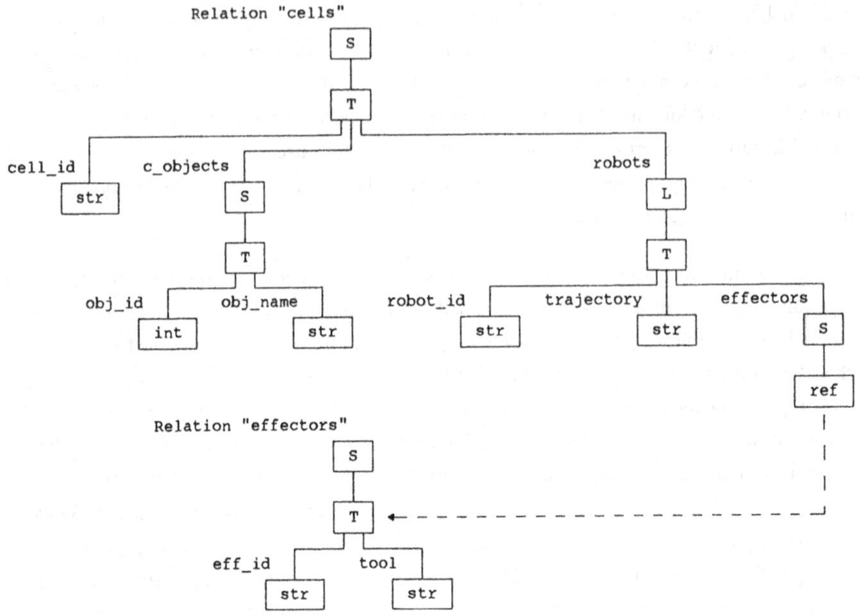

Figure 1. Non-Disjoint, Non-Recursive Complex Objects: Schema of the Relations "cells" and "effectors"

ences a complex object of a relation and never parts of any complex object. This assumption can be made without loss of generality, because conceptually each database schema can be easily transformed in order to fulfill this condition. Complex objects which do not contain shared data are stored within a single relation.

Figure 1 depicts the structure of the relations "cells" and "effectors" as an example for non-disjoint, non-recursive complex objects. S, L and T stands for set, list and (complex) tuple, respectively. The leaves of the schema trees consist of atomic data types without inner structure, e.g. strings (str), integers (int) or references to common data (ref). The dashed arrow indicates that each reference points to a specific effector - a tuple - within the relation "effectors". The attribute names are added to each node of the schema trees. The suffix "_id" of an attribute name indicates a key attribute. The relation "cells" models a manufacturing cell which contains different cell-objects. These cell-objects can be manufactured by some robots. The robots in the "robots" *list* are ordered, for instance, by "robot_id". The effectors (tools) which may be used by robots are stored within the relation "effectors", which in turn represents a library of effectors. *One effector may be used (shared) by different robots.* Some data of a complex object which models one manufacturing cell (i.e. some data of a complex object of complex object type "cells") are stored within relation "cells" (i.e. the data of a cell except the effector data), some within relation "effectors" (i.e. the effector data). So, a complex object can span data which are stored within more than one relation. The relations "cells" and "effectors" can be used to generate and to administrate manufacturing cells in automotive or aircraft industry [GFR87].

Recursive complex objects which can be ***disjoint*** as well as ***non-disjoint*** are well-suited for the modelling of bill-of-material-like data structures. In this paper, however, only non-recursive complex objects are

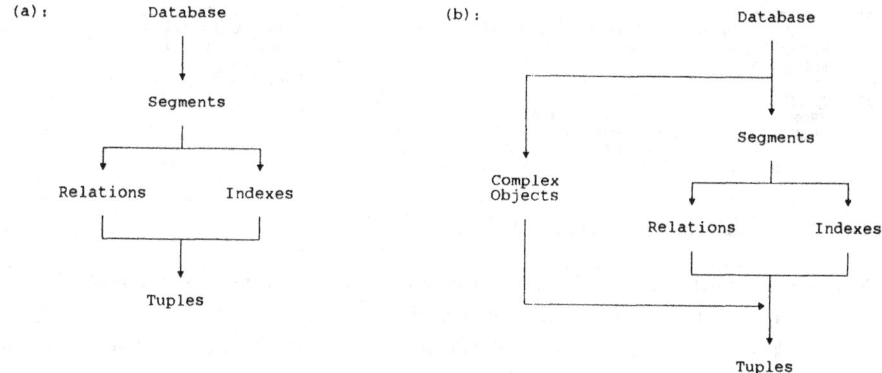

Figure 2. Granularity of Locks: Lock Graphs (DAG) of System R (a) and XSQL (b)

examined in detail because of space limitations. The consideration of recursive complex objects is subject of future work.

Some words on our terminology: The following discussion is based on the assumption that attribute values of a complex object may be atomic, or may consist of data of the same type, or may be composed of data of different types. Attribute values which consist of data of the same type (a set or a list) are called *homogeneously* structured. We use the term *heterogeneously* structured attribute values when an attribute value may be composed of data of different types; i.e. a (complex) tuple. In the example shown in Figure 1, for instance, "obj_id" is atomic, the set "c_objects" is homogeneously structured, and the tuple "c_objects" is heterogeneously structured.

3 Traditional Lock Techniques and their Shortcomings

3.1 Locking in System R and XSQL

In ***System R*** [Astr76], database, segment, relation, index and tuple have been chosen as lockable units. The lock graph of System R (Figure 2, (a)) can be interpreted as a *directed acyclic graph (DAG)* [GLP75, GLPT76]. The nodes of this lock graph represent the lockable units (for which locks can be requested); the edges indicate a "contained-in"-relationship. Each lockable unit can be locked in a certain mode: lock mode IS (Intention Share) or IX (Intention eXclusive) grants the right to lock a descendant node in mode S (Share) or X (eXclusive), respectively. Based on that lock graph, a protocol for explicitly requesting locks has been defined [GLP75, GLPT76]:

1. Before requesting an *S* or *IS lock* on a node, **at least one** parent node must be locked in IS (or a more restrictive) mode.
2. Before requesting an *X* or *IX lock* on a node, **all** parent nodes must be locked in IX (or a more restrictive) mode.
3. Locks must be released at the end of the transaction or in leaf-to-root order.

```
Q1:  SELECT o
     FROM   c IN cells, o IN c.c_objects
     WHERE  c.cell_id = 'c1'
     FOR READ

Q2:  SELECT r
     FROM   c IN cells, r IN c.roboters
     WHERE  c.cell_id = 'c1' AND
            r.robot_id = 'r1'
     FOR UPDATE

Q3:  SELECT r
     FROM   c IN cells, r IN c.robots
     WHERE  c.cell_id = 'c1' AND
            r.robot_id = 'r2'
     FOR UPDATE
```

Figure 3. Examples: Queries Q1, Q2 and Q3

A node is locked *explicitly* in mode S or X, if an S or X lock, respectively, has been granted on the corresponding node under the lock protocol mentioned above. Nodes can also be locked *implicitly*. A node is implicitly locked in *S mode* if **at least one** of its parents is locked in S (or X) mode; a node is implicitly locked in *X mode* if **all** its parents are locked in X mode. All these locks must be held, of course, by the same transaction.

To be able to use ***System R*** more efficiently in non-standard applications, it has been ***extended*** (among other things) to handle complex objects (XSQL [HaLo82, LoPl83, Lori85]). The throughput of database systems is heavily influenced by the size of the available lock granules [RiSt77]. Coarser lockable units lower the administrative overhead of locks and conflict tests, but also reduce the degree of concurrency which can be attained. The integration of complex objects into System R leads to some severe concurrency control problems: none of the available lockable units (Figure 2, (a)) is well-suited to synchronize access to complex objects. Because of this, the lock graph of System R has been extended by the granule "complex object" (Figure 2, (b)). In this way it is possible to lock a complex object with a single lock.

Complex objects which are checked-out by a user on a workstation get a ***long lock***. In contrast to traditional short locks, long locks must survive system shutdowns and system crashes. To simplify matters, it is assumed in this paper that for long locks IS, IX, S and X lock modes can be used as well. Special modes for long locks are discussed in more detail e.g. in [KSUW85].

3.2 Problems with Traditional (DAG Like) Lock Techniques

3.2.1 The Granule-Oriented Problem

In the applications described in [HaLo82] complex objects are always manipulated (checked-out, checked-in) *as a whole*. In that case, the lockable unit "complex objects" represents an appropriate compromise between concurrency and overhead. This technique, however, comes to its limit if transactions need only *parts* of complex objects. Query Q1 (Figure 3), for instance, is the request of a workstation user to check-out all c_objects of cell "c1" for read. With query Q2 another user on another workstation requests robot "r1" of cell "c1" for update. Both queries are written in a query language which is an extension of SQL[2]. Obviously, Q1 and Q2 access different parts of complex object "c1".

---

[2] Essentially, the query language is the Heidelberg Database Language (HDBL). HDBL is the query language of the Advanced Information Management Prototype (AIM-P) which is currently under development at the IBM Heidelberg Scientific Center. AIM-P is used to prototype and to simulate applications [Dada86, Dada88, Linn88].

Consequently, there exists no conflict at the *logical level*, and Q1 and Q2 could run simultaneously. Nevertheless, locking "cells" objects as a whole would serialize Q1 and Q2 unnecessarily. Locking each single tuple of a complex object, on the other hand, would lead to an immense concurrency control overhead, because one cell may contain hundreds of c_objects. *So, appropriate lock granules within the structure of complex objects are the basis for an efficient lock technique on complex objects.* As mentioned earlier, this is especially valid if long transactions are involved: Long locks on coarse granules (held by a long transaction) may unnecessarily block a large amount of data for a long time. Long locks on tuples of complex objects, however, may lead to a huge administrative overhead for a long time. Besides that, the potential conflict rate on shared data is extremely high. In the following, the problem alluded above is referred to as the ***granule-oriented problem***.

3.2.2 The Protocol-Oriented Problems

Beside the granule-oriented problem, ***protocol-oriented problems*** exist as well. A straightforward application of the traditional DAG lock protocol to non-disjoint complex objects may look as follows: Locks can be requested on granules within complex objects according to the rules of the traditional DAG lock protocol. This, however, leads to intolerable overhead when a node within shared data is requested *exclusively*: **all** parent nodes of the requested node must be determined and must be locked appropriately. For example, an effector (Figure 1) can be used by many different robots. To lock a certain effector exclusively (assuming that appropriate granules are available), all robots referencing the effector must have been locked previously. It is a very time-consuming task to find out which robots are affected. (Storing "backward pointers" within effectors to reference affected robots would lead to other severe drawbacks with regard to pointer maintenance, etc.) After *all* robots which share the effector are determined, each single robot (inclusive all its parent nodes) must be locked upon successful completion of all conflict tests. Even under the assumption that common data (e.g. libraries) are updated infrequently, a lock protocol for non-disjoint complex objects should be able to avoid the immense overhead described above. If the DAG requirement that all parents of a requested node (within common data) be locked before such a node may be requested in mode (I)X is given up, however, then implicit locks on common data become a problem.

In the traditional DAG lock protocol a node can be *locked implicitly* by locking its parent(s) in an appropriate mode. Locks on parents of a node are only visible by another transaction if the requested node is accessed by the other transaction via the locked nodes, i.e. on the same path. If the requested node is part of common data (e.g. an effector), however, another transaction can access the requested node via a graph (e.g. robot "r2") other than the one with the locks (e.g. robot "r1"). In this case, the second transaction would not see the implicit locks on the requested node within the first graph, and possible lock conflicts would not be detected. So, the database could be transformed into an inconsistent state. *A lock protocol for non-disjoint complex objects has to be able to synchronize all such "from-the-side access" to common data.*

3.2.3 The Authorization-Oriented Problem

A close cooperation of the concurrency control component and the authorization component (which administrates the access rights of all transactions (users)), can drastically increase the degree of concurrency; especially with regard to long locks on non-disjoint data. For example, if a transaction doesn't

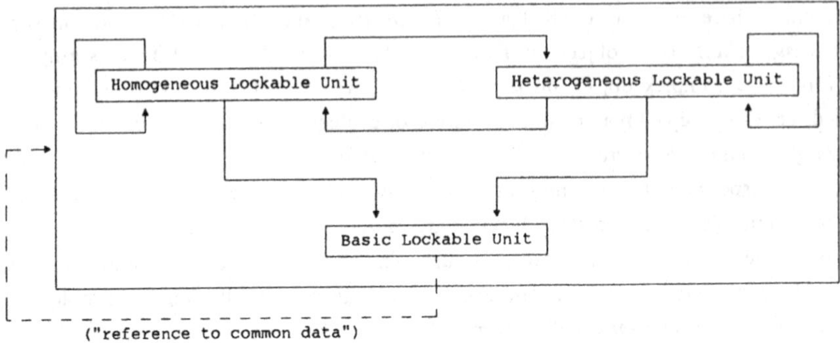

Figure 4. Granularity of Locks: General Lock Graph for Disjoint and Non-Disjoint Complex Objects

have the right to change any data within the effectors library it is never necessary for this transaction to hold (possibly for a long period of time) an explicit or implicit X lock on any effector, even if the transaction holds an X lock on a robot which references some effectors. It seems obligatory for a lock technique supporting non-disjoint complex objects to be able to exploit the above mentioned fact and to address effectively the ***authorization-oriented problem.***

4 Special Lock Techniques for Complex Objects

4.1 Overview

Access to complex objects can be synchronized by implementing the following steps: When a complex object type is defined, under use of the *general lock graph* (section 4.2) the corresponding *object-specific lock graph* (section 4.3) is constructed automatically. Each query to be processed is first *analyzed* to find out which attributes will be accessed, and which kind of access (read, update, ...) will be done. Then, "optimal" lock requests (i.e. the lock granules and their mode) are determined. The granule and mode information is stored within *query-specific lock graphs* (section 4.5). During *query execution*, the stored granule and mode information are obtained from the query-specific lock graphs, and locks are requested from a lock manager. The lock manager tests whether a certain lock request can be granted or not by observing certain *rules* (section 4.4). If a lock is granted, the corresponding data may be accessed.

The following discussion is based on the assumption that common data of non-disjoint complex objects may be bound to these objects via references. The implementation of these references (e.g. by using surrogates) has no influence on the general applicability of the lock technique proposed in this paper.

4.2 General Lock Graph for Disjoint and Non-Disjoint Complex Objects

To enable concurrent access of complex objects, the DAG lock graph presented in section 3.1 is extended in two areas. First, lock granules between tuple and complex object are needed (Figure 2, (b)). Second, lock graphs for complex objects must support *any* structure, since the structure and the "depth" of complex objects can vary from relation to relation. Figure 4 shows a ***general lock graph for disjoint and***

non-disjoint complex objects which meets both requirements. The nodes of that lock graph represent the lockable units, i.e. the lock granules. The *basic lockable units (BLU)* are the smallest lockable units[3]. *Homogeneous lockable units (HoLU)* consist of data of the same type (e.g. a set (relation) or a list of subobjects of the same type). *Heterogeneous lockable units (HeLU)* may be composed of subobjects of different types[4]. An example of a HeLU is a (complex) tuple which usually contains attributes of different types.

The solid lines in Figure 4 indicate that a lock granule may be composed of other lock granules, such as a complex object or relation which in turn may be composed of other (sub)objects or (sub)relations. Beside this, a BLU may be a reference to common data. The common data can be regarded as an independent complex object with its lockable units. We distinguish between the transition from one lock granule to another within non-shared data (solid lines), and the transition into shared data (dashed lines). These two kinds of transitions must be handled differently by the lock protocol being presented in order to address the protocol- and authorization-oriented problems.

The general lock graph supports lock granules within the hierarchy of complex objects of arbitrary structure. Hence, the *granule-oriented problem* is solved. For example, a *set* of *lists* of *integers* is treated by the lock manager as a HoLU composed of HoLUs which in turns consist of BLUs. In this case, the lockable units are the whole set, exactly one list, or in an extreme case, exactly one integer. The traditional lock graph of System R is a special case of the general lock graph: "database" can be regarded as a HeLU, "segments" as well, "relations" is a HoLU, and the "tuples" are the smallest lockable units, the BLUs[5].

4.3 Object-Specific Lock Graph

The object-specific lock graph of complex objects of a certain type contains the lockable units of the corresponding complex object type. For each complex object type, an ***object-specific lock graph*** can be constructed by using the general lock graph, catalog information, and simple derivation rules. The derivation rules specify how attribute types are transformed to lockable units. A possible set of derivation rules may be stated as follows:

1. An attribute of type "list" is transformed to a HoLU.
2. An attribute of type "set" is transformed to a HoLU.

---

[3] A BLU may be defined as an atomic attribute value (e.g. type integer, real). However, implementations of this concept would suffer greatly since atomic attribute locking would lead to an immense locking overhead. Hence, it is more *practical* to think of BLUs as comprised of one level of the hierarchy of a subobject within a complex object. For example, in the complex relation "cells", the attributes "obj_id" and "obj_name" could form one BLU. This BLU would be locked when either attribute is accessed by a transaction.

[4] The distinction between HoLUs and HeLUs is necessary for a proper mechanism to determine "optimal" lock requests. Section 4.5 contains a brief description of the underlying idea (i.e. the anticipation of lock escalations) of such a mechanism. For the purpose of the following discussion, however, HoLUs and HeLUs have the same properties.

[5] In this paper, indexes are not discussed.

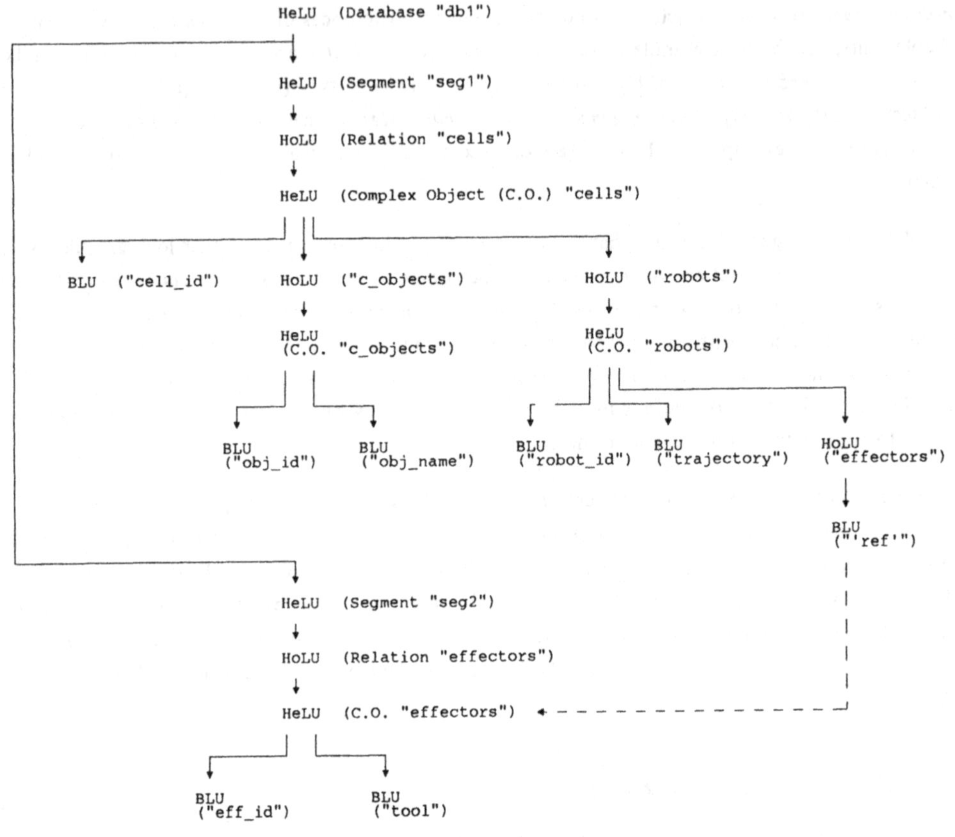

Figure 5. Object-Specific Lock Graph: Complex Relation "cells" and its Common Data ("effectors")

3. An attribute of type "(complex) tuple" is transformed to a HeLU.
4. An atomic attribute of any type is transformed to a BLU.

If complex object types have different structures, then their corresponding object-specific lock graphs differ structurally as well. Hence, allowances are made for the structure and depth of each complex objects type. If complex object types share data, the parts of the corresponding object-specific lock graphs which model the common data have the same structure. The fact that common data are modelled is indicated by dashed lines within each object-specific lock graph. In Figure 5 the object-specific lock graph of the complex object type "cells" can be found. The mapping between the nodes of this graph and the attributes of the corresponding schema (Figure 1) should be self-explanatory. In our example, we assume that both relations are stored within different segments of the same database.

4.4 *Rules for Explicitly Requesting Locks*

In the following, a protocol for requesting locks on object-specific lock graphs for disjoint as well as non-disjoint complex object types is proposed. Its basic idea is the inclusion of lock entry points into common data. Before the new lock protocol can be discussed, some additional definitions are required.

4.4.1 Definitions

All nodes which represent *non-shared* data and which are located between the relation node (inclusive) and the first nodes (inclusive) referencing common data, plus the parent nodes of the relation node (segment node and database node) form a structure called the ***outer unit*** of an object-specific lock graph. By analogy, the nodes which represent *shared* data and which are located between the root (inclusive) of a referenced complex object and the next nodes (inclusive) referencing common data or the end of the complex object form an ***inner unit***. Both inner and outer units can be regarded as complex objects. There is always *one outer unit*, and there may be *several inner units* within each object-specific lock graph. The root of a complex object which represents an inner unit is the ***entry point*** of that unit. An ***immediate parent*** of a node is the parent node from which the dependent node can be reached exclusively by following a single solid line (without crossing a unit boundary). A ***superunit*** consists of the present unit and all the immediate parents of its root (i.e. the immediate parent of its root, the immediate parent of the immediate parent of its root, and so on, up to and including the database node). Units (outer and inner ones) are always disjoint, whereas superunits are not. A reference to common data (a dashed line) represents the transition from one unit to another. Finally, a unit is called a ***(non-)modifiable unit*** of a transaction, if the transaction has (not) the right to modify the unit.

The definitions presented above are essential to understand the lock protocol proposed in the next section. The following example shall illustrate these definitions (Figure 6): The outer unit "cell c1" references inner unit "effector e1". The entry point into inner unit "effector e1" is the node "effector e1". The immediate parent of node "effector e1" is the node "Relation effectors". Node "effector e1" and all its immediate parents up to "Database db1" form a superunit. The node "o" within the outer unit "cell c1" references node "effector e1", but it is NOT the immediate parent of node "effector e1" (because of the dashed line). One can see that each node except the root has exactly one immediate parent - in other words, outer and inner units as well as superunits have hierarchical structure.

4.4.2 Lock Protocol

4.4.2.1 The Algorithm

The following protocol requests explicitly locks on object-specific lock graphs. It solves the *protocol-oriented problems*:

1. **IS Locks**, 2. **IX Locks**

Before requesting an IS/IX lock on a node which is a

root of an outer unit,

no other locks need be held by the transaction.

non-root node,

all the immediate parents of the requested node must be (at least) IS/IX locked by the transaction.

root of an inner unit (entry point),

the node which references that entry point and which has been passed through to access that entry point must be (at least) IS/IX locked by the transaction;

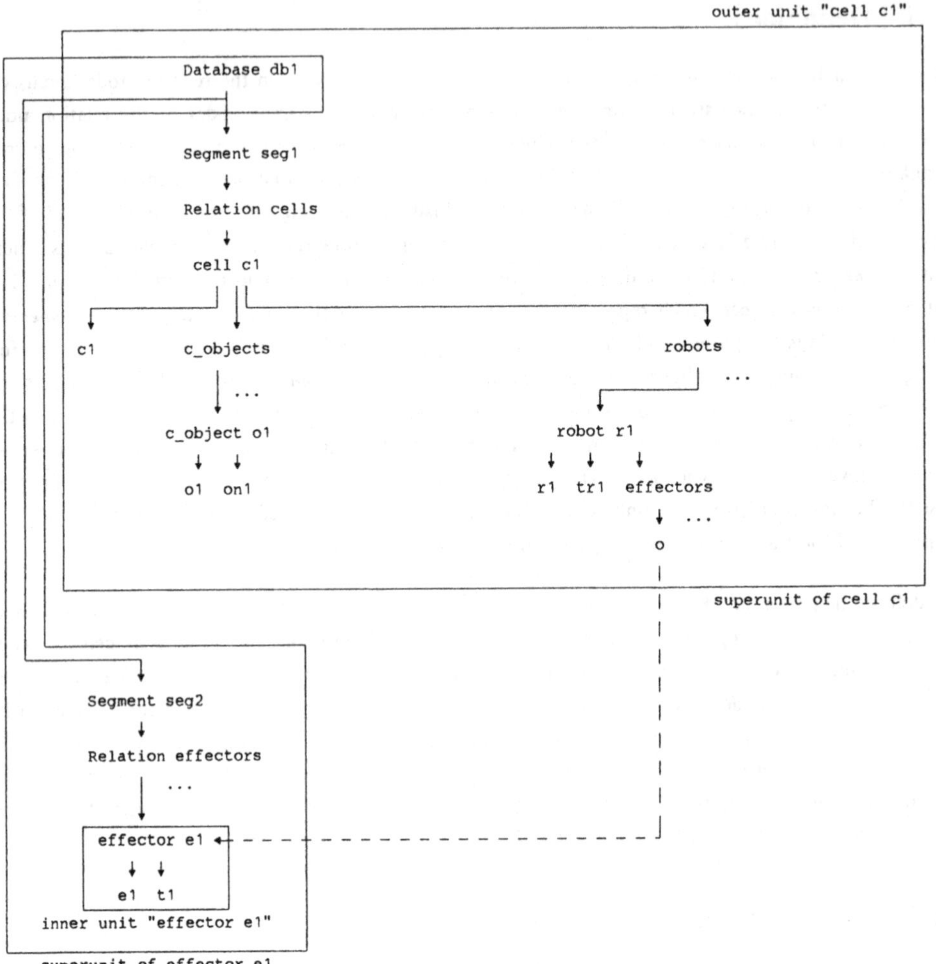

Figure 6. Example: Complex Object "cell c1" of Relation "cells" ("o" signifies a reference)

before *granting* the IS/IX lock, the concurrency control manager must (at least) IS/IX lock all immediate parents of the requested node (to the root of the superunit) for the transaction ("implicit upward propagation").

3. **S Locks**, 4. **X Locks**

Before requesting an S/X lock on a node which is a

root of an outer unit,

no other locks need be held by the transaction

non-root node,

all the immediate parents of the requested node must be (at least) IS/IX locked by the transaction

root of an inner unit (entry point),

the node which references that entry point and which has been passed through to access that entry point must be (at least) IS/IX locked by the transaction;
before *granting* the S/X lock, the concurrency control manager must (at least) IS/IX lock all immediate parents of the requested node (to the root of the superunit) for the transaction ("implicit upward propagation")

and in addition (to all of the above)

before *granting* the S/X lock on any node the concurrency control manager must (at least) S/X lock all entry points of lower (dependent) inner units accessible via the requested node for the transaction ("implicit downward propagation").

5. **Order of requesting and releasing locks**

Locks are *requested* starting at the root of a complex object in a root-to-leaf order;
locks are *released* in leaf-to-root order or at EOT in any order.

A slight modification of rule 4 solves the *authorization-oriented problem*:

4′. **X Locks**

Before requesting an X lock on a node which is a

root of an outer unit,

no other locks need be held by the transaction

non-root node,

all the immediate parents of the requested node must be (at least) IX locked by the transaction

root of an inner unit (entry point),

the node which references that entry point and which has been passed through to access that entry point must be (at least) IX locked by the transaction;
before *granting* the X lock, the concurrency control manager must (at least) IX lock all immediate parents of the requested node (to the root of the superunit) for the transaction ("implicit upward propagation")

and in addition (to all of the above)

before *granting* the X lock on any node the concurrency control manager must
(at least) X lock all roots of lower (dependent) *modifiable inner units* and
(at least) S lock all roots of lower (dependent) *non-modifiable inner units*
accessible via the requested node for the transaction ("implicit downward propagation").

The proposed lock protocol solves the **protocol-oriented problems** by granting a lock on an entry point only after all its immediate parents have been locked (*"implicit upward propagation"*), and by granting an S/X lock on any node only after all entry points of the lower (dependent) inner units accessible via the requested node have been locked (*"implicit downward propagation"*). Obviously, implicit *upward* propagation *does not* cross superunit boundaries; rather, it is done just within the same superunit. On the other hand, implicit *downward* propagation *does* cross superunit boundaries.

Furthermore, the **authorization-oriented problem** is solved by using lock modes which grant only as many rights as the transaction really needs (rule 4′).

All these goals are reached with an **acceptable overhead**: By accessing catalog or authorization information, the concurrency control manager can easily determine whether a requested node is a root of an outer unit, a non-root or a root of an inner unit (entry point), or whether a unit is or is not modifiable by a particular transaction. For example, all immediate parents of an entry point (upward propagation) can be determined with help of catalog information, since according to our assumption the immediate parent of each entry point is a relation node. It is also possible to determine in an easy way the entry points which are accessible via a requested node (downward propagation); this is done by a scan over all the existing references. Scanning these references and related entry points does not imply any additional run-time overhead, however, since the affected inner units have to be accessed anyway to read the data during query execution. Furthermore, during downward propagation locks are *only* requested for the *entry points* of the affected inner units, i.e. the number of the lock table entries is increased only moderately.

In case of disjoint complex objects no inner units exist. So, for disjoint complex objects the above lock protocol is identical to the traditional one presented in [GLPT76].

4.4.2.2 A Concrete Example

In the following ***example***[6] (Figure 7), the lock protocol described above is applied to query Q2 (Figure 3). Query Q2 selects robot "r1" for update. Now, an explicit X lock on "robot r1" is necessary. All immediate parents of non-root node "robot r1" must be IX locked before "robot r1" itself can be X locked. Hence, "Database db1" (the root of the outer unit "cells"), the non-root nodes "Segment seg1", "Relation cells", "cell c1" and list "robots" are IX locked in sequence (rule 2). The concurrency control manager notices that robot "r1" references common data ("effector e1" and "effector e2") within the relation "effectors". So, the concurrency control manager must request locks on the roots of these inner units ("effector e1" and "effector e2") for the requesting transaction. According to rule 4', S mode locks are sufficient to guarantee consistency assuming that the requesting transaction doesn't have the right to change any effector. Before the concurrency control manager can request S locks on "effector e1" and "effector e2", the first immediate parent of each of them as well as their paths to the root of the corresponding superunit must have been (at least) IS locked (rule 1). Only then can the concurrency control manager request an S lock on each "effector ..." (rule 3, 4'). As soon as all these locks are granted, the effectors referenced by robot "r1" can't be modified by other transactions. Then, the concurrency control manager can inform the requesting transaction that the X lock on "robot r1" was granted.

The locks held by the transaction which contains query Q2 are shown in Figure 7. This figure also contains the locks necessary to execute query Q3 under the protocol proposed above. Rule 4' allows Q2 and Q3 to run concurrently, although both queries touch effector "e2". The reason is that - according to our assumption - neither Q2 nor Q3 have the right to update relation "effectors".

---

[6] We assume that a mechanism exists to determine the ("optimal") lock requests (see section 4.5). The locks necessary to test a WHERE condition of a query are not treated in detail in this paper.

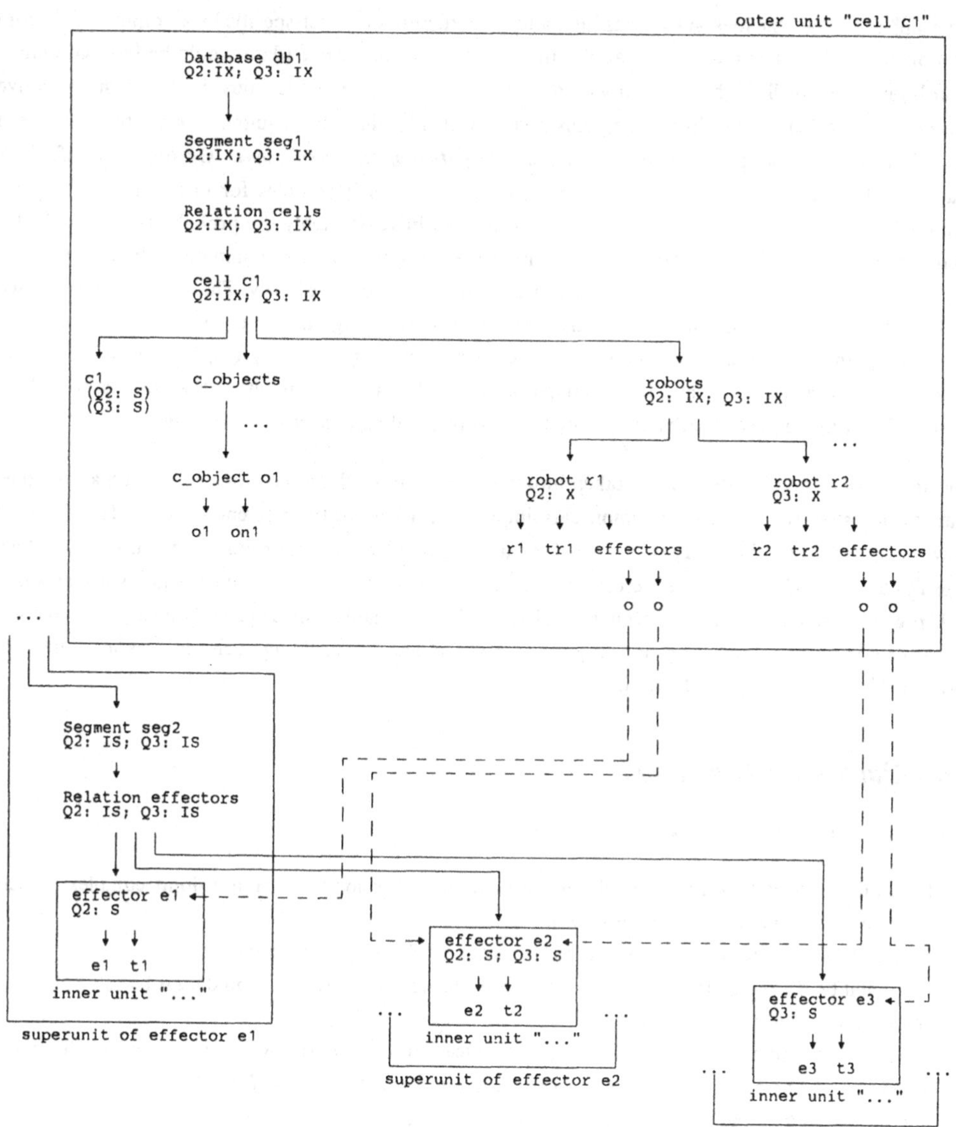

Figure 7. Example: Complex Object "c1" and the Locks held by the Queries Q2 and Q3

4.5 Determination of "Optimal" Lock Requests

Up to now, lock granules within disjoint and non-disjoint complex objects, and an appropriate protocol for requesting locks on such complex objects have been discussed. No word has been spent on the determination of "optimal" lock requests (i.e. the granule and its mode which should be requested in order to achieve the best overall throughput). Nevertheless, this question is essential for effective concurrency control. A mechanism to determine automatically "optimal" lock requests becomes mandatory given that the number of available lock granules is high and the structure of object-specific lock graphs differs from relation to relation. The requested granules must be neither too coarse (data would be blocked unnecessarily) nor too small (high overhead would result). Also, the lock modes must be the least restrictive necessary. A mechanism for disjoint complex objects which fulfills these requirements has been proposed in [HDKS89]. This mechanism is based on the ***anticipation of lock escalations***. On object-specific lock graphs, lock escalations (i.e. the trading of many locks on small granules for one lock on a coarser granule [Date85]) cause immense run-time overhead, and increase highly the probability for deadlocks. Hence, the number of lock escalations during the check-out phase should be minimized by requesting in advance appropriate granules which do not block so much data unnecessarily. The mechanism proposed in [HDKS89] determines during *query analysis* (i.e. before accessing any data) "optimal" lock requests. Then, the granule and mode information is stored within *query-specific lock graphs*. During *query execution*, locks are requested from a lock manager by using the information within the query-specific lock graphs. When the requested locks are granted, the corresponding data may be accessed.

The ***semantics*** of queries also has be taken into consideration. In the discussions above, it was assumed that the access of references to common data implies the access of the referenced data. This point of view, however, is not obligatory. Consider, for example, the deletion of a robot by a transaction which doesn't have the right to delete effectors. In this case, no locks on common data are necessary at all. A lock protocol which is able to exploit such details of the semantics of a query language can allow a higher degree of concurrency on non-disjoint complex objects. Imbedding such features into the proposed lock technique requires little effort.

4.6 Qualitative Evaluation

Advantages of the proposed lock technique are:

1. the availability of lock granules within the hierarchy of disjoint and non-disjoint complex objects (*solution of the granule-oriented problem*),
2. an acceptable overhead to lock common data exclusively, and at the same time,
3. the visibility of implicit locks; in particular, from-the-side access to common data is handled properly (*solution of the protocol-oriented problems*),
4. locking of common data in a mode which is the least restrictive necessary with regard to the rights a transaction has on common data (*solution of the authorization-oriented problem*),
5. the automatic determination of "optimal" lock requests,
6. the strict separation of these phases:
   a. Construction of Object-Specific Lock Graphs,
   b. Query Analysis:
      1) Determination of the "optimal" lock requests,
      2) Construction of the query-specific lock graph,
   c. Query Execution,
      Requesting locks by using the information within query-specific lock graphs,
7. the easy exploitation of the special properties of user defined data types and functions (cf. extensible database systems) by concurrency control (consequence of 6.).

Disadvantages of the proposed lock technique are:

1. some additional but small overhead to determine (only once) the object- and query-specific lock graph *before* the execution of a query and
2. some additional but small overhead when only disjoint complex objects are exclusively accessed by a transaction.

5 Summary, Conclusions and Future Work

In this paper, a ***lock technique for disjoint and non-disjoint complex objects*** has been proposed . It allows a high degree of concurrency on disjoint and non-disjoint complex objects, and it displays an acceptable overhead. The proposed technique is based on the use of lock granules within the hierarchy of complex objects. Special rules for requesting locks solve the problems which occur when different complex objects share data. Furthermore, the lock granules and the corresponding lock modes are determined automatically from a query and additional structural and statistical information [HDKS89]. This is done in a way which maximizes the expected throughput of the database system. The deeper complex objects are structured and/or the more abundant common data exist and/or the longer the transactions last and/or the more restrictive the required lock modes become, hence, the higher the benefit of the proposed technique promises to be.

Subjects for our future work are *simulations* with regard to the efficiency of the proposed technique, the integration of *indexes* into the proposed technique, a solution of the *phantom problem*, the projection of the proposed lock technique onto different *implementations of storage structures*, the extension of the proposed technique to *recursive complex objects*, the efficient *release of locks* ("de-escalation") and the integration of special *lock modes* for workstation-server environments [LoPl83, KSUW85]. In addition, we are considering *integrating* the proposed concepts into the *AIM-P prototype* [Dada88, Linn88].

Acknowledgement

The authors want to thank the members of the AIM-team, the colleagues at the University of Hagen - especially T. Berkel, P. Klahold, P. Pistor, N. Südkamp, and W. Wilkes - and H. Eckhardt for fruitful discussions and their valuable suggestions which helped to improve this paper.

References

Astr76 M. M. Astrahan, M. W. Blasgen, D. D. Chamberlin, K. P. Eswaran, J. N. Gray, P. P. Griffiths, W. F. King, R. A. Lorie, P. R. McJones, J. W. Mehl, G. R. Putzolu, I. L. Traiger, B. W. Wade, V. Watson, *System R: Relational Approach to Database Management*, ACM Transactions on Database Systems, Vol. 1, No. 2 (June 1976), pp. 97 - 137.

BaBu84 D. S. Batory, A. P. Buchmann, *Molecular Objects, Abstract Data Types, and Data Models: A Framework*, Proceedings 10th International Conference on Very Large Data Bases (Singapore; August 27 - 31, 1984), pp. 172 - 184.

BaSc77 R. Bayer, M. Schkolnick, *Concurrency of Operations on B-Trees*, Acta Informatica 9 (1977), pp. 1 - 21.

Dada86 P. Dadam, K. Küspert, F. Andersen, H. Blanken, R. Erbe, J. Günauer, V. Lum, P. Pistor, G. Walch, *A DBMS Prototype to Support Extended NF^2-Relations: An Integrated View on Flat Tables and Hierarchies*, Proceedings ACM SIGMOD (Washington; May 28 - 30, 1986), pp. 356 - 367.

Dada88 P. Dadam, *Advanced Information Management (AIM): Research in Extended Nested Relations*, IEEE Database Engineering, Special Issue on Nested Relations, Vol 11, No. 3 (September 1988), pp. 4 - 14.

Date85 C. J. Date, *An Introduction to Database Systems, Volume II, Third Edition*, Addison-Wesley Publishing Company, Inc.; ISBN 0-201-14474-3 (July 1985).

DiDa86 K. Dittrich, U. Dayal (eds.), *Proceedings International Workshop on Object-Oriented Database Systems; Pacific Grove, September 23 - 26, 1986;* IEEE Computer Society Press.

Ditt86 K. R. Dittrich, *Object-oriented Database Systems: The Notion and the Issues*, Proceedings International Workshop on Object-Oriented Database Systems (Pacific Grove; September 23 - 26, 1986), pp. 2 - 4.

Ditt88 K. R. Dittrich (ed.), *Advances in Object-Oriented Database Systems, Proceedings 2nd International Workshop on Object-Oriented Database Systems; Bad Münster am Stein-Ebernburg (FRG), September 27 - 30, 1988;* Lecture Notes in Computer Science 334; Springer-Verlag, ISBN 0-387-50345-5.

GFR87 E. Grill, J. Flittner, W. Rauch, *Integration of CAx via Relational Databases*, Information Management 1/87, pp. 54 - 64.

GLP75 J. N. Gray, R. A. Lorie, G. R. Putzolu, *Granularity of Locks in a Shared Data Base*, Proceedings International Conference on Very Large Data Bases (Framingham; September 22 - 24, 1975), pp. 428 - 451.

GLPT76 J. N. Gray, R. A. Lorie, G. R. Putzolu, I. L. Traiger, *Granularity of Locks and Degrees of Consistency in a Shared Data Base*, in: "Modelling in Database Management Systems", G. M. Nijssen (ed.), North Holland Publishing Company (1976), pp. 365 - 394.

HaLo82 R. L. Haskin, R. A. Lorie, *On Extending the Functions of a Relational Database System*, Proceedings ACM SIGMOD (Orlando; June 2-4, 1982), pp. 207 - 212.

HDKS89 U. Herrmann, P. Dadam, K. Küspert, G. Schlageter, *Locking of disjoint, non-recursive Complex Objects under use of Object- and Query-Specific Lock Graphs*, (in german), Proceedings "Datenbanksysteme in Büro, Technik und Wissenschaft"; Informatik-Fachberichte 204, T. Härder (ed.), Springer-Verlag (Zürich; March 01 - 03, 1989), pp. 98 - 113.

HHMM88 T. Härder, C. Hübel, K. Meyer-Wegener, B. Mitschang, *Processing and transaction concepts for cooperation of engineering workstations and a database server*, Data & Knowledge Engineering, Vol. 3, No. 2; Special Issue: First International Conference on Data and Knowledge Systems for Manufacturing and Engineering (September 1988), pp. 87 - 107.

HMMS87 T. Härder, K. Meyer-Wegener, B. Mitschang, A. Sikeler, *PRIMA - a DBMS Prototype Supporting Engineering Applications*, Proceedings 13th International Conference on Very Large Data Bases (Brighton; September 01 - 04, 1987), pp. 433 - 442.

KDG87 K. Küspert, P. Dadam, J. Günauer, *Cooperative Object Buffer Management in the Advanced Information Management Prototype*, Proceedings 13th International Conference on Very Large Data Bases (Brighton; September 01 - 04, 1987), pp. 483 - 492; also available as: Technical Report TR 87.02.002, IBM Scientific Center Heidelberg (Heidelberg, February 1987).

KLMP84 W. Kim, R. Lorie, D. McNabb, W. Plouffe, *A Transaction Mechanism for Engineering Design Databases*, Proceedings 10th International Conference on Very Large Data Bases (Singapore; August 27 - 31, 1984), pp. 355 - 362.

KSUW85 P. Klahold, G. Schlageter, R. Unland, W. Wilkes, *A Transaction Model Supporting Complex Applications in Integrated Information Systems*, Proceedings ACM SIGMOD (Austin; May 28 - 31, 1985), pp. 388 - 401.

KuRo81 H. T. Kung, J. T. Robinson, *On Optimistic Methods for Concurrency Control*, ACM Transactions on Database Systems, Vol. 6, No. 2 (June 1981), pp. 213 - 226.

Linn88 V. Linnemann, K. Küspert, P. Dadam, P. Pistor, R. Erbe, N. Südkamp, G. Walch, A. Kemper, M. Wallrath, *Design and Implementation of an Extensible Database Management System Supporting User Defined Data Types and Functions*, Proceedings 14th International Conference on Very Large Data Bases (Los Angeles; August 29 - September 01, 1988), pp. 294 - 305.

LoPl83 R. Lorie, W. Plouffe, *Complex Objects and Their Use in Design Transactions*, Proceedings ACM SIGMOD, Database Week, Engineering Design Applications (San Jose; May 23 - 26, 1983), pp. 115 - 121.

Lori85 R. Lorie, W. Kim, D. McNabb, W. Plouffe, A. Meier, *Supporting Complex Objects in a Relational System for Engineering Databases*, in "Query Processing in Database Systems"; W. Kim, D. S. Reiner, Don S. Batory (eds.); Springer-Verlag, ISBN 0-387-13831-5, pp. 145 - 155.

MeLo83 A. Meier, R. A. Lorie, *A Surrogate Concept for Engineering Databases*, Proceedings Ninth International Conference on Very Large Data Bases (Florence; October 31 - November 2, 1983); pp. 30 - 32.

Paul87 H.-B. Paul, H.-J. Schek, M. H. Scholl, G. Weikum, U. Deppisch, *Architecture and Implementation of the Darmstadt Database Kernel System*, Proceedings ACM SIGMOD (San Francisco; May 27 - 29, 1987), pp. 196 - 207.

PiAn86 P. Pistor, F. Andersen, *Designing a Generalized NF^2 Model with an SQL-Type Language Interface*, Proceedings 12th International Conference on Very Large Data Bases (Kyoto; August 25 - 28, 1986), pp. 278 - 288.

Rehm88 S. Rehm, T. Raupp, M. Ranft, R. Längle, M. Härtig, W. Gotthard, K. R. Dittrich, K. Abramowicz, *Support for Design Processes in a Structurally Object-Oriented Database System*, Proceedings 2nd International Workshop on Object-Oriented Database Systems (Bad Münster am Stein-Ebernburg (FRG); September 27 - 30, 1988), Lecture Notes in Computer Science 334, Springer-Verlag, pp. 80 - 97.

RiSt77 D. R. Ries, M. Stonebraker, *Effects of Locking Granularity in a Database Management System*, ACM Transactions on Database Systems, Vol. 2, No. 3 (September 1977), pp. 233 - 246.

ScSc86 H.-J. Schek, M. H. Scholl, *The Relational Model with Relation-Valued Attributes*, Information Systems, Vol. 11, No. 2 (1986), pp. 137 - 147.

WKS89 W. Wilkes, P. Klahold, G. Schlageter, *Complex and Composite Objects in CAD/CAM Databases*, Proceedings 5th IEEE International Conference on Data Engineering (Los Angeles; February 06 - 10, 1989), pp. 443 - 451.

MODELING PHYSICAL SYSTEMS BY COMPLEX STRUCTURAL OBJECTS AND COMPLEX FUNCTIONAL OBJECTS

Shamkant B. Navathe and A. Cornelio
Database Systems Research and Development Center
University of Florida, Gainesville, FL 32611, USA
e-mail: sham@ufl.edu.csnet

ABSTRACT

This paper describes the general properties of complex objects in engineering designs. There are two types of complex objects: (i) the complex structural objects which describe the physical composition of the design, and (ii) the complex functional objects which describe the behavior of the design and its components. Data manipulation operations on complex structural objects are governed by a set of structural invariants. Similarly, the validation of functional abstraction is governed by a set of functional invariants. The structure-function interactions are represented by interaction objects that describe a set of mappings. These three object types constitute the Structure-Function paradigm. The S-F paradigm can be used to represent engineering designs and active environments, monitor manufacturing operations and industrial processes, and carry out simulations.

1 INTRODUCTION

Object-oriented systems are rapidly becoming acceptable for modeling many non business applications, such as office information systems, [BAN87], engineering CAD/CAM, [KET85, KEM87], robotic workcell design [JAY88], spatial information, [DAY87], etc. The power of these modeling systems lies in their ability to represent the semantics of structures by including the operations along with the data. Inheritance of data and operations reduces the time spent in developing new applications by sharing previously developed code.

We have adapted the object-oriented paradigm (for engineering design applications) by modeling the physical configuration of a design by structural objects, the behavioral aspect of a design by functional objects and the interface between the structural and functional objects by interaction objects. We call this modeling principle as the Structure-Function paradigm, or **S-F paradigm.** The S-F paradigm preserves the structural and behavioral schemas of an application by modeling and abstracting the structures and functions independently and relating these schemas by a well defined interface. This paradigm provides a platform for (a) modeling and analyzing engineering designs, (b) representing manufacturing tasks, and (c) monitoring industrial processes. The reasons for proposing the S-F paradigm are briefly described below, [COR89b] provides an indepth analysis of the S-F paradigm. Our approach applies to any environment with physical objects having visible interfaces. This includes examples from software engineering, biological systems, and computer hardware.

In the engineering design domain, there are complex interactions between a system's structure and behavior. This interaction is further complicated because a structure can serve many functions (either independently or together) and a function can have many alternate structural implementations. For example, a resistor (structure) can function as a load, voltage to current converter, current to voltage converter, voltage bias, etc.; on the other hand, the function of lifting an object can be done by many alternate structures--robot, crane, fork-lift, etc. There is some work in artificial intelligence, where, for the sake of better reasoning, knowledge is modeled more precisely by separating functions from structures [DAV84]. In our approach, we explicitly represent the associative knowledge between structures and functions by interaction objects [COR89b].

Abstractions in the structural and functional domains for most realistic engineering applications are not isomorphic, i.e., a set of structures are aggregated according to their physical configuration and spatial locality, whereas functions are aggregated according to system behavior. Therefore, in the S-F paradigm, we extend the object oriented principle by autonomously abstracting the structural objects and the functional objects and then relating these domains by a well defined interface (made of interaction objects). We have shown with a real life robotic workcell design example in [COR90a] that the system naturally supports engineering design knowledge and simulation data. The other benefit that accrues from the S-F paradigm is the straight-forward integration of structural information with domain-specific application programs. This capability alleviates the most common bottleneck (of incompatible systems) in design automation. The details of this integration are the subject of ongoing research [COR90b].

An important characteristic of design information is that the structures and functions are aggregated to form complex structural objects [BAT84, BAT85] and complex functional objects. [KIM87a, KIM87b, KIM89] describes an object-oriented system for complex objects. In this paper, we show that the S-F paradigm extends the complex object definition of [KIM87b] by (a) including Assembly Relations (which are interconnection relationships among structural components) in the complex structural object definition along with the PART-OF relationship; (b) specifying the abstraction of complex structural objects in terms of the external features of its sub-structural objects; (c) defining complex functional objects and complex functional object hierarchies to model active data; and (d) validating the correctness of functional equivalence between two levels of a functional hierarchy.

Complex structural objects and complex functional objects are the primary constructs to model a design's structure and behavior in the S-F paradigm. In this paper, we concentrate on the properties of a complex structural object and propose data manipulation rules that are derived from a set of structural invariants. These invariants form the basis for inserting, deleting, and updating complex objects in a structural hierarchy. Similarly, the abstraction of complex functional objects is described by a set of functional invariants. Functional invariants formally state the correctness conditions between an abstract functional object and a set of sub-functional objects.

The focus of this paper is the definition and abstraction of complex structural and complex functional objects in the S-F paradigm. The next section briefly introduces the S-F paradigm. Section 3 describes complex structural objects. Section 4 describes complex functional objects. Section 5 is the conclusion.

2 THE S-F PARADIGM

The underlying principle of the S-F paradigm is to have three distinct types of objects: Structural, Functional, and Interaction. In this paper, our focus will be on the structural and functional objects.

A **Structural Object,** S, is a two-place tuple of features, S: <Es, Is> where Es are the *external features* of S and Is are the *internal features* of S. The external features are the interface properties such as surfaces, terminal pins, etc., that connect the structural object to other structural objects and to the external world. The internal features are denoted as Is: <Ps, Cs, Rs> where Ps is a set of properties or attributes of the structural object which include the state variables; Cs is a set of sub-structural object declarations; and Rs is a set of assembly relations that connect the external features of elements of Cs.

A **Functional Object,** F, is a two-place tuple, F:<Ef, If> where Ef and If are the *external features* and *internal features* of F. The external features refer to a set of input variables, INf, and a set of output variables, OUTf, and are denoted as Ef: <INf, OUTf>. The internal features consist of the state_output function(s), Pf, which consists of the state transfer function, Pfs, and the output function, Pfo, where Pf = Pfo • Pfs; a set of sub-functional object declarations, Cf; and a set of connection relations, Rf, (called control relations in [COR89a] and [COR90a]) that contain the relationship between elements in Cf. The internal features are denoted as If:<Pf, Cf, Rf>.

The state transfer function generates the new state of the system from the current state and the input variable values. The output function generates the outputs of the system from the current system state.

An **Interaction Object,** D, is a three-place tuple, D:<S, F, I>, where S is a set of structural object declarations, F is a set of functional object declarations and I is a set of mappings between structural and functional objects. This paper does not discuss Interaction objects, see [COR89a, COR89b, COR90a] for further details.

3 STRUCTURAL OBJECTS

3.1 INTRODUCTION

A structural object, S, is a complex object that represents the physical properties of an engineering component. Each engineering component or the physical aggregation of engineering components corresponds to a structural object. The definition of a structural object is based on features. A *feature* is a collection of *characteristics* that describe one discernible physical attribute of the object with which the designer or the manufacturing engineer works. For example, a Spindle of a Flow Control Valve consists of five features: three Steps, a Passage to pass liquid through, and a Key that locks the Spindle to a drive shaft, see Figure 1. The characteristics of the feature, Step_3, are its length and diameter. Features can be nested, e.g., the Key is contained in Step_1, and the Passage is contained in Step_2. Features also include the state variables of the structure, e.g., the 'Position' of the Spindle.

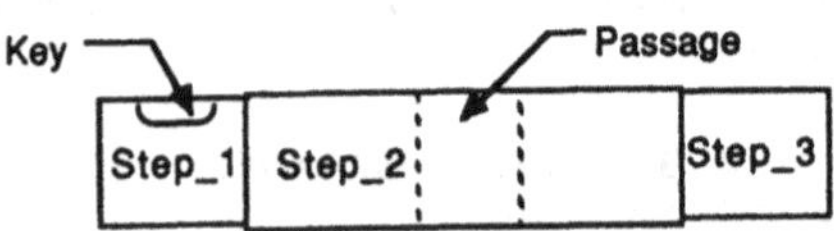

Figure 1. Spindle of a Flow Control Valve

The features of a structural object are divided into two distinct sets--external features and internal features. External features physically connect a structural object to other structural objects, and receive inputs and send outputs to the external world. The internal features are further classified into properties, component declarations, and assembly relations. Properties include features of the object like the designer's name, date, weight of object, etc., and the state variable definitions like flow rate, position of Spindle, etc. State variables take on values during simulation to describe the current state of the object. The default values for the state variables correspond to initial conditions. For example, a state variable for Spindle in a Flow Control Valve is 'Position' with a domain of {0..360} degrees and the default value of 0 degrees.

The component declaration defines the names (or object ids) of the sub-structural object. It describes the PART-OF relationship between a complex object and its component objects. For example, the Flow Control Valve consists of Spindle, Housing, Sealing Bush, Bearing Bush, and Threaded Bearing Bush. The Assembly Relations describe the physical associations among the components of the complex object. Each Assembly Relation consists of two parts: a set of physically interconnected object declarations, and the relationships among the external features of these objects.

3.2 STRUCTURAL OBJECT DEFINITION

This section illustrates the syntax for defining structural objects through an example. The DDL for structural objects follows the structural object definition in section 2. The DDL for a Flow Control Valve and one of its components, Spindle, are shown below. Line numbers are shown in the first column for quick reference.

```
DEFINE STRUCTURAL OBJECT: Spindle
        EXTERNAL FEATURES
3               Step_1:
                        diameter: real;
                        length: real;
6                       Key:
                                diameter: real;
                                depth: real;
9               Step_2:
                        diameter: real;
                        length: real;
12                      Passage:
                                diameter: real;
14              Step_3:
                        diameter: real;
                        length: real;

        INTERNAL FEATURES
                Ps:     /* properties */
19                      Position: {0..360} default 0;
                        material: string;
                        weight: real;

22              Cs:     /* components */
                        nil;

24              Rs:     /* assembly relations */
                        nil;
END STRUCTURAL OBJECT: Spindle.
```

```
DEFINE STRUCTURAL OBJECT: Flow_Control_Valve
      EXTERNAL FEATURES
29          inport:
                  #Housing:Inlet;
31          outport:
                  #Housing:Outlet;
33          control_port:
34                #Spindle:Step_1:
35                      length: real;

      INTERNAL FEATURES
            Ps:   /* properties */
38                Status: {ON, OFF} default OFF;
                  date: calendar;

            Cs:   /* components */
                  Housing;
                  Spindle;
                  Sealing Bush;
                  Bearing Bush;
                  Threaded Bearing Bush;

            Rs:   /* assembly relations */
                  R1: Spindle, s; Housing,h;
                        s:Step_1:diameter = h:S_Port:diameter - [1..5]mm;
49                R2: Spindle, s; Sealing_Bush, sb;
50                      s:Step_2:diameter = sb:in_diameter + [0.1..0.2]mm
END STRUCTURAL OBJECT: Flow_Control_Valve.
```

The structural object definition consists of different feature sections each describing one aspect of the structure. Primitive structural objects, e.g., Spindle, do not have component declarations and the assembly relations, see lines 22, 24. This is expected, as the assembly relations are only defined among component objects. The assembly relations relate the (characteristics of the) external features and the tolerance between these characteristics. For example, the assembly relation R2 (see line 49) between the Spindle and the Sealing_Bush declares that the diameter of Step_2 of the Spindle should be 0.1 to 0.2 mm larger than the inner diameter of the Sealing_Bush (see line 50). Assembly relations enforce structural consistency by propagating changes among the external features of the components.

3.3 FEATURE INHERITANCE IN STRUCTURAL OBJECTS

Structural objects are composed from other sub-structural objects. As all objects are composed of features, the external features of a complex object belong to the external features of its component objects. In this section we show that external features of a complex object selectively *inherit* the external features of its components and more importantly all the external features of a complex object belong to the external features of its components. Note that this inheritance works outward, *from the contained object to the containing object,* i.e., in a sense opposite of the typical inheritance in generalization hierarchies.

Continuing the above example, the external features of the Spindle are the Steps (lines 3, 9, 14), the Key (line 6), and the Passage (line 12); let the external features of the Housing (not shown) be the Inlet-Port, Outlet-Port, and a Control_opening through which the Spindle can receive input torque to control liquid flow. Referring to the Spindle and the Flow_Control_Valve definitions, the external features of the Flow Control Valve consist of the Inlet-Port and the Outlet-Port of the

Housing and Step_1 (along with the Key) of the Spindle (lines 3 to 8). These features of the Flow_Control_Valve are inherited from its substructural objects and are relabeled as inport (line 29), outport (line 31) and control_port (line 33) respectively. The Valve does not have any other external features. In the next section, we show that this relationship (i.e., external features of an object belongs to its components) is true for any physical system, and is specially obvious when the external features are clearly identified, as in circuit board assembly designs.

A complex object inherits (by default) all the *characteristics* of the inherited external features. In the above example, the characteristics of the external features of the Spindle, namely, diameter, length, and Key of Step_1 (lines 3 to 8), are also characteristics of the external features of the Flow Control Valve. The #object_name:feature_name construct in the external feature of the complex object (e.g., #Spindle:Step_1 in line 34) has been introduced to show that the complex object inherits from the sub-structural object (i.e., Spindle) all the characteristics of the feature (i.e., Step_1) including the subfeatures (i.e., the Key). Redefining a characteristic of an inherited feature amounts to overriding the inherited value from the sub-component object. For example, in the Flow_Control_Valve definition above, the length of the control_port, in line 35, (which is inherited from Step_1 of the Spindle) is redefined because it (the Flow Control Valve) only uses a subset of the length of Step_1 to interface with a drive shaft (note that, the actual length of Step_1 of the Spindle is unchanged). Similarly, characteristics can be deleted by redefining them in the parent object with the keyword NULL besides the definition.

3.4 ABSTRACTION BASED ON EXTERNAL FEATURES

This section formalizes the discussions above and presents a set of structural invariants that define (a) structural objects, and (b) the composition of the structural hierarchies. Structural aggregation, as stated earlier, is based on Assembly Relations and the PART-OF hierarchy. These invariants demonstrate that the PART-OF association and Assembly Relationships are essential in fully describing complex object hierarchies.

Let us start by formalizing the meaning of external features of a structural object. The external features of a primitive structural object, S_P, are denoted as

$$\xi(S_P) = \{e \mid e \epsilon Es \text{ and } S_P\!:<Es, Is>\} \qquad \text{(invariant\_1a)}$$

Where, $S_P\!:<Es, Is>$ is the structural object definition of S_P.

The external features of a complex structural object, S_A, are denoted as

$$\xi(S_A) \subseteq \bigcup_{C_j \,\epsilon\, Cs} \xi(C_j) \qquad \text{(invariant\_1b)}$$

where Cs is the set of sub-structural components of S_A, and $\xi{:}A \rightarrow E$, is a function returning the external features, Es, of object A. Invariants 1a and 1b together constitute the **Structural Composition Axiom.**

Invariant 1a states that the set of external features of a primitive object is directly determined from the object definition. Invariant 1b states that the set of external features of a complex structural object inherits a *subset* of the external features of *all* its sub-structural objects, C_j $(C_j \epsilon Cs)$. This definition is recursive and describes how a complex object is constructed from its components. Intuitively, the applicability of invariant 1b can be seen from Figure 2. Here, the structural object S_A is composed of three sub-structural objects C1, C2 and C3. The set of external features of all the sub-structural objects is given by

$Es_{C1,C2,C3} = \cup \{\{a, b, c\}, \{d, f\}, \{e, g\}\} = \{a, b, c, d, e, f, g\}$

The external features of the complex object S_A are $Es_{S_A} = \{a, f, g\}$ thus giving $Es_{S_A} \subseteq Es_{C1,C2,C3}$, as stated in invariant 1b.

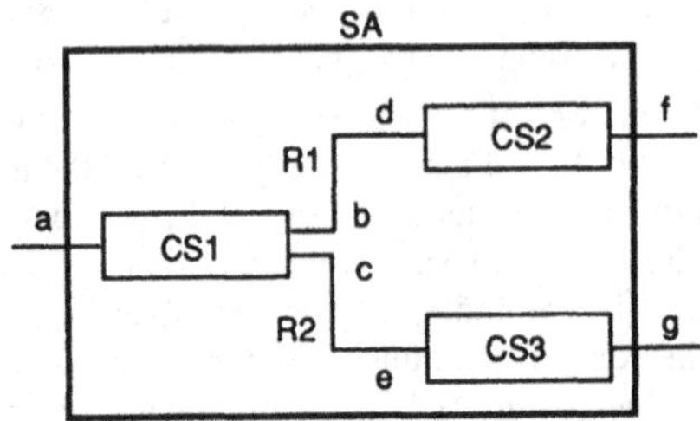

Figure 2. The structural object, S1, is composed of three sub-structural objects, CS1, CS2 and CS3. R1 and R2 are assembly relations between CS1, CS2 and CS1, CS3 respectively.

Invariant 1b is an inequality that defines the structure of complex object hierarchies. In engineering design, the semantics of aggregation (PART-OF) is closely tied to the semantics of interaction (Assembly Relations). The **External Feature Preservation Invariant** defines the structure of a complex structural object in terms of (a) the interactions among its components, and (b) the hierarchical aggregation of its components.

Let $\xi(C_j)$ represent the external features of C_j, where $C_j \in$ Cs, is a component of the complex structural object, S_A. Let $\xi(S_A)$ represent the external features of S_A. We define $\eta(R_i)$ to be the external features of the component objects, $C_j \in$ Cs, participating in the assembly relationship, R_i. These quantities are related by the External Feature Preservation Invariant as shown below:

$$\xi(S_A) \cup \{ \bigcup_{R_i \in Rs} \eta(R_i) \} = \bigcup_{C_j \in Cs} \xi(C_j) \qquad \text{(invariant\_2)}$$

Invariant 2 states that *all* external features of the sub-structural objects should either appear as the external features of the parent structural object, or participate in an assembly relation between the components, or both. This condition forms the basis for defining structural abstraction of complex structural objects by their external features.

To represent the general case, invariants 1 and 2 are modified such that the complex object, S_A, on the left hand side of each of these invariants is replaced by a set of objects, S. For example, invariant 2 is written as

$$\xi(S) \cup \{ \bigcup_{R_i \in Rs} \eta(R_i) \} = \bigcup_{C_j \in Cs} \xi(C_j) \qquad \text{(invariant\_2')}$$

A component object, C_j, can have several parents, allowing a directed cyclic graph (DAG) of structural objects. Such complex objects are useful where the same component has many parents, e.g., a shared power source of two or more distinct electric circuits, or a common wall shared by two houses, etc.

3.5 CONSISTENCY RULES FOR STRUCTURAL OBJECTS

The previous section formulated a set of invariants to define structural objects and structural aggregation. Based on these invariants we define a set of consistency rules for inserting, deleting and updating structural objects. The important rules for manipulating structural objects are summarized below:

(1) A complex object will see those external features (of the components) that are involved in (a) the assembly relations of the complex object; and (b) the external features of the complex object. Therefore, a parent complex object *uses* a subset of the external features of its components as its own external features and the remaining external features in the assembly relations definition among its components (by invariant 2').

(2) A complex object is built bottom-up from predefined (primitive or other complex) objects. The external features of a complex object cannot be updated (except as stated in condition (4) below) as these features physically belong to its components (by invariant 1b).

(3) Updates propagate among complex objects only when their external features are changed. Update propagation among components of a given parent complex object occurs via. the connection relations defined as a part of the parent object.

(4) The external features of a complex object, A, are updated only when these updates do not change the external features of any object declared as a component, Cj ϵ Cs, of A. Therefore the external features of a complex object, A, can be changed **if** these changes are the result of either (a) updating the assembly relations, Rs, of A, or (b) restricting the domain of one or more characteristics (of the external features), e.g., only using a part of the length of the Spindle in the Flow_Control_Valve. For all other cases, only the external features of the primitive objects can be changed (by invariants 1b and 2').

(5) By definition, any change to the internal features of a complex object is not visible to its parent complex object. However, changes to the internal features can trigger changes to the external features of the same object. For example, changes to an object's assembly relations may trigger updates to its external features. Any update to the external features are subject to conditions 2 and 4 above (by definition of Structural objects and invariant 1b).

(6) Changes to the external features of an object (complex or primitive), A, triggers updates to the complex object that contain A as a component (by invariant 2').

(7) The relationship among the components of a complex object can be updated by altering its (complex object) assembly relationship, Rs. These updates include the addition, or deletion of a component. Relationships among components can be redefined as long as these updates do not change the external features of the components, from condition 4 above (by invariant 2').

(8) The relationship between a complex object and its components should be consistently defined during the lifetime of the object, according to invariants 1a, 1b, and 2. Components participate in the *construction* of a complex object; whereas, a complex object *identifies* its components. Deleting a complex object will cause, by default, all the physical relationships among its components to be deleted. This results in the deletion of the PART-OF relation from the complex object to its components and assembly relations among the components. A cascaded delete of a complex object will delete the object and all its components recursively, with only the library (or primitive) components being retained. A complex object is undefined unless its components are defined (or, are expected to be defined later).

(9) The state variable values are updated only by the functional objects which simulate the behavior of the structural object (by the definition of structural objects, functional objects, and interaction objects).

4 FUNCTIONAL OBJECTS--ABSTRACTION AND VALIDATION

The second component of the S-F paradigm is the functional objects which model the behavior of the structural object. One of the tasks of the functional object is to model and thereby be able to simulate the behavior of the structure at different levels of abstraction. This section discusses the conditions for abstracting functional objects and demonstrates the abstraction by a simple example vis-a-vis these conditions.

Data abstractions are widely used in database modeling [SMI77, SCH80, HAM81, SU86] to represent large quantities of information in a uniform and concise manner. All these abstractions are defined on passive data and are called structural abstractions. A second category of abstraction, called *process abstraction* is useful for representing behavioral information of a domain and in simulating systems [FIS88]. Programming language research has developed *data type abstractions* based on the operational view of the data [LIS75, GUT77]. Recently, database research has employed these results to model operations on data [ONG84, COP84, AND87, STO87, SU90].

This section presents abstraction of functional objects. A formal definition of functional abstraction is given below. If a functional object F is the abstraction of a set of objects, Fi, then (a) equivalence is established between the external features of Fi and the external features of F; (b) state equivalence is established between F and the objects in Fi; and (c) behavioral equivalence is established between F and the objects in Fi.

(a) External Features Equivalence

External features equivalence of the components of Fi is defined as

$$HEAD(Fi) \subseteq \bigcup_{Fi \in F} INf(Fi) \qquad \text{(invariant\_4.1a)}$$

$$TAIL(Fi) \subseteq \bigcup_{Fi \in F} OUTf(Fi) \qquad \text{(invariant\_4.1b)}$$

Where HEAD(Fi) are the input variables of those elements of Fi that receive inputs from the external world; this does not include the inputs from the other elements of Fi. TAIL(Fi) are the output variables of those elements of Fi that send outputs to the external world; this does not include the outputs to other elements of Fi. The above invariants abstract (by taking a subset) the external features of the sub-functional objects to the external features of the parent object, F, i.e.,

$$INf(F) = HEAD(Fi) \text{ for } some\ i \qquad \text{(invariant\_4.2a)}$$

$$OUTf(F) = TAIL(Fi) \text{ for } some\ i \qquad \text{(invariant\_4.2b)}$$

(b) State Equivalence

A morphism between the state variables of F and its components should be established for functional abstraction. Let function α map the states of objects in Fi to the states in F. Then the relationship between the state_output functions, Pf_{Fi}, of Fi and state transfer function Pfs_F of F is described by a commutative diagram, Figure 3, such that

$$Pfs_F \bullet \alpha = \alpha \bullet Pf_{Fi} \qquad \text{(invariant\_4.3)}$$

Invariant 4.3 states that given an initial system (i.e., the functional objects in Fi have an associated set of structural objects in their initial states), the next state of F is determined either by: (a) mapping the initial state of Fi to F by α and then applying the state transfer function, Pfs_F (LHS); or (b) applying the state_output functions, Pf_{Fi} to get the new state of Fi and then mapping this new state to F by α (RHS).

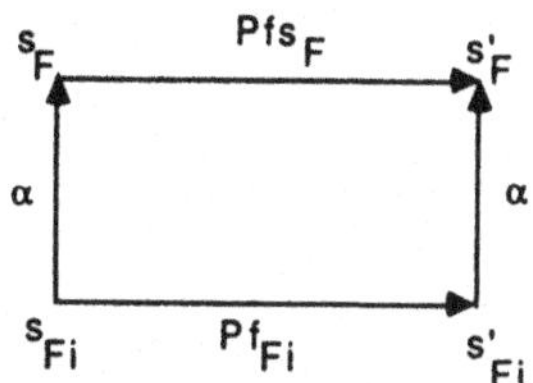

Figure 3. Equivalence between the states, s_F of the abstract functional object, F, and the states, s_{Fi} of the component functional objects in Fi.

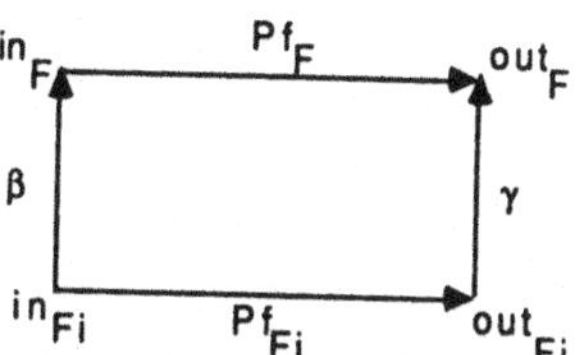

Figure 4. Behavior equivalence of functional objects. in and out are the input variables and the output variables of the abstract functional object, F, and the component functional objects in Fi.

(c) Behavioral Equivalence

A morphism between the input-output variables of F and its components should be established for functional abstraction. Let function β map the input values of objects in Fi to the input values of F, and let γ map the output values of the objects in Fi to the output values of F. Then the relationship between the state_output functions, Pf_{Fi}, of Fi and Pf_F of F is described by a commutative diagram, Figure 4, such that

$$Pf_F \bullet \beta = \gamma \bullet Pf_{Fi} \qquad \text{(invariant\_4.4)}$$

Invariant 4.4 states that given an initial system and a set of input values to Fi, the output values of F is determined either by: (a) mapping these inputs to F by β and then applying the state_output function, Pf_F (LHS); or (b) applying the state_output functions, Pf_{Fi} to get the new outputs of Fi and then mapping these new outputs to F by γ (RHS).

Notice that, from invariants 4.2a and 4.2b, the β and γ mappings correspond to the HEAD and TAIL functions respectively. Therefore, given a set of functional objects, Fi, and an abstract functional object, F, there exists a functional abstraction, F_{Fi}, from Fi to F if and only if, three sets of functions, α, β, and γ can be established such that

$$F_{Fi} = \{\alpha, \beta, \gamma\}.$$

To demonstrate the above concepts by example, we will show the equivalence between the functional objects of the top two levels of the functional hierarchy of a Flow Control Valve. The abstract function, "Transmit Liquid, F" is equivalent to the aggregation of the sub-functions "Pass Liquid, F1", "Vary Passage Dimensions, F2", and "Liquid Flow Control, F3", see Figure 5.a.

Consider the functional abstraction shown in Figure 5.b. The external features of the functional object F receive as input a flow rate, Fi, and torque, Ti, to generate the output flow rate, Fo. The state_output function of F, i.e., f_transmit, takes the input flow, input torque, and the current Status to generate the new Status of the Valve and the output flow, Fo. Status is the state variable defined in the structural object, Flow_Control_Valve (see section 3.2).

The rest of this section uses the above functional object definitions and Figure 5 to formally verify the abstraction conditions stated in invariants 4.1, 4.2, 4.3, and 4.4. Verification consists of three steps: (a) to show the external features equivalence, (b) to show behavioral equivalence, and (c) to show state equivalence.

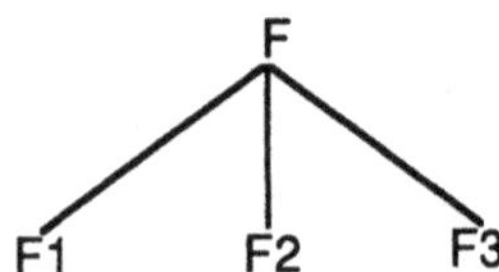

Figure 5.a Functional hierarchy for the Flow Control Valve

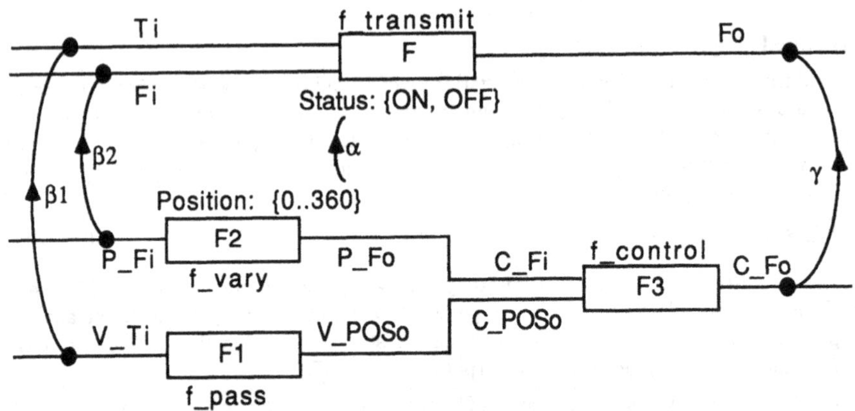

Figure 5.b Mappings between sub-functional objects F1, F2, F3 and the abstract functional object F. Status and Position are the state variables updated by F and F2 respectively. f_transmit, f_pass, f_vary, and f_control are the state_output functions of F, F1, F2, and F3 respectively.

Figure 5. Functional Abstraction

(a) To show **external features equivalence** of F1, F2, and F3 to the abstract object F.

(i) From F1, F2, and F3, the input features are

$$\bigcup_{Fi \in F} INf(Fi) = \bigcup_{Fi \in F} \{\{P\_Fi\}, \{V\_Ti\}, \{C\_Fi\}, \{C\_POSi\}\}$$
$$= \{P\_Fi, V\_Ti, C\_Fi, C\_POSi\}$$

(ii) Applying the HEAD function to the input features, we get

$$HEAD(Fi) = P\_Fi, V\_Ti \quad (1)$$

(iii) The input features of the abstract functional object, F, is given as

$$IN(F) = Fi, Ti \quad (2)$$

(iv) On examining (1), and (2), we find that (1) = (2). Therefore, giving HEAD(Fi) = IN(F), up to differences in variable labels. This result is directly verified from Figure 5.b. Similar analysis may be done for output features.

(b) To show **Behavioral equivalence** between F1, F2, and F3 and the abstract object F.

(i) Define the function β which maps the inputs of F1 and F2 to the inputs of F; and the function γ which maps the output of F3 to the output of F. Let $\beta = \{\beta 1, \beta 2\}$ where $\beta 1$ maps the inflow, P_Fi of functional object F1 to the inflow of the abstract functional object F, i.e., P_Fi = Fi. Similarly, $\beta 2$ maps the torque, V_Ti of functional object F2 to the torque of the abstract functional object F, i.e., V_Ti = Ti. The function γ maps the outflow, C_Fo of the functional object F3 to the outflow of the abstract functional object F, i.e., C_Fo = Fo.

(ii) According to the left hand side of invariant 4.4, apply β to the input values of Fi (i.e., P_Fi and V_Ti) to get the inputs for the state_output function, f_transmit, of F, and then apply f_transmit on these inputs:

f_transmit • β
→ f_transmit($\beta 1$, $\beta 2$)
→ f_transmit(Fi, Ti)
→ Fo

(iii) Apply the inputs to the state_output functions of F1 and F2, i.e., f_pass and f_vary and then use the connection relations to map the outputs of F1 and F2 to the input of F3, we then get the state_output function of F3 as f_control(C_Fi, C_POSi), which returns C_Fo. Apply γ to the output of f_control, to give Fo. According to the right hand side of invariant 4.4,

γ • f_control(C_Fi, C_POSi)
→ γ (C_Fo)
→ Fo

(c) To show **State Equivalence** between F1, F2, and F3 and the abstract object F.

(i) Define a state equivalence function, α, from the state variable, Position, of the sub-functional object, F2, to the state variable, Status, of the abstract functional object, F.

The state equivalence function (in this case) is a characteristic function that maps the state space of Position (i.e., 0 to 360 degrees) to the state space of Status (i.e., ON, OFF) such that if the Spindle's position is between 45 and 315 degrees the Flow Control Valve's Status is ON; otherwise the Valve is OFF.

(ii) Let the initial position of the Spindle = 0 degrees, and let the input torque, T, to the Valve move the Spindle by 50 degrees. Use α map the initial state of F2 to F; this gives the initial state of F as, Status = OFF.

(iii) Applying the state transfer function of F, on the initial state, Status = OFF, and the input torque, T, gives the new state of F as Status = ON.
(iv) Apply the state transfer function of F2, on the initial state, Position = 0, and the input torque, T, gives the new state of F2 as Position = 50.
(v) Map the new state of F2 to the state of F by α we get Status = ON, which is the same as obtained in step (iii).

5 CONCLUSION

This paper presented complex structural objects and complex functional objects using the S-F paradigm for modeling physical systems. Complex structural objects are made up of features which are divided into external and internal features. The abstraction of complex structural objects are based on the external features of the component structural objects and consists of the PART-OF relationships and the Assembly Relations. Complex functional objects are also made up of external features and internal features.

The notion of structural abstraction through external features, functional abstraction, and the S-F paradigm and its application are the main contributions of this paper. The advantage of the S-F paradigm is the flexibility with which it models complex behavior of systems. We have investigated the support of constraints to support simulation of complex systems, and have developed an integrated architecture to support databases, application programs, and user interfaces by using the S-F paradigm [COR89b]. The concepts presented in this paper can be illustrated on any object-oriented DBMS capable of managing complex objects.

Acknowledgements

The work is supported partially by Florida High Technology and Industry Council Grants UPN 85100316 and UPN 88092233.

References

[AND87] Andrews, T., and Harris, C., Combining Language and Database Advances in an Object-Oriented Development Environment, *Conference Proceedings on Object-Oriented Programming Systems, Languages and Applications,* OOPSLA, Orlando, Fl., October 1987, pp. 430-440.

[BAN87] Banerjee, J., Chou, H. T., Garza, J. F., Kim, W., Woelk, P., Ballou, N., and Kim, H. J., Data Model Issues for Object-Oriented Applications, *ACM Transactions on Office Information Systems,* Vol. 5, No. 1, January 1987, pp. 3-26.

[BAT84] Batory, D. S., and Buchmann, A. P., Molecular Objects, Abstract Data Types and Data Models: A Framework, *Proceedings of the Tenth International Conference on Very Large Data Bases,* Singapore, August 1984, pp. 172-184.

[BAT85] Batory, D. S., and Kim, W., Modeling Concepts for VLSI CAD Objects, *ACM Transactions on Database Systems,* Vol. 10, No. 3, September 1985, pp. 289-321.

[COP84] Copeland, G., and Maier, D., Making Smalltalk a Database System, *Proceedings of International Conference on Management of Data,* ACM SIGMOD, Boston, MA, June 1984, pp. 316-325.

[COR89a] Cornelio, A., and Navathe, S. B., Database Support for Engineering CAD and Simulation, *Proceedings of Second International Conference on Data and Knowledge Systems for Manufacturing and Engineering,* Gaitersberg, MD, October, 1989.

[COR89b] Cornelio, A., A Structure-Function Specification System For Engineering Designs and Simulation, Ph.D. thesis, University of Florida, Gainesville, Fl, 1989.

[COR90a] Cornelio, A., Navathe, S. B., and Doty, K. L., Extending Object-Oriented Concepts for Engineering Design and Simulation, to appear in *Proceedings of sixth International Conference on Data Engineering,* IEEE, Los Angeles, CA, February, 1990.

[COR90b] Cornelio, A., and Navathe, S. B., Integration and Cataloging of Engineering Design Information, to appear in *Proceedings of the first International Conference on Systems Integration,* Morristown, New Jersey, April, 1990.

[DAV84] Davis, R., Diagnostic Reasoning on Structure and Behavior, *Artificial Intelligence an International Journal,* Vol. 24, No. 1-3, December 1984, pp. 347-410.

[DAY87] Dayal, U., Dewitt, M., Goldhirsh, D., and Orenstein, J., PROBE Final Report, Technical Report CCA-87-02, CCA Corporation, December 1987.

[FIS88] Fishwick, P. A., Role of Process Abstraction in Simulation, *IEEE Transactions on Systems, Man, and Cybernetics,* Vol. 18, No. 1, January/February 1988, pp. 18-39.

[GUT77] Guttag, J. V., Abstract Data Types and the Development of Data Structures, *Communication of the ACM,* Vol. 20, No. 6, June 1977, pp. 396-404.

[HAM81] Hammer, M., and McLeod, D., Database Description with SDM: A Semantic Data Model, *ACM Transactions on Database Systems,* Vol. 6, No. 3, September 1981, pp. 351-386.

[JAY88] Jayaraman, R., and Levas, A., A Workcell Application Design Environment (WADE), to appear in NATO ASI series, Springer-Verlag, 1989.

[KEM87] Kemper, A., Lockemann, P., C., and Wallrath, M., An Object-Oriented Database System for Engineering Applications, *Proceedings of International Conference on Management of Data,* ACM SIGMOD, San Francisco, CA, May 1987, pp. 299-310.

[KET85] Ketabchi, M. A., On the Management of Computer Aided Design Databases, Ph.D. dissertation in Department of Information and Computer Science, University of Minnesota, November 1985.

[KIM87a] Kim, W., Chou, H. T., and Banerjee, J., Operations and Implementations of Composite Objects, *Proceedings of the Third International Conference on Data Engineering,* Los Angeles, CA, February 1987, pp. 626-633.

[KIM87b] Kim, W., Banerjee, J., Chou, H. T., Garza, J. F., and Woelk, D., Composite Object Support in an Object-Oriented Database System, *ACM Conference Proceedings of Object-Oriented Programming Systems, Languages and Applications,* OOPSLA, Orlando, Fl., October 1987, pp. 118-125.

[KIM89] Kim, W., Bartino, E., and Garza, J. F., Composite Objects Revisited, *Proceedings of the International Conference on the Management of Data,* ACM SIGMOD, Vol. 18, No. 2, Portland, Oregon, May 1989, pp. 337-347.

[LIS75] Liskov, B., and Zilles, S., Specification Techniques for Data Abstractions, *IEEE Transactions on Software Engineering,* SE-1, No. 1, March 1975, pp. 7-18.

[ONG84] Ong, J., Fogg, D., and Stonebraker, M., Implementation of Data Abstraction in the Relational Database System INGRES, *ACM-SIGMOD Record,* Vol.14, No. 1, March 1984, pp. 1-4.

[SCH80] Scheuermann, P., Schiffner, G., and Weber, H., Abstraction Capabilities and Invariant Properties Modelling Within the Entity-Relationship Approach, *Proceedings of the First E-R Conference, The ER Approach to Systems Analysis and Design,* Chen P. P. (editor), North-Holland Publishing Company, 1980, pp. 121-140.

[SMI77] Smith, J., and Smith, C., Database Abstractions: Aggregation and Generalization, *ACM Transactions on Database Systems,* Vol. 2, No. 2, June 1977, pp. 105-133.

[STO87] Stonebraker, M., Anton, J., and Hanson, E., Extending a Database System With Procedures, *ACM Transactions on Database Systems,* Vol. 12, No. 3, September 1987, pp. 350-367.

[SU86] Su, S. Y. W., Modeling Integrated Manufacturing Data With SAM*, *IEEE*Computer," Vol. 19, No. 1, January 1986, pp. 34-49.

[SU90] Su, S. Y. W., Krishnamurthy, V., and Lam, H., An Object-Oriented Semantic Association Model (OSAM*), to appear in *AI in Industrial Engineering and Manufacturing: Theoretical Issues and Applications,* S. Kumara, Kashyap, R. L., Soyster, A. L., (Editors), American Institute of Industrial Engineers, 1990.

Uniform Object Management

George Copeland, Michael Franklin*, Gerhard Weikum**
MCC
3500 West Balcones Center Drive
Austin, Texas 78759

Abstract

Most real–world applications require a capability for both general–purpose programming and database transactions on persistent data. Unfortunately, the implementation techniques for these capabilities are notoriously incompatible. Programming languages stress memory–resident transient data with a rich collection of data types, while database systems stress disk–resident persistent data with a limited collection of data types. Even in object–oriented database systems, combining these capabilities is traditionally done using a two–level storage model in which storage formats are quite different. This approach suffers from the performance overhead required to translate data between these two levels.

This paper describes the steps we have taken toward improving the simplicity and efficiency of applications by merging programming–language and database object management. Our approach includes using a single–level storage model, in which objects are represented as uniformly as possible, regardless of whether they are transient vs. persistent or resident in memory vs. disk. We illustrate the feasibility and performance advantages of this approach by describing our implementation experience and some performance measurements.

1 Introduction

During the past few years, a growing number of researchers have become aware of the chronic mismatch between programming languages and database systems [CM84, AB87, Ba88a]. Programming languages provide rich data types that can be accessed and manipulated in memory using simple language constructs (e.g., iteration, conditionals, assignment and pointer dereferencing), but do not typically provide support for persistent or shared data. On the other hand, the current generation of database systems offers efficient operations for concurrent retrieval and update of large amounts of persistent disk–resident data, but provides only limited data modeling and manipulation capabilities.

Since programming languages and database systems are both limited in the support they provide, neither by itself is sufficient for implementing complex applications that access shared persistent data. Two options are available to application programmers:

- directly calling operating system file services from their programs, or
- using an embedded database query language within their programs.

The first option places a complexity burden on the programmer to implement indexes for large objects, concurrency control and recovery. The second option places a complexity burden on the programmer due to the need to use (and debug) two separate languages. Both approaches cause significant complexity for the programmer due to the lack of uniformity of treatment of transient and persistent data.

Persistent programming languages [AB87] and object–oriented database systems [Dit86, Ba88a] are research directions that aim at providing a programming environment that is more uniform, easier to use and, therefore, more productive. Much of the work on these systems has focused on reducing

* Current Address: Computer Science Dept., University of Wisconsin, Madison, WI 53706, U.S.A.
** Current Address: ETH Zurich, Dept. Informatik, ETH–Zentrum, CH–8092 Zurich, Switzerland

complexity at the level of application programming. However, there are also important efficiency and complexity issues that must be addressed below the application level before such languages will be widely used. Of primary concern are efficient memory and disk management for complex structures and the reduction of the CPU costs of accessing and manipulating objects.

In the Bubba project [Bo88], we have taken the approach of using data uniformity to provide an efficient implementation technology for systems that manage large collections of complex, persistent data. By combining a "uniform object representation" (i.e., representation is orthogonal to persistence and to memory vs. disk residency) with a "single–level store" (i.e., representing all objects in a virtual address space), efficiency is gained by avoiding object translation and allowing objects to be accessed directly by the compiled application code. Disk and memory efficiency is gained by the careful design of these uniform structures. Our experience is that this approach not only simplifies the implementation of an object–oriented database programming system, but also leads to significant performance gains. The main intention of this paper is to show the feasibility and performance advantages of this approach.

Section 2 discusses the performance problems that existing approaches have encountered. Section 3 presents the main features of our approach. Section 4 outlines our implementation in the Bubba project. Section 5 illustrates the achieved performance advantages by giving the results of preliminary measurements. Section 6 concludes with a list of open issues that deserve further investigation.

2 Integrating Programming Languages and Persistent Objects

Optimization of disk access has long been a major performance concern in the design of database systems. Database systems attempt to minimize disk I/O by clustering logically related data and utilizing specialized access policies such as prefetching for sequential scans. Database systems also reduce I/O by placing restrictions on the sizes and/or structures of objects that can be stored in the database. Programming languages provide more general data structures and exploit virtual memory management to provide efficient access to in–memory objects, but do not provide efficient I/O and recovery. The result of this different emphasis between database systems and programming languages is that database structures are less efficient for in–memory use, while programming language structures cannot be used for persistent data.

Many systems have been built to address the mismatch between programming languages and database systems. Several of these systems have been developed using the notion of an "object buffer" or "in–memory object manager" (e.g., AIM [KDG87], Damokles [DGL87], DASDBS [Pa87], ObServer [SZR86], Orion [Kim88], Prima [HMMS87]). The basic idea is to transfer the complete result of a database query to the application program in a single step. Then, the application algorithms can process the retrieved objects without further interaction with the persistent data manager. Updates are performed on the object buffer and are propagated back to the persistent data manager again in a set–oriented mode. There are two basic philosophies that are used to manage the integration between disk–resident and memory–resident data:

- *Object Translation* – Objects are stored in a disk–based format and are translated into an in–memory format when they are faulted into memory (and vice–versa when they are written back to disk).
- *Disk–based Approach* – Database objects are kept in a disk–based format and are accessed in memory using that format. Programming language objects are represented either in the disk–based format or are kept in an in–memory format and segregated from the database objects.

We discuss these techniques below.

2.1 Object Translation

In systems employing object translation, disk-resident data is converted into an appropriate in-memory representation when it is faulted into memory (and converted back when it is written out). This is shown in Figure 1. This technique is typically used in situations in which data is read into memory initially and then operated on extensively. This technique has the advantage that database objects and transient programming language objects can appear to have the same format to the run-time environment.

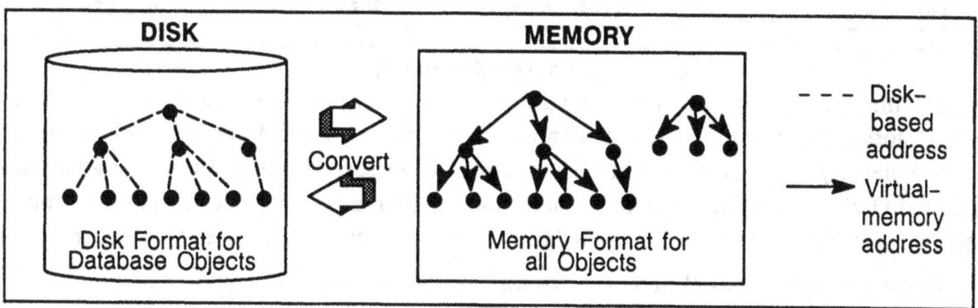

Figure 1 - Object Translation

There are three disadvantages of this approach. One is the complexity of maintaining the relationship between database objects and their in-memory copies [Kim88]. The second disadvantage is the performance cost of copying and converting objects when they are accessed or written out. It has been reported, based on practical experience (e.g., [KCB88],[JTTW88], [SPSW89]), that data translation from the page-oriented buffer pool of the database system into an object buffer representation can be a bottleneck in terms of CPU time consumption. A third disadvantage is that additional memory is required to maintain two buffers for the same data in different formats. This increases I/O.

The costs of this approach arise from the need to copy and convert objects from one format to the other whenever they cross the interface between the database system and the programming language. These data translation performance costs originate from three different sources:

- *Traversing objects* (i.e., conceptual pointer chasing) that are hierarchically structured and might be composed of thousands of atomic sub-objects, usually requiring interpretation of auxiliary structures (e.g., object headers and object table entries).
- *Converting data formats* between different representations of data values and, especially, (intra-) object references (e.g., from TIDs to virtual memory addresses or offsets).
- *Copying a potentially huge number of bytes* (up to several Megabytes) from memory to memory. The expense of copying may become increasingly critical because while technological advances promise drastic increases of CPU speed, memory latency improvements seem to be achievable on a much smaller scale.

2.2 The Disk-based Approach

Many systems attempt to avoid object translation costs by leaving data in its disk-oriented format even when it is read into memory (see Figure 2). Some of these systems (e.g., AIM, DASDBS, and EXODUS) hide these implementation formats, by encapsulating the object buffer and providing cursor functions for traversing objects. This approach is useful for systems that support relational or nested-relational data models because the cursor mechanism works well with the set-at-a-time access provided by such systems.

Systems that support complex objects (e.g., E [RC89], ODE [AG89],O_2[Ba88b], and Trellis/Owl [OBS86]) make more direct use of the disk-oriented structures by using disk-oriented pointers as

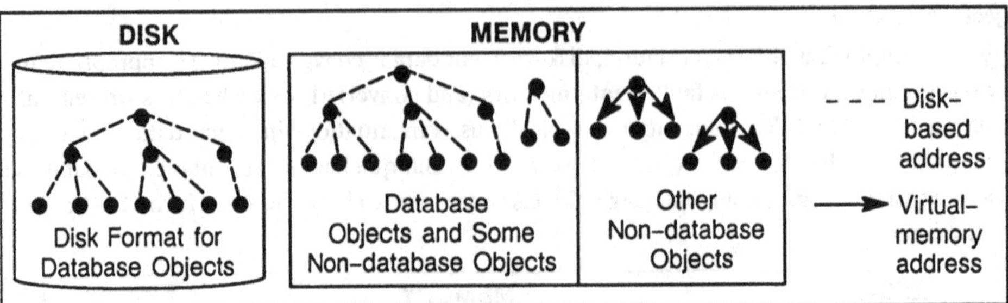

Figure 2 – Disk-based Approach

object identifiers and performing navigation using these identifiers. However, as they are built on a two-level storage architecture, these systems are forced to make a careful distinction between objects resident in memory vs. disk, and must be able to recognize and service "object faults". In some cases (e.g. E and ODE) the distinction between database objects (persistent objects) and other objects (transient objects) is shown explicitly in the language interface that is presented to the user.

2.3 Performance Implications of Both Approaches

Both of the described approaches incur costs that result from the difference in format between disk-resident and memory-resident data. These costs include object copying, format conversion, and inefficient pointer chasing. In addition, both of these approaches bypass the virtual memory support provided by their host operating systems. This results in the inability to exploit virtual-memory hardware and the potential for interference with the operating system such as "double buffering" [Tr82]. Using a two-level buffer management scheme, in which an object buffer and a conventional page buffer coexist, leads to several non-trivial problems related to the coordination of buffer replacements, update propagation, and query evaluation.

The usefulness of providing direct addressing to objects in the page buffer pool has been pointed out in the EXODUS project [CDRS86] for the special case of very long byte strings such as image data. Taking this performance requirement one step further, our approach demonstrates that using virtual memory addresses for all kinds of object references is indeed achievable.

A final cost that results from the above approaches is the difficulty of accessing objects directly from compiled code. Operating system virtual memory support allows compiled programs to access data as if it were completely in memory. By reimplementing the buffering policies above the operating system, this advantage is lost. Access to objects becomes more interpretive. However, as mentioned in [RC89], it is possible that smart compiler optimization techniques can reduce this problem somewhat.

3 Uniform Object Management In A Single-Level Store

Our approach to solving the performance and complexity issues that result from having separate formats for disk-based objects and memory-resident objects is to implement a uniform representation of objects using a single-level store. The idea of a homogeneously addressable single-level store into which permanent files are mapped can be traced back at least 20 years to the development of the Multics operating system [BCD72]. Its original motivation being to simplify programming by eliminating the discrepancy between file access and virtual memory addressing, it seems natural to rediscover this concept for a closer integration of programming languages, database systems, and operating systems.

3.1 The Case For A Single-Level Store

In the past, a number of criticisms of the single-level store approach have been raised. These include:

- *The virtual address space is too small to represent large databases* [Mo89]: This objection is rapidly becoming outdated by the increasing size of virtual address spaces (i.e., the predominance of 32 bit addresses and the near-term availability of 64 bit addresses). For example, the recently announced IBM ESA-370 architecture allows access to multiple address spaces resulting in addressability of up to 16 terabytes [SGS89].
- *Support for recovery is insufficient* [Tr82]: The usual recovery methods (e.g. Write Ahead Logs) require special support for fixing pages in memory and forcing pages to disk. These issues have been addressed in systems (e.g., the IBM 801 [CM88], the Bubba Operating System [CCF89] and others [Di84, Sp85, Th86]) by including adequate operating system support.
- *Buffer management is inefficient* [St81, Tr82]: This objection is due to the fact that operating system buffer management does not typically provide adequate support for database access patterns. Database-oriented buffer replacement policies [TG84] can be implemented using handshakes such as those provided by the systems mentioned above (e.g., fixing pages in memory and prefetching pages for scans).
- *Page table size is excessive* [St81]: This objection is becoming less significant as the cost/bit of memory decreases relative to disk. In Bubba, we also address this issue by having two page sizes: a small page as the unit of memory tables and a large disk block as the unit of disk tables. (The basic support provided by the Bubba Operating System is discussed in Section 4.2.)

As outlined above, a uniform object representation results in a reduction of the complexity of object management. In addition, significant performance advantages can be obtained by integrating a uniform object representation with a single-level store. These are:

- *Traversing objects faster:* A single-level store allows virtual memory addresses to be used as object references in both memory and disk. This makes traversing objects as cheap as possible by exploiting memory-management hardware support.
- *No format conversions:* Since there is only one object format and this format is memory-oriented rather than disk-oriented, complex objects that have been brought in from disk are directly accessible by compiled application code without requiring any format conversion. Note that programming-language virtual address representations for certain data types (e.g., large arrays or images) which are already efficient for disk I/O can be directly implemented.
- *Minimal object copying:* Objects can be accessed directly in the page buffers. This allows objects to be accessed without being copied.
- *Reduced disk I/O:* Since dual buffers are avoided, more memory is available to improve the buffer hit ratio.

3.2 Design Philosophy

Above we have outlined our motivation for choosing a single-level store as the basis for an object manager. The challenge in the design of such a system is to provide efficient access to *both persistent and transient objects*. A naive approach to implementing objects on the single-level store would be to simply treat the store as a "persistent heap". Space for persistent objects could be allocated from this heap in the same way that space for transient objects is allocated from a transient heap. Despite the apparent simplicity, this approach suffers from a number of performance-related problems:

- *By ignoring page and block boundaries, I/O could become excessive.* In the worst case, each access to a portion of a complex object could result in a disk I/O.
- *By ignoring page boundaries, main memory could become fragmented.* This could result in increased I/O.

- *By ignoring page boundaries, page locality could be reduced.* Poor page locality could result in excessive locking and data contention.
- *Overhead for maintaining pointer integrity could become excessive.* In a system with a large amount of data, the size of an object table could result in additional disk I/O to access portions of the object table on disk.

The above problems, in addition to others, have led most systems to rely on traditional database techniques when attempting to implement persistent objects. In such systems, page boundaries are a major consideration in the laying out of objects on disk. A strong point of these systems is that they provide cluster indexes as accelerators for large objects. These indexes allow fast access to portions of large objects, and avoid the pitfalls of indiscriminate I/Os that are problematic in the persistent heap approach. Also, in most systems, the format used for disk-resident objects is either offsets from the beginning of some object or indirections through an object table or slot array instead of virtual address pointers, thus minimizing pointer maintenance. However, these systems suffer from the performance problems outlined in Section 2.

The Bubba object manager design incorporates the advantages of both approaches:

- The entire database is mapped into a virtual address space shared by all transactions.
- Virtual memory addresses are used as pointers both in memory and on disk.
- Object formats for transient and persistent data are identical.
- Smaller objects are stored in a format that is directly accessible by the compiled transaction code.
- Larger objects are implemented with indexing and clustering that provide efficient disk access.

Compared to other object-oriented systems currently being developed in a single-level store (e.g., [Fo88]), our approach is unique by having a single uniform object format that avoids copying and conversions, yet can be directly accessed by the compiled application code. In addition to in-memory efficiency, the approach also addresses the need to efficiently access objects on disk. The IBM 801 project also investigated single-level store support for databases [CM88]. Our approach differs in that it provides direct support for large, dynamic persistent data (e.g., special support for indexing and clustering).

4 Implementation for Hierarchical Data

The Bubba project [Bo88] has addressed the objective of uniform object management on both the programming level and the implementation level. Bubba object management was designed to exploit the benefits of a single-level store while optimizing disk performance. Our approach was to first implement support for hierarchically structured data (i.e., nested sets) and then to extend this solution for general graph-structured data. In fact, as is described below, the current implementation allows persistent objects to have any number of transient parents and exactly one persistent parent. In this section, we briefly describe the object model that is supported by the Bubba system and the special features of the Bubba Operating System that provide the single-level store. We then describe, in more detail, the storage structures that are used to represent these objects and the algorithms used to manage objects during the execution of a transaction. Finally, we describe an approach to extending the architecture to support general graph-structured objects.

4.1 Object Model

The interface to Bubba is a language called FAD [BBKV87, DKV87], which can be viewed as an extension of relational functionality into a database programming language [AB87]. FAD has significantly improved data modeling and general-purpose programming capability over relational languages (e.g., SQL). FAD supports complex objects consisting of sets, tuples, and atoms, which can be nested to an arbitrary depth, as well as operations on these data types. There are no size constraints on FAD data. In addition, FAD provides flow-control primitives (e.g., while-do and if-then-else) and assignment to support general-purpose programming.

FAD treats transient and persistent data in a uniform way by providing the same structures and operations for both; that is, data types are orthogonal to persistence [AB87]. "Transient data" is visible only to the transaction that creates it and lives only for the lifetime of that transaction. Temporary query results are one example of transient data. "Persistent data" is visible to multiple transactions and exists beyond the life of any single transaction. Persistence in FAD is defined as reachability from a special persistent root object called "db". Logically, an object is made persistent by making it a child of an object that is already persistent. Likewise, an object is no longer persistent when it has no parents that are persistent objects.

Figure 3 shows an example of a complex object in a FAD schema, in which sets are indicated by curly braces and tuples are indicated by square brackets. The example consists of a database containing a set of Customer tuples, each containing atomic information about a Customer and a nested set of the Orders placed by the Customer. Each Order tuple contains atomic information as well as a nested set containing information about the Items ordered.

```
db = [ Customers: { [ CustCode: integer,
                      Address: string,
                      CreditLimit: dollars,
                      ...,
                      Orders: { [ OrderCode: integer,
                                  DateOrdered: date,
                                  ...,
                                  Items: { [ ItemCode: integer,
                                             Quantity: integer,
                                             Price: dollars ] } ] } ] } ]
```

Figure 3 – An Example Complex Object In FAD

When creating a physical schema (as opposed to the conceptual schema which provides a more logical view of the data) in FAD, the database designer can choose between normalizing the schema or directly representing the inherent nested structure of the database. Nesting objects has the obvious effect of enhancing performance for certain access patterns while degrading performance for others. The decision of how much nesting is appropriate in a particular database should be based on the expected workload for the application being supported.

4.2 The Single-Level Store Environment

For efficiency reasons, we have maintained uniformity between transient vs. persistent and memory vs. disk data as much as possible within the FAD compiler and the underlying system software. In some cases, we do this by avoiding differences, such as representing all data within a single-level store and using the same storage structures and operations for a given data type. In other cases, differences are required either for performance (e.g., indexing and physical data clustering for large objects) or for functionality (e.g., concurrency control and recovery). In these cases, we hide the differences within the lowest level of system software, so that they are transparent to compiled user programs. Indexing and clustering are hidden within the implementation of large objects. A default concurrency control mechanism using two-phase locking is provided that uses memory-management hardware support. Recovery from system crash is supported using a memory-resident shadowing mechanism employing safe RAM [CKKS89] and a copy-on-write workspace that also uses memory-management hardware support.

Bubba object management is one implementation of uniform object management on a single–level store (we do not claim it is the only viable approach). It takes advantage of functions provided by the Bubba Operating System[CCF89] such as implicit page locking for concurrency control and workspace management support for recovery. Although we believe that these features are an important asset in the construction of a single–level store, we realize that many systems builders do not have the luxury of extending their operating system. Fortunately, the basic ideas that have been outlined above require only the ability to map files into memory, to fix pages in memory, and to force pages to stable storage (i.e., disk or safe RAM). These capabilities are becoming more common [Bal87] and are supported in many extensions of UNIX and in Mach [Acc86, Tev87].

Bubba object management assumes that the entire database is mapped into the virtual address space of each executing transaction. A range of virtual addresses is reserved for this purpose called the "persistent partition". A separate range of virtual addresses, called the "transient partition", is used to contain objects that are created during the execution of the transaction. This approach is similar to the distinction between tenured objects and untenured objects in systems with generation–scavenging garbage collection [Un87]. The persistent partition is shared by all transaction executions. However, each transaction execution has its own transient partition which exists only for the life of that transaction execution. "Boxing" (i.e., garbage collection and data clustering) is performed at the end of a transaction in order to resolve the logical notion of persistence (i.e., reachability from the persistent root) with the physical notion of persistence (i.e., the persistent partition). During boxing, any newly created objects that have been attached to an object in the database are moved into the persistent partition.

In order to minimize disk I/O and reduce the size of disk mapping tables, a large disk "block" is used as the unit for disk tables (e.g., disk space allocation and indexes). The disk block size is the size of a disk track (e.g., 16K byte to 64K byte) (cf. [Sm85],[We89]). A smaller "page" (e.g., 512 byte) is used as the unit of main memory allocation, physical locking, and workspace management. Two types of pages can be allocated from the operating system: "data pages" and "system pages". When a data page in the persistent partition is accessed, it is automatically locked (by the operating system) and, if the page is dirty (i.e., an identical copy does not exist on disk), a workspace copy is created for the page using a copy–on–write mechanism. System pages are neither implicitly locked nor copied–on–write. An LRU algorithm is used for replacing pages in main memory; however, hooks are provided that allow pages to be fixed in memory or prefetched for scans (i.e., to augment the normal LRU page faulting mechanism).

4.3 Object Storage Structures

In this section, we describe the storage structures that were developed in order to efficiently implement the hierarchical FAD objects on our single–level store architecture. The design process was one in which the goal of directly supporting programming language data structures was traded off against the goal of efficiently managing large amounts of shared disk–resident data.

Bubba object management makes a distinction between "small" objects and "large" objects (cf. [KFC88]). In Bubba, small objects are those objects that are less than a disk block in size. The structure of a small object is known to the FAD compiler. That is, the code generated by the compiler can directly access the internals of small objects without calling the index mechanism. The page faulting, implicit locking, and workspace management provided by the operating system allow the compiled code to access objects without regard to whether they are persistent or transient or whether they are disk or memory resident.

Objects that are larger than a disk block can be stored using an index (either a B^+tree or hashed) which maps subobjects into disk blocks. For example, a large set of tuples could consist of a B^+tree that maps tuples into specific blocks based on the value of one of their attributes (e.g., a key). The tuples themselves could be stored as "small" objects within their assigned block. Objects that can be indexed are tagged to indicate whether they are stored using the "small" structure or indexed. When the compiled code detects that an object is indexed, it calls the index mechanism to access it. Since indexes are encapsulated within the index mechanism, the index mechanism is free to use various tricks (such as non–two–phase locking for indexes and prefetching of data blocks for scans) to optimize access to large objects. For both large and small objects, pointers are implemented using virtual addresses. Therefore, no translation of objects is necessary when reading from or writing to disk.

During a transaction, it is possible that a small object is grown to the point that it exceeds the size of a disk block (or likewise, a large object could shrink to below that size). In the current implementation, the small object is converted into a large object at the end of the transaction (in the "boxing phase" described in Section 4.4). Large objects that shrink are not currently converted into small objects.

Figure 4 shows an example of a large object whose index has two levels.The top level of the index (called the cluster index) maps sub–objects into blocks. The lowest level of the index (called the block index) is stored in the same block as the data that it indexes. Since data blocks are fairly large, the cluster index can typically fit in memory. (With a 16K byte block size, 1G byte of data would occupy approximately 65,000 blocks. Assuming 10 byte keys, 8 bytes overhead per entry, its cluster index would require only 1.2M bytes). In this way, access to any sub–object can usually be performed with at most one disk access. The indexes (shown in the shaded area of Figure 4) are kept on pages that are not implicitly locked upon access. These pages are protected using non–two–phase locking techniques [SG88]. The data area is made up of small pages that are implicitly locked when accessed.

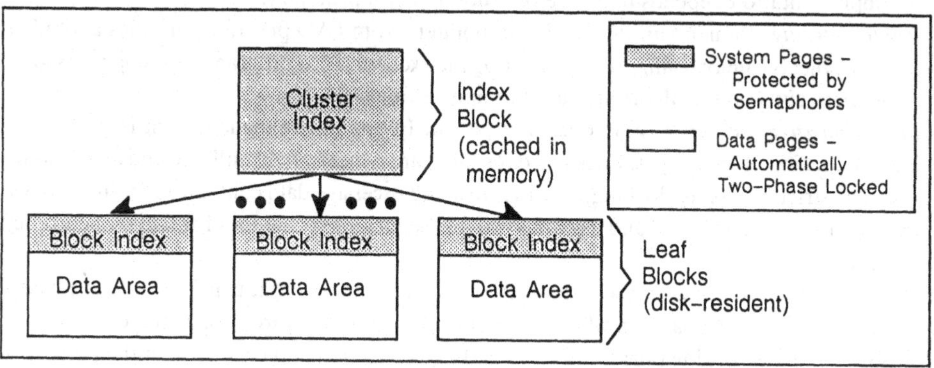

Figure 4 - A Large Object and Its Index

Figure 5 shows a simplified example of how objects are represented within the block of a large object. The example shows a block of a large Customer set from the example schema in Section 4.1. It contains two Customer tuples, one that fits entirely in the block, and one whose nested set of Orders is itself stored as a large set (because Customer n has made many Orders). Note that after obtaining a pointer to Customer 1, a compiled program could access the tuple directly without calling the index mechanism. A program accessing the tuple for Customer n would be able to access fields within the tuple directly but would need to call the index mechanism to access the large nested Order set.

The index mechanism's use of a structure that is sensitive to disk block boundaries supports efficient disk I/O. All of the subobjects of a particular object that fit in a block can be accessed with a

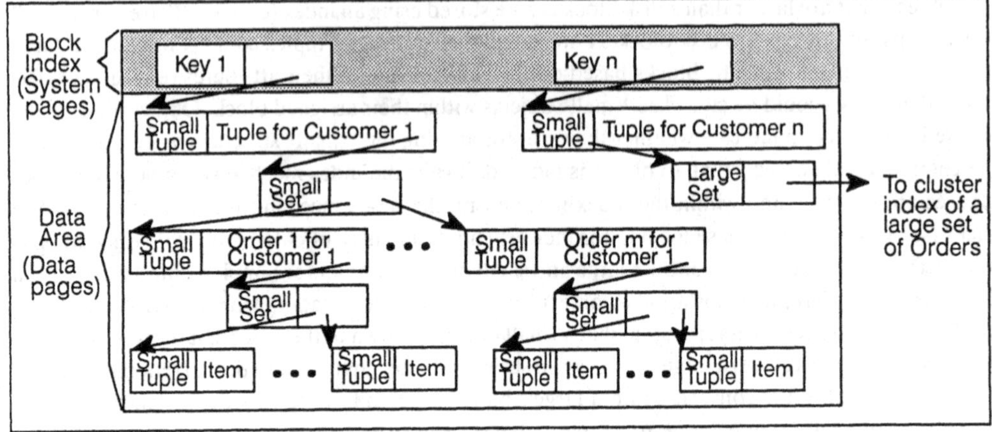

Figure 5 – Objects Within A Block Of A Large Customer Set

single disk I/O. Since the index mechanism encapsulates the structure of the indexes for large objects, it can perform non–two–phase locking on them, prefetch blocks when it seems appropriate (e.g., during sequential scans), and unlock pages early for "dirty" scans (i.e., when two–phase locking is not needed). In addition, the use of structures that are known to the compiler for objects up to the block size allows efficient direct access to many objects. We believe that this combination provides reasonable disk and in–memory efficiency.

4.4 Object Management Algorithms

Although the design of object management on a single–level store is conceptually simple, its successful implementation depends upon the resolution of two problems:

- *Pointer integrity*: To maintain the validity of pointers from FAD program variables and other objects, objects cannot change location during the execution of a program. This imposes significant constraints on the algorithms used to update objects.
- *Index concurrency control*: An important aspect of Bubba object management is the default implicit locking of data pages. Locks on data pages are typically held until the end of a transaction (i.e., strict two–phase locking). In order to avoid excessive data contention for indexes, we store them on system pages and use non–two–phase locking techniques for their concurrency control.

To address these problems, we use a transaction execution model that consists of three phases. These are: 1) the "execution phase" in which the transaction operations are applied to persistent and transient objects, 2) the "boxing phase" in which garbage collection and clustering of the persistent objects is performed, and 3) the "commit phase" in which changes to the persistent partition (i.e., the database) are made visible to other transactions.

The Execution Phase

During the execution phase, the operations of a transaction program are applied in the transaction's workspace. Any persistent objects that are accessed are brought into memory using the page faulting mechanism of the operating system and their pages are locked upon access.

For retrieval operations, objects that are brought into memory (typically by the page faulting mechanism) can be accessed directly using their virtual addresses. Pointers to such objects can be included in program variables and in transient objects. Therefore, retrieval operations can be done very efficiently (i.e., with no copying or data translation).

During the execution phase, all new objects are created in the transient partition. Objects are updated in place (subject to the copy–on–write workspace mechanism) with persistent and transient objects being updated in the same manner. The only distinction that is made is that an entry is made in a list for each update to an object in the persistent partition. This list is used to minimize the amount of data that must be traversed to do garbage collection and clustering in the next phase of the transaction. Because we used a partitioned address space, it is possible to determine if an object resides in the persistent partition simply by masking off the lower–order bits of its address.

Two restrictions are in effect during this phase. The first restriction is on object movement. If the size of an object is increased during this phase (e.g., as the result of an assignment), the object may have to be relocated. However, since there are potentially many references to the object, its address cannot be easily changed. This problem is solved by the use of "forwarding pointers". When an object is moved, a special marker is left in its place. This marker contains the address to where the object has been relocated. These forwarding pointers are cleaned up during the later phases of the transaction. Note that the use of forwarding pointers is needed only for variable–length objects. A bit in the tag of a variable–length object indicates whether the object is stored in–place or is forwarded. Currently, all accesses to variable–length objects check for forwarding pointers, however, a possible optimization is to allow the compiler to determine which objects require checking based on whether or not they have the possibility of being moved (e.g., a read–only transaction should never have to check for forwarding references).

Another restriction during this phase is that indexes can not be modified. This restriction is made to avoid recovery problems that would result from our use of non–two–phase locking for indexes. Index updates are deferred until the final phase of the transaction. The storage structures are designed so that they can be expanded without updating their indexes. For example, sets are stored as linked lists of "segments" (groups of pointers to elements) and the index for a set maps keys to segments (similar to the way a primary index maps keys to B^+tree blocks). A set can be expanded by adding segments to the linked list without having to make an entry in the set index. The elements in segments that are not in the index are reachable by following links from predecessors. The new segments can then be added to the index at a later time. This technique is similar to the B^{link} technique used for allowing concurrent access to B^+trees [LY81].

The Boxing Phase

At the end of the execution phase, the operations of the transaction have been applied and the persistent partition must be updated accordingly. In particular, it is possible that objects have been logically made persistent by making them children of persistent objects. However, as stated above, all objects created during the execution phase are created in the transient partition. During the boxing phase, the list of updates to persistent objects is processed, and any objects in the transient partition that are logically persistent are copied into the persistent partition.

During this phase, it is safe to move objects, because the transaction has completed its operations and the locking mechanism insures that no other transactions are accessing objects that have been updated by the transaction. Objects are copied into particular boxes based on clustering heuristics. The heuristics attempt to store small child objects within the same disk block as their parent. Objects that are larger than a disk block are indexed and stored in blocks that are near (on the disk) to the block containing their parent. If a small object does not fit into the block containing its parent, then that block is split using techniques similar to the splitting of B^+tree blocks. During this phase, operations that require updates to indexes are recorded in a log. These updates will be applied during the commit phase.

When all newly persistent objects have been moved into the persistent space, the entire transient partition can be discarded (it is released at the end of the transaction). Therefore, the amount of work done during the boxing phase is proportional to the amount of data added to the persistent partition rather than to the total amount of data created during the transaction. In this sense, the boxing phase works as a scavenging garbage collector [Un87]. Within the persistent partition, however, space that is contained by objects that are no longer reachable is reclaimed on a block by block basis when the block splitting algorithm is applied.

The Commit Phase

The commit phase is the final phase of transaction execution. In this phase, the indexes are updated, the workspace copies of modified data pages are installed in the persistent partition, and the locks on data pages are released. At the end of this phase, all of the modifications made to the persistent partition can be seen by other transactions.

4.5 Implementing Non–hierarchical Objects

As stated at the beginning of this section, the implemented system currently supports objects that are hierarchically structured (although multiple transient parents are allowed). The support of hierarchical structures simplified the implementation in several ways. In particular, it allowed us to avoid the need for an object table. In a system that contains large numbers of objects, an object table can result in significant overhead both in CPU costs (for bookkeeping) and disk I/O (because the table may be too large to keep it entirely memory resident). Many modern object–oriented programming language systems have done away with object tables (e.g., [Un87], [CW86]). However, this is done at the expense of clustering on disk.

For a system managing large amounts of persistent data, disk clustering is a crucial issue. Therefore, we are unable to adapt the programming–language techniques to our system. As a result, we have looked towards ways of making an object table more efficient. The approach that we plan to take is to use a "distributed object table". In this scheme, objects that are allowed to have multiple parents are referenced through an indirection that is stored in the same block as the object (similar to a slot in a B^+tree block). Objects can be moved within their block by simply updating the indirection pointer. When objects must be moved to a different block (e.g., for clustering reasons), the indirection is updated to point to an indirection in the new block. A background process cleans up these inter–block indirections. A possible optimization is to patch up pointers to inter–block indirections "on the fly" as they are accessed. This would allow commonly accessed paths to be optimized, hence reducing the frequency with which the background process must be run. However, the cost would be additional checking when following indirections.

A scheme that uses a similar type of distributed object table is described in [Mo89]. Our proposal differs in two ways. First, it pays strict attention to disk block boundaries and disk clustering in order to provide efficient I/O. Secondly, since it is implemented on the single–level store, it avoids many of the performance problems outlined in Section2.

5 Performance Experiments

To validate the viability of our approach and to gain initial quantitative insights into the expected performance advantages, we performed a number of experiments on a prototype system. This prototype was built on top of UNIX by simulating a single–level store in virtual memory. Integration of this prototype with the single–level store provided by the Bubba Operating System is currently under way.

The "Customer" database described in Section 4 served as the basis for our measurements. We generated a database consisting of 100 Customers, each of which had 100 Orders stored as a set–valued attribute, where each Order in turn consisted of 10 Items. The total storage size of one Item tuple was 26 bytes (including auxiliary structures), that of one Order 636 bytes, including its Items. For each Customer, the set of Orders was indexed and consumed 5 data blocks of 16 KB each. The total size of the database was approximately 10 MB, 8 MB of which was consumed by Orders.

As our workload we chose 3 retrieval operations and 1 update operation, following[Ca88]. In terms of our example schema, the operations can be described as follows:

GetItem: Given a Customer key and an Order key, find the first Item within the specified Order of the specified Customer, and print it (i.e., access a short sub-object reached by two random accesses along a hierarchical path from the root of a complex object).

GetOrd: Given a Customer key and an Order key, find the specified Order within the specified Customer, and print it (i.e., randomly access a relatively large complex sub-object of a randomly accessed complex object).

AllOrds: Given a Customer key, find all Orders of the specified Customer, and print them (i.e., access all sub-objects of a randomly accessed complex object, where the sub-objects again have a complex structure).

NewOrd: Given a Customer key, insert a new Order into the set of Orders of the specified Customer (i.e., create and insert a relatively large complex sub-object into a randomly accessed complex object).

GetItemP, GetOrdP, AllOrdsP: These are modified versions of *GetItem, GetOrd,* and *AllOrds*, where one atomic attribute is projected out of the retrieved Items or Orders, and only this attribute is printed.

CPU times for these operations were obtained by using a sampling-based monitor (the UNIX tool "gprof"). Each operation was run several thousand times, each time as a separate transaction. This technique ensures that the computed average times are sufficiently precise. For each operation, we analyzed the measured results, breaking its total CPU time down into several cost factors. Figure 6 shows the the total CPU time for each of the transactions and an approximate breakdown of the CPU cost by cost factor. The measurements were performed on a SUN-3/50 with 4 MB of main memory. These numbers demonstrate the following key observations:

- Printing the retrieved objects turned out to contribute by far the biggest costs. While printing is rather atypical for the processing of large complex objects in real-life applications, it clearly demonstrates the considerable costs of doing excessive object translation because objects must be converted to string format.
- For retrieval operations, no copying is necessary, nor are there any format conversions during the actual object access. This is true also for projections, which do not incur any significant additional costs in the implemented prototype.*
- The CPU costs of update operations, are dominated to a large extent by the amount of copying that is necessary during boxing.

On the average, it took approximately 6.5 milliseconds to copy an Order (e.g., a moderately complex object consuming 636 bytes of storage space in total). The main cost factor of object copying currently is the interpretation of auxiliary structures (e.g., small object headers) while traversing objects. Our storage structures give us the potential of compiling these steps directly into simple virtual memory pointer chasing. The current version of the FAD compiler does not fully exploit this potential. These costs will decrease with future versions of the compiler. The costs of the actual byte copying, on the other hand, have already reached a level at which they can hardly be reduced further. If we assume

*Note that the *AllOrds_P* function, unlike the other projections, required more work for the "object search", because it had to scan the order set for each customer, which is part of the printing for *AllOrds*.

	Printing		Object Search	Object Creation & Insertion	Object Copying	Boxing	Transaction Initiation & Termination	Total CPU Time (msec)
	String Output	Object Traversal & Conversion						
GetItem	12.6	16.3	40.6	--	--	--	29.6	13.5
GetOrd	53.3	34.5	7.9	--	--	--	2.9	69.6
AllOrds	54.1	45.6	0.1	--	--	--	0.2	4096.5
GetItemP	1.2	6.0	65.4	--	--	--	27.4	8.4
GetOrdP	2.5	6.0	66.3	--	--	--	25.3	8.3
AllOrdsP	24.1	49.7	23.8	--	--	--	2.4	70.2
NewOrd	--	--	4.2	30.9	30.9	29.4	4.4	47.3

Figure 6 - Cost of Object-Oriented Operations (% of CPU Time)

that a 16 KB block contains about 20 Orders and that copying such a complex object requires on the order of 1000 machine instructions, copying all objects of a block could take as long as reading the entire block from disk. Moreover, as the execution time of these instructions is increasingly limited by memory latency, this bottleneck will remain even with much faster CPUs.

Notice that in our approach these expensive copying steps are completely avoided for all retrieval operations. For update operations, copying is necessary during the boxing phase, and, in fact, it may be the case that even old objects have to be moved (i.e., copied) to achieve the desired clustering (e.g., by reorganizing or splitting blocks). While these costs seem to have their counterparts in any kind of object management architecture, systems that use an object buffer approach inherently suffer from the penalty of object copying also for retrieval operations. This means, for instance, that in our current implementation the CPU cost of the *GetOrd* operation (excluding printing) would be approximately doubled if our prototype system had an object buffer.

6 Conclusion

In this paper, we have presented an approach to uniform object management that is based on a single-level store. We have provided arguments that such an architecture achieves considerable performance gains by avoiding inefficiencies due to multiple object formats and incompatibility with operating system policies. A key factor in the design of such a system is the need to address the indexing and clustering of large objects on disk. Our prototype implementation has shown that the approach also simplifies the implementation of an object-oriented database system or a database programming language. It is because of this combination of performance advantages and simplicity that we regard the presented object management architecture as an important step in a promising direction. Nevertheless, there are several open issues that deserve further investigation.

An approach to reducing the update costs of a transaction could be to take boxing, which causes objects to be copied, out of a transaction's critical path, and allow a background demon to achieve the desired clustering. This, of course, requires that objects which are supposed to become persistent are initially created in the persistent partition, which in turn could be achieved by giving up the concept of a separate transient partition. Then, the task of the background boxer would, to a large extent, be that of a garbage collector.

Object copying is undesirable from a performance point of view. However, it is often regarded as a necessary evil for protection reasons, given the constraints and deficiencies of today's computing architectures. To avoid the "Trojan Horse" problem, the application code and the database system software typically reside in separate address spaces, that is, they have to be separate processes in most operating systems. Copying is inevitable in such an environment. We believe that rather than sacrificing performance, a better solution can be achieved by designing application development languages more carefully, e.g. by disallowing or restricting the direct use of virtual address pointers at the source code level. Then, a sophisticated compiler, that cannot be bypassed, could take care of the authorization issues by generating the necessary run–time checks. The FAD language and its compiler are a step in this direction.

Another issue is investigating different approaches for parallel machines. In the Bubba system, we use a single–level store architecture in each node of a shared–nothing system. An interesting alternative is the concept of a system–wide single–level store. This would allow object management to be as simple as in the centralized case. Proposals for such a globally shared single–level store can be found in the operating systems literature (e.g., [AK85]), but it is not clear what the performance impacts are. Also, an approach that allows access to multiple address spaces (e.g., [SGS89]) is a potential solution.

References

[AK85] D.A. Abramson, J.L. Keedy, *Implementing a Large Virtual Memory in a Distributed Computing System*, Hawaii Conf. on System Sciences, 1985.

[Acc86] M. Accetta, R. Baron, W. Bolosky, D. Golub, R. Rashid, A.Tevanian and M. Young, *Mach: a New Kernel Foundation For UNIX Development*, Summer USENIX Conf., 1986.

[AG89] R. Agrawal, N.H. Gehani, *ODE (Object Database and Environment): The Language and the Data Model*, SIGMOD Conf. 1989.

[AB87] M.P. Atkinson, O.P. Buneman, *Types and Persistence in Database Programming Languages*, ACM Computing Surveys 19,2 (1987).

[Bal87] R.M. Balzer, *Living In The Next–Generation Operating System*, IEEE Software, November, 1987.

[Ba88a] F. Bancilhon, *Object–Oriented Database Systems*, PODS Conf. 1988.

[Ba88b] F. Bancilhon et al, *The Design and Implementation of O₂, an Object–Oriented Database System*, 2nd Intl. Workshop on Object–Oriented Database Systems, 1988.

[BBKV87] F. Bancilhon, T. Briggs, S. Khoshafian, P. Valduriez, *FAD, a Powerful and Simple Database Language*, VLDB 1987.

[BCD72] A. Bensoussan, C.I. Clingen, R.C. Daley, *The Multics Virtual Memory: Concepts and Design*, CACM 15,5 (1972).

[Bo88] H. Boral, *Parallelism and Data Management*, 3rd Int. Conf. on Data and Knowledge Bases, 1988.

[CDRS86] M.J. Carey, D.J. DeWitt, J.E. Richardson, E.J. Shekita, *Object and File Management in the EXODUS Extensible Database System*, VLDB 1986.

[Ca88] R.G.G. Cattell, *Object–Oriented DBMS Performance Measurement*, 2nd Intl. Workshop on Object–Oriented Database Systems, 1988.

[CW86] P.J. Caudill and A. Wirfs–Brock, *A Third Generation Smalltalk–80 Implementation*, OOPSLA Conf., 1986.

[CM88] A. Chang, M.F. Mergen, *801 Storage: Architecture and Programming*, ACM TOCS 6,1 (1988).

[CCF89] L. Clay, G. Copeland, and M. Franklin, *UNIX Extensions for High Performance Transaction Processing*, USENIX Workshop on UNIX Transaction Processing, Pittsburgh, 1989.

[CM84] G. Copeland, D. Maier, *Making Smalltalk a Database System*, SIGMOD Conf., 1984.

[CKKS89] G. Copeland, T. Keller, R. Krishnamurthy, M. Smith, *The Case for Safe RAM*, VLDB 1989.

[DKV87] S. Danforth, S. Khoshafian, P. Valduriez, *FAD, A Database Programming Language, Revision 2*, MCC Technical Report DB–151–85Rev.2, Austin, 1987.

[Di84] H. Diel, N. Lenz, G. Kreissig, M. Scheible, B. Schoener, *Data Management Facilities of an Operating System Kernel*, SIGMOD Conf., 1984.

[Dit86] K.R. Dittrich, *Object–Oriented Database Systems: the Notion and the Issues*, 1st Intl. Workshop on Object–Oriented Database Systems, 1986.

[DGL87] K.R. Dittrich, W. Gotthard, P.C. Lockemann, *DAMOKLES– The Database System for the UNIBASE Software Engineering Environment*, IEEE Database Engineering 10,1 (1987).

[Fo88] S. Ford et al, *ZEITGEIST: Database Support for Object–Oriented Programming*, 2nd Intl. Workshop on Object–Oriented Database Systems, 1988.

[HMMS87] T. Haerder, K. Meyer–Wegener, B. Mitschang, A. Sikeler, *PRIMA– A DBMS Prototype Supporting Engineering Applications*, VLDB 1987.

[JTTW88] J. Joseph, S. Thatte, C. Thompson, D. Wells, Report on the Object–Oriented Database Workshop at the 1988 OOPSLA Conf., ACM SIGMOD Record 18,3 (1989)

[KFC88] S. Khoshafian, M.J. Franklin, M.J. Carey, *Storage Management for Persistent Complex Objects*, to appear in Information Systems.

[KCB88] W. Kim, H.T. Chou, J. Banerjee, *Operations and Implementation of Complex Objects*, IEEE Transactions on Software Engineering 14,7 (1988).

[Kim88] W. Kim, N. Ballou, J. Banerjee, H.T.Chou, J.F. Garza, D. Woelk, *Integrating an Object–Oriented Programming System with a Database System*, OOPSLA Conf., 1988.

[KDG87] K. Kuespert, P. Dadam, J. Guenauer, *Cooperative Object Buffer Management in the Advanced Information Management Prototype*, VLDB 1987.

[LY81] P. Lehman, S. Yao, *Efficient Locking for Concurrent Operations on B–Trees*, TODS 6,4 (1981).

[Mo89] J.E.B. Moss, *Addressing Large Distributed Collections of Persistent Objects: The Mneme Project's Approach*, 2nd Intl. Workshop on Database Programming Languages, Salishan Lodge, OR, 1989.

[OBS86] P. O'Brien, B. Bullis, C. Schaffert, *Persistent and Shared Objects in Trellis/Owl*, 1st Intl. Workshop on Object–Oriented Database Systems, 1986.

[Pa87] H.B. Paul, H.J. Schek, M.H. Scholl, G. Weikum, U. Deppisch, *Architecture and Implementation of the Darmstadt Database Kernel System*, SIGMOD Conf., 1987.

[RC89] J. Richardson and M. Carey, *Implementing Persistence in E Language*, Intl. Workshop on Persistent Object Systems, Newcastle, Australia, 1989

[SGS89] C.A. Scalzi, A.G. Ganek, R.J. Schmalz, *ESA/370: An Architecture for Multiple Virtual Address Space Access and Authorization,* IBM Systems Journal 28,1 (1989).

[SPSW89] H.–J. Schek, H.–B. Paul, M.H. Scholl, G. Weikum, *The DASDBS Project: Objectives, Experiences, and Future Prospects*, to appear in IEEE Transactions on Knowledge and Data Engineering.

[SG88] D. Shasha, N. Goodman, *Concurrent Search Structure Algorithms*, TODS 13,1 (1988).

[SZR86] A.H. Skarra, S.B. Zdonik, S.P. Reiss, *An Object Server for an Object–Oriented Database System*, 1st Intl. Workshop on Object–Oriented Database Systems, 1986.

[Sm85] Smith, A.J., *Disk Cache – Miss Ratio Analysis and Design Considerations*, ACM TOCS 3,3 (1985).

[Sp85] A.Z. Spector et al, *Support for Distributed Transactions in the TABS Prototype*, IEEE Transactions on Software Engineering 11,6 (1985).

[St81] M. Stonebraker, *Operating System Support for Database Management*, CACM 24,7 (1981).

[TG84] J.Z. Teng and R.A. Gumaer, *Managing IBM Database 2 Buffers to Maximize Performance*, IBM Systems Journal, 23,2 (1984).

[Tev87] A. Tevanian et al, *A UNIX Interface For Shared Memory And Memory Mapped Files Under Mach*, Summer USENIX Conf., Phoenix, 1987.

[Th86] S.M. Thatte, *Persistent Memory: A Storage Architecture for Object–Oriented Database Systems*, 1st Intl. Workshop on Object–Oriented Database Systems, 1986.

[Tr82] I.L. Traiger, *Virtual Memory Management for Database Systems*, ACM OS Review 16,4 (1982).

[Un87] D. Ungar, *The Design and Evaluation of a High Performance Smalltalk System*, MIT Press, 1987.

[We89] G. Weikum, *Set–Oriented Disk Access to Large Complex Objects*, Data Engineering Conf., 1989.

Exceeding the Limits of Polymorphism in Database Programming Languages

David Stemple
Leo Fegaras
Tim Sheard
Adolfo Socorro
Department of Computer and Information Science
University of Massachusetts at Amherst

Abstract

Database programming languages represent an attempt to merge the technologies of programming languages and database management in order to improve the development of data-intensive applications. One aspect of the research on database programming languages is an attempt to exploit polymorphism and higher order functions to integrate query algebra capabilities into programming languages. This has proved to be difficult especially in strongly and statically typed languages, due to the high level of polymorphism and reflection in database query languages. For example, the natural join operation of relational algebra requires examination of the types of the input relations to determine the match predicate and output type, neither of which are easily expressed in current polymorphic programming languages. These aspects of natural join require quite sophisticated polymorphism and some kind of reflection. The reflection must be powerful enough to allow the examination of the input types to determine the match function and to synthesize the output type. It is the difficulty in achieving such power parsimoniously that we examine in this paper.

1 Introduction

In order to discuss the issues of polymorphism and reflection crisply we first set out our goals and limit discussion to a few features and algebraic operations. The computational framework will be pure recursive functions over a few base types combined with tuple and set type constructors. Type constructors can be parametric, i. e., have free type variables, and functions can be both polymorphic and higher order. Section 2 describes the type and function definition environment in more detail.

The goals of language design that we will assume are:

- The type system should avoid asymmetry in the treatment of type constructors. For example, neither tuple nor relation types should be treated in any special manner, and type constructors should be composable with as few restrictions as possible.
- All expressions are to be strongly and statically typed. The only run-time type checking that should be required is for data received from external sources such as interactive users, files from outside the environment, and data received directly from other systems.
- The computational semantics should be kept as simple as possible. In particular, we will try to minimize run-time access to type details. This may be in some conflict with our first goal, if we allow limited access to certain type information.

It is in this context, a strongly and statically typed language with a minimum of run-time reflection (particularly access to and complex use of type details) and as uniform a type system as is practical, that we explore the limits of polymorphism. The benefits of strong and static type checking, such as avoidance of run-time errors, are well known, though their potential costs, for example, in terms of difficulty in exploratory programming, has not yet been determined. Uniformity is a common goal in language design and is thought to improve the usability of a language. The absence of run-time reflection seems to us to be in keeping with the desire to have strong typing with static checking, since if the types can be accessed, created and changed at run-time there will have to be run-time type checking. It also serves to promote both run-time efficiency and effective formal reasoning about systems specified in a language.

There are approaches which do not share these goals. For example, run-time reflective capabilities are the major objective of some work, e. g., [4,11] In other work, computation is actually performed on types[1]. The purpose of this paper is to explore ways of solving some language problems involving "type reflection" within the goals set out above. It is the limits of polymorphism in this context that we want to exceed.

We will concentrate on the basic relational algebra operations and the *nest* operation of nested relations. These operations give rise to surprising difficulties, and a simple, straightforward treatment meeting the design goals above seems unachievable using existing type systems and evaluation mechanisms. In Section 3 we discuss the problems of capturing such algebraic operators as polymorphic functions and some of the approaches to these problems.

In Section 4 we present a mechanism that can be added to a polymorphic type system to allow our example operators to be defined and statically type checked. We show how this mechanism achieves the reflection capability required to capture operations such as natural join and nest. The mechanism operates at compile-time and is not a part of the type system per se. If this capability were added to a language's type construction facility it would lead to a reflection requirement on the system's run-time computation: functions would have to access type definitions at run-time in order to perform their computations.

The features presented in this paper are part of the database system specification language, ADABTPL, being developed at the University of Massachusetts [2,9]. While we have not been overly concerned with the efficiency of code compiled from ADABTPL, since it is designed as a high level specification language, our concern for keeping its formal semantics simple in order to promote ease of formal reasoning [12,10] has led us to devise the mechanisms presented in this paper. We believe, however, that benefit may be gained from incorporating them into lower level database programming languages, such as Napier [6] or DBPL [5]. Another possibility is that their presence in a specification language such as ADABTPL can allow a simpler type system to be used safely in a lower level language so long as the specification language is used as the basis of sound transformations into lower level language programs. If this is true it adds to the motivation for using development paradigms that incorporate layers of refinement proceeding from specification languages down to programming languages.

2 The Type and Computational Environment

The type and computational environment in which we will discuss the issues of this paper is a fragment of the ADABTPL language. We will deal simply with two base types, **number** and **string**, whose details are of no import. We will also deal with two type constructors, **tuple** and **set**.

A tuple type definition will be written as in the following example.

```
person = consperson[name: string; age: number; address: string]
```

This defines a function, **consperson**, which constructs a value of this type from two strings and a number. The component names, **name**, **age** and **address**, stand for three functions from person values to strings, numbers and strings, respectively. Component names have no other meaning or special treatment in the language; they are just functions. The semantics of the tuple constructor and selector functions are the expected reciprocity equations, e. g.,

```
name(consperson(n, a, ad)) = n
```

It is this kind of axiomatic simplicity in the type semantics that we will try to preserve as we devise methods of capturing database features in a programming language.

To define a relation type over the person type, we write

```
personrel = set(person)
```

In order to define functions over a relation value of type **personrel** we need to have a variable of type **personrel**. We will not overload type names with instance denotations as is common in database systems. When defining functions an input variable will suffice. For example, we can define a **project** function for **personrel** values by

```
function perproject(r: personrel;
                    col: function(person)->alpha): set(alpha);
body
 if r = emptyset
    then emptyset
    else insert(col(choose(r)), perproject(rest(r), col))
end
```

The symbol **alpha** stands for a type variable that will be implicitly given in calls to **perproject** as the output type of a concrete projection function, **col**.

This example involves all the basic operations on values of set types: **emptyset**, **insert**, **choose** and **rest**. The function **choose** returns a value from its non-empty set input. It is not defined on **emptyset**. The **rest** function returns its input with the **choose** removed. The axiomatization of this type and mechanical reasoning over computations on it are discussed elsewhere [10].

To project a **personrel** value, in variable **persons**, on **name** we would write

```
perproject(persons, name)
```

This would return a set of strings. In a strictly typed environment, this result is not a relation. To make it a relation with a single column **name**, we can write, with a lack of sugar-coating that will be typical of the language of discourse in this paper,

```
perproject(persons, lambda(p:person)->[name: string]
                       ([name(p)]))
```

The second argument is a typed lambda function with one parameter of type **person** and an output which is a one component tuple whose component is named **name**. Its result is computed by applying **name** to the input **p** and making the returned value a tuple. The following example projects on **name** and **age**.

```
perproject(persons,
           lambda(p:person)-> [name: string; age: number]
             ([p.name, p.age]))
```

The dot notation is simply a way of applying a selector function, e. g., **p.name** stands for **name(p)**.

From these examples we can see that a completely generic **project** is easily defined using functional arguments to achieve a generic function definition as follows.

```
function project(s: set(alpha); f:function(alpha)-> beta):
     set(beta);
body
 if s = emptyset
    then emptyset
    else insert(f(choose(s)), project(rest(s), f))
end
```

This should be recognizable as a simple *map* function over sets.

The relational **select** function is also easily defined using these features.

```
function select(s: set(alpha);
                p: function(alpha)-> boolean):
                   set(alpha);
body
 if s = emptyset
    then emptyset
    else if p(choose(s))
            then insert(choose(s), select(rest(s), p))
            else select(rest(s), p)
end
```

Both **project** and **select** definitions allow calls to be statically checked for correct typing using reasonably simple algorithms. Note that we are assuming a type checking environment, i. e., an environment in which expressions are checked to see if they have types that are compatible with declared types, rather than a type inference approach as in ML or Machiavelli [7], in which the type inference algorithm is used to find a most general type for each expression. Various degrees of type inference can be used in a type checking environment. For example, in the ADABTPL type checking environment the types instantiated in a call to a polymorphic function are inferred from the arguments, rather than declared.

The basic parameters of the computational environment should be clear from these examples. We will deal with pure, recursive, total functions. All of our examples are functions that recursively traverse finite sets using **choose** and **rest**. For details of the full computational paradigm see [10].

3 Problematic Operations

In this section, we examine three problematic operations: *generic join*, *natural join* and *nest*. Each has a different level of a similar problem. The problem has to do with generating the type of the output and the details of the computation from the types of input arguments. We first examine the simplest of the three, generic join.

3.1 Generic join

An unproblematic generic join function can be written following the examples in the previous section as long as we are willing to specify both the match function and the concatenation function in each call. (The match function is a predicate that determines whether a pair of tuples is to be joined; the concatenation function is the means of combining them.) To simplify the definition we first define a function, **onejoin**, that joins one element with a set of elements.

```
function
 onejoin(t: alpha; s:set(beta);
        match:function(alpha,beta)->boolean;
        concat: function(alpha, beta)-> gamma):
                set(gamma);
body
   case s of
   emptyset: emptyset
     others: if match(t, choose(s))
             then
              insert(concat(t, choose(s)),
                    onejoin(t,rest(s),match,concat))
             else onejoin(t, rest(s), match, concat)
   end
end;

function
 join(s1   : set(alpha); s2: set(beta);
      match: function (alpha, beta)->boolean;
     concat: function(alpha, beta)-> gamma):
             set(gamma);
body
  case s1 of
  emptyset: emptyset
    others: union(
             onejoin(choose(s1), s2, match, concat),
             join(rest(s1), s2, match, concat))
  end
end;
```

The following gives an example of a call to this join.

```
rtuple = [a: ta; b: tb];
stuple = [a: ta; c: tc];
r: set(rtuple); s: set(stuple);
join(r, s,
     lambda(rt, st)(rt.a = st.a),
     lambda(rt, st)([rt.a, rt.b, st.c]),
```

It is difficult to specialize this join to a relational join in which the **concat** function is not a parameter but determined from the input relations. Synthesizing **concat** entails constructing the output type, since it is just set of the **concat** output type. There are two separate problems to be overcome in synthesizing **concat** functions: the construction of a "flat" tuple type (including an instance constructor function) from two tuple types and the problem of overlapping component names. **Note that the type construction occurs as a result of the compiler encountering a call to join, not as a result of a type definition statement.** This is not a type inference problem, since there is a function to be synthesized as well as a type to be inferred. We are not considering the easy problem of handwriting type and function definitions for any particular use of **join**.

Relational algebra interpreters solve this problem by implicit reflection: they have the capability of run-time access to the schema which contains all the relation type definitions. While this works, it is not in the spirit of static type-checking. The major problem in the context of general purpose database programming languages is orthogonally extending this reflection (run-time access to relation definitions) to all types in the type system. Uniform treatment of all types is a language design principle, and applying this principle to such a reflective capability yields a computational paradigm that is quite complex and in some dissonance with goals of strong typing.

Another approach is to encapsulate the component names in tuple values. One way of doing this is to define a tuple as a set of name value pairs. The set of attribute names paired with domain type names could also be attached to relations and accessed in generic functions. This too would work and does not suffer the problem of requiring uniform treatment in other types, since the attribute names are parts of the values and their manipulation is a part of the type specific behavior. This approach does complicate the implementation of tuples and sets of tuples. Whether this complication is preferable to the complications involved in successfully addressing the problem using general polymorphism features of a type system is not clear. The main question is whether there are general mechanisms that achieve acceptable solutions to this problem while adding little run-time or semantic complexity to a polymorphic type system. We prefer to consider alternatives to a complex tuple and relational value model before treating tuples and relations specially.

The previous approach is not to be confused with using tupling as the concatenation operation [8]. Tupling in a two-way join results in output tuples that are pairs, and access to the components of the input tuples needs to use two selectors since the tuple structure has increased in depth. The following typing is produced by this method.

```
rtuple = [a: ta; b: tb];
stuple = [a: ta; c: tc];
r: set(rtuple); s: set(stuple);
join(r, s, lambda(rt, st)(rt.a = st.a), left, right)
TYPED set([left: rtuple; right: stuple])
```

Yet another approach is taken in Machiavelli. In Machiavelli, "a language in the spirit of ML," functions that access tuples are given a polymorphic typing that achieves a degree of genericity that has been elusive in type inference environments. The type inferred for such functions involves constrained tuple types, and any tuple meeting the constraints are allowed as input and output of these functions. In addition to this sophisticated typing, Machiavelli contains a generalized relational join operation that implicitly accesses the types of input in order to perform its computation. This solution is elegant, but the full implementation and formal reasoning implications of it are not yet clear to us.

3.2 Natural join

For the generic join operation we first gave a full function that required both a match function and a concatenation function, and then considered the problem of synthesizing the concatenation function. The problem with natural join includes those of generic join, but adds two more: synthesizing the match function and eliminating components in the output type.

Natural join is performed by concatenating all matching pairs of tuples from two relations. A match is defined by equality on all the components that have the same name and type. These overlapping components are represented only once in the result of the join. The problem is to define this operation using normal facilities for defining polymorphic, higher order functions. We cannot see how this can be done.

The problem is that the match function depends on component names and their equality (as names). The computation of the output type also needs to access and compare names and types of components. Where the generic join could simply union component names to get the output component names, and deal with clashes in some way, natural join needs to get rid of clashes. Thus, natural join needs a more robust type construction capability even than generic join.

Though natural join requires more in type construction capabilities, it is still amenable to the methods outlined in the previous section for generic join.

3.3 Nesting

In the nested relational model [3] a relation may have a column or group of columns "nested" with values from the remaining columns that are associated with all the nested values. For example, consider the following relation, typed **set([A,B,C,D: number])**.

```
 A   B   C   D
<1,  1,  2,  3>
<2,  5,  3,  4>
<1,  1,  5,  3>
<3,  5,  3,  3>
```

Nesting **C** and **D** columns of this relation produces

```
<1,  1,  {<2, 3>, <5, 3>}>
<2,  5,  {<3, 4>}>
<3,  5,  {<3, 3>}>
```

But what is the type of this result? Does the third component have a name? How does it get it? Again, we are considering the case where there is no predefined type for this result. It is not reasonable to demand that a user write type definitions for all possible joins, projects and nests.

In order to define the operation of nesting, it is convenient to introduce a function that we use as a building block in ADABTPL. The function is the set version of what is often called *fold* in functional languages. The definition of this function, which we call **sfold**, is

```
function sfold(s: set(a);
               f: function(a, extratype)->b;
             acc: function(b, g)->g;
            base: g;
           extra: extratype): g;
body
  if s = emptyset
     then base
     else acc(f(choose(s), extra), sfold(rest(s),f,acc,base,extra));
end;
```

As an illustration of the use of **sfold** we define the aggregate function that sums a column of a relation by

```
sum(s, c) = sfold(s, c, plus, 0)
```

The extra parameter, **extra**, which can be instantiated by zero or any number of arguments, is an additional input to the **f** function in the body. This allows more robustness in the instantiations of **sfold** while avoiding any nesting of variable scopes. All variables inside a function are local. Avoiding nested variable scoping is important for facilitating mechanical reasoning about our functions.[10] [1]

We now define one version of **nest**.

[1] Another way of looking at the extra parameters is to consider them to be a limited form of the function's closure.

```
function nest(s: set(a);
              flat:function(a)->b;
              nst:function(a)->c): set([flatpart:b; nestedpart:set(c)]);
body
sfold(s,
      lambda(selement, extraset)
        ([flat(selement),
          project(select'(extraset,
                          lambda(e, sel)(flat(e)=flat(sel)),
                          selement),
                  nst)]),
      insert,
      emptyset,
      s)
end;
```

The **nest** function takes each element of a set and finds all other elements that have the same value returned for a function, **flat**, the nesting component. The elements whose parts are to be grouped are projected using another function, **nst**. The result of the project is then paired with the result of the function, **flat**, that selects the part of the tuple not to be nested, and this pair is inserted into the result. The same pair will be inserted once for each member of the select, but will be absorbed since insert is a set insert. The type of **nest**'s output is not yet what we would really like when nesting on multiple columns, but we will return to this and get it right at the end of the paper.

The following would nest the **c** and **d** components of a set of tuples, **r**, with **a**, **b**, **c** and **d** columns:

```
nest(r,
     lambda(rtuple)([rtuple.a, rtuple.b]),
     lambda(rtuple)([rtuple.c, rtuple.d]))
```

The result would be typed

```
set([flatpart:[-:ta; -: tb]; nestedpart:set([-:tc; -:td])])
```

where **ta**, **tb**, **tc** and **td** are the types of components **a**, **b**, **c** and **d** in the input. The dashes represent the fact that the components have no names. Such types arise naturally in tuple constants and projections using lambda functions. Values of these types can be used where structurally conforming values are required.

Note the use of extra parameters, in both **sfold** and in **select'**. The version of **select** used here, **select'**, has an extra parameter, employed as in **sfold** to keep all variables scoped locally in function bodies. It is used to make the select predicate use the current element of the input set in gathering the elements to be grouped. The extra parameter to **sfold**, the input set itself, is needed in order to make the selection work over the entire input set each time. Without it, the recursion would shrink the selection to the extent of the recursively shrunken input, **rest(s)**, and produce incorrect results.

From the previous discussion, it should be clear that **nest** is a problematic function to make truly generic. The version defined here is reasonably generic, though in the relational setting it requires the specification of both the column (or columns) which will not be nested and the columns to be nested. The normal nested relational operation only requires the specification of column or columns to be nested; the remaining columns "automatically" form the unnested columns of the nested relation.

The nest operation represents another case of a complex type construction being required when a call to a function is encountered. In this case the complement of a set of column names must be computed. Not only must a mechanism be devised for specifying the construction of types involving a complement of a set of function names (or its equivalent), we must also deal with the semantics of such computations in some manner, possibly by specifying run-time computation semantics. Again, we believe the latter should be avoided if possible due to the complexity that arises because of its higher order nature. (This goes beyond the complexity entailed in statically checked higher order functions.) Defining the semantics of a type system that includes the constructors necessary for dealing with such problems, even if the resulting computational semantics are kept simple, is a problem to be avoided, we believe.

4 A Type Extending Mechanism

More capability is needed in the type algebra outlined above (tuples, sets and parametric polymorphism) in order to capture the semantics of generic join, natural join, nest and unnest. However, it does not seem appropriate to keep adding type constructors to the type definition language in order to accomplish this. The semantics of new constructors would have to be defined and a means of building them into the type checking mechanism would also have to devised. Rather, new operations that examine the fine structure of types and compute parts of type definitions seem to be indicated. These operations could be layered on top of an existing type algebra, computed prior to the ordinary type checking and compilation, and also include side effects of defining new functions. It is to such an algebraic extension that we now turn, and we will address the problems of natural join and nest.

In this section we present a means of increasing the reflection capability of a language without complicating the type system or the computational semantics. The mechanism is a macro-like language extension that permits the definition of functions and types whose genericity exceeds current polymorphic capabilities. Macro definitions in this language can involve access to the type environment established at the time of macro calls and can even change the environment. However, all macro expansion is conceptually performed prior to type checking and all expansions are in the base language. This is how the type system and the computational semantics remain unchanged while more expressive capability is added to the language.

The macro capability involves a set of data structures for holding type definitions as a specification or program is scanned. The state of the type environment is accessible through a set of "macro-time" functions. Macro definitions can include these functions which cause computations to be performed over the type environment whenever macro calls are encountered and expanded.

There are several parts to an ADABTPL database specification: type definitions, function definitions, the database structure definition, database integrity constraints, and transaction definitions. ADABTPL macros need to have the capability of generating input to all of these components of a system specification in addition to the more traditional generation of inline expansions into source code. In order to address the issues raised in this paper, we will only need to use macros for generating inline expansions and function definitions, including the types of function input and output, from function calls.

4.1 Tuple retyping

As a first example, we will define a "simple" function for renaming the components of a tuple and generating a value that is component-wise equal to the input tuple. The reflection required here is twofold. The first allows component names (of the already defined tuple type), which refer to functions and are parts of the type definition, to be input to the (macro) function call. The second part of the reflection lies in the ability to give *parts* of a type definition (the new tuple type) as function inputs. The illusion is that the function has the computational ability to examine type definitions and inputs in order to compute and define new type definitions. The fact is that all such reflection is performed at compile time, allowing us to attain the goals that we set out at the beginning of the paper. We specify the details of compile-time reflection by using macro-time functions, whose names all start with $. If a macro-time function is unnested in other macro-time functions, then its evaluation is ADABTPL code included in the expansion of the macro.

```
macro comprename(tuplevalue:t;
          oldnames: list(identifier);
          newnames: list(identifier))
 ==
$newfunctiondefs

function $newname($f1)(tuplevalue: t):
    [$semicolonrepeat((oldnames newnames),
                      $lambda(oldname, newname)
                         (newname: $componenttype(t, oldname)))];
 body
 [$commarepeat(oldnames, $lambda(oldname)(tuplevalue.oldname))]
 end;

$inline

 $f1(tuplevalue)

endmacro;
```

This definition is for a macro, **comprename**, to be called in places where a function call is appropriate. Inputs to macros can have "meta-types", such as **list(identifier)**. The expansion will include two parts: a new function definition and an inline expansion. The latter will be a call to the new function defined in the first part. The new function name is generated by the macro-time function **$newname** whose input variable, **$f1**, can be used as a meta-variable for the name generated, as for example, in defining the inline expansion.

The function definition has two interesting parts, the definition of the output type and the definition of the body. The output type is generated by the macro-time function **$semicolon-repeat**. This function runs through lists applying a macro-time function, a lambda function in the example, and separates the results by semicolons. It is similar to Lisp *mapcar* except that the output is a linear string of the mapping function results separated by commas, rather than a new list. Multiple lists can be scanned in lock-step, in which case the first argument is a list of lists, e. g., **(oldnames newnames)**. In this example the lock-step feature is used to couple the new component names with the old components' types. The old components' types are generated by the macro-time function **$componenttype(t, oldname)**, which takes a tuple type and a component name and returns the type of the named component.

The inline expansion uses the comma analog to semicolon repeat. In this case only the **old-names** list is scanned.

The following shows an example use of the **comprename** macro. Macro arguments enclosed in parentheses are lists.

```
VAR x: [name: string; age: number];

 comprename(x, (name age), (pername perage))
```

This expands to the new function definition with a system generated name, that we will arbitrarily choose to be **f$1**:

```
function f$1(v: [name: string; age: number]):
                    [pername: string; perage: number];
body [v.name, v.age] end;
```

The inline expansion of the call is simply

```
f$1(x)
```

4.2 Natural join

In this section we will present a macro for natural join. It will only apply to pairs of tuple types with nonempty unique and overlapping component sets. Used otherwise it will generate output that will not type check at the macro-free level. This is not a weakness of macro capabilities, but a simplification for purposes of succinct illustration. One detail to notice is that both **lambda** and **$lambda** appear in the definition. This illustrates the difference between a run-time function (constant in this case), beginning with **lambda**, and a macro-time function, beginning with **$lambda**. The **$lambda** functions, like all macro-time functions, are executed during macro expansion, in this case during the execution of other macro-time functions, **$semicolonrepeat** and **$commarepeat**.

```
macro natjoin(r: set(tuple1type); s: set(tuple2type))
==
$newfunctiondefs
$let runique = $diff($compnamesandtypes(tuple1type),
                     $compnamesandtypes(tuple2type)),
     sunique = $diff($compnamesandtypes(tuple2type),
                     $compnamesandtypes(tuple1type)),
     overlap = $intersect($compnamesandtypes(tuple2type),
                          $compnamesandtypes(tuple1type))
in
function $newname($f1)
  (r: set(tuple1type); s: set(tuple2type)):
     set([$semicolonrepeat(runique, $lambda(runiquecol)(runiquecol));
          $semicolonrepeat(sunique, $lambda(suniquecol)(suniquecol));
          $semicolonrepeat(overlap, $lambda(overcol)(overcol))]);
body
 join(r,
      s,
      \the match function\
      lambda(rt, st)($listprojectfun(overlap, rt) =
                     $listprojectfun(overlap, st)),
      \the concat function\
      lambda(rt, st)
         ($commarepeat(runique,
                       $lambda(runiquecol)(rt.$compname(runiquecol))),
```

```
         $commarepeat(sunique,
                      $lambda(suniquecol)(st.$compname(suniquecol))),
         $commarepeat(overlap,
                      $lambda(overcol)(rt.$compname(overcol)))]))
end;

$inline
$f1(r, s)
endmacro;
```

We have used a number of special macro-time functions in this definition. These are built from a simple set of type definition access functions whose details are not too important. It is important to note that the output from macro expansions does not use these functions, nor does the type checking mechanism for such macro output need to synthesize either complex types or functions. The type reflection has been "compiled" out in the same way that run-time type checking has been avoided by compile-time processing in statically checked languages.

We will illustrate the semantics of the macro-time functions by the following example.

```
rtype = set([a:ta; b: tb; c: tc]);
stype = set([a: ta; d: td]);
VAR r: rtype; s: stype;
natjoin(r, s)

 EXPANSION in function definitions:
 function f$2(r: set([a:ta; b: tb; c: tc]);
              s: set([a: ta; d: td]))
                 : set([b: tb; c: tc; d: td; a: ta]);
 body
  join(r,
       s,
       lambda(rt, st)(rt.a = st.a),
       lambda(rt, st)
         ([rt.b, rt.c,
           st.d,
           rt.a]))
 end;

 EXPANSION inline:
 f$2(r, s)
```

The following outlines the meaning of the macro-time functions introduced in this example:

1. **$let** - not a function, but a way of factoring out complex expressions
2. **$compnamesandtypes(tt)** - a list of component names and types from a tuple type, **tt**, each in source form, e. g., `a: ta`
3. **$diff(l1, l2)** - list containing elements in first list, **l1**, that are not in the second list, **l2**
4. **$intersect(l1, l2)** - list intersection
5. **$listprojectfun(namelist, t)** - function with `t` as a parameter, that projects a tuple using the names taken from a list of tuple component types, **namelist**

6. **$compname(compnameandtype)** - gets the name of a component from a component name and type

These illustrate the kinds of computation over type information that is required to capture the semantics of generic algebraic operations typical of database systems, including those being proposed for object-oriented databases, e. g., in [8].

4.3 Nesting

In the case of natural join we needed to avoid duplicate names in the output tuples and construct a match function based on the overlap in component names of the input tuples. In nesting we need to construct a new tuple type, one of whose components is a set type. We also need to allow the passing of a name for the **set** component. The same features that were useful in capturing natural join can be used to model nesting.

Recall the **nest** function of Section 3.3. The header of the full function was

```
function nest(s: set(a);
              flat:function(a)->b;
              nst:function(a)->c): set([flatpart:b; nestedpart:set(c)]);
```

We would like to call a nest function with a list of the columns to be nested. For example, we want something like the following

```
rtype = set([a:ta; b: tb; c: tc; d: td]);
VAR r: rtype;
nest'(r, (c , d), grp)
```

to result in something equivalent to

```
nest(r, flat, nst)
```

where

```
flat(rtuple) = [rtuple.a, rtuple.b]
nst(rtuple) = [rtuple.c, rtuple.d]
```

but we want the type of the output to be

```
set([a: ta; b: tb; grp: set([c: tc; d: td])])
```

Note that this output type is not an instantiation of the output type of the nest function previously given. The variable length of nesting components is not expressible in the reference language we have been using. In the macro we will use to define a generic nest we will be able to generate the output type just given and synthesize the function that constructs the output values. To do this we will generate the body of individual nest functions by expanding the **flat(selement)** term in the **sfold** call constituting the body of the **nest** definition, i. e.,

```
sfold(s,
      lambda(selement, extraset)
        ([flat(selement),
          project(select(extraset,
                         lambda(e, sel)(flat(e)=flat(sel)),
                         selement),
                  nst)]),
      insert,
      emptyset,
      s)
```

We now give the macro definition for nest in two parts. The first part defines specific **flat** and **nst** functions.

```
macro nest(s: set(tupletype);
    nstnames:list(identifier);
     grpname: identifier)
==
$newfunctiondefs

\The nst function:\
function $newname($nst)
         (t: tupletype): $projidstype(nstnames, tupletype);
body
 [$commarepeat(nstnames, $lambda(nstname)(t.nstname))]
end;

\The flat function:\
$let flatnames = $diff($compnames(tupletype), nstnames)
in
function $newname($flat) (t: tupletype):
           $projidstype(flatnames, tupletype);
body
 [$commarepeat(flatnames, $lambda(flatame)(t.flatname))]
end;
```

The most interesting feature of this is the macro-time function, **$projidstype**. This function builds a tuple type expression from the subset of its second argument's component specifications, the subset being selected by the names in the first argument. For example,

```
$projidstype((a b),[a: ta; b: tb; c: tc; d: td]) = [a: ta; b: tb]
```

We now give the remainder of the **nest** macro definition.

```
\The nest function:\
$let nsttype =   $projidstype(nstnames, tupletype),
     flatnames = $diff($compnames(tupletype), nstnames),
     flattype =  $projidstype(flatnames, tupletype)
in
function $newname($nest)
           (s: set(tupletype);
         flat: function(tupletype)->flattype;
          nst: function(tupletype)->nsttype):
               set([$semicolonrepeat($compnamesandtypes(flattype),
                      $lambda(compnameandtype)(compnameandtype));
                    grpname:set(nsttype)]);
body
sfold(s,
      lambda(selement, extraset)
        ([$repeatcomma(flatnames, $lambda(flname)(selement.flname)),
          project(select(extraset,
                              lambda(e, sel)(flat(e)=flat(sel)),
```

```
                          selement),
                    nst)]),
        insert,
        emptyset,
        s)
end;

$inline
$nest(s, $flat , $nst)
endmacro;
```

In the example in Section 3.3, the function (macro) call would be

```
nest(s, (c d), cdgroup)
```

This would cause the generation of the following for **$flat** and **$nst**

```
function flat$1(rtuple: [a, b, c, d: number]):
  [a: number, b: number];
body [rtuple.a, rtuple.b] end;

function nst$1(rtuple:[a, b, c, d: number]):
  [c: number, d: number];
body [rtuple.c, rtuple.d] end;
```

The following specialized nest function would also be generated.

```
function nest$
           (s: set([a, b, c, d: number]);
         flat: function([a, b, c, d: number])->[a:number; b: number];
          nst: function([a, b, c, d: number])->[c:number; d: number]):
               set([a: number; b: number;
                    cdgroup:set([c: number; d: number])]);
body
sfold(s,
      lambda(selement, extraset)
        ([selement.a, selement.b,
          project(select(extraset,
                        lambda(e, sel)(flat(e)=flat(sel)),
                        selement),
                  nst)]),
      insert,
      emptyset,
      s)
end;
```

Note that the name of the nested part of the output, **cdgroup**, is not sent to the generated function, **nest$**, but appears instead in the output specification of **nest$**'s definition. Note also how the components that will not be nested are placed as the first components of the output tuples, instead of being in a nested tuple component, as in the function defined in Section 3.3. Thus, this function models exactly the nest function of the nested relational model.

While this is somewhat complex, it accurately reflects the amount of semantic loading that is contained in the nested relational nest operation. The computation of the value result is relatively straightforward, as evidenced by the **sfold** call, but its type computation for purposes of static type checking, represented by most of the rest of the macro definition, is complicated by the paucity of information given in a call.

5 Summary

The main purpose of this paper was to examine the issue of polymorphic and reflection requirements stemming from attempts to capture database algebra features in a statically type checked programming language. To this end we explored some of the problems of a few characteristic relational algebra operations. The problems involve the difficulty of generating new types from the types of input arguments, though in some cases, e. g., natural join and nest, functional input arguments also need to be synthesized. We outlined and illustrated a mechanism that addresses these problems in the context of three design strictures. The design constraints are uniformity in the type system, strong and static typing, and simple computational semantics.

Our examples include many macro-time generator functions that perform computations over type information. We have tried to demonstrate that carrying out these computations at (or prior to) compile-time is feasible without compromising the power to model very generic, set-oriented algebras. These functions encapsulate much of the processing done in interpretive query processors, most of which has to do with specializing built-in calculations to the types of inputs. We believe that performing these particular functions at compile-time need not interfere with query optimization efforts. Other applications of our facility are generating type-specific algorithms for testing the various equality relations between complex objects and producing browsers over complex objects.

The language features presented in this paper are designed to be part of the ADABTPL language. The macro facility is currenlty implemented in a kernel language that will become the core of a new ADABTPL implementation. The macro definition language in this paper is only for illustrating ways in which reflection and polymorphism issues can be addressed using macros, and are not the form that will be used in ADABTPL.

6 Acknowledgments

This paper is based on work supported by the National Science Foundation under grants IRI-8606424 and IRI 8822121, and a National Science Foundation Graduate Fellowship (for Adolfo Socorro). Support has also been received under the Office of Naval Research University Research Initiative contract, number N00014-86-K-0764.

References

[1] H. Ait-Kaci. *A lattice-theoretic approach to computations based on a calculus of partially-ordered type structures.* PhD thesis, Computer and Information Science Dept., Univ. of Pennsylvania, Philadelphia, 1984.

[2] L. Fegaras, T. Sheard, and D. Stemple. The ADABTPL Type System. In *Proceedings of the Second International Workshop on Database Programming Languages, Salishan, Oregon,* pages 243–254, 1989.

[3] G. Jaeschke and H. Shek. Remarks on the Algebra of Non First Normal Form Relations. In *Proceedings of the First ACM SIGACT-SIGMOD-SIGART Symposium on Principles of Database Systems, Los Angeles, California,* pages 124–137, 1982.

[4] P. Maes. Concepts and Experiments in Computational Reflection. *Proceedings of the Object-Oriented Programming Systems, Languages and Applications Conference, Orlando, Florida*, pages 147–155, October 1987.

[5] F. Matthes and J. Schmidt. The Type System of DBPL. In *Proceedings of the Second International Workshop on Database Programming Languages, Salishan, Oregon*, pages 255–260, 1989.

[6] R. Morrison, A. Brown, R. Carrick, R. Connor, A. Dearle, and M. P. Atkinson. The Napier Type System. In *Proceedings of the Workshop on Persistent Object Systems: Their Design, Implementation, and Use*, pages 253–269, 1989.

[7] A. Ohori, P. Buneman, and V. Breazu-Tannen. Database Programming in Machiavelli – A Polymorphic Language with Static Type Inference. In *Proceedings of the ACM-SIGMOD International Conference on Management of Data, Portland, Oregon*, pages 46–57, 1989.

[8] M. Shaw and S. Zdonik. An Object-Oriented Query Algebra. In *Proceedings of the Second International Workshop on Database Programming Languages, Salishan, Oregon*, pages 111–119, 1989.

[9] T. Sheard and D. Stemple. The Precise Control of Inheritance and the Inheritance of Theory in the ADABTPL Language. In *Proceedings of the IEEE International Conference on Computer Languages, Miami Beach, Florida*, pages 194–201, 1988.

[10] T. Sheard and D. Stemple. Automatic Verification of Database Transaction Safety. *ACM Transactions on Database Systems*, 12(3), September 1989.

[11] B. C. Smith. Reflection and Semantics in Lisp. *Proceedings of the Eleventh ACM Symposium on Principles of Programming Languages*, pages 23–35, January 1984.

[12] D. Stemple and T. Sheard. Database Theory for Supporting Specification-based Database System Development. In *Proceedings of the Eighth International Conference on Software Engineering*, pages 43–49, 1985.

[13] D. Stemple, A. Socorro, and T. Sheard. Formalizing Objects for Databases using ADABTPL. In K. R. Dittrich, editor, *Advances in Object-Oriented Database Systems*, pages 110–128. Springer-Verlag, 1988. Proceedings of the Second International Workshop on Object-Oriented Database Systems, Bad Muenster am Stein-Ebernburg, Germany.

SET OPERATIONS IN A DATA MODEL SUPPORTING COMPLEX OBJECTS

Elke A. Rundensteiner and Lubomir Bic

Information and Computer Science Department
University of California, Irvine
Irvine, CA 92717
Email: rundenst@ICS.UCI.EDU

Abstract

Class creation by set operations has largely been ignored in the literature. Precise semantics of set operations on complex objects require a clear distinction between the dual notions of a set and a type, both of which are present in a class. Our paper fills this gap by presenting a framework for executing set-theoretic operations on the class construct. The proposed set operations determine both the type description of the derived class as well as its set membership. For the former, we develop inheritance rules for property characteristics such as single- versus multi-valued and required versus optional. For the later, we borrow the object identity concept from data modeling research. Our framework allows for property inheritance among classes that are not necessarily is-a related.

1 Introduction

Most data models [1, 5, 4, 7] support a rich *class definition* facility based on restricting inherited properties, that is, special forms of the specialization and generalization abstractions [7, 4]. These derivations are *type-oriented* [2], i.e., they perform some operation on the type aspect of a class which then automatically implies a particular set relationship between the original and the derived class. On the other hand, the potential of set operations has largely been unexplored. The reason for that is that, while set operations on simple elements are well understood, precise semantics for set operations on complex objects have not yet been developed. Such definitions require a clear distinction between the dual notion of a class, which represents a *set* and also provides a *type* description. This distinction is usually blurred in the literature.

This paper presents a framework for executing set-theoretic operations on complex objects. We consider the four most common set operations – union, intersection, difference, and symmetric difference. Our approach is to extend set theory to the world of classes while preserving as much as possible of the well-known set-theoretic semantics. We borrow the concept of object identity from data modeling research for defining the effect of a set operation on the membership of a class. The type description of the resulting class is specified. For this, we design rules that describe how property characteristics are to be inherited through these set operations. The rules accommodate property characteristics such as multi-valued versus single-valued and required versus optional. For a more thorough discussion of our framework see [9].

The paper is organized as follows. Section 2 familiarizes the reader with conceptual data model terminology. In Section 3 we present definitions for set operations as well as rules for the inheritance of properties. Throughout this section we give pragmatic examples that support the usefulness of our framework. Some results are presented in Section 4. Related research is discussed in Section 5, whereas conclusions are presented in Section 6.

2 Types versus Sets

A key to the solution of well-defined set operations on complex objects is the explicit distinction between the type and set aspect of a class. Set operations on collections of untyped elements (mathematical sets) are well understood. Thus we have to study the effect of set operations on the type description of a class while preserving the semantics of the class's set notion.

2.1 Entities and Classes

An entity may be a simple or a complex object. An entity always consists of an identity and a state [6]. The identity is a globally unique reference which is not visible to the user. Each time a new entity is created, an identity is assigned to it by the system. In this paper, we use the entity's identifier as entity reference. To indicate that we refer to the identifier as such rather than the entity itself, we use the notation <entity reference>.id. The state of an entity corresponds to a collection of one or more property names and associated values. We refer to the properties (attributes) of an entity by < *property name* > (< *entity reference* >).

A class is formed by grouping together a collection of similar entities. The concept of a class serves a dual purpose: it does not only represents a collection of entities but it also provides a type description for all its members. The term type refers to the collection of properties associated with all entities that belong to that class. The set of properties of a class is specified by < *property name* >:< *domain* > [< *characteristics* >]. The domain can be any user-defined class of the model or a predefined base domain like an integer range. Characteristics are general descriptions of properties, for instance, whether a given property is required or optional. (More on this is presented later in this section.)

The following notation is used to refer to the properties of a class < *class name* > . < *property name* >. We refer to the domain of a property by **domain**(< *class name* > . < *property name* >). Given the previous example, we refer to the Name property of the class Person by Person.Name and we refer to the domain of this property by **domain**(Person.Name). We use the following predicate to test whether a property is defined for a class or not < *class name* > . < *property name* > ?. For instance, the predicate Person.Name? returns true if the Name property is defined for the class Person and false otherwise.

We use the set-theoretic predicate 'e ∈ C' to denote that the entity e is an *instance-of* the class C. The predicate 'e ∈ C' is solely based on the object identity of e [6]. An entity may take on values for different sets of properties when viewed as member of different classes. To refer to the properties of an entity as the participant in a particular class we use the following notation < *property name* > (< *entity reference* > **as** < *class name* >). For example, we assign the value $4,000 to the property Salary of the entity Jack in class Employee by "Salary(Jack **as** Employee) := $4,000".

2.2 Characteristics of Properties

Most object-oriented and semantic data models [4, 5] associate some or all of the following characteristics with each class property: (1) required versus optional; (2) identifying versus non-identifying; and (3) single- versus multi-valued.

If an entity is member of a class then it takes on some values (not equal 'undefined') for all properties defined for that class. The first characteristic distinguishes between required (mandatory) and non-required (optional) properties. Each entity of a class must have a value for its required properties, i.e., a value not equal 'unknown'. It may or may not have a value for the optional ones, i.e., its value may be 'unknown'. Note that if a property is not defined for a class, then the value of that property would be 'undefined', meaning not applicable, instead of 'unknown'.

The identifying characteristic corresponds to the concept of a key in relational database theory. It is not as important in advanced data models where the underlying concept of object identities allows entities to be identified independently of their values. It can however still be used by human users who wish to maintain their own unique values as entity references.

A property is defined to be either single- or multi-valued independent of the class for which it is initially introduced. If a property p is single-valued then for any entity e of class C, p(e **as** C) has to be an element of **domain**(C.p) or be unknown. If a property p is multi-valued then for any entity e of class C, p(e **as** C) is a subset of **domain**(C.p) or is unknown.

2.3 Class Relationships

Most existing systems ignore the set/type duality of the class construct and hence cannot provide clean semantics for set operations on classes. In the following, we disambiguate the meaning of class relationships which in the literature are generally referred to as subclass/superclass or "is-a" relationships by distinguishing between *subset/superset* and *subtype/supertype relationships.*

Definition 1 *The following set relationships can exist between two classes C1 and C2:*

1. *C1 is a* **subset** *of C2, denoted by* $C1 \subseteq C2$*, which is defined by* $C1 \subseteq C2 := (\forall\, e1)\ (\, e1 \in C1)\ ((\exists\ e2 \in C2)\ (e1.id = e2.id))$.
2. *C1 is a* **strict subset** *of C2, denoted by* $C1 \subset C2$*, as defined by* $C1 \subset C2 \iff (C1 \subseteq C2$ *and* $((\exists\ e)\ (e \in C2$ *and* $NOT(\ e \in C1))))$.
3. *C1 is* **set equivalent** *to C2, denoted by* $C1 \equiv^s C2$*, as defined by* $C1 \equiv^s C2 \iff (C1 \subseteq C2$ *and* $C2 \subseteq C1)$
4. *C1 is* **set inequivalent** *(set incompatible) with C2, denoted by* $C1 \not\equiv^s C2$*, as defined by* $C1 \not\equiv^s C2 \iff (\ NOT(C1 \subseteq C2)$ *and* $NOT(C2 \subseteq C1))$.

This definition is based strictly on object identity. It disregards the type description associated with the respective classes. Hence, the class C1 may have *more*, *less*, or *the same* number of attributes as C2.

Definition 2 *The following type relationships can exist between two classes C1 and C2:*

1. *C1 is a* **subtype** *of C2, denoted by* $C1 \preceq C2$*, as defined by* $C1 \preceq C2 := (\forall\ p)\ (\ C2.p?{=}true \Longrightarrow C1.p?{=}true\ )$ *and (* $\mathbf{domain}(C1.p) \subseteq \mathbf{domain}(C2.p)$ *).*
2. *C1 is a* **strict subtype** *of C2, denoted by* $C1 \prec C2$*, as defined by* $C1 \prec C2, \iff (\ C1 \preceq C2$ *and* $((\exists\ p)\ (\ C2.p?{=}true$ *and* $C1.p?{=}true$ *and (* $\mathbf{domain}(C1.p) \subset \mathbf{domain}(C2.p)))$ *or* $((\exists\ p)\ (\ C1.p?{=}true$ *and* $NOT(C2.p?{=}true)))))$.
3. *C1 being* **type equivalent** *to C2, denoted by* $C1 \equiv^t C2$*, is defined by* $C1 \equiv^t C2 \iff (C1 \preceq C2$ *and* $C2 \preceq C1)$.
4. *C1 is* **type inequivalent** *(type incompatible) with C2, denoted by* $C1 \not\equiv^t C2$*, which is defined by* $C1 \not\equiv^t C2 \iff (\ NOT(C1 \preceq C2)$ *and* $NOT(C2 \preceq C1))$.

The type relation does not make any assumptions about the corresponding class memberships. Hence, theoretically, a subtype could have *more, less,* or *the same* number of elements as its supertype, or their instances may even be totally unrelated.

The term *is-a* relationship has been misused to mean many different things [3]. We can now define the is-a relationship in terms of the two just defined class relationships.

Definition 3 *C1 is-a C2* $\Longleftrightarrow$ *C1* $\preceq$ *C2 and C1* $\subseteq$ *C2.*

Informally, we say that C1 is-a C2 if (1) every instance of C1 is an instance of C2 (the subset relationship) and (2) every property defined for C2 is also defined for C1 (the type relationship) [7]. If C1 is-a C2 and <C2.p? = true> and <**domain**(C2.p) := C2'> then C1 has the same property p, i.e., <C1.p? = true>, and < **domain**(C1.p) := C1'> with C1' is-a C2'.

3 Set Operations in Conceptual Data Models

3.1 Introduction

This section discusses how the set operations can be applied in conceptual data models. As mentioned earlier, set operations in conventional set theory are well understood, since the underlying objects are simple, i.e., are not typed and don't have any associated properties. When dealing with conceptual data models, typing becomes an issue. Determinating the type description of classes derived by set operations is related to the issue of property inheritance. The difference being that the inheritance of properties usually takes place between *two* classes while set operations always deal with three classes. In short, set operations are similar to the problem of multiple inheritance. The literature assumes that the inheritance of properties takes place between classes which stand in an is-a relationship to one another; this is not necessarily the case for classes derived by set operations. Below, we address the property inheritance problem by determining what characteristics properties of a derived class should have – once inherited. This leads to the development of general rules for property inheritance.

We assume the following naming convention: *The name of a property is prefixed by the name of the class for which it is initially defined.* Consequently, if a property is inherited from another class then its property name is prefixed by the name of the class in which it was originally defined. This convention guarantees the uniqueness of property values. Namely, if two classes define the same single-valued property, then an entity that appears in both cannot have two distinct values for it. The property value is either unknown in one of them or the two values are identical. The following two definitions are given to simplify the remainder of this section.

Definition 4 *Let p be a property. Let e be a member of C1 and/or C2. Then the operation COMBINE is defined as follows. If p is a single-valued property we have*

COMBINE(p(e **as** *C1), p(e* **as** *C2)) :=*

$$\begin{cases} \text{p(e \textbf{as} C1)} & \text{if } e \in \text{C1 and C1.p? and p(e \textbf{as} C1)} \neq \text{unknown} \\ \text{p(e \textbf{as} C2)} & \text{if } e \in \text{C2 and C2.p? and p(e \textbf{as} C2)} \neq \text{unknown} \\ \text{unknown} & \text{otherwise} \end{cases}$$

If p is a multi-valued property then COMBINE is defined as follows

COMBINE(p(e **as** *C1), p(e* **as** *C2)) :=*

$$
\begin{cases}
\text{p(e \textbf{as} C1)} \cup \text{p(e \textbf{as} C2)} & \text{if e} \in \text{C1 and C1.p? and p(e \textbf{as} C1)} \neq \text{unknown and} \\
 & \text{e} \in \text{C2 and C2.p? and p(e \textbf{as} C2)} \neq \text{unknown} \\
\text{p(e \textbf{as} C1)} & \text{if e} \in \text{C1 and C1.p? and p(e \textbf{as} C1)} \neq \text{unknown and} \\
 & \text{(e} \notin \text{C2 or NOT(C2.p?) or p(e \textbf{as} C2)} = \text{unknown)} \\
\text{p(e \textbf{as} C2)} & \text{if e} \in \text{C2 and C2.p? and p(e \textbf{as} C2)} \neq \text{unknown and} \\
 & \text{(e} \notin \text{C1 or NOT(C1.p?) or p(e \textbf{as} C1)} = \text{unknown)} \\
\text{unknown} & \text{otherwise}
\end{cases}
$$

It is understood that the union operation ($\cup$*) removes all duplicate values.*

The previous definition describes how a value is to be combined if it is inherited from more than one source - assuming the naming convention described in Section 2.2. Next, operations on type descriptions are introduced.

Definition 5 *Let C1 and C2 be two classes. Then, C1* $\bigvee$ *C2 := { p | C1.p? or C2.p? }. And, C1* $\bigwedge$ *C2 := { p | C1.p? and C2.p? }.*

Intuitively, C1 $\bigvee$ C2 denotes the collection of all properties defined for either C1 or C2. C1 $\bigwedge$ C2, on the other hand, consists of all properties common to the type description of both classes. Therefore we refer to the first operation as *collecting* and to the second as *extracting.*

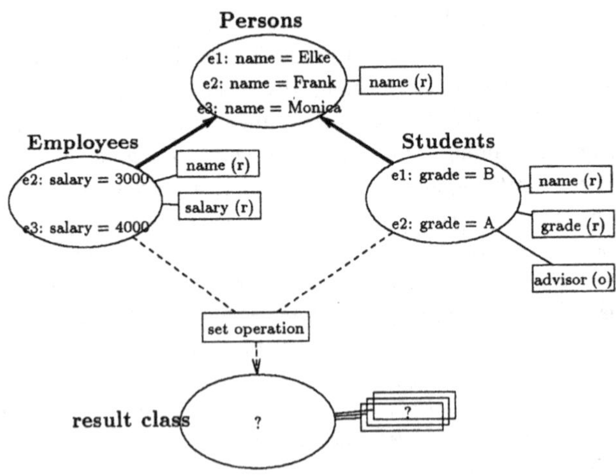

Figure 1: Template of a Derived Class.

In Figure 1 we present a template of a simple conceptual data model. It will be used for subsequent examples to show the result of the inherited type description as well as the membership of the derived class for each set operation. The examples are given to show the usefulness of the proposed procedures for the propagation of characteristics.

Example 1 *Figure 1 depicts the classes Employees and Students. Both classes are subclasses (by is-a relationship) of the Person class, which is depicted by solid dark arrows. The class Employees has two required properties, the inherited property Name and the newly defined property Salary. The class Students has two required and one optional property, namely, the inherited property Name, and the newly defined properties Grade and Advisor. The class containing the question mark represents the result of performing a set operation on the classes Employees and Students. Subsequent examples will instantiate the generic set operation to one of the possible four choices and show the corresponding result class.*

3.2 Difference Operations

We propose two types of difference operations. The first is derived automatically by the system while the second is determined by the user by specifying the desired type description. The property values of all entities included in the newly derived class will automatically be calculated once the type description of the new class has been established. This is correct for all set-theoretic operations and parallels the situation of set operations in conventional set theory.

Definition 6 *Let P be a collection of properties defined by* $P := \{p \mid C1.p? = true\}$. *The* **(automatic) difference** *of C1 with respect to C2, denoted by* $C1 \dot{-} C2$, *is defined by*

$C1 \dot{-} C2 := \{e \mid e \in C1 \text{ and } e \notin C2\}$

with $(\forall p \in P)\ ((C1 \dot{-} C2).p? := true)$

and $(\forall e \in C1 \dot{-} C2)\ (\forall p \in P)\ (p(e \textbf{ as } C1 \dot{-} C2) := p(e \textbf{ as } C1))$.

Definition 7 *Let P be as in the previous definition. The* **user-specified difference** *operation of C1 with respect to C2, denoted by* $C1 \ddot{-} C2$, *is specified by giving some* $Q \subseteq P$. *It is defined like the automatic difference except for replacing P with Q.*

There is an important difference between the just presented user-specified set operation and the user-specifiable subclass mechanism commonly found in the literature [4]. Here, the user has to specify the type description once - namely during the creation of the derived class. Thereafter, the class can be instantiated automatically by the system according to the semantics of the applied set difference operation. This contrasts with the user-specified subclass mechanism where the user has to explicitly insert all entities into the class.

Given these set definitions, we now study rules for the inheritance of property characteristics. We distinguish between single- and multi-valued properties. As described in Section 2.2, this characteristic once defined is fixed throughout the data model and thus does not change when a property is inherited by another class.

The second characteristic determines whether a property is identifying or not. The following simple rule is sufficient to describe the propagation of this characteristic from the base classes to the derived class.

Rule 1 *Let P1 and P2 be sets of identifying properties for C1 and C2, respectively. If C is a class resulting from the difference of C1 relative to C2 as defined by Definitions 6 and 7 then P1 will be identifying for C if inherited.*

C1	C2	C1 − C2
optional	-	optional
required	-	required
-	optional	-
-	required	-
optional	required	optional
required	optional	required
optional	optional	optional
required	required	required

Figure 2: Inheritance of Property Characteristics for a Derived Difference Class.

The previous rule is self-explanatory. The result class will contain only entities from the class C1. Hence if a set of properties P1 is sufficient to distinguish between all entities of C1 then it will also be sufficient to distinguish between the ones of a subset of C1, i.e., the difference class. Next we address the third characteristic which determines whether a property is required or non-required for a class.

Rule 2 *The table in Figure 2 lists the propagation rules for the inheritance of the required/optional characteristics of a class derived by a difference operation.*

The table is to be read as follows. The symbol "required" refers to a required property, "optional" refers to a not required (but existing) property, and "-" means that the particular property is not defined for that class. The third column gives the characteristic of the inherited property in the derived class C1 $\tilde{-}$ C2 or C1 $\dot{-}$ C2, based on the characteristics of the corresponding property in C1 and C2 (first and second column). The difference operations are not symmetric and hence the figure contains entries for all possible combinations. Every member of a difference class is also a member of C1. Therefore, all properties of C1 as well as their characteristics can be directly inherited by C1 $\tilde{-}$ C2 or C1 $\dot{-}$ C2. This explains why the third column of the table in Figure 2 is an exact copy of the first column.

Example 2 *The difference operation C1 $\dot{-}$ C2 defined in Definition 6 is applied to the conceptual data model shown in Figure 1. The result, shown in Figure 3, is a class that consists of all Persons who are Employees but not Students. Hence, all its elements are also members of the Employees class. Consequently, properties required for the Employees class , in this case, Name and Salary, are also required for the difference class. Properties of the Students class are not relevant to the resulting class since no entity of the result class would have any value for them. Hence, we choose the difference operation C1 $\dot{-}$ C2 as defined in Definition 6 over the operation C1 $\tilde{-}$ C2.*

3.3 Union Operations

Next, we distinguish three types of union operations. The type descriptions of first two are derived automatically by the system, whereas the third one is determined by the user.

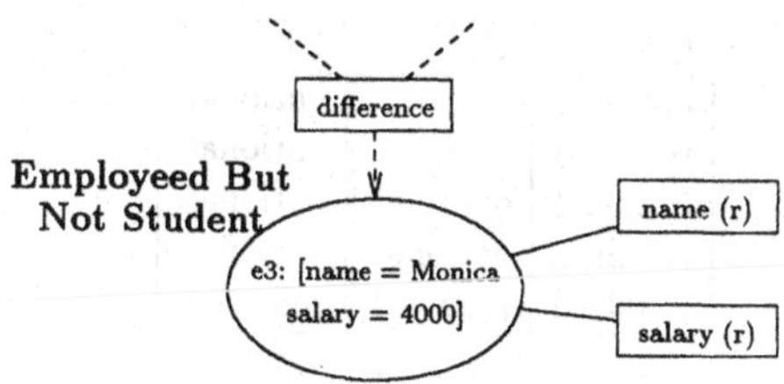

Figure 3: Derived Class Created by a Difference Operation.

Definition 8 *Let P be C1 $\bigvee$ C2. The first union operation of C1 and C2, denoted by C1 $\breve{\cup}$ C2, is called the* **collecting union**. *It is defined by*

$C1 \breve{\cup} C2 := \{e | e \in C2 \text{ or } e \in C2 \text{ or both}\}$

with $(\forall p \in P)\ ((C1 \breve{\cup} C2).p? := true)$

and $(\forall e \in C1 \breve{\cup} C2)\ (\forall p \in P)\ (p(e \textbf{ as } C1 \breve{\cup} C2) := COMBINE(p(e \textbf{ as } C1), p(e \textbf{ as } C2)))$.

Definition 9 *The second type of union operation of C1 and C2, denoted by C1 $\hat{\cup}$ C2, is called the* **extracting union**. *The extracting union is defined as in the previous definition except for replacing P with P := C1 $\bigwedge$ C2.*

Definition 10 *The user-specified union operation of C1 and C2, denoted by C1 $\tilde{\cup}$ C2, is defined by specifying a collection of properties Q with Q $\subseteq$ C1 $\bigvee$ C2. The definition of C1 $\tilde{\cup}$ C2 is equivalent to the one in Definition 8 with Q substituted for the symbol P.*

Note here that $\tilde{\cup}$ contains the other two union operations as special cases, since the user could choose the properties in the two cases as automatically derived by the system for $\breve{\cup}$ or $\hat{\cup}$.

Next, we study the general rules for property inheritance. As described in Section 2.2, the data model distinguishes between single- and multi-valued properties. This characteristic does not change when a property is inherited. Consequently, the rule of inheritance for this characteristic is trivial. The following rule describes the propagation of the identifying characteristic from the base classes to the derived class.

Rule 3 *Let P1 be a set of identifying properties for C1 and P2 a set of identifying properties for C2. If C is a class resulting from the union of C1 and C2 (any of the three union types) then P1 together with P2 will be identifying for C if both are inherited.*

The rule can best be explained with an example. Assume a situation similar to Figure 1 where the entities of the class Students are identified by the property Student-Id and the Employee entities by the property Employee-Id. Then, in the collection of Employees and Students each individual Student entity can be distinguished from all other Student entities by its Student-Id and from Employees entities by not having an Employee-Id. The converse is true for all Employee entities. If both properties are not inherited then some of the entities in the derived class may be indistinguishable to the user but the system is still able to distinguish them based on their object identities [6].

Rule 4 *The table in Figure 4 lists the general inheritance rules for the required/optional characteristic when deriving a class by one of the three union operations.*

C1	C2	C1 ∪ C2
optional	-	optional
required	-	optional
optional	optional	optional
required	optional	optional
required	required	required

Figure 4: Inheritance of Property Characteristics for a Derived Union Class.

Note that a property can only be required if it has been required for both base classes. In all other cases, it cannot be guaranteed that all entities will take on a value for a property and hence they can only be asserted as optional. Next, an example is given to demonstrate this inheritance mechanism.

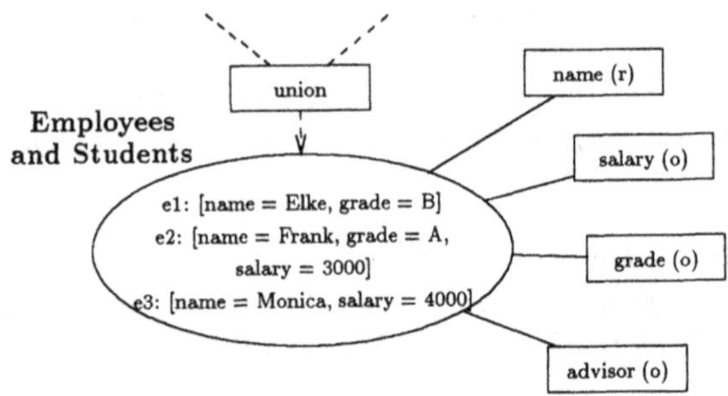

Figure 5: Derived Class Created by a Union Operation

Example 3 *The union operation C1 $\dot{\cup}$ C2 defined in Definition 8 has been applied to the situation in Figure 1; the result is shown in Figure 5. The new class consists of all those elements which were members of either the Employees or the Students class. Properties that were required for both classes can still be required for the resulting class, e.g., the inherited property Name. However, properties that were required for only one of these two classes can no longer be required. They can at best be optional in the new class. This is so since, for example, the person e1 does not have a value for the Salary property, even though the Salary property is required for the Employee class. The optional attributes must stay optional.*

3.4 Intersection Operations

Next we propose three types of intersection operations similar to the three unions. The first two again are automatically derived by the system. The third one is user-specified. The latter contains the other two as special cases.

Definition 11 *Let P be C1 $\vee$ C2. The intersection of C1 and C2, denoted by C1 $\hat{\cap}$ C2, is called the* **collecting intersection.** *It is defined by*

$C1 \hat{\cap} C2 := \{e | e \in C2 \text{ and } e \in C2\}$ *with* $(\forall p \in P)\ ((C1 \hat{\cap} C2).p? := true)$

and $(\forall e \in C1 \hat{\cap} C2)\ (\forall p \in P)\ (p(e \text{ as } C1 \hat{\cap} C2) := COMBINE(p(e \text{ as } C1), p(e \text{ as } C2)).$

Recall that if a property p is defined for both classes C1 and C2 then an entity which takes on values for p in both classes will have the same value in both cases.

Definition 12 *Let P now be C1 $\bigwedge$ C2. The second type of intersection of C1 and C2, denoted by C1 $\hat{\cap}$ C2, is defined by as in Definition 11 with the new meaning for P. It is called the* **extracting intersection.**

Definition 13 *The* **user-specified intersection** *operation of C1 and C2, denoted by C1 $\tilde{\cap}$ C2, is defined by specifying a collection of properties Q with Q $\subseteq$ C1 $\bigvee$ C2. The definition of C1 $\tilde{\cap}$ C2 is equivalent to the one in Definition 11 with Q substituted for the symbol P.*

The effect of the intersection operation on the characteristics of properties is evaluated next. Again, the single- and multi-valued property is fixed throughout the data model and therefore does not change when a property is inherited (Section 2.2). The identifying characteristic can be propagated from the base classes to the derived class by the following rule:

Rule 5 *Let P1 and P2 be sets of identifying properties for C1 and C2, respectively. If C is a class resulting from any of the three just defined intersection operations of C1 and C2 then P1 or P2 will be identifying for C if inherited.*

Again, the rule is self-explanatory. The result class will be a subset of both C1 and C2. Thus, if P1 is sufficient to distinguish between the entities of C1 then it is sufficient to uniquely identify them when they appear in a subset of C1, i.e., the derived class. The same is true for P2.

Rule 6 *Figure 6 gives the inheritance rules for the required/optional characteristic of properties defined for an intersection class.*

C1	C2	C1 ∩ C2
optional	-	optional
required	-	required
optional	optional	optional
required	optional	required
required	required	required

Figure 6: Property Inheritance of a Derived Intersection Class.

To summarize, a property can be required for the result class if and only if it is defined for both base classes and if it is required for at least one of them. In all other cases, the property can only be asserted to be optional. The following example uses the previous definition for property inheritance.

Example 4 *In Figure 7 the intersection operation C1 $\hat{\cap}$ C2 of Definition 12 has been applied to the situation in Figure 1. The new class consists of all Persons who are Employees and Students at the same time. Properties that were required for either of the two classes are also required for the resulting class, i.e., the inherited properties Name, Salary and Grade. This is a sensible rule since all members of the intersection class will be guaranteed to take on values for these properties. The optional attribute Advisor can still be optional.*

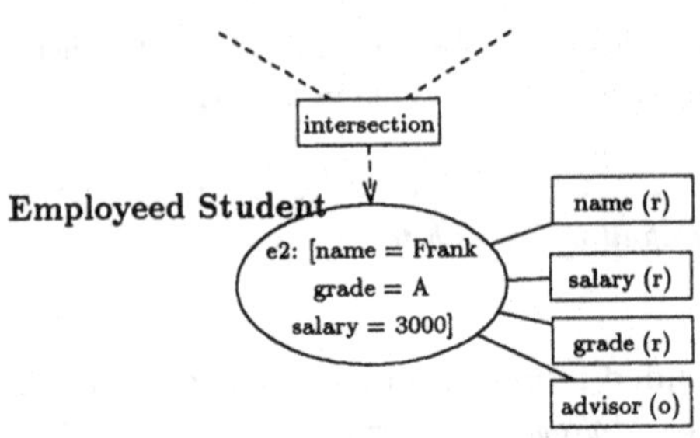

Figure 7: Derived Class Created by an Intersection Operation

3.5 Symmetric Difference Operations

Next we introduce three types of symmetric difference operations. In all three cases, the entities of the result class will come from exactly one of the two base classes. Consequently, no merging of properties by means of the COMBINE operation is needed - not even for multi-valued properties.

Definition 14 *Let P be C1* $\bigvee$ *C2. The symmetric difference of C1 and C2, C1* $\check{\Delta}$ *C2, is called the* **collecting symmetric difference**. *It is defined by*

$C1 \check{\Delta} C2 := \{e | e \in C1 \text{ or } e \in C2 \text{ but not both } \}$
with $(\forall\, p \in P)\ (\ (C1 \check{\Delta} C2).p? := true)$ *and* $(\forall\, e \in C1 \check{\Delta} C2)\ (\forall\, p \in P\ )$
$((e \in C1 \text{ and } C1.p? \Longrightarrow p(e \textbf{ as } C1 \check{\Delta} C2) := p(e \textbf{ as } C1)\ ) \text{ and}$
$(e \in C2 \text{ and } C2.p? \Longrightarrow p(e \textbf{ as } C1 \check{\Delta} C2) := p(e \textbf{ as } C2)\ ) \text{ and}$
$(((e \in C1 \text{ and } NOT(C1.p?)) \text{ or } (e \in C2 \text{ and } NOT(C2.p?))) \Longrightarrow p(e \textbf{ as } C1 \check{\Delta} C2) := unknown).$

Note that in the previous definition for all entities e of the result class at most one of the three predicates will be true since either e ∈ C1 or e ∈ C2 but not both.

Definition 15 *Let P be C1* $\bigwedge$ *C2. The symmetric difference of C1 and C2, C1* $\hat{\Delta}$ *C2, is called* **extracting**. *It is defined by*

$C1 \hat{\Delta} C2 := \{e | e \in C1 \text{ or } e \in C2 \text{ but not both } \} \text{ with } (\forall\, p \in P)\ (\ (C1 \hat{\Delta} C2).p? := true)$
and $(\forall\, e \in C1 \hat{\Delta} C2)\ (\forall\, p \in P\ )$
$((e \in C1 \Longrightarrow p(e \textbf{ as } C1 \hat{\Delta} C2) := p(e \textbf{ as } C1)\ ) \text{ and}$
$(e \in C2 \Longrightarrow p(e \textbf{ as } C1 \hat{\Delta} C2) := p(e \textbf{ as } C2)\ )\ ).$

In the previous definition, the properties in P are defined for both C1 and C2 and hence do not have to be tested.

Definition 16 *The* **user-specified symmetric difference** *operation of C1 and C2, denoted by C1* $\tilde{\Delta}$ *C2, is defined by specifying a collection of properties Q with* $Q \subseteq C1 \bigvee C2$. *The definition of C1* $\tilde{\Delta}$ *C2 is equivalent to the one in Definition 14 with the symbol P replaced by Q.*

For the same reasons mentioned earlier, the user-specified symmetric difference operation contains the other two automatic symmetric difference operations as special cases.

As described in Section 2.2, the single- and multi-valued property characteristic is fixed throughout the data model. Therefore, when a property is inherited it simply keeps its characteristic.

The second type of characteristic is whether a property is identifying or not. The following rule is sufficient to describe the propagation of this characteristic from the base classes to the derived class.

Rule 7 *Let P1 and P2 be sets of identifying properties for C1 and C2, respectively. If C is a class resulting from a symmetric difference of C1 and C2, then P1 together with P2 will be identifying for C if both are inherited by C.*

The rule of inheritance described in the previous rule can be justified by an argument similar to the one given for the union operation (rule 5).

C1	C2	C1 △ C2
optional	-	optional
required	-	optional
optional	optional	optional
required	optional	optional
required	required	required

Figure 8: Inheritance of Property Characteristics for a Derived Symmetric Difference Class.

Rule 8 *The inheritance of property characteristics for a derived symmetric difference class is defined by the rules described in the table of Figure 8.*

Again, a property can only be required in the new class if it has been required for both classes. In all other cases, it cannot be guaranteed that all entities of the result class will take on values for these properties.

Example 5 *The symmetric difference operation C1 $\dot{\triangle}$ C2 of Definition 14 is used in Figure 9. It results in a derived class that consists of all Persons who are Employees but not Students or Students but not Employees. Only properties which were required for both classes are required by rule 8. All others are optional. This is so since members of the result class will be exactly of one of the two types. For instance, the Salary property required for the entities of the Employees class could not be required in the result class since Student members of the latter would not have a value for it, and vice versa.*

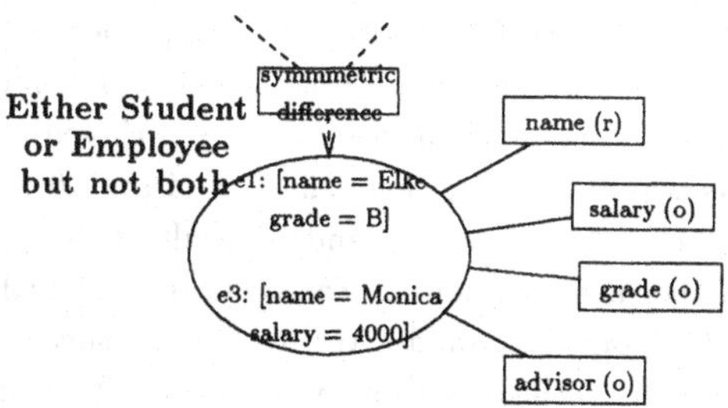

Figure 9: Derived Class Created by a Symmetric Difference Operation.

4 Set Operations and Class Relationships

In this section we investigate the consequences of performing a set operation: both, sets and types of the new and old classes obey certain relationships as shown below. We distinguish between several cases of user-specified set operations depending on the choice of the desired type description. The different choices for the type description of the resulting class, denoted by Q in Definitions 10, 13, and 16, result in distinct class relationships. Let $\check{P} = C1 \vee C2$ and $\hat{P} = C1 \wedge C2$. Let $P1 = \{p|C1.p?\}$ and $P2 = \{p|C2.p?\}$. Recall that always $Q \subseteq \check{P}$. Then the choices for Q are:

- case 1: $P1 \subseteq Q$ and $P2 \subseteq Q$ [$\Longrightarrow \check{P} = Q$];
- case 2: $P1 \subseteq Q$ and NOT($P2 \subseteq Q$);
- case 3: $P1 \supseteq Q$ and NOT($P2 \supseteq Q$);
- case 4: $P1 \supseteq Q$ and $P2 \supseteq Q$ [$\Longrightarrow Q \subseteq \hat{P}$];
- case 5: $P1 \not\equiv^{t} Q$ and $P2 \not\equiv^{t} Q$.

Case 1 models the situation of the first type of an automatic set operation (the collecting type) which collects all properties of C1 and C2. In case 2, Q contains all properties defined for C1 and possibly some (but not all) properties defined for C2. The three set operations (excluding the difference operation) are symmetric and hence the analogous situation obtained by exchanging C1 and C2 is also covered by case 2. Q of case 3 contains a subset of P1 and at least one of its elements is not in P2. Again, the converse situation is also included in this case, since C1 and C2 can by exchanged. Case 4 includes $Q = \hat{P}$, i.e., the second type of an automatic set operation which extracts all properties common to both C1 and C2 as a special case. Case 5 illustrates the case where there is no set relationship between P1 and Q (and P2 and Q). In order for that to occur, Q must contain some (but not all) elements of P1 which are not in P2, and some (but not all) elements of P2 which are not in P1.

In Figure 10 we list the set and type relationships which hold between the two classes C1 and C2 and the class derived by applying a set operation on them. We use the symbol R as abbreviation for the result class of the set operation. In the fifth column, an asterisk indicates cases that contradict the requirements of an "is-a" relationship. In other words, each such row models a situation that could not appear in a database built by applying only specialization and generalization operations. Our framework, on the other hand, allows for the inheritance of properties between classes which are not "is-a" related. We know of no other data model that has this capability.

This table shows clearly why the union definition of row 4 was chosen over the one in row 3 in the literature. Similarly, it shows why the intersection definition of row 10 was chosen over the one in row 11 in the literature. The reason is that rows 4 and 10 result in "is-a" relationships whereas the others don't. No violation of the "is-a" relationship can occur in the fourth block of Figure 10 since no type relationships hold. The complexity and diversity of the resulting relationships may partly be the reason for the lack of "user-specified" set operations in the literature. We wish to emphasize that the use of set operations for class creation results in class relationships that would not exist in a database schema build solely by specialization and generalization abstractions.

#	set operation	set relationships	type relationships	
1	$R = C1 - C2$	$R \subseteq C1$ and $R \not\equiv^s C2$	$R \equiv^t C1$ and $R \equiv^t C2$	
2	$R = C1 \tilde{-} C2$	$R \subseteq C1$ and $R \not\equiv^s C2$	$R \succeq C1$ and $R \succeq C2$	
3	$R = C1 \check{\cup} C2$	$R \supseteq C1$ and $R \supseteq C2$	$R \preceq C1$ and $R \preceq C2$	*
4	$R = C1 \hat{\cup} C2$	$R \supseteq C1$ and $R \supseteq C2$	$R \succeq C1$ and $R \succeq C2$	
5	$R = C1 \tilde{\cup} C2$	$R \supseteq C1$ and $R \supseteq C2$	case 1: $R \preceq C1$ and $R \preceq C2$	*
6		" "	case 2: $R \preceq C1$ and $R \not\equiv^t C2$	*
7		" "	case 3: $R \succeq C1$ and $R \not\equiv^t C2$	
8		" "	case 4: $R \succeq C1$ and $R \succeq C2$	
9		" "	case 5: $R \not\equiv^t C1$ and $R \not\equiv^t C2$	
10	$R = C1 \check{\cap} C2$	$R \subseteq C1$ and $R \subseteq C2$	$R \preceq C1$ and $R \preceq C2$	
11	$R = C1 \hat{\cap} C2$	$R \subseteq C1$ and $R \subseteq C2$	$R \succeq C1$ and $R \succeq C2$	*
12	$R = C1 \tilde{\cap} C2$	$R \subseteq C1$ and $R \subseteq C2$	case 1: $R \preceq C1$ and $R \preceq C2$	
13		" "	case 2: $R \preceq C1$ and $R \not\equiv^t C2$	
14		" "	case 3: $R \succeq C1$ and $R \not\equiv^t C2$	*
15		" "	case 4: $R \succeq C1$ and $R \succeq C2$	*
16		" "	case 5: $R \not\equiv^t C1$ and $R \not\equiv^t C2$	
17	$R = C1 \check{\Delta} C2$	$R \not\equiv^s C1$ and $R \not\equiv^s C2$	$R \preceq C1$ and $R \preceq C2$	
18	$R = C1 \hat{\Delta} C2$	$R \not\equiv^s C1$ and $R \not\equiv^s C2$	$R \succeq C1$ and $R \succeq C2$	
19	$R = C1 \tilde{\Delta} C2$	$R \not\equiv^s C1$ and $R \not\equiv^s C2$	case 1: $R \preceq C1$ and $R \preceq C2$	
20		" "	case 2: $R \preceq C1$ and $R \not\equiv^t C2$	
21		" "	case 3: $R \succeq C1$ and $R \not\equiv^t C2$	
22		" "	case 4: $R \succeq C1$ and $R \succeq C2$	
23		" "	case 5: $R \not\equiv^t C1$ and $R \not\equiv^t C2$	

Figure 10: Set-theoretic Operations and Resulting Set and Type Relationships.

5 Related Research

Some data models, in particular, most object-oriented models, define only type-oriented class operations. Others [7, 1] also include some limited repertoire of set operations on classes. Most of these approaches are, however, ad-hoc, as discussed below.

Hammer and McLeod [4] were among the first to propose different types of derivation mechanisms for subclasses. In SDM, they list four subclass connections, namely, attribute-defined, user-controllable, set-operator defined, and existence subclasses. However, their approach towards set-operator defined classes is limited in as much as only one of all possible interpretations is chosen for each set operation. The set operations considered in SDM [4] are union, intersection, and difference. The symmetric difference operation has not been utilized as a class derivation mechanism, since it never results in a "is-a" relationship. Most other existing data models [5] do not even consider the use of set operations.

SAM* by Su [10] consists of seven different abstractions, referred to as association types, that construct new classes out of existing ones. One abstraction, called generalization, creates a more general concept type out of existing ones. This generalization corresponds to a form of union operation, however, it is not clear how the type description of the resulting concept type is formed. This ambiguity arises from the fact that SAM* is value- rather than object-based. No set operations other than this union are considered in SAM*.

Property characteristics, such as, mandatory, single- or multi-valued, and others, have been proposed by several researchers [4, 7]. Property inheritance has been studied extensively in the context of type-oriented class creation operations. However, to our knowledge no one discusses the effect of class derivations by set operations on property characteristics. Inheritance of properties and their characteristics is generally studied only between is-a related classes, i.e., for generalization and specialization abstractions.

6 Conclusions

The contributions of this paper are summarized below. First, the paper presents sound definitions for set operations on the class construct. The semantics of set theory are preserved by these definitions: the resulting set relationships between classes correspond to those of set operations in set theory. A class derivation mechanism would not be well-defined without the specification of the exact treatment of characteristics of inherited properties (especially, when inherited from more than one class). Consequently, we develop rules that regulate the inheritance of properties and their associated characteristics. These rules take care of required versus optional, identifying versus non-identifying, and single- versus multi-valued properties.

In the literature, it is usually taken for granted that an is-a relationship must exist between base classes and a derived class. This assumption is unjustified since, for instance, the symmetric difference operation can never result in an is-a relationship. This problem has been avoided in other approaches by simply ignoring the existence of that set operation. As far as we know, the symmetric difference operation has never been utilized as a class derivation mechanism. Our approach, which allows for the symmetric difference operation, results in a data model where property inheritance proceeds along not necessarily is-a related class relationships.

References

[1] Abiteboul, S. and Hull, R. IFO: A Formal Semantic Database Model. *ACM TODS*, Dec. 1987, vol. 12, issue 4, 525–565.

[2] Atkinson, M. P., and Buneman, O. P., Types and Persistence In Database Programming Languages, *ACM Computing Surveys*, Vol. 19, No. 2, June 87, 105–190.

[3] Brachman, R. J., What IS-A is and isn't: An Analysis of Taxonomic Links in Semantic Networks, *Computer*, Oct. 83, 30 - 36.

[4] Hammer M. and McLeod D.J. Database Description with SDM: A Semantic Data Model. *ACM TODS*, vol. 6, no. 3, Sept. 1981, 351–386.

[5] Hull, R. and King, R. Semantic Database Modeling: Survey, Applications and Research Issues, *ACM Computing Surveys*, vol. 19, no. 3, Sept. 1987, 201–260.

[6] Khoshafian, S.N. and Copeland G.P., Object Identity, Sep. 1986, *Proc. OOPSLA'86*, ACM, 406–416.

[7] Mylopoulos, J., Bernstein, P.A., and Wong H.K.T. A Language Facility for Designing Database-Intensive Applications, June 1980, vol. 5, issue 2, *ACM TODS*, 185–207.

[8] Rundensteiner, E. A., and Bic, L., Aggregates in Possibilistic Databases, *VLDB'89*, Aug. 1989.

[9] Rundensteiner, E. A., and Bic, L., Set Operations in Semantic Data Models, Uni. of Cal, Irvine, Technical Report No. 89-22, June 1989.

[10] Su, Y. W. S., Modeling Integrated Manufacturing Data with SAM*, *Computer 19*, 1, 1986, 34 - 49.

Existentially Quantified Types as a Database Viewing Mechanism

Richard Connor, Alan Dearle, Ronald Morrison & Fred Brown

Department of Computational Science, University of St Andrews,
North Haugh, St Andrews, Scotland KY16 9SS

Abstract

In database management systems, viewing mechanisms have been used to provide conceptual support for the user and security for the overall system. By controlling the style of database use, views aid the user by concentrating on the area of interest, and the system by ensuring the integrity of the data.

In recent years, there have been a number of proposals for database or persistent programming languages. Such languages must be able to provide the facilities traditionally found in both database management systems and programming languages. In this paper we demonstrate how a persistent programming language, Napier88, can provide a viewing mechanism over persistent data by using existentially quantified types. The views, which may be generated dynamically, are statically type checked. The technique shown is applicable to any language which supports existentially quantified data types and a persistent store.

1 Introduction

Viewing mechanisms have been traditionally used in database systems both to provide security and as a conceptual support mechanism for the user. Views are an abstraction mechanism that allow the user to concentrate on a subset of types and values within the database schema whilst ignoring the details of the rest of the database. By concentrating the user on the view of current interest both security and conceptual support are achieved.

Persistent programming languages [ACO85,Mat85,ps87] integrate both the technology and methodology of programming languages and database management systems. One particular area of difficulty in this integration has been the friction caused by the type mechanisms of programming languages and databases being incompatible. Programming languages tend to provide strong, often static type systems with little to aid the expression or modelling of large uniform structure. Databases, on the other hand, are much more concerned with capturing this notion of bulk expression than with static or even strong typing. Both, however, are concerned with the integrity of the data.

Another area of difficulty in the integration of programming languages with database systems has been to demonstrate that the facilities found necessary in both systems are not lost or compromised by the integration. Viewing mechanisms which have been used so successfully in the database community have not found widespread acceptance in the programming language world. They therefore constitute a source of irritation in the above integration.

It is the intention of this paper to demonstrate how the facilities of the persistent programming language, Napier88 [MBC88], may be used to provide a viewing mechanism. Napier88 provides a strong polymorphic type system with existentially quantified types and a persistent store. In particular, it will be shown how existentially quantified types may be used to provide multiple views over objects whilst retaining static type checking.

2 Viewing mechanisms

Viewing mechanisms are traditionally used to provide security and information hiding. Indeed, in some relational database systems, such as INGRES [SWK76], a relational viewing mechanism is the only security mechanism available. A view relation is one which is defined over others to provide a subset of the database, usually at the same level of abstraction. A slightly higher level may be achieved by allowing relations to include derived data, for example, an age field in a view might abstract over a date of birth field in the schema.

Security provided by view relations is often restricted to simple information hiding by means of projection and selection. For example, if a clerk is not permitted to access a date of birth field, then the projected data may contain all the attributes with the exception of this one. If the clerk may not access any data about people under the age of twenty-one, then the view relation will be that formed by the appropriate selection.

Read-only security may be obtained in some database systems by restricting updates on view relations. Although this restriction is normally due to conceptual and implementation problems, rather than being a deliberate feature of a database system design, it may be used to some effect for this purpose. Some systems, for example IMS [IBM78], go further than this, and the database programmer can allow or disallow insertions, deletions, or modifications of data in view relations. This allows a fine grain of control for data protection purposes.

There are a number of problems associated with view relations. Often a new relation is created, with copied data. This means that updates (where permitted) to the view relation will not be reflected in the underlying relations, with the obvious loss of integrity. This problem may be partly solved by the use of delayed evaluation, where names are not evaluated until used in a query. This allows the database programmer to define views over the database schema before all of the data is in place.

Those systems where data copying does not occur seem to incur major integrity problems. For this reason, System R [ABC76] disallows updates on views which are constructed using a join operation. There is a more serious example in IMS, where deletion of a segment, if permitted, also deletes all descendant segments, including cases where they are not even a part of the view in question!

A much higher-level concept of a viewing mechanism is provided by the UMIST Abstract Data Store [Pow85]. This is a software tool which supports abstract data objects together with mechanisms for providing different views over them. The system provides a consistent graphical user interface which allows the user to directly manipulate objects via multiple views. Changes in objects are automatically reflected in other views since they contain no information about the state of objects, only the manner in which they are displayed. This provides a powerful tool for a user to build a store of objects which may be maintained and incremented interactively, and it seems possible that it may be sufficient for a surprisingly large class of problems. However, the inability to write general-purpose programs over the store must be seen as a major drawback for many applications.

3 Existentially quantified types in Napier88

Napier88 provides the existentially quantified types first described by Mitchell & Plotkin [MP85]. These types are often called abstract data types since the objects of such a type display some abstract behaviour that is independent of the representation type.

There are two important properties of the Napier88 abstract data types. The first is that users should not be allowed to break the abstraction via the abstract data type interface. Thus, once an abstract object is made, its representation type can never be rediscovered; it is truly abstract. The second property of these types is that they are statically type checked.

Abstract data types in Napier88 will be introduced by example. Care will be taken to explain the elements of the abstract data type in order that the reader is not lost in the syntax of Napier88.

The type declaration,

type TEST **is abstype**[i](value : i ; change : **proc**(i → i))

declares the identifier *TEST* as a type that is abstract. The identifier enclosed in square brackets is called the witness type and is the type that is abstracted over. There may be one or more witness types in any abstract data type. In this case, the abstract data type interface consists of an identifier *value* with the type *i* and an identifier *change* which is a procedure that takes a parameter of type *i* and returns a result of type *i*. This type is written **proc**(*i* → *i*).

To create an abstract data type the fields in the interface are initialised. For the above type *TEST* an object of type *i* and another of type **proc**(*i* → *i*), for some *i*, are required. There follows an example using the type integer as the representation type. Firstly, an increment procedure for integers may be written as,

let incInt = **proc**(x : **int** → **int**) ; x+1

The reserved word **let** declares an object, with the identifier *incInt* to be a procedure that takes an integer and returns the value incremented by 1.

Having created the *incInt* procedure it may be used as a *change* procedure in an instance of *TEST* by the following declaration,

let this = TEST[**int**](3,incInt)

which declares the object *this* to have the abstract type *TEST*, the concrete witness type **int**, the *value* field initialised to 3 and the *change* field initialised to the procedure *incInt*. Once the abstract data object is created, the user can never tell that the representation type is **int**. The object can only be used through its abstract interface.

The declaration,

let that = TEST[**int**](-42,incInt)

creates another abstract data object of the same type. However even although *this* and *that* have the same representation type the user may never discover this fact and cannot make use of it.

Finally,

let incReal = **proc**(x : **real** → **real**) ; x + 1.0

declares an increment procedure for real numbers, and,

let also = TEST[**real**](42.0,incReal)

declares another abstract data object with the same type, namely *TEST*, as *this* and *that* even although it has a different representation type.

These abstract data types display second order information hiding [CW85]. In first order information hiding a hidden object is encapsulated by scope and manipulated by procedures that do not mention the hidden object as parameters or results. In second order information hiding, the type of the hidden object is defined along with operations on it in an abstract interface. Thus it can be referred to in the abstract and instantiated with a concrete type. We will demonstrate some of the advantages of second order hiding later.

It should be mentioned here that Napier88 uses structural type equivalence semantics and therefore all abstract types with the same structure, and not just type name, are type equivalent. This property will be used in type checking across the persistent store for independently prepared program and data [ABM88].

As we have seen above, the representation type of different instances of an abstract data type may be different. Therefore the implementation must ensure that operations from one object are never applied to another. Also since, in general, the compiler cannot determine the representation type statically, the abstract data object may only apply its operations to itself. This is sufficient for static type checking.

To manipulate an abstract data object, the **use** clause is required. For example,

```
use this as X in
begin
    X( value ) := X( change )( X ( value ) )
end
```

defines a constant identifier, in this case *X*, for the abstract object, in this case *this*. The binding to the constant identifier is necessary for two reasons. Firstly, the object can be expressed as any legal expression and may therefore be anonymous. Secondly, for static type checking the compiler must be able to identify which instance of the object is being dereferenced: this is achieved by binding to an identifier which may not be updated. The body of the **use** clause alters the *value* field of the abstract data object by applying the *change* procedure with the *value* field as a parameter and assigning the result back to the *value* field.

A procedure to abstract over the abstract data type may be defined as follows:

```
let changeTEST = proc( A : TEST )
    use A as X in
        X( value ) : = X( change )( X ( value ) )
```

with calls,

```
changeTEST( this )
changeTEST( that )
changeTEST( also )
```

The *changeTest* procedure may be legally applied to any data object that is structurally equivalent to *TEST*, and changes the *value* field of the abstract data type by applying the *change* procedure to it.

This concludes the introduction to abstract data types except to mention that it is often useful to name the abstract witness types in a **use** clause. This can be achieved by placing their identifiers in square brackets after the constant binding identifier. However, no use will be made of this in this paper.

The essence of our viewing mechanism is to take a body of data, a database, place it in an abstract data type and give it to a user to manipulate in this abstract form. Since the same data or its subsets may be placed in many abstract data types it is possible to have many possible types or views on the same data. Most importantly the views can be statically type checked. We will give a detailed example of this later. For the present we will describe the environment mechanism of Napier88 for provision of a persistent store and a convenient mechanism for holding the data.

4 Environments in Napier88

In Napier88, environments are collections of bindings which may be extended or contracted under user control [Dea89]. Each binding contains an identifier, a value, a type and a constancy indicator. By manipulating the bindings in environments the user can control the name space of the data in the bindings. In particular, environments are used by convention in the persistent store as repositories for program and data that may be incrementally and independently generated. Thus, they are used in the construction and composition of systems out of components in the persistent store. Furthermore, the manner in which they are used controls the name space in the persistent store.

All environments belong to the same infinite union type, denoted by the type name **env**. To use the bindings in an environment a projection from the infinite union must take place.

Again environments will be introduced by example. To create an environment the standard procedure *environment* is called. It has the type:

proc(→ **env**)

Calling this procedure creates an environment containing no bindings. Adding a binding to an environment is the dynamic analogy of adding a declaration (binding) to a scope level. Indeed, it will be shown later how environments may be used to dynamically compose scope levels. Bindings are therefore added to an environment by declarations. For example,

let firstEnv = environment( )
in firstEnv **let** absInc = this

will create an environment, called *firstEnv*, and place the binding *absInc* with value *this*, which is the abstract data object defined above, in it. The environment records for each binding: the identifier, the value, the type and a constancy indicator. In this example, the environment will record: the identifier *absInc*, the value *this*, the type *TEST* and the constancy indicator **true**. The binding is added to the environment but not to the local scope.

Environments may be extended by further declarations and may be contracted by a **drop** clause which is not used here.

To use the bindings in an environment, a projection statement called a **use** clause is invoked. The environment **use** clause, which is different from the **use** clause for abstract data types, projects a binding into the local scope. For example,

use firstEnv **with** absInc : TEST **in** <clause>

binds the identifier *absInc* into scope as a declaration at the head of <clause>. The value of *absInc* is the value in the environment. Alterations to the value will alter the value in the environment.

The environment **use** clause need only specify the particular bindings that are to be used. Others that are present but not specifically mentioned are not in scope and therefore not usable within the <clause>.

As mentioned earlier, environments are used to impose structure on the persistent store. In accordance with the concept of orthogonal persistence [ABC83], all data objects in Napier88 may persist. For each incarnation of the Napier88 object store there is a root of persistence which may be obtained by calling the predefined procedure *PS* which has type:

proc(→ **env**)

Thus, the distinguished root of the persistent store graph is of type **env**. When a program is activated, the distinguished root will contain all the bindings for that universe. The standard bindings are defined for every system and one of these bindings contains the procedure used earlier to create environments. It is bound to the identifier *environment*. The following program illustrates the use of this procedure:

```
let ps = PS()
use ps with environment : proc ( → env ) in
begin
      let newEnv = environment()
      let this = TEST[ int ]( 3,proc( x : int → int ) ; x + 1 )
      in NewEnv let absInc = this
end
```

This program binds the root of persistence to the local identifier *ps*. The first **use** clause binds the identifier *environment* to the environment creation procedure in the root environment. Inside the body of the **use** clause this procedure is called to create a new (empty) environment. Finally a binding to *this*, denoted by *absInc*, is made in the newly created environment. The reader should note that the environment bound to *newEnv* is not yet persistent. Objects that persist beyond the activation of the unit that created them are those which the user has arranged to be reachable from the root of persistence. To determine this, the system computes the transitive closure of all objects starting with the root. Thus, in order to store objects in the persistent store the user has to alter or add bindings that can be reached from the distinguished root. In order to make the environment *newEnv* persist the above example may be rewritten as:

```
let ps = PS()
use ps with environment : proc ( → env ) in
begin                                          ! Create an environment, bound to localNewEnv
      let localNewEnv = environment()          ! in the local scope. Place 'this' in localNewEnv.
      let this = TEST[ int ]( 3,proc( x : int → int ) ; x + 1 )
      in localNewEnv let absInc = this
      in ps let newEnv = localNewEnv           ! Finally, bind localNewEnv to newEnv in ps.
end
```

At the end of this program the abstract data object *absInc* will be bound to the environment *newEnv* which is in the root environment.

The object may be retrieved from the persistent store and used by the following code:

```
use PS() with newEnv : env in
use newEnv with this : abstype[ i ]( value : i ; change : proc( i → i ) ) in
      use this as X in
      X( value ) := X( change )( X ( value ) )
```

Both abstract data types and environments will now be used to construct a viewing mechanism. The strategy is to place the raw data of a database in an environment or environments where it may persist. Within these environments, the data will be placed in an abstract data type that is appropriate to a particular view and that abstract data type stored in the persistent store. The views, or abstract data type interfaces may be exported to appropriate users. Since the raw data may be placed in many abstract data types, multiple views may be constructed and retained.

Higher order views may also be constructed by using existing views as components of the new abstract data types. These views may be used and made to persist in the usual way. Furthermore, database views often include a notion of looking at a subset of tuples or objects in a collection, in addition to limiting the protocol to individual objects. As the views described here are written in a general purpose programming language, this may be achieved by limiting the range of the procedure which retrieves the data from the database so that it does not return data which is outside the view in question.

5 Example of view construction

For a programming example, we will use a banking system in which customers have access to their accounts through autoteller machines. This poses the classic database problems of having a very large bulk of updatable data with different users requiring different operations on it. Here we will concentrate on views in the system. We shall restrict ourselves at first to the autoteller machines, which have different styles of access to accounts according to which bank the machine belongs. A customers own bank may have full access to an account whereas another bank may not access the customer's account balance, but must know if a withdrawal may be made.

5.1 Creating a concrete representation

We will begin by defining a concrete representation of a user account and the procedures that operate on that type. Here we are not interested in how the account data is stored (i.e. in a relation, a β-tree, etc.), and we will assume that we have previously declared a lookup function indexed by account number which returns the account associated with that account number.

We will implement an account using a record-like data structure which in Napier88 is called a structure. The structure type, called *account*, has three fields: *balance* which holds the account balance; *Limit* which contains the overdraft limit and *pin* which contains the password necessary to access the account. There is one instance of this type in the database for each user account.

One special instance of this type called *failAc* is created to use as a fail value. This is used in the *getAc* procedure if an illegal password is supplied when attempting to access an account.

Five procedures operate on the account directly, they are:

withdraw: This procedure checks to see that sufficient funds are in the specified account to make a withdrawal. If there are, the amount specified is debited from the account.

balance: This returns the balance of an account.

Limit: This returns the overdraft limit of an account, this is a negative number.

sufficient: This indicates whether sufficient funds are in an account to make a withdrawal of a specified amount.

getAc: This procedure interfaces with the persistent store, it looks up an account in an associative storage structure and checks the supplied password. If the password matches the *pin* field in the account, the account is returned, otherwise the fail value *failAc* is returned.

The Napier code necessary to implement the concrete type representations and the code to operate on the concrete type representation of an account is shown below:

```
type account is structure( balance,Limit : int ; pin : string )
let failAc = account( 0,0,"" )                    ! This is a fail value
let withdraw = proc( debit : int ; ac : account )  ! Withdraw debit pounds from ac.
begin
      let result = ac( balance ) - debit
      if result > ac( Limit ) and debit > 0 do ac( balance ) := result
end

let balance = proc( ac : account → int ) ; ac( balance )   ! Return the balance of account ac.
```

```
let Limit = proc( ac : account → int ) ; ac( Limit )        ! Return the credit limit of account ac.

let sufficient = proc( debit : int ; ac : account → bool )  ! Return whether or not debit pounds
      ac( balance ) - debit > ac( Limit )                   ! may be withdrawn from account ac.

let getAc = proc( accountNumber : int ;                     ! Look up the account number,
            passwd : string → account )                     ! check user password and if the
begin                                                       ! password matches the password in
      let new = lookup( accountNumber )                     ! the database return the account,
      if new( pin ) = passwd then new else failAc           ! otherwise return a fail value.
end
```

As mentioned earlier, we have made use of a predefined *lookup* procedure, as its implementation is of no interest in this context.

5.2 Placing concrete representations in the store

Of course, in a real bank there would be a requirement for the procedures and data defined above to persist over a long period of time. In order to achieve this in practice it is necessary to place them in the persistent store. We will assume that an environment called *bank* already exists in the root environment. The above example may be trivially rewritten as follows:

```
use PS() with bank : env in
begin
      let failAc = account( 0,0,"" )                        ! Must be declared both in local
      in bank let failAc = failAc                           ! scope and in bank environment

      in bank let withdraw = proc( debit : int ; ac : account ) ; ...   ! procedure body as above
      in bank let balance = proc( ac : account → int ) ; ...            ! procedure body as above
      in bank let Limit = proc( ac : account → int ) ; ...              ! procedure body as above
      in bank let sufficient = proc(     debit : int ;
                        ac : account → bool ) ; ...                     ! procedure body as above
      in bank let getAc = proc( accountNumber : int ;                   ! procedure body as above
                  passwd : string → account ) ; ...
end
```

Since the environment called *bank* is reachable from the persistent root the procedures will be saved when the program terminates. However, notice that if we allow programmers access to the concrete representations, the database will be vulnerable to misuse. For example, the unscrupulous programmer could write,

```
let myAc = getAc( 34589001,"3478" )
myAc( balance ) := myAc( balance ) + 1000000
```

yielding a net profit of one million pounds (a very high programmer productivity ratio of £500000/line). For this reason, it is necessary to protect the concrete representation with abstract interfaces. In the next section we will show how to do this.

5.3 Creating abstract view types

For the purpose of this example we will define two abstract data types which provide interfaces for the procedures shown in the last section. The first is to be used by an account holders own bank. The abstract type shown below, called *localTeller* has the following five fields:

failAc: is returned by *getAc* if a password check fails,

getAc: which will take as input an account number, and a secret password typed into the machine by the customer, and provided that the secret number is correct, return the representation of that account, otherwise it will return the fail value *failAc*,

withdraw: which will remove the amount specified from the account, unless there are insufficient funds, in which case it will do nothing,

balance : which returns the balance in the account, and,

Limit : which returns the account overdraft limit.

The type of *localTeller* is defined below:

```
type amount is int        ! an amount of money
type number is int        ! an account number
type passwd is int        ! a secret number

type localTeller is abstype[ ac ](   failAc   : ac
                                     getAc    : proc( number,passwd → ac )
                                     withdraw : proc( amount,ac )
                                     balance  : proc( ac → amount )
                                     Limit    : proc( ac → amount ) )
```

The concrete type named as *ac*, may never be discovered, therefore the programmer is forced to access accounts only using the procedures provided in the interface of the abstract data type. Notice that the fail value *failAc* appears in the interface of the abstract type. This permits the user of an instance of this abstract type to check for failure in the application of the *getAc* procedure. This is only possible because in Napier88 equality is defined over all types, including witness types. In Napier88, equality is always defined as identity.

Similarly, we can define another abstract type for use by another bank. Other banks are not allowed to discover a customers' balance or limit so a slightly different interface is required. In this type a procedure called *sufficient* is provided so that the bank may ensure that sufficient funds are available in the account. We may define the type *remoteTeller* as follows:

```
type remoteTeller is abstype[ ac ](   failAc     : ac
                                      getAc      : proc( number,passwd → ac )
                                      withdraw   : proc( amount,ac )
                                      sufficient : proc( amount,ac → bool ) )
```

5.4 Creating instances of views

Here, an instance of the type *localTeller* and an instance of the type *remoteTeller* are required to act as views over the single implementation shown in Section 5.2. This may be achieved by creating instances of the two types as follows:

```
use PS() with tellerEnv,bank : env in              ! We assume these environments have been
use bank with   failAc : account ;                 ! properly constructed and initialised
                withdraw : proc( int,account ) ;
                balance,
                Limit : proc( account → int ) ;
                sufficient : proc( int,account → bool ) ;
                getAc : proc( int,string → account ) in
begin
      in tellerEnv let local = localTeller[ account ](   failAc,
                                                        getAc,
                                                        withdraw,
                                                        balance,
                                                        Limit )
```

```
in tellerEnv let remote = remoteTeller[ account ]( failAc,
                                                   getAc,
                                                   withdraw,
                                                   sufficient )
end
```

The program extracts the procedures placed in the environment denoted by *bank* and creates an instance of the types *localTeller* and *remoteTeller*. These are initialised using the procedures from the *bank* environment. Therefore, using this technique, the level of procedural indirection normally found in viewing mechanisms is not required. Consequently there are both space and time advantages of this technique.

When this program terminates the two abstract objects denoted by *local* and *remote* in the environment denoted by *tellerEnv* will be committed to the persistent store, since they are within the transitive closure of the persistent root.

Although we have chosen to create the two abstract types used in this example in the same code segment this was not strictly necessary. Any programmer with access to the bank environment is free to create new abstract types which interface with the concrete types at any time in the future in a similar manner.

5.5 Using views

Two views of the database now exist in the environment called *tellerEnv* reachable from the root of persistence. In order to use the instance of *localTeller* in the *tellerEnv* the auto-teller programmer has only to write a main loop which uses the procedural interface correctly. This would look something like:

```
use PS() with tellerEnv : env in
use tellerEnv with local : localTeller in

use local as package in
begin
        let getAccount = package( getAc )
        let withdraw = package( withdraw )
        let findBalance = package( balance )
        let findLimit = package( Limit )

        ! code to use above procedures ...
end
```

Similarly, the instance of *remoteTeller* could be accessed as follows:

```
use PS() with tellerEnv : env in
use tellerEnv with remote : remoteTeller in
use remote as package in
begin
        let getAccount = package( getAc )
        let sufficient = package( sufficient )
        let withdraw = package( withdraw )


        ...
end
```

The interesting point here is that these procedures manipulate the same objects as those in the previous interface, and so provide a different view of them. If the account information is kept in a relational data structure, this is equivalent to a relational viewing mechanism: *getAc* is a relational select on a primary key. Notice that although the views update the same data, no integrity problems arise.

5.6 N-ary procedures

Suppose another function had been required from the auto-teller, so that a customer with two accounts may use the machine to transfer money from one to another. We can allow this by redefining the interface of *localTeller* as follows:

```
type localTeller is abstype[ ac ](   failAc      : ac
                                     getAc       : proc( number,passwd → ac )
                                     withdraw    : proc( amount,ac )
                                     transfer    : proc( amount,ac,ac )
                                     balance     : proc( ac → amount )
                                     Limit       : proc( ac → amount ) )
```

and by writing the *transfer* procedure in the module which places the interface procedures in the store as follows:

```
use PS() with bank : env in
begin

    let failAc = account( 0,0,"" )              ! Must be declared both in local
    in bank let failAc = failAc                 ! scope and in bank environment
    in bank let withdraw = proc( debit : int ; ac : account )
    begin
        let result = ac( balance ) - debit
        if result > ac( Limit ) and debit > 0 do ac( balance ) := result
    end

    in bank let balance = proc( ac : account → int ) ; ac( balance )

    in bank let Limit = proc( ac : account → int ) ; ac( Limit )

    in bank let sufficient = proc( debit : int ; ac : account → bool )
        ac( balance ) - debit > ac( Limit )

    in bank let transfer = proc( amount : int ; from,to : account )
    if amount > 0 and from( balance ) - amount > from( Limit ) do
    begin
        from( balance ) := from( balance ) - amount
        to( balance ) := to( balance ) + amount
    end

    in bank let getAc = proc(  accountNumber : int ;
                    passwd : string → account )
    begin
        let new = lookup( accountNumber )
        if new( pin ) = passwd then new else failAc
    end
end
```

The important difference between this new procedure, *transfer*, and those already discussed is that it is defined over more than one object of the witness type. This causes no problem with the definition of the interface, as the type of the operands is declared prior to the type of the procedure. Although the type is abstracted over, the parameters are bound to the same definition, and so are restricted to being the same representation type. Similarly, at the place where the procedure is written (within the scope of the representation type), it is written over two objects of the same type. If it were not, a type-checking error would be detected in the attempt to create the abstract type.

This example illustrates a major difference in power between first-order and second-order information hiding. With second-order, a type is abstracted over, and procedures may be defined over this type. With first-order hiding, it is the object itself which is hidden within its procedural interface. Procedures which operate over more than one such object may not be defined sensibly within this interface. Therefore any operations defined over two instances must be written at a higher level, using the interface. At best this creates syntactic noise and is inefficient at execution time. It also means that such operations are defined in the module which uses the abstract objects, rather than the module which creates them. Some examples, such as this one, are not possible to write without changing the original interface.

This example highlights another difference between this style of abstract data type and that used in the language ML. Although the use of the type is similar to an ML-style type, the definition of structural type equivalence allows objects of the type to be passed between different compilation units. This is not the case with ML abstract types, which are only compatible if they refer to the same instance of the type definition: construction and use by independently-prepared modules is not possible by this mechanism and must be achieved otherwise [Har85].

6 Privileged data access and incremental system construction

We have seen how abstract data types may be used in conjunction with environments to provide a safe and flexible viewing mechanism, of which viewing over a database style relation is a special case. We will now show another paradigm, which allows privileged users to access the raw data without danger of losing the integrity of the abstract interfaces. This solves some traditional problems associated with abstract data types, and shows a way towards some of the more general problems associated with system evolution and incremental system construction.

A problem exists with abstract data types in long-lived persistent systems if, when the abstract type is formed, access to the original representation of the data is lost. This is a requirement of these types for the purposes of safety and abstraction, but there is an underlying assumption that no access to the data will ever be required apart from that specified in the abstract interfaces. For a large body of persistent data this is unrealistic.

A serious problem occurs if an error leaves the database in an inconsistent state. In the banking example, this could happen if one of the auto-tellers develops a mechanical failure which prevents it from dispensing the requested money after the *withdraw* operation has been executed. The easiest way for such an error to be rectified is for a privileged user, such as the database administrator, to be allowed access to the concrete representation of the account and adjust the balance. If such access is not allowed, then an error may occur which leaves the database in an inconsistent state from which it is not possible to recover.

This kind of access may be treated as another view over the same data, with no abstraction in the interface. It may be achieved using the environment mechanism, by keeping the data representations in a known place in the persistent store as shown earlier; this also allows suitable abstraction for the programs which manipulate the concrete data.

To prevent unauthorised users from gaining access to the information contained in this environment, a password protection scheme may be used. So that the type of the data can not be discovered from a scan of the containing environment, this environment can be hidden inside a procedure which requires a password:

```
let makeSecretEnv = proc( password : string → proc( string → env ) )
begin
    let new = environment()

    proc( attempt : string → env )
        if attempt = password then new else fail
end

in dbAdmin let accountRepEnv = makeSecretEnv( "friend" )
```

Now the restricted definitions and data can be placed safely in this environment without fear of access by unprivileged users. This technique gives a result not dissimilar from the kind of module provided by Pebble [BL84] and a high level language analogy of capabilities [NW74].

This level of data access is also desirable for database programmers in other circumstances. It is not uncommon for a new operation to be required on data which is abstracted over: an example of this is if the procedure *transfer* described above became a requirement after the system had been installed. Although it may be possible to write such operations in a new user module, such use is often contrived and will always be inefficient. Using this technique, the database administrator may construct a new interface over the representation level of the data, with no associated loss of efficiency.

The above holds whether the new interface required is confined to adding an extra operation to one of the existing views, or whether an entire new view is necessary. The autoteller example given above could thus be added to an existing system, rather than being part of the design of the original system. Furthermore, none of the code would be any different from that shown, and programs which used the original interface would continue to work. This demonstrates the flexibility of this paradigm, and shows a way forward for the incremental construction of complex software systems.

7 Conclusions

We have demonstrated how the existentially quantified types of Napier88 may be used to provide a viewing mechanism over persistent data. Since one object may be a component of many existentially quantified objects, multiple views over the same data or database may be constructed.

We provide one example of constructing multiple views over a collection of bank accounts. Although we have not demonstrated it, it is possible to construct higher order views by imposing an existential interface over existing existential types.

We have also demonstrated that the technique for providing views and structuring the database can be used for data repair without compromising the abstract interfaces. Such a situation is similar to query processing in object-oriented databases where queries must have access to data in an object that is not available through the objects interface [BCD89].

The final attribute of the system is that the views are statically type checked.

8 Acknowledgements

We acknowledge discussions with Sandy Heiler and Stan Zdonik on viewing mechanisms in object-oriented databases which took place instead of some fluid dynamics experiments.

9 References

[ABC76] Astrahan M.M., Blasgen M.W., Chamberlin D.D., Eswaran K.P., Gray J.N., Griffiths P.P., King W.F., Lorie R.A., McJones P.R., Mehl J.W, Putzolu G.R., Traiger I.L., Waid B.W. & Watson V.
"System R: A Relational Approach to Data Management"
ACM TODS 1,2 (June 1976), pp 97-137.

[ABC83] Atkinson, M.P., Bailey, P.J., Chisholm, K.J., Cockshott, W.P. & Morrison, R.
"An Approach to Persistent Programming"
Computer Journal 26,4 (November 1983), pp 360-365.

[ABM88] Atkinson, M.P., Buneman, O.P. & Morrison, R.
"Binding and Type Checking in Database Programming Languages"
Computer Journal. 31,2 (1988), pp 99-109.

[ACO85] Albano, A., Cardelli, L. & Orsini, R.
"Galileo : A Strongly Typed Conceptual Language"
ACM TODS 10,2 (June 1985), pp 230-260.

[BCD89] Bancilhon, F., Cluet, S. & Delobel, C.
"A Query Language for the O_2 Object-Oriented Database System"
2nd International Workshop on Database Programming Languages, Salishan, Oregon Morgan & Kaufmann (1989), pp 122-138

[BL84] Burstall, R. & Lampson, B.
"A Kernal Language for Abstract Data Types and Modules"
Proc. international symposium on the semantics of data types, Sophia-Antipolis, France (1984). In **Lecture Notes in Computer Science**. 173. Springer-Verlag (1984).

[CW85] Cardelli, L. & Wegner, P.
"On Understanding Types, Data Abstraction and Polymorphism"
ACM Computing Surveys 17,4 (December 1985), pp 471-523.

[Dea89] Dearle A.
"Environments : A Flexible Binding Mechanism to Support System Evolution"
Proc. Hawaii International Conference on System Sciences (1989), pp 46-55 .

[Har85] Harper R.
"Modules and Persistence in Standard ML"
Proc Persistence Data Types Workshop, Appin, Scotland (1985) in **Data Types and Persistence** (Ed. Atkinson M.P., Buneman P. & Morrison R.) Springer-Verlag (1985), pp 21-30.

[IBM78] IMS/VS Publications
IBM, White Plains, N.Y. (1978).

[Mat85] Matthews, D.C.J.
"Poly Manual"
Technical Report 65, University of Cambridge, U.K. (1985).

[MBC88] Morrison, R., Brown, A.L., Connor, R.C.H. & Dearle, A.
"Napier88 Reference Manual"
Persistent Programming Research Report PPRR-77-89, University of St Andrews. (1989).

[MP85] Mitchell J.C. & Plotkin G.D.
"Abstract Types have Existential type"
ACM TOPLAS 10,3 (July 1988), pp 470-502.

[NW74] Needham R.M. & Walker R.D.
"Protection and Process management in the CAP computer"
Proc. International Workshop on Protection in Operating Systems. IRIA Rocquencourt, (August 1974), pp 155-160.

[Pow85] Powell M.S.
"Adding Programming Facilities to an Abstract Data Store"
Proc. Persistence Data Type Workshop, Appin, Scotland. Universities of Glasgow and St Andrews PPRR-16-85 (Ed. Atkinson M.P., Buneman P. & Morrison R.) (1985) pp139-160.

[ps87] "The PS-algol Reference Manual fourth edition", Universities of Glasgow and St.Andrews PPRR-12 (1987).

[SWK76] Stonebreaker M., Wong E., Kreps P, & Held G.
"The Design and Implementation of INGRES"
ACM TODS 1,3 (1976) pp 189-222.

Panel: Has Theory Brought Anything to Database Systems and Will It in the Future?

Moderator: David Maier
GIP Altaïr and Oregon Graduate Institute

This panel will fan the flames of the continuing arguments between Database Theory and Database Systems. To hear each side tell it, database theorists are frustrated mathematicians who wouldn't know a buffer pool if they fell in it, while database system researchers are ignorant hackers who couldn't care less for correctness, as long as their benchmarks run fast.

The panel will consist of an advocate and an apologist for database theory and for database systems. They will debate the past contributions of database theory to the development of database systems and the relevance of current theory to the real problems facing systems developers. The panelists will also try to divine the future and predict what will be the next hot areas for theoretical investigations and which areas of database systems would benefit most from application of theory.

Among the questions that the panelists might choose to ignore are:

- What affect has 18 years of data dependency theory had on the design of commercial database products?
- Is there any implemented database recovery algorithm that admits to a formal proof of correctness?
- Is the current flurry of activity in logic databases and recursive query processing really database theory, or simply programming language optimization?
- Will object-oriented database systems ever have a formal model as clean as the relational model?
- Should the next 30 concurrency control protocols or access methods be labeled theory or practice?
- What body of database theory is most underused by developers of current database systems?
- What areas of database systems design are most in need of formal foundations and theoretical analysis?

The HyperModel Benchmark

T. Lougenia Anderson
Servio Logic Development Corp., Beaverton, Oregon, USA

Arne J. Berre
Center for Industrial Research, Oslo, Norway

Moira Mallison
Tektronix Inc., Beaverton, Oregon, USA

Harry H. Porter, III
Portland State University, Portland, Oregon, USA

Bruce Schneider
Mentor Graphics, Beaverton, Oregon, USA

Abstract: *Database Management Systems are being developed to meet the complex data structure and functionality requirements of engineering applications. This paper describes an application-oriented strategy for evaluating engineering DBMSs based on a generic hypertext application. The hypertext application, which we call the HyperModel, consists of a schema and several operations described at a conceptual level, suitable for implementation on many different DBMSs. The results of running the HyperModel benchmark on two commercially available DBMSs (GemStone and Vbase) are presented and discussed.*

1. Introduction

As database systems are being developed and extended to meet the requirements of engineering applications, a need has arisen for a benchmark to check how well such systems meet various requirements. This paper describes the design of a benchmark, called the *HyperModel Benchmark*, and reports the preliminary results of running it on two Object-Oriented Database Management Systems (OO-DBMSs): Ontologic's Vbase system (Release 1.0) and Servio Logic's GemStone system (an early engineering release). Our implementations of the benchmark are public-domain and may be obtained from the third author.

Hypertext is a generic graph structure consisting of nodes and links. (Nodes may contain text or other kinds of data such as bitmaps; links are used to describe references between the nodes.) Examples of hypertext systems used in existing design environments are Neptune at Tektronix [6], and Tender/One Literate Programming System at SI (Center for Industrial Research) [10]. We picked the hypertext application for our benchmark because it is relatively simple to implement (any benchmark should be readily understood and implementable) and because it is representative of many of the requirements found in our analysis of engineering applications.

Our generic hypertext application (the HyperModel) extends the standard nodes-and-links data structure by adding two hierarchies over the nodes: the *parent/children* hierarchy and the *partOf/parts* hierarchy. At least one hierarchy is desirable since recursive structures and recursive query processing are common in design applications and the benchmark needs to reflect this. However, one hierarchy is not sufficient since it does not accurately model the design world (i.e., multiple hierarchies frequently exist over the same data structure) and one hierarchy is insufficient to evaluate various clustering strategies.

The *parent/children* hierarchy is a bi-directional aggregation relationship between a node and its children with 1-N cardinality. (The "/" separates the names of the two relationships, one for each direction.) The *partOf/parts* hierarchy is a bi-directional aggregation relationship between a node and its parts with M-N cardinality. In addition to being common in most design applications, a *partOf/parts* hierarchy has recently been suggested as a useful extension to other hypertext systems.

Typical hypertext applications have a strong interactive interface component for creating and editing the hypertext graphs and for editing the contents of nodes. Such an interface is not directly incorporated in our benchmark since it would be difficult to describe its functionality and to reproduce it on different systems. However, the benchmark does incorporate operations to test the performance of creating nodes and links and of editing their contents. Thus, it supports operations for retrieving the information that would be needed by an interactive hypertext front-end or by a formatting program.

The remainder of the paper is organized as follows. The next section outlines DBMS requirements for engineering applications. Section 3 examines existing benchmarks with respect to these requirements and argues for a new benchmark. Sections 4 and 5 describe the HyperModel benchmark's schema and operations. Section 6 returns to the requirements and analyzes the two systems within the framework provided. The final section outlines future directions. The results of running the benchmark on Vbase and GemStone can be found in the Appendix.

2. DBMS Requirements for Engineering Applications

The best evaluation and benchmark for a specific application can be achieved by implementing the complete application itself on different DBMSs and comparing the results. This is almost always too expensive. The next best alternative is to determine the requirements for a family of applications and to design a fairly simple generic application that incorporates these requirements. In addition to functionality and performance, other criteria, such as economic and market factors, must not be forgotten.

The design of the HyperModel application grew out of an analysis of DBMS requirements done earlier at Tektronix, Inc. as part of a study of the functionality and performance requirements of engineering applications [1]. In summary, we categorized the requirements of a DBMS for engineering applications as follows:

Data Model Requirements:
- (R1) Modeling of complex object structures.
- (R2) Description of different data types.
- (R3) Integration with application programming languages.
- (R4) Dynamic modifications to the database schema.
- (R5) Support for versions and variants.

System and Architecture Requirements:
- (R6) An architecture of workstations and servers.
- (R7) Performance suitable for interactive design applications.
- (R8) Concurrency control.
- (R9) Cooperation between users.
- (R10) Logging, backup and recovery.
- (R11) Access control.
- (R12) Ad-Hoc query language.

Similar DBMS requirements for engineering applications can be found in [3] and [9] Our hypothesis is that evaluating how well a database management system meets these requirements for a hypertext system will indicate how it well it will meet the requirements for a large set of engineering applications.

3. Existing Benchmark Designs

There are three well-known DBMS benchmarks, the Wisconsin relational benchmark [4], the Debit-Credit Transaction Throughput (TP1) benchmark [2], and the Sun "simple database operations" benchmark [5,13]. Unfortunately, none of these benchmarks provide enough data to be useful in a complete evaluation of DBMSs for engineering applications against our requirements list.

The Wisconsin benchmark has become the standard for relational databases. It is essentially a benchmark for query processing and, in particular, is aimed at selection-join query processing rather than at the higher level conceptual operations commonly found in engineering applications. The TP1 benchmark concentrates on monitoring system throughput for a large number of small transactions. However, engineering applications typically have a small number of long transactions.

The Sun benchmark paper states that most engineering applications involve simple database operations and that a benchmark must be built from these simple operations in order to evaluate its suitability for engineering applications[13]. The Sun benchmark incorporates the following seven operations: (1) Name Lookup, (2) Range Lookup, (3) Group Lookup, (4) Reference Lookup, (5) Record Insert, (6) Sequential Scan, and (7) Database Open. The database consists of *Documents* and *Persons* with a M-N relationship between them. Of the three prior benchmark designs, the Sun benchmark is the most similar to our own work. However, their data model is too simple to measure transitive closures and other traversal operations that are common in engineering applications. Also, many database systems support higher-level conceptual operations efficiently, so an evaluation involving only simple operations is insufficient. (For instance, can clustering of complex objects along an aggregation relationship make transitive closure operations perform more efficiently?) Finally, the *Person-Document* model does not show the problem of collaboration between multiple users editing parts of the same data structure.

The Sun benchmark is a good starting point, but we feel it would have more impact if cast in the context of a typical engineering application. Hence, the HyperModel benchmark uses an example data model with a more complex structure as well as a more explicit engineering flavor. It includes the same seven operations as the Sun benchmark, but adds additional operations to test transitive closure traversal as well as more complex "computational" functions.

4. The HyperModel Application

This section describes a conceptual schema for the HyperModel benchmark using the Object Modeling Technique (OMT) [12, 8]. In the OMT it is possible to describe Generalization/Specialization and Aggregation relationships. However, there is no notation for representing ordered relationships; we have added one here.

A HyperModel document consists of a number of sections and each section is represented by an object of type *Node*. There are two sub-types of *Node*: *TextNode* and *FormNode*. *Node* is not an "abstract" type; there are *Node* instances which are neither *TextNodes* nor *FormNodes*. There are 5 attributes (called *uniqueStr*, *ten*, *hundred*, *thousand*, and *million*) associated with each *Node*. In addition, a *TextNode* has a *text* attribute and a *FormNode* has a *bitmap*, *width*, and *height* attribute.

Nodes are interrelated by three relationships: the *parent/children* relationship, the *partOf/parts* relationship, and the *refTo/refFrom* relationship. The *parent/children* relationship is 1-N and is used to model the recursive aggregation structure of sections within a document. Furthermore, the children of a given parent are ordered. The *partOf/parts* relationship is an M-N relationship that is constrained to be hierarchical. That is, although parts may share subparts, the *partOf/parts* relationship is acyclic. Finally, the *refTo/refFrom* relationship is an arbitrary M-N relationship.

The *refTo/refFrom* relationship is designed to model Hypertext links, in which attributes are attached to each link to describe the offset (i.e., position) of each endpoint within a node. Associated with each *refTo/refFrom* link are two attributes: *offsetFrom* and *offsetTo*. For example, *offsetFrom* might represent the character position with in a *TextNode* of the tail of the link.

Considering the *parent/children* relationship, a document can be viewed as a tree. The internal nodes of the tree are instances of the class *Node* while the leaves are either *TextNodes* or *FormNodes* depending on their contents (text or bitMap).

In the schema (shown in Figure 1) lines represent bidirectional relationships, black circles represent a many-end of a relationship, and white circles represent a one-end. The arrow points towards the composite object in an aggregation relationship. A circle on the line means that the relationship should be ordered. Attributes are described inside a class object. The triangle on the lines between classes symbolizes generalization.

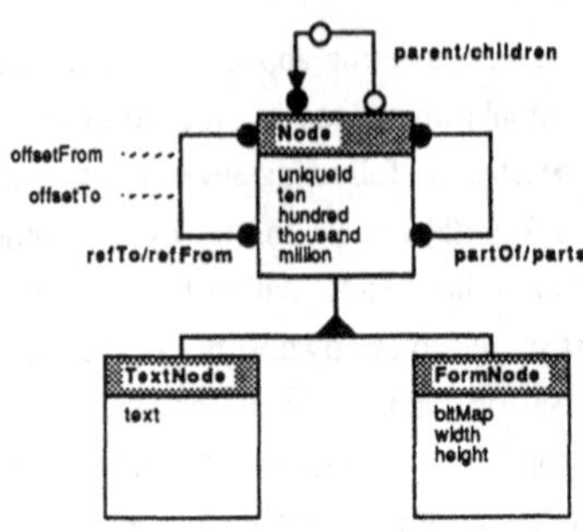

Figure 1. The HyperModel Schema

4.1. Test Database Generation

A HyperModel database consists of a single document which is comprised of a network of nodes with the relationships described above.

The test database has a fan-out of 5 nodes at each level in the tree structure described by the *parent/children* relation (see Figure 2). A document will normally contain 7 generations, numbered 0 through 6. The number of nodes in each generation is: 1 (generation 0), 5 (generation 1), 25 (generation 2), 125 (generation 3), 625 (generation 4), 3125 (generation 5), and 15625 (generation 6). By varying the number of generations in the document tree, the total number of *Nodes* in the database may be varied. (A database with *k* generations is referred to as a "level *k-1*" database.) The total number of nodes in a database is: 1 (level 0), 6 (level 1), 31 (level 2), 156 (level 3), 781 (level 4), 3906 (level 5), and 19531 (level 6). The benchmark must be run on level 4, level 5, and level 6 databases. For the future, the benchmark might be run against level 7 databases, which contain 97656 *Nodes*.

The *partOf/parts* relation is created by relating each node at level *k* to five randomly chosen[1] nodes from level *k+1* in the tree structure created by the *parent/children* relation. The number of *parent/children* relationships and *partOf/parts* relationships are both one less than the total number of nodes. The *refTo/refFrom* relation is

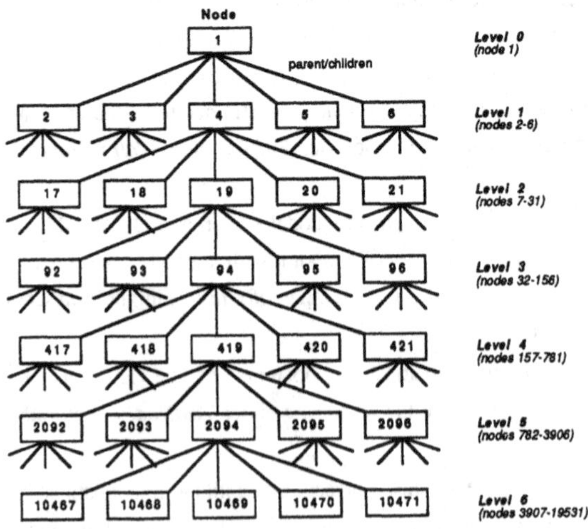

Figure 2. A Portion of the parent/children Hierarchy

[1] Whenever we use the term "random", we mean drawn from a uniform distribution over the appropriate interval.

created by visiting each node once and creating a reference to another node chosen randomly from the entire tree. The number of *refTo/refFrom* relationships is consequently equal to the number of nodes. The values of the *offsetTo* and *offsetFrom* attributes are initialized random integers between 0 and 10.

The *Nodes* are number sequentially, as shown in Figure 2, and the *uniqueId* attribute contains the unique integer value of each node. Each node also has four attributes called *ten, hundred, thousand* and *million.* Values are assigned to these attributes by randomly selecting integers from the corresponding interval (e.g., between one and ten for the *ten* attribute).

The lowest level consists of *TextNodes* and *FormNodes.* There is one *FormNode* per 125 *TextNodes*, giving 125 *FormNodes* and 15500 *TextNodes.* Each *TextNode* contains a text string of a random number (10-100) of words. Words are separated by a space and consist of a random number (1-10) of randomly chosen lowercase alphabetic characters. However, the first, middle and last word must be "version1". Each *FormNode* has a *bitMap* attribute which is initially white (all 0's), with a size varying randomly between 100x100 and 400x400 (but always a square).

If the system supports clustering, clustering must be done along the *parent/children* relationship for the benchmark. Since the data structure incorporates two hierarchies, it is possible to measure the effect on performance along the clustered hierarchy and to compare this to the performance along the non-clustered hierarchy.

5. The Operations

The Benchmark consists of 20 operations. To measure the time to perform each operation, the following sequence must be followed:

Setup: Prepare the inputs to the operations. The *NameLookup* operation, for example, requires 50 randomly selected integers. The *NameOIDLookup* operation requires the object ids (references to) 50 randomly selected nodes. The setup is not timed.

Cold Run: Run the operation 50 times, on the 50 inputs precomputed in the setup phase. Then, if the operation is an update operation, commit the changes once for all 50 operations.

Warm Run: Repeat the operation 50 times with the same inputs to test the effect of caching. Again, perform a commit if the operation was an update.

The entire cold run, including the commit (if any), is timed and the mean time per operation is computed by dividing by 50. Likewise, the mean time per operation for the warm run is computed and reported. Although the update operations are idempotent, in the sense that the warm run will undo the effects of the cold run, the time for the commit must be included in computing the mean time of the update operations. Needless to say, all 20 operations should be run on the same database: the database should not be reorganized or modified in any way between timing one operation and the next.

Many of the operations require a reference to (i.e., the object id of) a randomly selected node as input. These references might be generated by having a separate index mapping *uniqueIds* (integers) to object ids. In any case, for operations whose input is a randomly selected node, this generation of object references is done in the untimed setup phase. If an operation returns a result, we must be careful about whether or not we include the time to create returned objects. In our implementations, a result array was created in the (untimed) setup phase and then filled in with object ids (and other results) as necessary within the timed operations.

Next, we give a brief description of each operation. For each, we specify the implementation with respect to the HyperModel data structures, the input to the operation, and the output from the operation.

5.1. Name Lookup Operations

These operations retrieve an attribute of a node based on a reference to it. In the first operation, the object is specified by providing its unique integer-valued key (*uniqueId*) and in the other operation it is specified by providing a direct reference (i.e., an object id) for it. Indexing, which may speed-up the first operation, is permitted.

nameLookup()
Specification: Find the *Node* instance with *uniqueId* attribute equal to *n* and return the value of its *hundred* attribute.
Input: A random integer (*n*) between 1 and the number of nodes.
Output: The value of the *hundred* attribute for the corresponding node.

nameOIDLookup()
Specification: Find the *Node* instance with a given object id and return the value of its *hundred* attribute.
Input: A reference to a random node (i.e., an object id).
Output: The value of the *hundred* attribute for the corresponding node.

5.2. Range Lookup Operations

These operations find the nodes satisfying a range predicate based on the values of an attribute. The two range lookup operations have selectivity of 10% and 1% and allow for the use of an indexing mechanism on the *hundred* and *million* attributes.

rangeLookupHundred()
Specification: Get the set of all nodes that have the *hundred* attribute in the range x..x+9 (10% selectivity).
Input: A pair of numbers (x, x+9), where x is randomly selected from 1..91.
Output: The set of object ids for the nodes whose *hundred* attribute is in the given range.

rangeLookupMillion()
Specification: Get the set of all nodes that have the *million* attribute in the range x..x+9999 (1% selectivity).
Input: A pair of numbers (x, x+9999), where x is randomly selected from 1..990001.
Output: The set of object ids for nodes whose *million* attribute is in the given range.

5.3. Group Lookup Operations

These operations follow the *parent/children* relationship, the *partOf/parts* relationship and the *refTo/refFrom* relationship one level from a randomly selected node. The returned object should contain references to the nodes found.

groupLookup1N()
Specification: Get the *children* nodes of a random node.
Input: A reference to a randomly selected internal (i.e., non-leaf) node.
Output: A set of five object id's representing the *children* of the given node.

groupLookupMN()
Specification: Get the *parts* nodes of a random node.
Input: A reference to a randomly selected node.
Output: A set of five object id's representing the *parts* of the given node.

groupLookupMNAtt()
Specification: Get the node related to a given node by the *refTo/refFrom* relationship attribute *refTo*.
Input: A reference to a randomly selected node.
Output: The object id of the node referenced by the given node.

5.4. Reference Lookup Operations

This group of operations is similar to those in group lookup, except that the *parent/children* relationship, the *partOf/parts* relationship, and the *refTo/refFrom* relationship are followed in the inverse direction.

refLookup1N()

Specification: Given a node, find its *father* node.
Input: The object id of a random non-root node.
Output: The object id of the *father* of the given node.

refLookupMN()

Specification: Given a node, find the nodes it is a *partOf*.
Input: The object id of a randomly selected node.
Output: A set containing the object ids of the nodes it is a *partOf*.

refLookupMNAtt()

Specification: Get the nodes related to a given node by following the *refTo/refFrom* attribute *refFrom*.
Input: The object id of a randomly selected node.
Output: A set (possibly empty) containing the object ids representing the nodes that reference the given node.

5.4.1. Sequential Scan

This operation finds the total time to visit all of the nodes in the test database and access the *ten* attribute of each node. The database should be allowed to have other instances of class *Node* (e.g., a second copy of the test database) so the *instancesOf* property of the *Node* class (or an equivalent) cannot be used to iterate through its elements. If the database supports "contexts" or object spaces this may be used, but the requirement is that the application program must be able to simultaneously access other node objects not in the test database.

seqScan()

Specification: Get the *ten* attribute of each node in the test database, and add it to a running total.
Input: None.
Output: The sum of the *ten* attribute values over all the nodes in the database.

5.5. Closure Traversal Operations

These operations start with a random node and perform operations on the nodes transitively reachable by a certain relationship from the given node. These operations are defined to start at a specific node and to follow either the *parent/children* relationship, the *partOf/parts* relationship, or the *refTo/refFrom* relationship to a certain depth. The *parent/children* closure must preserve the order of the sub-node relationships, and deliver a list of references according to a pre-order traversal of the structure. The list should be in a form storable in the database. (This could for instance be used in a simple table of contents for the structure.)

closure1N()

Specification: Get a list of references to all nodes reachable from a random node on level 3 by following the *parent/children* relationship recursively to the leaves of the tree. The list should be ordered according to a pre-order traversal of the structure.
Input: The object id of a randomly selected node at level 3 in the *parent/children* hierarchy.
Output: A list of object ids for all nodes reachable from the given node by following the *parent/children* relationship recursively.

closureMN()

Specification: Get references to all nodes reachable from a random node on level 3 by following the *partOf/parts* relationship recursively to the leaves of the tree. Since clustering may be used for the *parent/children* relationship, it is assumed that this will take longer than *closure1N()*.
Input: The object id of a randomly selected node at level 3 in the *parent/children* hierarchy.
Output: A list of object ids for all nodes reachable from the given node by following the *partOf/parts*

relationship recursively.

closureMNAtt()

Specification: Specification: Get references to all nodes reachable from a random node on level 3 by following the *refTo/refFrom* relationship recursively to a depth of twenty-five – i.e. starting with the original node, visit twenty-five additional nodes by following the *refTo* relationship. (Recall that this relationship has a fan-out of one, not five as for the other two relationships.)

Input: The object id of a random node at level 3 in the *parent/children* hierarchy.

Output: A list of object ids for all nodes reachable from the given node by following the *refTo/refFrom* relationship recursively to a depth of twenty-five.

closure1NAttSum()

Specification: Get the sum of the *hundred* attribute for all nodes reachable from a random node on level 3 by following the *parent/child* relationship recursively to the leaves of the tree.

Input: The object id of random node at level 3 in the *parent/children* hierarchy.

Output: An integer representing the sum of the *hundred* attribute for all the nodes visited.

closure1NAttSet()

Specification: For all nodes reachable from a random node on level 3 by following the *parent/children* relationship recursively to the leaves of the tree, set the *hundred* attribute to ninety-nine minus the current value. (Note that by doing this twice the attribute is restored to its original value.)

Input: The object id of a random node at level 3 in the *parent/children* hierarchy.

Output: None. The nodes in the database will have been updated, however, so the commit time will be included.

closure1NPred()

Specification: Get references to all nodes reachable from a random node on level 3 by following the *parent/children* relationship recursively to the leaves of the tree. Exclude those nodes that have the *million* attribute in the range from x to x+9999. Also exclude the nodes that satisfy the predicate from further recursion (i.e., don't visit their children).

Input: The object id of a random node at level 3 in the *parent/children* hierarchy and a random integer in the range 1..990001.

Output: A set of node object id's that are reachable from the given node and that satisfy the predicate.

closureMNAttLinkSum()

Specification: Get a total, measured by summing the *offsetTo* attribute, for all nodes reachable from a random node on level 3 by following the *refTo/refFrom* relationship recursively to a depth of twenty-five (see definition of *closureMNAtt()* operation). Return a list of pairs containing the object reference and associated total.

Input: The object id of a random node at level 3 in the *parent/children* hierarchy.

Output: A set of pairs whose first elements are the node object id's that are reachable from the given node and whose second element is the value of the *offsetTo* attribute for the associated link (i.e., the *refTo/refFrom* relationship).

5.6. Editing Operations

These operations test the power of the database programming language and will determine whether any statements have to be executed in another programming language. These operations also determine the overhead to update a node, assuming that this node has just been updated by someone else. For both *FormNodes* and *TextNodes*, the node must be checked out if some system guarantee of exclusive write-access is not provided. For *TextNodes*, a sub-string is substituted while, for *FormNodes*, a selected sub-rectangle is inverted. The node is then released for others to update. The average time per node to perform the update is measured (including the time to retrieve and store the node).

textNodeEdit()

Specification: Get a random *TextNode* and substitute all three occurrences of sub-string "version1" with for approximately ninety-five percent of the implementation of the HyperModel benchmark. The text node population routines were the exception, and were written in C (random word generation is slow in OPAL due to inefficiencies in arithmetic).

(R4) Dynamic modifications to the database schema.

VBASE: New types may be added to the database, and migration of objects after a schema change is possible in some cases.

GEMSTONE: New types may be added to the database, but migration of objects after an attribute has been added to a type is not done.

(R5) Support for Versions and Variants.

VBASE, GEMSTONE: Versions and variants are not directly supported in either system though types may be created by the user to implement this functionality.

(R6) An architecture of workstations and servers.

VBASE: Version 1.0 is multi-user but runs only on a single processor.

GEMSTONE: GemStone is multi-user and has a client-server architecture, but is not fully distributed.[3] Thus, one can have multiple session processes running on different workstations directly accessing objects in a file over a network. A single monitor process controls object id allocation and the commit token.[4]

(R8) Concurrency Control.

VBASE: Version 1.0 supports a transaction mechanism for multiple users on a single processor and shared-memory, based on an optimistic concurrency control scheme.

GEMSTONE: There is an optimistic concurrency control scheme.

(R9) Cooperation between users.

VBASE: Synchronization primitives (lock, sequencer, and event count) may be used by the application programmer (similar to the use of semaphores). These might be building blocks for a long transaction mechanism. However an automatic abort occurring when one user reads something another has written may cause problems.

GEMSTONE: There is no support for long transactions. Also although there is a concurrency control mechanism that coordinates and controls simultaneous access to data, there are no explicit mechanisms implemented to enhance collaboration between multiple users on distributed workstations.

(R10) Logging, backup and recovery.

VBASE: The environment utilities contain backup and restore facilities.

GEMSTONE: The system supports online backup, and recovery is automatically done at startup if necessary. It is also possible to have more than one copy of the database online at one time (replicates).

(R11) Access control.

[3] The current HyperModel benchmark implementation is executing on a single processor. Since GemStone supports a client-server architecture, it is possible to implement a multi-workstation version as a simple extension to the current benchmark. Also, though the benchmark was done on a stand-alone Sun 3/60 there was a network error during the run that required restarting the system. This is because GemStone uses TCP/IP protocol to handle communication between the Gem and Stone processes even when running on a single system.

[4] The monitor process and associated file of objects are on a single node rather than being fully distributed.

the string "version-2" in the first (cold) run, then substitute back again in the second (warm) run. Note that the new string is one character longer.

Input: The object id of a randomly selected text node on the leaf level of the tree.

Output: None. The nodes in the database will have been updated, however.

formNodeEdit()

Specification: Invert a (50x50) subrectangle with corner points (25,25) and (75,75) in a randomly selected *FormNode*. To imitate an interactive editor session, do this 10 times on each node.

Input: The object id of a randomly selected *FormNode* on the leaf level of the tree.

Output: None, although the database will be updated.

5.7. Possible Extensions to the Operation Set

The HyperModel provides a useful framework within which to experiment with other operations that might prove useful in evaluating OO-DBMSs. Such additional benchmarking operations might include:

(1) Add a new type, *DrawNode*, or add an attribute to an existing type (to assess schema modification capabilities).

(2) Find the previous version or a specific version of a node (to assess version handling capabilities).

(3) Set the access to the nodes in a specific document to read-only or non-access for public (to check on access control).

6. Evaluation Against Requirements

This section revisits the requirements for engineering applications listed in Section 3 and comments briefly on the extent to which Vbase and GemStone satisfy them. There is not space for an in-depth analysis of the results and a discussion of the measured systems.

(R1) Modeling of complex object structures.

VBASE: The HyperModel is easily mappable to TDL. For the *partOf/parts* relationship the system automatically maintains the inverse whenever one of the relationships is updated. However, since the inverse relationship mechanism can only be specified for sets but not for lists, the *parent/children* aggregation relationship (which requires ordering) has to be handled explicitly. There is no special support for complex objects/aggregation relationship, but clustering may be specified at creation time.[2]

GEMSTONE: The HyperModel is easily mappable to OPAL. There is no explicit notion of inverse relationships in the system so that updates to both the *parent/children* relationship and *partOf/parts* relationship have to be managed explicitly. There is no special support for complex objects/aggregation relationship, but clustering may be specified at creation time (e.g., clustering was used along the *parent/children* relationship.)

(R2) Description of different data types.

VBASE, GEMSTONE: Since user-defined types can be created and array is a basic type, all the specified types are easily defined in both systems.

(R3) Integration with application programming languages.

VBASE: There is a natural integration with C through COP, but no support for C++, Smalltalk or other languages. The programmer needs to know 3 languages: C, COP and TDL.

GEMSTONE: There was a straightforward mapping from our initial prototype implementation in Smalltalk to OPAL. OPAL supports an interface to Smalltalk, C and Pascal through conversion routines. OPAL was used

[2] The clustering mechanism could be used, for example, to cluster nodes in the same aggregation hierarchy to possibly give better performance for some of the transitive closure queries. However, there was a documented error in Release 1.0 clustering and we did not attempt to use this feature for the benchmark.

VBASE: There are no access control facilities.

GEMSTONE: There are access control facilities, based on segments.

(R12) Ad-Hoc Query Language.

VBASE: There is a query language, Object SQL, with a "Select-From-Where" query style.

GEMSTONE: There is no query language interface.

7. Conclusions and Future Work

The HyperModel benchmark is a new benchmark specifically designed to test the performance of DBMSs developed or extended for engineering applications. However, we feel that it will also be useful to evaluate existing DBMS performance, particularly to test the performance of their programming languages interfaces. Furthermore, the HyperModel is also a good starting point to benchmark OO-DBMSs for applications other than engineering since it tests two of the most important features of OO-DBMSs: complex object representation and complex operation implementation.

The HyperModel has been implemented for Vbase and GemStone, and a prototype implementation was done for Smalltalk. A relational system implementation is currently being done following the methodology outlined in [12] and an implementation is in preparation for the Ontos system. There is also ongoing work to implement it on some of the recent European Object Management Systems, like Damokles [0] and PCTE-OMS [7].

A second aspect to be investigated is the impact of a multi-user environment on the design and results of the benchmark. We have done some experiments with multi-user aspects by starting up two or more HyperModel applications in parallel and running the operations as for the single user case. However, since the systems we have worked with support optimistic concurrency control, it is a problem to define update operations that do not conflict. This is an area for future work in the HyperModel benchmark design.

Finally, we have also run the Sun benchmark and a major portion of the Wisconsin benchmark for the two systems, Vbase and GemStone. There are differences in the results between the three benchmarks that need to be studied and explained. Basically, the question is: "What do the various benchmarks measure and how can they be used in concert to more accurately predict the performance of a particular application or mix of applications?"

Acknowledgements

This work was done while the authors were at Tektronix, and during the *Database Year 1987-88* sponsored by the Oregon Graduate Institute for Science and Technology (formerly Oregon Graduate Center) and the Oregon Center for Advanced Technology Education. A special thanks is due to Professor David Maier for arranging the *Database Year* and providing numerous valuable discussions for the benchmark design. Thanks also to Rick Cattell and the other participants at the "Workshop on Object-Oriented Database Benchmarking" in March 1988, arranged by the Oregon Database Forum. Arne J. Berre was sponsored by a fellowship from the Royal Norwegian Council for Scientific Research during the Database Year.

A. APPENDIX: Benchmark Results

To date, the HyperModel benchmark has been implemented on two systems: Release 1.0 of Ontologic's Vbase[5] and an engineering release of Servio Logic's GemStone. A prototype has also been implemented in Smalltalk. Implementations on Ontos, Relational Technology's Ingres, Sybase and a more recent release of GemStone are currently under way. This section reports on the results of the Vbase and GemStone implementations. We first note that the two OO-DBMSs evaluated did not meet all the requirements listed in Section 2. The current implementations of the benchmark reflect these deficiencies: you can't test what isn't there. We also recommend that the numbers presented below be taken as somewhat provisional; improvements in the accuracy of the existing implementations will be realized as the benchmarks are ported to a more current version of GemStone and to Ontos. Specific results are included in this report primarily to provide an example of the form in which benchmark results are to be reported.

Vbase and GemStone are both based on an object-oriented data model. Thus, for both systems, the Hyper-Model schema is mapped to four class definitions: *Node, TextNode, FormNode,* and *Link*. The *TextNode* and *FormNode* classes are subclasses of *Node*. The *Link* class is used to store the attributes *offsetTo* and *offsetFrom* for the *refFrom/refTo* relationship representing hypertext links. The *parent/children* relationship is implemented as a list in the parent and backward pointer in the child, while the *partOf/parts* relationship is implemented as two sets containing node references.

Though special care was taken to insure that the benchmark was implemented in a similar fashion on both systems, two main differences still exist in the final result. These differences are due to indexing and to message sends vs. procedure calls. First, Vbase provides no built-in indexing mechanism to support range queries while GemStone provides general-purpose indexing based on B-trees. To lessen the effect of this, a simple hashed array was used to implement the index in Vbase.[6] This gave Vbase an advantage since the hashing scheme was tailored to the query rather than being general purpose. Also, GemStone's indexing mechanism was slightly slower than expected. Second, though Vbase is an OO-DBMS, it is possible to use procedure calls rather than message sends to increase performance. This was done for the benchmark implementation. We were not aware that a similar, well-documented, structural access facility is available through the C interface to GemStone that, in some cases, has significant performance advantages over the message-send paradigm available in OPAL. Thus, we intend to recode the Vbase and GemStone benchmarks using both the message-send and procedure-call interfaces to determine the effect of this difference.

We feel that benchmark results are only comparable if the benchmarks are run on the same machine. These results were produced on a Sun 3/60 with Sun/OS 3.4 and 12 MB of memory, a 141 MB Micropolis 1355 disk drive, an 86 MB Fujitsu 2243AS disk drive, and swap space of 45 MB. The Micropolis disk contained the system executables and swap space, while the Fujitsu disk contained the data space. The cache size for GemStone is fixed and is approximately 1.5 MB for the release tested. The Vbase cache size is variable and was set at 4 MB. (The benchmark requires the cache size to be no larger than 4 MB.) The benchmark was run for the level 4 and level 5 test databases for both GemStone and Vbase. However, the full level 6 test was completed only for GemStone because of problems encountered in loading the level 6 database in Vbase. In particular, the temporary file space used in database creation exceeded the 60 MB available on the Micropolis disk. (It is possible that more frequent commits during loading could have alleviated this problem.) The following shows the size of the empty (kernel) database and of the three different test databases, with 781 (Level 4), 3906 (Level 5), and 19531 (Level 6) nodes, respectively.

Database Size in MB				
System	Empty	Level 4	Level 5	Level 6
Vbase	5.5	8.6	20.1	
GemStone	1.1	2.4	6.5	27.0

A.1. Database Creation

Time for object and relationship creation was measured when the test databases were created. Note that since each node is represented by 6 or more objects, a correspondingly higher number of objects is present in the test database. The measured time is split into time for internal and leaf node creation with corresponding commits, and time for the creation of the different relationships. Node creation also includes time to initialize all node attributes and to update appropriate indexing structures. For each case, the total elapsed time is divided by the corresponding number of nodes or of relationships created. (For example, for the *parent/children* relationship, the link between a

[5] Ontologic is now marketing a second generation OO-DBMS, called Ontos, which features a C++ language binding.

[6] The programmer would have to build and maintain this index for every indexed collection, since this is not provided by the system.

node and its five children is counted as one relationship.) The numbers reported below are thus the average time in milliseconds to create an instance of a node or of a relationship of the indicated type.

Create Internal Nodes (milliseconds/node)						
System	Level 4	Commit	Level 5	Commit	Level 6	Commit
Vbase	1356.3	208.2	1262.9	521.6		
GemStone	115.0	51.9	114.1	20.1	145.2	8.1

Create Leaf Nodes (milliseconds/node)						
System	Level 4	Commit	Level 5	Commit	Level 6	Commit
Vbase	1571.5	236.5	3329.0	715.7		
GemStone	176.0	27.2	198.9	13.4	230.1	6.4

Create parent/children Relationship (milliseconds/relationship)						
System	Level 4	Commit	Level 5	Commit	Level 6	Commit
Vbase	35.0	180.2	56.2	550.3		
GemStone	7.9	11.0	13.3	6.0	24.5	3.6

Create partOf/parts Relationship (milliseconds/relationship)						
System	Level 4	Commit	Level 5	Commit	Level 6	Commit
Vbase	72.4	159.3	203.5	492.1		
GemStone	43.7	13.1	149.0	8.1	880.5	2.9

Create refTo/refFrom Relationship (milliseconds/relationship)						
System	Level 4	Commit	Level 5	Commit	Level 6	Commit
Vbase	243.1	188.5	400.8	611.5		
GemStone	95.4	16.5	261.3	7.9	583.4	3.7

A.2. Benchmark Operations

In the tables that follow, we report the results of running the benchmark operations on level 4 and level 5 test databases for the two OO-DBMSs and the results of running the operations on a level 6 GemStone database. The heading "4-cold" is the cold run time on the level 4 database, and so on. Each number is the mean time to perform the operation, computed by averaging over the 50 operations as described earlier.

A.2.1. Name Lookup Operations

Name Lookup (milliseconds/operation)						
System	4-cold	4-warm	5-cold	5-warm	6-cold	6-warm
Vbase	80.0	12.4	152.8	12.0		
GemStone	66.0	8.0	92.0	11.2	332.4	8.8

Name OID Lookup (milliseconds/operation)						
System	4-cold	4-warm	5-cold	5-warm	6-cold	6-warm
Vbase	46.8	2.4	141.6	2.4		
GemStone	30.0	7.2	33.6	13.6	73.8	7.8

A.2.2. Range Lookup Operations

Range Lookup - Million (milliseconds/operation)						
System	4-cold	4-warm	5-cold	5-warm	6-cold	6-warm
Vbase	105.5	77.9	96.1	57.9		
GemStone	28.2	26.6	30.8	27.2	108.6	96.5

A.2.3. Group Lookup Operations

Group Lookup 1-N (milliseconds/operation)						
System	4-cold	4-warm	5-cold	5-warm	6-cold	6-warm
Vbase	8.2	1.4	28.6	1.3		
GemStone	33.0	12.4	98.2	10.0	232.4	13.8

Group Lookup M-N Attribute (milliseconds/operation)						
System	4-cold	4-warm	5-cold	5-warm	6-cold	6-warm
Vbase	91.6	9.6	241.2	9.2		
GemStone	102.8	100.6	264.8	47.6	1228.4	230.8

A.2.4. Reference Lookup Operations

Reference Lookup 1-N (milliseconds/operation)						
System	4-cold	4-warm	5-cold	5-warm	6-cold	6-warm
Vbase	51.2	2.4	133.2	2.8		
GemStone	46.4	8.0	113.2	11.6	344.2	30.0

Reference Lookup M-N Attribute (milliseconds/operation)						
System	4-cold	4-warm	5-cold	5-warm	6-cold	6-warm
Vbase	89.8	9.1	285.0	11.0		
GemStone	127.4	63.3	275.3	45.5	922.3	172.3

A.2.5. Sequential Scan

Sequential Scan (milliseconds/operation)						
System	4-cold	4-warm	5-cold	5-warm	6-cold	6-warm
Vbase	3.2	2.9	11.3	10.5		
GemStone	6.3	6.6	8.1	7.6	12.5	13.0

A.2.6. Closure Traversal Operations

Closure 1-N (milliseconds/operation)						
System	4-cold	4-warm	5-cold	5-warm	6-cold	6-warm
Vbase	33.9	16.0	35.4	15.9		
GemStone	20.9	12.7	25.6	22.1	62.7	26.9

Closure M-N (milliseconds/operation)						
System	4-cold	4-warm	5-cold	5-warm	6-cold	6-warm
Vbase	44.4	17.8	76.2	58.9		
GemStone	24.6	17.9	65.0	52.3	261.7	129.6

Closure M-N Attribute (milliseconds/operation)						
System	4-cold	4-warm	5-cold	5-warm	6-cold	6-warm
Vbase	27.8	20.4	66.9	20.4		
GemStone	38.9	29.7	102.0	88.2	594.0	214.0

Closure 1NAttSum (milliseconds/operation)						
System	4-cold	4-warm	5-cold	5-warm	6-cold	6-warm
Vbase	23.4	7.3	24.5	7.3		
GemStone	20.2	5.0	24.5	21.0	54.8	25.7

Closure 1NAttSet (milliseconds/operation)						
System	4-cold	4-warm	5-cold	5-warm	6-cold	6-warm
Vbase	210.9	198.4	469.7	467.2		
GemStone	41.2	22.0	57.0	44.1	190.0	123.0

Closure 1NPred (milliseconds/operation)						
System	4-cold	4-warm	5-cold	5-warm	6-cold	6-warm
Vbase	37.5	18.3	37.1	18.4		
GemStone	24.9	15.5	25.3	22.9	66.9	32.0

Closure MNAttLinkSum (milliseconds/operation)						
System	4-cold	4-warm	5-cold	5-warm	6-cold	6-warm
Vbase	31.0	22.5	65.3	22.5		
GemStone	42.4	37.2	105.5	92.0	631.8	253.1

A.2.7. Editing Operations

TextNode Edit (milliseconds/operation)						
System	4-cold	4-warm	5-cold	5-warm	6-cold	6-warm
Vbase	252.4	145.6	1347.6	996.8		
GemStone	134.6	60.8	176.4	58.8	573.6	70.0

FormNode Edit (milliseconds/operation)						
System	4-cold	4-warm	5-cold	5-warm	6-cold	6-warm
Vbase	3841.2	3728.4	4222.8	3722.4		
GemStone	382.8	345.6	525.6	392.8	1261.6	558.4

1. T.L. Anderson, J. Besemer, and E.F. Ecklund, *DBMS Requirements for Engineering Applications*, Tektronix Internal Report and forthcoming paper (June 1987).
2. Anon and et al., ''A Measure of Transaction Processing Power,'' *Datamation* **31**(7)(April 1985).
3. P. Bernstein, ''Database System Support for Software Engineering - An Extended Abstract,'' in *Proceedings of the 9th International Conference on Software Engineering*, , Monterey, California (April 1987).
4. D. Bitton, D. DeWitt, and C. Turbyfill, *Benchmarking Database Systems - A Systematic Approach*, University of Wisconsin-Madison, Technical Report #526 (December 1983).
5. R.G.G. Cattell, ''Object-Oriented DBMS Performance Measurement,'' pp. Springer-Verlag in *Advances in Object-Oriented Database Systems — Proceedings of the Second International Workshop on Object-Oriented Database Systems*, ed. K.R. Dittrich,, Bad Munster am Stein-Ebernburg, FRG (September 1988).
6. J. Conklin, N. Delisle, and M. Schwartz, ''Neptune: A Hypertext System for CAD Applications,'' *IEEE Computer*, (May 1986).
7. F. Gallo, R. Minot, and I. Thomas, P. Garg, and W. Scacchi, ''On Designing Intelligent Hypertext Systems for Information Management in Software Engineering,'' in *Proceedings of Hypertext'87*, , Chapel Hill, North Carolina (November 1987).
8. M. Loomis and J. Rumbaugh, ''An Object-Modeling Technique for Conceptual Design,'' in *ECOOP-87*, ().
9. D. Maier and D. Price, ''Data Model Requirements for Engineering Applications,'' in *Proceedings of the 1st International Workshop on Expert Database Systems*, , Kiawah Island, South Carolina (October 1984).
10. Reenskaug, T., *The Tender/One Environment*, Center for Industrial Research, Technical Report 86-15, Oslo, Norway (1986).
11. W. Rubenstein, M. Kubicar, and R. Cattell, ''Benchmarking Simple Database Operations,'' in *Proceedings of the 1987 ACM SIGMOD International Conference on the Management of Data*, , San Francisco, California (May 1987).
12. K. Dittrich, W. Gotthard, and P. Lockemann, ''DAMOKLES - A Database System for Software Engineering Environments,'' in *Proceedings of IFIP Workshop on Advanced Programming Environments*, , Trondheim, Norway (June 1986).
13. M. Blaha, W. Premerlani, and J. Rumbaugh, ''Relational Database Design Using an Object-Oriented Methodology,'' *Communications of the Association for Computing Machinery* **31**(4)(April 1988).

LISPO$_2$: a Persistent Object-Oriented Lisp

Gilles Barbedette
Altaïr
BP105
78153 Le Chesnay Cedex

Abstract

Large and complex design applications such as CASE, office automation and knowledge based applications require sophisticated development environments supporting modeling, persistence and evolution of complex objects. This paper presents a brief overview of a persistent object-oriented LISP named LISPO$_2$ combining both language and database facilities. LISPO$_2$ is a Lisp-based environment providing the O$_2$ object-oriented data model extended with the notions of constructor and exception. Persistence is achieved through the use of a persistent name space. These features centered around an interpreter facilitate quick prototyping of applications.

1 Introduction

In order to support new application domains such as CASE, office automation or knowledge bases, a development environment has to provide both modeling power and database facilities. The former requires the representation and manipulation of complex objects (programs, documents, rules...), while the latter requires sharing and persistence between program invocations.

Databases and programming languages have tried separately to cope with these types of applications. Traditional database systems support persistence, but fail to model objects either in their structural or behavioral complexity. For instance, first normal form relational systems do not deal with structural complexity. Moreover, to express complex behavior, application programmers have to use a query language embedded in a programming language. They are thus faced with the well known "impedance mismatch" problem [Cope84]: they have to learn two different languages and map continuously their different models.

In contrast, programming languages, in particular object-oriented languages [Gold83] [Stro86] [Meye88], offer powerful features such as encapsulation, inheritance and exception handling that ease the design, implementation and evolution of modular and robust applications. However they support only a limited form of persistence through the use of files. Therefore the programmer has to flatten the highly interconnected in-core data structure onto the linear format of files. These error-prone conversions interfere with the application logic, decreasing programmer productivity.

Recently, efforts to integrate database and programming languages have come either from database people producing object-oriented databases [Banc88], [Bane87], [Andr87], and [Maie86] or from programming language people producing persistent languages [Schm77], [Atki81], and [Alba85]. These efforts focus on eliminating the major bottleneck to programmer productivity in such systems: the impedance mismatch.

LISPO$_2$ belongs in this trend. It is a Lisp-based language devoted to supporting incremental and

interactive design of applications. It provides the programmer with object orientation to cope with complex design and persistence facilities to deal with data lifetime.
$LISPO_2$ is developed within the Altaïr project whose objective is to build a multi-language object-oriented database system called O_2. This system provides a data model [Lécl89a] with which the programmer can design an application schema and, for the time being, two languages, namely $BASICO_2$ and CO_2 [Lécl89b], used to implement the behavioral part of the application. However $LISPO_2$ should be distinguished from $BASICO_2$ and CO_2. The latter are intended to be used in an industrial environment while the former is designed to experiment with object orientation and persistence. Hence, although it retains the advantages of the O_2 data model, $LISPO_2$ is autonomous and is developed following the LISP philosophy using bootstrapping techniques, i.e. almost all the system is implemented using the language. Hence, it offers the flexible architecture needed in an experimentation environment.
The remainder of the paper is organized as follows. Section 2 introduces the object-oriented features of the language. Section 3 is devoted to the integration of persistence in the language. This is followed, in Section 4, by a brief outline of the implementation. Section 5 compares $LISPO_2$ with other related approaches. Finally, we conclude by indicating future plans.

2 Object-Oriented Features

Although several object-oriented languages [Stro86], [Gold83], [Meye88] and databases [Care88], [Andr87], [Bane87], [Banc88] have appeared, there is no universal consensus on the term "object-oriented" [Wegn87]. Its meaning ranges from "prototype based" [Lieb86] to "class based with inheritance" [Stro86]. $LISPO_2$ belongs to the family of languages where the term object-oriented implies the conjunction of encapsulation, class and inheritance. This section gives an informal presentation of how these notions are defined and used in the $LISPO_2$ language. Additional features such as tailored object creation and exception handling are also described. We illustrate them by means of a simple example. This application concerns the management of a flying club whose members have a passion for antique airplanes.

2.1 Objects and Classes, Values and Types

To manage the complexity of applications, any modern programming language provides the programmer with both abstract and concrete representation of data. Data abstraction allows the programmer to model and organize information of the real world naturally in term of its functionality without concentrating on its implementation. In contrast, concrete representation is generally used to structure the implementation of data.
$LISPO_2$ is an object-oriented language and thus offers data abstraction through *objects*. Objects encapsulate a state via an operational interface. Object manipulation is achieved through *operations* and not by directly accessing its internal state.
On the other hand, $LISPO_2$ also supports unencapsulated data. These are *values*. They are used both at an implementation level to represent object states and at a modeling level whenever data abstraction is not useful. Thus, an object can be seen as a capsule built around a value. While objects are manipulated by operations, values are manipulated by *operators*. Figure 1 shows how we can represent the parts of an airplane as objects. It presents a wheel object whose encapsulated value is an aggregate containing the name of the part, the set of parts of which it is a component

and its supplier. Objects are denoted using identifiers in italics. Values are either simple as the string "wheel", or complex as the set (**setof** *landing-gear*).

$LISPO_2$ is a class-based object-oriented language, i.e. each object is generated by (is an instance of) a *class*. A class describes the structure (state) and behavior (operations) of its instances. Just as classes are object descriptors, *types* are value descriptors. For instance the type associated with the value encapsulated by the object *wheel* in Figure 1 is shown in Figure 2. Classes are denoted with capital letters. Classes are defined using a **defclass** command as shown in Figure 3 where bold font is used for reserved words. This class definition consists of three clauses:

- The **type** clause:
  Since objects encapsulate values, each class definition introduces a type describing the structure abstracted by its instances. A type in $LISPO_2$ is either an atomic type (integer, string, float...), or a complex type built from other types and classes using the tuple, set and list constructors. Tuple types offer aggregation. Set types represent collections without duplicates. List types support indexable and homogeneous collections as opposed to LISP lists which are head and tail access oriented, and heterogeneous.

- The **operations** clause:
  The **operations** clause describes the operational interface through which the rest of the world can manipulate instances of the class PART. It just specifies the operations. An operation specification, called a *signature*, consists of its name and the type/class of the arguments and result. The keyword **virtual** states that the operation specified cannot be implemented using only the information provided in class PART. This is further explained in Section 2.2.

- The **has-extension** clause:
  This provides automatic grouping of all created instances of the class into a set. It permits easy operations on all instances of that class. Section 2.4 further details this point.

The class PART definition shows the benefit of providing both type and class as modeling tools. To constrain the attribute "is-part-of", we use the type (**setof** COMPLEX-PART) instead of a class (say SETOF-COMPLEX-PART). Indeed, since the PART class defines an abstraction, the "is-part-of" attribute will be manipulated only by its operations. It is already protected and we do not see the advantage of defining another abstraction level. In addition, the "is-part-of" attribute appears to be just a set of parts and not a high level application concept such as the part concept. Hence it does not need to be described by a class. In contrast, using a SETOF-COMPLEX-PART class, would lead to an increasing complexity (and decreasing performance) in the manipulations since we would have to define and use operations on an object instead of direct operators on a value.

In languages such as Smalltalk [Gold83] where a class is the only modeling tool, natural complex values are simulated through objects. This leads to the definition of unnecessary classes and to a kind of "pollution" of the abstract space.

The object/value duality is inherited from the O_2 model presented in [Lécl89a] with a notable difference. In $LISPO_2$, the duality relies on the fact that objects are encapsulated and values are not. In the O_2 model, values are neither encapsulated nor shared. In $LISPO_2$, values are sharable because LISP is a language whose semantics is based on reference, i.e. all LISP data have an identity. Since objects and values are LISP data, they can be shared.

```
wheel = (tupleof
            (model-name "wheel")
            (is-part-of (setof landing-gear))
            (supplier darlington))
```

Figure 1: A wheel part

```
(tupleof
    (model-name string)
    (is-part-of (setof COMPLEX-PART))
    (supplier SUPPLIER))
```

Figure 2: Type describing the value encapsulated by *wheel*

```
(defclass PART
        ; definition of the type associated with the class
        (type (tupleof
                    (name string)
                    (is-part-of (setof COMPLEX-PART))
                    (supplier SUPPLIER)))
        ; definition of the operational interface
        (operations
            (virtual cost () (return integer))
            (virtual mass () (return integer)))
        ; automatic extension option
        has-extension)
```

Figure 3: Class PART definition

```
(defclass COMPLEX-PART
        ; list the classes from which the class inherits
        (PART)
        (type (tupleof
                (assembly-cost integer)
                (components (setof (tupleof
                                        (quantity integer)
                                        (part PART))))))
        (operations
           (cost () (return integer))
           (mass () (return integer)))
        has-extension)

(defclass BASIC-PART
        (PART)
        (type (tupleof
                (cost integer r)
                (mass integer r)))
        has-extension)
```

Figure 4: Complex and Basic part definitions

2.2 Inheritance

Classes are more than just abstract data types. They are related each other through inheritance links. It enables the modeling of semantic generalization/specialization relationships occurring between objects in the application (e.g. an employee is a person, or a complex part is a part). A subclass inherits the structure and behavior specified by its superclasses. Moreover it can either redefine or extend them.

To have a more realistic model of airplane parts, we now define the two subclasses of PART that describe respectively complex and basic parts (see Figure 4). The class COMPLEX-PART is said to inherit from the class PART. Hence, the programmer simply specifies in the subclass the additional attributes and operations. This leads to an incremental modeling style where only differences from existing concepts are specified.

Notice the structural complexity of the type associated with the class COMPLEX-PART. With complex types, we model the "complex objects" (which are in fact pure complex values) provided by extensions of relational systems allowing relation-valued attributes as in [Dada86].

In the class BASIC-PART, the cost and mass are stored as attributes. Hence, the cost and mass operations are just attribute extraction operations. They are implicitly defined using the readable (r) option which automatically generates a read access operation for an attribute.

The **operations** clause of class COMPLEX-PART redefines explicitly the mass and cost operations defined as "virtual" in class PART. The class PART simply introduces functional properties of parts in their generality. It defines an abstract interface differently implemented in class COMPLEX-PART and BASIC-PART. This facility allows the inclusion in the language of classes that are pure interface specification. Such classes are useful as inheritance roots, since they represent the concept that is implemented differently in the subclasses. A similar feature can be found in the abstract classes of Smalltalk [Gold83] or the deferred facility of Eiffel [Meye88].

if T is an atomic type
then T' is an atomic type and T = T'

if T = (**setof** E) (resp. (**listof** E)),
then T' is set structured i.e. (**setof** E') (resp. list structured i.e. (**listof** E'))
and E' is a subtype of E.

if T is tuple structured i.e. of the form (**tupleof** (a_1 TA_1) ... (a_n TA_n))
then T' is tuple structured i.e. (**tupleof** (a_1 TA'_1) ... (a_m TA'_m))
$m \geq$ n and $\forall$ i $\in$ [1, ..., n] TA'_i is a subtype of TA_i

if T is a class,
then T' is a class and T' is a subclass of T.

Figure 5: Subtyping rules asserting that T' is a subtype of T

In LISPO$_2$, inheritance is based on subtyping and behavior refinement. If a class C' inherits from a class C, then the type of C' must be a subtype of the type of C. Figure 5 gives a syntactic definition of subtyping. For a formal description of the O$_2$ semantics of subtyping, the reader is referred to [Lécl89a]. In addition, C' may extend or redefine the operations offered by C. Redefinition occurs when C' defines an operation already defined in C. In that case, the operation of C' must have the same number of arguments as the one of C. Moreover the types of the arguments and result specified in the operation of C' must be subtypes of those specified in the operation of C.

Intuitively, these inheritance constraints ensure that a subclass introduces more information either by specializing or extending the information (structural or behavioral) provided by its superclasses. Since the core of an application is the class hierarchy, inheritance based on subtyping allows the immediate detection of errors due to establishing a subclass relationship between two unrelated concepts. Moreover it allows static type checking of operations as explained in Section 2.6.

In the part example, we use simple inheritance. LISPO$_2$ also supports multiple inheritance, i.e. a class may inherit from several direct superclasses. We illustrate this point with the example of the flying club members given in Figure 6 (where we omit the type specifications for clarity). They are categorized into general club members, pilots and mechanics, each category being modeled with a class. Each club member has a status operation returning the category to which he/she belongs. Let us assume that some new members can both repair and pilot (maybe different) airplanes. To model this situation, we want to define a PILOT-MECHANIC class which inherits both from PILOT and MECHANIC. Unfortunately, such a definition leads to an inheritance conflict. Indeed, the PILOT and MECHANIC classes both have a status operation. Therefore, there is a name conflict in the PILOT-MECHANIC class. The programmer has to solve it explicitly, either by choosing which operation to inherit (the one from PILOT or the one from MECHANIC) or by defining a new local operation as shown in Figure 6.

Unlike some systems such as ORION [Bane87], we do not rely on the order of the superclasses given in the class definition to solve the conflict. We believe that this solution does not offer a clear view of the inheritance paths (who inherits from whom) when the class hierarchy becomes

```
(defclass MEMBER
    (PERSON)
    (operations
        (status () (return string)))) ; the general status is "member"

(defclass PILOT
    (MEMBER)
    (operations
        (status () (return string)))) ; the status is "pilot"

(defclass MECHANIC
    (MEMBER)
    (operations
        (status () (return string)))) ; the status is "mechanic"

(defclass PILOT-MECHANIC
    ; multiple inheritance
    (PILOT MECHANIC)
    (operations
        (status () (return string)))) ; the status is "pilot and mechanic"
```

Figure 6: Classes representing club members

complex. Moreover, schema manipulations such as adding an operation or a superclass change the inherited operation and thus affect unpredictably the behavior of existing programs.
Notice that, if the status operation were defined only in the MEMBER class, adding the PILOT-MECHANIC class would not lead to a name conflict. Inheriting the same operation from two different paths is not a name conflict.

2.3 Operation Implementations: Methods

Operations are just the specifications of the behavior provided by a class. For each operation defined in a class, there is a *method* that implements it. Methods are coded in LISP extended with object and value manipulation expressions. For instance, the method shown in Figure 7 computes the cost of a complex part. Within methods defined in a class, the programmer can manipulate the internal representation of an instance of this class. For this, he/she needs a means to pass from an object to its associated value, i.e. to break encapsulation: this is the *disencapsulate* operator. If "x" is a variable denoting an object, then "x." denotes its value.
Besides disencapsulation, operations are the only way to act upon objects. Applying an operation to an object consists in *sending a message* to it. Following Smalltalk terminology, the object is called the *receiver*. Message passing is expressed using brackets. In a method, the receiver of the message is automatically bound to the pseudo variable **self**.
While objects are capsules and are manipulated through operations, values are not encapsulated and are manipulated using predefined operators. For example, the **get-field** operator allows the attribute extraction of a tuple value. Thus, the expression "[(**get-field** component 'part) cost]" extracts the object stored in the attribute part and sends it the cost message. Attribute names are not denotable values of the language. This would prevent the static type checking of

```
(defmethod (COMPLEX-PART cost) ()
   ; initialization of the result with the assembly cost
   (let ((cost self.assembly-cost))
      ; iterate over the components of the complex part and accumulate their cost
      (foreach ((component self.components))
         (setq cost (+ cost
         ; multiply the quantity by the cost of the part
                     (* (get-field component 'quantity)
                        [(get-field component 'part) cost]))))
      ; return the total cost
      cost))
```

Figure 7: Cost method for a complex part

methods. Therefore attribute names must appear as constants. This explains the quote ' used in LISP to represent constants. Since tuple-structured objects are frequently used, we offer a short notation for extracting attributes of tuple values encapsulated in objects. Hence the expression "**self**.assembly-cost" is equivalent to "(**get-field self**. 'assembly-cost)".

A notable operator on collection values (sets or lists) is the **foreach** iterator. It binds a temporary variable to each element of the collection and executes its body in this environment until a condition is satisfied or the end of the collection is reached.

We can now describe the body of the *complex cost* method. It iterates over the composition of the complex part, which is a set of tuple values. Each tuple value contains a component part and a quantity representing the number of times the part is involved in the composition of the complex part. Thus, each iteration computes the additional cost induced by the current component multiplying the cost the component part by its quantity.

A complex part can be made from basic parts and other complex ones. However, in the component cost computation i.e. "[(**get-field** component 'part) cost]", such a discrimination does not appear. This is because the system calls at run time the relevant method depending on whether the receiver is a basic or a complex part. This automatic method dispatching depending on the class of the receiver is called *late-binding*. It ensures the extensibility of the complex cost computation. Suppose that we introduce a new kind of part by defining a new subclass of PART. All we have to do is to define a cost operation local to the new class. The complex cost operation will still be correct for complex parts made from instances of this new class *without having to be recompiled.* Thus, the late binding facility ensures the reuse of methods for incoming classes.

2.4 Object Creation: Constructor

Assume that the name of a part is a key. Thus, when a part is created, the programmer implementing the part abstraction has to check that there is not an already existing part with the same name. Those checks cannot be included in an operation because nothing forces the *clients* of PART (i.e. the classes that reference the class PART in their methods) to call it. Moreover, it is logically bound to object creation. Therefore, we provide the programmer with the ability of tailoring the object creation in order to perform some precondition checks and some attribute initializations. This is the role of constructors. A constructor is introduced by the **maker** clause in the class definition as shown in Figure 8. As for operations, only a specification is given. The constructor implementation is defined separately as shown in Figure 9. As with **self**, **new** is a pseudo variable automatically bound to a new instance of the class.

In order to know if a conflicting part exists, there must be a container of all created parts up to now. This is the role of the class extension. A class extension records all created instances of a class. The three part classes are declared with extension. Since a basic (or complex) part is also a part, it is a member of both the BASIC-PART (or COMPLEX-PART) and PART extensions. Inheritance between classes induces a set inclusion between their extensions. Therefore, we retrieve in the PART extension all the complex and basic parts. Hence, the "part-already-exist?" predicate can be implemented as described in Figure 9. Declaring the class PART with extension generates a function named PART-extent. When called, it returns the set of all parts created. Finding a conflict is just iterating over this set and checking for name equality.

ORION [Bane87] also offers a class extension mechanism. For each user-defined class C, a class SETOF-C is created with two instances representing respectively the set of the "direct" instances of C and the set of the instances of C and of its subclasses. Our approach differs from the one of ORION in a number of points. In $LISPO_2$ the extension mechanism is not automatic. The programmer has the choice of declaring a class with extension or not. This avoids the management of unnecessary extensions. Moreover class extensions are values (not objects). They are accessed through a function call and, thus, distinguished from "normal" values and protected from accidental updates. Finally, the $LISPO_2$ class extension gathers both the direct instances of the class and the instances of its subclasses, enforcing the natural set inclusion semantics of inheritance as defined in the O_2 data model [Lécl89a].

2.5 Coping with Faults: Exceptions

If a user of the part abstraction wants to create a basic part with a name that already exists, an exception is raised by the BASIC-PART constructor using the **raise-exception** statement (see Figure 9). When an operation or a constructor cannot perform its task, it warns its caller by raising an exception and terminates its execution. The caller must provide a handler for this exception. If it does not want to cope with it, it can simply raise it again. Exceptions in $LISPO_2$ are objects, instances of exception classes as in VBASE [Andr87]. Thus, raising an exception creates an instance of such a class. The state of an exception is used to pass some information from the signaler to the handler. Moreover, inheritance can be used for defining a hierarchy of exceptions. Figure 10 shows the definition of the ALREADY-DEFINED-PART exception class and an example of an exception handler. Notice that the handler uses operations to access information.

2.6 Type Checking Methods

The development environment of $LISPO_2$ offers both an interpreter and a compiler performing respectively dynamic and static type checking of the object-oriented expressions (value manipulations, message passing, object creation, disencapsulation and exception handling) occurring in methods. The interpreter supports the dynamics and debugging facilities needed in the first stages of development and traditionally associated with Lisp languages. Variables can be untyped enabling the programmer to defer typing decisions. Therefore, methods work as long as the objects bound to the variables respond to messages. However if, during a message passing, there is no pending operation in the receiver class, the execution is suspended and the programmer can

```
(defclass BASIC-PART
        (PART)
        (type (tupleof
                    (cost integer r)
                    (mass integer r)))
        (maker (string integer integer SUPPLIER))
        has-extension)
```

Figure 8: Complete BASIC-PART class definition

```
(defmaker BASIC-PART (name mass cost supplier)
    (let (conflicting-part)
      ; does the part already exist ?
      (if (setq conflicting-part (part-already-exist? name))
         ; yes, it is an error, raise an exception
         (raise-exception ALREADY-DEFINED-PART name conflicting-part)
         ; no, fill the attributes
         (setq new.name name) ... )))

(defun part-already-exist? (part-name)
    (let (found)
      ; iterate over all created parts until we find a conflict
      (foreach ((part (PART-extent)) found)
          (setq found (eqstring part-name [part name])))
      found))
```

Figure 9: Constructor of class BASIC-PART

```
; exception class definition
(defexception ALREADY-DEFINED-PART
    (type (tupleof
              (part-name string r)
              (conflicting-part PART r)))
    (maker (string PART)))

; example of a handler
(with-exception
    (setq part (make-BASIC-PART "seat" 123 15 supplier))
(handle
    ((ex ALREADY-DEFINED-PART)
     (print "conflict with part " [ex conflicting-part print]))))
```

Figure 10: Exception class definition and exception handling

either define *an operation and a method* on the fly, or give a result.
Once design decisions have been frozen, the programmer can invoke the compiler on methods. It performs static type checking of the O_2 expressions and catches any inconsistencies of the method with regard to the schema (unknown classes or operations for instance). For this task, the type checker must know the static types associated with the variables involved in those expressions. Most of them can be inferred from the formal arguments of the method (typed in the operation signature), **self** and constructor applications. However, type declarations of variables or functions used may be necessary.
The type checking algorithm is similar to the one of Trellis/Owl [Scha86]. Each variable (a formal argument or a local variable) can be assigned an expression whose type is a subtype of its (declared or inferred) type. The static type checking also catches the most common source of run time errors in object-oriented languages, which is message passing with an unknown operation. For each message passing expression the type checker searches for an operation in the static class of the receiver and checks that the type of the actual arguments are subtypes of those specified in the signature. In addition, the static analysis of method checks for encapsulation. Within a method, the disencapsulation notation can be used only in an expression whose type is the class defining it or one of its superclasses.

3 Integrating Persistence Facilities in the Language

This section concentrates on issues raised by integrating persistence in the language from an application programmer's point of view. Section 4.1 gives an overview of the implementation aspects. When trying to integrate persistence in a language, the designer is faced with two design goals:

- Eliminate the "impedance mismatch":
  Persistence facilities of LISPO_2 must fit naturally in the underlying LISP language model. The amount of semantic and syntactic extensions needed must be as little as possible. In particular, the way that data persist between program invocations must not be too different from the way the transient data survive during program invocation. Since in LISP, the programmer does not explicitly destroy his/her data, explicit store or delete commands have to be avoided.

- Persistence must be orthogonal to type:
  Every entity of the language has the right to persist without additional programming cost. Notice that the second goal is not subsumed by the first. Some languages such as CO_2 [Lécl89b] or PASCAL/R [Schm77] deal with persistence by providing the programmer with type and operations syntactically and semantically well integrated with the host language. Thus, they eliminate the "impedance mismatch" but do not fulfill orthogonality because data of some host types cannot persist (everything that is not a relation in PASCAL/R and a C struct in CO_2 for instance).
  In particular, we do not restrict persistence to O_2 data (objects and values). We believe that complex applications will result in a mix of object-oriented implementation using O_2 data and conventional procedural implementation using LISP data (such as lists and vectors).

Once the objectives are set, let us see how persistence is used by the programmer. We introduce persistence as an extension of the lifetime of LISP data. Due to the automatic storage management

```
; definition of a database variable
(defdbvar mass-memory (listof (tupleof
                                        (part COMPLEX-PART)
                                        (mass float))))

(defmethod (COMPLEX-PART mass) ()
    (let (mass)
        ; see if the mass has already been computed
        (foreach ((cell #:db:mass-memory) mass)
            (if (eq (get-field cell 'part) self)
                (setq mass (get-field cell 'mass))))
        (unless mass
            ; not yet memorized, compute and memorize the mass
            (setq mass [self mass])
            (list-insert #:db:mass-memory 0 (make-tuple (part self) (mass mass))))
        mass))
```

Figure 11: Complex cost method using a cache

provided by Lisp systems through garbage collection, data are alive during a program execution if they are referenced (directly or indirectly) by a set of roots (usually the symbol table and the stack). Extending this view leads to a definition of some persistent roots. Those roots are database variables and class extensions. Hence, we introduce a persistent name space including all defined classes and database variables. Everything in the closure of class extensions and database variables is persistent.

For instance, to reduce the time spent to compute the mass of a complex part, we can declare a database variable whose role is to cache the mass already computed (like the memorizing facility given in [Atki87]). Figure 11 gives the new implementation of the cost method. The first command defines a database variable called mass-memory. Its purpose is to register the parts with their computed mass and to act as a cache during the computation of masses. Defining a database variable simply introduces an entry in the persistent name space. Persistent variables are referenced in methods using the LISP name space syntax. Hence the name #:db:mass-memory means the variable mass-memory defined in the db name space (i.e. the persistent name space). Persistent variables are used in the same way as ordinary variables.

A major database feature that we cannot easily map onto a language concept is the notion of transaction supporting both concurrency and recovery. Thus we just provide the programmer with the top level command (i.e. a command that the programmer can only call at the top level of the interpreter) **with-transaction**. It begins a transaction scope, in which **abort-transaction** and **commit-transaction** have the usual semantics.

4 System Design

The implementation includes three layers: the persistent layer presenting an interface with a system providing database facilities, an object layer supporting the object-oriented extension and an application layer offering some predefined toolkits (for the time being a user interface and a programming environment kernel). We outline very briefly the first two layers.

4.1 The Persistent Layer

Since we do not want to "reinvent the wheel", we need a layer that allows us to use some existing persistent facilities ranging from the UNIX file system to a sophisticated object server such as the O_2 one [Vele89]. Therefore, we adopt the virtual machine approach used in several language implementations [Gold83] [Rees87] to facilitate portability. This virtual machine defines storage structures and reading/writing transformations from main memory representation to those storage structures. There is one storage structure for each O_2 atomic type and constructor, for LISP data types (list, vector, ...) and schema information (classes, types, operations, database variables and methods). We use storage buckets to group logically related objects together. For pure LISP data, those buckets are filled in a depth first manner. In the development environment, we use the same approach for the O_2 objects and values. We plan to use this notion of storage buckets to implement clustering for an application. Every entity is tagged by its descriptor and a particular storage bucket is devoted to the storage of classes together with their types, operations and methods.

To handle transfer from persistent to main memory, we use a two address space model as in [Atki81]. Every persistent entity has a Persistent Identifier, pid in short. A persistence table associates pids with main memory entities. The object fault mechanism detects the use of a pid as a memory address and if necessary loads the object. It preserves identity and sharing.

Garbage collection in main memory deals only with data not reachable from this table (pure LISP data or objects) and uses a stop and copy algorithm. Since we do not handle references coming from persistent to main memory, there may be some objects in the table which become unreachable from the persistent roots. In this case, the commit generates some garbage on disk. The benefit is that garbage collection and commit do not perform disk accesses and thus are fast. The disk garbage is recovered in a batch way.

4.2 The Object Layer

This layer supports the implementation of the object extension. An object is represented as a pair consisting of a class and its value. Values are tagged by their types. Tuple values are implemented using contiguous memory. Lists (resp. sets) are B-trees allowing fast indexing (resp. fast insertion and membership checking). These B-trees also contain a header recording all classes appearing in the collection and the first object of each class in the collection. Objects of the same class are chained together. When there is an iteration containing a message passing expression, this organization permits late-binding once for each class in the collection and not once for each element of the collection.

The late-binding implementation uses the fact that the Schema Manager expands the operations of a class to its subclasses. Hence, each class contains all the operations (inherited or locally defined) that can be applied on its instances. Therefore message passing extracts the class of the receiver object, looks for an operation in this class and invokes its associated method.

To implement the Schema Manager, we use a classical bootstrap technique in Lisp environments. Classes, types, operations and methods are implemented as objects and thus described by meta-classes. This allows us to implement all the schema manipulations as operations on those objects. For instance, there is a subtype operation defined as virtual in the TYPE class and redefined in the ATOMIC-TYPE, SET-TYPE, LIST-TYPE, TUPLE-TYPE and CLASS classes. This bootstrap has allowed us to implement the system quickly and to evaluate the advantages of the language in the development of a complex application: the system itself. Moreover the metalevel eases the extension of the language since adding a type constructor is just adding a metaclass.

5 Related Work

Recently there has been a great deal of work aiming at integrating programming language and database features. From the programming language field, several attempts have been made to extend a language with orthogonal persistence. This was pioneered by PS-ALGOL [Atki81]. We use similar techniques to implement the persistent layer. PS-ALGOL however does not support object orientation with classes and inheritance.

LOOM [Kael86] provides Smalltalk-80 with an object-oriented virtual memory including transparent object faulting. But it does not support database features like transactions. Moreover Smalltalk does not offer a clear semantic of (simple) inheritance and in the standard version [Gold83], there is no static type checking. The closest work is PCLOS [Paep88], a persistent extension of the Common Lisp Object System [Demi87]. Persistent facilities are offered through an interface that may be ported to several storage managers (including Iris's [Fish87]). However, only the CLOS objects are allowed to persist and not pure LISP data. Moreover, the CLOS model is similar to Smalltalk and does not provide inheritance based on subtyping.

Object-oriented databases tend to reduce or eliminate the impedance mismatch. Gemstone [Maie86] provides database functionalities to Smalltalk including transactions, queries, and distribution. Based on Smalltalk, Gemstone provides only simple inheritance and does not model complex values directly.

ORION [Bane87] is a complete database system based on LISP extended with object orientation. Name conflicts raised by multiple inheritance are solved implicitly by the system based on the declared order of the superclasses. In LISPO_2, we choose to notify the programmer of all name conflicts and let him/her explicitly solve them.

A last interesting point of comparison is the object/value duality provided by several systems. In LISPO_2 this duality relies on the fact that objects are encapsulated and values are not, but both can be shared. This distinguishes LISPO_2 from the pure O_2 data model exposed in [Lécl89a] where values are neither shared nor encapsulated. In contrast, ORION [Kim87] does not offer values but unshared objects named *dependent objects*, the class notion being the single modeling tool.

6 Future Work

We have implemented a first version of LISPO_2. It includes all the features presented. The Schema manager, the programming environment tools and the method and application compilers are implemented using LISPO_2. They are currently serving as benchmarks to evaluate the performance of this first implementation. The persistent layer is implemented on top of the Unix file system. Therefore it supports only a simple form of recovery and no concurrency at all. We are considering its implementation using the O_2 storage manager [Vele89].

Some future work directions result from the first evaluations. Our own programming experience with LISPO_2 encourages us to provide the programmer with a development methodology. Encapsulation and inheritance can be seen as useful design tools and thus as tools they can be misused or underused. Without guidelines, it is quite easy to design complex and deep class hierarchies.

We are currently defining a top-down methodology starting from an informal specification of the application and leading step by step to its implementation and test strategy. Of course this methodology will be supported by tools in the programming environment.
Operations are the unique way to act upon objects and we do believe in encapsulation as a good development principle. However, functional decomposition of methods leads to a number of simple operations that are just data structure manipulations. Those operations will (and sometimes should) never be redefined in subclasses. Letting the programmer state explicitly which operations are "redefinable" offers a clear view of the points of flexibility of his/her design. Moreover, the late binding overhead only occurs for those operations. Therefore we should obtain benefits both at the conceptual and implementation levels. Such a feature will be introduced in the next version of the language.
At a physical level, we plan to integrate a clustering mechanism in the application compiler based on the application schema and on the access patterns relying in methods.

7 Acknowledgments

We wish to thank F. Bancilhon, P. Richard and the referees for their careful reading of this paper.

References

[Alba85] A. Albano, L. Cardelli and R. Orsini, "Galileo: a Strongly-Typed, Interactive Conceptual Language", *ACM Trans. on Database Syst.*, 10(2), June 1985.

[Andr87] T. Andrews and C. Harris, "Combining Language and Database Advances in an Object-Oriented Development Environment", *Proc. 2nd OOPSLA Conf.*, Orlando 1987.

[Atki81] M. Atkinson, "PS-ALGOL: an Algol with a Persistent Heap", *Sigplan Notices*, 17(7), July 1981.

[Atki87] M. Atkinson and P. Buneman, "Types and Persistence in Database Programming Languages", *ACM Computing Surveys*, June 1987.

[Banc88] F. Bancilhon, G. Barbedette, V. Benzaken, C. Delobel, S. Gamerman, C. Lécluse, P. Pfeffer, P. Richard and F. Velez, "The Design and Implementation of O_2, an Object-Oriented Database System", *in Advances in Object-Oriented Database Systems, Springer-Verlag*, 1988.

[Bane87] J. Banerjee, H.T. Chou, J. Garza, W. Kim, D. Woelk, N. Ballou and H.J. Kim, "Data Model Issues for Object Oriented Applications", *ACM Trans. Office Info. Syst.* 5(1), January 1987.

[Care88] M. Carey, D. DeWitt and S. Vandenberg, "A Data Model and Query Language for EXODUS", *Proc. SIGMOD Conf.*, Chicago 1988.

[Cope84] G. Copeland and D. Maier, "Making Smalltalk a Database System", *Proc. SIGMOD Conf.*, Boston 1984.

[Dada86] P. Dadam et al., " A DBMS Prototype to Support Extended NF^2 Relations: An Integrated View of Flat Tables and Hierarchies", *Proc. SIGMOD Conf.*, Washington, 1986.

[Demi87] L.G. Demichiel and R.P. Gabriel, "The Common Lisp Object System: An Overview", Proc. 1st ECOOP Conf., Paris 1987.

[Fish87] D. Fishman et al., "Iris: an Object-Oriented Database Management System", *ACM Trans. Office Info. Syst.* 5(1), January 1987.

[Gold83] A. Goldberg and D. Robson, "Smalltalk 80: The Language and its Implementation", *Addison-Wesley*, 1983.

[Kael86] T. Kaehler, "Virtual Memory on a Narrow Machine for an Object-Oriented Language", *Proc. 1st OOPSLA Conf.*, Portland 1986.

[Kim87] W. Kim, J. Banerjee, H.T. Chou, J.F. Garza and D. Woelk, "Composite Object Support in an Object Oriented Database System", *Proc. 2nd OOPSLA Conf.*, Orlando 1987.

[Lécl89a] C. Lécluse and P. Richard, "Modeling Complex Structures in Object-Oriented Databases", *Proc. PODS Conf.*, Philadelphia 1989.

[Lécl89b] C. Lécluse and P. Richard, "The O_2 Database Programming Language", *Proc. VLDB Conf.*, Amsterdam 1989.

[Lieb86] H. Lieberman, "Using Prototypical Objects to Implement Shared Behavior in Object Oriented Systems", *Proc. 1st OOPSLA Conf.*, Portland 1986.

[Maie86] D. Maier, J. Stein, A. Otis and A. Purdy, "Development of an Object-Oriented DBMS", *Proc. 1st OOPSLA Conf.*, Portland 1986.

[Meye88] B. Meyer, "Object Oriented Software Construction", *Prentice Hall*, 1988.

[Paep88] A. Paepcke, "PCLOS: A Flexible Implementation of CLOS Persistence", *Proc. 2nd ECOOP Conf.*, Oslo 1988.

[Rees87] M. Rees and D. Robson, "Practical Compiling with Pascal-S", *Addison-Wesley*, 1987.

[Scha86] G. Schaffert, T. Cooper, B. Bullis, M. Killian and C. Wilpolt, "An Introduction to Trellis/Owl", *Proc. 1st OOPSLA Conf.*, Portland 1986.

[Schm77] J.W Schmidt, "Some High Level Language Constructs for Data of Type Relation", *ACM Trans. Database Syst.* 2(3), September 1977.

[Stro86] B. Stroustrup, "The C++ Programming Language", *Addison-Wesley*, 1986.

[Vele89] F. Velez, G. Bernard and V. Darnis, "The O_2 Object Manager: an Overview", *Proc. VLDB Conf.*, Amsterdam 1989.

[Wegn87] P. Wegner, "Dimensions of an Object-Based Language Design", *Proc. 2nd OOPSLA Conf.*, Orlando 1987.

The Iris Kernel Architecture

Peter Lyngbæk
Kevin Wilkinson
Waqar Hasan

Hewlett-Packard Laboratories
1501 Page Mill Road
Palo Alto, CA 94304

ABSTRACT

We describe an architecture for a database system based on an object/function model. The architecture efficiently supports the evaluation of functional expressions. The goal of the architecture is to provide a database system that is powerful enough to support the definition of functions and procedures that implement the semantics of the data model. The architecture has been implemented to support the Iris Database System.

1 Introduction

Iris is an object-oriented database management system being developed at Hewlett-Packard Laboratories [FBB+89] [FBC+87]. One of its goals is to enhance database programmer productivity by developing an expressive data model. Another goal is to provide generalized database support for the development and integration of future applications in areas such as engineering information management, engineering test and measurement, telecommunications, office information, knowledge-based systems, and hardware and software design. These applications require a rich set of capabilities that are not supported by the current generation (i.e., relational) DBMSs.

Figure 1 illustrates the major components of the Iris system. Central to the figure is the Iris Kernel, the retrieval and update processor of the DBMS. The Iris Kernel implements the Iris data model [LK86] which is an object and function model that supports structural as well as behavioral abstractions. Retrievals and updates are written as functional expressions. Extensibility is provided by allowing users to define new functions. The functions may be implemented as stored tables or derived as computations. The computations may be expressed either as Iris functional expressions or as foreign functions in a general-purpose programming language, such as C. The Iris Kernel is further described in Section 3.

Like most other database systems, Iris is accessible via stand-alone interactive interfaces or interfaces embedded in programming languages. All interfaces are built as clients of the Iris Kernel. A client formats a request as an Iris expression and then calls an Iris Kernel entry point that evaluates the expression and returns the result which is also formatted as an Iris expression. Currently, two interactive interfaces are supported. One interactive interface, Object SQL (OSQL), is an object-oriented extension to SQL. The second interactive interface is the Graphical Editor. It is an X-Windows-based system that allows users to retrieve and update function values and metadata with graphical and forms-based displays.

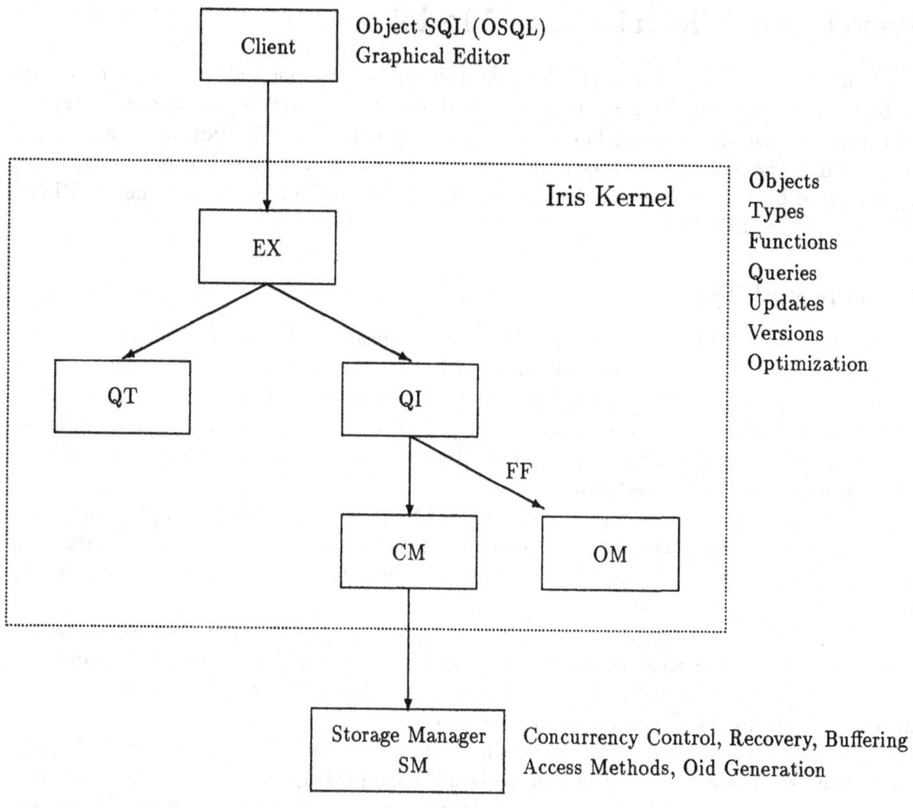

Figure 1: *Iris System Components*

One of the long-term goals of the Iris project is to be able to define and implement the Iris model in terms of its own functions [LK86]. This provides a conceptual simplicity with the result that the implementation of the system is easier to understand and maintain. It is also easier to prototype new operations with such a system because data model operations can be prototyped as ordinary database functions. An added advantage is that it will be possible to optimize and type check data model operations like ordinary database functions.

Since the essence of the Iris data model is function application, the Iris Kernel has been architected around the single operation of invoking a function. In addition, the Kernel may call itself recursively so that data model operations may invoke other data model operations. This flexibility permits the customization of Iris operations and allows us to experiment with different semantics of, for example, multiple inheritance, versioning, and complex objects with little re-implementation effort.

The emphasis of this paper is to describe the Iris Kernel architecture. Section 2 gives a brief overview of the Iris Data Model, Section 3 describes the Iris Kernel architecture and its components, Section 4 describes how the architecture processes an example request, and Section 5 provides some concluding remarks. An Initial draft of the material presented in this paper has appeared in [LW89a].

2 Overview of the Iris Data Model

The Iris Database System is based on a semantic data model that supports abstract data types. Its roots can be found in previous work on Daplex [Shi81] and Taxis [MBW80]. A number of recent data models, such as PDM [MD86] and Fugue [HZ88], also share many similarities with the Iris Data Model. The Iris data model contains three important constructs: *objects*, *types* and *functions*. These are briefly described below. A more complete description of the Iris Data Model and the Iris DBMS may be found in [LK86, FBB+89].

2.1 Objects and Types

Objects in Iris represent entities and concepts from the application domain being modeled. Some objects such as integers, strings, and lists are self identifying. Those are called *literal* objects. There is a fixed set of literal objects, that is each literal type has a fixed extension.

A *surrogate* object is represented by a system-generated, unique, immutable *object identifier* or *oid*. Examples of surrogate objects include system objects, such as types and functions, and user objects, such as employees and departments.

Types have unique names and are used to categorize objects into sets that are capable of participating in a specific set of functions. Objects serve as arguments to functions and may be returned as results of functions. A function may only be applied to objects that have the types required by the function.

Types are organized in an acyclic type graph that represents generalization and specialization. The type graph models inheritance in Iris. A type may be declared to be a subtype of other types (its supertypes). A function defined on a given type is also defined on all its subtypes. Objects that are instances of a type are also instances of its supertypes.

User objects may belong to any set of user defined types. In addition, objects may gain and lose types dynamically. For example, an object representing a given person may be created as an instance of the Employee type. Later it may lose the Employee type and acquire the type Retiree. When that happens, all the functions defined on Retiree become applicable to the object and the functions on Employee become inapplicable. This feature enables us to support database evolution better than other object-oriented systems in which the types of an object may be specified only at the time the object is created.

Objects in Iris may be versioned. An object being versioned is represented by a *generic* object instance and a set of distinct *version* object instances corresponding to each version of the object. By default, objects are not versioned, i.e. they have the type `UnVersioned`. The Iris versioning mechanism is further described in [BM88].

2.2 Functions

Attributes of objects, relationships among objects, and computations on objects are expressed in terms of functions. Iris functions are defined over types, they may be many-valued and, unlike mathematical functions, they may have side-effects. In Iris, the declaration of a function is separated from its implementation. This provides a degree of data independence. This section discusses function declaration and Section 2.4 discusses function implementation.

In order to support stepwise refinement of functions, function names may be overloaded, i.e. functions defined on different types may be given identical names. When a function call is issued using an overloaded function name, a specific function is selected for invocation. Iris chooses the function that is defined on the most specific types of the actual arguments.

A type can be characterized by the collection of functions defined on it. The Employee type might have the following functions defined over it:

```
JobTitle:   Employee → String
EmpDept:    Employee → Department
SalHist:    Employee ↠ Integer × Date
ChangeJob:  Employee × String × Department → Boolean
```

If Smith is working as a software engineer in the Toolkit Department then the function values are as follows (references to surrogate objects are denoted by italics):

JobTitle(*Smith*) = 'Software Engineer';

EmpDept(*Smith*) = *Toolkit*;

The SalHist function is many-valued. It is also an example of a function with multiple result types. Each result is a pair of salary and date objects, where the salary is represented by an integer. The date indicates when the salary was changed. If Smith was hired on 3/1/87 with a monthly salary of $3000 and given a raise of $300 on 3/1/88 then the salary history function has the following value:

SalHist(*Smith*) = [<3000, *3/1/87*>, <3300, *3/1/88*>]

Note that the dates are represented by surrogate object identifiers (they are in italics). Thus, there are, presumably, functions on date objects that materialize parts or all of the date, e.g. month, day and year functions.

In Iris, we use the term *procedure* to refer to a function whose implementation has side-effects. The function ChangeJob is an example of a procedure and is also a function with multiple argument types. Let us assume that it may be used to change the job title and department of an employee. The promotion of Smith to Project Manger in the Applications Department can be reflected in the database by the following invocation:

ChangeJob(*Smith*, ''Project Manager'', *Applications*)

In Iris, a new function is *declared* by specifying its name, the types of its argument and result parameters and, optionally, names for the arguments and results:[1]

create function ChangeJob(Employee , Charstring , Department) → Boolean

Before a function may be invoked, an *implementation* must be specified. For example ChangeJob may be implemented as follows:

```
implement function ChangeJob(Employee emp, Charstring ttl,
                                          Department dep) → Boolean as
     begin
          set JobTitle(emp) = ttl;
          set EmpDept(emp) = dep;
     end;
```

The implementation of functions is described in more detail in Section 2.4.

[1]For readability, subsequent examples will be expressed in OSQL [FBB+89]. Keywords of this language appear in bold font. Keep in mind, however, that OSQL is parsing each statement into a functional expression that invokes an Iris system or user function.

2.3 Database Updates and Retrievals

Properties of objects can be modified by changing the values of functions. For example, the following operation will add another salary and date pair to Smith's salary history:

```
add Salhist(Smith) = <3800, 1/1/89>;
```

In addition to setting and adding function values, one or more values may be removed from the value-set of a many-valued function. The ability to update a function's values depends on its implementation. In general, functions whose values are stored as a table can always be updated. However, functions whose values are computed may or may not be updatable (see Section 2.4).

The database can be queried by using the OSQL `select` statement and specifying a list of results, a list of existentially quantified variables, and a predicate expression. The result list contains variables and function invocations. The predicate may use variables, constants (object identifiers or literals), nested function applications, and comparison operators. Query execution causes the existential variables to be instantiated. The result list is then used to compute a result value for each tuple of the instantiated existential variables. The collection of all result values is returned as a bag.

The following statement retrieves all the dates on which Smith's salary was modified:

```
select d
for each Date d, Integer s
where SalHist( Smith ) = <s, d>;
```

and the statement:

```
select Manager( Smith );
```

returns Smith's manager.

Retrievals must be side-effect free, i.e. they may not invoke procedures.

2.4 Function Implementation

So far, we have discussed the declaration of functions and their use in retrievals and updates. An important additional characteristic of a function is its *implementation* or *body*, that is, the specification of its behavior. The implementation of the function is compiled and optimized into an internal format that is then stored in the system catalog. When the function is later invoked, the compiled representation is retrieved and interpreted.

Iris supports three methods of function implementation: Stored, Derived, and Foreign. A stored implementation explicitly maintains the extension of the function as a stored table in the database. Derived and foreign implementations are alternative methods for computing function values.

Stored Functions

The extension of a function may be explicitly maintained by storing the mapping of corresponding argument and result values as tuples in a database table. Since the storage manager does not support nested structures, the result of a many-valued function is stored as several tuples with identical argument values.

To improve performance, functions with the same argument types may be clustered in a single table by extending the tuple width to include result columns for each of the functions. As illustrated in Section 2.3, stored functions may be updated by using the OSQL `set` and `add` statements. There is also a `remove` statement that is not shown. A formal treatment of the mapping of Iris functions to relational tables may be found in [LV87].

Derived Functions

Derived functions are functions that are computed by evaluating an Iris expression. The expression is defined in terms of other functions and may represent a retrieval or an update. As an example of a retrieval function, the `select` statement in Section 2.3 could represent the body of a derived function with zero arguments that retrieves the dates on which Smith's salary was modified.

A function may also be derived as a sequence of updates, which defines a procedure. An example is the ChangeJob function shown in Section 2.2. Procedures themselves may not be updated.

A derived function without side-effects may be thought of as a view of the stored data. The semantics of updates to such a function are not always well-defined. However, in those cases where Iris can solve the "view update" problem, the update actions are automatically inferred by Iris. For example, functions that are derived as inverses of stored functions are updatable.

Foreign Functions

A foreign function is implemented as a subroutine written in some general-purpose programming language and compiled outside of Iris. The implementation of the foreign function must adhere to certain interface conventions. Beyond that, the implementation is a black box with respect to the rest of the system.

This has three consequences. First, it is impossible to determine at compile time whether the implementation has side-effects. For this reason, users must specify whether or not their foreign function has side-effects. Second, foreign functions cannot be updated. Third, the implementation of foreign functions cannot be optimized by Iris. However, their usage can, potentially, be optimized. For example, given a foreign function that computes simple arithmetic over two numbers, rules could be added to evaluate the result at compile time if the operands are constants.

Foreign functions provide flexibility and extensibility. Since the Iris database language is not computationally complete, there are certain computations that cannot be expressed as derived functions. Foreign functions provide a mechanism for incorporating such computations into the system. Furthermore, an existing program can be integrated with Iris through the foreign function mechanism either by modifying the program to adhere to the foreign function calling conventions or by writing new foreign functions to provide an interface to the existing program.

Foreign functions pose a potential security problem since the executable code of a foreign function is linked to the Iris executable. A higher level of security can be provided if the foreign functions execute in their own processes. This capability has already been prototyped.

Foreign functions and the mechanisms with which they are supported in Iris are described in detail in [CL88].

2.5 Iris System Objects

In Iris, types and functions are also objects. They are instances of the system types, `Type` and `Function`, respectively. Like user-defined types, system types have functions defined on them. The collection of system types and functions model the Iris metadata and the Iris data model operations.

System functions are used to retrieve and update metadata and user data. Examples of retrieval functions include, `FunctionArgcount`, that returns the number of arguments of a function, `SubTypes`, that returns the subtypes of a type, and `FunctionBody`, that retrieves the compiled representation of a function. *System procedures* correspond to the operations of the data model are used to update metadata and user data. Examples of system procedures include `ObjectCreate`, to create a new object, `FunctionDelete`, to delete a function and `IndexCreate`, to create an index.

`Select` and `Update` are two important system functions that may be used to access metadata or user data. `Select` is the system function that corresponds to the OSQL `select` statement illustrated in Section 2.3. `Update` is used to modify function values. It corresponds to the OSQL `set`, `add` and `remove` statements.

As with user functions, system functions (and procedures) may have either stored, derived or foreign implementations. Currently, there are a number of *system foreign functions.* These exist either because their functionality cannot be expressed as Iris functional expressions or they are more efficiently implemented as foreign functions. Most system procedures are implemented as foreign functions. System foreign functions are also used to implement transaction support, e.g., `XactCommit` and `XactRollback`, and facilities for source code tracing and timing.

In order to compile and execute functions, the Iris Kernel needs access to metadata (a system catalog) that describes the database schema. The Iris system catalog is maintained as a collection of stored system functions. Since certain system functions are frequently accessed together, most of the functions for a particular type of object are horizontally clustered on the same table. For example, the *function* table stores the `FunctionName`, `FunctionArgcount`, and `FunctionRescount` functions, among others. The current system catalog consists of approximately 100 functions horizontally clustered in 15 tables.

3 Iris Kernel Architecture

The Iris kernel is a program that implements the Iris data model. The architecture described in this section was devised after experimenting with an earlier prototype. In the initial prototype, the data model operations were implemented as separate kernel entry points rather than as Iris functions. Therefore they could not be invoked inside Iris expressions which made it hard to define complex procedures that involved several data model operations. In the current architecture data model operations are true Iris functions.

In the current architecture, the kernel is accessed via a single entry point that serves as a function call evaluator. Iris requests are formatted as functional expressions. Each node in an Iris expression is self-identifying and consists of a header and some data fields. The header defines the node type.[2] The possible node types are: object identifier, variable, function call and one node type for each Iris literal type (i.e. *integer*, *real*, *boolean*, *string*, *binary*, *bag*, *list*). The results of a request are also formatted as Iris expressions.

All user and system functions are invoked via function call expressions, including such basic functions as comparison or equality checking. The kernel is organized as a collection of software modules. They are layered as illustrated in Figure 1.

The top-level module, EX (the Executive), implements the kernel entry points and controls the interaction between the kernel and an Iris client. For each request, it calls the query translator, QT, to construct a relational algebra tree for the request [DS89]. It then passes the relational algebra tree to the query interpreter, QI, to yield the results. The query interpreter obtains its results from the storage manager, SM, or from foreign functions. The Object Manager, OM, is a collection of system foreign functions that implement the data model operations.

The Cache Manager, CM, is an intermediate layer between the Iris kernel and the Storage Manager. It provides prefetching and cache management for data retrieval and data updates between the kernel and SM. The Storage Manager provides access to shared, stored tables, transaction management, recovery, and buffering. The remainder of this section describes the Iris kernel modules in more detail.

3.1 Iris Executive

The Executive module, EX, manages interaction between the Iris kernel and its clients. It provides an external interface to clients, accepts requests and returns results to the client. The EX module implements the server loop of: *accept request*, *execute request*, *send reply*. A request consists of a functional expression, a result buffer and an error buffer. The result buffer is filled with the

[2]This is a distinct notion from an object type. Node types merely identify interface data structures.

result objects generated by evaluating the expression tree. The error buffer is used to return errors encountered during the processing of the request.

Request processing consists of two steps: compile and interpret. The compilation step, performed by the QT module, converts the functional expression into an extended relational algebra tree. The relational algebra tree is then passed to the query interpreter, QI, which traverses the tree and produces the result objects for the request.

Note that the current version of Iris differs from other expression tree evaluators (e.g. LISP) in that Iris does not contain a sophisticated *eval-apply* loop. The conventional eval-apply algorithm operates on expression trees by first *evaluating* the arguments of a function call, then *applying* the function to the results of the argument evaluation. In the current Iris, every request expression tree must be rooted by a function call and the function call arguments must be constants. Thus, the Iris *eval* operation is trivial since the function arguments need no evaluation.

Actually, Iris permits specific arguments to some system functions to be non-constant. Currently, these are treated as special-case exceptions. For example, the *select-expression* argument to the `Select` system function may be an arbitrary expression tree containing variables and nested function calls.

We plan to extend Iris in the future by first allowing any function call argument to be a nested function call and later by allowing variables. However, the semantics of such expression trees remain to be defined. Conventional *eval-apply* algorithms may not be consistent with Iris semantics. For example, Iris expressions may be bag-valued or may be re-ordered by query optimization.

Iris result objects are also formatted as expression trees. However, a result expression tree consists entirely of constant nodes (i.e., literals or oids). The content and structure of the result tree depend on the function invoked by the request expression tree. For example, invocation of the `ObjCreate` system procedure (create an object) would return an expression tree consisting of a single node, an object identifier. However, invoking a multi-valued function or a function with more than one result type returns a bag or a list, respectively. For example, the `Select` system procedure (find a collection of objects) returns a bag of objects.

In the course of processing a request, the Iris kernel may need to invoke itself, recursively. This is done for two reasons. First, the kernel accesses the Iris metadata through the same system functions provided to external clients. For example, to retrieve the object identifier for a named function, QT must construct an expression to call the appropriate system function and invoke an EX entry point.

The second reason for recursive kernel calls is that some system procedures and functions may be defined in terms of other system functions. For example, creating a function involves updates to several stored system functions. When such a system procedure is implemented as a system foreign function, it must recursively call the kernel in order to invoke the other system functions.

3.2 Query Translator

The Iris Query Translator, QT, is responsible for translating Iris requests into extended relational algebra trees. A request to the Iris kernel is formatted as an Iris functional expression, or *F-tree*. The nodes of an F-tree include function calls, variables, and literal nodes. The query translation process consists of three main steps. First, the F-tree is converted to a canonical form. This involves a series of tree transformations that are done to simplify subsequent transformations. For example, nested function calls are unnested by introducing auxiliary variables. Type checking is also performed. The actual arguments in a function call must match or be subtypes of the corresponding formal argument types.

The second step converts the canonical F-tree to an extended relational algebra tree known as an *R-tree*. This is a mechanical process in which function calls are replaced by their implementations (which are, themselves, R-trees). For example, comparison function calls (e.g. equal, not-equal, less-than, etc.) are converted to relational algebra filter[3] operators. The logical function, *And*, is

[3]In order to distinguish the Iris system function, `Select`, from the select operator of the relational algebra, the

converted to a cross-product operator.

The resulting R-tree consists of nodes for the relational algebra operations of project, filter and cross-product. To increase the functionality of the Query Interpreter, there are some additional nodes. A *temp-table* node creates and, optionally, sorts a temporary table. An *update* node modifies an existing table. A *sequence* node executes each of its subtrees in turn. A *foreign function* node invokes the executable code that is the implementation of a foreign function.

The leaves of an R-tree actually generate the data that is processed by the other nodes. A leaf may be either a table node or a foreign function node. A table node retrieves the contents of a Storage Manager table. A projection list and predicate can be associated with the table node to reduce the number of tuples retrieved. A foreign function node simply invokes a foreign function.

The semantics of the tree are that results of a child node are sent to the parent node for subsequent processing. For example, a project node above a table node would filter out columns returned by the project node. Joins are specified by placing a filter node above a cross-product node to compare the columns of the underlying cross-product.[4]

The final, and most complex, step is to optimize the R-tree. The optimizer is rule-based. Each rule consists of a test predicate and a transformation routine. The test predicate takes an R-tree node as an argument and if the predicate evaluates to true, the transformation routine is invoked. The predicate might test the relative position of a node (e.g., filter node above a project node) or the state of a node (e.g., cross-product node has only one input). The possible transformations include deleting the node, moving it above or below another node, or replacing the node with a new R-tree fragment. As in [DG87], the system must be recompiled whenever the rules are modified.

Rules are organized into rule-sets which, together, accomplish a specific task. For example, one rule-set contains all rules concerned with simplifying constant expressions (e.g., constant propagation and folding). Optimization is accomplished by traversing the entire R-tree for each rule-set. During the traversal, at a given node, any rule in the current rule set may be fired if its test predicate is true.

The optimization steps (i.e., rule-sets) can be roughly described as follows. There is an initial rule set that converts the R-tree to a canonical form. The canonical form consists of a number of query blocks. A query block consists of a project node above a filter node above a cross-product node (any one of these nodes is optional). A leaf of a query block may be either a table node, a foreign function node or another query block. A query block may be rooted by a temp-table node, an update node or a sequence node.

A second rule-set eliminates redundant joins. This has the effect of reducing the number of tables in a cross-product. A third rule set is concerned with simplifying expressions. A fourth rule set reorders the underlying tables in a cross-product node to reduce the execution time. A fifth rule set handles Storage Manager-specific optimizations, for example, finding project and filter operations that can be performed by the Storage Manager.

The final (optimized) R-tree is then sent to the Query Interpreter which processes the query and returns the result to the user. However, the R-tree may not represent a query but may, instead, be the newly defined body of a derived function. In this case, the R-tree is simply stored in the database system catalog for later retrieval when compiling queries that reference the derived function.

The Query Translator is flexible and can accommodate any optimization that can be expressed in terms of a predicate test on a node and a tree transformation. Of particular interest is the ability to optimize the usage of foreign functions. As a simple example, given a foreign function that computes simple arithmetic over two numbers, rules could be written to evaluate the result at compile time if the operands are constants.

---

term, *filter operator,* will be used to denote the latter.

[4]Of course, joins are rarely executed this way because the filter predicate is typically pushed down below the cross-product to produce a nested-loops join.

3.3 Query Interpreter

The Query Interpreter module, QI, evaluates an extended relation algebra tree (R-tree) which yields a collection of tuples that become the result objects for the request expression tree. The Query Interpreter traverses the R-tree and pipes data between parent and child nodes. Conceptually, each node in the R-tree may be viewed as a scan object and it must implement three operations: *open*, *next*, and *close*.

An *open*, *next*, or *close* operation may call the Query Interpreter, recursively, to evaluate a sub-tree. For example, given a project node, the portion of the R-tree below the project node represents the source of the tuples for the project operation. Thus, an *open* operation on a project node must recursively open the sub-tree in order to get its input tuples. The leaf nodes of the tree are the data sources. An *open* operation on a table node creates a Storage Manager scan.

The *next* operation returns the next tuple in the pipeline. A *next* operation on a table node results in a call to the Storage Manager to fetch the next tuple in the previously opened scan. Similarly, a *next* operation on a foreign function node will invoke the foreign function to generate the next tuple value.

Note that a *next* operation on an update node has side-effects. For this reason, if the subtree of an update node references the stored table that is being updated, the update tuples are spooled into a temporary table. This prevents cycles in the data pipeline. Typically, the result tuple for an update operation is a single boolean value indicating success or failure.

3.4 Object Manager

The semantics of some Iris system functions can be defined and implemented in terms of other Iris system functions. Essentially, this is the job of the Iris Object Manager. It is a collection of system foreign functions. These functions provide services that are essential to Iris but whose implementations either cannot be expressed as a stored or derived Iris function or are more efficient written in an external programming language. For example, type creation is a system foreign function. It involves creating a typing function and updating several stored system functions. Such a complex update is difficult to express as a relational algebra expression. Another example is a system function that returns the time of day.

In the current version of Iris, most of the system procedures (system functions that update the metadata) are implemented as foreign functions. These system procedures call the Storage Manager directly (bypassing the cache) to update the stored system functions. As the number and complexity of the system procedures has increased, the direct SM calls have become a problem. Because the Storage Manager is called from many places in the Object Manager, it will be difficult to modify Iris to use a different Storage Manager. Making Iris independent of any particular storage subsystem is a long-term goal.

A second problem with direct Storage Manager calls is that the semantics of an operation are hidden inside the procedure. Thus, it is not possible to optimize the procedure. In addition, it means that Iris is not self-describing.

Thus, the next step is to reimplement the Iris system procedures as extended relational algebra expressions. An initial step along these lines has been taken. An *update* node and a *sequence* node have been added to the set of R-tree nodes. These nodes are currently used only to modify user functions. The next step is to use these nodes to update the system tables. Then, a complex system procedures could be implemented as a derived function using a sequence of updates to individual stored system functions. This work is currently under investigation. It may require the addition of more relational algebra nodes, e.g. a branching node.

3.5 Cache Manager

The Iris Cache Manager, CM, implements a general-purpose caching facility between the Iris kernel and the Storage Manager. The Cache Manager maintains two types of caches: a *tuple cache* and a *predicate cache*. The tuple cache is used to cache tuples from individual tables. A table may have at most one tuple cache. A table cache is accessed via a column of the table and that column must be declared as either uniquely-valued or *multi-valued*. If a column is declared as multi-valued, the cache ensures that whenever a given value of that column occurs in the cache, all tuples of the table with the same column value will also occur in the cache. This guarantees that when a cache hit on a multi-valued column occurs, the scan can be entirely satisfied from the cache without having to invoke the Storage Manager. This permits the effective caching of multi-valued functions.

When a scan is opened, the scan will be directed at a tuple cache if the table has a tuple cache and: *(1)* the scan has an equality predicate on a column with a unique index, or *(2)* the scan has an equality predicate on a multi-valued column. The Cache Manager can only support caching on one multi-valued column per table cache (although the underlying table may have several multi-valued columns).

A table may have many predicate caches. A predicate cache contains tuples from a table that satisfy a particular predicate. Thus, a predicate cache has an associated predicate and projection list. An open-scan operation will be directed at a predicate cache if the scan's predicate and projection list match the predicate and projection list of the cache.

The tuple cache is primarily intended to support caching of system tables. However, user tables may also be cached in this way. The predicate cache is useful in caching intermediate results during query processing.

Information in that cache is always kept consistent with the storage manager. If an update request is too complicated to preserve cache consistency, the table will be automatically uncached.

3.6 Storage Manager

The Iris Storage Manager is (currently) a conventional relational storage subsystem, namely that of HP-SQL [HP-]. HP-SQL's Storage Manager is very similar to System R's RSS [BE77]. It provides associative access and update capabilities to a single relation at a time and includes transaction support.

Tables can be created and dropped at any time. The system supports transactions with savepoints and restores to savepoints, concurrency control, logging and recovery, archiving, indexing and buffer management. It provides tuple-at-a-time processing with commands to retrieve, update, insert and delete tuples. Indexes allow users to access the tuples of a table in a predefined order. Additionally, a predicate over column values can be defined to qualify tuples during retrieval.

One of the basic functions of the Storage Manager is the retrieval of tuples from tables. A retrieval request includes a table identifier and may include a filter predicate, a projection list and a preferred access method. The Storage Manager begins by opening a scan on the table. The scan specifies any projection list, filter predicate and whether the scan should be sequential or via an access method. The filter predicate is composed of conjunctions and disjunctions of operators applied to constants and column values. Subsequent calls to the storage manager can be used to extract tuples from the scan one or several at a time.

4 Example

To provide a better understanding of the Iris architecture, we describe how the Kernel processes a request for compiling and storing the body of a derived function. Function derivation is the task of the system procedure, `FunDerive`, which is implemented as an OM foreign function. To invoke this procedure, a request expression is built containing a single call node with a function identifier of

"FunDerive" and an argument list specifying the name of the function to be compiled and a query expression defining the function derivation.

The request expression is then passed to an Iris entry point in the Executive. The Executive immediately passes the request expression to the Query Translator for compilation. QT checks the argument types, retrieves the R-tree implementation for "FunDerive" and substitutes the actual arguments for the formal arguments.

Since this request was a simple function call with constant arguments, QT uses its fastpath and no further optimization of the R-tree is required. In this case, the R-tree is a single foreign function node that calls the OM foreign function that implements `FunDerive`.

QT returns the R-tree to the Executive which then passes the tree to the Query Interpreter to produce the result values. QI simply invokes the foreign function and returns the result that is the object identifier of the newly created type. Thus, the real work of function derivation is done in the foreign function.

The `FunDerive` foreign function performs the following actions. It first performs some sanity checks that the function exists and does not already have an implementation specified. This is done by a recursive kernel call that invokes the appropriate system function for the relevant metadata. Next, it must call QT to compile the function body into a relational algebra tree. This is done by building an expression that calls the `Select` system function. The arguments to `Select` are a list of result variables and their types, a list of existential variables and their types, a *distinct* flag and a *select-expression.* The select-expression is itself an expression tree containing function calls, variables and constants.

The semantics of `Select` may be roughly described as follows. The result and existential variables are bound to the cross-product of the extensions of their types. For each binding of the variables, the select-expression is evaluated to produce a bag of result objects that is then projected on the result variables. These partial results are accumulated and the entire collection is returned to the user as one large result bag. If the *distinct* flag is `True`, duplicates are eliminated from the final result bag.

Note that the *select-expression* can be any object, including another function call. This is one case where the arguments to a function call may be non-constant. The remainder of the compilation task is more complicated than the simple parameter substitution in the previous example.

QT considers `Select` an *intrinsic* system function. The intrinsic system functions are those that QT can compile directly into a relational algebra tree unlike `FunDerive` for example, which has a R-tree that identifies the object code that implements the foreign function. Examples of other intrinsic system functions include `FunUpdate`[5], `Sequence`, `And`, and the six comparison operators (i.e. `Equal`, `NotEqual`, `LessThan`, etc.).

For `Select`, compilation proceeds as follows. First, the select-expression is converted to a simplified form in which function calls are unnested. This may result in the introduction of auxiliary variables for the results of the nested function call. The select-expression is then converted to an R-tree by replacing all function calls by their stored implementations and substituting the actual parameters. This is described in more detail in Section 3.2.

The R-tree is then checked to ensure that all declared variables are bound to a column value of their declared type. If a variable is not bound, the R-tree is joined with the extension of the type of the variable. Of course, this is only possible for types with finite extensions, e.g. unbound integer variables cause an error. Finally, a project node is prefixed to the R-tree to guarantee that the result variables of the `Select` appear in the correct order in the result tuples.

The initial R-tree is then optimized to remove unnecessary joins and to push project and filter operations as far as possible down the R-tree (i.e. into the Storage Manager, if possible). The R-tree is then returned to the FunDerive foreign function which then updates the system function that returns the implementation of a function.

[5]`FunUpdate` updates stored user functions.

5 Conclusions

We have proposed a new architecture for the Iris database system. The architecture provides a generalized function evaluator. Database requests of any kind, including queries, updates, and data definitions, are presented to the evaluator as functional expressions. The evaluator executes a request by first compiling it into an extended relational algebra and then interpreting it. The extended algebra supports database updates and foreign functions, i.e., invocation and evaluation of user-defined programs. Experiences in implementing and using the Iris architecture are reported in [WLH89].

To provide adequate performance, database functions may be stored in a compiled and optimized form. In that case, the compilation process consists of obtaining the compiled function representation from disk or a special function cache. The process of interpreting the compiled function can be improved by caching the stored database tables being accessed by the function. This mechanism is crucial to the performance of system catalog accesses. The architecture may be extended with a function value cache. Such a cache would simplify the compilation and interpretation steps of function evaluation in cases where the result of the evaluation could be provided by the cache.

The generalized function evaluation mechanism greatly simplifies the system structure as it is used both for external user requests and for internal requests to the cached system dictionary. The system catalog, for example, requires no special implementation, but is provided as a collection of database functions which are queried and updated just like ordinary user functions.

The Iris System facilitates the prototyping of new model semantics and functionalities. In order to implement new model semantics, the structure of the system catalog may have to be changed. This is easily done by the addition or removal of functions. Procedures can be implemented as derived or foreign functions. Foreign functions are defined by programs, e.g., C programs, which may call the function evaluator. Derived functions are defined in terms of other functions by an Iris database language expression. Derived functions may be optimized by the database system, but their power is restricted by the current extended relational algebra.

We expect to do a lot of experimentation in such areas as authorization, complex objects, versioning, overloading, late binding, monitors and triggers. In addition, two main research directions have been identified. One is to extend and generalize the Iris model and language to allow most application code to be written in OSQL. That way a large amount of code sharing and reuse can be obtained. Some of the interesting research topics include optimization of database programs with side-effects, optimization of database requests against multiple, possibly different storage managers, and using the language to support declarative integrity constraints.

The other research direction is to increase the functionality and power of the Iris client interface, i.e. the parts of Iris running on a client machine. In order to better utilize local resources, the Iris interpreter must dynamically decide whether to interpret a given request locally (using locally cached data and possibly extending the cache in the process), send the entire request to the server for interpretation, or possibly split the request into several parts some of which are evaluated locally and others remotely. Some of the interesting research topics include copy management (for example by using database monitors [Ris89]), checkin/checkout mechanisms, and data clustering techniques.

Acknowledgements

Many members of the Database Technology Department at HP Labs contributed to and influenced the design of the described architecture. We acknowledge the assistance of Jurgen Annevelink, Tim Connors, Jim Davis, Charles Hoch, Bill Kent, Marie-Anne Neimat, and Ming-Chien Shan.

References

[BE77] M. W. Blasgen and K. P. Eswaran. Storage and Access in Relation Databases. *IBM Systems Journal*, 16(4):363–377, 1977.

[BM88] D. Beech and B. Mahbod. Generalized Version Control in an Object-Oriented Database. In *Proceedings of IEEE Data Engineering Conference*, February 1988.

[CL88] T. Connors and P. Lyngbaek. Providing Uninform Access to Heterogeneous Information Bases. In Klaus Dittrich, editor, *Lecture Notes in Computer Science 334, Advances in Object-Oriented Database Systems*. Springer-Verlag, September 1988.

[DG87] D. J. Dewitt and G. Graefe. The EXODUS Optimizer Generator. In *Proceedings of ACM-SIGMOD International Conference on Management of Data*, pages 160–172, 1987.

[DS89] N. Derrett and M. C. Shan. Rule-Based Query Optimization in Iris. In *Proceedings of ACM Annual Computer Science Conference*, Louisville, Kentucky, February 1989.

[Fis+89] D. H. Fishman et al. Overview of the Iris DBMS. In W. Kim and F. H. Lochovsky, editors, *Object-Oriented Languages, Applications, and Databases*. Addison-Wesley Publishing Company, 1989.

[Fis+87] D. H. Fishman et al. Iris: An Object-Oriented Database Management System. *ACM Transactions on Office Information Systems*, 5(1), January 1987.

[HP-] Hewlett-Packard Company. *HP-SQL Reference Manual*. Part Number 36217-90001.

[HZ88] S. Heiler and S. Zdonik. Views, Data Abstraction, and Inheritance in the FUGUE Data Model. In Klaus Dittrich, editor, *Lecture Notes in Computer Science 334, Advances in Object-Oriented Database Systems*. Springer-Verlag, September 1988.

[LK86] P. Lyngbaek and W. Kent. A Data Modeling Methodology for the Design and Implementation of Information Systems. In *Proceedings of 1986 International Workshop on Object-Oriented Database Systems*, Pacific Grove, California, September 1986.

[LV87] P. Lyngbaek and V. Vianu. Mapping a Semantic Data Model to the Relational Model. In *Proceedings of ACM-SIGMOD International Conference on Management of Data*, San Francisco, California, May 1987.

[LW89a] P. Lyngbaek and W. K. Wilkinson. An Overview of the Iris Kernel Architecture. In G. Blair, J. Gallagher, D. Hutchinson, and D. Shepherd, editors, *Object-Oriented Programming Systems*, London, UK, 1989. Pitman Publishing.

[LW89b] P. Lyngbaek and W. K. Wilkinson. The Architecture of a Persistent Object System. In *Proceedings of an International Workshop on Persistent Object Systems*, Newcastle, Australia, January 1989.

[MBW80] J. Mylopoulos, P. A. Bernstein, and H. K. T. Wong. A Language Facility for Designing Database-Intensive Applications. *ACM Transactions on Database Systems*, 5(2), June 1980.

[MD86] F. Manola and U. Dayal. PDM: An Object-Oriented Data Model. In *Proceedings of 1986 International Workshop on Object-Oriented Database Systems*, Pacific Grove, California, September 1986.

[Ris89] T. Risch. Monitoring database objects. In *Proceedings of the Fifteenth International Conference on Very Large Data Bases*, Amsterdam, The Netherlands, August 1989.

[Shi81] D. Shipman. The Functional Data Model and the Data Language DAPLEX. *ACM Transactions on Database Systems*, 6(1), September 1981.

[WLH89] K. Wilkinson, P. Lyngbaek, and W. Hasan. The Iris Architecture and Implementation. *IEEE Transactions on Knowledge and Data Engineering*, December 1989.

Integrating Concurrency Control into an Object-Oriented Database System

Michèle Cart, Jean Ferrié
Université de Montpellier / CRIM (ura CNRS)
860 rue de St Priest, 34090 Montpellier (France)

Abstract

In this paper, we describe the problems involved in integrating concurrency control into object-oriented database systems. The object-oriented approach places specific constraints on concurrency between transactions, which we discuss. We then propose an adaptation of the locking technique to satisfy them, without unnecessarily restricting concurrency. Finally, we analyse in detail the impacts of both the transaction model and the locking granularity imposed by the underlying system. The solutions proposed are illustrated with the O2 system developed by the Altaïr GIP.

INTRODUCTION

Construction of object-oriented database systems, such as Orion [4], Iris [12], O2 [3], GBase, Gemstone, etc ..., is now a challenge. These systems [2] make it possible to deal with complex objects, both shared and persistent, that are usable through specific operations. They can easily be extended by creating new object classes and by reusing inherited existing methods and redefining them with overriding and late binding properties. It is also essential that they support multiple concurrent users, but few studies have been published on concurrency control (CC) in such systems.

We describe three aspects of CC in an object-oriented DBMS. We first indicate the constraints placed on concurrency by the object-oriented approach, with respect to a classical DBMS, namely : complex objects, objects (instances) grouped together into classes, multiple inheritance, specific operations (methods) on classes and instances with richer semantics than the usual read and write operations. These constraints make it necessary to extend the principles of classical CC [7] in order to serialize transactions.

We then propose an adaptation of the locking technique to satisfy the constraints of object-oriented CC. A particular adaptation has been implemented in the Orion system [14], which minimizes the number of locks requested by a transaction, by using implicit locking. Nevertheless, the restricted number of lock-types used in the system does not allow exploitation of all possible parallelism in an object-oriented approach. Our proposal does not have this shortcoming. We also consider the particular synchronization required when creating and deleting instances so that phantom objects can be avoided [11], [15].

Finally, we investigate the integration of such aspects with regard to an underlying system, providing transaction management and synchronization associated with a given granularity. We study the constraints placed on concurrency by the underlying system in the object-oriented approach, taking phantom objects into account. More specifically, the impact of both the locking granularity and the transaction model (single or multi-level) is analyzed in detail. We show that potential concurrency is best exploited with a multi-level transaction model.

To illustrate our study of concurrency control, we use the O2 system [3], an object-oriented DBMS currently being implemented by the Altaïr group. The description of the O2 system given here does not

---

This research was supported in part by Altaïr GIP contract n° 88-8.

necessarily correspond to its current state of implementation, nor are the solutions we propose necessarily those that will be kept in the project.

The paper is organized as follows. Section 1 presents transactions and O2 objects, giving a physical representation of O2 objects and a hierarchy of abstraction levels that plays a significant part in concurrency control. Section 2 specifies constraints inherent in the object-oriented approach when dealing with classes and multiple inheritance relationships ; we show how to satisfy them using a locking technique. The following sections raise the problem of integrating this method into the system used to support O2 objects. We investigate possible solutions in accordance with the transaction model and the properties of physical objects supporting O2 objects.

1. THE O2 SYSTEM

1.1 User transactions and O2 objects

In the O2 system [1], [3], [17], [18], [22] a user can create O2 objects and make them persistent and accessible to other users ; he can also consult, modify and delete them. O2 objects are either **classes** or **instances**. A class defines an equivalence relationship between instances used through the same **methods**. Morever, all the instances belonging to the same class are based on the same model. Therefore, a class determines properties which specify the structure (i.e. the attributes) of instances of the class and the set of methods usable with any instance of the class. Generally classes are not independent. Using **multiple inheritance**, a new class may be constructed from one or several other existing classes.

The user names objects by means of an identifier called an **external name**. The methods used to manipulate objects (classes or instances) resemble procedures and also have an external name. A user source program consists of a succession of method invocations on O2 objects. The hierarchical construction of classes and instances in the O2 system means that the methods consist themselves of a succession of method invocations on other objects.

At compile time, each external name of an object is translated into an **internal name** oid, locating the object representation ; the internal name of an instance is noted iid and that of a class, tid. Similarly, the external name of a method is translated into an intermediate name, noted mcode ; this intermediate name is used at run time to determine, using a dynamic binding phase, the code associated with the invoked method. The same method name may in fact correspond to several possible computations depending on the class the manipulated instance belongs to. The same holds for attributes.

When simplifying, the program resulting from compilation consists of a succession of method invocations, denoted by their mcode, and performed on objects (classes or instances) denoted by oid. This program is called an O2 transaction.

$\underline{\text{begin}}$ . . . $oid_i.mcode_k$; . . . $oid_j.mcode_l$; . . . $\underline{\text{end}}$

Figure 1. An O2 transaction.

The following classical properties [16] are associated with an O2 transaction : (1) integrity, (2) "all or none" effect (failure atomicity), (3) isolation from effects due to concurrent execution with other transactions (concurrency atomicity), (4) persistence of a transaction's effects once committed. The transaction programmer is responsible for the integrity property, whereas the system assures the other three. In this study we limit ourselves to implementing property 3 without considering properties 2 and 4, which are related to fault tolerance.

The property of isolation from effects due to concurrency is achieved by transactions **serializability**. This criterion may be costly if transactions are long, thereby inducing excessive rejects or waiting. In this case, non-serializable schedules could be accepted [13], [21], [9] using the semantics of transactions, objects or methods.

1.2 Representation of O2 objects

1.21 File structure

O2 objects are represented in files supplied by the underlying system. A **file**, named f, is composed of a set of **pages** of the same size. The page is the transfer unit between disk and main memory. A page p is located by the pair <f, p>. Moreover, pages support **records** of which there are two types :

- the short record, which is smaller than (or the same size as) the page, so that several short records can be grouped within a page ;
- the long record spread over several pages, the first page specifying the others supporting the record.

Each page contains a table describing records so that the address of the rth record within the page is given by the rth table entry. Record r within page p of file f is located by the triplet <f, p, r >.

The hierarchical structure binding these objects (files, pages, and records) results from their hierarchical designation as shown in figure 2.

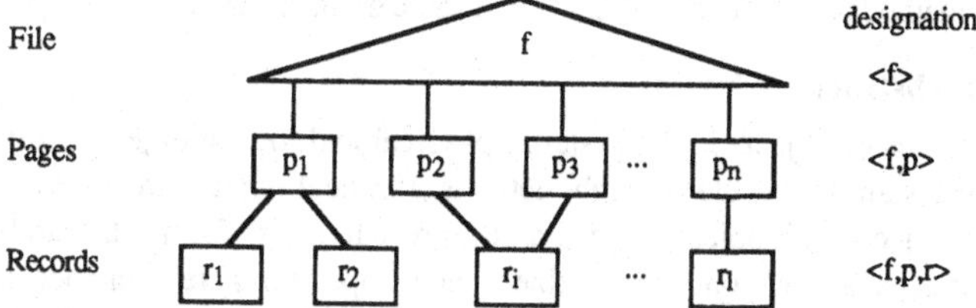

Figure 2. Hierarchical designation of objects managed by the file system.

1.22 Designation and representation of O2 objects

O2 objects are not duplicated, so that only one representation exists for any object. Broadly speaking an O2 object is represented in only one record and its internal name oid is the record name <f, p, r >.

Instances of a class may be constructed from either primitive items (integer, string,...) or from instances belonging to the same class or to different ones. The constructors **tuple** or **set** express this composition. When an instance refers to other instances iid_j, iid_k,.., its representation contains the names iid_j and iid_k of these instances but not their representations. These principles are illustrated in the following example [1].

Example 1. Representation of an instance of the class "movie".
Let us consider the class "movie", specified using the class "person". Thus the structure of the instance "Casablanca" of the class "movie" is the following.

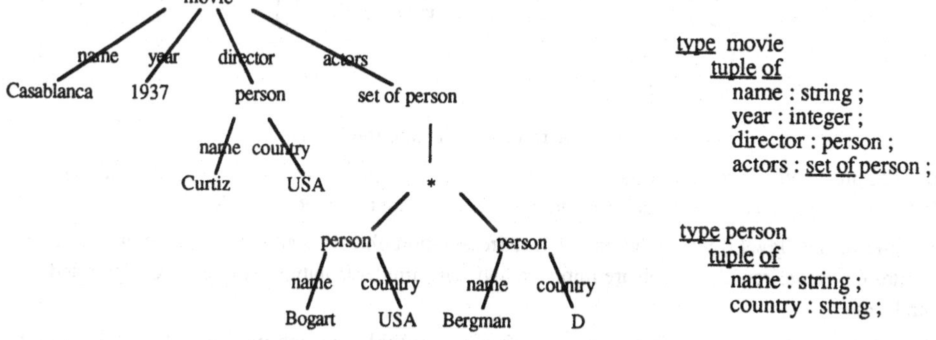

Specifically, the instance "Casablanca" is a tuple composed of :

- the instance "Curtiz" of the class "person",
- an instance of class "set of person", composed itself of the instances "Bogart" and "Bergman".

Each instance is represented in a different record, as follows :

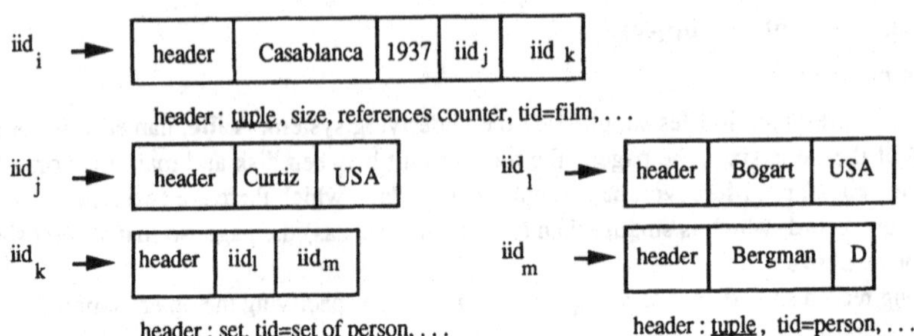

We call the **representation** of the instance "Casablanca", the single record named by iid_i. The other records constitute representations of other instances.

Similarly, the representation of the class tid contains the structure (i.e. the attributes) of instances of this class and the list of methods defined on this class and usable on its instances.

1.3 Hierarchy of abstraction levels

There are two categories of objects in the system : physical and logical objects. Logical objects are O2 objects (classes and instances) usable through methods. Physical objects are pages and representations. The three **types** of objects (O2 objects, pages and representations) form a hierarchy with 3 levels of abstraction, such that at each level, one type of object and its operations are implemented.

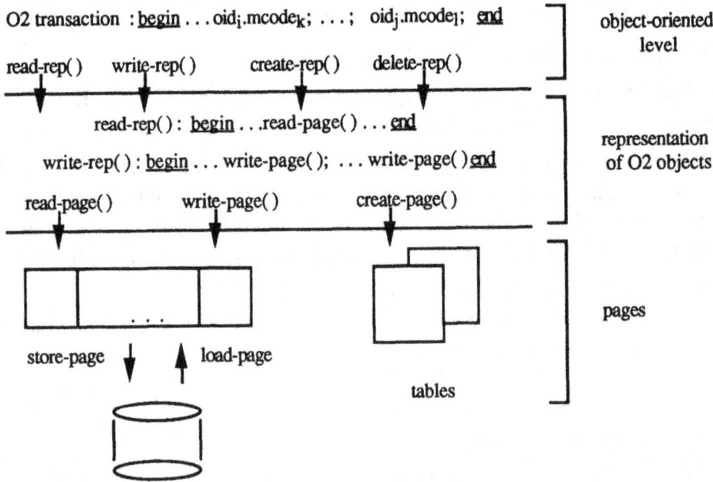

Figure 3. Hierarchy of abstraction levels.

At the bottom level (page level) the page objects and the operations read-page and write-page are implemented. Page transfers between disk and main memory are managed at this level.

At the intermediate level (representation level) representation objects usable through the operations read-rep, write-rep, create-rep, delete-rep are implemented. This implementation requires pages supplied by the bottom level.

Finally, at the top level (O2 object level) are O2 objects usable through methods. The invocation of a method on an O2 object involves accessing its representation by means of the operations read-rep and write-rep.

Thus, any O2 transaction request, even a simple one, involves activity of the underlying system (accesses to pages containing representations, to internal tables, etc.,) which must be taken into account in concurrency control and recovery.

2. CONSTRAINTS UPON CONCURRENCY IN THE OBJECT-ORIENTED APPROACH

2.1 Underlying structures

In an object-oriented system, controlling accesses to object representations is not sufficient to achieve concurrency control. Specific constraints must be taken into account, due to the fact that each object belongs to a class and due to the inheritance property between classes. Classes and instances are not independent insofar as each instance belongs to a particular class. Clustering instances into classes is represented by a 3-level tree, called an **instance tree**, whose leaves are instances and the intermediate nodes the classes they belong to. Similarly classes are not independent of each other, due to the multiple inheritance relationship. The **class graph** expresses this dependency. Thus, with each class C is associated the set of its superclasses, denoted SC(C) ; these are classes whose properties are directly or indirectly inherited by C. Similarly, the set of subclasses of C, denoted sc(C), contains classes which, directly or not, inherit properties from C.

Lastly, instances are not independent of each other insofar as an instance i may take on as the value for an attribute any instance i'.

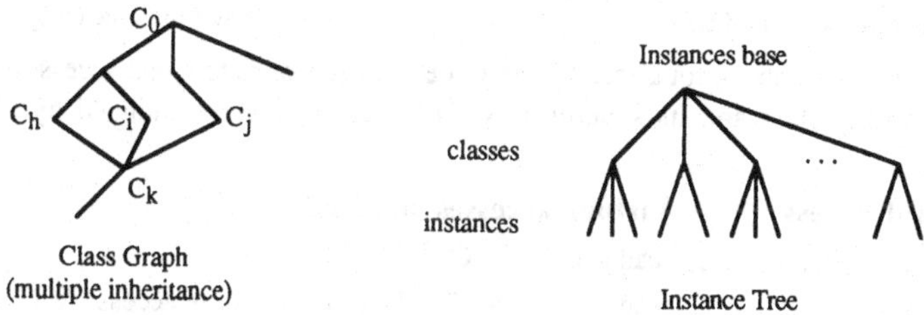

Figure 4. Class graph and instance tree.

2.2 Classification of methods on classes and instances

Classes and instances can be accessed through methods. Those performed on instances essentially consist of consultation and modification of an attribute value. Among those performed on classes, are the following : consult the class definition, add / delete an attribute as well as a method in a class, change the domain of an attribute of a class, change the code of a method in a class and change the inheritance relationship between classes.

Each method, depending on whether it only consults object representation or both consults and modifies it, is considered to be either a reading or a writing method. We emphasize the fact that a method m performed on an object O, is classified as a reading or a writing method according to its effects on the representation of O exclusively. The effects induced on the representation of the component objects of O are not considered. They will be felt through the methods invoked by m on the components of O.

We also distinguish methods depending on whether they are performed on a class or an instance. Lastly, for requirements of CC, methods are classified into 4 categories :

- read-c and write-c performed on classes,
- read-i and write-i performed on instances.

Creation and deletion methods on classes or instances, pose the problem of phantom objects, which will be considered below.

2.3 Compatibility of methods

Real and virtual access

We call a **real access** to an O2 object, an access to its representation resulting from the invocation of a method on this object by a transaction. Because of dependency among objects, a real access to an object may concern other objects, though not requiring access to their representation. For those objects, we will speak of **virtual access**. For instance, applying a method to an instance i induces a real access to i and a virtual one to the class of i as well as to its superclasses, since i inherits their properties.

For each real access, the induced virtual accesses are the following. Reading some class C, through read-c(C), corresponds to a real read access to C and a virtual read access to its superclasses. Similarly, writing a class C, through write-c(C), corresponds to a real write access to C as well as a virtual read access to all its superclasses and a write access to its subclasses.

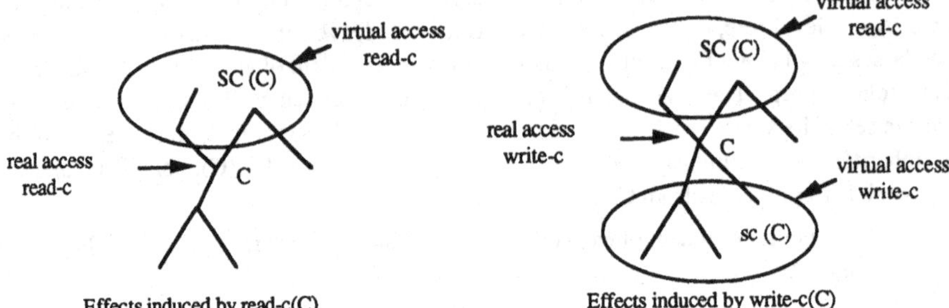

Effects induced by read-c(C) — Effects induced by write-c(C)

Reading or writing an instance, through read-i and write-i, corresponds to a real access to the instance and a virtual access to the class and its superclasses. The virtual accesses induced by a real access are summarized below.

Real access	**Virtual accesses induced**
read-c(C)	read access : $\forall$ C' $\in$ SC(C)
write-c(C)	read access : $\forall$ C' $\in$ SC(C) and write access : $\forall$ C" $\in$ sc(C)
read-i(i) i $\in$ C . .	read access : $\forall$ C' $\in$ C $\cup$ SC(C)
write-i(i) i $\in$ C . .	read access : $\forall$ C' $\in$ C $\cup$ SC(C)

Compatibility of methods

Two methods are compatible if they can be executed concurrently without having to be controlled. In other words, the effects produced by one do not interfere with those produced by the other. Compatibility of two methods depends on whether they involve real or virtual accesses to common objects. When there are common objects, compatibility results from the semantics of read and write : only read methods are compatible. For instance, reading a class C that induces a virtual read access to its superclasses is not compatible with writing a superclass of C. Figures 5 and 6 summarize compatibilities among the methods.

	class C		C' $\in$ sc(C)		C" $\in$ SC(C)	
	read-c(C)	write-c(C)	read-c(C')	write-c(C')	read-c(C")	write-c(C")
read-c(C)	--	N	--	--	--	N
write-c(C)	N	N	N	N	--	N
read-i(i) i $\in$ C	--	N	--	--	--	N
write-i(i) i $\in$ C	--	N	--	--	--	N

Legend : -- = compatible, N = incompatible

Figure 5. Compatibility of methods on classes and instances.

	$i \in C$		$i' \in C'$ and $C' \in sc(C)$		$i'' \in C''$ and $C'' \in SC(C)$	
	read-i(i)	write-i(i)	read-i(i')	write-i(i')	read-i(i")	write-i(i")
read-i(i) $i \in C$	--	N	--	--	--	--
write-i(i) $i \in C$	N	N	--	--	--	--

Figure 6. Compatibility of methods on instances.

2.4 Access control of classes and instances

In this section, we describe the principles of concurrency control on O2 objects based on locking, while disregarding the physical objects that support them. We consider two independent **types of locks**, C and I, to control classes and instances, respectively. Depending on whether the object has to be read or written (really or virtually), two **modes** are distinguished for each type of locks : the R mode for reading and the W mode for writing. Lock compatibility is shown in figure 7.

on classes	C_R	C_W
C_R	--	N
C_W	N	N

on instances	I_R	I_W
I_R	--	N
I_W	N	N

Legend :

-- : compatible

N : incompatible

Figure 7. Lock compatibility.

Integration of control into the execution schema is shown in Figure 8. Each time a method is invoked on some object, the following actions take place. If the object is a class, locks on classes (C-type locks) are requested for the real and virtual acceses. If the object is an instance, a lock on the instance (I-type lock) is requested for the real access as well as locks on classes (C-type lock) for virtual accesses. In any case, control of a real access only takes place after virtual accesses to the classes are completed. When all the locks have been granted, the code of the method is run.

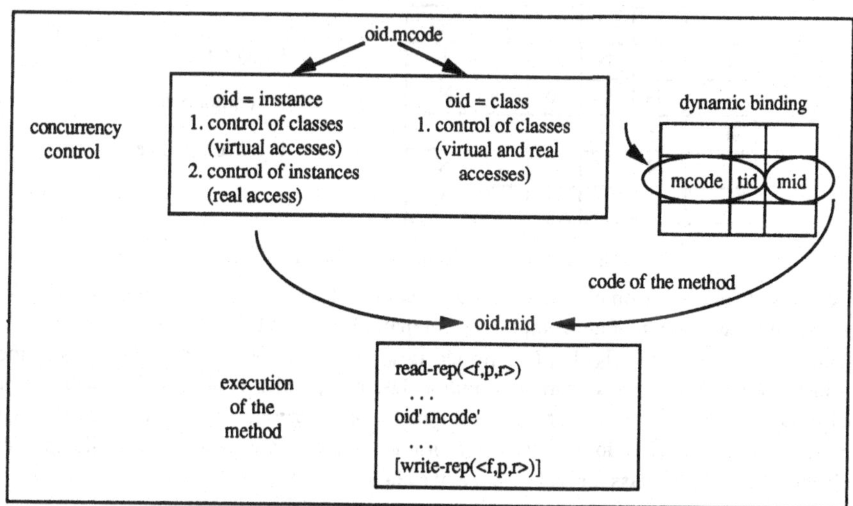

Figure 8. Concurrency control location when a method is invoked.

From a practical point of view, the control of virtual accesses to the superclasses, whose aim is to protect them from concurrent writing, is redundant. Indeed, as a superclass C' of the class C cannot be written before the virtual accesses to its subclasses have been controlled, and as C is a subclass of C', concurrent writing of C' will not occur. For these reasons locks on superclasses do not have to be requested.

Locks granted to a transaction are held until commitment. To prevent risks of deadlock, locks on classes must be requested in the same order. This can be achieved by accessing the class graph in a predefined order (for instance, downward traversal from the root, from the left to the right).

Object-oriented CC cannot be considered without taking underlying abstraction levels into account. In sections 3 to 5, we discuss physical objects supporting O2 objects and show their impact on CC.

2.5 Creation and deletion of instances

A phantom is an object whose creation (or deletion) by some transaction has not been perceived by a concurrent one that follows it in the serialization order. The result is that isolation of transactions is no longer ensured. The phantom problem is more easily solved by taking into account the grouping of instances into classes. This consists in controlling any access to an instance using the instance tree while applying the hierarchical locking protocol [15]. We briefly describe its use in an object-oriented system.

As all the locks are used to control accesses to instances, they are of the I-type. Moreover, there are five lock modes R, W, IR, IW and RIW. An instance can be **explicitly** locked only in the R (or W) mode to indicate whether it has to be read (or written). On the other hand a class can be locked (with an I-type lock) in any of the five modes. The **intentional** read mode IR (or write mode IW) on a class means that some instances of the class are or will be explicitly locked in the R or W mode. An R (or W) mode implies that all the instances of the class are **implicitly** locked in the R (or W) mode ; it prevents them from being written (or read / written) by another concurrent transaction. Lastly, an RIW mode on a class associates effects of both modes R and IW. Before placing an explicit lock (I_R or I_W) on an instance an intentional lock (I_{IR} or I_{IW}) must be placed on its class.

With this protocol, the phantom problem is solved merely by requiring a transaction that has to create or delete some instance, to hold an I_W lock on its class ; thus, creation (or deletion) will be done in mutual exclusion with any transaction that manipulates other instances of this class. On the other hand, minimizing the number of locks for a transaction that has to access all the instances of a class is achieved by explicitly locking (with I_R or I_W locks) the class rather than each instance separately.

	I_R	I_W	I_{IR}	I_{IW}	I_{RIW}
I_R	--	N	--	N	N
I_W	N	N	N	N	N
I_{IR}	--	N	--	--	--
I_{IW}	N	N	--	--	N
I_{RIW}	N	N	--	N	N

Legend :

-- : compatible

N : incompatible

Figure 9. Compatibility of I-lock modes.

I_R, I_W, I_{IR}, I_{IW} and I_{RIW} locks on classes must not be confused with C_R and C_W locks, since they have a different meaning and are in fact completely compatible. C_R and C_W locks control access to the representation of a class, while I_R, I_W, I_{IR}, I_{IW} and I_{RIW} locks control access to instances of the class. Thus, an instance-write can run concurrently with a class-read, which is not possible with the protocol described in Orion [14]. Indeed, in our protocol, transaction T_1 can hold both a C_R lock on class C for virtual access and an I_W (or I_{IW}) lock on the class for real access to an instance of C, while transaction T_2 holds a C_R lock on the same class for real access to the class.

2.6 Creation and deletion of classes

When creating and deleting classes, the class graph is used to avoid phantoms. For instance, creating class C_k as a direct subclass of C_i and C_j, is checked as a writing of these classes and is therefore controlled by a

C_W lock. Any transaction that uses the class being created, has to request a lock on its superclasses and is prevented from holding it as long as the transaction that created the class is not committed. Deleting a class C_k is also managed as a writing of all its superclasses.

3. OBJECT AND OPERATION PROPERTIES EXPLOITED BY THE CONCURRENCY CONTROL

O2 objects are built from physical objects supplied by the system and CC implementation has to take this into account. Objects (whether logical or physical) and their operations can be characterized by properties that are exploited by CC. We specify them below.

3.1 Primitive and constructed objects

An object is defined by its representation and the operations that can be performed on it. For the requirements of concurrency control we separate **primitive** and **constructed** objects.

Operations defined on primitive objects satisfy the following two properties :

1) an operation performed on any primitive object has no effect on the representation of other primitive objects,

2) concurrent operations on the same primitive object are run serially ; they are referred to as **indivisible** operations.

A constructed object is made from existing ones, whether primitive or constructed. In the following, a constructed object means an object (at some level i) made from one or several objects at lower level (i-1). From this point of view, O2 objects obtained using various constructors (tuple, set, etc.,) are not considered to be constructed objects. The operations defined on a constructed object are built from operations defined on the component objects. The two properties verified by primitive objects are not necessarily satisfied by constructed ones. An operation on a constructed object may indeed affect another constructed one when there is a common object in their representation (such as object z in Fig. 10).

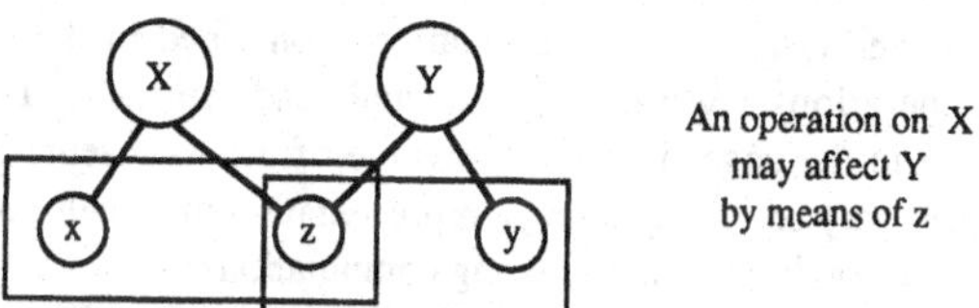

Figure 10. Example of constructed objects.

Operations on constructed objects are not necessarily indivisible but have to be **atomic** (i.e. as if indivisible) to ensure their isolation. In the O2 system, we consider pages as primitive objects and representations as objects built from pages.

3.2 Compatibility and commutativity between operations

The parallelism allowed by concurrency control depends to a large extent on the properties of compatibility and commutativity between operations defined on the objects.

Let X be a primitive or constructed object that is usable through a set of operations $\{OP_1, ..., OP_n\}$.The pair of operations (OP_i,OP_j) has the property of **compatibility** if, whatever the initial state of object X and the concurrent execution of these operations by two different transactions, the effects on the object X and on the transactions are the same. In other words, two compatible operations may be performed concurrently without having to be controlled. For instance, readings are compatible. When two operations are not compatible, commutativity may be used, which is a weaker property.

The ordered pair of operations $(OP_i;OP_j)$ has the property of **commutativity** [10] if, whatever the initial state of object X, execution of operation OP_i by transaction T_1 followed by execution of operation OP_j by transaction T_2 has the same final effect on the object and the same results for the transactions as the execution in the reverse order (OP_j followed by OP_i). This definition can be more concisely formulated as follows :

$$\forall X_i \quad T_1.OP_i(X) \,;\, T_2.OP_j(X) \sim T_2.OP_j(X) \,;\, T_1.OP_i(X)$$

where X_i is the initial state of X

$\sim$ signifies that both executions give the same final state for object X and the same results for transactions.

It should be noted that compatible operations always commute. It is also possible to take call and return parameters into account to express conditional commutativity between operations [20], [9].

3.3 Independence of objects at the same abstraction level

We discuss below the significance of the independence of constructed objects when a multi-level transaction model is used. Assume that X and Y are two objects at the same abstraction level, usable through the sets of operations O_x and O_y respectively. X and Y are said to be **independent** if, whatever the initial state of X, Y and whatever the operations $OP_x \in O_x$ and $OP_y \in O_y$, the execution of OP_x by transaction T_1 followed by the execution of OP_y by transaction T_2 gives the same final states of objects X, Y and the same results for the transactions as the execution in the reverse order (OP_y followed by OP_x). The independence of objects X and Y can be more concisely expressed as follows :

$$\forall X_i, \forall Y_i \qquad \forall OP_x, \forall OP_y \qquad T_1.OP_x(X) \,;\, T_2.OP_y(Y) \sim T_2.OP_y(Y) \,;\, T_1.OP_x(X)$$

where X_i and Y_i are the initial states of X and Y, respectively.

Primitive objects are naturally independent since an operation on a primitive object has no effect on the representation of another primitive object. As for constructed objects, if they are obtained from independent and distinct objects at lower level, they are themselves independent. If they share common objects at lower level in their representation, they are independent on condition that all pairs of operations defined on the common objects commute. For instance, in Figure 10, if x, y, z are independent and if all pairs of operations defined on z commute, then X and Y are independent. On the other hand, the following example shows a situation where constructed objects are not independent.

Example 2. Suppose that r_1 and r_2 are two representations contained in the same page. They may be manipulated through the operations : write-rep(r_i, ...) and read-rep(r_i,@). The return value @ is the address of the representation in the page (it is not the value of the representation). We assume that the length of a representation may vary so that updating a representation may cause other representations to be moved in the page. Given these conditions the following computations :

T_1.write-rep(r_1, ...) ; T_2.read-rep(r_2,@) and T_2.read-rep(r_2,@') ; T_1.write-rep(r_1, ...)

do not always give the same effects. Indeed when updating r_1 causes r_2 to be moved in the page, the final effect on the page remains the same but the effect on the transaction that invoked read-rep is different (@≠@'). The result is that r_1 and r_2 are not independent.

4. IMPACT OF A ONE-LEVEL TRANSACTION MODEL

A one-level transaction [7] is modeled as a set of indivisible operations op_i on primitive objects. In the O2 system, primitive objects are pages ; pages are provided with a locking mechanism that we call **physical locking** as opposed to **logical locking** defined on classes and instances. Given these conditions object-oriented CC can be obtained either by using only physical locking on pages, or by combining physical and logical locking. The consequences of these two approaches are discussed in the following section.

4.1 Physical locking

When physical locking is used alone, running transactions are controlled at the page level only : when methods are invoked on O2 objects, only induced operations on pages are taken into account by the CC. Thus the page is the only granule concerned by a lock request. In the following discussion locks placed on pages are considered to be P-type locks. P_R or P_W lock is used depending on the nature of operation (read or write page). All locks needed to satisfy the requirements of the object-oriented approach are translated into locks on pages that contain the representations. With 2PL locking [11], pages (and therefore the objects they contain) remain locked until the end of the transaction. If pages simultanously contain instance and classe representations, concurrency is then severely decreased since it is not possible for different transactions to read the definition of a class C and to update an instance i (with $i \in C$ or $i \notin C$) concurrently if the representations belong to the same page. This consideration must be taken into account when placing objects in pages.

In any case, two transactions cannot concurrently use different instances if they are represented in the same page and the lock modes on the page are incompatible.

4.2 Physical and logical locking

The use of logical locks to satisfy the constraints of the object-oriented approach (see section 2) may be combined with the use of physical locks on pages. A logical lock is associated with the oid of an O2 object and must be requested by the transaction for any virtual or real access to the object. In the case of a real access to an object, the physical lock that controls the page containing its representation must be requested once the logical lock is held.

Serializability of transactions is achieved by releasing logical locks at the end of the transaction (2PL on logical locks). As for a physical lock, it may be released either at the end of the transaction (2PL on physical locks), or at the end of the operation read-page or write-page on the page ; in this case physical locks are called short locks. The former solution has the same drawbacks as in 4.1 while the latter one avoids them. It uses a physical lock as a means of performing operations on pages in mutual exclusion so that read-page and write-page are made atomic. In fact, this technique used in the Orion system [14] amounts to a 2-level transaction model (cf. section 5). However, although it takes the object-oriented approach into account, it does not allow a full exploitation of it ; specifically, as we will see below, it does not take advantage of methods commutativity (to increase concurrency). Finally it should be noted that the use of logical locks with a one-level transaction model allows implementation of the 2PL hierarchical protocol to solve the phantom problem.

5. IMPACT OF A MULTI-LEVEL TRANSACTION MODEL

5.1 Multi-level transaction

This model, which is based on nested transactions [5], [6] takes the different abstraction levels into account. It follows directly from the hierarchical construction of operations and objects as presented in 1.3. A transaction is modeled as a sequence of operations on objects provided at a given level of abstraction. An operation may be regarded in turn as a transaction invoking operations defined on objects at lower level.

Figure 11 shows the decomposition of operations in the O2 system and the nested transactions involved in an O2 transaction. Three levels of transaction are considered :

1. transactions at the object-oriented level corresponding to the O2 transactions :

   $T_{O2} \equiv$ begin ... $oid_i.mcode_k$; ... $oid_j.mcode_l$; ... end

2. transactions at the method level ; each method m is taken as a transaction T_m :

   $T_m \equiv$ begin $op_i(x)$;...; $op_j(y)$ end

   where x, y are representations of classes and instances named by a triplet <f,p,r>

   and $op_i, op_j \in$ {read-rep, write-rep, create-rep, delete-rep}

3. transactions at the representation level ; an operation on a representation (read-rep, ...) corresponds to a transaction T_r :

   $T_r \equiv$ begin $op_k(z)$;...; $op_l(w)$ end

   where z, w are pages named by a pair <f,p> and $op_k, op_l \in$ {read-page, write-page}.

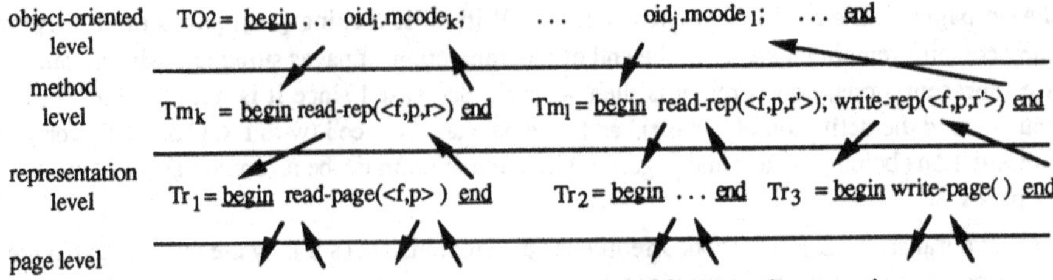

Figure 11. An O2 transaction represented by nested transactions.

The advantage of multi-level transactions over one-level transactions is that the semantics of both operations and objects can be exploited at each level of abstraction. Thus, dependencies due to conflicts on primitive objects can be eliminated. The following examples illustrate this idea.

Example 3. Exploiting objects independence.

Let r_1 and r_2 be representations contained in the same page p. Reading and writing a representation is expressed in terms of operations on the page, as follows :

read-rep(r) = begin ... read-page(p) ... end and write-rep(r) = begin ... write-page(p) ... end

The operation read-rep is assumed to return the value of the representation (and not the address in the page). Let us consider a concurrent execution in which transaction T_1 reads r_1 and transaction T_2 writes r_2. Accesses to the page p are made in the following order : T_1.read-page(p) ; T_2.write-page(p). It entails the dependency T_1.read-rep(r_1) -> T_2.write-rep(r_2) due to the conflict on p. If we exploit the fact that representations r_1 and r_2 are independent, it follows that the execution T_1.read-rep(r_1) ; T_2.write-rep(r_2) has the same effects on both representations r_1, r_2 and the transactions (information read by T_1 is the same) as the execution in the reverse order, T_2.write-rep(r_2) ; T_1.read-rep(r_1). Thus, the dependency T_1 -> T_2 can be eliminated.

Example 4. Exploiting operations commutativity.

Let A and B be two objects of the bank account class. They may be used through the operations (i.e. methods) credit et debit. These operations are expressed in terms of read-rep / write-rep. For instance :

credit(A) = begin read-rep(A) ; ... ; write-rep(A) .. end .

Consider a concurrent execution where transactions T_1 and T_2 transfer money from one bank account to another.

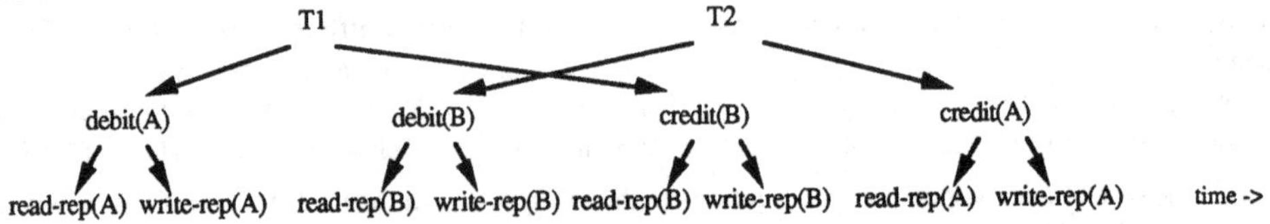

This execution leads to dependencies T_1->T_2 et T_2->T_1 due to conflicts on the representations of A and B so that the transactions are not serializable. But if we consider the semantics of credit and debit, we find that the pair of operations (debit ; credit) verifies the commutativity property [10]. Since in the execution above these operations are atomic, it is possible to apply this property so that the dependencies between T_1 and T_2 disappear and the transactions become serializable.

The multi-level transactions theory [19], [6] states that a concurrent execution of transactions is correct (i.e. top-level transactions are serializable) if the transactions at each level are serializable and if the serialization orders of the different levels are compatible. This result is obtained by proceeding iteratively from the lowest level. Once the serializability of transactions at a given level is achieved, transactions are then considered to be atomic operations invoked by higher level transactions that in turn have to be serialized (using operations commutativity and objects independence).

In practice, serializability is obtained at each level by the same CC methods as for one-level transactions. However, all these methods set up dependencies between transactions from conflicts due to shared objects.

This leads to a limitation concerning the modeling of objects, which has not been sufficiently discussed in the literature ; we examine the problem in the following section.

Necessity of objects independence

Let X, Y, Z be objects usable through operation OP and built from primitive objects x, y, z, w used through operation op ; we suppose that w is an object common to representations of X, Y, Z, and the pair of operations (op ; op) does not satisfy the commutativity property. Operation OP corresponds, according to the object on which it is performed, to the following actions :

OP(X) = <u>begin</u> op(x) ; op(w) <u>end</u>

OP(Y) = <u>begin</u> op(y) ; op(w) <u>end</u>

OP(Z) = <u>begin</u> op(z) ; op(w) <u>end</u>

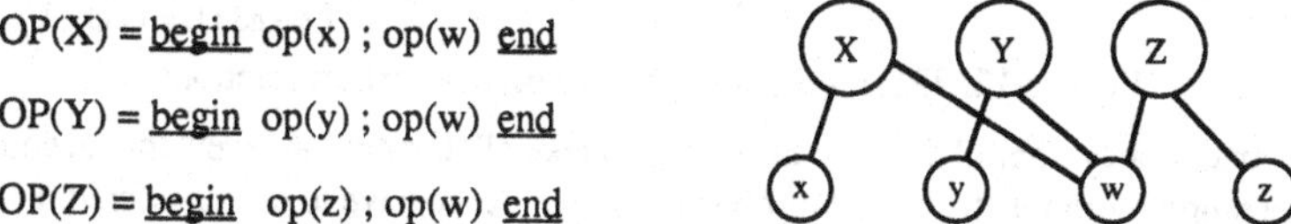

Let T_1 and T_2 be the transactions :

$T_1 \equiv$ <u>begin</u> ... OP(X) ; ... ; OP(Z) <u>end</u> and $T_2 \equiv$ <u>begin</u> ... OP(Y) ; ... <u>end</u>

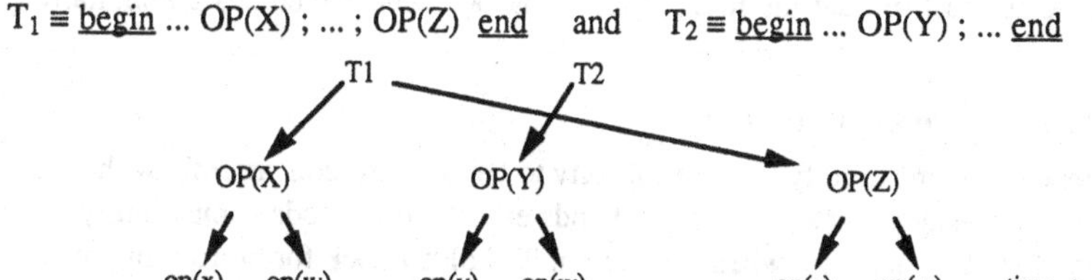

Let us consider the concurrent execution given by the tree above. To determine whether T_1 and T_2 are serializable, we first consider operations OP as transactions that invoke operations op. They are serializable (their execution is performed serially) and the dependencies due to conflicts on w are : OP(X) -> OP(Y) -> OP(Z). As the operations OP are atomic, we then examine transactions T_1 and T_2 considering that operations OP are invoked in the order : OP(X); OP(Y); OP(Z). Whatever CC method (in particular 2PL) is used, dependencies between transactions arise from conflicts on shared objects ; the result is that T_1 and T_2 do not conflict and are therefore serializable (equivalence with $T_1;T_2$ ou $T_2;T_1$). The problem here is that the method ignores dependencies resulting from operations on objects at lower levels. These dependencies may be ignored only if the semantics of the objects shows that they are independent. If that is not the case, transactions T_1 and T_2 are not serializable.

In practice, the objective is then to prove objects independence (at each level), allowing use of the multi-level transaction model. Independence (cf. 3.3) is ensured in the following cases :

a) when objects are constructed from distinct and independent objects at lower level ;

b) when objects share some common objects in their representation and these common objects are only used by operations that commute.

5.2 Multi-level two phase locking

Assuming that the objects at each level are independent, transactions serializability can be achieved at each level by the 2PL protocol. This implies that some types of locks have been defined at each level to control accesses to the objects of this level :

- I and C type locks are used to control O2 objects,
- R-type locks are used to control representations,
- P-type locks are used to control pages.

Figure 12 shows the different levels of locking. In the absence of deadlock, the 2PL protocol ensures that serialization orders of the different levels are compatible. It should be emphasized that a page is locked only during execution of an operation on a representation within the page. The representation of an object is locked during execution of a method while an O2 object is locked until the end of the O2 transaction.

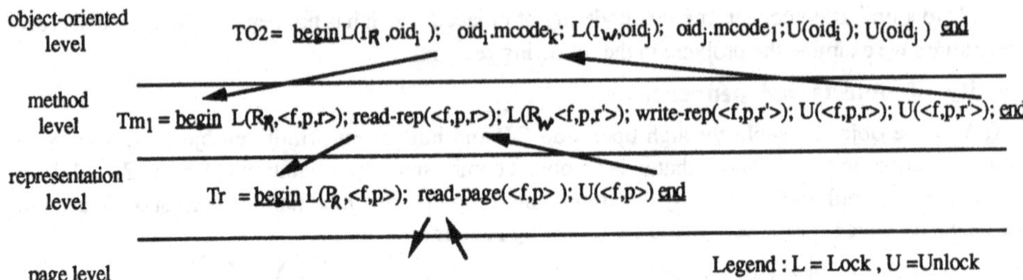

Figure 12. 2PL protocol applied to multi-level transactions.

In multi-level concurrency control, it is not necessary to take all abstraction levels into account. Only those that involve operations commutativity and/or objects independence have to be considered. For instance, it is of no interest to consider the representation abstraction level if each representation fills the whole page. Similarly, there is no interest to take the method level into account if methods commutativity is not exploited.

5.3 Exploiting methods commutativity

In section 2, only methods compatibility (i.e. the capacity to be executed concurrently without control) is used by the CC, and lock mode compatibility corresponds exactly to methods compatibility. Thus, if m_1 and m_2 are two incompatible methods, when transaction T1 holds a lock for performing m_1 it impedes transaction T2 from acquiring the lock for performing m_2 ; T2 has to wait until the commitment of T1.

However, although methods m_1 and m_2 are not compatible, they may be commutative. In this case, provided that methods m_1 and m_2 are atomic, the fact that transaction T1 holds the lock for performing m_1 no longer prevents transaction T2 from obtaining the lock for performing m_2. The waiting by T2 is eliminated but method atomicity has to be ensured. It may be obtained either by serial execution (in mutual exclusion) or by a serializable one.

The following example shows how to take advantage of methods commutativity when using multi-level locking. Suppose we want to exploit the commutativity of debit and credit methods presented in example 4. New modes associated with I-type locks have to be defined and included into the compatibility table - a DEB mode for debit and a CRED mode for credit. In particular these two lock modes are compatible since the methods they are associated with are commutative. Thus, a bank account object is locked until the commitment of the transaction that invoked the credit / debit method but as the I_{DEB} and I_{CRED} locks are compatible, this provides a higher degree of parallelism.

The atomicity of debit and credit methods at run time has to be ensured by performing the sequences of operations : read-rep( ) . . ; write-rep( ) relative to credit and debit methods either in mutual exclusion or in a serializable way. In this case a method is seen as a transaction and serializability can be achieved using R-type locks on the representation. Thus, incompatible but commutative methods may be performed concurrently provided that their atomicity is ensured. This is a great advantage over mutual exclusion when methods are long.

6. CONCLUSION

We have shown here that the structural properties of objects in an object-oriented database impose requirements on concurrency control if the dynamic creation, deletion and update of classes are to be performed concurrently with the creation, deletion, consultation and update of instances. These requirements can be expressed in terms of compatibility and can be implemented with a locking protocol. The problem arising when adaptating to the underlying system used to support object representations has been studied. The transaction model provided by this system and the locking granularity it imposes are determining features when a high degree of parallelism is needed. The multi-level transaction model seems best suited to fully exploiting potential parallelism, especially methods commutativity. However, recovery must be adequately managed, which has not been addressed in this paper.

ACKNOWLEDGMENTS

We would like to thank Michel Scholl and Fernando Velez for providing helpful explanations of the O2 system.

REFERENCES

[1] Bancilhon F., BenzakenV., Delobel C., Velez F. *The O2 Object Manager Architecture Version V1*. Rapport Technique Altaïr 14-87, novembre 1987.

[2] Bancilhon F. *Object-Oriented Database Systems*. Proc. 7th ACM Symposium on Principles of Database Systems (SIGART / SIGMOD / SIGACT), Austin, march1988, pp. 152-162.

[3] Bancilhon F., Barbedette G., BenzakenV., Delobel C., Gamerman S., Lécluse C., Pfeffer P., Richard P., Velez F. *The Design and Implementation of O2 an Object-Oriented Database System*. Proc. OODBS 2 Workshop, Badmunster, september 1988; in Advances in Object-Oriented Database Systems, Springer Verlag.

[4] Banerjee J., Kim H.J., Kim W., Korth H.F. *Semantics and Implementation of Schema Evolution in Object-Oriented Databases*. Proc. ACM SIGMOD Conference on Management of Data, San Francisco, may 1987, pp. 311-322.

[5] Beeri C., Schek H.J., Weikum G. *Multi-Level Transaction Management, Theoretical Art or Practical Need ?* Proc. Int. Conference on Extending Database Technology, Venice, march 1988, pp. 134-155.

[6] Beeri C., Bernstein Ph., Goodman N. *A Model for Concurrency in Nested Transactions Systems*. Journal of the ACM, vol. 36, n° 2, april 1989, pp. 230-267.

[7] Bernstein P.A., Hadzilacos V., Goodman N. *Concurrency control and recovery in database systems*. Addison-Wesley Publishing, Reading, Mass., 1987.

[8] Carey M.J. *Granularity Hierarchies in Concurrency Control*. Proc. 2nd ACM SIGACT-SIGMOD Symposium on Principles of Data base Systems, Atlanta, march 1983, pp. 156-165.

[9] Cart M., Ferrié J., Richy H. *Le contrôle de concurrence des transactions dans les environnements orientés-objets*. Actes 4è Journées Bases de Données Avancées, Bénodet, mai 1988, pp. 117-138.

[10] Cart M., Ferrié J., Richy H. *Contrôle de l'exécution de transactions concurrentes*. Technique et Science Informatique, vol. 8, n° 3, juin 1989, pp. 225-240.

[11] Eswaran K.P., Gray J.N., Lorie A., Traiger I.L. *The notions of consistency and predicate locks in data base system*. Comm. ACM, vol. 19, n° 11, nov. 1976, pp. 624-633.

[12] Fishman D. H. et al. *Iris : An Object-Oriented Database Management System*. ACM Transactions on Office Information Systems, vol. 5, n° 1, january 1987, pp. 48-69.

[13] Garcia-Molina H. *Using semantic knowledge for transaction processing in a distributed database*. ACM Transactions on Database Systems, vol. 8, n°2, june 1983, pp. 186-213.

[14] Garza J.F., Kim W. *Transaction management in an object-oriented database system*. Proc. Int. Conference on Management of Data (ACM-SIGMOD 88), Chicago, june 1988, pp. 37-45.

[15] Gray J. *Notes on Database Operating Systems*. in Operating Systems : an Advanced Course, Lectures Notes in Computer Science, Springer-Verlag, 1979.

[16] Haerder T., Reuter A. *Principles of transaction-oriented database recovery*. ACM Computing Survey, vol. 15, n°4, december 1983, pp. 287-317.

[17] Lécluse C., Richard R., Velez F. *O2, an Object-Oriented Data Model*. Proc. Int. Conference on Management of Data (ACM-SIGMOD 88), Chicago, june 1988.

[18] Lécluse C., Richard R. *Modeling Complex Structures in Object-Oriented Databases*. Proc. 8th ACM Symposium on Principles of Data Base Systems (PODS), Philadelphia, march 1989.

[19] Martin B.E. *Modeling Concurrent Activities with Nested Objects*. Proc. 7th Int. Conference on Distributed Computing Systems, Berlin, september 1987, pp. 432-439.

[20] Schwarz P.M., Spector A.Z. *Synchronizing shared abstract types*. ACM Transactions on Computer Systems, vol. 2, n°3, august 1984, pp. 223-250.

[21] Sha L. *Modular concurrency control and failure recovery - Consistency, correctness and optimality*. Ph.D. dissertation, Dept. of Computer Science, Carnegie-Mellon University, march 1985.

[22] Velez F., Bernard G., Darnis V. *The O2 Object Manager : an Overview*. Proc. 15th Int. Conference on Very Large Data Bases, Amsterdam, august 1989, pp. 357-366.

[23] Woelk D., Kim W. *Multimedia information management in an object-oriented database system*. Proc. 13th Int. Conference on Very Large Data Bases, Brighton, sept. 1987, pp. 319-329.

Representation of the Historical Information Necessary for Temporal Integrity Monitoring

K. Hülsmann*, G. Saake

Informatik, Abt. Datenbanken, Technische Universität, PF 3329, D-3300 Braunschweig

Abstract

Temporal integrity constraints describe long-term data dependencies to be respected by correct database evolutions. Such temporal constraints can be monitored by a runtime evaluation of corresponding transitions of an equivalent finite automaton for each substitution of the free constraint variables with database objects. The current states of the automaton are the historical information necessary for temporal integrity monitoring. This paper presents techniques for decreasing the amount of historical information by monitoring automata for whole sets of substitutions instead of single substitutions thus enabling a monitoring even for large sets of monitored substitutions.

1. Introduction

Temporal integrity of a database means the satisfaction of long-term data dependencies by the database evolution. This notion is a generalization of transitional integrity by looking at whole database state sequences instead of handling only database state transitions as it is done with transitional assertions [Ch76, Vi83]. Whereas several authors propose the use of temporal constraints especially in conceptual modelling of database applications [Se80, ELG84, Ku84, SFNC84, SaL89], our working group was apparently the first starting with the design of an integrity monitor for temporal integrity to be implemented as part of a database management system [LEG85, LiS87, SaL87, Sa88, HüS89].

Temporal constraints are usually formulated in a predicate logic extended by temporal operators resulting in a *temporal logic* [MaP81, Kr87]. It was well known for propositional temporal logic that temporal formulae can be transformed into finite automata accepting exactly those state sequences satisfying the formula (for algorithms see [MaW84, LiS87, Sa88, Li89]). If we forbid variable quantifiers outside of temporal operators and assume free variables as universally quantified, we can use these techniques also for temporal integrity monitoring. The validity of a temporal formula is then checked by runtime simulation of such a finite automaton (having predicate logic formulae as transition conditions) for each relevant substitution of the free variables (see chapter 2. and 3.). For a given substitution, the current state of the automaton simulation is the minimally necessary historical information for the evaluation of the temporal constraint (after automaton minimization).

The basic task of temporal integrity monitoring is therefore the runtime handling of the current automaton states and the performing of automaton state transitions after database transactions. For temporal integrity monitoring, especially the following critical problems arise:

1. Since the automaton simulation has to be performed for all substitutions, the amount of historical information (the current state of the automaton for each substitution) may easily exceed the given storage capabilities. For formulae having a free variable of a data sort

* K. Hülsmann's work is supported by Deutsche Forschungsgemeinschaft (AZ: En 184/1-1)

(integer for example), the set of substitutions to be considered in monitoring may even become infinite.

2. As it is also a known problem in usual database constraint monitoring, a preselection of automaton / substitution combinations depending on the current transaction is necessary to reach an acceptable performance of the database management system. In the non-temporal case, several approaches were suggested for tackling this problem. So, Hsu and Imilienski propose a method for reducing the checking space of a constraint [HsI85] whereas [Ni82, LIT85] and [KoSS87] deal with methods for simplification and efficient evaluation of constraints, respectively. These approaches seem to be extensible for the temporal case.

This paper is devoted to solutions for the first mentioned problem. In the second chapter, the basic notations and definitions for temporal integrity monitoring are introduced. In the third chapter, there are described the basic notations and definitions for a compact representation of historical information. Subsequently, the concept of integrity monitoring based on this approach is outlined in the fourth chapter. Chapter five contains some remarks on analysis possibilities for constraints and enhancement of the monitoring concepts. In chapter six, we summarize our results and sketch our future plans.

2. Monitoring Temporal Integrity using Transition Graphs

We omit in this paper the introduction of temporal logic as a formal language for temporal database constraints as well as the formal derivation of the automata from temporal formula, because both are not essential for the results presented herein. The interested reader can find this in detail in [LiS87, Sa88, Li89, HüS89, SaL89].

We assume a logic signature containing sorts, functions and predicates determined by a suitable schema of a data model. A database state is an interpretation of this signature by sort carriers and function / predicates on these carriers. The dynamic evolution of a database is given by a sequence $\underline{\sigma}=\langle\sigma_0,\sigma_1,\ldots\rangle$ of such database states, where the carriers of the database object sorts may vary due to object insertions and deletions. The pure data sorts (integer, string, ...) have in all states the same interpretation. Since we want to observe the behaviour of fixed database objects during the run of time, we additionally assume that our data model offers a *time-independent object identification mechanism*, be it by database keys [EDG86] or by surrogates. This is necessary, since the other object properties may change due to update transactions.

Having a time-independent object identification, we can define *global substitutions* for state sequences which in their turn are sequences of usual variable substitutions with elements of the related sort carriers.

definition 2.1: If a global substitution $\underline{\vartheta}$ has at some time i a local substitution ϑ_i with currently existing database objects (wrt a set of variables X), the other local substitutions ϑ_j are defined as follows:

$$\vartheta_j := \begin{cases} \vartheta_i & \text{iff all substituted objects } \vartheta_i(x),\ x\in X, \text{ exist in } \sigma_j \\ \bot & \text{otherwise} \end{cases}$$

The equality of substitutions is defined over the time-independent object identification mechanism. The set of all possible global substitutions $\underline{\vartheta}$ for given variables X is denoted by $\underline{\Theta}(X)$. For a local substitution ϑ, FIRST(ϑ) denotes the index i of the first state where the corresponding global substituition has a local substitution $\vartheta_i = \vartheta$. □

Global substitutions fix the variable to carrier element binding as far as the elements exist in the carriers, so enabling the observation of object properties during the existence interval of the substituted object. The existence interval of an object, i.e. the subsequence of the whole database evolution between its insertion and its deletion, is called *life cycle* of the object. Such life cycles are assumed to be in general of a finite length. We use this notation also for substitutions if we refer to those subsequences where all substituted objects do exist.

A temporal constraint (expressed by an automaton) has to be satisfied by the database evolution during the life cycles of all substitutions of the variables occurring free in the state transitions formulae of the automaton. Such an automaton is called *transition graph* and defined as follows:

definition 2.2: A *transition graph* $T = (N, E, \nu, \eta, m_0, F)$ consists of

a directed graph $G=(N,E)$ with nodes N and edges E,
a *node labelling* ν with temporal formulae,
an *edge labelling* η with predicate logic formulae,
an *initial node* m_0 and
a set of *final nodes* $F \subseteq N$. □

The node labelling gives the possible current monitoring states of the temporal constraint in terms of temporal formulae. A special node is the *error node* labelled with **false** indicating a constraint violation. The node labelling results from the construction of such graphs from descriptive temporal database constraints. As mentioned before, we concentrate on the technical handling of transition graphs in a monitoring component and do not consider the link to temporal logic formulae.

The stepwise evaluation of a state sequence using a transition graph automaton is formalized by the definition of transitions between nodes depending on the current value of the edge labels. Therefore, the evaluation proceeding is based on the construction of *paths* through the graph with edge labels valid in the related state. As known from finite automata, it is only necessary to consider the end points of such correct paths; those end points are contained in the so-called *current marking*.

definition 2.3: The *current marking* $m_T(i,\underline{\sigma},\underline{\vartheta})$ at time i for a state sequence $\underline{\sigma}$ and a global substitution $=\langle\vartheta_0,\vartheta_1,\ldots\rangle$ of the free variables is defined as follows:

$$m_T(i,\underline{\sigma},\underline{\vartheta}) = \bot \qquad \text{for } i < \text{FIRST}(\vartheta) \text{ or } \vartheta_i=\bot$$

$$m_T(\text{FIRST}(\vartheta),\underline{\sigma},\underline{\vartheta}) = m_0$$

$$m_T(i+1,\underline{\sigma},\underline{\vartheta}) = \text{trans}(m_T(i,\underline{\sigma},\underline{\vartheta}),\sigma_i,\vartheta_i) \qquad \text{for } i \geq \text{FIRST}(\vartheta)$$

where

$$\text{trans}(L,\sigma,\vartheta) = \{n \in N \mid (\exists l \in L): (l,n) \in E \wedge (\sigma,\vartheta) \models \eta((l,n))\}$$

The expression $(\sigma,\vartheta)\models\varphi$ means 'φ is valid in the state σ under the substitution ϑ'. The substitution ϑ is the local substition with existing database objects uniquely determined by the global substitution $\underline{\vartheta}$. The function 'trans' is called *transition rule* and formalizes the state transitions of the automaton. 'trans' applied on an undefined marking, i.e. $m_T(i,\underline{\sigma},\underline{\vartheta}) = \bot$, yields again an undefined marking as result. □

Transition graphs are a special sort of non-deterministic finite automata where the transition rule defines the state transition function. Following this point of view, we define a few useful properties of transition graphs in analogy to finite automata.

definition 2.4: A transition graph *accepts* a finite (!) state sequence, iff the last marking contains a final node, i.e. iff $m_T(|\underline{\sigma}|, \underline{\sigma}, \underline{\vartheta}) \cap F \neq \emptyset$ □

definition 2.5: A transition graph is called *deterministic*, if at each time at most one node is marked, i.e. iff for each two different nodes l and l' directly reachable from a node n :

$$\eta((n,l)) \wedge \eta((n,l')) \equiv \textbf{false}$$

A transition graph is called *complete*, iff for each node n a valid transition to a node exists, i.e. iff for each node $n \in N$: $\textbf{true} \equiv \bigvee_{(n,l)\in E} \eta((n,l))$ □

In deterministic and complete transition graphs, the current marking for a substitution contains always exactly one node. According to well-known results from automata theory, every transition graph can be equivalently transformed into a complete and deterministic graph.

As a last property of transition graphs, we say that a transition graph is *reduced*, if each edge label is satisfiable and at each node a path through the graph starts leading to a final node (with exception of the error node).

For temporal integrity monitoring, we have at a certain point of time a finite database state sequence describing the database history until the current state. We say that this sequence is *provisionally accepted* by a (reduced) transition graph iff

for each current possible substitution of the free variables, the current marking is not equal to the error node;

for each possible 'historical' substitution, i.e. for substitutions with in the meanwhile deleted objects, the substitution life cycle was accepted by the graph.

Herein, the computation of the markings starts with the insertion of the substituted objects into the database. The provisional acceptance of the database history is the basic principle of runtime monitoring of temporal integrity. Since the future database evolution is in principle open, one can only check the final validity of the temporal constraints for in the meanwhile deleted objects, and for the other substitutions one has to perform an optimistical handling of the constraints.

example 2.6: The following transition graphs are example automata for simple temporal constraints. The first one requires that at some state of the sequence the formula p(x) becomes valid; whereas the complementary second graph requires that p(x) must be valid in all states. The initial node is marked with m_0, whereas final nodes are highlighted by double borders. Both graphs are complete and deterministic.

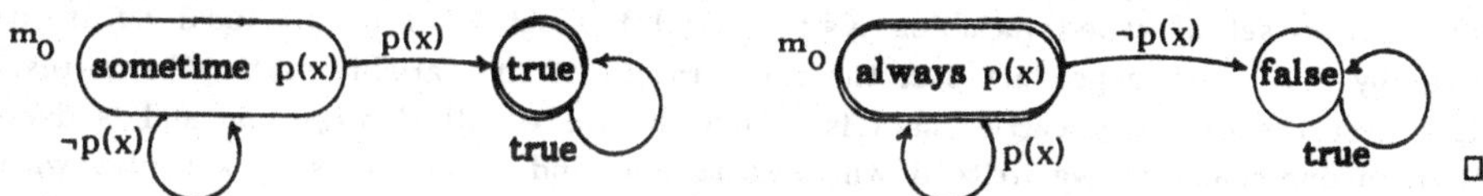

□

The nodes are labelled with simple temporal formulae surely being understandable without a detailed explanation of the used temporal logic operators. The node labelled by **sometime** p(x) is non-final, this means that a sequence termination is only allowed after leaving the node by a transition. After once reaching the non-final error node labelled with **false**, a sequence acceptance is impossible because a future transition leading to a final node is impossible.

By the use of transition graphs, long term data dependencies like the admissible evolution of a person's salary are expressible.

example 2.7: We consider the following temporal constraint:

"Historical salaries of a person may not exceed the present salary unless the corresponding employers are different."

For this constraint we have the following transition graph with the initial marking $m_0 = \{\langle 1\rangle\}$. The free variables are P, E and s of the types PERSON, ENTERPRISE and **integer**.

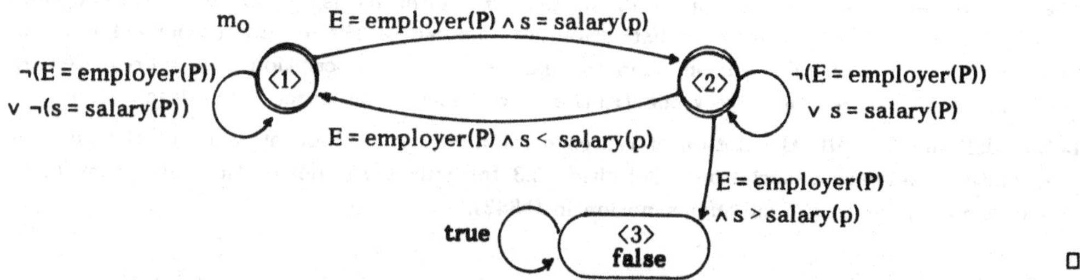

□

For the nodes ⟨1⟩ and ⟨2⟩ the temporal logic labels can be found in the appendix.

Initially every substitution for the variables P, E and s has the marking {⟨1⟩}. If a person P is employed at an enterprise E and earns a salary s, the corresponding substitution obtains the new marking {⟨2⟩}. The marking {⟨2⟩} means that whenever P is employed at E the salary must not fall under s. This is indicated by the edge from ⟨2⟩ to the error node ⟨3⟩. Whenever the salary P earns at E is higher than s, it suffices to assure this condition for the higher salary. Therefore there is an edge from ⟨2⟩ to ⟨1⟩.

3 Substitutions and Descriptions

A crucial point for temporal integrity monitoring in practice is representing the markings of substitutions to be stored as historical information. In principle, for each global substitution $\underline{\vartheta}$ and each state σ_i within the life cycle of $\underline{\vartheta}$, the current marking $m_T(i,\underline{\sigma},\underline{\vartheta})$ must be represented somehow in the database. Storing explicitly the set of all local substitutions with their markings is not practical or even impossible if some of the free variables refer to sorts with infinite carriers. So in example 2.7 the set of all substitutions consists of

$$|\mathrm{PERSON}| \times |\mathrm{ENTERPRISE}| \times |\mathbf{integer}|$$

where |...| denotes the (local) extension of the corresponding object or data sort. For tackling this problem, [Li89] proposes to reduce the set of explicitliy stored substitutions by introducing default markings. In this paper, we generalize this approach and define the notion of *description* for referring to substitution sets instead of single substitutions. Therefore a placeholder *, assumed to be not contained in any of the carrier sets, is introduced. A carrier set extended by a placeholder is called an extended carrier.

For a given set of typed variables $X = \{x_1,\ldots, x_k\}$ the set $\Theta(X)$ of all local substitutions is given by the cartesian product over the sort carriers of the variable sorts. The cartesian product over the extended carrier sets is called the set of all *descriptions* and is denoted by $\Delta(X)$. In our examples we write down substitutions and descriptions as k-tuples with round and square brackets, respectively. For a given local substitution ϑ or a description D, $\vartheta(x)$ or D(x) denote the element the variable x is substituted by in ϑ or D, respectively.

The following definition formalizes which substitutions are *described* by a given description.

definition 3.1: Let there be a variable set X and a description $D \in \Delta(X)$. The set |D| of the substitutions *described* by D is defined as follows:

$$|D| = \{\vartheta \mid \vartheta \in \Theta(X) \wedge \forall x \in X: [(D(x) \neq *) \Rightarrow (\vartheta(x) = D(x))]\}$$ □

So, a description describes all substitutions matching the variables not replaced by the placeholder. As a special case, the description substituting every variable by the placeholder, i.e. the description [*,...,*], describes the whole set $\Theta(X)$.

example 3.2: For the description [Miller, *, *] over the variables in $X = \{P, E, s\}$ from example 2.7 there holds:

$$|[\mathrm{Miller}, *, *]| = \{\mathrm{Miller}\} \times |\mathrm{ENTERPRISE}| \times |\mathbf{integer}|$$ □

The idea of description based monitoring of temporal integrity is to represent substitutions by descriptions and thus handling substitution sets instead of single substitutions. For regaining the marking of a substitution from the marking of the description it is represented by, there has to be assured that every substitution is represented by exactly one description.

Before defining formally the notion of representation we have a look at some of the possible interrelations between descriptions. Definition 3.3 formalizes for descriptions different kinds of inclusion similar to the subsumes-notion in [Ni82].

definition 3.3: Let $\mathfrak{D}$ denote a set of descriptions over a set of variables X. For a description $D \in \mathfrak{D}$ and a description $D' \in \Delta(X)$ holds

(1) D' is a *refinement* of D, $D' \subseteq D$, iff for each variable $x \in X$ holds:
$D(x) \neq * \Rightarrow D'(x) = D(x)$

(2) D' is a *genuine refinement* of D, $D' \subset D$, iff $D' \subseteq D$ and $D' \neq D$

(3) D' is a *direct refinement* of D in $\mathfrak{D}$, $D' \sqsubset D$ in $\mathfrak{D}$, iff
$D' \subset D$ and there is no $D'' \in \mathfrak{D}$ such that $D' \subset D'' \subset D$ □

In some situtations we prefer to talk about *inclusion*, *genuine inclusion* or *direct inclusion*, respectively. Another relation between descriptions is *intersection* formalized in definition 3.4.

definition 3.4 (intersection): Let D and D' be two descriptions over a given set X of variables.

(1) $D \cap D'$ is *well defined* iff $\forall x \in X: (D(x) = D'(x)) \vee (D(x) = *) \vee (D'(x) = *)$

(2) if $D \cap D'$ is well defined then $D \cap D'$ is determined by the following equation:

$$D \cap D'(x) = \begin{cases} D(x) & \text{if } D'(x) = * \\ D'(x) & \text{else} \end{cases} \qquad \text{for each } x \in X$$

otherwise $D \cap D' = \perp$

(3) a well defined intersection $D \cap D'$ is a *genuine intersection* of D and D' if
$D \cap D' \neq D$ and $D \cap D' \neq D'$. □

We say a description set $\mathfrak{D}$ is *closed under* $\cap$ iff for any two descriptions $D, D' \in \mathfrak{D}$ with $D \cap D'$ well-defined, the intersection $D \cap D'$ is contained in $\mathfrak{D}$. With close($\mathfrak{D}$) we denote the $\cap$-closure of $\mathfrak{D}$. The closure close ($\mathfrak{D}$) can be easily determined by adding to the increasing set $\mathfrak{D}$ all well-defined intersections of its elements until no changes are possible.

example 3.5: We again consider descriptions over our variable set {P, E, s}. For the descriptions in $\mathfrak{D}$ = {[Miller, *, *], [Miller, Jones&Co, *], [Miller, Jones&Co, 3000], [*, Jones&Co, *]} we have the following relations:

[Miller, *, *] $\subseteq$ [Miller, *, *]
[Miller, Jones&Co, 3000] $\subseteq$ [Miller, *, *]
[Miller, Jones&Co, 3000] $\subset$ [Miller, *, *]
but [Miller, *, *] $\not\subset$ [Miller, *, *]
[Miller, Jones&Co, *] $\sqsubset$ [Miller, *, *] in $\mathfrak{D}$
but [Miller, Jones&Co, 3000] $\not\sqsubset$ [Miller, *, *] in $\mathfrak{D}$
[*, Jones&Co, *] $\cap$ [Miller, *, *] = [Miller, Jones&Co, *] □

Let us remark that $\mathfrak{D}$ is closed or, in other words, $\mathfrak{D}$ = close($\mathfrak{D}$), i.e. $\mathfrak{D}$ contains every well-defined intersection of any pair of its elements.

The essential link between description sets and the set of all local substitutions $\Theta(X)$ is the notion of *representation* formalized in definition 3.6.

definition 3.6: Let X be a variable set and let $\mathfrak{D} \subseteq \Delta(X)$ denote a set of descriptions. $D \in \mathfrak{D}$ *represents* a given substitution $\vartheta \in \Theta(X)$ iff $\vartheta \in |D|$ and additionally holds that there is no description $D' \in \mathfrak{D}$ such that $D' \subset D$ and $\vartheta \in |D'|$.
For $D \in \mathfrak{D}$, $\langle D \rangle_{\mathfrak{D}}$ is the set of substitutions represented by D with respect to $\mathfrak{D}$. □

This means intuitively that each substitution is represented by the descriptions describing it in the most exact way.

example 3.7: For $\mathfrak{D}$ = {[Miller, *, *], [Miller, Jones&Co, *]} there holds:
$\langle$[Miller, *, *]$\rangle_{\mathfrak{D}}$ = |[Miller, *, *]| − |[Miller, Jones&Co, *]| □

Description sets providing a unique representation of every local description are called *partitions*. Obviously, partitions are exactly what we need for description based temporal integrity monitoring. In this context, closed description sets have the nice property that every substitution is represented by at most one description in the set. The existence of more than one such description is impossible, because their intersection would describe the common substitutions in a more exact way, which contradicts the definition of representation. So, if a closed description set contains for every local substitution a description representing it, then so it is a partition. This result is fixed in the following proposition.

proposition 3.8: Let there be a variable set X and a description set $\mathfrak{D} \subseteq \Delta(X)$ such that every substitution in $\Theta(X)$ has a description in $\mathfrak{D}$ describing it. Then holds:

$\mathfrak{D}$ closed $\Rightarrow$ $\mathfrak{D}$ is a partition of $\Theta(X)$ □

Whereas being a partition is a semantic property depending on the current extensions of object sorts, the property of being closed is of syntactical nature only depending on the description set itself. This is particularly useful when performing some minor changes on a partition $\mathfrak{D}$ like adding some new descriptions $D_1, \ldots, D_n$. In this case we obtain a new partition $\mathfrak{D}'$ by computing the closure of $\mathfrak{D} \cup \{D_1, \ldots, D_n\}$.

4. Monitoring Algorithm

In this chapter we outline the concepts of description based monitoring of temporal integrity. Let us begin with the general task of temporal integrity monitoring. The background is given by a database signature and a state sequence $\underline{\sigma} = \langle \sigma_0, \sigma_2, \ldots \rangle$. Temporal integrity constraints are given by transition graphs T. A graph refers to a set $X = \{x_1, x_2, \ldots x_k\}$ of variables occurring free in some of its edge labels. According to the state sequence $\underline{\sigma}$, we have a sequence of substitution sets $\underline{\Theta}(X) = \langle \Theta_0(X), \Theta_1(X), \ldots \rangle$ such that for each database state σ_i, $\Theta_i(X)$ contains all possible substitutions for the variables in X. Additionally, there is a marking m_T relating each substitution in each state of its life cycle to a set of transition graph nodes. Subsequent markings for a substitution are related by the transition rule trans (definition 2.3).

The essential task of an integrity monitor is to assure that no life cycle of some substitution terminates unless its marking contains a final node and that no marking of some substitution is empty or contains as its only element the error node, respectively. Therefore the monitor subsequently computes the marking for the substitutions according to the transition rule.

4.1. Description Based Monitoring

In our approach, substitutions are represented by descripitions. So, we have a sequence $\underline{\Delta}(X) = \langle \Delta_1(X), \Delta_2(X), \ldots \rangle$ of possible descriptions $\Delta_i(X)$ over X in database states σ_i. For representing the substitutions, there is a sequence of description sets $\underline{\mathfrak{D}} = \langle \mathfrak{D}_1, \mathfrak{D}_2, \ldots \rangle$ with $\mathfrak{D}_i \subseteq \Delta_i(X)$ and a marking $m_T(i, \underline{\sigma}, D)$ for each description $D \in \mathfrak{D}_i$ such that

(i) $\mathfrak{D}_i$ is a partition of $\Theta_i(X)$ and

(ii) $\forall D \in \mathfrak{D}_i\, \forall \underline{\vartheta} \in \underline{\Theta} : \vartheta_i \in \langle D \rangle_{\mathfrak{D}_i} \Rightarrow m_T(i, \underline{\sigma}, \underline{\vartheta}) = m_T(i, \underline{\sigma}, D)$

If these properties are provided we say $\mathfrak{D}_i$ is a *marking preserving partitioning* of $\Theta_i(X)$. This is the correctness criterion for description based monitoring.

So, description based monitoring is characterized by a stepwise computing of new partitions and their markings.

In this paper, we present an algorithm performing this task in an incremental way, i.e. by manipulating the partition $\mathfrak{D}_i$ for an old database state σ_i to obtain another partition $\mathfrak{D}_{i+1}$ for the new state σ_{i+1}. Doing so, special attention has to be paid to the starting and ending points of substitution life cycles. So, there can be distinguished three phases the monitor has to run through after database state transitions.

(1) Adjustment of the previous partition to the current substitution set
(2) Performing of node transitions
(3) Violation test

During the adjustment phase the previous description set $\mathfrak{D}_i$ is updated according to insertions or deletions of database objects. The resulting set $\mathfrak{D}'_{i+1}$ is a partition of the new current substitution set $\Theta_{i+1}(X)$ but it is not necessarily a marking preserving partitioning for the new state σ_{i+1}.

Adjustment is done by deleting descriptions referring to deleted objects and adding descriptions and their initial markings for substitutions that begin to exist. Phase (2) is a manipulation of the adjusted description set resulting in a marking preserving partitioning for σ_{i+1}. Phase (3) checks whether there are any substitutions represented by some description with an empty marking or with a marking containing the error node.

The rest of this chapter is dedicated to the activities performed in phase (2). The point is that not for all substitutions represented by some description in $\mathfrak{D}_i$ there necessarily results the same marking for state σ_{i+1}. Therefore we can distinguish the following properties of descriptions.

definition 4.1: Let there be a variable set X and a description set $\mathfrak{D} \subseteq \Delta_{i+1}(X)$ with some marking. We say $D \in \mathfrak{D}$ with marking m is *convergent in* $\mathfrak{D}$ wrt σ_i iff for all substitutions ϑ with ϑ_{i+1} in $\langle D \rangle_{\mathfrak{D}}$, the same node set results from trans(m, σ_i, ϑ). Otherwise we call D *divergent in* $\mathfrak{D}$ wrt σ_i. □

If all descriptions in an adjusted partition $\mathfrak{D}'_{i+1}$ are convergent in $\mathfrak{D}'_{i+1}$, we obtain a marking preserving partitioning of $\Theta_{i+1}(X)$ just by setting $\mathfrak{D}_{i+1} := \mathfrak{D}'_{i+1}$ and updating the marking according to the transition rule for the represented substitutions. In general, however, there are some divergent descriptions in the partition such that there must be generated a new partition $\mathfrak{D}_{i+1}$.

The main idea for doing this is to replace each divergent descriptions by a set of descriptions which are convergent. Such a set is called an *expansion* of the description. The notion of expansions is defined formally in the following definition.

definition 4.2: Let $\mathfrak{D}'_{i+1}$ be a partition of $\Theta_{i+1}(X)$ with an old marking referring to the previous database state σ_i. Given a description $D \in \mathfrak{D}'_{i+1}$ and set $\mathfrak{D}_D = \{D_1, D_2, \ldots\}$, we say $\mathfrak{D}_D$ is an *expansion of D wrt to* σ_{i+1} iff the following conditions are provided:

(a) for each $D_j \in \mathfrak{D}_D$ holds (i) $D_j \sqsubset D$ in $\mathfrak{D}'_{i+1}$ or $D_j = D$
and (ii) $m_T(i, \varrho, D_j) = m_T(i, \varrho, D)$
and (iii) D_j is convergent in $\mathfrak{D}_D \cup \{D\}$ wrt σ_{i+1}

(b) every substitution in $\langle D \rangle_{\mathfrak{D}'_{i+1}}$ is represented by a single description $D_j \in \mathfrak{D}_D$ □

For a convergent description D the singleton {D} is an expansion of D. In algorithm 4.3 there is presented the general proceeding of computing new partitions.

algorithm 4.3: Let $\mathfrak{D}'_{i+1}$ be a partition of $\Theta_{i+1}(X)$ with an old marking referring to state σ_i.

begin

(1) Set $\mathfrak{D}_{i+1} = \text{close}\left(\bigcup_{D \in \mathfrak{D}'_{i+1}} \mathfrak{D}_D\right)$

where $\mathfrak{D}_D$ is an expansion of D wrt σ_{i+1}

(2) **for each** $D \in \mathfrak{D}_{i+1}$

do set $m_T(i, \varrho, D) := m_T(i, \varrho, D_F)$

where $D_F \in \mathfrak{D}'_{i+1}$ is the origin description of D

od

end □

The origin description of $D \in \mathfrak{D}_{i+1}$ is the description $D_F \in \mathfrak{D}'_{i+1}$ from which D is descending. In case D is an element of $\mathfrak{D}'_{i+1}$, the origin desciption D_F is given by D itself. Otherwise, D_F is some description D' in $\mathfrak{D}'_{i+1}$ such that $D \sqsubset D'$ in $\mathfrak{D}'_{i+1}$. There exists exactly one such D' because D is a refinement of some element in the closed set $\mathfrak{D}'_{i+1}$. So in both cases the origin description D_F is uniquely determined. Please note that for each $D \in \mathfrak{D}_{i+1}$ and the corresponding description $D_F \in \mathfrak{D}'_{i+1}$ there holds:

$$\langle D \rangle_{\mathfrak{D}_{i+1}} \subseteq \langle D_F \rangle_{\mathfrak{D}'_{i+1}}$$

So, the descriptions representing a given substitution in $\mathfrak{D}_{i+1}$ and in $\mathfrak{D}'_{i+1}$ have both the same marking.

For the descriptions in $\mathfrak{D}_{i+1}$ we can prove the following proposition.

proposition 4.4: Let $\mathfrak{D}_i$ be a marking preserving partitioning. Let $\mathfrak{D}_{i+1}$ and its marking be computed according to algorithm 4.3 from the adjusted partition $\mathfrak{D}'_{i+1}$. Then each description $D \in \mathfrak{D}_{i+1}$ is convergent in $\mathfrak{D}_{i+1}$. □

Proposition 4.4 allows to complete algorithm 4.3 by a third step determining the current marking for the descriptions in $\mathfrak{D}_{i+1}$ thus resulting in a marking preserving partitioning of $\Theta_{i+1}(X)$. Thus completed, this algorithm correctly performs the generation of marking preserving partitionings.

4.2 Generation of Expansions

The general proceeding of description based monitoring is essentially based on generating expansions and performing node transitions for descriptions. In this section we explain how to generate expansions and how a transition rule for descriptions is defined. Both solutions base on a validity concept for descriptions allowing a syntactical evaluation of edge labels for descriptions, i.e. an evaluation not referring to the represented substitutions.

The edge labellings of a transition graph are propositional logic formulae over a given set of ground formulae. The ground formulae are arbitrary predicate logic formulae over the given database signature possibly containing free variables.

For our further discussion, we assume the considered transition graph automatons to be transformed into the following form:

(i) The edge labels are in a disjunctive normal form over the ground formulae, i.e. the labels have the form

$$\alpha_1 \vee \ldots \vee \alpha_n \text{ with } \alpha_i = A_{i_1} \wedge \ldots \wedge A_{i_k}$$

where the A_{i_j} are negated or non-negated ground formulae.

(ii) For each node, the disjunction of the labels for the outgoing edges can be reduced to **true** by propositional logic simplification (syntactical characterization of complete transition graphs).

(iii) For each two different nodes l and l' directly reachable from a node n, propositional logic simplification reduces the formula $\eta((n, l)) \wedge \eta((n, l'))$ to **false**. (syntactical characterization of deterministic transition graphs).

Definition 4.5 formalizes validity of formulae for descriptions.

definition 4.5: Let there be a set X of variables and a set of ground formulae with free variables in X. Let A be a ground formula and $D \in \Delta_i(X)$. Then we define

$(\sigma_i, D) \models A$ iff (i) for all variables x occurring free in A there holds: $D(x) \neq *$
(ii) A is true in state σ_i if each free occurrence of a variable x in A is substituted by $D(x)$. □

Arbitrary propositional formulae over a set of ground formuale are evaluated by evaluating the ground formulae and combining the results according to the formula structure.

Please note that a negated ground formulae $\neg A$ is evaluated to true if either some of its free variables are substituted with * or if A is evaluated to **false**. So, $(\sigma_i, D) \models \neg A$ does not necessarily imply validity of $\neg A$ for each represented substitution.

The main idea of generating expansions is to generate descriptions providing validity of edge formulae.

In definition 4.6 we define how to generate refinements for a conjunction of ground formulae.

definition 4.6: Let $\mathfrak{D}$ with a given marking be a partition of $\Theta_{i+1}(X)$ for a variable set X. Let α be be a conjunction of ground formulae whose free variables are contained in X. For a description $D \in \mathfrak{D}$ with marking $m_T(i, \varrho, D) = \{n\}$, the description set $exp(D, m_T(i, \varrho, D), \sigma_i, \alpha)$ is defined as follows:

$D' \in exp(D, m_T(i, \varrho, D), \sigma_i, \alpha)$

iff - $(\sigma_{i+1}, D') \models \alpha$

- $D' \sqsubset D$ in $\mathfrak{D}$ or $D' = D$

- $\forall x \in X$: $D'(x) \neq *$ iff $D(x) \neq *$ or x occurs free in some non-negated ground formula of α □

So, each description in 'exp...' provides validity of α and substitutes all those variables with * which do not occur free in some non-negated ground formula and which are substituted by * in the original description.

Please note that the substitutions represented by some description in 'exp...' not necessarily provide validity of α (because of the negated ground formulae in α), i.e. the descriptions in 'exp...' are not necessarily convergent. However, if α is valid for a substitution ϑ, there is a description in 'exp...' representing it.

Definition 4.7 provides a syntactical characterization of expansions.

definition 4.7: For a given transition graph with the properties (i) to (iii) and a variable set X let $\mathfrak{D}$ with a given old marking be a partition of $\Theta_{i+1}(X)$. Let $D \in \mathfrak{D}$ be a description with old marking {n}. Further let C be the set of all conjunctions occurring in labels of the edges starting in n. Then we define:

$$expand(D, \{n\}, \sigma_{i+1}) := close\Big(\bigcup_{\alpha \in C} exp(D, \{n\}, \sigma_{i+1}, \alpha)\Big)$$ □

The following proposition says that 'expand...' is an expansion according to definition 4.2.

proposition 4.8: Given the same preconditions as in definition 4.7. Then holds:

(i) $expand(D, \{n\}, \sigma_{i+1})$ is an expansion of D wrt σ_{i+1}

(ii) for each description $D' \in expand(D, \{n\}, \sigma_{i+1})$ and each substitution ϑ represented by D' there holds:

$(\sigma_{i+1}, \vartheta) \models \eta((n,l))$ iff $(\sigma_{i+1}, D') \models \eta((n,l))$

where l is a node reachable via some edge from n. □

The function 'expand' together with the validity concept for descriptions give rise to a "syntactical way" of generating convergent description sets and evaluating edge labels.

Let us have a brief look at the proof idea of this proposition. A detailed proof can be found in [HüS 89].

The major part of a proof for (i) is to prove convergence for the generated descriptions. Convergence is a special case of part (ii) of the proposition.

It was already stated that for a single conjunction α, the descriptions in $exp(D, \{n\}, \sigma_{i+1}, \alpha)$ are not necessarily convergent. Thus convergence of the descriptions in expand(...) results from generating the set exp(...) for each conjunction in each edge label. The proof of this property is essentially based on the fact that the underlying transition graphs obey the syntactical characterization of complete and deterministic transition graphs.

5. Monitor Enhancements

Similar to static constraints, there are being developped approaches for analysis and minimization of temporal integrity monitoring. So, [Li88] suggests to integrate integrity monitoring into transaction specification whereas [Sa88] proposes to integrate transaction analysis into a centralized monitoring. These approaches apply to description based monitoring, too. But there can be done additional efforts in that direction with respect to the aspects of being description based.

Finiteness of description sets

Although descriptions enable a finite representation of infinite substitution sets, it is still possible that description sets in their turn become infinite, or reach a finite but unmanageable extent. Whether this problem occurs or not depends on the underlying transition graph.

The problem is that the graph may contain ground formulae causing the generation of "too large" refinement sets, like the ground formula '$x \geq 0$'. Such formulae may not be employed for generating refinements, i.e. we have to make some restrictions on the contexts in which these formulae occur in a transition graph.

We assume that for each ground formula A occurring in some edge label of a transition graph there is fixed the set of *definable variables* denoted by def(A). The *non-definable variables* of A denoted by ndef(A) are the free variables of A not in def(A).

So, a ground formula A may only be used for generating refinements if its non-definable variables are already predefined in the description to be expanded. The set def(A) must be fixed that way that an "allowed" generation of refinements does not yield "too much" descriptions. What "too much" means, however is to be decided by the database designer. For the ground formula '$x \geq 0$', she or he would probably define $def(x \geq 0) = \emptyset$.

The *relevant variables* of a transition graph node n denoted by rv(n) is the maximal set of variables which are not substituted by * in any description possibly reaching n. This means for each description D reaching a node n there holds:

$$x \in rv(n) \Rightarrow D(x) \neq *$$

The relevant variables of a node can be determined by analyzing the paths touching that node. For the initial node, the relevant variables are set to X_0 which is the maximal set of variables not substituted by * for any description in the initial partition $\mathfrak{D}_0$.

The restrictions to be made on transition graphs are formalized in the following definition.

definition 5.1: Let T be a transition graph fulfilling conditions (i) to (iii) stated in section 4.2. Then T is *coherent* iff for each node of the graph and for each conjunction α in the label of some outgoing edge there holds:

There is some ordering $A_1,\ldots,A_k$ on the non-negated ground formulae in α such that

$$ndef(A_i) \subseteq \bigcup_{j<i} def(A_j) \cup rv(n) \quad ; \quad \text{for } i = 1,\ldots,k$$ □

Coherent transition graphs assure that the ground formulae occur in admissible contexts. Similar to the range restricted property in [Ni82], the coherence of a transition graph provides the free variables to be bound to a sufficiently small set of explicit values. If a transition graph is not coherent, description based monitoring is in general not possible without exceeding storage limitations.

Deleting descriptions

The algorithm presented in chapter 4 successively computes partitions by expanding descriptions, i.e. by generating additional descriptions. However, it is also possible to delete a description D from a marking preserving partitioning $\mathfrak{D}_i$ if the following conditions hold:

There exists a description $D' \in \mathfrak{D}_i$ such that

(a) D' is the only description in $\mathfrak{D}_i$ with $D \sqsubset D'$ in $\mathfrak{D}_i$

(b) $m_T(i, \underline{\sigma}, D) = m_T(i, \underline{\sigma}, D')$ □

The description set $\mathfrak{D}_i$-{D} is then a marking preserving partitioning of Θ_i, too, because condition (a) provides every substitution represented by D in $\mathfrak{D}_i$ to be represented by D' in $\mathfrak{D}_i$ - {D}. So the monitoring algorithm can be extended by a reorganization part removing superfluous descriptions.

Further Optimizations

Further optimizations result from integration of computing the closure and new marking into the expansion procedure. Thus the algorithm generates expansions, computes intersections of new and old descriptions and evaluates edge formulae for new descriptions succesively for all descriptions.

For computing intersections, there must only be considered the refinements of the expanded description [HüS89]. Thus we can decrease the expense for computing closures.

Other optimizations result from properties of transition graphs. Some graphs contain edges with the property that the refinements generated according to conjunctions in its labels do not intersect with other descriptions (see the example in the appendix). So, for these descriptions, there can be omitted the costly procedure of computing intersections. Another possible property of edges is that all descriptions whose marking results from validity of such an edge's label are deletable.

Algorithms for detecting such edges are presented in [Hü88].

6. Conclusions

Temporal integrity constraints describe long-term data dependencies to be respected by correct database evolutions. Such temporal constraints can be monitored by a runtime evaluation of the corresponding transitions of a so-called transition graph. This has to be done for each substitution of the free constraint variables with database objects. Transition graphs can be constructed from descriptive specifications of constraints in temporal logic. The historical information is given by the node markings for the substitutions of the variables occurring in the constraint specification. In this paper, there are presented techniques for compact representation of large substitution sets thus enabling integrity monitoring for very large or even infinite substitution sets. The basic concept is to represent whole substitution sets instead of single substitutions by so-called descriptions.

Special kinds of description sets are partitions of the underlying substitution sets. The basic concept of description based monitoring is to compute marking preserving partitionings of substitution sets according to the evaluation of node transitions. This is based on a validity concept of non-temporal formulae for descriptions.

Although the presented algorithm performs a centralized, global integrity monitoring, it appears to be possible to integrate the presented concepts into a transaction-local monitoring as proposed in [Li88].

Our future activities are to integrate the presented approach of temporal integrity monitoring into the database design and prototyping environment CADDY currently being implemented at our working group ([EHHLE89]). Tools for constructing transition graphs and for integrity monitoring (still not description based) are currently being implemented. Our next step is to integrate the presented method of description based monitoring by providing the system with a description handling component.

7. References

[Ch76] Chamberlin, D.D. et al.: SEQUEL 2: A Unified Approach to Data Definition, Manipulation and Control. IBM Journal. Res. Dev. 20. 1976. 560-576.

[EDG86] Ehrich, H.-D., Drosten, K., Gogolla, M.: Towards an Algebraic Semantics for Database Specification. Proc. IFIP Work. Conf. on Knowledge and Data "DS-2". Albufeira (Portugal) 1986 (R.A. Meersmann, et al., eds.), North-Holland Amsterdam 1988, 119-135.

[EHHLE] Engels, G., Hohenstein, U., Hülsmann, K., Löhr-Richter, P., Ehrich, H.-D.: CADDY: Computer Aided Design of Non-Standard Databases. To appear in Proc. of the Int. Conf. on System Development Environments & Factories. Berlin 1989.

[ELG84] Ehrich, H.-D., Lipeck, U.W., Gogolla, M.: Specification, Semantics and Enforcement of Dynamic Database Constraints. Proc. Int. Conf. VLDB. Singapore 1984, 301-308.

[FiS88] Fiadeiro, J., Sernadas, A.: Specification and Verification of Database Dynamics. Acta Informatica. Vol.25, Fasc.6, 1988, 625-661.

[HsI85] Hsu, A., Imielinsky, T.: Integrity Checking for Multiple Updates. SIGMOD 1985, 152-168.

[Hü88] Hülsmann, K.: Entwurf eines Systems zur Überwachung dynamischer Integritätsbedingungen *(Design of a system for monitoring dynamic integrity constraints; in German)*. Diplomarbeit, TU Braunschweig 1988.

[HüS89] Hülsmann, K., Saake, G.: Theoretical Foundations of Handling Large Substitution Sets in Temporal Integrity Monitoring. Informatik-Bericht Nr.89-04, TU Braunschweig 1989.

[KoSS87] Kowalski, R., Sadri, F., Soper, P.: Integrity Checking in Deductive Databases. In Proc. 19th Int. Conf. VLDB, 1987, 61-69.

[Kr87] Kröger, F.: Temporal Logic of Programs. Springer-Verlag, Berlin 1987.

[Ku84] Kung, C.H.: A Temporal Framework for Database Specification and Verification. VLDB 1984, 91-99.

[LEG85] Lipeck, U.W., Ehrich, H.-D., Gogolla, M.: Specifying Admissibility of Dynamic Database Behaviour Using Temporal Logic. Proc. IFIP Work. Conf. on Theoretical and Formal Aspects of Information Systems (A. Sernadas et al., eds.). LNCS 326, North-Holland, Amsterdam 1985, 145-157.

[Li88] Lipeck, U.W.: Transformation of Dynamic Integrity Constraints into Transaction Specifications. Proc. 2nd Int. Conf. on Database Theory (M.Gyssen et al., eds.). LNCS 326, Springer-Verlag, Berlin 1988, 322-337.

[Li89] Lipeck, U.W.: Zur dynamischen Integrität von Datenbanken: Grundlagen der Spezifikation und Überwachung *(On dynamic integrity of databases: foundations of specification and supervision; in German)*. Habilitationsschrift, TU Braunschweig 1988, Informatik-Fachbericht Nr. 209, Springer-Verlag, Berlin 1989.

[LiS87] Lipeck, U.W., Saake, G.: Monitoring Dynamic Integrity Constraints Based on Temporal Logic. Information Systems, Vol.12, No.3, 1987, 255-269.

[LlT85] Lloyd,J.W.; Topor, R.W.: A Basis for Deductive Database Systems. J. Logic Programming, 2, 1985, 93-109.

[MaP81] Manna, Z., Pnueli, A.: Verification of Concurrent Programs: The Temporal Framework. in: The Correctness Problem in Computer Science (R.S.Boyer et al., eds.). Academic Press London 1981, 215-273.

[MaW84] Manna, Z., Wolper, P.: Synthesis of Communicating Processes from Temporal Logic Specifications. ACM Trans. on Programming Languages and Systems. Vol.6, 1984, 68-93..

[Ni82] Nicolas, J.-M.: Logic for Improving Integrity Checking in Relational Data Bases. Acta Informatica, 18, 1982, 227-253.

[Sa88] Saake, G.: Spezifikation, Semantik und Überwachung von Objektlebensläufen in Datenbanken *(Specification, semantics and supervision of object life cycles in databases; in German).* Dissertation. Informatik-Skript Nr.20, TU Braunschweig 1988.

[SaL87] Saake, G., Lipeck, U.W: Foundations of Temporal Integrity Monitoring. Proc. IFIP WG 8.1 Conf. on "Temporal Aspects in Information Systems" TAIS (C.Rolland et al., eds.), Sophia-Antipolis 1987, North-Holland, Amsterdam 1988, 235-249.

[SaL89] Saake, G., Lipeck, U.W.: Using Finite-Linear Temporal Logic for Specifying Database Dynamics. In Proc. CSL'88 2nd Workshop ComputerScience Logic (E.Börger, H. Kleine Büning, M.M. Richter, Eds), Duisburg 1988, LNCS 385, Springer-Verlag 1989, 288-300.

[Se80] Sernadas, A.:Temporal Aspects of Logical Procedure Definition. Information Systems 5, 1980, 167-187.

[SFNC84] Schiel,U., Furtado, A.L., Neuhold, E.J., Casanova, M.A.: Towards Multilevel and Modular Conceptual Schema Specifications. Information Systems 9, 1984, 43-57.

[Vi83] Vianu, V.: Dynamic Constraints and Database Evolution. Proc. 2nd ACM SIGACT-SIGMOD Symp. on Princ. of Database Systems (Atlanta), ACM, New York 1983, 389-399

Appendix

An Example

We demonstrate our monitoring algorithm for the constraint in example 2.7.:

> "Historical salaries of a person may not exceed the present salary unless the corresponding employers are different."

temporal logic formulation:

```
↑       always (E = employer(P) ∧ s = salary(P) ⇒
|   ↑           (E = employer(P) ⇒ ¬ (s > salary(P))
φ   ψ           until E = employer(P) ∧ s < salary(P)
|   ↓           )
↓            )
```

free variables: X = {E, P, w} with P: PERSON; E: ENTERPRISE; w : integer;

ground formulae: BF = {E=employer(P), s = salary(P), s<salary(P), s>salary(P)}

transition graph:

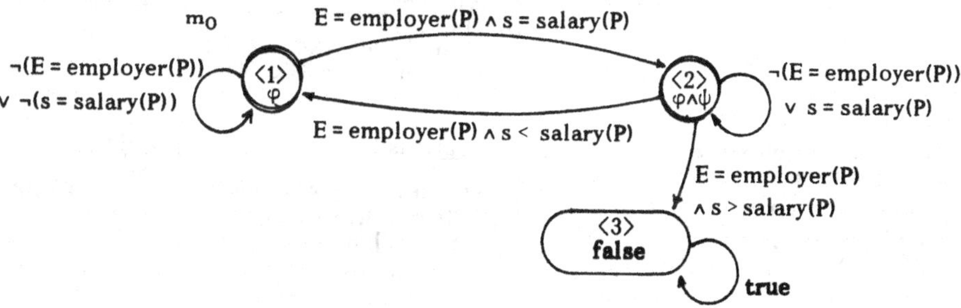

definable variables: def(E=employer(P) = {E, P}; def(s = salary(P)) = {s, P}; def(s<salary(P)) = { }; def(s>salary(P)) = { }

relevant variables: rv(⟨1⟩) = { }   rv(⟨2⟩) = {E, P, w}   rv(⟨3⟩) = {E, P, w}

For these parameters we obtain that T is coherent.

Evolution of the database:

extension of object types

|PERSON| = {Smith, Miller}
|ENTERPRISE| = {Jones&Co, Brown&Co}

For Smith, we have the evolution

state	employer (Smith)	salary(Smith)
0	Jones&Co	3000
1	Brown&Co	2500
2	Brown&Co	3000
3	Jones&Co	2500

Miller remains unemployed all the time. Thus, if P is substituted by Miller there is no substitution for the variable E that satisfies the basic formula 'E = employer(P)'.

Work of the monitor:

initialization of the initial partition:

descriptions	marking
D_1 = [*, *, *]	⟨1⟩

Step 1: expand(D_1,{⟨1⟩},σ_1) = {D_1, D_2}

descriptions	marking
D_1 = [*, *, *]	⟨1⟩
D_2 = [Smith, Jones&Co, 3000]	⟨2⟩

Step 2: Smith is now employed at Brown&Co with salary 2500.

expand(D_1,{⟨1⟩},σ_2) = {D_1, D_3}
expand(D_2,{⟨2⟩},σ_2) = {D_2}

descriptions	marking
D_1 = [*, *, *]	⟨1⟩
D_2 = [Smith, Jones&Co, 3000]	⟨2⟩
D_3 = [Smith, Brown&Co, 2500]	⟨2⟩

Step 3: Smith is now employed at Brown&Co with salary 3000.

expand(D_1,{⟨1⟩},σ_3) = {D_1, D_4}
expand(D_2,{⟨2⟩},σ_3) = {D_2}
expand(D_3,{⟨2⟩},σ_3) = {D_3}

descriptions	marking
D_1 = [*, *, *]	⟨1⟩
D_2 = [Smith, Jones&Co, 3000]	⟨2⟩
D_3 = [Smith, Brown&Co, 2500]	⟨1⟩
D_4 = [Smith, Brown&Co, 3000]	⟨2⟩

Because the salary of Smith is now higher than 2500, description D_3 passes to node ⟨1⟩. Since D_3 and the only description including it, i.e. D_1, are both associated to the same node, we can delete D_3. The result is:

descriptions	marking
D_1 = [*, *, *]	⟨1⟩
D_2 = [Smith, Jones&Co, 3000]	⟨2⟩
D_4 = [Smith, Brown&Co, 3000]	⟨2⟩

Step 4: Smith is now employed at Jones&Co with salary 2500.

expand(D_1,{⟨1⟩},σ_4) = {D_1, D_5}
expand(D_2,{⟨2⟩},σ_4) = {D_2}
expand(D_4,{⟨2⟩},σ_4) = {D_4}

descriptions	marking	
D_1 = [*, *, *]	⟨1⟩	
D_2 = [Smith, Jones&Co, 3000]	⟨3⟩	ERROR
D_4 = [Smith, Brown&Co, 3000]	⟨2⟩	
D_5 = [Smith, Jones&Co, 2500]	⟨2⟩	

The current salary of Smith is now lower than his earnings the same enterprise some states before. Thus the constraint is violated.

During all the time, the monitor only keeps for each person and the enterprises she/he was employed at the information about the maximum salaries she/he earned at that enterprise. This is the minimal information to be stored for monitoring this constraint by a monitor or any other realization.

Making an Object-Oriented DBMS Active: Design, Implementation, and Evaluation of a Prototype†

Sharma Chakravarthy
Computer and Information Scienced Department and
Database Systems Research and Development Center
University of Florida, Gainesville FL 32611
Email: sharma@ufl.edu

Susan Nesson
Lotus Development Corporation
55 Cambridge Parkway
Cambridge, MA 02142.

Abstract

Extant databases are passive in nature and offer little or no support for automatically monitoring conditions defined over the state of the database. In fact such a capability is central for a variety of applications requiring timely and time-constrained data management and processing (e.g., cooperative processing, process control, air traffic control, threat analysis).

Traditionally, the effect of condition monitoring has been realized either by encoding condition evaluation as part of the application program or by polling the database (periodically) for condition evaluation. This paper explores a third alternative, viz. *active* condition monitoring from an object-oriented design perspective. The focus of this paper is on the design and implementation of *active* condition monitoring functionality for an object-oriented Database Management System (DBMS) and its evaluation: performance comparison with polling, influence of implementation strategies on performance, and identification of opportunities for optimization.

1. Introduction

Although the concept of condition monitoring is not new (ON conditions in programming languages and early DBMS's, and signals in operating systems), there is a genuine need for providing a similar capability having well-defined semantics and satisfying the efficiency requirements of DBMSs. A large class of applications, such as process control, threat assessment and analysis, monitoring of intensive care units, air traffic control, and cooperative processing, that require database support need to react (often subject to timing-constraints) to a variety of conditions that are defined over the database state and events that change the state of the database. Traditionally, DBMSs are passive. Hence, the effect of condition monitoring is achieved either by encoding condition evaluation as part of the application program (equivalent to posing external queries) or by polling the database (periodically) to detect whether any of the conditions have become true. Neither of these approaches is satisfactory. Encoding condition evaluation within the application program not only transfers the burden -- of determining the conditions, formulating queries for these conditions, and the time of their evaluation -- to the application programmer but also interferes with

† This work was carried out when the authors were with Xerox Advanced Information Technology (previously Advanced Information Technology Division of Computer Corporation of America), 4 Cambridge Center, Cambridge, MA 02142. This work was supported by the Defense Advanced Research Projects Agency and by Rome Air Development Center under contract No. F30602-87-C-0029. The views and conclusions contained in this paper are those of the authors and do not necessarily represent the official policies of the Defense Advanced Research Projects Agency, the Rome Air Development Center, or the U.S. Government.

the application development. Furthermore, optimization of such conditions is extremely difficult. Polling results in wasted resources and in addition the user now has to determine the frequency of polling which is dependent on a variety of parameters including the frequency of update, timeliness (the time window within which the condition needs to be detected).

Recent research on active databases [STON86, STON87, DARN87, DITT86] is aimed at supporting new capabilities (e.g., alerters, triggers, situation-action rules) and techniques for their optimization (e.g., lazy, eager, overlapped execution). Active capability is being viewed as a unifying mechanism for supporting a number of DBMS functionality, such as integrity/security enforcement, maintenance of materialized (e.g., view) data, constraint management, and rule-based inferencing. On the other hand, AI systems have traditionally used *daemons* for asynchronous execution. LOOPS [BOBR83] and KEE [INTE85] have incorporated active values as a new paradigm that generalizes asynchronous rule processing. However, these systems do support sharing, consistency, and concurrent execution of transactions.

The goals of this effort are to design and implement active functionality for an object-oriented DBMS to facilitate the evaluation of this new approach and gain additional insights into its performance and optimization to feed into the HiPAC project [CHAK89, DAYA88b], investigated at XAIT. Specifically, the emphasis is towards answering basic questions, such as *is active condition monitoring always better than polling?, should polling be retained as a viable alternative?, and what issues need to be considered when an existing DBMS is made active?* than an in-depth performance evaluation. For this purpose, a prototype[1] object-oriented DBMS was designed and implemented on a Symbolics machine using Symbolics Common Lisp and flavors. This prototype was modularly extended to include active objects for supporting automatic condition monitoring in addition to other DBMS functions. Needless to say that transaction processing and concurrency control were not included in the prototype.

The remainder of this paper is structured as follows. Section 2 briefly describes the implementation of an object-oriented DBMS using Symbolics Flavors. Section 3 discusses the design and implementation of active objects and the functionality of the resulting prototype. Section 4 describes the evaluation of the prototype. It also provides an analysis of the observed results. Section 5 contains conclusions.

2. Symbolics Implementation of a Prototype OODBMS

For the purposes of this effort, a subset of PROBE[2], excluding spatial/temporal objects and recursion, was designed and implemented on Symbolics using Common Lisp and its object-oriented extension, Flavors. In this version stored and virtual relations are supported. A generalization of relational algebra is used as the query language. The algebra consists of relational operators (such as select, project natural join etc.) with suitable extensions (apply-and-append for example) to support the PROBE object classes. The system is composed of a hierarchy of objects and operations on objects. For example, relation is an object consisting of file objects, attribute objects and other instance variables. These objects are in turn built using other objects. Figure 2.1 shows the object hierarchy (including the objects introduced for active condition monitoring) used for supporting the

[1]The prototype has the functionality of a subset of PROBE — a passive, extensible DBMS developed at CCA [DAYA87a].

[2]PROBE [MANO86, ROSE86, DAYA87a, DAYA87b], supports a rich data model incorporating spatial/temporal objects as well as recursion at the kernel level. The Probe Data Model (PDM) provides *objects* and *functions* as basic constructs. An *object* is used to represent a real world object. *Functions* can be applied to objects to obtain properties of objects, invoke operations on objects, and describe relationships among objects. Objects and functions are manipulated through an algebra that is a generalization of the relational algebra.

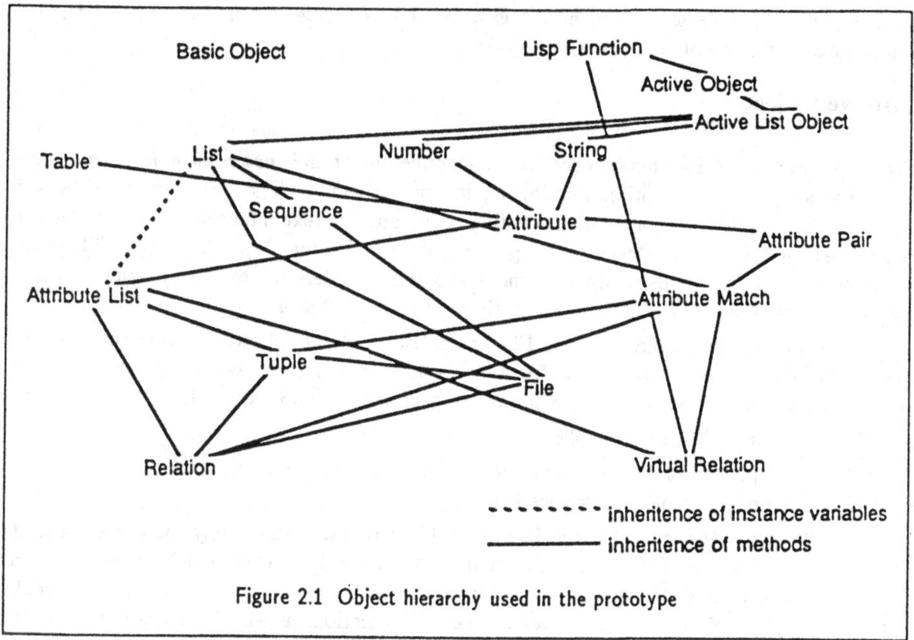

Figure 2.1 Object hierarchy used in the prototype

relational model. Basic object of Figure 2.1 is inherited by all other objects (not shown to keep the diagram comprehensible).

A simple user interface that embeds algebra operators in LISP has been implemented. It allows the use of lists, strings, numbers, and conditional expressions using LISP syntax instead of objects and functions.

3. Design of an Active OODBMS

The conceptual ingredients of condition monitoring are: events, conditions, and actions. An event is an indicator of a happening (recognized by the system or signaled by an application program/user). For example, events such as an arithmetic overflow or a timer underflow are recognized by the hardware whereas events corresponding tp updates (e.g., insert, delete, and modify) are detected by the DBMS software. A condition is a predicate over the database state that evaluates to a boolean value. (In the presence of free variables, the predicate is false if there are no bindings to the free variables.) Actions are operations to be performed when an event occurs and the condition associated with the event evaluates to true. Actions can be arbitrary programs. Actions, conditions and events can be packaged in various ways.

Situation-action rules (henceforth rules) have been used to group a condition and its associated action. One or more rules can be associated with a specific event. When an event occurs, one or more conditions are evaluated and corresponding action(s) invoked.

Our design assumes that a set of primitive events (such as read, write, execution of a function, clock event) on objects can be detected by the underlying system (either the operating system or the kernel of a DBMS). These events are independent of the model and the object classes in the system. Model and object specific events can be built from these events as we will demonstrate later. A condition and its associated action is packaged as a rule in our prototype and is implemented as instances of an object class (*active-object*).

3.1. Active Objects

We have introduced two new object classes - *active-object* and *activelist-object* which provide the basis for supporting condition monitoring in the prototype. The object class *active-object* encompasses the functionality of a rule including scope and context information. The object class *activelist-object* has been introduced to support multiple rules for a specific event. These object classes along with the methods defined on them and the handlers for read and write events provide all the necessary mechanisms for making the prototype DBMS *active*.

The *active-object* is a Common Lisp Flavor consisting of the following components: *local* - to hold the value of an object, *readfn* - a function to be executed on a read event, *writefn* - a function to be executed on a write event, *relation-id, tuple-id* - context variables (for the relational model)[3] , and *hist-vars* - history variables.

The *local* component of an *active-object* is a place holder for storing the value of the data object with which an *active-object* instance is associated.

The *readfn* stores the rule (in the form of a LISP function that may include calls to database operations) to be executed on a read event. When an object, with which an *active-object* is associated, is read the *readfn* of the active-object is executed, passing the current value of *local*, the context, and history variables as parameters. The read function, usually, returns the value of the object as its final action. A NIL *readfn* value is interpreted as a no-op and the value of *local* is immediately returned. Similarly, the *writefn* is a function to be executed when the object (with which the *active-object* is associated) is assigned a new value. The final action of a write function usually changes the value of *local*. Again, a NIL *writefn* value immediately assigns new value to *local*.

The *relation-* and *tuple- ids* are essentially variables providing the context in the form of the relation and the tuple identification, respectively. Storing references to the relation and the tuple provides context for the *active-object*'s read and write functions. The context information has several potential uses. First, the name, type, and the details of the object can be extracted from the tuple or the relation. Such accesses are often part of a triggered action. Second, the information in the tuple or relation may be used in computation performed by the read and/or write functions. Finally , it is useful to know the relation instance or the tuple instance containing the active object in order to pass it to a function called from within the rule. In our applications, we use the context information in all these ways.

The history variables can be used for a variety of purposes. Specifically, they can be used for optimization by storing materialized data and for optimizing rule evaluation.

The *activelist-object* is also a Common Lisp Flavor consisting of a list of *active-object* instances. For the sake of uniformity, an *activelist-object* is always used to make an object *active*.

3.2. Semantics of Active Objects

The semantics of an *active-object* can be easily inferred from the way *readfn* and *writefn* are invocated. The semantics of nested active objects is as follows. For read events, the *readfn*'s are

[3]The discussion is cast in the relational framework for comparison purposes, although the design is object-oriented.

executed inside out. In other words, the first operation is a read of *local* which may result in executing a nested *active-object*. The value of *local* generated for the innermost *local* is passed to the outer level *readfn* and so forth. Analogously, for write events, the *writefn*'s are executed outside in. Functions for both read and write events can be nested to arbitrary levels.

In the case of multiple rules, if rules are to be executed one at a time, then a 'conflict resolution' strategy is required to choose the appropriate rule. If multiple rules can be executed when an event occurs, they can be executed concurrently. In either case ordering of the rules based on some criterion (e.g., priority) is useful. In the prototype, the read and write functions of an active object are executed in the order in which they appear. The implementation of read function assumes that at least one of them will return the value of the object and the first non-NIL value returned is used as the value of the object. For multiple write functions, each of them is executed in the order specified. In this case, it is assumed that values are kept consistent by the functions. Other strategies for evaluating multiple rules are possible.

A set of methods are defined over the object classes introduced above. They include methods for: creating *active-object* instances, associating them with attributes and tuples of a relation, activating and deactivating them, and executing rules for read and write events.

3.3. Implementation of Event Handlers

In order to perform condition monitoring effectively and efficiently, events of interest (read and write on object instances in our case) need to be recognized. Recognition of events at the class level simplifies implementation as the method will be inherited by all the instances of the object class.

Choice of the strategy for implementing event handlers was based upon: simplicity of the technique (without sacrificing the functionality of the resulting system), ease of implementation (one that would not require extensive modifications to existing code), and ease of maintenance (a single version of code which can be made active incrementally).

The following alternatives were considered: i) define our own access functions for components of object classes of interest, ii) use error signaling system to get control of the occurrence of an event, iii) use before- and after-daemons to get control of the occurrence of an event, iv) use Whoppers to intercept the invocation of methods.

The first three options (listed above) were rejected as they did not satisfy our criteria. The first option violated the ease of implementation and ease of maintenance criteria. The second option is mostly used for debugging and lacked the generality required for our purpose. The third alternative does not permit the binding of variables during the execution of a method. Also, this mechanism does not provide the flexibility of not invoking the method for which they are defined.

The last alternative provided the type of control and at the level that satisfied our objectives. Whoppers provide a means for wrapping code *around* any method. Furthermore, it is a general mechanism that permits one to gain control prior to the execution of any method (both system defined as well user defined) and permits passing of parameters to the actual method itself. This mechanism is superior to other alternatives in providing a lexical scope within which the actual method itself can be invoked (optionally, of course) and local variables can be created and passed as parameters. In additions, Whoppers delay the detection of triggers as far as possible thereby reducing the overhead incurred for condition monitoring.

Whoppers need to be defined as a separate function for each flavor whose components are active. One has to only load the Whopper definitions in order to make objects active in this scheme and hence does not require any change to existing code. Furthermore object instances can be made active incrementally. Figure 3.1 shows the definition of string-object and Whoppers for read and write methods.

```
;;; definition of stringobj object class (flavor)
(defflavor stringobj (string)
        (obj)
  :initable-instance-variables
  :readable-instance-variables
  :locatable-instance-variables
  :writable-instance-variables)
;;; a whopper around the read function of string component of stringobj
(defwhopper (stringobj-string stringobj) ()
  (if (typep string ◇activelistobj)
      (p_triggerreadfns string)
      (continue-whopper)))
;;; a whopper around write function of string component of stringobj
(defwhopper ((setf stringobj-string) stringobj) (new-string)
  (if (typep string ◇activelistobj)
      (p_triggerwritefns string new-string)
      (continue-whopper  new-string)))
```

Figure 3.1 A Sample Whopper

3.4. Functionality of the Resulting System

Au Incorporation of active objects into a passive DBMS dramatically enhances the capabilities of the DBMS. We indicate below how active objects of the prototype support the following..

Triggers/alerters: The prototype supports triggers and alerters. For a relational DBMS, triggers/alerters can be associated with: an attribute instance (by associating an active object with an attribute instance), a tuple instance (by associating an active object with a tuple instance), an attribute name (by associating an active object with an attribute name to be associated with every instance of that attribute), and a relation instance (by associating an active object with a relation name to be associated with every tuple of that relation).

In order to support the last two, an *activelist-object* is maintained for each attribute of a relation which stores the active objects to be associated when a tuple is inserted into the relation. Similarly, active objects to be associated with the tuples of a relation are stored as part of the relation. This information is used when a tuple is inserted (deleted) into (from) a relation.

Multiple and nested rules: Multiple rules and nesting of rules (one active object invoking methods of other active objects including recursive invocation) are readily supported in our prototype. The mechanism used for nested rules is the same as the one used for supporting a rule in the first place and hence no special treatment is needed for handling nested rules.

Forward/Backward Chaining: The prototype supports both backward and forward chaining. The function associated with a read event can be used to support backward chaining (read on a virtual field or a virtual tuple) using the history variable to indicate whether the local value need to be computed or not. The function associated with the write event simulates forward chaining and alerters. Embedded reads in rules cause deeper backward chaining. It is assumed that the functions defined as part of active objects are well-behaved (i.e., there are no self references generating infinite loops).

Optimization: The prototype can also be used to implement materialization, lazy, eager, and one-shot rule evaluation techniques. History variable mentioned earlier plays a key role in this regard. The computations encoded in *readfn* and *writefn* can be distributed differently and intermediate results can be stored in history variables. Currently, the functions are not analyzed/processed by the system and hence lazy and eager evaluations have to be encoded by the implementor of these functions judiciously. However, with a higher-level user interface these functions can be generated to exploit lazy, eager, and one-shot evaluation.

Active Relational DBMS: Data manipulation operators are built in terms of the basic events supported by the system. That is, relational level operations cause the corresponding basic events which in turn execute the functions associated with the events. For example, a modify operation on an active field value (or field values) of a relation will activate the write functions associated with the corresponding fields. Similarly, a read on an active field (or field values) will activate the read function associated with the corresponding field (or field values).

4. Evaluation

In this section we compare monitoring of conditions using active objects and polling. We first describe the scenario used. We then analytically compare polling and active objects and predict their behavior. Finally, we conduct several simulations and analyze the observed behavior resulting in identifying potential optimization opportunities.

4.1. Scenario and Measurements

The scenario used for the purposes of comparison is a simulation of a simple command and control application. In this application, the database is populated with various kinds of platforms (such as airborne, naval, and submarine) which are are converging towards the stationary platform. The stationary platform is monitoring the movement of all the platforms around it to determine the threat posed by other platforms based on the distance of a platform from itself. The application simulates updates to the position of the platforms in a way that moves the platforms toward the stationary platform at specified rates. When, during the simulation, the distance becomes less than a certain threshold value (which is distinct for each class of platforms and there are three thresholds for each class) the commander is alerted by displaying the appropriate alert code on the console.

The database consists of three relations - *friendly-platforms* - for the stationary platform (having its name, X, and Y coordinates), *hostile-platforms* - for the rest of the platforms (having their name, class, X and Y coordinates) and *thresholds* - for the thresholds (having the platform class and the threshold values - three for each class). Each tuple of *hostile-platform* relation is made active. Functions corresponding to write events obtain the appropriate threshold value based on the class of the platform and compare the distance computed with the threshold values to determine whether there is a change in the alert code. Graphic updates are performed by triggers for active values using the same functions used for updating graphics for polling.

For comparing the performance of polling and active objects, the following were measured at run time using the system clock on Symbolics. *computations* - the number of times a rule is executed, *comp-time* - the sum of times spent in executing rules, for a given number of updates, *polling-time* - the amount of time spent in polling (only for polling), and *total-time* - total time taken to run a fixed number of simulated updates.

The parameters input for each experiment are: strategy (polling or active), number of hostile platforms, number of updates, and polling interval. The *hostile-platforms* relation is populated with X and Y coordinate values generated randomly making sure that none of the platforms is within the threshold to start with. After setting up the initial graphics, specified number of updates are performed in a loop measuring the values indicated above. At the end of the experiment the values are displayed. A running average of the above values is also computed and displayed.

All measurements used for plotting graphs in this paper are the average of at least two simulations. We also eliminated the effect of paging objects from secondary storage by discarding initial simulations until the measurements stabilized. Hence most of the readings should reflect simulations with the database resident in the main memory.[4]

4.2. Expected Behavior

Of the values measured, *computations* is a measure which is independent of the way in which tuples are accessed in a relation. For active objects the number of computations is the same as the number of updates (assuming that all tuples in the relation are active) and is independent of the size of the relation. For polling, it is directly proportional to size of the relation and inversely proportional to the time interval of polling. The crossover point of these curves (when number of tuples and the computations are plotted on the X- and Y- axis respectively) is a function of the size of the relation and the polling frequency.

Analytically, suppose N is the number of tuples in a relation, u is the update interval (of tuples) for the relation (average), and p is the polling interval. The polling interval is defined as the time between the beginning of one polling cycle to the beginning of the next polling cycle (a polling cycle corresponds to scanning the relation and evaluating the conditions associated with each tuple). The number of computations over a time period T for active objects is $\frac{T}{u}$. The number of computations for polling is $\frac{T}{p}*N$. They are equal when $p = N*u$. For a fixed u, p increases directly with respect to N and hence the timeliness of detection (which is inversely proportional to p) is directly dependent on the size of the relation in the case of polling. If the same timeliness of detection is to be maintained as N increases, the amount of computation increases in every polling cycle which may give rise to thrashing (i.e., losing updates). The system will thrash if p is less than the time it takes to perform N computations, i.e., if $p \leq N*a$, where a is the time it takes to perform an action (ignoring the access time of the tuple for the time being). The system can also thrash when conditions are monitored actively, if $u \leq a$. But the size of the relation does not have any impact in this case. Ideally, p should be large enough not only to perform all the computations in one polling cycle but should also allow updates to occur after the polling cycle. If in each polling interval p, x units of time is left after performing N1 operations (N1 is the size of the relation) and if the size of the relation were to increase to N2, the new and old relation sizes are related

[4]Readings of time reported in this paper need to be qualified further. First, time measurements reported here are not comparable to DBMS benchmarks (in terms of number of transactions per second) as the implementation is a prototype on Symbolics. Furthermore, the conclusions drawn in this paper do *not* depend upon on absolute values of execution time, but instead depend upon relative values (for polling and active objects) and hence are valid in our opinion. The prototype primarily used for demonstrating the active capability *visually* uses graphics and manipulation of graphic icons (using expensive operations such as drawing and erasing line segments) extensively. In addition, time is measured with a granularity of i/60th of a second and not in microseconds.

(assuming p is same) by the equation $N2 = N1 + O(\frac{x}{a})$. Note that the two sizes are related additively (and not multiplicatively) and the computation performed for each tuple (a) is a significant factor. Preferably, the ratio x/a should be chosen to accommodate the expected size of the relation. As a increases, x need to be increased losing timeliness of detection as a result.

A similar analysis indicates that, for active objects, the *total-time* (or even the *comp-time*) should not be influenced by the size of a relation. However, our initial measurement of *total-time* (shown in Figure 4.1) clearly indicated the dependence of the operation on the size of the relation. It was not difficult to trace this anomaly to the implementation of our update operation which retrieved tuples sequentially instead of using a direct access.

The above observation implies the significance of physical database design in the presence of active values. The physical database design is influenced by the rules and their association with data objects. A relation which may not need indexing when the database is passive have to be indexed (on one or more attributes) when the same database is made active.

In response to the above behavior we implemented a set of operators that were based on object identifiers (or cursors). Cursors can be used to access tuples directly from relations without having to scan the entire relation. Results obtained using the revised implementation are discussed below.

4.3. Comparison with Polling

Simulation 1: 200 database updates were executed. For polling, intervals of 2, 5, and 10 seconds were considered. In this experiment, we measured the *total-time* to run the simulation as the

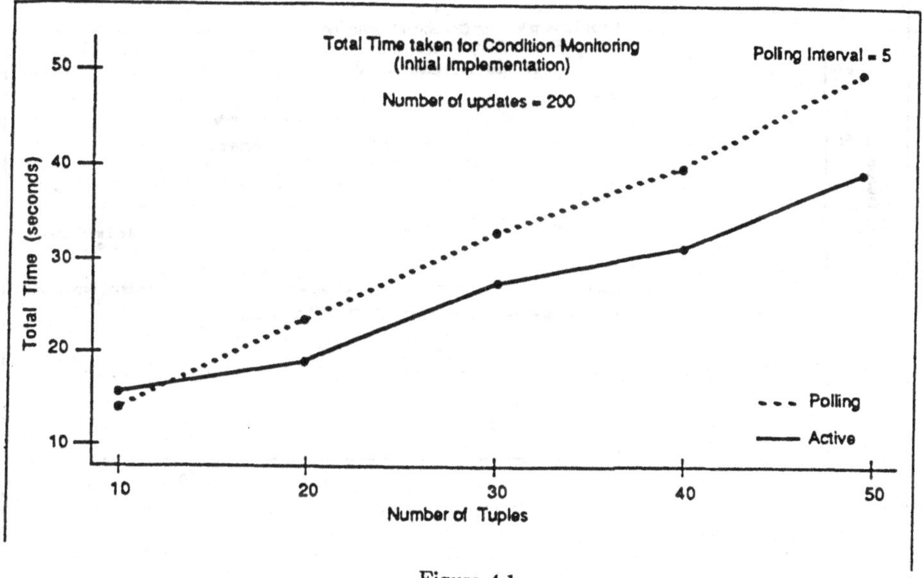

Figure 4.1

number of platforms in the database increases. In agreement with our analysis, the *total-time* for active values is flat (as shown in Figure 4.2) and does not seem to be influenced by the size of the relation. As expected, the *total-time* increases with the decrease of polling intervals as can be inferred from the graph. The curves for polling seem to diverge and the *total-time* spent on polling and active monitoring are more pronounced as the number of tuples increase and the polling intervals decrease. Note that the *total-time* used in this simulation *includes* the overhead incurred for the execution of active objects (Whoppers in our case). The effect of the overhead does not appear to be significant for the number of updates and the size of the relation used in this simulation.

The measurements obtained from this simulation also indicate that active condition monitoring is better than polling beyond the crossover point. In general, crossover point shifts towards the Y-axis (non-linearly) as the polling interval decreases. This strengthened our initial conjecture that although active condition monitoring is often better than polling, the decision for choosing a strategy (polling or active objects) has to be based upon the various parameters of the application at hand.

Simulation 2: 200 database updates on 30 platforms were conducted. In the polling case, the polling interval is varied from 1 to 10 seconds. In this simulation, we measured the fraction of the *total-time* used for condition monitoring as the polling interval varied. Figure 4.3 shows the the polling interval (in seconds) on the X-axis and the fraction (as a percentage) of the *total-time* spent on condition monitoring on the Y-axis. In this experiment, the overhead for active condition monitoring *does not* come into the picture enabling us to compare the waste of resources in the case of polling as compared to active condition monitoring. It can be easily observed from the graph that as the polling interval decreases, the fraction of time spent on condition monitoring increases almost exponentially.

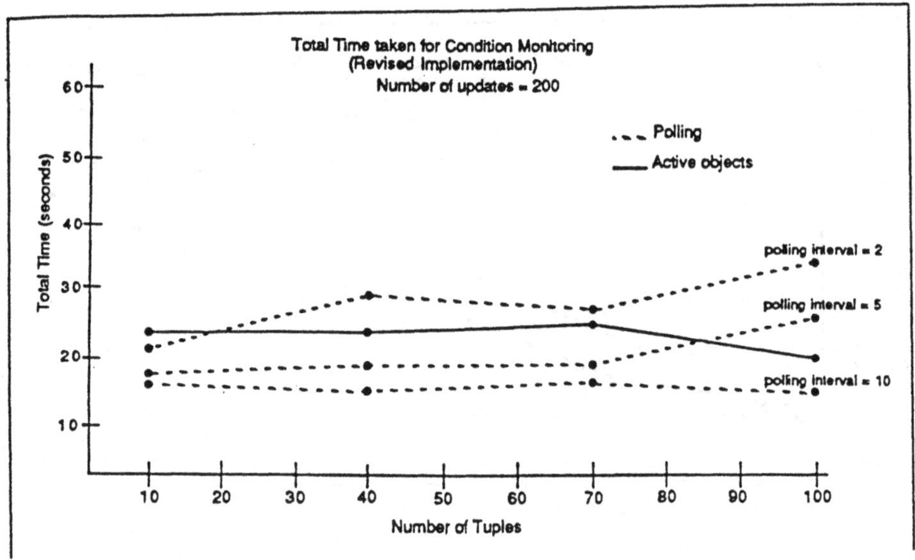

Figure 4.2

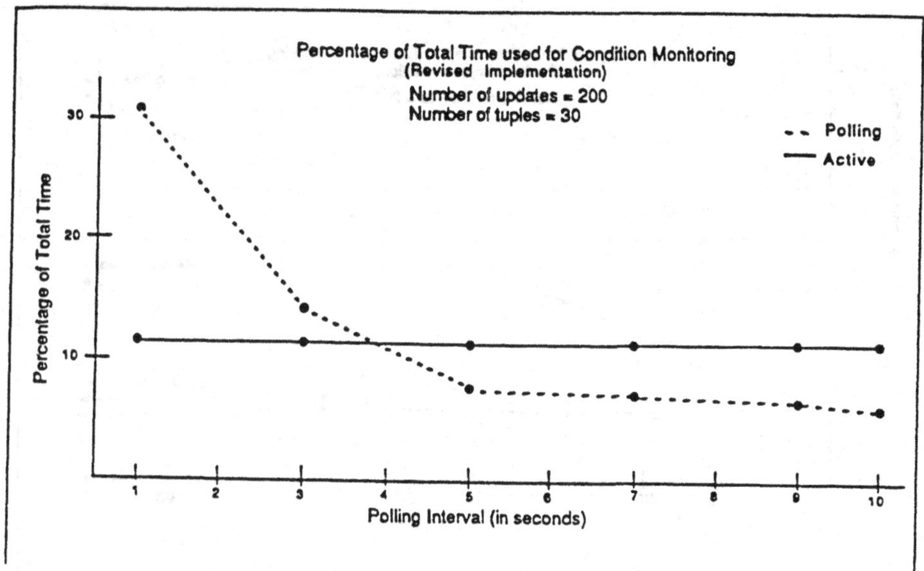

Figure 4.3

The results of the above simulation clearly demonstrate two limiting aspects of polling, namely, waste of resources and the timeliness of detection. These are conflicting requirements and hence have to be balanced against application needs. In real-time (time critical) applications, the lack of timeliness may not be acceptable. On the other hand, the increased overhead of polling at very short time intervals may not be tolerable.

Polling, by its nature, involves excessive computation to support timely notification. However, even with a very small polling interval, the notification of a condition being met in the database is not ideal. On the other hand, the timeliness of notification approaches the ideal for active objects. There is no need to wait for the next polling cycle, however soon that might be.

Simulation 3: In this simulation, we measured the fraction of time spent on condition monitoring as the number of platforms in the database increases. For active objects, the fraction of time spent on condition monitoring does not change significantly as number of platforms in the database increases. For polling, on the other hand, the fraction of time spent on condition monitoring does increase as the number of platforms increases. This result reflects the fact that more work is done in polling a large number of objects, other things being equal.

This simulation strongly indicates a subtle aspect of polling. Note that the crossover points in Figure 4.4 occur much earlier than those in Figure 4.2. While the same fraction of the total time is spent on condition monitoring in active objects (as indicated by a flat line), for polling, the fraction increases with the increase in the number of tuples indicating that the condition is evaluated for all the tuples *whether they were changed or not.* This strongly suggests that there is potential for optimizing polling to reduce the overhead.

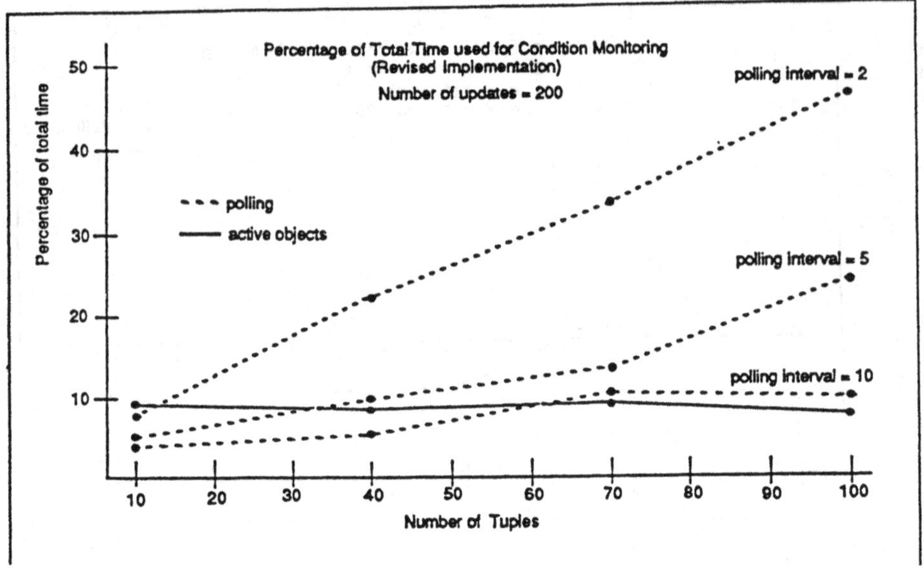

Figure 4.4

4.4. Analysis of Simulation Results

Below, we analyze the results of the above simulations and identify opportunities for improving the performance of both active objects and polling. The following analysis assumes that polling and active condition monitoring are being carried out on a relation where all the tuples are assumed to be active.

For a relation of size N, the amount of time spent during the time interval T using the polling technique is $\frac{T}{p}$ *(access time for (N_{un} + N_{ch}) tuples + (N_{un} + N_{ch})*a), where $\frac{T}{p}$ represents the number of polling cycles and the expression in the outermost parenthesis indicates the computing time during each polling cycle. N_{un} and N_{ch} represent the number of tuples that were not changed and the number of tuples that were actually changed, respectively, after the previous polling cycle. Clearly, $N = N_{un} + N_{ch}$. For active condition monitoring the above can be expressed as (access time for $\frac{T}{u}$ tuples + $\frac{T}{u}$ *a). Assuming that T_u *a and T_p *(N_c *a) are same (i.e., the same amount of work is done for tuples that were really changed in both cases, though it is likely to be less for polling as several changes may get grouped for each polling cycle), any optimization that can be incorporated for evaluating the conditions can be done for both techniques.

Simulations with revised implementation eliminated the dependency of the access time for $\frac{T}{u}$ tuples. However, for polling there are still additional overheads in the form of access time for (N_{un} + N_{ch}) tuples and N_{un} *a and this accounts for the observed results in Figures 4.2 to 4.4. Access time for N tuples was measured as *polling-time* (though not shown in any of the Figures) which increased with the number of tuples multiplicative factor of $\frac{T}{p}$.

The above analysis indicates that the polling technique used for condition monitoring can be improved in at least two ways: by reducing the access time in each polling cycle and by reducing or eliminating the condition evaluation on tuples that have not changed in a way to affect the outcome of the condition. These two improvements are further elaborated in the next section.

5. Conclusions

The results presented in this paper confirm our initial hypothesis that active monitoring is, in general, better than polling when the relation being monitored is large or when timely response is important. However, our simulations strongly indicate that a naive implementation of active objects (or making a passive DBMS active without taking the physical redesign into consideration or adding active capability without analyzing the implementation of operations) will not provide the performance advantage that one would expect of active condition monitoring. In addition, there is clear indication that polling is better than active condition monitoring below the crossover point substantiating retention of polling as one of the strategies. Pragmatically, an active DBMS should intelligently choose from among a set of strategies to reduce the waste of resources and increase the timeliness of condition detection. An DBMS should also be capable of dynamically restructuring the physical access to support active objects.

Typically, polling is implemented by scanning the entire relation during each polling cycle. The analysis of simulated results suggested opportunities for reducing the amount of work done during a polling cycle. First, the access time can be reduced by employing direct access techniques such as indexing for those tuples that have been modified from the previous polling cycle. Second, the time spent on condition evaluation can be reduced by storing some information as part of the tuples which can be used for deciding whether the condition should be evaluated at all. Though this optimization can be easily made part of condition evaluation, it will add an additional burden, of incorporating this into the code, on the implementor.

6. Acknowledgements

We would like to thank Umeshwar Dayal for many fruitful discussions during the course of this task and for insightful comments which improved the presentation of this paper. The implementation reported in this paper was carried out on a Symbolics machine given to CCA on loan by Symbolics Inc. We gratefully acknowledge the support Symbolics Inc. provided us during the course of the task reported in this paper.

7. References

[BOBR83] Bobrow, D. G., Stefik, M., "The Loops Manual", Intelligent Systems laboratory, Xerox Corporation, 1983.

[CHAK89] S. Chakravarthy, B. Blaustein, et al, "HiPAC: A Research Project in Active, Time-Constrained Database Management", Final Technical Report, Xerox Advanced Information Technology Division, July 1989.

[DARN87] Darnovsky. M., and Bowman, J., "TRANSACT-SQL USER'S GUIDE", Document 3231-2.1, Sybase Inc., 1987.

[DAYA88a] Dayal, U., et al., "The HiPAC Project: Combining Active Databases and Timing Constraints", ACM Sigmod Record, March 1988.

[DAYA88b] Dayal, U., et al., "HiPAC: A Research Project in Active, Time-Constrained Database Management", Interim Report (CCA-88-02), June 1988.

[DAYA87a] Dayal, U., Goldhirsch, D., Orenstein, J., and DeWitt, M., "PROBE Final Report", Draft, CCA, November 1987.

[DAYA87b] Dayal, U., et al., "Overview of PROBE: An Object-Oriented, Extensible Database System", To appear in IEEE Expert.

[DITT86] Dittrich, K. R., Kotz, A. M., and Mulle, J. A., "An Event/Trigger Mechanism to Enforce Complex Consistency Constraints in Design Databases", SIGMOD Record, Vol. 15, No. 3, 1986, pp. 22-36.

[INTE85] IntelliCorp, "KEE Software Development System User's Manual", IntelliCorp, Mountain View, 1985.

[MANO86] Manola, F. A., and Dayal, U., "PDM: An Object-Oriented data Model", Proceedings of International Workshop on Object-Oriented Database Systems, 1986.

[ROSE86] Rosenthal, A., Heiler, S., Dayal, U., and Manola, F. A., "Traversal Recursion: A Practical approach to Supporting Recursive Applications", Proceedings ACM SIGMOD, 1986.

[STON86] Stonebraker, M., Rowe, L., "The Design of POSTGRES", Proceedings of ACM-SIGMOD, 1986, pp. 340-355.

[STON87] Stonebraker, M., Hanson, M., and Potamianos, S., "A Rule manager for Relational database Systems", Technical Report, Dept. of Electrical Engineering and Computer Science, Univ. of California, Berkeley, 1987.

A Theory for Rule Triggering Systems*

Yuli Zhou Meichun Hsu
Aiken Computation Laboratory
Harvard University, Cambridge, MA 02138

Abstract

We define and study the family of RTS's, each appearing in the form of a relational database extended with a set of production-like rules with forward-chained operational semantics.

The syntax and operational semantics of RTS's are first defined, which provide a simple model for rule triggering systems. Operationally rules behave like concurrent processes which update the database's state. A computation of a RTS is then a sequence of states induced by firing rules in some order, which terminates in a fixed point. When a RTS has more than one rule, there may be multiple computations from the same state, and they may terminate in different fixed points.

The RTS's that have determinate computational behavior are identified as those computing unique fixed points. We give an easy-to-check sufficient condition that detects RTS's that may fail to belong to this class.

1 Introduction

The active database management systems make use of condition-action rules. These rules can perform operations when certain conditions on the database are satisfied, therefore they are convenient for implementing various DBMS functionalities such as maintaining data integrity, automatic recomputation of defined data, performing inference, etc.

With the introduction of rules into a database system, additional processing and updates in a database may be triggered by "user-proposed" updates. We call a set of rules with forward chaining semantics a *rule triggering system*. In this paper, we define and study the properties of a *family* of simple rule triggering systems (RTS's).

Based on the relational data model and first order predicate calculus, RTS's are simple yet quite general in scope. Our goal in this paper is twofold: Firstly, we would like to define the syntax and the semantics of RTS's to serve as a simple model for rule triggering systems, in which we can formulate and study various properties concerning their computational behavior. Secondly, we would like to identify some properties that are of practical importance; to this end, we identify a

*This work is supported in part by the US Department of Navy, Space and Naval Warfare Systems Command and Defense Advance Research Projects agency under contract N00039-88-Q-0163, and the National Science Foundation under grant NSF-44-782-10-7687-2-30

sub-family of RTS's which are guaranteed to have *determinate* behavior, and give an easy-to-check sufficient condition to test for membership of RTS's in this sub-family.

1.1 Background

Various rule triggering systems have appeared in the literature. Many are primarily concerned with implementing active DBMS functionalities such as condition monitoring ([3],[6],[2]), automatic recomputation of materialized views ([1]), maintenance of integrity constraints, and derivation of data ([5], [14], [4]). Other systems exist for AI applications, such as OPS5 ([7]) and some other expert systems.

Several models for executing rules have been proposed. Hipac ([8]) incorporates an extensive execution model, in which various "coupling-modes" are identified. These modes specify how the activities of firing rules (i.e., condition evaluation, action execution, etc.) are embedded in the overall DBMS operations. For instance, the *decoupled execution* of rules treats the triggered actions as separate transactions, which is also used in AP5 and CPLEX ([9]) for their *automation rules.* In System R as well as in HiPAC, triggered actions can also be executed before the end of the execution of a user-proposed update request. In other words, upon the invocation of an operation, a triggered action can be executed *immediately* without being deferred to the end of the user request. The immediate execution is also assumed in triggers supported in Sybase ([15]). In POSTGRES ([14]), the execution semantics is influenced by the rules' *evaluation strategy*, which can be either eager evaluation or lazy evaluation.

In all the rule triggering systems, the issue of concurrent firing of rules must be addressed. Most systems assume that if multiple rules are triggered at the same time, then the system will decide arbitrarily which one to execute first. The nested transaction model in [11] is found to be appropriate in defining the correct semantics of concurrent execution of rules and thus allows for non-determinism ([8]). Some systems supplement the non-deterministic scheme with a *conflict resolution* policy. POSTGRES and OPS-5 employ a *priority* scheme, in which the system chooses the rule which has the highest priority. If two rules have the same priority, then one is chosen randomly.

1.2 RTS

A RTS is a relational database extended with production-like rules, in which the collection of rules is called the rule base. A rule can be regarded as a conditional update: Given a database state $\mathbf{s}$, it updates $\mathbf{s}$ to $\mathbf{s}'$ if certain condition is true of $\mathbf{s}$. Performing the update action is also called *firing* the rule. Once state $\mathbf{s}'$ is computed, rules in the rule base are applied again, this time to $\mathbf{s}'$.

Similar to a computation in a production system, a computation of RTS is a sequence of state transitions caused by firing rules in the rule base in an arbitrary order:

$$\mathbf{s}_1 \xrightarrow{\alpha_1} \mathbf{s}_2 \xrightarrow{\alpha_2} \cdots \xrightarrow{\alpha_k} \mathbf{s}_k \xrightarrow{\alpha_{k+1}} \cdots$$

the sequence will terminate in $\mathbf{s}_n$ if $\mathbf{s}_n$ is a fixed point of all the rules considered as functions mapping states to states.

To understand how the above sequence is embedded in the overall operations of DBMS, let $\mathbf{s}$ be a database state which is changed to $\mathbf{s}_0$ by a user transaction T. It is at the end of the user transaction that the rule triggering sequence is started. If the rule triggering sequence terminates in $\mathbf{s}_n$, the database makes a transition from $\mathbf{s}$ to $\mathbf{s}' = \mathbf{s}_n$, which is considered one atomic unit. Therefore, the operation of RTS logically extends the effect of a user transaction T, which can be depicted in the following diagram:

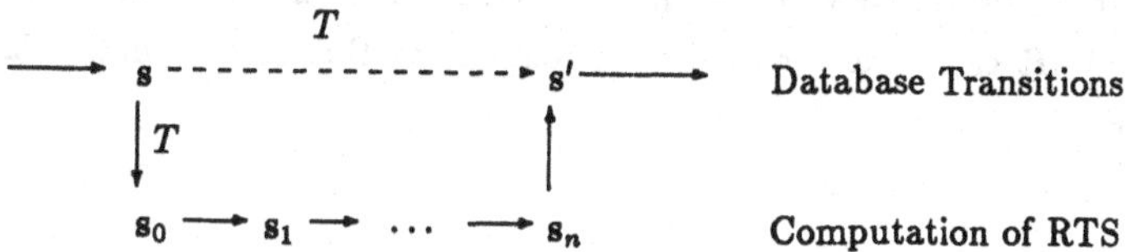

Obviously the embedded sequence corresponding to each transaction T is generally not unique, which raises the question of the uniqueness of the final state $\mathbf{s}'$. A RTS is said to have determinate computational behavior if for each $\mathbf{s}$ the corresponding $\mathbf{s}'$ is unique. This means that the RTS will compute unique fixed points regardless of the order in which rules are fired.

The above picture is only a simplified version of a RTS computation. In fact, the transient states $\mathbf{s}_k, k \geq 0$ are partitioned into a pair $\mathbf{s}_k = (\mathbf{s}, \mathbf{u}_k)$, where $\mathbf{s}$ is the original database state, $\mathbf{u}_0$ the effect of the user transaction T, and $\mathbf{u}_k, k > 0$ the accumulated update of firing rules. In this way rules can refer not only to the current state (obtained by applying $\mathbf{u}_k$ to $\mathbf{s}$) but also to the original state $\mathbf{s}$ and the change $\mathbf{u}_k$. This partition has been used extensively for the purpose of incrementally evaluating rule conditions and specifying transitional constraints ([1], [12], [4]).

The above picture also says that we have focused on *coupled execution* of rules (i.e., triggered actions are considered part of the same transaction). However, the framework described in this paper should be applicable to the study of the properties of *decoupled* rules as well. We do not dwell on this issue further in this paper.

The rest of the paper is organized as follows: In Section 2 we define the syntax and operational semantics of RTS's. In section 3 we develop a condition of noninterference that guarantees that a RTS will compute unique fixed points, as well as a simple method to test for interference. Section 4 is a brief summary of the paper.

2 RTS — Syntax and Semantics

In this section we briefly outline the structure of RTS's. A RTS can be represented as a triple $\langle \mathbf{R}, \Gamma, \tau \rangle$, where $\mathbf{R}$ is the *database* (a finite set of relation variables), Γ the *rule base* (a finite set of rules) and τ the *triggering mechanism* that executes rules. We describe the necessary notations that will serve as a definition of RTS's syntax and semantics.

2.1 Syntax

2.1.1 Relations

Let **R** be a database. Each relation variable $R \in \mathbf{R}$ has an arity $a(R)$, which is a positive integer. R may have a value $v(R)$, which is a $a(R)$-ary relation (a set of tuples of length $a(R)$).

For each $R \in \mathbf{R}$, we introduce two *update relation variables* ^+R and ^-R, holding increments and decrements to R, respectively. Both ^+R and ^-R have the same arity as that of R. Let $\Delta_{\mathbf{R}}$ (or simply Δ where **R** can be understood from context) be the set of update relation variables associated with **R**.

2.1.2 Rules

Let Γ be a rule base. All rules in Γ have the form

$$\delta x_1, x_2, \ldots, x_n.F \rightarrow U$$

where F is a first order predicate formula and U a sequence of assertions and deletions. $\delta x_1, x_2, \ldots, x_n$ is called the δ-prefix, which lists all the free variables in F, and by convention they subsume those in U. It can be omitted in case F is closed. F is also called the *condition* or the *LHS* of the rule, U the *action* or the *RHS* of the rule.

Expressions in the form

$$R(t_1, t_2, \ldots, t_n)$$

where $R \in \mathbf{R} \cup \Delta$ and $t_i, 1 \leq i \leq n$ is either a constant or a variable are called *atomic formulas*. The class of first order predicate formulas is formed inductively on the base of atomic formulas, such that if F and G are two formulas, then so are the following:

$$\neg F,\ F \wedge G,\ F \vee G,\ F \rightarrow G,\ \forall x F,\ \exists x F.$$

Assertions and deletions are expressions of the forms (respectively):

$$\text{++}R(t_1, t_2, \ldots, t_n), \quad \text{--}R(t_1, t_2, \ldots, t_n)$$

where $R \in \mathbf{R}$.

If F does not contain variables, then it is *ground*. Let $fv(F)$ be the set of variables that occur free in F, F is said to be *closed* if $fv(F) = \emptyset$. We will adopt the notation of writing a formula F that is not closed as $F(x_1, x_2, \ldots, x_n)$, which makes explicit the free variables $x_1, x_2, \ldots, x_n$ in F. $F(c_1, c_2, \ldots, c_n)$ then is the formula obtained by substituting c_i for x_i, $1 \leq i \leq n$. The same notation and terminology will be used on assertions and deletions where applicable.

Example 1 Suppose we have a database

$$\mathbf{R} = \{P(parent, child), A(ancestor, person)\},$$

where A is normally the transitive closure of P. This agreement can be destroyed, however, when a user tries to update P but not A. Therefore we want to write a rule base that recomputes A each time P is updated.

To deal with the case where user updates arrive in the form of assertions only, we can use the rule base $\{\alpha_1, \alpha_2, \alpha_3, \alpha_4\}$ where

$$\begin{aligned}
\alpha_1 &= \delta x, y.{}^+P(x,y) \rightarrow {++}A(x,y) \\
\alpha_2 &= \delta x, y.\exists z A(x,z) \wedge {}^+A(z,y) \rightarrow {++}A(x,y) \\
\alpha_3 &= \delta x, y.\exists z {}^+A(x,z) \wedge A(z,y) \rightarrow {++}A(x,y) \\
\alpha_4 &= \delta x, y.\exists z {}^+A(x,z) \wedge {}^+A(z,y) \rightarrow {++}A(x,y)
\end{aligned}$$

Upon an user update, α_1 will copy to A all the tuples added to P, and α_2–α_4 will add to A all tuples implied by transitivity. □

2.2 Semantics

2.2.1 States and Updates

A database $\mathbf{R}$ with its value bindings is commonly called a *state*. If $\mathbf{R} = \{R_1, R_2, \ldots, R_n\}$, then a state can be represented as a vector of n relational values

$$\mathbf{s} = (r_1\ r_2\ \cdots\ r_n)$$

where $r_i = v(R_i), 1 \leq i \leq n$. We shall call Δ with its value binding an *update*, represented by the array

$$\mathbf{u} = \begin{pmatrix} p_1 & p_2 & \cdots & p_n \\ q_1 & q_2 & \cdots & q_n \end{pmatrix}$$

where $p_i = v({}^+R_i)$ and $q_i = v({}^-R_i)$, $1 \leq i \leq n$. Applying $\mathbf{u}$ to $\mathbf{s}$ we get the new state

$$\mathbf{u}(\mathbf{s}) = (r_1 \cup p_1 - q_1 \quad r_2 \cup p_2 - q_2 \quad \cdots \quad r_n \cup p_n - q_n).$$

2.2.2 Rules as Functions

Given any closed formula F, a state $\mathbf{s}$ and an update $\mathbf{u}$ form an *interpretation* for F, in which the truth of F can be determined in the usual way. Let $fv(F) = \{x_1, x_2, \ldots, x_n\}$. We define the evaluation of F in $\mathbf{s}$ and $\mathbf{u}$, denoted $\mathcal{E}[F(x_1, x_2, \ldots, x_n)]\mathbf{su}$, as the set of tuples $(c_1, c_2, \ldots, c_n)$ such that $F(c_1, c_2, \ldots, c_n)$ is true in $\mathbf{s}$ and $\mathbf{u}$. First order formulas used in this way form essentially the relational domain calculus (cf. [16]).

A sequence U of ground assertions or deletions is actually an update

$$\begin{pmatrix} p_1 & p_2 & \cdots & p_n \\ q_1 & q_2 & \cdots & q_n \end{pmatrix}$$

where

$$\begin{cases} (c_1\ c_2\ \cdots\ c_n) \in p_i & \text{if } {++}P_i(c_1, c_2, \ldots, c_n) \in U \\ (c_1\ c_2\ \cdots\ c_n) \in q_i & \text{if } {--}P_i(c_1, c_2, \ldots, c_n) \in U. \end{cases}$$

Let $fv(U) = \{x_1, x_2, \ldots, x_n\}$ and therefore we can write U as $U(x_1, x_2, \ldots, x_n)$. We denote by $U[c_1, c_2, \ldots, c_n]$ the update obtained from U when each x_i is replaced by c_i, $1 \leq i \leq n$.

A rule α defines a function f_α such that

$$f_\alpha(\mathbf{s},\mathbf{u}) = \mathbf{u} \cup \bigcup_{(c_1\ c_2\ \cdots\ c_n)\in\mathcal{E}[F(x_1,x_2,\ldots,x_n)]\mathbf{su}} U[c_1,c_2,\ldots,c_n],$$

where the operator $\cup$ stands for component-wise set union. From now on we will simply denote f_α as α.

2.3 The Rule-Triggering Process

With the previous notations we can now explain the process of rule triggering. Let $\langle \mathbf{R}, \Gamma, \tau \rangle$ be a RTS. At any state $\mathbf{s}$, when a user submitted transaction T arrives, let its initial effect be summarized as an update $\mathbf{u}_0$. The rule triggering mechanism τ computes some sequence of updates

$$\mathbf{u}_k = \alpha_k(\mathbf{s}, \mathbf{u}_{k-1}), k > 0$$

where $\alpha_1, \alpha_2, \ldots, \alpha_k, \ldots$ are chosen from Γ in some unspecified manner, until a fixed point $\mathbf{u}_n$ is reached. $\mathbf{u}_n$ is said to be a *fixed point of* Γ *at* $\mathbf{s}$ iff $\forall\ \alpha \in \Gamma\ \alpha(\mathbf{s}, \mathbf{u}_n) = \mathbf{u}_n$. $\mathbf{u}_n$ is then applied to $\mathbf{s}$ to get a new database state $\mathbf{s}'$.

Example 2 Let us continue with example 1. Suppose the database is originally empty (i.e., $v(P) = v(A) = \emptyset$), and the user tries to update the database by $++P(Mary, John), ++P(Smith, Mary)$. Our rule base will compute the sequence:

$$\begin{pmatrix} \{(Mary, John) & \emptyset \\ (Smith, Mary)\} & \\ \emptyset & \emptyset \end{pmatrix} \xrightarrow{\alpha_1} \begin{pmatrix} \{(Mary, John) & \{(Mary, John) \\ (Smith, Mary)\} & (Smith, Mary)\} \\ \emptyset & \emptyset \end{pmatrix}$$

$$\downarrow \alpha_4$$

$$\begin{pmatrix} & \{(Mary, John) \\ \{(Mary, John) & (Smith, Mary) \\ (Smith, Mary)\} & (Smith, John)\} \\ \emptyset & \emptyset \end{pmatrix}$$

When the final update is applied, we get the new state

$$\begin{cases} P = \{(Mary, John), (Smith, Mary)\} \\ A = \{(Mary, John), (Smith, Mary), (Smith, John)\} \end{cases}$$ □

2.3.1 Contradictory Updates

One problem associated with the sequence $\{\mathbf{u}_k\}$ is the potential introduction of contradictory updates. For every

$$\mathbf{u} = \begin{pmatrix} p_1 & p_2 & \cdots & p_n \\ q_1 & q_2 & \cdots & q_n \end{pmatrix},$$

if $\exists\ 1 \leq i \leq n\ p_i \cap q_i \neq \emptyset$, then $\mathbf{u}$ is said to be *contradictory*. We will follow a convention of AP5 ([4]) that aborts the triggering process whenever the accumulative update becomes contradictory. From this we gain the benefit of reduced complexity, due to the fact that $\{\mathbf{u}_k\}$ will be monotonically increasing.

Many questions can now be asked about the computational behavior of a RTS, as the triggering process defined previously is neither deterministic nor guaranteed to terminate. This is the problem we will address in the next section. We will first define, for each rule base Γ, a transition relation $\rightarrow_\Gamma$ in which all computation sequences of τ can be traced. We then proceed to develop a series of conditions, under which τ is guaranteed to compute unique fixed points (i.e., from each $(\mathbf{s}, \mathbf{u}_0)$, τ computes the same $\mathbf{u}_n$, if exists, no matter which sequence is followed).

3 The Computational Behavior of RTS's

3.1 Notations and Definitions

We will build on the material presented in section 2 and define some additional notations which will help us in analyzing the computational behavior of RTS's.

3.1.1 The Lattice of Updates

Let $\mathbf{D}$ be some domain of constants from which all the n-ary relations ($n > 0$) are constructed as subsets of $\mathbf{D}^n$. Let $\mathbf{S}$ be the class of states, $\mathbf{U}$ be the class of updates as introduced in the previous section, i.e.,

$$\begin{cases} \mathbf{S} &= \{(r_1\ r_2\ \cdots\ r_n) \mid r_i \subseteq \mathbf{D}^{\alpha(R_i)}, |r_i| < \infty, 1 \le i \le n\} \\ \mathbf{U} &= \{\begin{pmatrix} p_1 & p_2 & \cdots & p_n \\ q_1 & q_2 & \cdots & q_n \end{pmatrix} \mid p_i, q_i \subseteq \mathbf{D}^{\alpha(R_i)}, |p_i|, |q_i| < \infty, 1 \le i \le n\}. \end{cases}$$

Notice that since the values of database relations have to be finite, all states and updates are finite.

Certain properties of $\mathbf{U}$ are important to us: $\mathbf{U}$ is a *partial order* with the ordering relation $\subseteq$ (the component-wise set inclusion), and it is a *lattice* with the two operations of $\cup$ (component-wise union) and $\cap$ (component-wise intersection).

In section 2 we have adopted the convention to abort the triggering process whenever the accumulative update becomes contradictory, therefore there is no need in $\mathbf{U}$ to keep contradictory updates separate. We will identify all of them to $\top$, and the resulting class of updates will be denoted by $\mathbf{U}_\top$:

$$\mathbf{U}_\top = \{\begin{pmatrix} p_1 & p_2 & \cdots & p_n \\ q_1 & q_2 & \cdots & q_n \end{pmatrix} \mid p_i, q_i \subseteq \mathbf{D}^{\alpha(R_i)}, |p_i|, |q_i| < \infty, p_i \cap q_i = \emptyset, 1 \le i \le n\} \cup \{\top\}.$$

As one can see, $\top$ has to be the supremum element of $\mathbf{U}_\top$, i.e., $\forall\ \mathbf{u} \in \mathbf{U}_\top\ \mathbf{u} \subseteq \top$. $\mathbf{U}_\top$ is still a lattice, but has a different structure (In particular, $\mathbf{U}$ is distributive, but $\mathbf{U}_\top$ is not).

3.1.2 The Transition Relation

Given a rule base Γ, a better view of the triggering process can be provided if we expand the computation of τ on all its choices. This is defined as the *transition relation* of Γ, denoted $\rightarrow_\Gamma$: $\mathbf{S} \times \mathbf{U}_\top \rightarrow \mathbf{S} \times \mathbf{U}_\top$, such that

$$(\mathbf{s}, \mathbf{u}) \rightarrow_\Gamma (\mathbf{s}, \mathbf{u}') \iff \exists\ \alpha \in \Gamma\ \mathbf{u}' = \alpha(\mathbf{s}, \mathbf{u}) \neq \mathbf{u}.$$

When Γ can be understood from context, we will simply write $\rightarrow$ for $\rightarrow_\Gamma$. To simplify our notation, let us write $\mathbf{u} \rightarrow_s \mathbf{u}'$ as equivalent to $(\mathbf{s},\mathbf{u}) \rightarrow (\mathbf{s},\mathbf{u}')$. Due to the the way rules are defined, a transition sequence

$$\mathbf{u}_0 \rightarrow_s \mathbf{u}_1 \rightarrow_s \cdots \rightarrow_s \mathbf{u}_k \rightarrow_s \cdots$$

must also be a *chain*, i.e.,

$$\mathbf{u}_0 \subset \mathbf{u}_1 \subset \cdots \subset \mathbf{u}_k \subset \cdots.$$

It is said to *terminate* in $\mathbf{u}_n$ iff $\nexists\, \mathbf{u}'$ such that $\mathbf{u}_n \rightarrow_s \mathbf{u}'$, i.e., iff $\mathbf{u}_n$ is a fixed point of Γ at s.

Remark Recall that we introduced $\top$ to let a transition sequence abort as soon as it becomes contradictory, which is indeed the case since $\top$ is always a fixed point. Now *aborting* is completely characterized as *terminating in* $\top$.

$\rightarrow$ can be seen as a reduction relation in the sense of [10]. We realize that the question of termination translates into whether $\rightarrow$ is Noetherian, and the question of unique fixed point translates into whether $\rightarrow$ has the unique fixed point property, whose stronger form is stated as confluence or the Church-Roser property in [10].

3.1.3 Termination and the Unique Fixed Point Property

$\rightarrow$ is said to be *Noetherian* if every transition sequence is finite. In this case we also say $\rightarrow$ is *terminating*. Since each transition sequence is a chain, $\rightarrow$ is terminating iff each transition sequence

$$\mathbf{u}_0 \rightarrow_s \mathbf{u}_1 \rightarrow_s \cdots \rightarrow_s \mathbf{u}_k \rightarrow_s \cdots$$

has a finite upper bound. This happens to be the case with every $\rightarrow_\Gamma$ defined by some rule base Γ introduced in section 2. The reason is simple: each $(\mathbf{s},\mathbf{u}_0)$ is finite and hence contain finite number of symbols. The rule base is also finite, and rules can not construct new symbols (for instance, generate integers). Therefore every sequence $\{\mathbf{u}_k\}$ from $(\mathbf{s},\mathbf{u}_0)$ is upper-bounded by $\mathbf{u}_{max}$, where $\mathbf{u}_{max}$ is the largest update that can be constructed using symbols in $\mathbf{s},\mathbf{u}_0$ and Γ. Obviously $\mathbf{u}_{max}$ has to be finite. We will state the above as the following fact:

Fact 1 *Every* $\rightarrow_\Gamma$ *is terminating.*

$\rightarrow$ is said to have the *unique fixed point property* (UFP) iff $\forall\, \mathbf{s},\mathbf{u}_0$, if $\exists$ a terminating transition sequence from $(\mathbf{s},\mathbf{u}_0)$ to $(\mathbf{s},\mathbf{u}_n)$, then every transition sequence from $(\mathbf{s},\mathbf{u}_0)$ terminates in $(\mathbf{s},\mathbf{u}_n)$.

Our task now is to define conditions that result in restricted families of rule bases whose transition relations have UFP. We would like to make these conditions as less restrictive as possible.

3.2 The Family of Monotonic Rule Bases

We shall see how the concept of monotonic functions will help us in achieving our goal. A rule α is *monotonic* (in the update) iff $\forall \mathbf{s},\mathbf{u},\mathbf{v}$, if $\mathbf{u} \subseteq \mathbf{v}$ then $\alpha(\mathbf{s},\mathbf{u}) \subseteq \alpha(\mathbf{s},\mathbf{v})$. Monotonic rules are interesting to us since it preserves the partial ordering $\subseteq$ between updates. This, together with the fact that every transition sequence is a chain, will force $\rightarrow$ to have UFP as we are going to prove shortly.

The monotonicity condition above can best be illustrated by the following diagram:

$$\begin{array}{ccc} \mathbf{u} & \subseteq & \mathbf{v} \\ \downarrow^{\alpha} & & \downarrow^{\alpha} \\ \mathbf{u}' & \subseteq & \mathbf{v}' \end{array}$$

A rule base Γ will be called *monotonic* iff all rules in Γ are monotonic. All monotonic rule bases have UFP, as stated in the following theorem:

Theorem 1 *If Γ is monotonic, then $\rightarrow_\Gamma$ has UFP.*

Proof Let $\mathbf{s}, \mathbf{u}_0$ be any state and update. Suppose there exists a transition sequence

$$\mathbf{u}_0 \rightarrow_s \mathbf{u}_1 \rightarrow_s \cdots \rightarrow_s \mathbf{u}_n$$

where $\mathbf{u}_n$ is a fixed point. Let

$$\mathbf{v}_0 = \mathbf{u}_0 \xrightarrow{\alpha_1}_s \mathbf{v}_1 \xrightarrow{\alpha_2}_s \cdots \xrightarrow{\alpha_m}_s \mathbf{v}_m$$

be any sequence from $\mathbf{u}_0$, where $\mathbf{v}_k = \alpha_k(\mathbf{s}, \mathbf{v}_{k-1})$, which terminates in $\mathbf{v}_m$. We show $\mathbf{v}_m = \mathbf{u}_n$.

First notice that $\forall\, 0 \leq k \leq m$, $\mathbf{v}_k \subseteq \mathbf{u}_n$: since $\mathbf{v}_0 = \mathbf{u}_0 \subseteq \mathbf{u}_n$, applying α_1 to both sides, we have $\mathbf{v}_1 \subseteq \mathbf{u}_n$ by the fact that α_1 is monotonic and $\mathbf{u}_n$ is a fixed point. The rest follows by induction. In other words, $\mathbf{u}_n$ is an upper bound for $\mathbf{v}_k, 0 \leq k \leq m$, in particular $\mathbf{v}_m \subseteq \mathbf{u}_n$.

By a symmetrical argument, since $\mathbf{v}_m$ is a fixed point, it is an upper bound for $\mathbf{u}_l, 0 \leq l \leq n$ and $\mathbf{u}_n \subseteq \mathbf{v}_m$. This completes our proof that $\mathbf{v}_m = \mathbf{u}_n$.

$$\begin{array}{ccc} \mathbf{u}_0 & \subseteq & \mathbf{u}_n \\ \downarrow^{\alpha_1} & & \downarrow^{\alpha_1} \\ \mathbf{v}_1 & \subseteq & \mathbf{u}_n \\ \downarrow^{\alpha_2} & & \downarrow^{\alpha_2} \\ \vdots & \vdots & \vdots \\ \downarrow^{\alpha_m} & & \downarrow^{\alpha_m} \\ \mathbf{v}_m & \subseteq & \mathbf{u}_n \end{array} \quad + \quad \begin{array}{ccc} \mathbf{u}_0 & \subseteq & \mathbf{v}_m \\ \downarrow & & \downarrow \\ \mathbf{u}_1 & \subseteq & \mathbf{v}_m \\ \downarrow & & \downarrow \\ \vdots & \vdots & \vdots \\ \downarrow & & \downarrow \\ \mathbf{u}_n & \subseteq & \mathbf{v}_m \end{array} \quad \Longrightarrow \quad \mathbf{v}_m = \mathbf{u}_n$$

□

Example 3 The class of horn clauses used extensively in deductive databases appear in their rule form as

$$\delta x_1, x_2, \ldots, x_n.A'_1 \wedge A'_2 \wedge \cdots \wedge A'_m \rightarrow {+\!+}B$$

where $A'_i = (A_i \vee {}^+A_i)$, and $A_i, 1 \leq i \leq m$, and B are atomic formulas.

It is obvious that all horn clause rule bases are monotonic. Following theorem 1, all of them compute unique fixed points. Therefore we have shown, using another approach, the well known result in [17], namely, a set of horn clauses defines a least fixed point. □

3.3 The Family of Interference-free Rule Bases

Obviously rule bases that are not monotonic do not necessarily have a transition relation that does not have UFP. For instance, if each rule in a rule base Γ works on a "segregated" part of the database, so that there is no interaction among them, the order of firing rules can not make any difference on the final state. It follows that we can weaken the monotonicity condition to allow some of the nonmonotonic rules to be used in Γ, while still guarantee $\rightarrow_\Gamma$ to have UFP.

The question that should be asked now is: in what situation does nonmonotonicity not matter (i.e., will not destroy UFP)? The key to the answer lies obviously in the interaction among the rules in a rule base. In a rule base, interaction among rules creates *data dependencies*. Rules rely on these dependencies to exchange information, the same way as procedures rely on parameter passing.

3.3.1 Dependency among Rules

Recall that we have defined a rule α to be a function from $\mathbf{S} \times \mathbf{U}_\mathsf{T}$ to $\mathbf{U}_\mathsf{T}$, and

$$\Delta = \{{}^+R_1, {}^+R_2, \ldots, {}^+R_n\} \cup \{{}^-R_1, {}^-R_2, \ldots, {}^-R_n\}$$

is the set of update relation variables. Fixing a state, α can be seen as a function in these $2n$ variables, which make up the components of an update $\mathbf{u}$. Rules interact by reading and augmenting these variables, thereby creating data dependency among themselves.

Given a rule

$$\alpha = \delta x_1, x_2, \ldots, x_n.F \rightarrow U,$$

let us define the *read set* of α, denoted $\mathbf{Rd}(\alpha)$, as the set of variables $R \in \Delta$ such that R occurs in F. Similarly let us define the *write set* of α (denoted $\mathbf{Wt}(\alpha)$) to be the set of variables occurring in U:

$$\begin{cases} \mathbf{Rd}(\alpha) &= \{R \mid R \in \Delta \wedge R \text{ occurs in } LHS(\alpha)\} \\ \mathbf{Wt}(\alpha) &= \{R \mid R \in \Delta \wedge R \text{ occurs in } RHS(\alpha)\}. \end{cases}$$

A rule β can be said to *depend on* another rule α iff β reads what α writes, i.e., $\mathbf{Rd}(\beta) \cap \mathbf{Wt}(\alpha) \neq \emptyset$.

3.3.2 Local Monotonicity

We will use each update relation variable $R \in \Delta$ as a projection function $\mathbf{U}_\mathsf{T} \rightarrow \mathbf{U}_\mathsf{T}$, i.e., $R(\mathbf{u})$ is obtained from $\mathbf{u}$ by erasing to $\emptyset$ all its components not corresponding to R. For every $X \subseteq \Delta$ we define

$$X(\mathbf{u}) = \bigcup_{R \in X} R(\mathbf{u}).$$

We want to examine how monotonicity can be intertwined with dependency. Let α be a rule and $X \subseteq \Delta$. α is said to be *monotonic* in X iff $\forall\, \mathbf{s}, \mathbf{u}, \mathbf{v}$ where $\mathbf{u} \subseteq \mathbf{v}$ and $\mathbf{v} - \mathbf{u} \subseteq X(\mathbf{v} - \mathbf{u})$, we have $\alpha(\mathbf{s}, \mathbf{u}) \subseteq \alpha(\mathbf{s}, \mathbf{v})$. In other words, α is monotonic in X if it preserves the ordering $\mathbf{u} \subseteq \mathbf{v}$ whenever the difference $\mathbf{v} - \mathbf{u}$ lies entirely in X.

If α is monotonic in $\{R\}$, we say it is monotonic in R, and R is said to be a *monotonic variable* of α. Let $\mathrm{Mon}(\alpha)$ denote the set of monotonic variables of α. $\Delta - M(\alpha)$ will be called the set of *nonmonotonic variables* of α and denoted $\mathrm{Non}(\alpha)$

The question of where α is monotonic is completely determined by its monotonic variables, as stated by the following lemma.

Lemma 1 *α is monotonic in X iff $X \subseteq \mathbf{Mon}(\alpha)$.*

Proof The only-if part is obvious. We will prove the following statement: "If α is monotonic in X, R, then α is monotonic in $X \cup \{R\}$." The if part will follow by induction.

Assume α is monotonic in X and R. Let $X' = X \cup \{R\}$. Then for all $\mathbf{u}, \mathbf{v}$ such that $\mathbf{u} \subseteq \mathbf{v}$ and $\mathbf{v} - \mathbf{u} \subseteq X'(\mathbf{v} - \mathbf{u})$, we have

$$\mathbf{u} \subseteq \mathbf{u}' = \mathbf{u} \cup X(\mathbf{v} - \mathbf{u}) \subseteq \mathbf{v}.$$

Since $\mathbf{u}' - \mathbf{u} \subseteq X(\mathbf{u}' - \mathbf{u})$ and $\mathbf{v} - \mathbf{u}' \subseteq R(\mathbf{v} - \mathbf{u}')$, we have

$$f(\mathbf{u}) \subseteq f(\mathbf{u}') \subseteq f(\mathbf{v}).$$

□

3.3.3 Interference among Rules

We now return to our original question, namely, in what situation does nonmonotonicity not matter? If α is not monotonic, let X be its set of nonmonotonic variables. Obviously if no rule in the rule base writes to X, then so far as the transition relation is concerned the nonmonotonicity of α will not be visible and therefore harmless. It is the other situation, namely, when X can be written to by some other rule, that will create multiple fixed points. We will capture the latter as interference.

Let α and β be rules. We say α *interferes with* β iff α writes to some nonmonotonic variable of β, i.e., $\mathbf{Wt}(\alpha) \cap \mathbf{Non}(\beta) \neq \emptyset$. Interference turns out to be the kind of interaction among rules that may destroy UFP, as shown by the following examples.

Example 4

1. To rephrase a frequently used example of interfering rules, let the database be {Bird(name), Penguin(name), CanFly(name)}. The rule base $\{\gamma_1, \gamma_2\}$ where

$$\begin{aligned} \gamma_1 &= \delta x.{}^{+}Bird(x) \wedge \neg(Penguin(x) \vee {}^{+}Penguin(x)) \rightarrow {+\!+}CanFly(x) \\ \gamma_2 &= {}^{+}Bird(tweety) \rightarrow {+\!+}Penguin(tweety) \end{aligned}$$

has γ_2 interfering with γ_1. If we start with an empty database and let $\mathbf{u}_0 = {+\!+}Bird(tweety)$, then two fixed points may be computed:

$$\begin{array}{ccc} \begin{array}{ccc} \mathbf{B} & \mathbf{P} & \mathbf{CF} \\ \{tweety\} & \emptyset & \emptyset \\ \emptyset & \emptyset & \emptyset \end{array} & \xrightarrow{\gamma_2} & \begin{pmatrix} \{tweety\} & \{tweety\} & \emptyset \\ \emptyset & \emptyset & \emptyset \end{pmatrix} \\ \downarrow \gamma_1 & & \\ \begin{pmatrix} \{tweety\} & \emptyset & \{tweety\} \\ \emptyset & \emptyset & \emptyset \end{pmatrix} & \xrightarrow{\gamma_2} & \begin{pmatrix} \{tweety\} & \{tweety\} & \{tweety\} \\ \emptyset & \emptyset & \emptyset \end{pmatrix} \end{array}$$

2. Consider a database of students and courses they take. It has three relations S(student-name), C(course-title) and T(student-name, course-title). We can enforce the "referential integrity constraint" on the database, which requires that all the student names and course

titles referenced in T should be contained in S and C, respectively. This is done by the following rules:

$$\begin{aligned}\beta_1 &= \delta x, y.^{-}S(x) \wedge T(x,y) \rightarrow {-}{-}T(x,y)\\ \beta_2 &= \delta x, y.^{-}C(y) \wedge T(x,y) \rightarrow {-}{-}T(x,y)\\ \beta_3 &= \delta x, y.^{+}T(x,y) \wedge \neg((S(x) \vee {}^{+}S(x)) \wedge (C(y) \vee {}^{+}C(y))) \rightarrow {-}{-}T(x,y)\end{aligned}$$

β_1, β_2 delete references to student names and course titles when they are deleted. β_3 will cause an abort if a tuple (a,b) is added to T but either a or b is undefined, by deleting (a,b). For the case dealt with by β_3, we can also add a to S and b to C, if they are not already there, using the rule

$$\beta_4 \;=\; \delta x, y.^{+}T(x,y) \wedge \neg((S(x) \vee {}^{+}S(x)) \wedge (C(y) \vee {}^{+}C(y))) \rightarrow {+}{+}S(x), {+}{+}C(y)$$

Now if we use β_1–β_4 as a rule base, then we are sure to have inconsistent behavior: the rule base may compute either $(\top)$ (firing β_3 first) or something else (firing β_4 first).

This is because β_4 interferes with β_3: the write set of β_4 is obviously $\{^{+}S, {}^{+}C\}$, in which β_3 is not monotonic. Notice when β_4 is fired first, β_3's LHS will be made false, which stops β_3 from being fired. □

Let Γ be a rule base. If $\forall\, \alpha, \beta \in \Gamma$, α does not interfere with β, then Γ is said to be *interference-free*. Similar to theorem 1, we have

Theorem 2 *If Γ is interference-free, then $\rightarrow_\Gamma$ has UFP.*

Proof Let

$$\mathbf{u}_0 \xrightarrow{\alpha_1}{}_{s} \mathbf{u}_1 \xrightarrow{\alpha_2}{}_{s} \cdots \xrightarrow{\alpha_n}{}_{s} \mathbf{u}_n$$

be a terminating sequence, let

$$\mathbf{v}_0 = \mathbf{u}_0 \xrightarrow{\beta_1}{}_{s} \mathbf{v}_1 \xrightarrow{\beta_2}{}_{s} \cdots \xrightarrow{\beta_m}{}_{s} \mathbf{v}_m$$

be any sequence from $\mathbf{u}_0$, which must terminate in $\mathbf{v}_m$ for some $m \geq 0$, and let

$$X = \bigcup_{i=0}^{n} \mathbf{Wt}(\alpha_i).$$

Notice that $\forall\, 0 \leq k \leq m\ \mathbf{v}_k \subseteq \mathbf{u}_n$: It is clear that $\mathbf{v}_0 \subseteq \mathbf{u}_n$ and $\mathbf{u}_n - \mathbf{v}_0 \subseteq X(\mathbf{u}_n - \mathbf{v}_0)$ ($\alpha_i, 1 \leq i \leq n$ could not have written something outside of their write sets). Since none of $\alpha_l, 1 \leq l \leq n$ interferes with β_1, β_1 is monotonic in X. Applying β_1 we have $\mathbf{v}_1 \subseteq \mathbf{u}_n$. The rest follows by induction. Therefore by an argument similar to that for theorem 1, we have $\mathbf{v}_m = \mathbf{u}_n$. □

Notice that if Γ is monotonic, then it is interference-free. The converse is obviously not true, by the following counter example. Therefore the family of interference-free rule bases contains all the monotonic rule bases as a proper subset.

Example 5 The rules $\beta_1, \beta_2, \beta_3$ in example 4.2 form a rule base that is not monotonic but interference-free, the nonmonotonic rule being β_3. The write set of both β_1 and β_2 is $\{^{-}T\}$, in which β_3 is monotonic (in fact ^{-}T is not in the read set of β_3). □

3.4 Checking for Interference

Given two rules α and β, we know α interferes with β iff $\mathbf{Wt}(\alpha) \cap \mathrm{Non}(\beta) \neq \emptyset$. Since the write set of a rule is easy to determine, it follows that if we can tell which of the variables in a rule is nonmonotonic, then we have an effective way of checking for interference.

Let $\alpha = \delta x_1, x_2, \ldots, x_n.F \rightarrow U$ be a rule. Let us say $\mathcal{E}[F]$ is monotonic in $R \in \Delta$ iff $\forall\, \mathbf{s}, \mathbf{u}, \mathbf{u}'$ we have $\mathcal{E}[F]\mathbf{su} \subseteq \mathcal{E}[F]\mathbf{s}(\mathbf{u} \cup R(\mathbf{u}'))$. It is clear that if $\mathcal{E}[F]$ is monotonic in R, then so will be α. Let $\mathrm{Non}(F)$ be the set of variables in which $\mathcal{E}[F]$ is not monotonic. We have:

Lemma 2 $\mathrm{Non}(\alpha) \subseteq \mathrm{Non}(LHS(\alpha))$.

As one might have suspected, the variables in which $\mathcal{E}[F]$ is not monotonic are restricted to those that occur "negatively" in F. Roughly, R occurs negatively in F if the matrix of F (obtained by removing all quantifiers) can be written as

$$G \vee \neg R(t_1, t_2, \ldots, t_n) \wedge H.$$

Let us consider the special case where F does not contain any quantifiers, so that it can be converted easily to its conjunctive normal form F_n. We realize that if $R \in \Delta$ does not occur as some negation $\neg R(t_1, t_2, \ldots, t_n)$ in F_n, then $\mathcal{E}[F_n]$ must be monotonic in R. On the other hand if R occurs as some negation in F_n, then almost certainly $\mathcal{E}[F_n]$ will not be monotonic in R.

The above suggests that we can approximate the nonmonotonic variables of F by its "negative" variables. Simulating the process where negation signs are moved inside by applications of de Morgan's law, we define inductively the notion of R occurring positively in F (denoted $P(R,F)$) and negatively in F (denoted $N(R,F)$) as the following:

1. $P(R, R(t_1, t_2, \ldots, t_n)) = \mathit{true}$, $N(R, \neg R(t_1, t_2, \ldots, t_n)) = \mathit{true}$.
2. $P(R, F \wedge G) = P(R,F) \vee P(R,G)$, $N(R, F \wedge G) = N(R,F) \vee N(R,G)$
3. $P(R, F \vee G) = P(R,F) \vee P(R,G)$, $N(R, F \vee G) = N(R,F) \vee N(R,G)$
4. $P(R, F \rightarrow G) = N(R,F) \vee P(R,G)$, $N(R, F \rightarrow G) = P(R,F) \vee N(R,G)$
5. $P(R, \forall x F) = P(R,F)$, $N(R, \forall x F) = N(R,F)$
6. $P(R, \exists x F) = P(R,F)$, $N(R, \exists x F) = N(R,F)$

Given a formula F, its set of negative variables is defined as

$$\mathrm{Neg}(F) = \{R \mid R \in \Delta, N(R,F) = \mathit{true}\}.$$

Lemma 3 $\mathrm{Non}(F) \subseteq \mathrm{Neg}(F)$.

Proof P and N are defined to meet the following conditions: For all $\mathbf{s}, \mathbf{u}$ and $\mathbf{u}'$,

$$\begin{cases} P(R,F) \neq \mathit{true} & \Longrightarrow \quad E[F]\mathbf{s}(\mathbf{u} \cup R(\mathbf{u}')) \subseteq E[F]\mathbf{su} \\ N(R,F) \neq \mathit{true} & \Longrightarrow \quad E[F]\mathbf{su} \subseteq E[F]\mathbf{s}(\mathbf{u} \cup R(\mathbf{u}')) \end{cases}$$

This can be shown by induction on the structure of F. The second condition means that if R does not occur negatively in F, then $\mathcal{E}[F]$ is monotonic in R. It follows that every nonmonotonic variable of F must occur negatively in F, i.e., $\mathrm{Non}(F) \subseteq \mathbf{Neg}(F)$. □

The following is a direct consequence of lemma 2 and lemma 3:

Theorem 3 *Let α and β be two rules. If $\mathbf{W}t(\alpha) \cap \mathbf{N}eg(LHS(\beta)) = \emptyset$, then α does not interfere with β.*

The above theorem can be used as a basis for interference checking, i.e., given a rule base Γ, we can check to see whether none of the rules writes to some negative variable, which guarantees Γ to be interference-free.

4 Summary

We have proposed a family of RTS's as a model for simple rule triggering systems. Our modeling is abstract in the sense that it does not imply any specific concurrency or implementation decisions; such things are *latent* in the model. The mathematical semantics enables us, however, to study more closely the computational behavior of rules in terms of their interdependencies. We have shown how the sub-family of RTS's that compute unique fixed points can be approximately identified by the condition of noninterference, and how the potential presence of interference can be easily checked. This result can have practical importance in managing rule-based systems.

Acknowledgement

We would like to thank Professor T. E. Cheatham, who initiated and supervised this work. Much of our research has been influenced by his strong conviction that a more rigorous model of rule systems is needed. We'd also wish to thank D. Cohen of ISI, U. of Southern California for helping the first author to get acquainted with AP5, which provided the basic structure for RTS.

5 References

1. J. A. Blakeley et al, Efficiently Updating Materialized Views. *Proc. 1986 ACM SIGMOD Conference on Management of Data*, 61–71.

2. P. Buneman, E. Clemons, Efficiently Monitoring Relational Databases. *ACM Trans. on Database Systems* vol. 4 No. 3 (Sept. 1979), 368–382.

3. D. D. Chamberlain et al, SEQUEL 2: A Unified Approach to Data Definition, Manipulation, and Control. *IBM Journal of Research and Development*, Vol. 20, No. 6 (November 1976).

4. D. Cohen, Automatic Compilation of Logical Specifications into Efficient Programs. In *Proc. 5th National Conference on Artificial Intelligence*, August 1986.

5. C. J. Date, *An Introduction to Database Systems, Volume II.* Addison-Wesley, Reading, Mass. 1983.

6. K. P. Eswaran. Specifications, Implementations, and Interactions of a Trigger Subsystem in an Integrated Data Base System. *IBM Research Report RJ1820* (August 1976).

7. C. L. Forgy, Rete: A Fast Algorithm for the Many Pattern/Many Object Pattern Match Problem. *Artificial Intelligence* 19 (1982) 17–37.

8. M. Hsu, R. Ladin and D. McCarthy, An Execution Model for Active Data Base Management Systems. *Proc. 3rd International Conference on Data and Knowledge Bases*, June 1988.

9. M. Hsu, T. E. Cheatham, Rule Execution in CPLEX: A Persistent Objectbase. *Proc. 2nd International Workshop on Object Oriented Database Systems*, September, 1988.

10. Gerard Huet, Confluent Reductions: Abstract Properties and Applications to Term Rewriting Systems. *JACM*, Vol. 27, No. 4, 1980, 797-821.

11. J. Moss, *Nested Transactions: An Approach To Reliable Distributed Computing.* MIT Laboratory for Computer Science, MIT/LCS/TR-260 (1981).

12. J. M. Nicolas, K. Yazdanian, Integrity Checking in Deductive Databases. In H. Gallaire, J. Minker (ed.) *Logic and Data Bases*, 325–344. Plenum Press, 1978.

13. D. A. Schmidt, *Denotational Semantics: a Methodology for Language Development.* Allyn and Bacon, Newton, Mass., 1986.

14. M. Stonebraker et al, A Rule Manager For Relational Database Systems. *The POSTGRES Papers*, Univ. of California, Berkeley, Ca. Electronics Research Lab, Memo No. UCB/ERL M86/85 (1986).

15. Sybase, Inc. *Transact-SQL User's Guide.* (1987).

16. Jeffrey. D. Ullman, *Principles of Database Systems.* 2nd ed., Computer Science Press, 1982.

17. M. H. Van Emden, R. A. Kowalski, The Semantics of Predicate Logic as a Programming Language. J. ACM **23**:4, 1976, 733–742.

A PRAGMATIC APPROACH FOR INTEGRATING DATA MANAGEMENT AND TASKS MANAGEMENT : MODELLING AND IMPLEMENTATION ISSUES

Francisca Antunes[a], Sean Baker[b], Brian Caulfield[b], Mauricio Lopez[c], Mark Sheppard[b]

ABSTRACT : This paper outlines a particular approach to monitoring and responding to events by automatically starting activities and building sets of activities into office procedures that define long lived work sequences that many office workers could take part in. This is comprehensively achieved by integrating this support with an information server. Three aspects are discussed : the model, the language, the implementation.

1. INTRODUCTION

The work reported here was done as part of the design and implementation of a database server providing the advanced functions required in office environments. Rather than implementing an office information system for a particular kind of office, we have built an Office Information Server (OIS) that provides basic functions for the integrated handling of classical data, documents and tasks. Although developed in the context of an office information server, the task management functions are applicable in any domain where computed aided management of tasks is needed.

The model adopted to describe office tasks is similar to those used in other research projects [Ell79], [Chu84], [Bra83]. It is based on the concepts of **Activity** and **Procedure**. An Activity is a sequence of operations which perform a particular task in the office. An activity is enabled for execution when an associated precondition, expressed in terms of database changes or database states, becomes true. Unstructured applications, very prevalent in the office environment, can then be modelled as sets of activities more or less interrelated through their preconditions. Structured applications can be modelled using the concept of Procedure by which activities can be organized as a directed graph expressing sequencing, parallelism or synchronisation of activities. Other features of the model include automatic and manual starting of enabled activities and the association of a computer program with an activity. Providing procedures and both automatic and manual activities enables a continuous range of applications to be modelled ranging from unstructured to very structured.

The most important issues addressed by the project in the area of task management are :

- The **integration of the concepts of activity and procedure**, and their management functions, with the data model and manipulation language. This has significant implications for the architecture of the system.

- The **expressive power of activity and procedure preconditions** and their efficient evaluation in a database environment.

(a) Laboratoire de Génie Informatique, (c) Centre de Recherche BULL : Unité Mixte BULL IMAG, ZI de Mayencin, 2, rue Vignate, 38610 Gières, France ;

(b) Distributed System Group, Dept. of Computer Science, Trinity College, Dublin 2 Ireland

• The **control and persistent execution** of procedures.

The data model chosen has a small number of concepts and instead of specifically building in activity and procedure concepts to give a larger model, we have defined the dynamic aspects in terms of the existing data model concepts. Activities and procedures are therefore **predefined entity types** specified using the standard DDL but having a particular semantics, i.e., treated specially by the implementation. The basic concepts of the resulting model are presented in Section 2.1, and the mechanism supporting the persistent control of activities and procedures is discussed in Section 4.2.

Although it was desirable to keep the number of special language constructs to a minimum, a sublanguage to describe the structure of procedures as a **directed graph of activities** was introduced. This allows office procedures to be monitored and controlled as cohesive units rather than just as collections of activities related by their actions and preconditions. The alternative is to have sets of individual activities reacting to, what the system views as, independent events. The sublanguage, called OPL3, is a database concurrent programming language, and is presented in Section 2.1.

It is important that precondition evaluation does not become a bottleneck in the system given that they have to be evaluated whenever the database is updated. Therefore, we have developed a **mechanism** to (i) compile preconditions at definition time in order to obtain good performance at evaluation time; (ii) to closely couple the evaluation of preconditions to the execution of updates in order to minimize the number of database accesses; and (iii) to coordinate precondition evaluation with transaction commitment in order to avoid enabling activities within subsquently aborted transactions. This mechanism is more fully described in Section 4.1.

In order to allow preconditions with high expressive power, the precondition language is a **superset of the DML**. This not only provides for powerful and easily written preconditions, but it also forms the basis for a method of matching update statements to preconditions so that the set of preconditions that can potentially be enabled by an update can be efficiently determined. Determining whether an update has actually enabled a precondition again uses the matching so that the number of accesses to the database can be minimised, and eliminated in some cases. A characterization of update statements and preconditions as well as a complete set of matching rules are presented in Section 3.

2. SUPPORT FOR TASK MANAGEMENT

2.1. Modelling Concepts

The OIS uses a functional semantic data model, FM [Sac87], which is interesting in two ways : it is based on a minimum number of concepts (entities and facts) and has a powerful inference mechanism. Only the former need interest us here. Entity types form a specialisation hierarchy, and several types, like integer, string and document, are predefined in the system. Facts are unnamed relationships between entity types, e.g.,

DEFINE [Salesman,Contract]

This defines functions Salesman.Contract and Contract.Salesman that are used in query and update statements. The functions can be specified to be single or multivalued, and total or partial. Unlike Daplex [Shi81] inverse functions do not need to be explicitly defined. Facts, and therefore functions, are inherited through the specialisation hierarchy. Panel 1of Figure 1 gives an example of a conceptual schema.

In the general case, a fact declaration like [Man, Woman] is not enough if it is desired to express several kinds of relationship between Man and Woman. A complete fact declaration is [Husband: Man, Wife: Woman] which defines the functions Woman.Husband -> Man and its inverse Man.Wife -> Woman.

The data manipulation language, FML [Lop87] [Ped88], has a SQL-like syntax. The following query retrieves information about salesmen that are related to sales worth more than 5000

```
SELECT Salesman.Name, Salesman.Sale.Number, Salesman.Sale.Amount
WHERE  Salesman.Sale.Amount > 5000
```

or using explicit variables

```
SELECT s1.Name, s2.Number, s2.Amount
FROM   Salesman s1.Sale s2
WHERE  s2.Amount > 5000
```

A new salesman entity, with the name 'Jones', can be inserted by

```
INSERT  Salesman  WITH  Name = "Jones"
```

The entity can be related to a particular sale by inserting a fact

```
INSERT  [Salesman, Sale]
WHERE  Salesman.Name = "Jones"  and  Sale.Number = 301
```

Existing facts can be modified using the ASSERT statement, and entities and facts can be deleted using DELETE. See also the examples in Panel 3 of Figure 1.

Rather than extending this model with a large number of concepts necessary to handle office procedures, we have modelled them using the concepts of entity and fact. This has many advantages, among these are that definitions of activity and procedure data can be given using the standard DDL, and the status of activities and procedures can be queried and modified using the standard DML. This reduces the complexity for users as well as for the implementation. We have also used this approach in modeling documents [Ber88].

Office procedure classes are templates from which procedure instances are created when required. For example, a procedure class 'Car_Sale' would have a **precondition** which specifies that a 'Car_Sale' procedure should be created whenever a customer wishes to buy a car. The precondition could be written to be fulfilled when a new 'sale' entity is created. This new entity is like a parameter to the procedure, and is known as its '**focal entity**' [Sir82] [Ham83]. Focal entities are FM entities which may be created and manipulated through the DML as normal, and should have facts relating them to all of the entities specific to the procedure. In a similar fashion, activity classes are templates used to create activities, that is, the individual programs or actions in a procedure. Activities also have focal entities; normally they are some entity related to the procedure's focal entity (or simply the procedure's focal entity itself).

These concepts are implemented as **predefined types** in the OIS. The following approach has been taken because FM has a clear distinction between types and instances which results in a two level classification hierarchy. 'Procedure_class' is the type of all procedures classes in the system, that is, the descriptive level. Each instance of it is related by facts to the data required to describe that class of procedure. 'Procedure' is the type of all currently created

CONCEPTUAL SCHEMA

STATIC SCHEMA

Panel 1

Name : String
Number : Integer
Amount : Integer
Salary : Integer
Person : Entity
Customer : Person
Employee : Person
Salesman : Employee
Order : Document
Contract : Document
[Person, Name]
[Employee, Salary]
[Contract, Number]
[Sale, Number]
[Sale, Amount]
[Sale, Contract]
[Sale, Order]
[Sale, Customer]
[Sale, Salesman]

DYNAMIC SCHEMA

Panel 2

Class_Status : ("Loaded","Unloaded")
Status : ("Enabled", "Started", ...)
Start_Mode : ('Manual", "Automatic")

Program, Site_Name : String
Description : Text
Fe_Type : Type
FE : Entity

Activity concept

Activity_Class : Entity
Activity : Entity
[Activity_Class, Activity]
[Activity_Class, Name]
[Activity_Class, Description]
[Activity_Class, Precondition]
[Activity_Class, Fe_Type]
[Activity_Class, Class_Status]
[Activity_Class, Start_Mode]
[Activity_Class, Program]
[Activity_Class, Site_Name]
[Activity, Status]
[Activity, FE]

Procedure concept

Procedure_Class : Entity
Prcedure : Entity
[Procedure_Class, Procedure]
[Procedure_Class, Name]
[Procedure_Class, Description]
[Procedure_Class, Precondition]
[Procedure_Class, Fe_Type]
[Procedure_Class, Class_Status]
[Procedure_Class, Schema]
[Procedure, Status]
[Procedure, FE]

DATA MANIPULATION LANGUAGE

Panel 3

Insert Salesman
With Name = "Viriato"

Insert [Sale, Order]
Where Sale.Number =
12
And Order.Number =
123

Select Name
From Salesman
Where Salary > 15000

Panel 4

Insert Activity_Class
With Name = "Bonus"
And Description = "This..."
And Fe_Type = Customer
And Precondition = **Test**
Insert [Sale, Customer]
Where Sale.Amount
> 5000
And...

Select Fe_Type
From Activity-class
Where Name = "Bonus"

Panel 5

Insert Procedure_Class
With Name = "Car_Sale"
And Description = "A procedure ..."
And Fe_Type = Sale
And Precondition =
Test Insert Sale
And Schema =
Begin-Schema
Get_Customer_Details (Customer:
Sale.Customer)
Generate_Contract (Contract:
Sale.Contract)
Cobegin
Check_Contract (...)
|| Send_Order_Manufacturer(...)
Coend
...

OPCL

Panel 6

Load Activity-Class
Where Name = "Bonus"

Start Activity
Where Activity-Class.
Name = "Bonus"
And FE.Name="Viriato"

Panel 7

Unload Procedure-Class
Where Fe-Type = "Sale"

Abort Procedure
Where Procedure-Class.
Name ="Car-Sale"
And FE.Number = 5055

Figure n° 1 - Activity and Procedure Definition and Manipulation

procedures, and each instance of it is related by a fact to its 'Procedure_Class'. This is the executable level. Each instance of 'Procedure' also has a status and a focal entity. Similarly 'Activity_Class' and 'Activity' are predefined types. The corresponding FM schema is shown in Panel 2 of Figure 1.

The creation of an 'Activity_Class' (Panel 4) or 'Procedure_Class' (Panel 5) is done using the standard 'INSERT-WITH' FML statement and involves specifying its related facts. Note that a procedure_class's specification includes its 'Schema'; this specifies, in a language called OPL3, the structure and make up of the procedure. The simple 'Car_Sale' procedure class might be defined as shown in Panel 5 of Figure 1. Note that the focal entities of the activity are specified as parameters, for example the focal entity of the Get_Customer_Details activity is a Customer and is related to the focal entity of the procedure (Sale) by the function Sale.Customer (hence we write Customer: Sale.Customer).

For flexibility, the **Program** (identified by a file name) associated with activity classes may be coded in any programming language (including the DML), and may use the facilities of the DML for locking and recovery support. Activities are said to be 'enabled' when their precondition is fulfilled. Activities with an associated Program can be 'automatic' or 'manual'. **Automatic** activities are 'started' (i.e., run) once they become enabled; **manual** activities remain 'enabled' until explicitly 'started' by a user or application (using the START statement). Activities with no Program can also be specified and then the action associated with an activity is wholly the responsibility of a user, thus facilitating ad-hoc tasks. Such activities are always 'manual'.

Note that an activity class need not form part of any procedure schema. However, only through the procedure mechanism which groups activities into an identifiable unit, can the proper level of abstraction be achieved, allowing users to control and monitor long lived tasks. Using these concepts we distinguish three levels of support. Unstructured tasks are modelled as manual activities without associated programs (Level 1) with increasing structure leading to more automatic activities with associated programs (Level 2) and finally these activities being bound together into a procedure (Level 3).

Since procedure classes, procedures, activity classes and activities are FM entities, they can be queried using normal FML queries, For example,

```
SELECT Activity.FE.Number
WHERE  Activity.Activity_Class.Name = "Check_Contract"
AND    Activity.Status = "Enabled"
```

selects the focal entity (Contract) number of all activities of the 'Check_Contract' class that are now enabled for execution.

Despite wishing to avoid making major additions to FM, we have introduced the language OPL3 to specify a procedure class's schema. This language provides means to execute a set of activities sequentially ('BEGIN' statement, an example is given in Panel 5 of Figure 1), to start a number of activities in parallel ('COBEGIN' statement, see Panel 5), to repeat a statement list ('WHILE' statement), to proccess a set of entities in the same way ('FOREACH' statement) and to non-deterministically selects one, and only one, statement list of a set ('AWAIT' statement). An example of this last statement is :

```
AWAIT  <statement sequence 1>
  ||   <statement sequence 2> ...
AWEND
```

2.2. Office Procedure Control Language

The Office Procedure Control Language (OPCL) provides a set of statements to manage and control procedures and activities. These primitives provide the user with a means of activating/deactivating (LOAD/UNLOAD) procedure and activity classes, starting, ending, aborting and failing activity and procedure instances (START/END/ABORT/FAIL), and suspending and resuming (SUSPEND/RESUME) procedure instances. The syntax of these statements closely matches that of the FML Select statement. For example, the following statement starts the execution of all 'Register_Customer' activities whose application forms have been validated.

```
START   Activity
WHERE   Name = "Register_Customer"
AND     Application_Form.Status = "Validated"
```

Choosing such a syntax for OPCL statements simplifies the implementation since the FML compiler was easily modified to accept them.

Note that three statements are provided to terminate an activity. END indicates successful completion, ABORT implies an error in the execution of the activity, while FAIL may be called (by an appropriately privileged user) to terminate the execution of a range of activities.

Finally, a precondition is only monitored if the related activity or procedure class is LOADed as follows :

```
LOAD    Procedure_Class
WHERE   Name = "Customer_Audit"
```

This will initiate active monitoring of the classes precondition. To reduce complexity, LOADing a procedure has the side effect of loading any activity classes associated to it. UNLOADing a procedure UNLOADs any of its activities not also related to other loaded procedures. Panel 6 and 7 of Figure 1 provide some examples.

2.3. Integration of OP and Transaction Support

Like any other application, activities may use the OIS's locking and transaction support, described in [DOE87] [Ped88]. However, neither activities nor procedures are implicitly transactional, except in so far as all DML statements are transactions. Two potentially desirable features are not provided : locks and transactions that may span a number of activities in a procedure.

Providing the former would have required the implementation of persistent locks to cater for machine crashes. Instead, we rely on the access rights control mechanism whereby access to particular entities can be granted to users playing a given role in the office : this is by its nature presistent. This approach is less efficient, but it works well in an environment where most entities are either locked for short periods, or are controlled for an extended period by a user fulfilling a particular role within the office.

The provision of transaction rollback across activity boundaries would also overly complicate the implementation, and, in any case, is unlikely to be required often since activities are natural units of office work. If such rollback is required, it must be performed by the procedure itself, using compensating actions. This is made much easier, if all of the procedure's activities are written as transactions, and if the version management facilities are used.

To atomically update both the data changed by an activity and the persistent control of the procedure the activity is in, the END statement completes the activity and also commits any outstanding transactions. For completeness, the ABORT statement also aborts any outstanding transactions, but this is not strictly necessary as the transactions could be aborted by the ABORT_TRANSACTION statement and if a crash occurred before the END activity statement the activity would be aborted automatically by the system.

2.4. Comparison with Related Work

It is useful to consider the alternative ways in which the office procedure support might have been developed. The alternatives can be divided into conventional programming languages, database programming (or access) languages, persistent programming languages, and special purpose office modeling languages.

Conventional programming languages, would certainly have been powerful enough to describe office procedures, but would have suffered from many drawbacks. Not least among these is the notorious difficulty in accessing databases through embedded query languages like SQL or 'dynamic SQL'. In any case, development work would still have been required since most existing language extensions work with the relational model. Furthermore, the focal entity paradigm, precondition monitoring and the work of automatically starting procedures and stepping through them (starting activities) would also have had to be implemented. Similarly, persistence of control over office procedures would require additional work.

The second approach of using a **special purpose database access language** would have solved the first problem listed above, but none of the others. Examples of these include Pascal/R [Sch77] and DBPL [Mal83], both of which use the relational data model. A seemingly attractive combination would be a database access language and a trigger mechanism for monitoring preconditions. The resulting system would have lacked one important feature; the unit identity of office procedures. It is very beneficial to be able to view office procedures as a whole rather than just as collections of activities with triggers associated with each. Persistence of control would also have to be added. Languages such as Galileo would have provided an integrated semantic data modeling facility and programming language but the specific office procedure facilities would have to be added.

Recently, **active databases** such as HiPAC [Day89] have been developed. This system provides a trigger mechanism and could be a candidate to develop future OIS. Nevertheless, HiPAC would still have required the implementation of the whole procedure concept. It also insists that 'actions' (activities) must be transactional, while our system makes no such restriction.

Persistent programming languages (e.g. PS-ALGOL [PPR85], Napier) would have provided persistence of control. Procedures would be implemented as (active) objects that survived crashes. Again, precondition monitoring and further data modeling facilities, would have to be added. The 'await' statement in particular would have to be implemented and integrated into the system. An important consideration is that since we expect a large number of procedure and activity instances (but relatively few procedure classes) we cannot use a system that represents active objects by heavy-weight processes. Our system would only create a process per currently running activity, with other activities and procedures being represented only by non-volatile data. The main cost is in precondition monitoring, but this is shared among all instances of a procedure or activity class.

Finally, many **modelling languages** (e.g. Information Control Nets, Predicate Transition Networks, Office Analysis Methodology) are suitable for describing long lived work sequences; indeed our design has been heavily influenced by them. Our aim was to provide a more programmer oriented system that was integrated with a particular data model and to implement a system for running, monitoring and controlling office procedures rather than just describing them.

3. PRECONDITION SPECIFICATION AND MATCHING

Preconditions are expressed in a language very similar to the DML, actually a superset of it, giving a number of obvious advantages. For example the precondition

```
TEST INSERT  [Sale s, Customer FE]
     WHERE  s.amount > 5000
```

is similar to a DML INSERT statement (Section 2). This become a precondition when it is related to, say, an activity class through the [Activity_Class, Precondition] fact. It is fulfilled whenever a relationship is created between a customer and a sale worth over 5000. The special variable FE indicates that the focal entity of the activity to be created is to be the customer. Time constraints can be expressed using entities that represent the time and date.

When an update is made to the database, it is important to only evaluate preconditions that are directly related to the update. The update form (insert fact, delete entity, ...) is matched against the precondition forms, and the types of entities updated are also matched against those in preconditions. The correspondence is not purely syntactic since the type hierarchy must be taken into account. Also the above precondition can be fulfilled by inserting a new customer or sale, or changing an existing sale.

Figure 2 gives rules for matching update forms (u1..u6) to precondition forms (p1..p6). The notation used is : ai and ei denote entity classes; gi and fi denote functions. Thus ai.gj means the function gj applied to the entity ai (Section 2). $(ai.gj)^{-1}$ is the inverse function of ai.gj. G(ai) and S(ai) denote the sets of generalisations and specialisations of ai respectively. H(ai) denotes the union of G(ai) and S(ai). Comparison and set operators (=, <, >, IN,..) are denoted by op. Remember that in the general case, a fact like [g2:a1, g1:a2] defines functions a1.g1 -> a2 and a2.g2 -> a1 (see the Man-Woman example in section 2).

The semantics of updates imply : an entity insertion includes some fact insertions; an entity deletion includes some fact deletions; an assertion includes fact insertions and fact deletions. Consequently, a fact insertion precondition is matched by entity insertions and assertions, and a fact deletion precondition is matched by entity deletions and assertions.

To illustrate the matching rules assume the static schema shown in Fig. 1 Panel 1 extended with the definitions Vehicle: entity; Car_Salesman: Salesman; [Employee, Vehicle]. Salesman inherits the new fact so the function Salesman.Vehicle is valid. The only function defined on Vehicle is Vehicle.Employee; thus Vehicle.Salesman does not exist. Updates of the form INSERT Salesman WITH Vehicle, and ASSERT Salesman.Vehicle match preconditions of the form TEST INSERT [Employee, Vehicle]. The update ASSERT Salesman.Vehicle matches preconditions of the form TEST DELETE [Employee, Vehicle], and TEST ASSERT

UPDATE FORM

u1 - Entity Insertion
Create an instance of a1 with values for functions g1,...,gm
Insert a1
With g1 = ... **And** ...
And gm = ...

u2 - Fact Insertion
Create a fact between already existing entities
Insert [g2:a1, g1:a2]
From ...
Where ...

u3 - Specialisation Insertion
Insert existing entities from entity type a2 into a specialised entity type a1
Insert a1
From a2 **Where** ...

u4 - Entity Deletion
Delete a1 instances (implies deleting all facts of a1)
Delete a1
From ...
Where ...

u5 - Fact Deletion
Delete facts between entities a1, a2
Delete [g2:a1, g1:a2]
From ...
Where ...

u6 - Assertion
Change the values of functions a1.g1, ..., a1.gm
Assert a1.g1 = ...
... a1.gm = ...
From ...**Where** ...

PRECONDITION FORM

p1 - Entity Insertion
Test Insert e1
With f1 = ... **And** ...
And fn = ...

p2 - Fact Insertion
Test Insert [f2:e1, f1:e2]
From ...
Where ...

p3 - Specialisation Insertion
Test Insert e1
From e2
Where ...

p4 - Entity Deletion
Test Delete e1
From ...
Where ...

p5 - Fact Deletion
Test Delete [f2:e1, f1:e2]
From ...
Where ...

p6 - Assertion
Test Assert e1.f1 = ...
... e1.fm = ...
From ...**Where ...**

MATCH RULES

Rule for p1
p1 is matched by an update only if
1. the update form is u1 AND
2. e1 $\in$ {a1, G(a1)} AND
3. {f1, ...,fn} $\subset$ {g1, ...gm}

Rule for p2
p2 is matched by an update only if
(1. the update form is u2 AND
2. {e1.f1, e2.f2} $\equiv$ {H(a1).g1, H(a2).g2})
OR
(3. the update form is u1 AND
4. ($\exists$i) a1.gi $\in$ {e1.f1, e2.f2, S(e1).f1, S(e2).f2})
OR
(5. the update form is u6 AND
6. ($\exists$i) a1.gi $\in$ {H(e1).f1, H(e2).f2})

Rule for p3
p3 is matched by an update only if
1. the update form is u3 AND
2. e1 $\in$ {a1, G(a1)} AND
3. e2 $\in$ {a2, G(a2)}

Rule for p4
p4 is matched by an update only if :
1. the update form is u4 AND
2. e1 $\in$ {a1, G(a1)}

Rule for p5
p5 is matched by an update only if
(1. the update form is u5 AND
2. {e1.f1, e2.f2} $\equiv$ {H(a1).g1, H(a2).g2})
OR
(3. the update form is u4 AND
4. ($\exists$h) (a1.h $\in$ {H(e1).f1, e2.f2, S(e1).f1, S(e2).f2} AND {$(a1.h)^{-1}$, $(S(a1).h)^{-1}$} $\subset$ {e1.f1,e2.f2}))
OR
(5. the update form is u6 AND
6. ($\exists$i) a1.gi $\in$ {H(e1).f1, H(e2).f2})

Rule for p6
p3 is matched by an update only if
1. the update form is u6 AND
2. ($\exists$i) a1.gi $\in$ {H(e1).f1, $(H(e1).f1)^{-1}$ })

Figure n° 2 - Match Rules

Car_Salesman.Vehicle. Updates of the form DELETE Employee and DELETE Person match preconditions of the form TEST DELETE [Employee, Vehicle], and TEST DELETE Employee; but these precondition forms are not matched by updates of the form DELETE Salesman.

The kind of preconditions discussed above are called '**change preconditions**' because they are expressed in terms of database updates. It is also useful and convenient in many cases to be able to express preconditions purely in terms of databases states; this kind of preconditions is called '**state preconditions**' and the following is an example :

```
TEST STATE  Contrat
      WHERE Number = NULL
```

The general form of state preconditions is 'TEST STATE <type> WHERE <condition>' and they are fulfilled when the condition becomes true for an entity of this <type>. The difference in semantics with change preconditions is as follows. Once change preconditions become fulfilled they remain fulfilled until the associated activity or procedure is started. In other words, once the change has ocurred (and is committed) the precondition remains fulfilled. State preconditions on the other hand can be fulfilled and subsequently become false. The system reevaluates state preconditions before starting an activity. For manual activities this means that the system reevaluates the precondition when the START statement is executed. For automatic activities within a procedure, its state preconditions has to be rechecked when it becomes the current activity to run. Also, a state precondition will be tested on each iteration of the loop and will be fulfilled if the condition evaluates to true; in comparison repeated changes must occur to the database for a change condition to be repeatedly fulfilled. This difference between change and state preconditions desappears for procedures and automatic activities that are not part of any procedure.

Change and state preconditions are selected for evaluation and evaluated in the same way given that state conditions can only become true due to database updates.

4. IMPLEMENTATION OF OFFICE PROCEDURE SUPPORT

The OIS is a server providing services to the higher level parts of the automated office. Its interface, defined using the Courier RPC facility, centers mainly around an operation that passes a statement, in the form of a string, to the OIS and returns a response. The current prototype uses the facilities of a RDBMS (Oracle running on UNIX) to store the data definitions and extensional data; both normal and task information are stored in this way. This allows FM statements to be translated into SQL. A session process, which compiles queries and interprets the resulting object code, is created per active client application, and these share single instances of the manager processes shown in Fig 3. Data definition statements are translated into calls to either the Catalog Manager or the Office Procedure Catalog Manager. Data manipulation statements that query any data or modify only non-task data are translated into execution plans that are composed of SQL statements and operations on the Transaction Manager. These plans are executed by the session process's interpreter module. OPCL statements modify task states and are translated into calls to the OP Execution Manager which is responsible for the creation and controlling of activities and procedures as detailed in Section 4.2. Preconditions are monitored by the Precondition Evaluator which is actually part of each session process, as explained in Section 4.1.

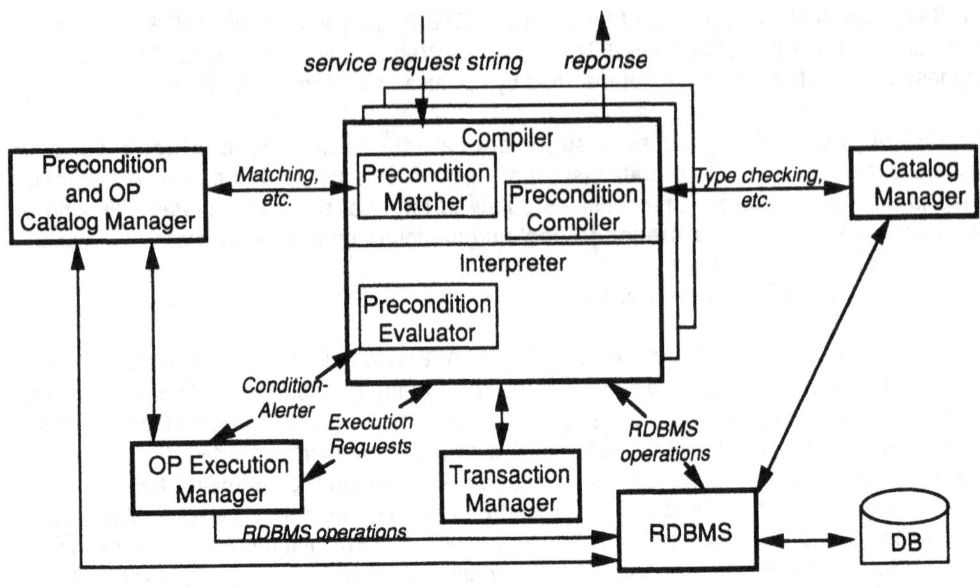

Figure n°3 - OIS Architecture

4.1 Precondition Processing

There are two aspects to precondition processing : **compilation** and **evaluation**. When an activity class is defined its precondition is compiled and stored in the Office Procedure Catalog. When an update is made on the database the subset of preconditions that could be fulfilled is determined and these are evaluated. Compilation reduces the work required for both the subset selection and the evaluation. Evaluation is integrated with the execution of the update in order to further reduce the cost of subset selection and to reduce the number of database accesses during evaluation. A prototype Precondition Evaluator has been implemented with the following features :

- Since the precondition language and FML are very similar language the FML compiler can be used to parse and perform semantic analysis as well as to generate the optimised selection statements needed for precondition evaluation.

- The compiled preconditions are buffered in main memory by the Office Procedure Catalog Manager.

- **Update compilation and precondition selection are integrated**. Compilation of update statements requires the translator to request schema and storage details from the catalog. This data is also required while matching preconditions and updates (Section 3), but since the Precondition Evaluator is part of each session process the data need only be requested once.

- Similarly **update execution and precondition evaluation are integrated** in the following ways :

a. Executing an update includes accessing the data to update which is in general the same data involved in the precondition. Therefore, this data is shared with the precondition evaluator to reduce database accesses.

b. The constants that appear in the updates and preconditions are used to help determine whether parts of the precondition are true or false without accessing the database.

c. In the case of deletion and modification (ASSERT) statements, a main memory recovery log is used to hold a 'before image' of the update information. This log is used by the Predicate Evaluator to further reduce database accesses.

- The clauses of a precondition are evaluated in order of increasing cost, where cost is a function of the complexity of the clause and whether it requires accessing data in the update statement, in the recovery log or in the database.

- During a transaction the precondition evaluator maintains a memory resident list of enabled activities (and their associated focal entities) that have been fulfilled by changes to the database made by the transaction. If the transaction aborts, the list is discarded (this occurs naturally if the system crashes). If it commits, the system writes the information concerning the newly enabled activities into the database and then notifies the OP Execution Manager using a 'Condition-Alerter' message (see section 4.2). The write operation is atomic with the commit of the transaction. Since a system crashmay occur before the 'Condition-Alerter' message has been processed, the OP Execution Manager retrieves the list of enabled activities from the database wheneverthe system reboots. There is no inheritance of locks from the transaction to the enabled activities since this would require the implementation of persistent locks (remember that the system could crash between the enabling of the activity and it actually starting). The protection facility can be used in some cases to provide an inefficient but conceptually clean alternative. Inheritance of locks is provided in HIPAC but unfortunately the commit of the transaction is delayed until all enabled activities have completed. We do support inheritance of locks from an application that starts a manual activity to the activity itself (Section 4.2).

4.2. Execution and Control of Activities and Procedures

The Office Procedure Execution Manager is responsible for

- controlling the enabling and starting of activities and procedures, and storing their status in a relation so that it can be queried by itself as well as by applications,
- maintaining persistent threads of control within office procedure instances.

The first main function is to process messages of two types

a. **Condition-Alerts** from the Precondition Evaluator informing it that a new activity/procedure is to be created because a precondition has become true for a particular entity (which becomes the focal entity for the activity/procedure). If the condition alert concerns a manual activity it awaits a START statement from an application. Alternatively, if it is an automatic activity the OP Execution Manager issues an internal START statement with the effect described in point (b) below. Finally, if it is a procedure (all procedures are automatic) it is marked as 'started' and its first activity is run if this is automatic and has no precondition. If its first activity is not of this form it is treated as described later.

b. Execution Requests from the interpreter as part of the execution of OPCL statements. As an example, when a request to start an activity is received its status is updated to 'started' and a process is created to run the associated 'Program', if it exists. There is a special value of 'Site-Name' that indicates that the activity should be run on the same machine as the application that invokes the START statement and inherit locks from it.

The second main function of the OP Execution Manager is the maintenance of **multiple threads of control** in multiple instances of an office procedure class. When a procedure is defined (Section 2.1) a schema tree is generated and stored that describes its OPL3 program. When the OP Execution Manager is informed that an activity has completed, it determines the next activity to run using the schema tree for the activity's procedure class. If this has a state precondition it immediately evaluates the precondition (by making a SELECT on the database). If the activity has a change precondition, then the OP Execution Manager determines if it is 'enabled' by searching the list of enabled activities maintained in the database. If found to be enabled, the activity is started if automatic, or if manual it awaits a START statement. If not, it awaits a 'Condition-Alerter' from the Precondition Evaluator before 'enabling' or 'starting' the activity.

Initially, a newly created instance has one thread of control (in effect, the number of a node in the schema tree), but use of the Cobegin or For statements require the system to maintain a set of threads per instance, and join multiple threads into one on completion of these parallel statements. A complexity that arises here is that two threads in a set could concurrently refer to different nodes that none the less contain activities of the same activity class. If the focal entities are also the same then it is unclear whether to run the activity twice, or just once and in the latter case whether to progress both threads or just one. We have decided to run it once and progress both threads, but realise that it would be better to have postconditions associated with the activities and only progress the threads if the postconditions become true. There is also an enforced restriction that prevents an activity class being stand-alone as well as being used in a procedure. An activity class can however appear in any number of procedure classes.

5. CONCLUSION

A number of improvements could be made to the current system. Possibly, the most serious is the lack of finer control over procedures. This would enable an appropriately privileged user to allow an instance of a procedure to follow a different path than that described in its schema, for example to skip an activity or go back to a previous state. This might be necessary to handle unforeseen circumstances or exceptions. Another area requiring further study is the modification of a procedure's schema when there are instances in existence (but perhaps not currently running). The system, though easy for programmers to use, is not suitable in itself for use by non-programmers. A graphical front-end may well increase its suitability, but such considerations are outside the scope of the project.

Though there are advantages in allowing activities to be written in any language, it may also be interesting to investigate a single language providing all of the advantages of OPL3 (see section 2.1) and those of a conventional programming language.

Acknowledgment

This work was partly funded by the CEC Esprit Programme. We would like to thank the rest of the DOEOIS project team at Bull, TCD, ICL, Fh.G., LGI IMAG and Univ of Stuttgart. In particular Guy Standen, Michael Rathgeb, Ann Barry, Christian Lenne and Esperanza Pedraza. We gratefully acknowledge the comments made by the paper's reviewer.

6. REFERENCES

[Ant89] Francisca Antunes, Mauricio Lopez; "A Mechanism for Efficient Evaluation of Activity Preconditions in a Database Environment"; 5th Base de Données Avancées Conf., Genève, 26-28 Sept. 89

[Bra83] G. Bracchi, B. Pernici; "SOS : A Conceptual Model for Office Information Systems"; Proc. ACM SIGMOD Conf., San Jose, California, 83; Also SOGMOD RECORD Vol. 18, N° 2, pp. 251-224, Sept. 86

[Ber88] Paul Berard, Claudia Jiminez, José Valdeni de Lima, Jean Pierre Martin; "Traitement des documents dans l'OIS. Spécifications Version1"; DOEOIS : ESPRIT Project 231, BUL-DH-10.01 Mars 88

[Chu84] K. L. Chung; "An Extended TAXIS Compiler"; M. Sc. Thesis, Dept. of Computer Science, University of Toronto, Jan.84; Also CSRG Technical Note 37, 84

[Cau88] Brian Caulfield; "Office Procedure Manual"; DOEOIS : ESPRIT Project 231, OIS-OP-01.0, Jan. 88

[Day89] Umeshwar dayal, dennis R. McCarthy; "The Architecture of an Active Data Base Management System"; Proc. ACM-SIGMOD Conf., Portland, Oregon, May31-June 2

[DOE87] DOEOIS; "OIS Transaction Support"; DOEOIS : ESPRIT Project 231, Apr. 87

[Ell79] C. A. Ellis; "Information Control Nets : A Mathmatical Model for Office Information Flow"; Conference on Simulation, Measurement and Modelling of Computer Science, pp. 152-168, Boulder, Aug. 79

[Ham83] M. Hammer, S. R. Kunin, M. A. Sirbu, J. B. Sutherland, C. L. Zarmer; "Office Analysis : Methodology and Case Studies"; Report MIT/LCS/TR-289, Massachusetts Institute of Technology, Laboratory for Computer Science, 83

[Lop87] Mauricio Lopez; "Data Definition and Data Manipulation Services"; DOEOIS : ESPRIT Project 231, OIS-DM-01, Jan.87

[Mal83] M. Mall, J.W. Schmidt; "Abstraction Mechanism for Database Programming"; ACM SIGPLAN Vol. 18, N° 6 June 83

[Ped88] Esperanza Pedraza; "SGBDs Sémantiques pour un Environment Bureautique : Intégrité et Gestion des Transactions"; Thèse de Docteur Ingénieur, Université Joseph Fourrier, Grenoble, Nov. 88

[PPR85] Persistent Programming Research Group; "The PS-Algol Reference Manual"; 2nd Ed. Tech. Report PPR-12-85, Dept of Computer Science , Univ. of Glasgow, Glasgow 85

[Sac86] G. Sacco; "The Fact Model : a Semantic Model for Complex Databases"; ESPRIT : DOEOIS Project 231, OIS-DM-01.0, Sept. 86; Proc.ETW Conf., Sept. 87

[Sch77] J. W. Schmidt; "Some High Level Language Constructs for Data of Type Relation"; ACM Trans. Database Systems, Vol. 2, N° 3, pp 147-261, Sept. 77

[Shi81] David W. Shipman; "The Functional Data Model and the Data Language DAPLEX"; ACM Transactions on database Systems, Vol. 6, N° 1, pp. 140-173, Mars 81

[Sir82] M. A. Sirbu and al.; "OAM : An Office Analysis Methodology"; Office Automation Conf. Digest, AFIPS, 82

The Reuse and Modification of Rulebases by Predicate Substitution

Anthony J. Bonner Tomasz Imielinski

Rutgers University
Department of Computer Science
New Brunswick, NJ 08903
United States

Abstract

We propose a method for reusing and modifying a deductive database. The need for such techniques occurs when new rulebased applications differ only slightly from existing ones or when an application is to be incrementally updated. Such techniques are particularly important when reprogramming is expensive or unreliable. In order to facilitate reuse we extend deductive database systems by the concept of predicate substitution. In this way, during query evaluation, not only variables, but also predicates can be substituted. Substitution increases the expressive power of Datalog. Not only does data complexity increase from *PTIME* to *EXPTIME*, but substitution also allows large sets of Datalog rules to be succinctly expressed. The paper provides a proof and model theory for this language, including a fixpoint semantics.

1 Introduction

This paper proposes a method for reusing and modifying a deductive database. The need for such techniques occurs when new rulebased applications differ only slightly from existing ones or when an application is to be incrementally updated. Such techniques are particularly important when reprogramming is expensive or unreliable. Unfortunately, these issues have not yet received significant attention in the deductive database literature. This paper attempts to address them.

We focus on a particular class of modifications which we call *predicate substitutions*. The idea is to reuse and modify a set of rules by substituting one predicate symbol for another. To this end, we introduce a modal-like notation $A(x)[P/Q]$ which we call a *predicate with substitution*. Intuitively, this expression means, "replace P by Q in the definition of A". To take the simplest example, suppose that A is defined by the following rules:

$$A(x) \leftarrow B(x,y), P(x), P(y).$$
$$A(x) \leftarrow C(x), P(x).$$

where B and C are base predicates. Then the expression $A(x)[P/Q]$ is treated a new predicate symbol defined by the following rules.

$$A(x)[P/Q] \leftarrow B(x,y), Q(x), Q(y).$$
$$A(x)[P/Q] \leftarrow C(x), Q(x).$$

Conceptually, these rules are generated automatically and do not have to be supplied by the user.

Like ordinary predicates, predicates with substitution can be used in the body of rules, as in the rule $B(x) \leftarrow A(x)[P/Q]$. In the case when A is defined by a large number of rules, generating the definition of $A(x)[P/Q]$ by hand could be an expensive and unreliable task. Additionally, it could double the size of the rulebase. In this way, rules with substitution can be viewed as a short-hand notation for describing rulebases without substitution. This conciseness is achieved by reusing and modifying rule sets, possibly many times. In fact, by having recursion through substitution, it is possible to reuse and modify rules an unbounded number of times. Using this idea, we show that a *finite* set of rules with substitution can describe an *infinite* set of rules without.

We believe that substitution is a principle which can be applied to logic-based languages generally in order to facilitate reuse and modification. In this paper, however, we focus on Horn logics and on Datalog in particular. Several examples are given to illustrate the idea of substitution and its utility. Substitution is then defined precisely and an inference system is developed for Horn rules with substitution.

The issue of semantics is also addressed. First, a semantics is developed in which Horn rulebases *without* substitution are the models for Horn rulebases *with* substitution. This captures, in a model-theoretic way, the view of this paper: that rulebases with substitution are a short-hand notation for rulebases without. The inference system for substitution is shown to be sound and complete with respect to this semantics.

As in the theory of Horn logic [8, 1], we complement the model-theoretic semantics with a fixpoint semantics. We define a monotonic "T-operator" which can be applied to a rulebase in a bottom-up fashion, generating the minimal model (or least fixpoint) piece-by-piece. In Horn logic, the T-operator takes a database as input and returns another database as output. In our logic, the T-operator takes a Horn rulebase as input and returns another Horn rulebase as output. Starting with the empty rulebase, the T-operator is applied over-and-over again until the minimal model is generated. Each application of the operator expands rules with substitution into equivalent Horn rules. If there is recursion through substitution, it may take infinitely many applications to generate all the Horn rules in the minimal model. Because the operator is continuous, however, any particular Horn rule will be generated in a finite number of applications. In this way, the Horn rules represented by a rulebase with substitution can be materialized.

In the function-free case, predicate substitution increases the power of Horn logic. Whereas the complexity of Datalog (i.e., function-free Horn logic) is complete for PTIME, the complexity of Datalog augmented with substitution is complete for EXPTIME. Although a proof of this result is beyond the scope of this paper, we present an example showing that the data complexity is NP-hard. Syntactically, this boost in expressive power comes about from recursion through substitution. Semantically, this increased power has an interesting interpretation: When a Datalog rulebase with substitution is EXPTIME-complete, it represents an *infinite* Datalog rulebase *without* substitution. Furthermore, this infinite Datalog rulebase is not equivalent to any finite one. In such cases, substitution provides an extremely concise notation for representing a set of Datalog rules.

1.1 Applications

In this section, we present an example of how predicate substitution can be used, and we discuss several other possible applications. In the example, a module of rules for solving a graph problem is described. The idea is to reuse and modify this general-purpose module in order to solve certain problems in airline flight reservations.

Let G be a weighted graph in which each edge has an associated cost. Given a path between two nodes, the cost of the path is the sum of the weights on each edge. Let R be a set of rules which for any pair of nodes x and y, computes the minimum cost of all the paths from x to y. The rules R will have two base predicates (i.e., input predicates): $Edge(x, y)$, meaning that there is an edge from x to y in the graph; and $Weight(x, y, w)$, meaning that the edge from x to y has weight w. The output predicate of R is $MinCost(x, y, w)$ where w is the minimum cost of a path from node x to node y.

Suppose now that we wish to use the set of rules R in an airline reservation system. The graph G now represents flight connections in the United States. We would like to reuse the rules R for many different notions of cost. In particular, we would like to know the following three parameters for the connections between Tucson, Arizona and Bismarck, North Dakota: (*i*) the smallest number of stopovers, (*ii*) the minimum flying time, and (*iii*) the minimum price. For this purpose, we can reuse the module R, substituting the following predicates for the predicate $Weight$:

- $W_1(x, y, w)$ where w is 1 if x and y are directly connected, and 0 otherwise. In this case, we want to calculate the minimum number of stopovers.
- $W_2(x, y, w)$ where w is the price of a direct flight from x to y (here we assume that the global cost of the connection is a sum of individual costs). In this case, we want to calculate the minimum price.
- $W_3(x, y, w)$ where w is the flying time for a direct flight from x to y. In this case, we want to calculate the minimum flying time.

Using these three different predicates, we can reuse the minimum-cost module by simply writing the following rules:

$$MinStopovers(x, y, w) \leftarrow MinCost(x, y, w)[Weight/W_1]$$
$$MinPrice(x, y, w) \leftarrow MinCost(x, y, w)[Weight/W_2]$$
$$MinFlyingTime(x, y, w) \leftarrow MinCost(x, y, w)[Weight/W_3]$$

In each case, the rules in the module R are copied and modified so that $Weight$ is replaced by W_i. In this way, a possibly complex and large module R does not have to be rewritten every time it is reused.

The above example is typical of a class of applications in which a module is to be used repeatedly with different inputs. In such cases, we simply "plug in" different definitions for the base predicates of the module. In this way, for instance, a module for matrix multiplication could be reused many times for different types of matrices or even different types of multiplication (integer, real, complex, etc.)

In addition, rules with substitution seem well suited to the reuse and modification of expert database systems. Such systems have a variety of applications, such as computer-based medical and legal consultation systems. Kowalski and Sergot, for instance, have encoded the British Nationality Act in Prolog, and McCarty and

Sridharan have developed expert systems for reasoning about contract law and corporate tax law [5]. As laws are amended, such systems have to be updated. For instance, sections of the income tax act could be amended to treat residents as citizens. In this case, every occurrence of "citizen" could be replaced by a new predicate meaning "citizen or resident". Similarly, other bodies of law could be amended to replace the predicate "male" by "person". Such updates could easily be expressed and implemented with predicate substitutions.

The need to often reuse and modify existing rule bases occurs in rulebased specifications of the operations of large enterprises, such as big corporations, computer operating systems or various legal systems, such as tax-law, citizenship law etc. When changes are small, it simply does not make sense to rewrite possibly-huge rulebased specifications. It is definitely more attractive to reuse as much as possible of the old definition.

From the above examples it may appear that adding the principle of substitution does not increase the expressive power of a language. We show later that this is not the case. In fact, the data complexity of Datalog with substitution is complete for EXPTIME. To illustrate this increased power, section 2.2 shows a set of rules which use recursion through predicate substitution to solve an NP-complete problem—a task impossible for Datalog, unless P = NP.

2 Inference with Predicate Substitution

This section formalizes the notion of predicate substitution. In particular, the syntax of predicates and rules with substitution is defined and an inference system is described. The description of inference is initially informal and is given in terms of a copy-and-substitute mechanism. Several examples are presented. Finally, the mechanism is defined precisely and an axiomatization is given.

Definition 1 *Every atomic formula is a predicate with substitution. Furthermore, if α is a predicate with substitution, then so is $\alpha[P/Q]$, where P and Q are predicate symbols of equal arity.*

Expressions of the form $[P/Q]$ shall be called *predicate substitutions*, or simply *substitutions*. They should be distinguished from the more familiar form of substitution in which terms are substituted for variables. For instance, in the expression $\{u/f(x), v/y\}$, the terms $f(x)$ and y are to be substituted for the variables u and v, resp. We call these expressions *term substitutions* to distinguish them from predicate substitutions. Throughout this paper, the symbol $[\theta]$ shall denote a predicate substitution and σ shall denote a term substitution.

Definition 2 *(Rules) A rule with substitution is an expression of the form $\beta \leftarrow \beta_1 ... \beta_k$ where β and each β_i are predicates with substitution. If β is atomic, then the rule is called a Horn rule with substitution.*

From the database perspective, a rulebased system consists of two parts: a set of rules, called the *rulebase*; and a set of ground atomic formulas, called the *database*. This dichotomy leads naturally to two types of relations: *base relations* and *derived relations*. A base relation is defined by the database, and an derived relation is defined by the rulebase. The division of relations in this way is common in deductive databases. Furthermore, by separating the rulebase from the database in this way, we are able to treat the rulebase as a mapping from base relations to derived relations. Substitution is then a composition of one map with another.

To represent these two types of relations, we use two types of predicate symbols: base and derived. Base predicate symbols are used to construct the atomic formulas in the database but may not appear in the heads of rules. Conversely, derived predicate symbols may appear in the heads of rules but may not appear in the database.

We treat predicates with substitution as derived predicates. For instance, the expression $A(x)[P/Q]$ is treated as just another derived predicate. This predicate has a special meaning however: The rules defining $A(x)[P/Q]$ must be identical to the rules defining $A(x)$ except that P is replaced everywhere by Q.

To be more precise, we define the intension of $A(x)[P/Q]$ in terms of a copy-and-substitute mechanism. First, we copy all the rules in the rulebase, and in this copy, each predicate $B(x)$ is given a new name $B(x)[P/Q]$.[1] In this way, the original rulebase and its copy can co-exist as a single rulebase without interfering with each other. Second, each occurrence of $P(\overline{x})[P/Q]$ in the premises of these rules is replaced by $Q(\overline{x})$. In this way, substitution is carried out. Finally, for all base predicates $B(\overline{x})$, the new predicate $B(\overline{x})[P/Q]$ is replaced by $B(\overline{x})$. In this way, the new rulebase is able to access the database. The result is a rulebase which is identical to the original except that P has been replaced everywhere by Q; and instead of defining $A(x)$, the new rulebase defines $A(x)[P/Q]$, for every derived predicate A.

[1]We could equally well use the notation $B'(x)$ instead of $B(x)[P/Q]$. The latter notation simply provides a systematic way of providing new and distinct predicate names for each substitution.

Example 1. Let S be the following rulebase, where B and C are base predicates:

$$A(x) \leftarrow B(x), P(x).$$
$$A(x) \leftarrow C(x,y), P(x), P(y).$$

Then the expression $A(x)[P/Q]$ is treated a new predicate symbol defined by the following rules.

$$A(x)[P/Q] \leftarrow B(x), Q(x).$$
$$A(x)[P/Q] \leftarrow C(x,y), Q(x), Q(y).$$

Notice that the definition of $A(x)[P/Q]$ is identical to the definition of $A(x)$ except that P has been replaced by Q in the premise of every rule. Conceptually, these rules are generated automatically; and in particular, they do not have to be supplied by the user. □

The above example is the simplest possible in that there is only one derived predicate and no recursion. The next two examples illustrate the substitute-and-copy mechanism for slightly more complex rulebases.

Example 2. Let S be the following rulebase, where C and D are base predicates:

$$A(x) \leftarrow P(x), C(x,y), B(y).$$
$$B(x) \leftarrow D(x,y), P(y).$$

Then the predicates $A(x)[P/Q]$ and $B(x)[P/Q]$ are defined by the following rules:

$$A(x)[P/Q] \leftarrow Q(x), C(x,y), B(y)[P/Q].$$
$$B(x)[P/Q] \leftarrow D(x,y), Q(y).$$

Since these rules are to be treated classically, we can make the following inference:

$$A(x)[P/Q] \leftarrow Q(x), C(x,y), D(y,z), Q(z).$$

□

Example 3. Let S be the following rulebase, where C is a base predicate:

$$A(x) \leftarrow P(x), C(x,y), A(y)$$
$$A(x) \leftarrow P(x)$$

The following rules then define the predicate $A(x)[P/Q]$:

$$A(x)[P/Q] \leftarrow Q(x), C(x,y), A(y)[P/Q]$$
$$A(x)[P/Q] \leftarrow Q(x)$$

Since these rules are to be treated classically, we can make the following inferences (among others):

$$A(x)[P/Q] \leftarrow Q(x), C(x,y), Q(y)$$
$$A(x)[P/Q] \leftarrow Q(x), C(x,y), Q(y), C(y,z), Q(z)$$

□

The idea of copying rules, renaming predicates and making substitutions applies to Horn rulebases with substitution as well as to those without. Furthermore, the idea can be applied recursively; that is, once predicates such as $A(x)[P/Q]$ have been defined, they can be used to define more complex predicates such as $A(x)[P/Q][R/S]$. These two ideas are illustrated in the next example.

Example 4. Let S be the following rulebase, where Q and R are base predicates:

$$A(x) \leftarrow B(x)[P/Q]$$
$$B(x) \leftarrow P(x), R(x).$$

We then get the following rules:

$$A(x)[R/S] \leftarrow B(x)[P/Q][R/S]$$
$$B(x)[P/Q] \leftarrow Q(x), R(x).$$
$$B(x)[P/Q][R/S] \leftarrow Q(x), S(x).$$

Since these rules are to be treated classically, we can make the following inferences:

$$A(x) \leftarrow Q(x), R(x).$$
$$A(x)[R/S] \leftarrow Q(x), S(x).$$

□

The copy-and-substitute mechanism outlined above describes informally the idea of substitution for Horn rules with substitution. The following definition makes the idea precise.

Definition 3 *Let S be a Horn rulebase with substitution. Then S^* is the set of rules with substitution constructed from S as follows:*[2]

1. *$S \subseteq S^*$*
2. *If $\beta \leftarrow \beta_1 ... \beta_n$ is in S^*, then $\beta[\theta] \leftarrow \beta_1[\theta]...\beta_n[\theta]$ is in S^* for every predicate substitution $[\theta]$.*
3. *The rule $P(\overline{x})[P/Q] \leftarrow Q(\overline{x})$ is in S^* for every substitution $[P/Q]$.*
4. *The rule $B(\overline{x})[P/Q] \leftarrow B(\overline{x})$ is in S^* for every substitution $[P/Q]$ and every base predicate $B \neq P$.*

The second item in the definition of S^* ensures that for every rule defining β there is a copy of the rule in S^* defining $\beta[\theta]$. The third item carries out the substitution $[P/Q]$, so that every occurrence of $P(\overline{x})[P/Q]$ is replaced by $Q(\overline{x})$. The fourth item ignores the substitution when it is applied to base predicates not equal to P, so that every occurrence of $B(\overline{x})[P/Q]$ is replaced by $B(\overline{x})$. The rulebase S^* thus represents the result of all possible copy-and-substitute operations. As such, it provides a complete definition of all possible predicates with substitution.

It is not enough, however, to simply generate Horn rules. To be useful, a rulebase must be augmented with a database and the rules used to infer new atomic formulas. Having generated S^*, we now treat it as a set of Horn rules and apply it to a database using classical inference.

Definition 4 *Suppose β is a predicate with substitution, S is a Horn rulebase with substitution,*

[2]To be precise, S^* is the smallest set of rules closed under these operations.

and DB is a database. Then,[3]

$$\mathcal{S}, DB \vdash \beta \quad \textit{iff} \quad \mathcal{S}^* \cup DB \vdash_c \beta$$

Example 5. Suppose DB consists of the atoms $Q(a)$, $S(a)$, $Q(b)$, $R(b)$, $P(b)$. Applying rulebase $\mathcal{S}$ from example 4 to this database gives the following inferences (among others):

$$\mathcal{S}, DB \vdash A(b) \qquad \mathcal{S}, DB \vdash A(a)[P/Q]$$
$$\mathcal{S}, DB \vdash B(b)$$

□

The set of rules $\mathcal{S}^*$ is infinite and contains an infinite number of distinct predicate symbols. As the next example shows, this is because substitution is not idempotent; that is, in general, $A(x)[B/C][B/C]$ is not the same as $A(x)[B/C]$. Thus, from a finite set of predicate symbols, it is possible to create new and distinct predicates whose names have arbitrarily length, such as $A(x)[B/C][B/C][B/C]$. Because of this, $\mathcal{S}^*$ contains an infinite number of distinct predicate symbols and is itself infinite.

Example 6. Suppose $\mathcal{S}$ consists of the following two rules, where B and P are base predicates:

$$A(x) \leftarrow P(x)$$
$$Q(x) \leftarrow B(x,y), P(y)$$

The predicates $A(x)[P/Q]$, $A(x)[P/Q][P/Q]$ and $A(x)[P/Q][P/Q][P/Q]$ are then defined as follows:

$$A(x)[P/Q] \leftarrow Q(x)$$
$$A(x)[P/Q][P/Q] \leftarrow B(x,y), Q(y)$$
$$A(x)[P/Q][P/Q][P/Q] \leftarrow B(x,y), B(y,z), Q(z)$$

In general, the definition of $A(x)[P/Q]^i$ is different from the definition of $A(x)[P/Q]^{i+1}$, and so they denote distinct predicates. In other words, substitution is not idempotent. □

[3]In this definition and in the rest of the paper, the symbol $\vdash_c$ denotes classical inference, where all free variables are universally quantified.

2.1 An Axiomatization

Because $\mathcal{S}^*$ is infinite, its value is largely conceptual; that is, it provides a concise definition of inference with substitution. To actually perform inference, however, it is impractical to first generate $\mathcal{S}^*$ and then invoke classical inference procedures. This section offers a more practical alternative by providing a finite axiomatization which is sound and complete. The inference system below can be operated in either a top-down or a bottom-up manner. When operated top-down, it attempts only those substitutions which are relevant to proving its current goal.

Lemma 1 *Let β be a predicate with substitution, $\mathcal{S}$ a Horn rulebase with substitution, and DB a database. Then $\mathcal{S}, DB \vdash \beta$ iff β can be inferred from the following inference system:*

Axioms:

1. *For every substitution $[P/Q]$,* $P(\bar{x})[P/Q] \leftarrow Q(\bar{x})$
2. *For every substitution $[P/Q]$ and every base predicate $B \neq P$,* $B(\bar{x})[P/Q] \leftarrow B(\bar{x})$
3. *Every rule in $\mathcal{S}$.*
4. *Every atomic formula in DB.*

Inference Rules:

1. *For any predicate substitution $[\theta]$,*
$$\frac{\beta \leftarrow \beta_1 ... \beta_n}{\beta[\theta] \leftarrow \beta_1[\theta] ... \beta_n[\theta]}$$
2. *For any term substitution σ,*
$$\frac{\beta \leftarrow \beta_1 ... \beta_n}{(\beta \leftarrow \beta_1 ... \beta_n)\sigma}$$
3. *Modus Ponens:*
$$\frac{\beta_1 \; ... \; \beta_n \qquad \beta \leftarrow \beta_1 ... \beta_n}{\beta}$$

Given a predicate β, the first inference rule effectively makes copies of the rules defining β in order to derive rules defining $\beta[\theta]$. The first two axioms come directly from the definition of S^*. The other axioms and inference rules are familiar from classical logic: the second inference rule makes all instances of a rule available for inference, and the third rule applies rules to atomic facts to infer more atomic facts.

2.2 The Power of Substitution

In the function-free case, predicate substitution increases the power of Horn logic. Whereas the complexity of Datalog (i.e., function-free Horn logic) is complete for PTIME, the complexity of Datalog augmented with substitution is complete for EXPTIME. Syntactically, this boost in expressive power comes about from recursion through substitution. Although a proof of this result is beyond the scope of this paper, this section presents an example in which rules with predicate substitution are used to solve an NP-complete problem—a task impossible for Datalog, unless P = NP.

Given a combinational circuit (i.e., a logic network without feedback), it is NP-complete to determine whether the output of the circuit can ever have the value 1.[4] We construct a Datalog program with substitution that generates all possible input values and computes the output value for each one. The program has three parts: (*i*) a set of Horn rules which evaluates the output of the circuit for a given set of input values, (*ii*) a set of Horn rules which generates the next input set from the current input set, and (*iii*) a set of rules with substitution that replaces the current input set with the next input set.

[4] The satisfiability of propositional formulas can be reduced to this problem in a straightforward way.

The circuit itself is encoded as a database. There are many ways in which this can be done. For instance, constant symbols can denote wires and predicates can denote circuit connections. Thus, the predicate $Nor(x, y, z)$ could mean that wire x is the output of a nor-gate whose input wires are y and z. Similarly, the values on wires can be represented by the binary predicate $Val(x, y)$, which means that wire x has value y, where y is either 0 or 1.

(*i*) Given such a representation of the circuit and a set of input values, it is not difficult to write a set of Datalog rules to compute the output value of the circuit. In particular one can define a zero-ary predicate $Test$ which is true iff the output value is 1. For each circuit, the value of $Test$ will depend upon the circuit's input values, that is, upon the predicate $Val(x, y)$. The rules defining $Test$ are independent of the database (i.e., of the circuit).

(*ii*) If the circuit contains n input lines, then any set of input values can be encoded as an n-bit binary number. Thus, to generate all possible input sets, we can build a binary counter from 0 to $2^n - 1$. Each input line then corresponds to a binary digit. Suppose that u_i is the value of the ith input line. The entire input to the circuit is then represented by the binary number $u_1...u_n$, which is represented by the following atomic formulas:

$$Val(a_1, u_1),\ Val(a_2, u_2)\ ...\ Val(a_n, u_n)$$

where a_i denotes the ith input line. We use the predicate $Val^+(x, y)$ to represent the successor of the binary number represented by Val. In particular, if $v_1...v_n$ is the successor of $u_1...u_n$, then it is represented by the following atomic formulas:

$$Val^+(a_1, v_1),\ Val^+(a_2, v_2)\ ...\ Val^+(a_n, v_n)$$

It is not difficult to write a set of Datalog rules which given the relation Val will generate the relation Val^+. In this way, given a binary number, we can increment it by one.

By using predicate substitution, we can compute larger increments. For instance, the predicate $Val^+[Val/Val^+]$ increments the binary number Val by two. The rules defining this predicate are identical to the rules defining Val^+ except that all the predicates are given new names, and in particular, the predicate Val is replaced by Val^+. Thus, $Val^+[Val/Val^+]$ is computed from Val^+, which in turn is computed from Val. In this way, the Horn rules for computing a single increment are reused and modified to produce rules which compute a double increment.

The substitution $[Val/Val^+]$ can be applied over and over again to produce rules for computing larger and larger increments. Thus, the predicates $Val^+[Val/Val^+]$, and $Val^+[Val/Val^+][Val/Val^+]$ represent increments of two and three, resp. Conceptually, each additional application of the substitution $[Val/Val^+]$ generates a new copy of the rules defining Val^+, with the output of one copy being used as the input for the next. Each such copy produces an additional increment of one.

(*iii*) Given a set of input values, the Horn rules described in (*i*) infer the atom $Test$ iff the output of the circuit is 1. By using the rules in (*ii*) and predicate substitution, we can test the output value of the circuit for any subsequent set of input values. For instance, the predicate $Test[Val/Val^+]$ is true iff the output of the circuit is 1 on the *next* set of input values.

If the predicate Val represents the number 0, then we can test the circuit for all input values. For instance, suppose the circuit has four input lines, each of them 0. $Test$ is then true iff the output is 1 on the input 0000. In addition, $Test[Val/Val^+]$ is true iff the output is 1 on the input 0001, and $Test[Val/Val^+][Val/Val^+]$ is true iff the output is 1 on input 0010. In general, the predicate $Test[Val/Val^+]^i$ is true iff the output of the circuit is 1 when the input is i (in binary). In this way, we can test the output of the circuit for any set of consecutive input values. The following four rules, for example, infer the atom Sat iff the output of the circuit is 1 for one of the input sets 0000, 0001, 0010 or 0011.

$$Sat \leftarrow Test$$
$$Sat \leftarrow Test[Val/Val^+]$$
$$Sat \leftarrow Test[Val/Val^+][Val/Val^+]$$
$$Sat \leftarrow Test[Val/Val^+][Val/Val^+][Val/Val^+]$$

By using recursion through substitution, it is possible to test the circuit for all possible input sets. The rules below do precisely this. In particular, they infer the atom Sat iff the output of the circuit is 1 for some set of inputs.

$$Sat \leftarrow Sat[Val/Val^+]$$
$$Sat \leftarrow Test$$

Intuitively, this recursion can be unfolded to produce an infinite set of Datalog rules. For instance, the first four levels of recursion produce the four Datalog rules above plus a Datalog definition of the predicates $Test[Val/Val^+]^i$. After unfolding, each of these predicates is treated as a predicate of classical logic. In this way, the definitions of $Test$ and Val^+ are reused and modified over and over again to produce an infinitely large Datalog rulebase.

Notice that there is no *finite* set of Datalog rules which is equivalent to this rulebase, unless P = NP. This is because the above rules with substitution solve an NP-complete problem, whereas Datalog rules can only solve problems in P. In this way, substitution offers a succinct notation for describing Horn rulebases. In this case, a finite rulebase with substitution describes an infinite Datalog rulebase.

3 Horn Semantics

Given a set of Horn rules S *without* substitution, it is relatively clear what the rulebase S^* means. For such rulebases, the copy-and-substitute mechanism of definition 3 produces a set of Horn rules for $A(x)[B/C]$ in terms of the Horn rules for $A(x)$. Intuitively, the definition of $A(x)[P/Q]$ is identical to that of $A(x)$ except that P is replaced everywhere by Q. The meaning is less clear, however, when the rulebase S contains rules with substitution, especially when there is recursion through substitution. In the rule $A(x) \leftarrow B(x,y), A(y)[P/Q]$, for instance, the definitions of $A(x)$ and of $A(x)[P/Q]$ are circular. What does the expression $A(x)[P/Q]$ mean in such cases? Section 2 provided a proof-theoretic meaning. This section provides a model-theoretic one.

3.1 Models and Entailment

A model in our semantics is a Horn rulebase (without substitution). Not only do such rulebases provide a non-circular definition for predicates with substitution, they also support the idea that a rulebase with substitution is a shorthand notation for a (possibly larger) Horn rulebase, which the user might have written had he had the time, space and inclination.

Definition 5 *An interpretation is a set R of Horn rules without substitution.*

Rules with substitution are intended to be a shorthand notation for a set of Horn rules. Suppose, for instance, that S contains the rule $A(x) \leftarrow B(x)[P/Q]$. S^* then determines how this rule can be expanded into Horn rules. In particular, suppose that S^* contains the following two rules, where f is a unary function symbol:

$$B(x)[P/Q] \leftarrow C(x,y), D(y).$$
$$B(fx)[P/Q] \leftarrow E(x)$$

Then the rule $A(x) \leftarrow B(x)[P/Q]$ can be expanded into the following two Horn rules:

$$\begin{array}{l} A(x) \leftarrow C(x,y), D(y). \\ A(fx) \leftarrow E(x) \end{array} \qquad (1)$$

This suggests what it means for a Horn rulebase R to be a model of a rulebase with substitution S. In this example, if R does not contain the two rules (1), then we shall say that R is not a model of S. The following definition formalizes the idea that premises with substitution should be unfolded in the natural way.

Definition 6 *(Satisfaction) Let R be a set of Horn rules, let α be an atomic formula, and let $\beta_1 ... \beta_n$ be predicates with substitution. Then, $R \models \alpha \leftarrow \beta_1 ... \beta_n$ iff for all term substitutions σ, and all strings of atomic formulas γ, $R \models_c \alpha\sigma \leftarrow \gamma$ whenever $R^* \models_c \beta_i\sigma \leftarrow \gamma$ for each $1 \le i \le n$.*

If S is a rulebase with substitution and R is a Horn rulebase, then we say that R satisfies S iff R satisfies each rule in S. In this case, we also say that R is a *model* of S.

Note that the definition of satisfaction involves the rulebase R^*. Because R is Horn rulebase without substitution, the intuitive meaning of R^* is provided in a straightforward way by the copy-and-substitute mechanism.

The following example shows models of a rulebase in which recursion occurs through substitution. Note that recursive rules may have non-recursive models.

Example 7. Suppose S consists of the following two rules, where B and C are base predicates:

$$A(x) \leftarrow B(x)$$
$$A(x) \leftarrow A(x)[B/C]$$

Then both of the following are models of S, where D is a base predicate:

$$R_1 = \begin{cases} A(x) \leftarrow B(x) \\ A(x) \leftarrow C(x) \end{cases}$$

$$R_2 = \begin{cases} A(x) \leftarrow B(x) \\ A(x) \leftarrow C(x) \\ A(x) \leftarrow D(x,y), C(y). \end{cases}$$

To see this, note that in R_1^*, the predicate $A(x)[B/C]$ is defined by the following rule:

$$A(x)[B/C] \leftarrow C(x)$$

and that in R_2^*, it is defined by the following two rules:

$$A(x)[B/C] \leftarrow C(x)$$
$$A(x)[B/C] \leftarrow D(x,y), C(y).$$

Thus, in either rulebase, any expansion of the rule $A(x) \leftarrow A(x)[B/C]$ will only produce rules which are already in the rulebase. Thus both rulebases satisfy $A(x) \leftarrow A(x)[B/C]$. Similarly, both rulebases satisfy $A(x) \leftarrow B(x)$. Thus, both R_1 and R_2 are Horn models of S. □

It is worthwhile noting that satisfaction is not monotonic in R. That is, if $R_1 \subseteq R_2$, then in general it is not true that if $R_1 \models \alpha \leftarrow \beta$ then $R_2 \models \alpha \leftarrow \beta$. This should not be surprising, since satisfaction is not generally monotonic in logical systems. In classical logic, for instance, if s_1 and s_2 are first-order structures and $s_1 \subseteq s_2$, then it is not necessarily true that if $s_1 \models_c \psi$ then $s_2 \models_c \psi$, for an arbitrary first-order sentence ψ.

As in section 2, our goal is not to derive rules, but to apply rules to a database to derive atomic formulas. Thus, given a rulebase with substitution S and a database DB, we need a semantic characterization of logical entailment. The following definitions provide exactly this.

Definition 7 *Let R be a set of Horn rules, β a predicate with substitution, and DB a database. Then $R, DB \models \beta$ iff $R^* \cup DB \models_c \beta$.*

Definition 8 *(Entailment) Suppose S is a set of rules with substitution, DB is a database for S, and β is a predicate with substitution. Then, $S, DB \models \beta$ iff $R, DB \models \beta$ for every Horn model R of S.*

The inference system of section 2 is sound and complete with respect to this semantics. That is, we have the following theorem, whose proof is omitted for reasons of space.

Theorem 1 *Suppose β is a predicate with substitution, S is a Horn rulebase with substitution, and DB is a database. Then,*

$$S, DB \models \beta \quad \textit{iff} \quad S, DB \vdash \beta$$

4 Fixpoint Semantics

As in the theory of Horn logic [8, 1], we complement the model-theoretic semantics with a fixpoint semantics. In particular, we define a monotonic "T-operator" which can be applied to a rulebase in a bottom-up fashion, generating the minimal model (or least fixpoint) piece-by-piece. In Horn logic, the T-operator takes a database as input and returns another database as output. In our logic, the input and output of the T-operator is a Horn rulebase. Starting with the empty rulebase, the T-operator is applied over-and-over again until the minimal model is generated. Each application of the operator expands rules with substitution into equivalent Horn rules. If there is recursion through substitution, it may take infinitely many applications to generate all the Horn rules in the minimal model. However, because the operator is continuous, any particular

Horn rule will be generated in a finite number of applications. In this way, the Horn rules represented by a rulebase with substitution can be materialized.

Formally, the set of Horn rulebases (i.e., the interpretations of rulebases with substitution) is viewed as a lattice, and the T-operator maps one element of this lattice onto another element. The operator is then shown to be monotone and continuous, and the Tarski fixpoint theorem [6] is applied in the usual way. A precise statement of definitions and results is provided. Several examples are given of the application of the T-operator to actual rulebases, illustrating the way in which each application of the operator "unfolds" rules with substitution to produce equivalent Horn rules. When no more unfolding is possible, the least fixpoint has been reached.

Lemma 2 *The set of Horn rulebases (without substitution) forms a complete lattice under the following operations:*

- $R_1 \leq R_2$ *iff* $R_2 \models_c R_1$
- $R_1 \sqcup R_2 = R_1 \cup R_2$.
- $R_1 \sqcap R_2 = \{\phi \mid R_1 \models_c \phi$ *and* $R_2 \models_c \phi\}$ *where each* ϕ *is a Horn rule.*

Note that if R_1 and R_2 are classically equivalent, then $R_1 \leq R_2$ and $R_2 \leq R_1$, so that $R_1 = R_2$ in the lattice. It is reasonable to treat equivalent rulebases as equal since if R_1 and R_2 are equivalent, then for any rulebase with substitution $\mathcal{S}$, R_1 is a model of $\mathcal{S}$ iff R_2 is.

Definition 9 *(T-operator) Let* $\mathcal{S}$ *be a Horn rulebase with substitution, and let* R *be a Horn rulebase (without substitution). Then*

$$T_{\mathcal{S}}(R) = \cup_\sigma\{ \alpha\sigma \leftarrow \gamma \mid \alpha \leftarrow \beta_1 ... \beta_n \in \mathcal{S} \text{ and } R \models \beta_i\sigma \leftarrow \gamma \text{ for each } i\}$$

where each σ *is a term substitution, and each* γ *is a list of atomic formulas.*

A fixpoint of $T_{\mathcal{S}}$ is a Horn rulebase R such that $T_{\mathcal{S}}(R) \leq R$. Our first result says that R is a Horn model of $\mathcal{S}$ iff it is a fixpoint of $T_{\mathcal{S}}$. The proof is straightforward.

Lemma 3 $R \models \mathcal{S}$ *iff* $T_{\mathcal{S}}(R) \leq R$

Thus, as in the fixpoint semantics of Horn logic, we can study the models of a rulebase by studying the fixpoint structure of its T-operator.

Lemma 4 $T_{\mathcal{S}}$ *is a monotonic operator. That is, if* $R_1 \leq R_2$ *then* $T_{\mathcal{S}}(R_1) \leq T_{\mathcal{S}}(R_2)$.

Corollary 1 $T_{\mathcal{S}}$ *has a unique minimal fixpoint* $lfp(T_{\mathcal{S}})$.

Since every fixpoint is a model (and vice-versa), this shows that a rulebase with substitution $\mathcal{S}$ has a unique minimal model. The minimal model contains all the important information about $\mathcal{S}$, as the following corollary shows.

Corollary 2 *Let* $\mathcal{S}$ *be a Horn rulebase with substitution,* β *be a predicate with substitution, and DB be a database. Then,*

$$\mathcal{S}, DB \models \beta \quad \textit{iff} \quad lfp(T_{\mathcal{S}}), DB \models \beta$$

By showing that it is continuous, the T-operator can be used to construct the least fixpoint.

Lemma 5 $T_{\mathcal{S}}$ *is a continuous operator. i.e., If* $R_1 \leq R_2 \leq R_3$ ..., *then* $T_{\mathcal{S}}(\cup_i R_i) = \cup_i T_{\mathcal{S}}(R_i)$.

Theorem 2 $lfp(T_{\mathcal{S}}) = T^*(\{\}) = \cup_i T^i_{\mathcal{S}}(\{\})$

This theorem says that the least fixpoint can be constructed in a bottom-up, iterative fashion by starting with the empty rulebase and applying the operator T_S to it over and over again until there are no more changes. In general, this will take infinitely many iterations and $lfp(T_S)$ itself will be infinitely large. However, only finitely many iterations are needed to determine whether a particular Horn rule is in $lfp(T_S)$.

4.1 Examples

As the operator T_S is applied over-and-over again, the substitution rules in S are expanded into equivalent Horn rules. The first application of T_S extracts the Horn rules in S. These rules then act as seeds for the generation of new Horn rules. Thus, the second application of T_S combines these Horn rules with the substitution rules in S to generate new Horn rules. The third application then combines these new Horn rules with the substitution rules to generate still more Horn rules. When no new Horn rules can be generated in this fashion, the least fixpoint has been computed. The examples below illustrate this bit-by-bit conversion of substitution rules into Horn rules.

In general, $T_S^{i-1}(\{\}) \subseteq T_S^i(\{\})$; so for the purpose of the examples below, we define $\Delta T_S^i(\{\}) = T_S^i(\{\}) - T_S^{i-1}(\{\})$. $\Delta T_S^i(\{\})$ is the set of new Horn rules created by the ith application of T_S.

Example 8. Suppose the rulebase S consists of the following three rules, where B, C and D are base predicates:

$$A(x) \leftarrow B(x), C(x).$$
$$A(x) \leftarrow D(x,y), C(x), C(y).$$
$$A'(x) \leftarrow A(x)[C/C']$$

It then takes two applications of the operator T_S to generate the minimal model of S. That is, $lfp(T_S) = T_S^2(\{\})$. This model consists of four Horn rules, generated as follows:

$$\left.\begin{array}{l} A(x) \leftarrow B(x), C(x). \\ A(x) \leftarrow D(x,y), C(x), C(y). \end{array}\right\} \in T_S^1(\{\})$$

$$\left.\begin{array}{l} A'(x) \leftarrow B(x), C'(x). \\ A'(x) \leftarrow D(x,y), C'(x), C'(y). \end{array}\right\} \in \Delta T_S^2(\{\})$$

Thus, the definition of the predicate A' is the same as the definition of A except that C has been replaced everywhere by C'. □

Typically, not all the substitution rules in S will be applicable during each application of the operator T_S. At first, only a few substitution rules may be applicable. However, as more and more Horn rules are generated, more and more substitutions become available for conversion into Horn rules. This is illustrated by the following propositional example.

Example 9. Suppose the rulebase S consists of the following $n+1$ rules, where each B_i is a base predicate:

$$A_1 \leftarrow B_1, B_2, B_3 ... B_n.$$
$$A_2 \leftarrow A_1[B_1/C_1]$$
$$A_3 \leftarrow A_2[B_2/C_2]$$
$$\cdots$$
$$A_{n+1} \leftarrow A_n[B_n/C_n]$$

It then takes $n+1$ applications of the operator T_S to generate the minimal model of S. That is, $lfp(T_S) = T_S^{n+1}(\{\})$. This model consists of $n+1$ Horn rules, generated as follows:

$$\begin{array}{rcl} A_1 \leftarrow B_1, B_2, B_3 ... B_n. & \in & T_S^1(\{\}) \\ A_2 \leftarrow C_1, B_2, B_3 ... B_n. & \in & \Delta T_S^2(\{\}) \\ A_3 \leftarrow C_1, C_2, B_3 ... B_n. & \in & \Delta T_S^3(\{\}) \\ & \cdots & \\ A_{n+1} \leftarrow C_1, C_2, C_3 ... C_n. & \in & \Delta T_S^{n+1}(\{\}) \end{array}$$

The $i + 1^{st}$ application of T_S effectively makes a copy of the rule defining A_i, substitutes C_i for

B_i in the premise, and then uses this as the definition of a new predicate A_{i+1}. □

In general, when there is recursion through substitution, the minimal model of $\mathcal{S}$ will be infinite, and generating this model will require an infinite number of iterations of the operator $T_{\mathcal{S}}$. Unlike the previous examples, the next example cannot be terminated after a finite number of iterations.

Example 10. Suppose the rulebase $\mathcal{S}$ consists of the following three rules:

$$A(x) \leftarrow B(x,a), B(x,b).$$
$$A(x) \leftarrow A(x)[B/B']$$
$$B'(x,y) \leftarrow B(x,fy)$$

where f is a unary function symbol. Then,

$$\begin{array}{ll} \textit{if} & A(x) \leftarrow B(x,y), B(x,z) \in T^i_{\mathcal{S}}(\{\}) \\ \textit{then} & A(x) \leftarrow B(x,fy), B(x,fz) \in T^{i+1}_{\mathcal{S}}(\{\}) \end{array}$$

Thus,

$$\begin{array}{l} A(x) \leftarrow B(x,a), B(x,b). \in T^1_{\mathcal{S}}(\{\}) \\ A(x) \leftarrow B(x,fa), B(x,fb). \in \Delta T^2_{\mathcal{S}}(\{\}) \\ A(x) \leftarrow B(x,f^2a), B(x,f^2b). \in \Delta T^3_{\mathcal{S}}(\{\}) \\ \ldots \\ A(x) \leftarrow B(x,f^ia), B(x,f^ib). \in \Delta T^i_{\mathcal{S}}(\{\}) \\ \ldots \end{array}$$

□

5 Concluding Remarks

We believe that substitution is a principle which can be applied to logic-based languages generally in order to facilitate reuse and modification. In this paper, however, we focused on Horn logics and on Datalog in particular. Several examples were given to illustrate the idea of substitution and its utility.

We established formal proof and model theories for Horn logic with predicate substitution. In particular, we developed (in our opinion) natural semantics in which an ordinary set of substitution-free rules is a model of a set of rules with substitution. This corresponds to the intuition that rules with substitution are written by a user who has rules without substitution "in mind," rules which he might have written if he had enough space. This is similar to the view taken of ordinary Datalog rules, in which the user has an "intended model" in mind (the least fixpoint of the rules), which he would have written if he had enough space. Hence, it can be argued that by moving from Datalog to Datalog-with-substitution, we achieve an upgrade similar to that of going from relational algebra to Datalog.

Substitution adds a great deal of power to Datalog. Whereas the complexity of Datalog is complete for $PTIME$, the complexity of Datalog augmented with substitution is complete for $EXPTIME$. An example was presented showing that its data complexity is NP-hard. Syntactically, this boost in expressive power comes about from recursion through substitution. Semantically, this increased power has an interesting interpretation: When a Datalog rulebase with substitution is $EXPTIME$-complete, it represents an *infinite* Datalog rulebase without substitution. Furthermore, this infinite Datalog rulebase is not equivalent to any finite one. In such cases, substitution provides an extremely concise notation for representing a set of Datalog rules.

We view predicate substitution as a principle which in order to facilitate the reuse and modification of deductive rules, has to be added to logic-based languages. Predicate substitution can be implemented in several existing formalisms: state variables (with unary function symbols), complex objects, or Prolog. However, predicate substitution assures reusability with the minimal possible cost (i.e. with a minimal increase in expressive power). Besides, we see Datalog with predicate substitution as a natural *specification language* facilitating reuse. Indeed, we insist that the concept of predicate substitution is a more natural specification vehicle for reusability than the concepts of state variable or complex objects.

In this paper, we studied the complexity and expressive power of Datalog with substitution; but we plan to investigate the effect of substitution on other languages, such as the various extensions of Datalog with complex objects [4, 7, 2], as well as extensions of Datalog which allow restricted use of function symbols, as in [3].

References

[1] K.R. Apt and M.H. Van Emden. Contributions to the Theory of Logic Programming. *Journal of the ACM*, 29(3):841–862, 1982.

[2] C. Beeri, S. Naqvi, and R. Ramakrishnan. Sets and negation in a logic database language (LDL). In *Proceedings of the ACM Symposium on the Principles of Database Systems (PODS)*, San Diego, CA, 1987.

[3] J. Chomicki and T. Imielinski. Relational specification of infinite query answers. In *Proceedings of the International Conference on Management of Data (SIGMOD)*, Portland, Oregon, May 1989.

[4] G.M. Kuper. Logic programming with sets. In *Proceedings of the ACM Symposium on the Principles of Database Systems (PODS)*, San Diego, CA, 1987.

[5] L.T. McCarty and N.S. Sridharan. The Representation of an Evolving System of Legal Concepts. II. prototypes and deformations. In *Proceedings of the Seventh IJCAI*, pages 246–253, 1981.

[6] A. Tarski. A Lattice-Theoretical Fixpoint Theorem and its Applications. *Pacific Journal of Mathematics*, 5:285–309, 1955.

[7] S. Tsur and C. Zaniolo. LDL: A logic-based data-language. In *Proceedings of the International Conference on Very Large Databases (VLDB)*, Kyoto, Japan, 1986.

[8] M.H. Van Emden and R.A. Kowalski. The Semantics of Predicate Logic as a Programming Language. *Journal of the ACM*, 23(4):733–742, 1976.

Panel:

"Why are object-oriented folks producing systems, while deductive folks are producing papers ?"

Panel Chairperson: *Michele Missikoff (CNR, Italy)*

This panel will discuss and compare the relative advances of two of the most lively subfields of the database field: object-oriented database systems and deductive database systems. Topics to be discussed by the panelists include (i) are the two fields competitive or complementary? (ii) what is the status of advancement of the two respective fields? and (iii) do they address specific and different applications or markets?

Vol. 379: A. Kreczmar, G. Mirkowska (Eds.), Mathematical Foundations of Computer Science 1989. Proceedings, 1989. VIII, 605 pages. 1989.

Vol. 380: J. Csirik, J. Demetrovics, F. Gécseg (Eds.), Fundamentals of Computation Theory. Proceedings, 1989. XI, 493 pages. 1989.

Vol. 381: J. Dassow, J. Kelemen (Eds.), Machines, Languages, and Complexity. Proceedings, 1988. VI, 244 pages. 1989.

Vol. 382: F. Dehne, J.-R. Sack, N. Santoro (Eds.), Algorithms and Data Structures. WADS '89. Proceedings, 1989. IX, 592 pages. 1989.

Vol. 383: K. Furukawa, H. Tanaka, T. Fujisaki (Eds.), Logic Programming '88. Proceedings, 1988. VII, 251 pages. 1989 (Subseries LNAI).

Vol. 384: G.A. van Zee, J.G.G. van de Vorst (Eds.), Parallel Computing 1988. Proceedings, 1988. V, 135 pages. 1989.

Vol. 385: E. Börger, H. Kleine Büning, M.M. Richter (Eds.), CSL '88. Proceedings, 1988. VI, 399 pages. 1989.

Vol. 386: J.E. Pin (Ed.), Formal Properties of Finite Automata and Applications. Proceedings, 1988. VIII, 260 pages. 1989.

Vol. 387: C. Ghezzi, J. A. McDermid (Eds.), ESEC '89. 2nd European Software Engineering Conference. Proceedings, 1989. VI, 496 pages. 1989.

Vol. 388: G. Cohen, J. Wolfmann (Eds.), Coding Theory and Applications. Proceedings, 1988. IX, 329 pages. 1989.

Vol. 389: D.H. Pitt, D.E. Rydeheard, P. Dybjer, A.M. Pitts, A. Poigné (Eds.), Category Theory and Computer Science. Proceedings, 1989. VI, 365 pages. 1989.

Vol. 390: J.P. Martins, E.M. Morgado (Eds.), EPIA 89. Proceedings, 1989. XII, 400 pages. 1989 (Subseries LNAI).

Vol. 391: J.-D. Boissonnat, J.-P. Laumond (Eds.), Geometry and Robotics. Proceedings, 1988. VI, 413 pages. 1989.

Vol. 392: J.-C. Bermond, M. Raynal (Eds.), Distributed Algorithms. Proceedings, 1989. VI, 315 pages. 1989.

Vol. 393: H. Ehrig, H. Herrlich, H.-J. Kreowski, G. Preuß (Eds.), Categorical Methods in Computer Science. VI, 350 pages. 1989.

Vol. 394: M. Wirsing, J.A. Bergstra (Eds.), Algebraic Methods: Theory, Tools and Applications. VI, 558 pages. 1989.

Vol. 395: M. Schmidt-Schauß, Computational Aspects of an Order-Sorted Logic with Term Declarations. VIII, 171 pages. 1989. (Subseries LNAI).

Vol. 396: T.A. Berson, T. Beth (Eds.), Local Area Network Security. Proceedings, 1989. IX, 152 pages. 1989.

Vol. 397: K.P. Jantke (Ed.), Analogical and Inductive Inference. Proceedings, 1989. IX, 338 pages. 1989. (Subseries LNAI).

Vol. 398: B. Banieqbal, H. Barringer, A. Pnueli (Eds.), Temporal Logic in Specification. Proceedings, 1987. VI, 448 pages. 1989.

Vol. 399: V. Cantoni, R. Creutzburg, S. Levialdi, G. Wolf (Eds.), Recent Issues in Pattern Analysis and Recognition. VII, 400 pages. 1989.

Vol. 400: R. Klein, Concrete and Abstract Voronoi Diagrams. IV, 167 pages. 1989.

Vol. 401: H. Djidjev (Ed.), Optimal Algorithms. Proceedings, 1989. VI, 308 pages. 1989.

Vol. 402: T.P. Bagchi, V.K. Chaudhri, Interactive Relational Database Design. XI, 186 pages. 1989.

Vol. 403: S. Goldwasser (Ed.), Advances in Cryptology – CRYPTO '88. Proceedings, 1988. XI, 591 pages. 1990.

Vol. 404: J. Beer, Concepts, Design, and Performance Analysis of a Parallel Prolog Machine. VI, 128 pages. 1989.

Vol. 405: C.E. Veni Madhavan (Ed.), Foundations of Software Technology and Theoretical Computer Science. Proceedings, 1989. VIII, 339 pages. 1989.

Vol. 407: J. Sifakis (Ed.), Automatic Verification Methods for Finite State Systems. Proceedings, 1989. VII, 382 pages. 1990.

Vol. 408: M. Leeser, G. Brown (Eds.) Hardware Specification, Verification and Synthesis: Mathematical Aspects. Proceedings, 1989. VI, 402 pages. 1990.

Vol. 409: A. Buchmann, O. Günther, T.R. Smith, Y.-F. Wang (Eds.), Design and Implementation of Large Spatial Databases. Proceedings, 1989. IX, 364 pages. 1990.

Vol. 410: F. Pichler, R. Moreno-Diaz (Eds.), Computer Aided Systems Theory – EUROCAST '89. Proceedings, 1989. VII, 427 pages. 1990.

Vol. 411: M. Nagl (Ed.), Graph-Theoretic Concepts in Computer Science. Proceedings, 1989. VII, 374 pages. 1990.

Vol. 412: L.B. Almeida, C.J. Wellekens (Eds.), Neural Networks. Proceedings, 1990. IX, 276 pages. 1990.

Vol. 413: R. Lenz, Group Theoretical Methods in Image Processing. VIII, 139 pages. 1990.

Vol. 414: A. Kreczmar, A. Salwicki (Eds.), LOGLAN '88 – Report on the Programming Language. X, 133 pages. 1990.

Vol. 415: C. Choffrut, T. Lengauer (Eds.), STACS 90. Proceedings, 1990. VI, 312 pages. 1990.

Vol. 416: F. Bancilhon, C. Thanos, D. Tsichritzis (Eds.), Advances in Database Technology – EDBT '90. Proceedings, 1990. IX, 452 pages. 1990.

This series reports new developments in computer science research and teaching – quickly, informally and at a high level. The type of material considered for publication includes preliminary drafts of original papers and monographs, technical reports of high quality and broad interest, advanced level lectures, reports of meetings, provided they are of exceptional interest and focused on a single topic. The timeliness of a manuscript is more important than its form which may be unfinished or tentative. If possible, a subject index should be included. Publication of Lecture Notes is intended as a service to the international computer science community, in that a commercial publisher, Springer-Verlag, can offer a wide distribution of documents which would otherwise have a restricted readership. Once published and copyrighted, they can be documented in the scientific literature.

Manuscripts

Manuscripts should be no less than 100 and preferably no more than 500 pages in length.

They are reproduced by a photographic process and therefore must be typed with extreme care. Symbols not on the typewriter should be inserted by hand in indelible black ink. Corrections to the typescript should be made by pasting in the new text or painting out errors with white correction fluid. Authors receive 75 free copies and are free to use the material in other publications. The typescript is reduced slightly in size during reproduction; best results will not be obtained unless the text on any one page is kept within the overall limit of 18 x 26.5 cm (7 x 10½ inches). On request, the publisher will supply special paper with the typing area outlined.

Manuscripts should be sent to Prof. G. Goos, GMD Forschungsstelle an der Universität Karlsruhe, Haid- und Neu-Str. 7, 7500 Karlsruhe 1, Germany, Prof. J. Hartmanis, Cornell University, Dept. of Computer Science, Ithaca, NY/USA 14850, or directly to Springer-Verlag Heidelberg.

Springer-Verlag, Heidelberger Platz 3, D-1000 Berlin 33
Springer-Verlag, Tiergartenstraße 17, D-6900 Heidelberg 1
Springer-Verlag, 175 Fifth Avenue, New York, NY 10010/USA
Springer-Verlag, 37-3, Hongo 3-chome, Bunkyo-ku, Tokyo 113, Japan

---

ISBN 3-540-52291-3
ISBN 0-387-52291-3